CW01457220

THE EXECUTIVE IN THE CONSTITUTION

THE EXECUTIVE IN THE CONSTITUTION

Structure, Autonomy, and Internal Control

TERENCE DAINTITH

and

ALAN PAGE

UNIVERSITY PRESS

This book has been printed digitally and produced in a standard specification in order to ensure its continuing availability

OXFORD
UNIVERSITY PRESS

Great Clarendon Street, Oxford OX2 6DP

Oxford University Press is a department of the University of Oxford. It furthers the University's objective of excellence in research, scholarship, and education by publishing worldwide in

Oxford New York

Auckland Bangkok Buenos Aires Cape Town Chennai Dar es Salaam Delhi Hong Kong Istanbul Karachi Kolkata Kuala Lumpur Madrid Melbourne Mexico City Mumbai Nairobi São Paulo Shanghai Taipei Tokyo Toronto

Oxford is a registered trade mark of Oxford University Press in the UK and in certain other countries

Published in the United States
by Oxford University Press Inc., New York

Reprinted 2004

ISBN 0-19-826870-X

Preface

Most of the research for this book was carried out with the assistance of a grant (No. L 124251003) from the Economic and Social Research Council, within the framework of its 'Whitehall' programme. This support enabled one of us to get a year away from teaching (though alas not from all the other kinds of professional obligation which today form part of academic life), and secured invaluable research assistance for us both. We profited greatly from the cross-disciplinary contacts fostered by the programme, and owe particular thanks to its Director, Professor Rod Rhodes, for the energetic and responsive way in which he did his job and for the practical help he gave us.

The book is a mixture of joint and individual efforts. The structure embodies our common view—not easily arrived at—of how best to approach the organization and analysis of a mass of material whose constitutional and indeed legal reference points are often far from obvious. Within that structure we have divided responsibility for drafting chapters broadly according to subject-matter. Daintith is responsible for the introduction and the chapters on financial and legal resources, with the exception of the chapter on legislation, Page for the chapters on the executive, the civil service, legislation, the Citizen's Charter and open government, and the conclusion. All drafts, however, have been the subject of intensive discussion between us, and we each accept responsibility for the whole work, and for each other's mistakes as well as our own.

The 'Whitehall' programme has been both a reflection and an occasion of an increasing willingness in the United Kingdom executive to open its actions and thoughts to public scrutiny in a way we should have found hard to imagine even ten years ago. Occasional strictures about continuing areas of reticence should not be read as ingratitude for the extensive access and co-operation we have enjoyed within the executive. We have greatly appreciated the willingness of many senior civil servants and others in public service to devote considerable time, in interviews, in correspondence, and in seminars, to informing us and to discussing our ideas and questions. Following a convention which is not yet outmoded, we do not name them, but trust that they will recognize in the pages that follow both the essential character of their contribution and our gratitude to them for providing it.

Two people we can name, whose contribution has likewise been indispensable, are Cecilia O'Leary and Chris Willis, our research assistants on the project. Our respective institutions, the Institute of Advanced Legal Studies in the University of London, and the Department of Law in the University of Dundee, have supported us in a variety of ways. In two workshops held at the Institute we were able to discuss our ideas in comparative, inter-disciplinary, and professional contexts, and to learn many lessons from the comments and criticisms of the participants.

Our families, whom we love dearly, have lived with this project for longer than they might have wished (though hardly longer than bitter experience must have taught them to expect), and are to be thanked for sustaining throughout an attitude of benevolent neutrality towards our activities. Finally, we wish to add a word of appreciation to the distinguished Scottish chef, David Wilson. It was at his restaurant in Fife, on a singularly dark and stormy winter's night in 1994, that we decided to write this book. The optimism needed to form such a resolution owed much, if not everything, to the warmth of his hospitality and the excellence of his food and wine, and we gladly acknowledge his contribution.

T.D.
A.P.

December 1998
London and Dundee

Contents

List of abbreviations xv
Table of statutes, regulations, etc. xvii
United Kingdom statutes xvii
United Kingdom regulations xviii
EC treaties, regulations, directives etc. xix
Table of cases xxi
United Kingdom courts xxi
Cases from other courts xxiii
Chapter 1 The executive in the constitution 1
I Introduction 1
II Why is the executive important? 2
1 The executive in shadow 2
2 External controls and the compliance principle 3
3 The plural executive 6
III Why is the executive neglected? 10
1 The political background 10
2 The separation of powers 10
3 The Crown 12
4 The lack of 'real' law 13
IV Positive constitutional theory 15
1 The constitution as empirical record 16
2 The constitution as one 'grand idea' 16
3 The constitution as fiction 17
4 The constitution as a structure of values 18
V The executive in a resource-based theory of the constitution 19
Chapter 2 The executive in constitutional law 26
I Introduction 26
II The Crown 27
III The ministerial department 28
1 The principle of departmental autonomy 29
2 The establishment of departments 32
3 Departmental powers 33
4 The Ministers of the Crown Act 36
IV Hollowing out the department 37
1 Next Steps agencies 37
1.1 Status of agencies 39
1.2 Mode of establishment 39

1.3 Relationship with sponsor departments 41
1.3.1 Strategic management 41
1.3.2 Framework documents 41
1.3.3 Targets 42
1.3.4 Agency chief executives 43
1.4 Agency reviews 45
2 Contracting out 46
2.1 The Deregulation and Contracting Out Act 47
3 Non-departmental public bodies 49
V The cabinet and ministry 51
1 The cabinet 51
1.1 'Cabinet business' 52
1.2 The Cabinet Secretariat 54
2 Strengthening the 'centre' 54
VI Conclusion 57
Chapter 3 The civil service 59
I Introduction 59
II The legal basis of control 62
III The organization of control 65
1 The Treasury 65
2 The Cabinet Office 66
3 The Office of the Civil Service Commissioners 69
4 Departments and agencies 71
4.1 The principal establishments officer 71
4.2 Delegated responsibilities 72
4.3 'Cabinet Office requirements' 73
4.4 The Senior Civil Service 75
4.4.1 The central pay framework 75
4.4.2 Personal contracts 76
IV Recruitment 78
1 Audited self-regulation 78
2 The recruitment principles 78
3 Commissioners' approval 80
4 'SASC Group' appointments 82
5 Exceptions 83
6 Compliance and audit 84
7 'Central requirements' 86
V Conduct and discipline 86
1 Standards of conduct 86
1.1 The central framework 87
1.2 The Civil Service Code 91
1.3 The Armstrong memorandum 94
1.4 Departmental and agency rules 95

2 Discipline 96
3 Ministerial conduct 97
4 Appeals 98
VI Conclusions 101
Chapter 4 The financial resources of government: institutions 104
I Introduction: the constitutional dimension 104
II The constitutional structure 107
III The institutions of the executive 109
1 The Treasury 109
1.1 Tasks and organization 110
1.2 History 113
1.3 Powers 116
1.3.1 Issuance of public funds 117
1.3.2 Supervision of expenditure of funds 118
1.3.3 Control of access to Parliament 120
1.3.4 Conclusion 122
2 Control of resources otherwise than by the Treasury 123
3 The spending Departments 126
3.1 The Accounting Officer 126
3.2 The Finance Division, and the Principal Finance Officer (PFO) 129
4 Executive agencies and trading funds 132
4.1 History 132
4.2 Creation 133
4.3 Types 134
4.3.1 Government trading funds 135
4.3.2 Agencies with their own Vote 136
4.3.3 Other agencies 137
5 Central responsibilities for accountancy and internal audit 137
Chapter 5 The financial resources of government: allocation and appropriation 140
I Introduction: a plurality of systems 140
II The Public Expenditure Survey system 143
1 History 143
2 The public expenditure total 144
3 Fitting Departmental activities to public expenditure plans 148
4 Results 151
5 PES in Parliament 152
5.1 In general 152
5.2 The Code of Fiscal Stability 153

5.3 Departmental reports 154
III The supply system 155
1 The supply cycle 155
2 The estimates 159
2.1 Structure and control 159
2.2 Simplification and alignment with PES 162
IV Resource accounting and budgeting 164
1 In general 164
2 Resource accounting 165
3 Resource budgeting 166
Chapter 6 The financial resources of government: monitoring and control 169
I In general: criteria, constraints, concepts 169
1 Introduction 169
2 Legislative, parliamentary, and internal rules 170
3 Regularity, propriety and value for money 171
3.1 Regularity 171
3.2 Propriety 173
3.3 Value for money 175
3.4 Conclusion 176
II Treasury authorizations and delegations 177
1 Introduction 177
2 From approvals to delegations 177
3 Virement 180
4 Establishments 181
5 New works and services 182
III Cash control 183
1 Cash limits and supplementary estimates 183
2 The Reserve and the Contingencies Fund 186
3 Running costs control 188
IV Control and sanctions 190
1 A self-enforcing system? 190
2 Links with external controls: Parliament 193
2.1 The Comptroller and Auditor-General and the National Audit Office 193
2.2 Treasury–NAO relations 195
3 Links with external controls: the law and the courts 199
Chapter 7 The organization of the legal function in government 207
I Introduction 207
1 The salience of legality 207
2 Whose legality? 208
3 Legality as a professional specialism 210
4 Legal tasks in government 212

II The development of the structure for government legal work 214
III The current structure of legal services 217
1 The Treasury Solicitor's Department 217
2 The Parliamentary Counsel Office 221
3 The Crown Prosecution Service and the Serious Fraud Office 221
4 The Legal Secretariat to the Law Officers 222
5 Law reform 223
6 Departmental legal services 223
7 Scotland and Wales 228
8 Northern Ireland 230
9 General comments 230
IV The Law Officers: history and status 231
1 The English Law Officers 231
2 The Scottish Law Officers 236
3 Conclusion 239
Chapter 8 Legislation 240
I Introduction 240
II Machinery and purposes 241
1 Primary legislation 241
1.1 Determining legislative priorities 242
1.2 'Better legislation' 245
1.3 Policy clearance 246
1.4 Drafting 250
1.4.1 The PCO's monopoly 251
1.4.2 Ministerial responsibility 251
1.4.3 Drafting authority 252
1.4.4 Relations with instructing departments 253
1.4.5 Counsel as guardians of legal values 254
1.4.6 The role of the Law Officers 256
2 Subordinate legislation 258
2.1 The Statutory Instruments Act 1946 258
2.2 Departmental practice 259
2.3 Parliamentary scrutiny 260
2.4 The changing character of subordinate legislation 263
III The impact of Europe 264
1 The negotiation and implementation of EU law 265
1.1 EC law-making 265
1.2 Giving effect to EC obligations 266
1.2.1 Central co-ordination 266
1.2.2 PCO scrutiny 267

2 The impact on domestic law-making 268
2.1 European Community law 268
2.2 The European Convention on Human Rights 269
IV Burdens on Business 271
1 Machinery 272
2 Mechanisms 273
2.1 Regulatory appraisal and regulatory impact assessments 274
2.2 Principles of good regulation 277
2.3 Deregulation orders 278
2.4 Secondary legislation 279
2.5 EC legislation 280
V Conclusions 285

Chapter 9 Litigation and legal advice: co-ordination and control 287
I The Law Officers, criminal prosecutions, and civil litigation 287
1 The general constitutional position 287
2 The exercise of the Law Officers' powers 290
3 The appointment of counsel 295
II The Law Officers as the government's chief legal advisers 297
1 Introduction 297
2 Law Officers' opinions: their nature 298
3 Asking for advice 302
4 Confidentiality, dissemination, and impact 309
4.1 Disclosure outside government 309
4.2 Dissemination within government 313
III Cabinet Office co-ordination in legal matters 315
1 In general 315
2 On European law 316
IV Co-ordination within the framework of the Government Legal Service 319

Chapter 10 Executive legality: constitutional background and current issues 323
I Legality: pluralism and centralization 323
II Constitutional roots of our present system 325
1 Ministerial responsibility 325
2 Executive subservience to the judiciary 326
3 Executive dominance of Parliament 331
III The changing context 332
1 Administrative heterogeneity 332

2 The rise and rise of judicial review 335
2.1 Expansion in scope and depth 335
2.2 Positive reactions 336
2.3 Negative reactions 337
2.4 Underlying problems 338
IV Change within the executive 340
1 Litigation strategy 341
2 The executive in legal debate 343
3 The ethics of government lawyering 345
4 Conclusion 347
Chapter 11 Better government: charter standards, open government and good administration 348
I Introduction 348
II The Citizen's Charter and Service First 349
1 A non-statutory initiative 350
2 Principles of public service delivery 351
3 Delivering the principles 352
3.1 Charter standards 354
3.2 Performance audit 357
3.3 Charter standards: conclusions 357
4 Complaints procedures 358
4.1 Redress 361
4.2 Systems improvement 365
4.3 Complaints procedures: conclusions 366
III Access to official information 367
1 The Code of Practice 367
2 Towards a Freedom of Information Act 372
IV External controls on standards of administration 373
1 Parliament 373
1.1 The Parliamentary Commissioner for Administration 373
1.2 Other parliamentary checks 376
2 The courts 377
3 The Council on Tribunals 378
V Conclusion 378
Chapter 12 Conclusions: internal control in a plural executive 380
I Introduction 380
II Trends in internal control 381
1 The traditional system 381
2 Growth and change 383
2.1 Forces for change 383
2.2 Co-ordination versus centralization 383
2.3 Formalization 386

III Internal control and external controls 388
1 Executive reliance on external control: Parliament 388
2 Executive reliance on external control: the courts 391
3 The dependence of external controls on internal control 392
IV The constitutional significance of internal control 393
Bibliography 399
1 Books and articles 399
2 Parliamentary and other official papers 413
Index 425

List of Abbreviations

AME	Annually managed expenditure: a public expenditure aggregate
APA	Audit Policy and Advice Team within FMRA (below)
CA	Central Accountancy Team within FMRA (below)
CPS	Crown Prosecution Service
CSD	Civil Service Department
CSR	Comprehensive spending review
DART	Development of Accountancy Resources Team within FMRA (below)
DEL	Departmental expenditure limits: a public expenditure aggregate
DEO	Cabinet Office letter to departments beginning 'Dear Establishment Officer'
DETR	Department of Environment, Transport and the Regions
DfEE	Department for Education and Employment
DH	Department of Health
DAO letter	Treasury letter to Department on financial issues beginning 'Dear Accounting Officer'
DPP	Director of Public Prosecutions
DSS	Department of Social Security
DTI	Department of Trade and Industry
EC	European Community or European Communities
ECA	European Communities Act 1972
ECHR	European Convention on Human Rights
EDX	Cabinet committee on public expenditure (1992–1997)
EEC	European Economic Community
EMU	Economic and Monetary Union
ESA	European System of Accounts
EU	European Union
FCO	Foreign and Commonwealth Office
FMI	Financial Management Initiative
FMRA	Financial Management, Reporting and Audit Directorate of the Treasury
GDP	Gross domestic product
GEMS	General expenditure monitoring system
GGE	'General government expenditure': a public expenditure aggregate
GGE(X)	Another public expenditure aggregate, incorporating only some elements of GGE
GLS	Government Legal Service
GLSLG	Government Legal Service Liaison Group
HMSO	Her Majesty's Stationery Office
LAD	Lord Advocate's Department
LCD	Lord Chancellor's Department
LMU	Lawyers' Management Unit
MAFF	Ministry of Agriculture, Fisheries and Food
MoD	Ministry of Defence
NAO	National Audit Office

NCT	'New control total': a public expenditure aggregate
NDPB	Non-Departmental public body
ODA	Overseas Development Administration
OFTEL	Office of Telecommunications Regulation
OFWAT	Office of Water Regulation
OMCS	Office of the Minister for the Civil Service
OPS	Office of Public Service
OPSS	Office of Public Service and Science
PCA	Parliamentary Commissioner for Administration
PCO	Parliamentary Counsel Office
PEFO	Principal Establishment and Finance Officer
PEO	Principal Establishment Officer
PES	Public Expenditure Survey
PFO	Principal Finance Officer
PII	Public interest immunity
PSA	Public Service Agreement
PSX	Cabinet committee on public services and public expenditure (1998–)
PX	Cabinet committee on public expenditure (1997–98)
RAB	Resource Accounting and Budgeting
SASC	Senior Appointments Selection Committee
SFO	Serious Fraud Office
SSRB	Senior Salaries Review Body
TEU	Treaty on European Union
TME	Total managed expenditure: a public expenditure aggregate
TOA	Treasury Officer of Accounts
TSol	Treasury Solicitor's Department
VAT	Value Added Tax
VFM	Value for money

Table of Statutes, Regulations, etc.

United Kingdom Statutes

Animal Health Act 1981 (1981, c. 22) 345
Appropriation Act 1862 (25 and 26 Vict., c. 71) 183
Bank of England Act 1998 (1998, c. 11) 30, 113
Bill of Rights 1689 (1 Will. and Mary sess. 2, ch. 2) 23, 34, 104
British Nationality Act 1981 (1981, c. 61) 340
Civil Service (Management Functions) Act 1992 (1992, c. 61) 64, 67, 72–4, 389
Competition and Service (Utilities) Act 1992 (1992, c. 43) 350
Continental Shelf Act 1964 (1964, c. 29) 178
Contingencies Fund Act 1974 (1974, c. 18) 170, 186–7
Crime and Punishment (Scotland) Act 1997 (1997, c. 48) 253
Crime (Sentences) Act 1997 (1997, c. 43) 253
Criminal Justice Act 1987 (1987, c. 38) 222, 288
Criminal Justice Act 1988 (1988, c. 33) 291
Criminal Procedure and Investigations Act 1996 (1996, c. 25) 291, 295, 332
Crown Estate Act 1961 (9 and 10 Eliz. 2, c. 55) 168
Crown Lands Act 1702 (1 Anne, St. 2, c. 18) 167
Crown Proceedings Act 1947 (10 and 11 Geo. 6, c. 44) 34, 212, 334
Customs and Excise Management Act 1979 (1979, c. 2) 63, 292–3
Deregulation and Contracting Out Act 1994 (1994, c. 40) 47–9, 271, 273, 279, 389
Education (Schools) Act 1992 (1992, c. 38) 350
Environmental Protection Act 1990 (1990, c. 43) 254
European Communities Act 1972 (1972, c. 68) 232, 266–7, 280–1, 283, 396
Exchequer and Audit Departments Act 1866 (29 and 30 Vict., c. 39) 112, 116–21, 126, 132, 141–2, 160, 164, 166, 170–1, 177, 193–5
Exchequer and Audit Departments Act 1921 (11 and 12 Geo. 5, c. 52) 112, 119, 132, 171–2, 193–5
Export and Investment Guarantees Act 1991 (1991, c. 67) 204
Finance Act 1998 (1998, c. 36) 106, 251
Financial Services Act 1986 (1986, c. 60) 280
Government of Wales Act 1998 (1998, c. 38) 60, 103
Government Trading Funds Act 1973 (1973, c. 63) 135–6
Government Trading Funds Act 1990 (1990, c. 30) 135–6, 389
Health and Safety at Work etc. Act 1974 (1974, c. 37) 253
Historic Buildings and Ancient Monuments Act 1953 (1 and 2 Eliz. 2, c. 49) 167–8
Import, Export and Customs Powers (Defence) Act 1939 (2 and 3 Geo. 6, c. 69) 243
Inland Revenue Regulation Act 1890 (53 and 54 Vict., c. 21) 292
Insolvency Act 1985 (1985, c. 65) 212
Law Commissions Act 1965 (1965, c. 22) 223
Law Officers Act 1944 (7 and 8 Geo. 5, c. 25) 223, 236
Law Officers Act 1997 (1997, c. 60) 222, 233, 236

Law Officers' Fees Act 1872 (35 and 36 Vict., c. 70)....233
Local Government Act 1992 (1992, c. 19)....350
Ministerial and Other Salaries Act 1972 (1972, c. 3)....33
Ministers of the Crown (Transfer of Functions) Act 1946 (9 and 10 Geo. 6, c. 31)....36–7
Ministers of the Crown Act 1964 (1964, c. 98)....30, 32, 37
Ministers of the Crown Act 1975 (1975, c. 26).... 28, 32, 37, 64
Ministry of Health Act 1919 (9 and 10 Geo. 5, c. 21)....34
Ministry of Pensions Act 1916 (6 and 7 Geo. 5, c. 65)....33
National Audit Act 1983 (1983, c. 44)....141, 170, 175, 193–5
National Health Service (Invalid Direction) Act 1980 (1980, c. 15)....302
National Loans Act 1968 (1968, c. 13)....120, 170
Northern Ireland Act 1998 (1998, c. 47)....230
Northern Ireland Constitution Act 1973 (1973, c. 36)....230
Oil Taxation Act 1975 (1975, c. 22)....157
Overseas Development and Co-operation Act 1980 (1980, c. 63)....35, 172, 204
Parliamentary Commissioner Act 1967 (1967, c. 13)....373
Petroleum (Production) Act 1934 (24 and 25 Geo. 5, c. 36)....178
Prosecution of Offences Act 1879 (42 and 43 Vict. c. 22)....222
Prosecution of Offences Act 1985 (1985, c. 23)....221, 288–9, 291
Public Interest Disclosure Act 1998 (1998, c. 23)....101
Scotland Act 1998 (1998, c. 45)....29, 60, 103, 236
Secretary for Scotland Act 1885 (48 and 49 Vict. c. 61)....237
Secretary for Scotland Act 1887 (50 and 51 Vict. c. 52)....237
Social Security Act 1986 (1986, c. 50)....201
Statutory Instruments Act 1946 (9 and 19 Geo. 6, c. 36)....258–9
Supreme Court (Offices) Act 1997 (1997, c. 69)....213
Telecommunication Act 1984 (1984, c. 12)....31
Treasury Solicitor Act 1876 (39 and 40 Vict. c. 18)....218
Tribunals and Inquiries Act 1992 (1992, c. 53)....378
Value Added Tax Act 1994 (1994, c. 23)....14
Water Industry Act 1991 (1991, c. 56)....30

United Kingdom regulations

Prerogative Orders in Council

Civil Service Order in Council 1870....78–9, 384
Civil Service Order in Council of 22 July 1920....66–7
Civil Service Order in Council 1995.... 67, 70, 78, 80–1, 83–4, 100
Civil Service (Amendment) Order in Council 1997....83, 94
Civil Service Commissioners Order in Council 1855....69
Diplomatic Service Order in Council 1995....61, 67

Statutory instruments

Minister for the Civil Service Order 1968, SI 1968 No. 1656....56, 66–7
Prosecution of Offences Regulations 1946, SI 1946 No. 1467....288
Prosecution of Offences Regulations 1978, SI 1978 No. 1357....288
Secretary of State for Environment, Transport and the Regions Order 1997, SI 1997 No. 2971....32

Transfer of Functions (Minister for the Civil Service and Treasury) Order 1981, SI 1981 No. 1670 66
Transfer of Functions (Treasury and Minister for the Civil Service) Order 1995, SI 1995 No. 269 66
Transfer of Undertakings (Protection of Employment) Regulations 1981, SI 1981 No. 1794; amended, Trade Union Reform and Employment Rights Act 1993 320

EC Treaties, Regulations, Directives, etc.

Acquired Rights Directive 1977, Directive 77/187/EEC, OJ 1977 L61/26 320
Council Regulation on the application of the protocol on the excessive deficit procedure, Regulation 3605/93/EC, OJ 1993 L332/7 146
Treaty establishing the European Economic Community 1957, as amended Treaty on European Union 1992 .... 146–7, 317

Table of Cases

United Kingdom courts

Agee v Secretary of State for Scotland 1977 SLT (Notes) 54 33
Associated Provincial Picture Houses v Wednesbury Corporation [1948] 1 KB 223 .... 338, 342
Attorney-General v De Keyser's Royal Hotel Ltd [1920] AC 508 .... 35, 64
Attorney-General v Lord Advocate (1834), 2 Cl. & Fin. 481; 6 ER 1236 238
Berko v SAFE, unreported industrial tribunal decision of 16 April 1998 71
British Broadcasting Corporation v Johns [1965] Ch. 32 13
Burmah Oil Co. (Burma Trading) Ltd. v Lord Advocate 1964 SLT 218 (HL); [1965] AC 75 23
Carltona Ltd v Commissioners of Works [1943] 2 All ER 560 .... 40–1, 47
Case of Proclamations (1611), 12 Co. Rep. 74 .... 23, 34
Cooper v The Queen (1880) 14 Ch D 311 64
Council of Civil Service Unions v Minister for the Civil Service [1985] AC 374 .... 64, 77, 335, 392
D v National Society for the Prevention of Cruelty to Children [1978] AC 171 212
Department of Health v Bruce, *The Times*, 31 December 1992 71
Dyson v Attorney-General [1911] 1 KB 410 200
Gilbert v Corporation of Trinity House (1886) 17 QBD 795 13
Gillick v West Norfolk and Wisbech Area Health Authority [1986] AC 112 335
Gouriet v Union of Post Office Workers [1978] AC 435; [1977] 3 All ER 70 232
Harrison v Bush 1855 5 F&B 344 33
H. Lavender v Minister of Housing and Local Government [1970] 3 All ER 871, [1970] 1 WLR 1231 .... 31, 40
HM Advocate v Copeland 1988 SLT 249 40
International Railway Co. v Niagara Power Commission [1941] AC 328 13
Ironmonger v Dyne (1928) 44 TLR 497 .... 87, 91
Laker Airways Ltd v Department of Trade [1977] QB 643 335
Lewisham MB and Town Clerk v Roberts [1949] 2 KB 608 40
M. v Home Office [1994] 1 AC 377 .... 13, 27, 320, 327, 337, 343
Ex parte Napier (1852), 18 QB 692; 118 ER 261 200
Nixon v AG [1931] AC 184 64
O'Reilly v Mackman [1983] 2 AC 237 338
Pepper v Hart [1993] AC 593; [1993] 1 All ER 42 321
Pergau Dam case: see *R v Secretary of State for Foreign and Commonwealth Affairs, ex parte World Development Movement Ltd.*
R v Civil Service Appeal Board, ex parte Bruce [1988] 3 All ER 686, QBD; [1989] 2 All ER 907, CA 77
R v Criminal Injuries Compensation Board, ex parte Lain [1967] 2 QB 864 ... 335, 349
R v Criminal Injuries Compensation Board, ex parte P [1995] 1 All ER 869 (CA). 203
R v Department of Social Security ex parte Overdrive Credit Card Ltd [1991] STC 129. 329–30

R v Employment Secretary, ex parte Equal Opportunities Commission [1995] 1 AC 1. 249
R v Fisher [1903] AC 158 (Privy Council) 203–4
R v Gloucestershire County Council, ex parte Berry [1997] AC 584 203
R v Greater Birmingham Supplementary Benefits Appeal Tribunal, ex parte Simper [1974] QB 543 328
R v Inland Revenue Commissioners, ex parte Camacq Corporation [1989] STC 785 330
R v Inland Revenue Commissioners, ex parte Unilever plc [1996] STC 681 296
R v Lancashire County Council, ex parte Huddleston [1986] 2 All ER 941 336
R v Lord Chancellor, ex parte Witham [1997] 2 All ER 779 296
R v Lord Chancellor's Department, ex parte Nangle [1992] 1 All ER 897 .... 77, 392
R v Lords Commissioners of the Treasury (1872), L.R. 7 Q.B. 387 .... 200, 203, 328
R v Lords Commissioners of the Treasury, ex parte Hand (1836), 4 Ad. and El. 984, 111 ER 1053 280
R v Lords Commissioners of the Treasury, ex parte Smyth (1835), 4 Ad. and El. 285; 111 ER 794 200
R v Lords Commissioners of the Treasury, ex parte Walmsley (1861) 1 Best and Smith 31, 121 ER 644 200
R v Maguire [1992] QB 936 291
R v Secretary of State for the Environment, ex parte Brent London Borough Council [1982] QB 593 342
R v Secretary of State for the Environment, ex parte Greenwich London Borough Council [1989] COD 530 338
R v Secretary of State for Foreign Affairs, ex parte World Development Movement Ltd ('Pergau Dam') [1995] 1 WLR 386; [1995] 1 All ER 611 .... 35–6, 169, 172, 204, 330, 335
R v Secretary of State for the Home Department, ex parte Brind [1991] 1 AC 696. 342
R v Secretary of State for the Home Department, ex parte Fire Brigades Union [1995] 2 All ER 243 (HL); [1995] 1 All ER 887 (CA) 36, 204, 335
R v Secretary of State for the Home Department, ex parte Leech [1994] QB 198 ... 342
R v Secretary of State for the Home Department, ex parte Fayed [1997] 1 All ER 228. .... 296, 339–40
R v Secretary of State for the Home Department, ex parte Oladehinde [1991] 1 AC 254. 40
R v Secretary of State for Social Services, ex parte Cotton, The Times, 5 August and 14 December 1985 262
R v Secretary of State for Social Services, ex parte Lewisham, Lambeth and Southwark LBCs, The Times, 26 February 1980 (Divisional Court, Woolf J) 302
R v Secretary of State for Social Services, ex parte Sherwin, unreported 16 February 1996 (Divisional Court, Kennedy LJ, Latham J) 40
R v Secretary of State for Trade, ex parte Chris International Foods Ltd, unreported 4 March 1983 (Divisional Court, Hodgson J) 31
R v Secretary of State for Trade and Industry, ex parte Unison [1996] ICR 1003 281
R v Secretary of State for Transport, ex parte Pegasus Holdings (London) Ltd [1988] 1 WLR 990 342
R v Skinner [1968] 2 QB 700 40
R v Ward [1993] 1 WLR 619; [1993] 2 All ER 557 291

R v West London Supplementary Benefit Appeal Tribunal, ex parte Wyatt [1978] 1 WLR 240 328
In re T (a minor), House of Lords, 20 May 1998 203
Town Investments Ltd v Department of the Environment [1978] AC 359 ..... 13, 26–7

Other courts

Ahmed and others v The United Kingdom (European Court of Human Rights, 2 September 1998) 90, 392
Brasserie du Pecheur SA v Germany; R v Secretary of State for Transport, ex parte Factortame Ltd ('Factortame III'), joined Cases C-46/93 and C-48/93, [1996] ECR I-1029; [1996] All ER (EC) 301; [1996] CEC 295 (European Court of Justice, 5 March 1996) 319
Fisher v R (1901), 26 Victoria LR 781 (Supreme Court of Victoria) 204
Fisscher v Voorhuis Hengelo BV, Case C-128/93, [1994] ECR I-4583; [1995] ICR 635 (European Court of Justice, 28 September 1994) 319
Francovich v Italy, Cases C-6/90 and C-9/90, [1991] ECR I-5357; [1995] ICR 772 (European Court of Justice, 19 November 1991) 319
Marbury v Madison, 1 Cranch 137; 2 L. Ed. 60 (United States Supreme Court 1803) 19
R v Secretary of State for Transport, ex parte Factortame Ltd, Case C-221/89 [1991] ECR I-3905; [1992] QB 680 (European Court of Justice 25 July 1991) 343
Vroege v NCIV Instituut voor Volkshuisvesting BV, Case C-57/93, [1994] ECR I-4583; [1995] ICR 635 (European Court of Justice, 28 September 1994) 319

1
The Executive in the Constitution

I INTRODUCTION

This book is about the executive in the United Kingdom and its place in constitutional law. In it we investigate the central executive—the part of government that consists of ministers and civil servants organized in the great departments of state. We examine the structure of the executive, and the ways in which it co-ordinates and controls the actions of its component parts; and we try to explain the constitutional significance of what we find. We think that this is a rather unusual enterprise. The last book-length treatments of executive government by United Kingdom constitutional lawyers appeared—so far as we are aware—in the nineteen-thirties (Jennings [1936] 1959*a*; Keith 1938). The importance of the subject seems obvious, but its long-term neglect suggests that it would be wise to begin by spelling out its significance in constitutional terms. The reader who simply wants to know what the executive government is and how it regulates itself can turn at this point to Chapter 2 and those that follow it. The reader who wants to know why it is constitutionally important to know these things will, we hope, read on as we try to answer three questions.

First, why is analysis of the internal structure and co-ordination of the executive important to an understanding of our constitution?

Second, if it is important (and we shall obviously say it is), why has it been neglected for so long?

Third, how may such an analysis be related to a positive theory of our constitution? How can we sort out what is constitutionally significant about the executive from what is not?

Before we answer these questions, a further piece of specification may be useful. We naturally feel that the analysis we have to offer in this work should affect the way in which people think about the United Kingdom constitution. In particular, we want to influence the thinking of constitutional lawyers, and the book is therefore written in their language and uses concepts familiar to them such as democratic accountability and the rule of law. We do not attempt to analyse the executive's structure and co-ordinating activity in terms of any particular economic or social theory, but this does not mean that we accept the received theories of constitutional lawyers as adequate to the needs of intelligent constitutional discussion. In the course of this chapter, therefore, we both review such theories and attempt to show both how influential concepts such as the separation of powers are challenged by modern socio-economic theory, and how ideas drawn from such theory may enrich the analytical apparatus which constitutional lawyers might use.

Implicit in this approach is the view that the constitutional order is neither self-contained nor *sui generis*. The borderline between what is and is not a constitutional issue is not given *a priori* but has to be constructed and constantly adjusted by each society, whether explicitly (in societies which give themselves codified constitutions) or implicitly (as in our own case). As a corollary, we make no assumption that the questions which arise for determination within that border are different in nature from those arising outside it, and we therefore assume, at least *ex ante*, that the same types of analysis, drawn from general social and economic theory, are applicable in both areas. Most writing by constitutional lawyers in the United Kingdom appears to us to start from the opposite position, though there are important recent exceptions (e.g. Loughlin 1992).

II WHY IS THE EXECUTIVE IMPORTANT?

1 The executive in shadow

The executive governs us; it comprises the individuals—mostly ministers and civil servants—who actually control, from day to day, the state's instruments of coercion, wealth and information (Daintith 1997*a*). The idea that it might not be constitutionally important would seem too bizarre to mention, were it not for the fact that the literature of constitutional law is remarkably reticent on the subject. The standard texts go on at length about the *arcana* of royal prerogative and its relationship with statutory powers. They offer careful analysis of ministerial responsibility to Parliament. They even show interest in the rather 'political' subject of the relative influence of Prime Minister and Cabinet. Yet their treatment of the formal structure of government is perfunctory, even grudging: a few pages usually suffice to deal with the status and powers of ministers and departments, with a nod at the special position of Secretaries of State (e.g. Bradley and Ewing 1997: 298–305).

Reading these standard texts, one seems always only to glimpse the executive; to see it, in some sense, as the reflection of some other organ's concerns and functions. Departmental action is viewed through the prism of how ministers account to Parliament; executive action generally (including, in this case, the behaviour of local authorities as well as central government) is also observed through the distorting mirror of judicial review, with its parade of instances of bad and unlawful administration. Responding to judicial and parliamentary evaluation, within the confines of a collective responsibility likewise conceived in parliamentary terms, sometimes appears to be the very *work* of government, as opposed to the constitutional *discipline* to which that work must be subject. This, dominant, approach to United Kingdom constitutional law has been characterized as 'red light theory' (Harlow and Rawlings 1997), or as 'normativism', either 'liberal' or 'conservative' (Loughlin 1992). Its lack of interest in how government gets and maintains the means to govern renders it, in our view, a seriously incomplete account of our constitutional structure. Effective government is a highly problematical pursuit.

We certainly do not deny the over-riding importance of these parliamentary and judicial constraints. Indeed, we shall argue in this book that the way the executive works is being significantly changed by the shifting balance in the relative importance of these disciplines, and by the arrival of new constraints, like the law of the European Community, which now permeates almost every area of government. Unless, however, we look inside the executive, we cannot begin to understand how these traditional and new constraints really operate—or if indeed they work at all. Through proper analysis, we shall find that there is a close interdependence between such controls on the executive, which we will broadly describe as 'external', and the 'internal' controls which operate within it as part of the necessary processes of co-ordination and control entailed by its particular structure.

2 External controls and the compliance principle

One way of appreciating how this interdependence might function in practice is by taking a detour into a different field: the world of finance. Financial firms, from banks to commodities traders, have become subject to an increasingly complex mass of regulation, as their businesses have become larger, more multi-functional (what were banks are often now financial conglomerates), multi-national in their scope, instantaneous and continuous in their dealings, and exposed to significantly higher levels of client and own-account risk. An almost universal response to this phenomenon has been to underline the concern of management with regulatory compliance through the appointment of compliance officers within such firms. Their job is not just to check whether the firm is complying with the mass of national and transnational regulation to which it is subject, but much more important, to develop, install, and monitor structures and processes for everyday decision-making which minimize the risk of regulatory breach. The compliance officer, in other words, attempts to ensure that there exist effective internal controls. If he does his job, the firm will keep out of trouble with the official regulators; indeed, assuming that official regulation is economically rational, the conduct which ensures this may also operate to the firm's general commercial benefit, as by enhancing its reputation of reliability and honesty among investors.

A commitment to an effective system of internal control is not only a necessity if a firm is to thrive in highly regulated financial markets; it is also a pre-condition if a complex official system of regulation is to work. Modern financial regulation depends crucially on the reporting by financial operators of large amounts of information which can be quickly scrutinized for anomalies; on complaints; and on occasional inspection activities. Regulatory authorizations focus on entry to business, not on day-to-day transactions. Modern regulators, in other words, have no capacity to supervise the day-to-day behaviour of financial businesses. If therefore firms do not have appropriate control and business systems, official regulation will simply break down.

For 'financial firm', we can readily substitute 'executive government'. Parliament and the courts, in exercising their constitutional control functions, find themselves very much in the position of the modern financial regulator. With one important exception, in the field of expenditure audit (below, pp. 193–9), they have no capacity for continuous supervision. They rely on analogous mechanisms of large-scale information transmission, and on reactive response to complaints (whether political, administrative, or legal) and to anomalous events. Their scope for following up their interventions is strictly limited. In consequence, the effectiveness with which the values of democratic accountability and of legality are implemented in the British system depends in large measure upon the executive's being so organized and controlled as to achieve those ends. Without such organization and control, Parliament and the courts might say all the right things; indeed, by reason of the fact that there would be innumerable breaches of the relevant principles, they would be led to say them far more often than they presently do; but such utterances would not get translated effectively into corrective action and preventive re-design of systems of behaviour.

These characteristics, of financial enterprise and its regulation on the one hand, and political enterprise and its control on the other, may each be seen as an expression of a very general idea that different social sub-systems—such as law, finance, and government—operating autonomously and according to different principles, are incapable of controlling one another's operations. Control signals emitted by one system can only be acted upon by another once translated into its own operational codes, a process which may transform them out of all recognition (Teubner 1992; compare Dunsire 1978). One means of minimizing such distortion and enabling sub-systems to interact effectively is by means of 'structural coupling', that is, the creation within such sub-systems of mechanisms which in some way reproduce the operations of other sub-systems and are therefore capable of reflecting and responding to their messages. The compliance function within financial enterprises, and the control and co-ordination mechanisms within central government which are the subject of our study, may be seen as examples of such structural coupling.

This general lesson of systems theory, that effective constitutional control of government by the other 'powers'—legislative and judicial—of the State depends on the executive's own structure and internal controls, is largely ignored by constitutional law thinking, which has tended to approach issues of control in a partial and distorted way. Consider the debate about ministerial responsibility. There is ample evidence for the proposition that this particularly British manifestation of the idea of democratic accountability of government has, since the middle of the last century, been a powerful influence shaping both the organization of government and the way it copes with the increasing mass and complexity of business. It produced a government of departments identified by function and organized as multi-layered structures which emphasize vertical transmission of information and opinion, and offer greater sensitivity to the *political* dimensions of routine administration than to other qualities such as efficiency (Royal Commission on the Civil Service 1914: 82–3; Parris 1969: chs. III and IV). Constitutional lawyers, however, have tended to neglect this structural coupling between executive organization and the procedures of parliamentary accountability in favour of issues of blame and sanction for ministers, issues which are largely irrelevant to the control system. The contemporary crisis of ministerial responsibility has little to do with blame and sanction either, but may be seen as deriving from governmental attempts to break away, for reasons of efficiency and effectiveness, from the old structures and internal controls, without acknowledging the inconsistency of these moves with the traditional procedures and concepts which constitute the external, parliamentary control (see further below, pp. 44–5). In this area there is at least debate about the importance of internal structures, in which constitutional lawyers are beginning hesitantly to join (Freedland 1995; 1996); elsewhere, notably in regard to judicial control, effectiveness is something which lawyers seem to prefer not to think or talk about. A prophet occasionally cries in the wilderness (Harlow 1976; Richardson and Sunkin 1996), but others are too busy with doctrinal chatter to hear.

3 The plural executive

A key element of the compliance function in any complex organization is its capacity to ensure that decisions taken at the centre are in fact carried out across the organization. This most basic aspect of internal control cannot be taken for granted. In the United States context, Wilson and Rachel asked in 1977 how far public agencies could produce desired social effects when the end in view required that one government agency modify the behaviour of another. They thought that this was likely to be very difficult: so difficult, in fact, that they ended by suggesting that except in certain cases—where change was not seen as threatening agency autonomy, or where it could be backed by monopoly control of a necessary resource—it might be easier for public agencies to change the behaviour of private actors than that of other public agencies (Wilson and Rachal 1977).

Any constitutional lawyer in Britain who read these interesting reflections at the time might well have been inclined to put them aside as inapplicable to a country which, after all, had a unified executive, unencumbered (in 1977 if not now) with 'independent' executive agencies, and cemented together under an unchallenged leader by the convention of collective responsibility and the discipline, and common conviction, of party politics. To do so would have been a mistake. The fact is that the United Kingdom executive is more plural than unitary. This may seem an odd way to put the matter. It is necessary because law and convention speak with different voices on the issue. Indeed, law treats the executive as both plural (operationally) and unitary (conceptually). We explore these positions in detail in our next chapter. Here, the key point to emphasize is that our executive (while still conceived of as the unitary Crown) is made up of departments, and it is normally to the heads of these departments (who are usually but not invariably ministers), and not to the government as a whole, that powers, and resources, are allocated by law.

This feature of our constitution may, as we have said, be fleetingly noticed in the textbooks, but given that they are written by lawyers, its significance is curiously underplayed. Instead, the emphasis is placed on the political capacities of control and co-ordination possessed by Cabinet and Prime Minister (below, pp. 22–3, 51–7). It is, however, precisely this dispersion of legal powers which makes those capacities vital to orderly government. The legal powers of the government as a whole are confined to those—important but rather few—which are vested in 'Her Majesty in Council' or simply in 'Her Majesty' and which will be exercised on the advice of Prime Minister and (perhaps) Cabinet. The Prime Minister, acting as such, has no legal powers, though we should acknowledge that his conventional power over his government has the legal base of the Sovereign's rights to appoint and dismiss her own ministers, to summon and dissolve Parliament, and other such prerogatives, whose exercise he determines. A further support for this power is the portfolio he has held as Minister for the Civil Service since control was transferred away from the Treasury in 1968 (below, pp. 65–9). Other central capacities which have some legal support, such as control of the public revenue, reside in a department—in this case the Treasury (below, Chapters 4–6).

The distribution of most of a government's powers and functions among its component departments in this way, with little or no countervailing central legal power, is unusual in modern constitutional practice. The United States, with its independent regulatory agencies, might appear a much more plural administration than that of the United Kingdom; in fact, if we restrict our attention to the core executive, the United States government is among the most unitary, the constitution providing simply that 'the Executive Power shall be vested in a President of the United States of America' (Constitution, article II.1). Just how far this restricts legislative ordering of the structure of government is open to argument (compare Calabresi and Rhodes 1992 with Lessig and Sunstein 1994), but the President's legal power of direction of his Cabinet is not in issue. Elsewhere legislative attribution of functions to ministries, as in Italy, is balanced by giving the President of the Council of Ministers powers to direct the general policy of the government and to maintain the unity of its political and administrative approach (Constitution of Italy 1948, art. 95); or—as in France—the Prime Minister is given a general power of direction, in a constitutional framework which leaves the legal organization of government in its own hands (Constitution of 1958, arts. 21, 34, and 37). Only in Thailand have we come across a structure where executive power is, in strictly legal terms, more dispersed than in the United Kingdom (Bunnag 1992).

In making these comparisons we do not want to suggest that the shape of the formal law is the only factor determining the unity or plurality of the executive at the national level. What really matters, perhaps, as the determinant of the essentially plural and non-hierarchical nature of the United Kingdom executive, is the long-established fact of the distribution of the tools of government among the different departments, and the entrenched habit of their utilization on this basis. Law, especially when it emanates from Parliament (legislation) rather than from within the executive (prerogative Orders in Council), formalizes this situation, demands that changes to the distribution of functions are likewise formal and legal, and legitimates the specific interests of the department when they come into conflict with collective policy requirements.

The executive thus structured faces a chronic, and serious, problem of control of its component parts by the 'centre'. This adds a further dimension to the compliance problem already identified as a reason for looking within the executive. Legally speaking, what courts and Parliament seek to control is not a compact monolith, but a loosely structured conglomerate, with a number of co-ordinate *loci* of power and responsibility, the departments. Could democratic and legal control be effective if each such department's compliance arrangements, and responses to Parliament and courts, were entirely its own affair? Aside from the multiplication of efforts that this would involve, it would imply the avoidance of responsibility by government as a whole for the failings of one of its component parts, an outcome rejected by Parliament at least since the party system of government developed, if not earlier. If our constitution is to work, therefore, external control procedures need to be completed not just by appropriate compliance arrangements within each department, but by a system of co-ordination and control of those arrangements by the 'centre' of the executive itself.

Two examples, to be developed in detail later in this book, will show how the internal co-ordination of the executive is coupled—well or badly—with external controls.

First, legal advice (below, Chapters 7, 9). Most major departments have their own legal services. Smaller ones (and the defence departments) share the services of the Treasury Solicitor; but the Treasury Solicitor also does litigation for some (but not all) of the major departments too. There can be divergences between the advice given by legal services to their departments on similar matters. The Attorney-General, a minister, is legal adviser to the government as a whole; but whether he gets the opportunity to give advice depends on whether he is consulted by the relevant minister or ministers. Where is the obligation to consult defined and laid down? In the internal document, *The Ministerial Code* (Cabinet Office 1997*d*) (formerly *Questions of Procedure for Ministers*), which rests on the Prime Minister's conventional authority and whose contents were, until 1992, a state secret. Once given, the advice is confidential to the department which receives it. Indeed, because it is the minister and the department who are responsible for the decision to which the advice refers, the very fact of seeking the Attorney's advice is, by convention, not to be disclosed outside the executive, since to do so might dilute the minister's responsibility. These considerations are highly relevant to the operation of judicial review. They place obstacles in the way of forming and diffusing collective government views on administrative law issues, and they mean that any such views cannot be made publicly available other than through arguments presented within specific litigation, unless government makes a special decision to do so (as on Rhodesian sanctions, on aspects of the first Maastricht Treaty, on public interest immunity after the Matrix Churchill affair). Even within the litigation framework, the Treasury Solicitor's Department, which handles most of it, may find that different departmental clients maintain different views. Exceptionally, within the field of EU law, there is machinery for making collective or centralized decisions on legal advice. Doubtless this reflects the binding and non-appealable nature of decisions of the European Court of Justice; that is to say, it represents a response of the system to the demands of a new and powerful system of control. Structural modifications to the machinery of government legal advice, reflecting the growing power of the domestic judicial review system, have come more slowly, but as we shall see, are now occurring.

A second example is offered by public expenditure information (below, Chapter 5). Parliament has long relied on the Treasury to furnish consistent and useful information, especially within the framework of estimates procedure, through which it might exercise its function of granting supply. Thus the Treasury has presented the estimates of most of the civil departments since the mid-nineteenth century (revenue and defence came later). But the Treasury, in its pursuit of value for money, wants both to make departments take greater responsibility for their own efficiency by delegation of its financial controls, and to increase its own (and hence, it would argue, Parliament's) control over the economic efficiency of departmental policy and administration by introducing new formats for financial information and new principles of accounting and budgeting (based on resources and accruals, not cash). Very much a matter of management: but this process involves switching a lot of detailed information from the estimates (a Treasury responsibility) to annual departmental reports, designed by departments and presented by them to Parliament, albeit under Treasury supervision. House of Commons Select Committees, both general (the Treasury Committee and the Public Accounts Committee) and departmental, have been most exercised about this, because they fear that this relaxation of control within the executive will lead to variation of departmental practice, difficulty in linking estimates and reports, loss of objectivity, loss of information relevant to public audit, and so on.

Examples of this kind, in which there are strong reciprocal effects between low-visibility executive norms (who owns legal advice? who controls the content of expenditure information?) and the operation of traditional controls, are multiplied in the chapters that follow. The next question we should consider here is why the visibility of these executive norms should have remained so low.

III WHY IS THE EXECUTIVE NEGLECTED?

1 The political background

We have already suggested that the preoccupation with parliamentary and judicial controls as a subject of constitutional law, rather than with the activity and organization of government that is the subject of control, exemplifies the dominant tendency in constitutional law writing over the last hundred years in Britain. If we ask why writers in this tradition should view the executive much as Victorians viewed the mentally ill, as an object of restraint rather than of analysis, always at risk of 'running amok' (Wade and Forsyth 1994: 5), fear and mistrust may suggest themselves as an answer. The 'age of collectivism' was seen by Dicey as an age of danger, precisely because of the powers of social control accumulating to the executive (Dicey 1905). The consequences of this liberal suspicion of the developing welfare state have been projected, via the clarity and force of Dicey's legal analysis, into the core literature and attitudes of constitutional law, so that the essentially political shaping of its agenda is now all but invisible.

While it is the political and philosophical background of 'red light theory' which most clearly distinguishes it from alternative writings in constitutional law ('green light theory' or functionalism, as most notably represented by Laski, Jennings and Robson in the nineteen-thirties (Loughlin 1992)), the sublimation of the executive as a topic of analysis in that theory is not purely a matter of political dislike. A variety of features of long-established constitutional doctrine combine as deterrents to any lawyer tempted to look within the black box of the executive.

2 The separation of powers

The first of these is the doctrine of the separation of powers. The issue here is not that of the conformity of the United Kingdom constitution with the normative requirements of the doctrine. There are obvious difficulties in arguing that a constitution incorporating the principle of parliamentary government, in which the leadership of the majority party in the House of Commons directs the action of the executive, manifests such conformity. Only the judiciary's position in relation to other organs of government seems to approximate to those characteristics of independence, and of mutual constraint through checks and balances, that the doctrine demands. None the less, the influence of the doctrine on constitutional law thinking may be judged by the fact that even those who question its relevance to the United Kingdom often do so from the standpoint established by the doctrine itself: that is to say,

Montesquieu's idea that the primary classification of the organs of government in Britain could, as a matter of empirical observation, be made in accordance with the schema of executive, legislative and judicial functions (Montesquieu [1748] 1989: Book XI, ch. 6; cf. Vile 1967: ch. IV). What the critics call into question, whether with bold strokes (Marshall 1971: ch. V) or in fine detail (Bradley and Ewing 1997: ch. 5), is the nature of relations between the different organs of government; they do not challenge the broad characterization of functions nor the drawing of the key dividing lines between organs of government which results from it.

Even as no more than a crude labelling system for the organs of government, however, separation of powers is today called into question by new social theories such as public choice theory (Mueller 1989), which applies economic analysis to political action and is based on the premise that 'the basic motivational structure of the individual agent is viewed as constant across institutional settings, at least in the short term' (Brennan and Hamlin 1996: 607). In other words, people pursue their own self-interest, whether they are arms dealers or judges, civil servants or footballers, politicians or actors. The more sophisticated proponents of public choice do not deny that the self-interest of one who chooses public service may be differently structured from that of one who, say, goes into commerce, particularly in terms of the ordering of such goods as money, power, prestige, and the satisfactions of altruism. The theory does, however, warn, in our view rightly, against the assumption that institutional frameworks—such as those marked off by the separation of powers—necessarily either represent or produce distinctive behaviour or preferences in those who work within them. It asks us not to assume that civil servants and ministers are always hungry for power whereas judges are inspired only by disinterested concern for the rule of law.

The idea that 'perverse' motivations—such as the desire to obtain personal enrichment from office—might cut across the boundaries drawn by the separation of powers has to some extent been officially recognized in the shape of the Committee on Standards in Public Life, established in 1994. The Committee is concerned with the standards of conduct of all 'holders of public office'. It gave early consideration to questions of personal enrichment by Members of Parliament as well as by civil servants and ministers, and in the course of that inquiry promulgated a set of principles which apply indifferently across the public service (Committee on Standards in Public Life 1995: 14). Judges, however, apparently continue to enjoy an official presumption of possession of the virtues (such as honesty and integrity) urged on others by the Committee; its terms of reference define 'holders of public office' in a way which appears inappropriate to describe the judiciary.

Public choice theory, therefore, invites us, as a minimum, to avoid preconceptions about the impact of institutions, in other words to go behind the façade of the separation of powers and to examine, objectively, the characteristics of the organs labelled according to the traditional scheme. Constitutions, like economies, develop by division of labour. From specialization of tasks within the ruler's household, Western states have proceeded to erect some of those tasks into 'offices' of varying degrees of permanence and independence, and to develop particular kinds of institutions—councils, courts—to carry on others. The process of evolution did not stop in 1748 with the publication of Montesquieu's *L'Esprit des lois*, but continues vigorously today, as the spread to Europe of the device of the independent administrative agency vividly demonstrates (Prosser 1997; Cassese and Franchini 1996; Garcia Llovet 1993). Within that process, any stable pattern of specialization creates separations between agents and between functions, and implies a complex structure of dependency and autonomy. The control functions that interest us may be located anywhere in such a structure: they are not the monopoly of courts and legislatures.

While the trinity of executive, legislative, and judicial functions may be the most powerful rationalization of the specialization process that has yet been offered, it cannot by itself capture the overall significance of any given structure of government for constitutional values such as democracy or accountability. Nor does its application tell us much about individual institutions. To say that audit of public expenditure was a judicial function in the fourteenth century, an executive one in the eighteenth, and a legislative one in the twentieth, tells us little if anything about how, how well, and in whose interest, it was carried on. We should therefore resist the easy assumption that the allocations of powers and functions *within* each of the organizational blocs identified by separation of powers doctrine are less significant to the protection of constitutional values than are the relations *between* those blocs. Other possible systems for the diffusion and balancing of public power may well have equal practical importance (Mitchell 1964: 31–8; Griffith and Street 1952: 15–16). Devolution of governmental functions—to Scotland, Wales, to London—is an obvious current case. Functional allocations of power and resources within the national level of executive government are no less important.

3 The Crown

That constitutional lawyers think of the United Kingdom executive as quintessentially unitary must also be due, in significant measure, to the obfuscatory concept of 'the Crown', and to the power of its hold over the legal mind by reason of its very difficulty and obscurity. From the medieval arguments about the King's two bodies (Kantorowicz 1957) to those of the last hundred years as to what might, or might not, be an 'emanation of the Crown',[1] lawyers in the United Kingdom have wrestled with the problem of the legal personification of the government as a whole; and have generally been defeated. The arena for this struggle has been one common to many jurisdictions: the need to set borderlines capable of clearly identifying the composition and actions of the state and hence the circumstances in which the privileges appropriate to state action should apply in disputes about matters like property, contracts, and non-contractual liability. The difficulties of deploying, for this purpose, a medieval conceit with early modern embellishments (such as the notion of the Crown as 'corporation sole': Maitland 1900, 1901), seem to have blinded lawyers to the significance of the mode of legal ordering of the executive in modern times, with its tendency to assign legal rights and duties to specific members of the government, rather than to that government as a whole. Instead of seeing such assignments as a direct reflection of the changing political conception of the state—a conception evolving towards plurality as a guarantee of effective democratic accountability—they have construed them, until very recently, as a kind of puzzle or paradox, alien to the inherited conceptual apparatus of 'the Crown' yet somehow to be fitted into it (see *Town Investments v Department of the Environment* 1978; Harlow 1980; and compare *M v Home Office* 1994). The pluralist tendency does not eliminate the utility of a legal conception of 'the central government', of 'the state' or of the 'public' as a whole (Marshall 1971: ch. II), though there are hopeful signs that lawyers may now be ready to think about these concepts in the light of principle and reality rather than in the obscurity of Crown learning (Allison 1997). So doing, they may be better able to appreciate the full constitutional import of the rules articulating structure and powers within the executive.

4 The lack of 'real' law

Another reason for the impression of legal unity is the low visibility of the legal rules which allocate functions, powers, and resources within the executive. The rules are a mixture of common law, Orders in Council, and legislation (both statute and statutory instruments); but even those of the latter type, most familiar to lawyers generally, are seldom such as

[1] The term was apparently coined by Mr Justice Day in *Gilbert v Corporation of Trinity House* (1886: 801); for disapproving references to its vagueness, see *International Railway Co. v Niagara Power Commission* (1941) and Lord Justice Diplock in *British Broadcasting Corporation v Johns* (1965: 81–2).

to be the object of litigation and judicial enforcement. British legal scholars, steeped in the common law, regularly play down the significance of such 'imperfect' legal rules, neglecting the considerable weight that their legal status may none the less carry in intra-governmental argument and decision-making (Daintith 1988: 16–20). David, looking across the channel from France, even suggests that in traditional theory, 'the rule contained in the statute will only be finally accepted and fully incorporated into English law when it has been applied and interpreted by the courts', and that this perspective neglects a new body of statutory administrative or *public officers' law* (as opposed to *lawyers' law*) (David and Brierley 1985: 385–6: emphasis in original). Once one moves away from questions of the structure of the executive to consider its internal control, 'real' (judicially-enforceable) law fades even further from view. In the United Kingdom, unlike continental neighbours such as France (Wiener 1996) or Italy (Cassese 1996), the vehicle of expression of such central control seldom takes the form of formal law; the appearance of such formal rules may be a sign that an external discipline, such as requirements of European Community law, has come into play. Thus the EC requirement that for the sake of transparency, government departments pay VAT on some transactions with other government departments gave rise to the Value Added Tax Act 1994, s. 41, and to various implementing rules published—unusually—in the *London Gazette*, the nearest thing we have in the United Kingdom to an *Official Journal*. Most of our material, however, is in the shape of informal guidance, minutes, even letters. Seldom does it rise to the dignity of a Command Paper; often it is not published outside government; sometimes it is still secret.

Constitutional lawyers are unaccustomed to the handling of such material, an activity which one has described, with evident distaste, as 'rummaging about in the publications of government departments and parliamentary officers and committees' (Brazier 1992: 281). How do we find our way amidst this mass of paper when, by definition, we cannot rely on familiar rules of identification and classification of legal norms? when, indeed, even the normative nature of some of the material may be in doubt? To have confidence in dealing with such material one would need the assurance of a solid positive theory of the constitution: a theory, that is, of what the constitution is, as opposed to what it ought to be. Positive theory should tell us why particular political and governmental phenomena should attract the epithet 'constitutional'. We argue, and here we come to the third of our initial questions, that the dominant trends in positive constitutional theory in Britain do not support, indeed are sometimes hostile to, treatment of the internal control of the executive as a subject of constitutional scholarship.

IV POSITIVE CONSTITUTIONAL THEORY

I divide the world
into two main classes—
those who perpetually
divide
the world
into two main classes;
and those who don't.
I prefer
The latter.

(From C. Kent Wright's anthology, *Nectar in a Nutshell* (1944))

Despite this pithy warning, let us try to divide British constitutional writers into four main classes by reference to the positive theory they espouse. We shall call them, purely for ease of reference, foxes, hedgehogs, rude little boys, and Humpty Dumpties.

For most of the twentieth century, the dominant mode of writing by constitutional lawyers has been descriptive (Daintith 1991). The description mixes historical development, current or not-so-current practice, relevant legislative and other rules, and relevant judicial decisions, in an effort to convey to lawyers, in a vocabulary they can understand, what actually happens in the discharge of the relevant branch or function of government. While what happens (or might be expected to happen) is often expressed in the form of legal rules, the normative emphasis of the writing is weak. Changes are recorded as they occur, and new practice is absorbed into the account without a great deal of discussion of its compatibility with existing rules or principles. Where important changes occur and are not reversed, the constitution may be said to be changing, much as one might record a townscape as changing, as old buildings come down and new ones are built, roads are rerouted and public spaces rearranged. There is little sense of tension between what the constitution might require and what is actually done, of its functioning as an overarching structure of norms.

Such writing does not always clearly articulate its theoretical bases, but if we probe a little we may identify two alternative theories of the constitution which might explain it. We refer to their respective holders in terms of the fable of the fox and the hedgehog. The fox, it will be recalled, knew many things, but the hedgehog knew one big thing. Critics of these orthodoxies can likewise be conveniently referred to in terms of rhyme and fable.

1 The constitution as empirical record

Foxes propound a unique British understanding of constitutions. Elsewhere, the constitution is a fundamental and comprehensive normative statement of how the nation's government must be carried on: a collective affirmation and expression of political values, which is itself a source of guarantees that those values will be respected. By contrast, the people of the United Kingdom have never felt the need to set down the principles and structure of its government in a comprehensive and ordered way. Even at times of revolution, crisis, and radical change, a partial restatement—of what was changing or to be changed—is all that has been thought necessary. The United Kingdom 'constitution' is different not just in its patchwork appearance, but in its basic nature: not a set of fundamental norms of government, but an empirical record of how the country is in fact governed. It reflects, after the fact, the decisions we may take about changing our system of government, such as—to take a recent example—shifting power from democratic local authorities to technocratic 'quangos'; it does not, as do other constitutions, provide the normative framework in which such decisions must be taken. That framework has been provided, instead, by political values which are sufficiently deeply enracinated and broadly shared to be confidently applied—by legislators, judges, ministers—to issues as they arise without the artificial constraint of constitutional reference. Dicey's third sense of the rule of law, that the general principles of the constitution are 'the result of the judicial decisions determining the rights of private persons in particular cases brought before the courts' (Dicey 1959: 195), encapsulates this style of thinking (see also Bryce 1901: vol. I 145–254).

2 The constitution as one 'grand idea'

Constitutional hedgehogs have a different reason for treating the constitution as a structure of facts rather than of norms. They find, in the United Kingdom constitution, a key normative principle which, by its very nature, pre-empts the possibility of any other principles of equal status—or, for that matter, of any status superior to that of ordinary legislation. For most writers this is, of course, the principle of parliamentary sovereignty. On this view, since there is no legal check on Parliament's capacity to change by legislation any existing law or practice, propositions about, say, the 'constitutional' relations of central and local government (as in Elliott 1981*b*) can only be understood as being descriptive of existing practice and values, since they enjoy no greater protection against change than any other norm—as we have recently seen (Loughlin 1994). Indeed, it is argued by Grant that any other understanding admits the danger of 'an unhappy process of inductive reasoning in which description unconsciously becomes translated into norm, and in which constitutional "conventions" are invented to serve the political arguments of the day' (Grant 1989: 254).

A maverick among hedgehogs is John Griffith, who in 1963, to the confusion of students ploughing through their standard texts, coined the phrase 'if it works, it's constitutional' (Griffith 1963), and who in 1979 went on to proclaim (1979: 19) 'Everything that happens is constitutional. And if nothing were to happen, that would be constitutional also.' Though these appear as statements of an extreme descriptivist slant—even effectiveness has been abandoned as a test by 1979—they are in fact associated with a slightly less parsimonious account of a core normative structure for the constitution than that normally offered in the shape of parliamentary sovereignty. This account is unorthodox in placing the executive, not Parliament, at the centre of discussion. It treats as the 'heart' of the constitution the right of the government to take any action it thinks necessary for the proper government of the United Kingdom, subject to not infringing legal rights except so far as permitted by statute and prerogative, to the need for the legislative consent of Parliament for any change in the law and, perhaps also to be seen as part of this core, to compliance with applicable European Community law (Griffith 1979: 15). While the emphasis on executive initiative makes this a much more realistic representation of United Kingdom government than is evoked by parliamentary sovereignty, its author shares with Grant the aim of debunking any claims to discover constitutional norms outside the extremely skeletal structure he describes.

3 The constitution as fiction

In recent decades the dominance of these tendencies has waned under sustained attack. The first group of critics have been likened—by one of their number—to the little boy in the fairy tale who noticed that the emperor had no clothes on and, being unsophisticated, said so, to general embarrassment. These people react to both foxes and hedgehogs by saying that for the British to think their government is clothed in a constitution is pure self-deception. Some, like Ridley, argue that we have never had a 'real' constitution, that is, an act establishing or constituting our system of government, made by an authority outside and above the order it constitutes, having an authority superior to that of other laws, and being entrenched in some way against ordinary processes of legal change (Ridley 1988). The immense range of historical and contemporary national constitutional practice renders suspect, however, any such attempt to claim that a particular form of constitution is somehow more authentic than others (Wolf-Phillips 1972). An alternative formulation is to say that what the foxes describe did once have real normative force, of the kind claimed for the rule of law by Dicey, but that political and social change have now completely eroded it (Johnson 1977: ch. 3; Siedentop 1990). In both cases the suggestion is that we cannot today rely upon the constitutional—or better, non-constitutional—practice of the past; a new constitutional settlement is needed, which should be formal and explicit (cf. Institute for Public Policy Research 1993).

4 The constitution as a structure of values

A second critical tendency takes a step beyond the position of the rude little boys, asserting the existence, in and for the United Kingdom, of a constitution which is not merely descriptive in character. It may not meet the formal criteria advanced by Ridley, but it functions as a true system of obligations laid on public actors. It is to be discovered and defined through the delineation of a number of basic principles or values which, it is alleged, inhere in our constitution, and against which actual legal rules, or constitutional conventions or practice, are to be measured. These procedures present some of the problems which troubled Alice when she met Humpty Dumpty in *Alice through the Looking Glass* ('when *I* use a word, it means just what I choose it to mean'). Those who argue in this way rely on a number of different theoretical bases, such as collective consumption theory (McAuslan 1983), immanent critique (Harden and Lewis 1986), or a theory of the nature of law (Allan 1993). Their selection of values or principles, varying from one author to another, is inherently open to question (Daintith 1993). Chosen values, like 'open and accountable government' (Harden and Lewis 1986), or 'openness, fairness and impartiality' (McAuslan 1988), may not be precise enough to guide decision-making in practice or to test its legitimacy.

Despite these difficulties, it is clear that this is the only one of the four approaches so far described which might be capable both of accommodating norms of executive self-management as part of the constitution and of providing tests for distinguishing them from bureaucratic and political disciplines. Constitutional foxes and hedgehogs both believe that it is irrelevant or impossible, in the United Kingdom, to define a system of constitutional norms; rude little boys say that there exist no norms to be identified. To attempt this book would be pointless without the belief that norms generated within the executive might properly form part of the constitution. We think that the Humpty Dumpties are right to be convinced of the existence of a United Kingdom constitution which consists of a stable and effective set of norms, diverse both in form and in weight, and of much greater richness than the crude monoliths offered by traditional theory. In particular, we see no reason to follow the hedgehogs in denying the adjective 'constitutional' both to norms that are not wholly immune to modification by parliamentary legislation and to norms which may not be susceptible to third-party (especially judicial) enforcement.

On the first point, we remark, by way of example, that the structural constraints on legislative alteration of certain norms (such as the limits on what legislation Parliament may consider in the absence of a recommendation from the executive: below, pp. 108–9) are the equivalent of provisions which figure prominently in codified constitutions. A neglected task of constitutional lawyers in Britain is to identify those constraints and test their strength. On the second, we note that the possibility of third-party enforcement is not in general a pre-requisite either of the existence of a norm as such nor even of its effectiveness. This is readily recognized in constitutions, and in constitutional scholarship, outside the United Kingdom. True, the tide is now running in favour of enforcement through constitutional courts, but we should not forget how recently they have arrived on the scene in Europe (Cappelletti 1984), nor the fact that in the home of constitutional judicial review (*Marbury v Madison* (1803)), debate about the significance and effect of executive and legislative interpretation of their own—and each other's—constitutional competences is still very much alive (Alito *et al.* 1993). More generally, the idea of self-enforcing norms is now a commonplace in social science analyses of legal obligations (Telser 1980). There is nothing incongruous or utopian in arguing, as does Harden (1991), that Parliament's legislative authority might be subject to constitutional restriction, notwithstanding the inability of the courts to review legislation. (Whether it actually is so subject, and if so what the restrictions are, are trickier matters.)

V THE EXECUTIVE IN A RESOURCE-BASED THEORY OF THE CONSTITUTION

We therefore need to provide an account of co-ordination and control within the executive in terms of its constitutional significance, without falling into the trap of writing our own personal constitution for the United Kingdom. Unlike the Humpty Dumpties, we do not think that this task can be attempted through the identification of constitutional principles and values. Such principles and values are, of necessity, normative in nature. How can one say whether a given principle or value forms part of our *positive* constitution? One approach is to ask for some process of official declaration—by a Royal Commission, perhaps (Brazier 1992)—though even here the issue of acceptance is not straightforward. The Nolan Committee's 'Seven Principles of Public Life'—selflessness, integrity, objectivity, accountability, openness, honesty, leadership—represent a ringing declaration, but are they 'official'? Neither the House of Commons nor the government referred to them in its responses to the report (Oliver 1995). Pending such a definitive declaration, the question whether a principle or value has been received as a norm of that constitution must be a matter for empirical enquiry. In a country lacking a codified constitution, such an enquiry raises questions of extraordinary difficulty, notably as to the criteria of reception that should be viewed as sufficient. If the criteria are formal (if, for example, we say that a single legislative reference suffices to import a principle), then this approach may be indistinguishable from one of pure description. If the criteria are substantive (a certain period of acceptance? a certain degree of popular consent? etc.), the constitutional explorer finds herself forced to provide further justifications for their selection, as well as evidentiary rules, in what can easily become an infinite regression of argument.

We do not intend, by raising these objections, to question the essential place of values in constitutional discourse. We would expect constitutional lawyers to be energetic proponents of the protection of human rights and of democracy, of openness and fairness in government, even—why not?—of efficiency and effectiveness in government; to argue about the extent to which existing legal and other rules reflect such values; and to seek change when the rules fail to do so. All this, however, is the discourse of critique and reform, and our objection is only to reliance on values and principles to underpin a *positive* theory of the constitution, a theory of what it is as opposed to what it ought to be. Our preferred approach, therefore, is to address ourselves directly to the task of finding empirical evidence of constitutional rules. In the sphere of the executive, as we have already indicated, such rules may as often be informal, or based on established practice, as formal. Our assumption will be that in the absence of discernible conflicts with rules of superior status (which is not necessarily a simple concept in the United Kingdom legal order), or of inconsistency with rules and practices of similar weight, these rules do in fact form a coherent ensemble which represents a part of the United Kingdom constitution. Subject therefore to the acceptance of general principles relating to the hierarchy of legal sources, this is a strictly inductive approach; we make no assumptions as to the existence or operation of general principles, though we expect to find many such principles made manifest in the rules and practices we examine. Broadly speaking, therefore, we view our task as expository of the constitution in an area hitherto little studied, and leave to others the task of suggesting improvements or reforms in the light of preferred principles or values.

Even this limited enterprise, restricted to the elucidation of the positive constitution in this area, cannot go forward in a satisfactory way unless it is grounded on some coherent positive theory. This is not just a matter of intellectual coherence; a positive theory is also imperative as a guide to determining whether particular rules or practices are of constitutional significance or not. *Our approach to this issue is grounded in the conception of the state as an associative enterprise for the control of a territory in the interests of the security and well-being of its people, and of the constitution of the state as a set of rules for obtaining, allocating, and deploying the resources it requires for this purpose.* States are, of course, not the only forms of associative enterprise, nor, in our view, are they innately supreme as forms of such enterprise. Such paramountcy as they enjoy is due to the fundamental nature of the services they perform, notably in providing the conditions of material and economic security, and to the monopoly in the use (or threat of use) of physical force that this provision entails. Today, however, it is clear (as perhaps it was not fifty or a hundred years ago) that this paramountcy is under threat from a variety of sources. The increasing powers and range of functions possessed by the international and regional economic organizations like the European Union or the World Trade Organization; the power obtained by private financial operators, individually or collectively, through the creation of means for the instantaneous worldwide transmission of both information and wealth; and the acceptance of global standards of conduct in many areas such as pollution and human rights, are but a few of these (Sassen 1996; Strange 1996).

While the idea of the state as one among many forms of social enterprise has considerable value as a corrective to claims of an exclusive legitimacy in the exercise of power, and has contributed productively to economic theories of constitutional development, its particular importance for us is the emphasis it gives to two facts: first, that the state, like all other enterprises, requires resources in order to fulfil its (self-appointed) tasks (Montemartini 1900; Auster and Silver 1979); and second, that without stable rules determining how those resources are to be obtained, allocated, and deployed, it is unlikely to enjoy much success or to develop very far (North 1981; North and Weingast 1989; McGuire and Olsen 1996). We have developed in some detail elsewhere the notion that the powers of the state derive from its possession of the means to exercise force, of wealth, and of means of information and persuasion, along with the idea that these resources are independent of any particular system of law (Daintith 1997*a*).

The resources are in other words *pre-constitutional*; they will be found in every state, whether despotic or democratic, and it is the manner in which they are organized by the constitution which will determine the state's political characteristics. It follows that our resource-based definition of a constitution is in no way prescriptive of its content, and admits totalitarian constitutions alongside liberal ones, autocratic constitutions alongside democratic ones. Such characteristics are a function of the constitution's rules about the obtaining and deployment of resources. A constitution will be seen as autocratic and oppressive if it permits the acquisition of state wealth through taxation without popular consent, democratic (in this respect at least) if it insists for this purpose on authorization by an elected legislature. A constitution will be seen to place a different value on free speech and assembly according to whether it envisages the application of state force to protect them, or merely forbids its application to restrict them, or indeed envisages or mandates such restrictive application.

Stable rules for the control and management of the executive's resources thus constitute the object of our inquiry. This definition may look more all-inclusive than it really is, so a little further elaboration may be excusable.

'Stable rules', as discussion earlier will have hinted, are not in our view limited to formal legal rules. 'Constitutional conventions' are included: or at least, such of them as can be described, in the formulations of Wheare (1953: 10) and Jennings (1959*b*: ch. III), as being followed out of a sense of obligation, as opposed to representing mere usage or working practice. Some of the rules we describe in this book may indeed look very different from the examples of constitutional conventions commonly given; but though the inner regulation of the government's public expenditure system doubtless lacks both the glamour and the grandeur of the rules (if rules they be) governing the selection of a Prime Minister in a hung Parliament, it may arguably possess greater influence on the democratic control of governmental policy choices.

On the other hand, not everything in the ordinary books of constitutional law, nor everything that is important, or perhaps even crucial, to the way a particular government works, can be brought within the rubric of 'stable rules'. The most notable exception is perhaps the day-to-day working of the Cabinet system, a source of endless fascination for political scientists and—with less obvious justification—for constitutional lawyers too. People bring a variety of concerns to the study of the way the Cabinet system works and the relative power and influence of its participants: some want to make broad characterizations of the British 'system of government' in terms of its 'Prime Ministerial' or 'Cabinet' character (Mackintosh 1962; Crossman 1972); some want to expose specific bits of bad practice to inspection and thereby to improve modes of government decision-making (Foster and Plowden 1996: chs. 10, 11; Foster 1997). In either case the material with which they grapple has little normative content; it is about the way a particular administration—which really means a particular Prime Minister—sets out to tackle the job of co-ordinating the work of government. Some Prime Ministers, like Mr Blair (1997–) may make much of their intentions in this respect, some little; most, not excluding Mrs Thatcher (1979–90), find that the practices they install do not necessarily produce the results they anticipated (Mount 1992; James 1994; Jones 1992). In themselves, these constantly shifting styles of work of Cabinet and Prime Minister—what papers circulate, what committees meet, what Cabinet gets to consider or decide—fall clearly on the non-constitutional side of the line Ferdinand Mount draws between the proper concerns of the constitutionalist, and the organization of the executive: 'making government work better' (Mount 1992: 156). We do not discuss them. Our topic is rather the structure of lasting rules and institutions within which these co-ordination styles are exercised. Those lasting rules of course evolve, both through deliberate change to accommodate the way a particular administration wants to go about its work, and through the solidification of practice accepted over time in sets of precedents, of which what is now called the *Ministerial Code* is the pre-eminent example (Cabinet Office 1997*d*: Lee 1986). In this way the working practices (and the working mistakes) of one generation in government may shape the constitutional environment of the next.

In a comprehensive discussion of the constitution it would be important to analyse its basis in the deployment and control of resources from first principles, demonstrating, for example, how long-standing and still fundamental constitutional rules developed as responses to resource-related issues. Examples would be the attempt at democratic control of executive maintenance of the means of exercising force, through the requirement of annual legislative approval of maintenance of a standing army (Bill of Rights 1689), or the early assertion of parliamentary control over taxation as a means of supplementing established sources of royal wealth (ibid.). But since we are not trying to write constitutional history, and aim to concentrate on the executive's management of its resources *within the framework of 'external' constitutional controls*, we propose to adopt a more synthetic approach in which we focus on resources in the terms on which they are today accessible to the executive. It is, for example, a well-established principle that the executive cannot coerce its subjects, save in highly exceptional circumstances of extreme necessity (*Case of Proclamations* 1611; *Burmah Oil Co. (Burma Trading) Ltd v Lord Advocate* 1964), without the authority of parliamentary legislation. In practical terms, therefore, and under our specific constitution as it exists today, law, rather than force, is the resource to which the executive must get access. While starting from resources as the raw material of the United Kingdom's constitutional organization, we therefore assume, in laying out the general plan of our discussion, the institutions through which those resources are obtained. Chapter 2 thus addresses the allocation of resources in the most general terms, by considering the rules, both internal and external to the executive, that discipline its organizational structure. We then go on to consider successively the *personnel* of the executive (Chapter 3), its use of *funds* (Chapters 4–6), its *legal institutions* (Chapter 7), and their activities in *law-making* (Chapter 8) and in *legal advice and interpretation* (Chapters 9–10). Such a tripartite division (people, money, laws) has also been used for the analysis of substantive policies of government, which may at different times and under different circumstances find it easier to deploy one kind of resource than another, or may regularly employ them in complex combinations (Rose 1982; Hood 1983).

In conducting our own analysis we shall naturally make reference to the basic constitutional rules—such as legislative consent both to taxation and appropriation of public funds—which condition the whole action of the executive; but our aim is not to discuss those rules for their own sake, but for the way in which they support or constrain the executive's internal organization and regulation of its actions. We shall also notice (Chapter 11) that the executive may adopt systems of internal control—such as the Citizen's Charter programme and the Code of Open Government—which cut right across the use of different kinds of resources, and which may be seen as possibly complementing, possibly substituting for, related external controls traditionally operated by Parliament and the courts.

Throughout our discussion, we shall be looking for evidence (or refutation) of the characteristics of the executive and its internal ordering which seem to be of particular significance to the United Kingdom constitution. We have already signalled the importance which may attach to the plural character of the central executive (above, pp. 6–9), its articulation as a series of co-ordinate functional authorities. We address the way this characteristic affects control of different resources, and how it is affected in its turn by the changes to departmental structures and functions engendered by the 'new public management' in the form of executive agencies and contracting out of tasks. Likewise, we have noted the apparent informality and low legal visibility of the executive's internal ordering processes (above, pp. 13–14); we shall see if these persist amid the 'legalizing' environments of the European Union and of judicial review. A third theme, identified in our opening pages (above, pp. 3–5), is of the possible interdependence between the internal controls which are our subject and the more familiar external controls by courts and Parliament. How extensive is that interdependence? how symmetrical? Do the judicial power and the legislative power stand in the same relationship to the executive in this respect? These are the key issues to which we shall return in our conclusions in Chapter 12.

2
The Executive in Constitutional Law

I INTRODUCTION

Arriving at a satisfactory understanding of the internal control function within executive government requires an analysis of the legal structure and status of the executive branch under the constitution. The purpose of this chapter is to provide that analysis. An immediate difficulty we face is that the term 'the executive' is 'barely known to the law' (*Town Investments Ltd v Department of Environment* 1978: at 398, per Lord Simon of Glaisdale), which has continued to use the language of Queen and Crown to signify an executive which has been transformed almost out of all recognition since the seventeenth and eighteenth centuries. The executive, Maitland famously observed, is not 'a legal organization. Of course I do not mean it is an illegal organization; rather I should prefer to say it is an extra-legal organization: the law does not condemn it, but it does not recognize it—knows nothing about it' (1908: 387). The explanation for the law's failure to recognize 'what we are apt to consider an organ of the state second only in importance to Parliament' (Maitland 1908: 388) lies in the fact that, as we indicated in the previous chapter, the functions of modern government have been laid not on the executive as a whole but on 'a heterogeneous collection of ministers, officers, and authorities exercising a mass of apparently unrelated miscellaneous functions' (Jennings 1959*a*: 90). It is with these various authorities therefore that we are mainly concerned in this chapter. In the main part of the chapter we concentrate on what traditionally has been the most prominent of these authorities—the ministerial department. We then look at the changes which have been wrought in the internal organization of departments over the last decade or so as a result of the restructuring of parts of departments as Next Steps or executive agencies and the contracting out of departmental functions to private contractors; before examining in the final section of the chapter the 'extra-legal organization of cabinet and ministry' through which the 'requisite harmony' in executive action is meant to be secured (Maitland 1908: 417). We begin, however, with the Crown.

II THE CROWN

The term 'the Crown' is used in a variety of senses. In its narrowest meaning it refers to 'a piece of jewelled headgear under guard at the Tower of London' (*Town Investments Ltd v Department of Environment* 1978: at 397, per Lord Simon of Glaisdale); in its broadest it is as close as the constitution comes to a notion of the state; indeed the failure to develop a theory of the state is commonly attributed to the existence of the concept of the Crown (Dyson 1980: 37–42). In between these extremes it may refer to the monarch personally, the Queen or King for the time being, or to the executive itself (*M v Home Office* 1994: at 395, per Lord Templeman). In the *Town Investments* case, Lord Diplock suggested that it would be better, 'instead of speaking of "the Crown", to speak of "the government"—a term appropriate to embrace both *collectively and individually* all of the ministers of the Crown and parliamentary secretaries under whose direction the administrative work of government is carried on by the civil servants in the various government departments' (1978: at 381, emphasis added); but the notion of the Crown as executive continues to find favour alongside that of the Crown as monarch (e.g. *M v Home Office* 1994).

The Crown is often said to be 'one and indivisible'. The legal significance of this doctrine, however, is far from clear; for nearly all purposes the idea is said to be 'thoroughly misleading' (Hogg 1989: 10). Certainly, it is impossible to reconcile with legal ordering of the executive branch, which as we have observed vests functions in departments and other authorities rather than the executive as whole. On occasion the courts have been prepared to lift the corporate veil and treat the executive as a unity (e.g. *Town Investments Ltd v Department of Environment* 1978), but across much of what it does the executive is indisputably plural rather than unitary. In a system in which the pull towards 'severalness' (below, pp. 60–1) exerts a persistent influence, however, we should not underestimate the Crown's significance as a source of unity, as well as continuity and stability. One of the most obvious expressions of its significance in this regard is the fact that the business of government is carried on in its name by ministers and civil servants who are all servants of the Crown. The Crown's significance as a source of unity and continuity may be as much psychological as practical, but it does not follow that it is unimportant. The civil service, for example, is said to regard loyalty to the Crown as 'a great deal more than a mere shibboleth' (Mount 1992: 107).

Of more tangible significance for our purposes is the fact that the Crown is also the source of the executive's prerogative powers, i.e. the powers unique to the executive which the courts recognize it as possessing for the purpose of carrying on the business of government.[1] These include the creation of new offices and the regulation of the civil service, powers of continuing significance in the internal organization and control of the executive branch. The modern executive, Chester points out, derived immense practical advantage from its inheritance of these powers. In particular, it was relieved of the need to obtain them from Parliament in the form of legislation, which in the case of the right to declare war, for example, 'would almost certainly have been difficult to draft and controversial in passage' (1981: 82). It is of course open to Parliament to restrict the prerogative. But given that it is dominated by the executive it is unlikely to do so, except at the executive's initiative, and as a general rule statutes do not expressly supersede the prerogative, there being little obvious incentive for the executive to limit its capacities in this way. Thus the powers conferred by the Ministers of the Crown Act 1975 are without prejudice to 'any power exercisable by virtue of the prerogative power of the Crown in relation to the functions of Ministers of the Crown' (s. 5(5)).

III THE MINISTERIAL DEPARTMENT

> It is now certain, for better or for worse, that the Haldane Committee were correct in their tacit assumption that the departments exist in their own right as elements in the constitution.
>
> (Mackenzie 1957: 88)

The ministerial department is the 'effective unit of government' (Bridges 1966: 117). As we have remarked, a legal analysis of the internal ordering of the executive branch reveals the executive power as fragmented among a number of different kinds of authority. Among these authorities ministerial departments stand out by reason of the extent of the powers, prerogative as well as statutory, legislative as well as administrative, to which they have access, and their power to institute and defend legal proceedings. The ministerial department came to the fore during the middle years of the nineteenth century when it replaced the board of public officials as the preferred form of executive organization (Willson 1955; Parris 1969: ch. III). (The replacement of boards by departments was not reflected in constitutional usage which continued to describe

[1] Some commentators define the prerogative more broadly to include all the executive's non-statutory powers. Dicey, for example, defined the prerogative as 'the residue of discretionary or arbitrary authority, which at any given time is legally left in the hands of the Crown' (1959: 424). Contrast Blackstone: 'the word prerogative can only be applied to those rights and capacities which the king enjoys alone, in contradistinction to others, and not to those which he enjoys in common with any of his subjects' (1783: 239).

departments as boards—e.g. the Local Government Board created in 1871 or the Board of Education formed in 1899.) The department superseded the board for the simple reason that it enabled power to be concentrated in the ministerial head of the department who could in turn be held responsible for the exercise of that power to Parliament. It was therefore thought to offer the best prospect of ensuring the responsiveness of the administration to parliamentary and public opinion. The essence of the idea of individual ministerial responsibility on which the department was founded, Willson explains, was the

> happy conjunction of its two main features, the concentration of administrative power and therefore of responsibility in one person and the presence of that person in Parliament. Parliament can see in the persons of some of its Members the embodiment of administrative authority. The ministers can be attacked, questioned, advised, warned or entreated with all the warm intimacy which is only possible in personal contact and which is diluted if not destroyed by the abstraction of a collegiate authority. (Willson 1955: 54–5)

Once this idea had been accepted in practice, the ministerial department quickly supplanted the board as the preferred form of executive organization. 'We are so far from thinking that the importance of a service to the community is prima facie a reason for making those who administer it immune from ordinary Parliamentary criticism', the Haldane Committee warned, 'that we feel that all such proposals should be most carefully scrutinised, and that there should be no omission, in the case of any particular service, of those safeguards *which Ministerial responsibility to Parliament alone provides*' (Ministry of Reconstruction 1918: Pt I, para. 33, emphasis added).

1 The principle of departmental autonomy

The significance of departments within the machinery of government stems principally from the practice of vesting functions in them, more precisely in their ministerial heads, rather than the executive as a whole. 'In the British constitution, government is ministerial government. Powers and duties are laid on ministers, not on the prime minister' (Jones 1987: 64). We may contrast the Scotland Act 1998, establishing the devolved Scottish executive and Parliament, under which functions are for the most part vested in the executive as a whole rather than individual ministers. By the time the need arose to supplement the prerogative powers, Chester explains, it was generally accepted that the king acted on the advice of his ministers and that a particular minister was responsible for advice in a particular field. It was more 'open and direct', therefore, and more in keeping with the increasing emphasis on individual ministerial responsibility for new powers and duties to be conferred, not on the king, but on the minister who would have to administer them and to take public responsibility for their performance (1981: 93–4). While some important functions are vested in 'Her Majesty in Council' or simply in 'Her Majesty' (such as the appointment of the Governor and Directors of the Bank of England: Bank of England Act 1998, section 1(2)), the vast majority are vested in departments. Across most of what it does, therefore, the executive is plural rather than unitary.

The fact that functions are vested directly in departments rather than the executive as a whole is important to an understanding of the way in which the executive works. Also important is the fact that it is rare for ministers to be subject to any higher authority in the exercise of the functions entrusted to them. 'Theoretically, the responsibility of each individual minister for the policy pursued in his own department rests upon him alone. No other minister—not even the Prime Minister—has any legal power to override him' (Anderson 1946: 148). 'It is the Secretary of State who is the power in the land. Cabinets and Prime Ministers can only encourage or discourage him in his course; they cannot instruct. This may sound like a formal distinction. It is, in practice a very real one when a department wants to dig its heels in' (Mount 1992: 149). Were ministers to be routinely subject to a higher authority in the exercise of their functions it would obviously cut across the idea that they were responsible for their exercise to Parliament. Again, there are or have been exceptions. When departments were established by statute (below, pp. 32–3), it was normal practice to give the Treasury control over the number of their staff and their remuneration (e.g. Ministers of the Crown Act 1964, Sched. 1; Woods 1956: 119), but as we shall see, few existing ministerial departments have been so established. Such provisions are rather more common, of course, in relation to non-ministerial departments such as OFTEL or OFWAT (Telecommunications Act 1984, s. 1(5); Water Industry Act 1991, Sched. 1, para. 2).

The upshot is that departments enjoy a greater degree of autonomy within the executive branch than is commonly acknowledged by the constitutional textbooks, by reason of the fact that their functions are vested directly in them and they are as a general rule subject to no higher authority in the exercise of those functions. That autonomy has been reinforced by the courts, which have insisted in accordance with the underlying theory of ministerial responsibility that it is for each department and each department alone to exercise the functions entrusted to it, so that their exercise at the direction of another department, or their delegation to another department without authorization, is liable to be struck down as unlawful. In the *Lavender* case, a decision by the Ministry of Housing and Local Government to dismiss an appeal against the refusal of an application for planning permission to which the Ministry of Agriculture, Fisheries and Food was opposed was successfully challenged on the ground that the decision was in fact that of the Minister of Agriculture and not, as was required by the statute, that of the Minister of Housing and Local Government. (*H. Lavender v Minister of Housing and Local Government* 1970; *R v Secretary of State for Trade, ex parte Chris International Foods Ltd* 1983; for comment on the latter case, see Scott 1996: C1.122–31; see too Cabinet Office 1997*d*: para. 42). It is therefore for the individual department on which functions are conferred and no one else to exercise those functions.

Departmental autonomy within the executive branch also derives support from the underlying principle of individual ministerial responsibility. We are familiar with the use of the principle as a shield against outside intervention in the running of the department on the argument that such intervention would be incompatible with the responsibility of the minister to Parliament. The appointment of a Parliamentary Ombudsman to investigate complaints of maladministration, for example, was initially opposed on the grounds that it would not be possible to reconcile with the principle of ministerial responsibility to Parliament and could seriously interfere with the prompt and efficient dispatch of public business. More recently, it was claimed that ministers must retain responsibility for making and terminating public appointments 'in order to retain accountability to Parliament' (Committee on Standards in Public Life 1995: para. 4.26). It is not difficult to envisage the same argument being used internally to resist control from other parts of the executive. One reason why the appointment of ministerial 'overlords' has not been a success in British government is because of the uncertainties over control and accountability to which they have given rise (Chester and Willson 1968: 313–14; Jennings 1959*a*: 80–1; below, p. 55). Intended to ensure the democratic accountability of the administration, the doctrine of individual ministerial responsibility thus also 'helps to sustain departmental autonomy' (Burch and Holliday 1996: 52).

This does not mean that there are no mechanisms by which tensions between the individual responsibilities of ministers and the collective interest of government may be resolved (below, pp. 51–7). It does mean, however, that departments occupy an exceptionally powerful position within the executive branch, one which as we shall see is further buttressed by the fact that as well as being individually responsible to Parliament their ministerial heads are also members of the central executive authority, the Cabinet (below, pp. 51–4).

2 The establishment of departments

Some departments owe their existence to the prerogative, others to statute. The oldest departments such as the Treasury and the Home Office are 'expressions of the royal prerogative'; the legal authority for their existence derives from 'the constitutional usage of an earlier age when all executive power resided in the King' (Robson 1950: 90). The period of the statutory creation of departments, from the middle years of the nineteenth century to the nineteen-sixties, coincided with the major period of growth in the functions of modern government. The modern Departments of Health, Social Security, Education and Employment, Agriculture, Fisheries and Food, and Environment, Transport and the Regions, for example, all trace their origins to statute. When after the Second World War powers were first taken to transfer functions between departments by ministerial order it was anticipated that new departments would continue to be established by statute (418 HC Debs., col. 458, Herbert Morrison, 25 January 1946). Practice since the nineteen-sixties, however, has favoured creating an additional Secretary of State—an exercise of the prerogative—and transferring the requisite functions to the new Secretary of State by statutory transfer of function order made under what is now the Ministers of the Crown Act 1975 (e.g. Secretary of State for Environment, Transport and the Regions Order 1997; for the Ministers of the Crown Act, see below, pp. 36–7). The last ministerial departments created by statute were the Ministries of Land and Natural Resources, Overseas Development, and Technology, which were created by the Ministers of the Crown Act 1964. None of these still exists as an independent department: the Ministry of Land and Natural Resources was dissolved in 1967 and its functions 'returned' to the Ministry of Housing and Local Government and the Welsh Office; while the Ministries of Overseas Development and Technology were absorbed into the Foreign and Commonwealth Office and the Department of Trade and Industry respectively in 1970 (since when the Ministry of Overseas Development has been twice re-created, most recently as the Department for International Development). At the same time as creating a new department it is common to incorporate the Secretary of State, usually in the form of a corporation sole, so that the department can hold property, enter into contracts, and sue and be sued in its own name and not that of the Crown.

Two reasons may be identified for this shift from statute to the prerogative as the basis of executive organization. The practical one is that it economizes on the need for legislation, including transfer of functions orders under the Ministers of the Crown Act in so far as functions are vested in 'the Secretary of State', as has increasingly become the case (Simcock 1992: 548–9) rather than a named minister. In law the office of Secretary of State is treated as one and indivisible, with the consequence that each Secretary of State is capable of exercising any of the functions of the departments that make up the office (other than functions conferred on a named Secretary of State). *Harrison v Bush* 1855 and *Agee v Secretary of State for Scotland* 1977 are commonly cited as authority for this proposition, but it was in fact decided by Parliament (Simcock: 544–7). Once functions are vested in the Secretary of State therefore, by statute or transfer of functions order, there is no need to further transfer functions between the different ministers holding the office. The human reason is that it appealed to the vanity of ministers who preferred to be Secretaries of State rather than common or garden ministers; it also served to distinguish them from 'Ministers of State' who had by the nineteen-sixties become much more common. The abruptness and scale of the change may be gauged from the Ministerial and other Salaries Act 1972, which increased from nine to 19 the maximum number of Secretaries of State to whom salaries could be paid. Two ministerial titles were retained—those of Minister of Agriculture, Fisheries and Food, and President of the Board of Trade—both for reasons connected with the holding of property overseas. There was an element of irony therefore in Michael Heseltine's decision to revive the 'more old fashioned, if grandiose' title of 'President of the Board of Trade' (Crick 1997: 380), in place of the modern 'Secretary of State for Trade and Industry', as a way, presumably, of distinguishing himself from the by now common herd of Secretaries of State.

The establishment of departments in the exercise of the prerogative was described to us as 'a major expansion in the modern use of the prerogative'. If we assume that Parliament is more interested in functions than machinery, probably not too much significance ought to be attached to this reassertion of the older theory of governmental power as inherent in the executive. In contrast to their statutory predecessors the new prerogative departments are the product of the reallocation of existing functions rather than the assumption of new ones. Nevertheless it is illustrative of a preference on the part of the modern executive for relying on its inherent powers wherever possible, one which we will find replicated in other contexts (see below, pp. 39–40).

3 Departmental powers

Departments' powers are not confined to those conferred on ministers by legislation. The theory is that ministers are creatures of the prerogative not statute, even though there have been statutes authorizing, and in at least one case requiring (Ministry of Pensions Act 1916, s. 1), their appointment; who may, 'as agents of the Crown, exercise any of the powers which the Crown has power to exercise (which are generally those of an ordinary person), except so far as they are precluded from doing so by statute' (Treasury 1989*a*: para. 2.2.1). The principle is that 'the Crown—and Ministers of the Crown as its agents—can do anything an ordinary person can do provided that there is no statute to the contrary and Parliament has voted the money' (Office of Public Service 1996*a*: Annex C4, para. 16). Unlike statutory bodies therefore ministers' powers are not confined to those conferred on them by statute. When departments were established by statute it was the practice to include in the 'machinery' Act a 'fanfare' provision indicating the general scope of a minister's duties, but this was not intended to imply that any action taken outside the terms of the provision was necessarily *ultra vires*.

> The doctrine of *ultra vires* may apply to a Minister who exceeds his statutory powers or acts without powers in such a way as to injure a citizen in respect of his property or person. It does not apply where no such injury is committed, even if the particular act is not within the scope of the minister's functions as laid down by statute. (Robson 1950: 9; for an example of a fanfare section, see the Ministry of Health Act 1919, s. 2)

Nor were such provisions intended to be judicially enforceable (Crown Proceedings Act 1947, s. 2(2)).

A minister's common law capacities, supplemented by the prerogative, however, can only take a department so far. The Glorious Revolution brought to an end the use of the prerogative to raise taxes or to change the law (*Case of Proclamations* 1611, Bill of Rights 1689, art. 4). Taxation is the particular concern of the Treasury. Spending departments, for their part, have had recourse to parliamentary legislation for two main purposes—to change the law, including to empower them to do things they would otherwise be legally unable to do, and to obtain statutory authority for continuing expenditure. The latter purpose derives not from any legal obligation—the annual Appropriation Act provides legal authority for voted expenditure (Treasury 1989*a*: para. 2.2.6)—but from a 1932 Concordat between the Treasury and the Public Accounts Committee of the House of Commons in which it was agreed that as a matter of constitutional propriety rather than strict legality, terms whose interpretation and context we examine below (pp. 170–6), continuing expenditure should be based on statutorily defined powers and duties rather than solely on the authorization of the annual Appropriation Act, even though the latter is sufficient to satisfy the constitutional requirement of parliamentary authorization for spending. While such legislation provides specific statutory authority for continuing expenditure in the sense of defining the powers and duties in the exercise of which it is incurred, it does not provide the money, 'which must be, and can only be, given year by year by means of the Supply Estimates and the confirming Appropriation Act' (Treasury 1989*a*: para. 2.2.5).

Given that there is no necessity for legislation in this latter category—that it is a matter of constitutional propriety rather than strict legality—its legal significance is an interesting question. Take it away and a department would not be acting unlawfully; but is the same true if a department misinterprets or otherwise fails to observe the limits the legislation purports to impose? Does the impulse to legislation in other words matter, or is it the fact of legislation that is decisive? Although there have been at least two decided cases with a bearing on this question, we are not aware that it has been discussed. The following propositions, however, seem sustainable:

1. Where there is permanent statutory authority for expenditure, the power to incur expenditure subject only to the authority of the Appropriation Act is by analogy with the *De Keyser's Royal Hotel* case (*Attorney-General v De Keyser's Royal Hotel Ltd* 1920) extinguished. To hold otherwise would be to render the legislation devoid of purpose. What matters is not why the government asked Parliament to legislate: what matters is that Parliament did so. The *Pergau Dam* case (*R v Secretary of State for Foreign and Commonwealth Affairs, ex parte World Development Movement Ltd* 1995) may be read as confirmation of this. In that case the Divisional Court held the provision of financial assistance to a dam and hydro-electric power station in Malaysia *ultra vires* the Overseas Development and Co-operation Act 1980. The question of the relationship between the legislation and the Department's power to incur expenditure subject only to the authority of the Appropriation Act does not appear to have been raised or discussed.

2. The limits imposed by such legislation can, however, be temporarily overridden by means of the annual Appropriation Act, applying the principle *lex posterior derogat priori*. This is the view on which the Treasury has proceeded (Treasury 1989*a*: Annex 2.1, para. 3), and faced with a conflict between permanent spending legislation and a subsequent Appropriation Act there seems little question that the courts would be bound to give effect to the latter.

3. If the legislation is repealed, rather than amended, the power to incur expenditure subject only to the authority of the Appropriation Act revives.

While it would seem therefore that it is competent to Parliament in effect to extend powers specifically limited by statute by means of the Appropriation Act, 'constitutional propriety' is also said to require that such extensions should be regularized at the earliest possible date by amending legislation, unless they are of 'a purely emergency or non-continuing character' (Treasury 1989*a*: Annex 2.1, para. 3). The Treasury's expectation is therefore that amending legislation should be brought forward rather than that extensions should continue to be overridden by means of the Appropriation Act (Treasury 1989*a*: paras. 2.2.8 and 2.2.10).

The crucial question is of course who can enforce the limits imposed by permanent spending legislation. Before the *Pergau Dam* case, it was assumed, without necessarily having been discussed (above, p. 34), that the limits were administratively rather than judicially enforceable, a matter for the Treasury and the Public Accounts Committee of the House of Commons rather than the courts. The *Pergau Dam* case showed that assumption to be false. It is a measure of the latitude afforded modern government by the extent of the statutory powers vested in it that it was nevertheless able to uncover good statutory authority elsewhere for much of the expenditure (Comptroller and Auditor General 1995: and below, pp. 204–5). At the same time, however, we may wonder whether, when the costs in increased exposure to judicial review are added to those in legislative time, the effects of judicial intervention in cases like *Pergau Dam* and the *Fire Brigades Union*, will not be to weaken the executive's commitment to the statutory definition of departmental spending powers. As yet there is little indication of this happening. The *de minimis* threshold below which permanent authority for recurrent expenditure is not required has been raised, but the Treasury's commitment to the Concordat appears essentially unchanged (cf. Harden, White and Hollingsworth 1996: 664 n. 14). Were the rigour with which observance of the Concordat is insisted on internally to diminish, the result would be a further lessening in Parliament's role in defining the structure and functions of the executive branch.

4 The Ministers of the Crown Act

The vesting of functions in departments rather than the executive as a whole creates a need for machinery to authorize the transfer of functions between departments consequent upon changes in the machinery of government. Were functions not to be transferred, their exercise by a person other than the person on whom they were originally conferred, save where that person is a Secretary of State and they are being transferred to another Secretary of State, would be liable to be struck down by the courts as unlawful (above, pp. 30–1). Before the Ministers of the Crown (Transfer of Functions) Act 1946, the only generally available means by which functions could be transferred was primary legislation. That Act, which was the product of the need to reorganize the machinery of government along peacetime lines, made provision for the transfer of functions between offices and departments by order subject to negative resolution procedure, giving the executive the same flexibility, it was said, in relation to the transfer of statutory powers as it enjoyed in relation to the transfer of prerogative powers (Chester and Willson 1968: 335; but see below, pp. 64–5). The Act also made provision for the dissolution of departments by order subject to affirmative resolution procedure (ss. 1(1) (b), 5(1)), but not for the establishment of new departments, which it was anticipated would continue to be effected by primary legislation (above, p. 32). The Act was amended in 1964 and 1974 before being consolidated by the Ministers of the Crown Act 1975. As we have seen, the revival of the device of the Secretary of State has reduced the need to resort to the Act for the purpose of the transfer of functions.

IV HOLLOWING OUT THE DEPARTMENT

1 Next Steps agencies

Next Steps or executive agencies are the most significant development to have taken place in the machinery of government this century. They are a product of the Ibbs Report (Efficiency Unit 1988), a scrutiny by the Efficiency Unit commissioned by the Prime Minister in 1986 to assess the progress of management reforms in the Civil Service since the launch of the Financial Management Initiative four years earlier aimed at improving the allocation, management, and control of resources throughout central government (Cabinet Office 1982: paras. 13–16, Appendix 3) (below, pp. 124–5). The scrutiny was asked to identify the remaining obstacles to better management and efficiency, and to report to the Prime Minister on what further measures should be taken (Efficiency Unit 1988: Annex C). It found that some progress had been made—principally as a result of manpower cuts and the introduction of budgeting systems—but that substantial obstacles to further progress remained. Not enough attention was paid to the delivery of services, as opposed to policy and ministerial support, even though 95 per cent of civil servants worked in service delivery or executive functions; there was a shortage of management skills and of experience of working in service delivery functions among senior civil servants; there was too much emphasis on spending money, and not enough on getting results—outputs were neglected; and the Civil Service was managed as a single organization, with common rules for financial management and personnel management, despite its size (it employed 600,000 people) and the diversity of its activities (Efficiency Unit 1988: Annex B). The scrutiny argued that greater priority needed to be given in the organization of government to the effective delivery of services, to which end it recommended that 'agencies' should be established to carry out the executive functions of government within a policy and resources framework set by departments (Efficiency Unit 1988: paras. 17, 19).

In February 1988, after a 'lengthy written concordat' had been negotiated between the Treasury and the Prime Minister's Office over the implications of reform for the control of public expenditure (Lawson 1993: 392; Burch and Holliday 1996: 229; and below, pp. 132–4), the Prime Minister announced that the Government had accepted the scrutiny's main recommendations, and decided that, to the greatest extent practicable, the executive functions of government, as distinct from policy advice, should be carried out by agencies 'generally within the civil service'. Each agency would be headed by a chief executive who would have delegated responsibility for day-to-day matters within a framework of policy objectives and resources set by the responsible Minister, in consultation with the Treasury (127 HC Debs., col. 114, Margaret Thatcher, 18 February 1988).

Shortly after the initiative was launched it was estimated that within a decade around three quarters of the civil service would be working in agencies rather than departments. This target was reached in 1997. In September 1998, nearly 377,500 civil servants, 76% of the total, were working in 138 agencies and four departments operating 'on Next Steps lines'.[2] The agencies range in size from the Social Security Benefits Agency (over 66,000 staff) to Wilton Park (35 staff), with responsibilities as diverse as weather forecasting, managing prisons, issuing driving licences, issuing passports, and providing support services to the armed forces. The four departments which operate on Next Steps lines are HM Customs and Excise, the Inland Revenue, the Crown Prosecution Service, and the Serious Fraud Office. A further 19 organizations have been identified as candidates for agency status; and 11 former agencies have been privatized (Next Steps Briefing Note: September 1998).

With the target for the percentage of civil servants working under Next Steps arrangements achieved, the Labour Government announced in March 1998 a switch in emphasis from the creation of agencies to performance. The emphasis on agency creation during the initial phase of the initiative, it argued, had overshadowed the need for continuous

[2] Where departments 'operate on Next Steps lines', the work of the department is carried out by a number of individual offices, each of which has agreed a 'framework document' (below) setting out the statutory, policy, and resources framework within which it operates and its relationship with the rest of the department.

improvement in the delivery of services. The agency creation phase of the initiative would therefore be ended and a new phase launched with the emphasis on performance. A small number of agencies would continue to be created, but the primary focus would be on improving the quality, efficiency and convenience to users of agency services (308 HC Debs., cols. *272–3*, written answers 12 March 1998).

1.1 Status of agencies

Significant though agencies are, they do not detract from the legal primacy of the department in the organization of government. A handful of agencies, including the Treasury Solicitor's Department, National Savings, and the Public Record Office, are departments in their own right (for a full list, see Cabinet Office (Office of Public Service) 1998*a*: Introduction). What these agencies have in common is that they are non-ministerial departments, i.e. their functions are vested in a single office-holder or board rather than as is more common a minister. Most agencies, however, are administrative arrangements within departments rather than separate legal entities; the functions they exercise remain vested in their sponsor departments rather than directly in them. Agencies differ in these respects from (executive) non-departmental public bodies, an earlier alternative to the departmental form of organization, which are legally separate from departments and which exercise functions vested directly in them (below, pp. 49–50).

1.2 Mode of establishment

As it concerned administrative arrangements within departments, the establishment of agencies was not considered to require legislation. Ibbs seemingly favoured 'a change in the British constitution, by law if necessary, to quash the fiction that ministers can be genuinely responsible for *everything* done by officials in their name' (Hennessy 1990: 620, original emphasis). In its published version, the report itself was somewhat less forthright, recommending that consideration should be given to the enactment of legislation where, as would generally be the case, it was necessary to change the arrangements for formal accountability for operations currently carried out within departments (Efficiency Unit 1988: para. 23, Annex A). In legal terms, divesting ministers of operational responsibility for the work of agencies would have required the formal reallocation of these responsibilities. As we have seen, the vesting of functions in ministers is both a consequence and a cause of ministerial responsibility: it is because ministers can be held responsible that functions are vested in them; it is because functions are vested in them that they are held responsible. The Government, however, set its face against any changes in accountability for the work of agencies, the Prime Minister emphasizing that 'Ministers will continue to account to Parliament for all the work of their Departments, including the agencies' (127 HC Debs., col. 1151, Margaret Thatcher, 18 February 1988) and proceeded on the theory, by then also applied as we have seen to the establishment of departments, that the internal organization of departments was a matter for the executive itself and not therefore something which required legislation. As we shall see in later chapters, Parliament's involvement in other aspects of public service reforms such as the Citizen's Charter or the Code of Practice on Access to Government Information has been equally limited (below, pp. 350–1, 368).

The theory that the internal organization of departments is a matter for the executive itself, i.e. for ministers, finds judicial support in a line of cases in which the courts have refused to strike down decisions on the basis that they were taken not personally by the ministers to whom they were entrusted but by officials in their departments. Public business could not be carried on, Lord Greene MR pointed out in the first of these cases, *Carltona Ltd v Commissioners of Works,* if ministerial functions were not normally exercised under the authority of ministers by responsible officials in departments. Constitutionally, the decision of an official was the decision of the relevant minister for which he was responsible to Parliament. Ministers' responsibility to Parliament gave them an incentive to ensure that important duties were entrusted to experienced officials. If they failed to do so, Parliament, rather than the courts, was the place 'where complaint must be made against them' (*Carltona Ltd v Commissioners of Works* 1943: 563; *Lewisham MB and Town Clerk v Roberts* 1949; *R v Skinner* 1968; *R v Secretary of State for the Home Department, ex parte Oladehinde* 1991; for Scotland, see *HM Advocate v Copeland* 1988).

Some commentators have doubted whether the *Carltona* principle—that it is not unlawful for officials to exercise functions conferred on ministers—is sufficient to support the establishment of agencies. Freedland questions whether the exercise of discretion has not been devolved so far into 'a separate decision-making complex' that the principle can no longer protect its exercise against the non-delegation rule, i.e. the rule against the delegation of powers without express or implied statutory sanction (Freedland 1996: 30). The courts, however, have shown little inclination to become involved in questions of the internal organization and management of departments (*R v Secretary of State for Social Services, ex parte Sherwin* 1996). This is in seeming contrast to the diligence with which they have policed the allocation of functions within the executive as a whole (see e.g. *Lavender and Son Ltd v MHLG* 1970 above, pp. 30–1); both stances, however, are equally consistent with giving effect to the intention of Parliament. Were *Carltona* to be overturned, or its ambit restricted, legislation would then become necessary.

Although the Conservative Government did not seek legislative approval for the establishment of agencies, it did maintain a dialogue with the House of Commons Treasury and Civil Service Committee and, following its establishment, the Public Service Committee over civil service management reform, mindful no doubt of the additional leverage which parliamentary approval in the form of select committee endorsement offered it in negotiations with individual departments and might offer in possible argument before the courts.

1.3 Relationship with sponsor departments

1.3.1 'Strategic management'

Agencies are essentially about increasing 'the capacity of ministers to control the work of civil servants where it most matters, in the setting of policy guidelines and standards of performance' (Jones and Burnham 1995: 178). What is commonly termed the 'strategic management' of agencies embraces responsibility for the policy framework within which each agency operates, for determining its strategic objectives, for setting its annual key financial and performance targets, and for monitoring its performance against those targets (Office of Public Service 1996*a*: Section B, para. 2). Thus the Secretary of State for Social Security allocates resources to the Social Security Benefits Agency and sets the annual targets which it is expected to achieve; he agrees the Agency's standards of service, its strategies and objectives, and its annual Business Plan (Department of Social Security Benefits Agency 1995). The Lord Chancellor allocates resources to the Court Service and approves its corporate and business plans, including its key targets (Court Service 1995); and the Home Secretary allocates resources to the Passport Agency and is responsible for determining policy in relation to the Agency, agreeing its corporate and business plans, and its performance targets (United Kingdom Passport Agency 1996).

1.3.2 Framework documents

The relationship between an agency and its sponsor department is governed by a 'framework document', which defines the aims and objectives of the agency and the division of responsibilities between it and the department, and sets the principles of its management, accountability, measures of performance, and resources and personnel regime (Efficiency Unit 1991: para. 2.3). An agency's framework document is agreed by the agency itself, its sponsor department, the Next Steps Team in the Cabinet Office, and the Treasury. Although a framework document has been likened by an agency chief executive to 'a bill of rights' for his agency (Treasury and Civil Service Committee 1994*a*: para. 157), framework documents have no formal legal status. One consequence of the fact that they are not legally binding is that agencies lack any guarantees of their autonomy in the shape of restrictions on the controls exercisable over them by departments akin to those enjoyed by executive non-departmental public bodies or indeed departments themselves.

As its description indicates, an agency's framework document provides no more than a framework. The detail which is lacking is provided by the agency's corporate and business plans. The corporate plan sets out the agency's main strategies, objectives, and projected resource requirements for the medium term, usually the three following years. It is up-dated annually. The business plan sets out more specific objectives, targets, performance measures, and financial plans for the forthcoming financial year. Both documents are prepared by the agency chief executive for approval by the minister (Office of Public Service 1996*a*: Section D, paras. 4–5).

1.3.3 Targets

Targets are a 'key aspect' of the relationship between departments and agencies. A consortium project set up to develop guidelines on best practice in the strategic management of agencies described targets as 'a major driver of performance—what-gets-measured-is-what-gets-done—and therefore setting the right set of targets is of critical importance to the overall strategy of the agency and its contribution to departmental objectives' (Next Steps Team 1995*a*: Appendix 4, p. 68). Four types of target are employed: volume of output targets, also referred to as throughput targets, which are suitable for only certain types of agency; quality of service targets; financial performance targets; and efficiency targets (Treasury 1992*c*: paras. 6, 8, and 24). The consortium project identified six 'good practice principles' applicable to the design of targets:

focus—key targets should be few in number—four to seven—to ensure the right degree of focus from managers;

balance—targets should form a balanced package to cover dimensions of output, time, quality, and cost. They need to cover the breadth of an organization's activities, to avoid resources being re-directed towards areas where performance can be easily measured, and away from areas where measurement is more difficult (Cabinet Office 1994*a*: para. 3.8);

clarity—targets should be simple and precise: each definition should be explicit leaving no room for argument. A lack of clarity can suit what the consortium project described as 'success conspiracies', which arise where neither departments nor agencies want agencies to be seen to be failing to achieve their key targets (Next Steps Team 1995*a*: p. 82);

results—targets should be measures of output rather than input. They should be concerned with what is achieved with resources, not with measuring those resources;

strategic perspective—the priorities / objectives set out in the organization's long-term strategic plans should be used to set targets; and

relevance—targets should be set at an appropriate degree of detail for managers' needs (Next Steps Team 1995*a*: Appendix 4; 1995*b*: ch. 5).

The consortium project identified a further set of principles applicable to the setting (as opposed to the design) of targets:

stretch—targets should be stretching but achievable and fair. Some respondents to the consortium project pointed out that the expectation, common to both central and sponsor departments, that agencies should meet all their targets inevitably affects what targets are set. Both agencies and departments seek to establish 'safe' targets, as it is in neither of their interests for targets not to be met (Next Steps Team 1995*a*: p. 70);

stakeholder interests—the interests of all stakeholders should be considered in setting and reviewing targets;*optimum levels*—a view should be taken of the optimum value for targets. Targets should not necessarily be tightened year-on-year, as the optimal level may have been reached and increasing the target may involve disproportionate cost;

objectivity—to overcome any lack of independence and objectivity in target setting, targets should be scrutinized by a ministerial advisory board with non-executive members and stakeholder representatives;

comparisons—in seeking to set stretching targets, comparisons should be made with other organizations seen as good performers;

practicality and cost effectiveness—targets should not be chosen which cannot be assessed practically and cost effectively; and

continuity—there needs to be an element of comparability over time (Next Steps Team 1995*a*: Appendix 4; 1995*b*: ch. 5).

The one 'overriding feature' of target setting was that targets should be simple and published widely. The emphasis should be on getting the right set of targets and then using them effectively. Practical approaches which provide the right amount of meaningful information should always be preferred to complex review and measurement (Next Steps Team 1995*b*: p. 39).

1.3.4 Agency chief executives

Agency chief executives have delegated responsibility for the day-to-day operations of agencies within the policy and resources framework set by departments. In some framework documents the minister's approval of the corporate or business plan is described as the source of the chief executive's authority. The Secretary of State's approval of the Benefits Agency's business plan, for example, is said to constitute authority for the chief executive to conduct the operations of the agency accordingly (Department of Social Security Benefits Agency 1995), while the Lord Chancellor's approval of the Court Service's corporate plan is said to provide formal authority for the chief executive to act in accordance with the plan (Court Service 1995). In others the framework document itself is described as the source of authority: 'the chief executive may, within his or her delegated authorities under this document make such changes to the organisation as he or she considers necessary to maintain and improve the operating efficiency and overall performance of the agency' (Valuation Office Agency 1995: para. 3.5). In yet others the chief executive's authority appears to derive from both sources: the Scottish Prison Service's framework document constitutes the 'main authority' for the chief executive to conduct the operations of the Service (Scottish Prison Service 1993: para. 1.4), while approval of its business plan constitutes 'the authority' for the chief executive to conduct its operations and forms the basis against which its performance will be judged (Scottish Prison Service 1993: para. 6.4). But however the source is defined, the *Agency Chief Executive's Handbook* adds the crucial gloss that 'the use of the word "delegated" is in the everyday management sense, not implying a formal delegation of power or a change to the framework within which Ministers account to Parliament' (Office of Public Service 1996*a*: Section B, Introduction).

The strategic approach to agency management implies that having settled the policy and resources framework within which an agency is to operate and the targets it is to achieve the minister should then leave the achievement of those targets to the chief executive—he or she should adopt a hands-off approach and not intervene in matters of day-to-day concern. Ibbs saw the operational independence of chief executives as crucial to the success of Next Steps:

> . . . once the policy objectives and budgets within the framework are set, the management of the agency should then have as much independence as possible in deciding how those objectives are met. . . . The presumption must be that, provided management is operating within the strategic direction set by Ministers, it must be left as free as possible within that framework. (Efficiency Unit 1988: para. 21; Efficiency Unit 1991: para. 2.11)

Framework documents acknowledge the importance of agencies' operational independence. Thus the Secretary of State for Social Security, it is said, does not normally become involved in the day-to-day management of the Contributions Agency (Department of Social Security Contributions Agency 1994: para. 2.2); the Secretary of State for Scotland does not normally intervene in the day-to-day management of Historic Scotland (Historic Scotland 1994: para. 2.3); and the Home Secretary does not normally become involved in the day-to-day management of the Passport Agency (United Kingdom Passport Agency 1996: para. 4.1.1). These documents do not, however, exclude the possibility of ministerial intervention. Nor indeed could they so long as functions remain vested in ministers. The ministerial foreword to the 1997 Next Steps Report is unequivocal: 'Management responsibilities are delegated to Chief Executives in accordance with the terms of their framework documents, but Ministers retain the right to look at, to question and, if necessary, intervene in the operation of their agencies if public or Parliamentary concerns require this. The revolution achieved by Next Steps should be a managerial and not a constitutional one' (Cabinet Office (Office of Public Service) 1998*a*: Foreword).

The risk is of course that ministers will be led through parliamentary or other pressures to intervene, to the possible detriment of purposes for which agencies have been established. Short of a willingness to accept that the responsibility of ministers for the work of agencies should be limited, however, it is difficult to see how this risk can be avoided. Proposals for reform have been put forward, but MPs no less than Ministers remain insistent that the establishment of agencies should involve no reduction in the responsibility of ministers to Parliament. The Ministerial Code provides that 'Ministers have a duty to Parliament to account, and be held to account, for the policies, decisions, and actions of their Departments and Next Steps Agencies' (Cabinet Office 1997*d*: para. 1. ii); since when the Labour Government has declared one of its key objectives as being to dispel the confusion that had been allowed to grow up about the extent of ministers' accountability for the work of their agencies. Management delegations are to be maintained in order to deliver the benefits of the Next Steps approach, but ministers are to demonstrate by their close interest in performance that the creation of agencies does not affect ministerial accountability to Parliament (Cabinet Office (Office of Public Service) 1998*a*: Foreword). So long as it continues to be insisted that accountability can only be secured through holding ministers responsible, the vulnerability of agencies to ministerial intervention will remain.

1.4 Agency reviews

It is government policy that agencies should be periodically reviewed, normally after five years; the first of the Conservative Government's Civil Service White Papers announced an increase in the period between reviews—from three to five years, with the aim of providing a more stable framework in which departments and agencies would be able to plan ahead to improve performance (Cabinet Office 1994*a*: para. 3.22). A review comprises three elements: an evaluation of the arrangements under which the agency operates as set out in the framework document and of the agency's performance; a re-examination of the 'prior options', i.e. the options of abolition, privatization, and contracting out that were (in theory) considered before the agency was created, which may or may not lead to a decision in favour of retaining agency status; and, assuming that ministers agree that agency status remains appropriate, a revision of the framework document to reflect the agency's agreed objectives and managerial arrangements and any increased flexibilities. As at launch, the decision on the future status of the agency has to be agreed by the Cabinet Office and the Treasury (Office of Public Service 1996*a*: Annex F1, para. 26).

2 Contracting out

Government has always procured services through contract (Turpin 1972). In its Competing for Quality initiative, launched in November 1991, however, the Conservative Government sought a significant increase in the volume and range of public services exposed to competition as a means of improving public services and value for money (Treasury 1991*b*). The range of services subject to 'market testing' was to be extended beyond ancillary support services such as catering and cleaning to areas such as legal services 'closer to the heart of government' (Treasury 1991*b*: para. 12). Departments were at first required to set annual targets for areas of activity to be market tested (Treasury 1991*b*: p. 8). Subsequently, however, they were given greater freedom to tailor the use made of market testing and contracting out to their own circumstances (Cabinet Office 1994*a*: paras. 3.2–3.3; Efficiency and Effectiveness Group 1995). An Efficiency Unit scrutiny of the implementation of the initiative carried out in 1995 found that without a central 'kick start' the desired step change in the level of competition would not have been achieved, but that outcomes could have been significantly improved had the centre and departments adopted a more 'strategic and flexible' approach to agreeing targets (Efficiency Unit 1996: para. 5.3). It reported that the greater freedom given to departments by the efficiency planning framework was universally welcomed (Efficiency Unit 1996: paras. 5.60–5.61; see further below, pp. 188–90).

In November 1997, the new Labour Government announced twelve 'Guiding Principles' for use by departments when considering market testing and contracting out of their services. Under the principles, which are grounded in 'pragmatism not dogmatism', market testing and contracting out are to be used where they offer 'better value for money', which is defined as 'better quality services at optimal cost'. Existing plans for market testing and contracting out were therefore expected to proceed unless ministers were satisfied that, in the particular circumstances of an individual case, better value for money could be achieved by other means, which would enable a department to live within its running costs ceilings. This judgement was to be based on a robust and objective comparison of the particular market test or contracting out exercise and the alternative means available (300 HC Debs., cols. *94–5,* written answers 4 November 1997; see, too, Efficiency Unit 1998*a* and *b*).

2.1 The Deregulation and Contracting Out Act

In contrast to the setting up of Next Steps agencies, the contracting out of *statutory* functions has required the legislative sanction of Parliament. (The contracting out of non-statutory functions does not require Parliamentary approval because the functions have not been conferred by Parliament.) This is because the *Carltona* principle is confined to the exercise of functions on behalf of ministers by *civil servants,* leaving the contracting out of statutory functions to private contractors vulnerable to being struck down by the courts as an unlawful delegation of power. In its second report on the Citizen's Charter, the Government revealed that some activities had had to be withdrawn from the current Competing for Quality programme because of statutory obstacles to contracting them out (Cabinet Office 1994*b*: p. 95).

Part II of the Deregulation and Contracting Out Act 1994 empowers a minister to specify by order statutory functions as eligible for contracting out. The effect of an order is not to contract out the functions specified but to permit them to be carried out by a contractor authorized by the relevant minister or office holder (s. 69(2)). The definition of an office holder includes the holders of offices created or continued in existence by Act of Parliament and the holders of offices whose salaries are paid out of money provided by Parliament (s. 79(1)). Before an order specifying the functions of an office holder as eligible for contracting out is made, the office holder must be consulted (s. 69(3)). Orders are subject to affirmative resolution procedure (s. 77(2)). Parliament's approval in the form of a resolution of both Houses must therefore be obtained before a function may be contracted out.

The Act does not give the executive *carte blanche* to contract out statutory functions. Excluded from the scope of the order-making power are a number of constitutionally sensitive functions:

> those the exercise of which would constitute the exercise of jurisdiction of any court or tribunal which exercises the 'judicial power of the State';
>
> those the exercise or failure to exercise which would necessarily interfere with or otherwise affect the liberty of the individual;
>
> powers or rights of entry, search or seizure; and
>
> powers or duties to make subordinate legislation. (s. 71(1))

'The implication of these exceptions', the Cabinet Secretary suggested to a House of Lords inquiry into the public service, 'is that there are certain functions (judicial, law-making, interference with liberty and entry or seizure of property), where overall accountability for the function without actually carrying it out is not enough, and it would be unsatisfactory for the Minister, local authority or office-holder to arrange for people who are not public servants to act on their behalf' (House of Lords Select Committee on the Public Service 1998: para. 233). Also excluded from the scope of the power, in recognition of the 'constitutional separation' of Parliament and the executive, are the functions of the Comptroller and Auditor General, the Parliamentary Ombudsman, and the Health Service Ombudsman (s. 79(1)). Nor, in deference to the expressed intention of Parliament, may functions that require to be exercised by a minister or office holder personally be contracted out under the Act (s. 69(1)).

The Act is facilitative. It removes obstacles to contracting out functions but does not require them to be contracted out. It is for individual ministers and statutory office holders to determine the extent to which functions are contracted out. Where functions are contracted out, the Act fixes the minister or office-holder with responsibility for anything done or omitted to be done in their exercise by the contractor, with the principal exception of breaches of the criminal law (s. 72(2)). This provision was included to head off the criticism that contracting out would enable ministers or office-holders to hide behind contractors. A contractor may be authorized to carry out functions for a maximum of ten years (s. 69(5)(a)). A minister or office holder, however, retains the right to revoke an authorization at any time (s. 69(5)(b)). If an order specifying a function as eligible for contracting out or an authorization is revoked during the term of a contract, the contract is treated as repudiated rather than frustrated (s. 73(2)). This protects the contractor against the risk that the minister or office holder might revoke the order or authorization in an attempt to avoid the provisions of the contract in respect of termination. The fact that contracted out functions may be resumed at any time, however, means that, like agencification, contracting out does not detract from the legal primacy of the department in the organization of government.

3 Non-departmental public bodies

A non-departmental public body is a body 'which has a role in the processes of national government, but is not a government department or part of one, and accordingly operates to a greater or lesser extent at arm's length from Ministers' (Cabinet Office and Treasury 1992: para. 1.2.1). NDPBs are conventionally divided into three main categories—bodies with executive, administrative, regulatory or commercial functions, generally described as 'executive NDPBs'; advisory committees and commissions, i.e. bodies set up by ministers to advise them and their departments on matters within their sphere of interest; and tribunals and other judicial bodies, i.e. bodies which, independently of the executive, decide the rights and obligations of private citizens towards each other or towards a government department or other public authority. A number of public sector bodies are not treated as NDPBs, including the residuary nationalized industries, health authorities and hospital trusts (Cabinet Office and Treasury 1992: Appendix A).

Non-departmental public bodies are an earlier alternative to the departmental form of organization—the 'old style of devolution' as opposed to new style represented by agencies (213 HC Debs., col. 459, William Waldegrave, 5 November 1992). Their emergence during the early years of the twentieth century marked a revival of the board form of administration which the ministerial department had replaced. Willson attributed its revival to a reluctance to increase still further the amount of administrative power vested in the political executive, coupled with a desire to insulate some functions from the political process, and to the view that the orthodox administrative department, accountable to Parliament for everything which it did, was an unsuitable instrument for participation in economic activity: 'its organisation was too inflexible and its personnel too cautious to achieve the requisite degree of initiative and efficiency' (Willson 1955: 55). These considerations continue to feature prominently among the reasons advanced for conferring functions on NDPBs rather than departments, which stress their importance as a means of involving outside interests and expertise in advisory or executive functions and of insulating functions from the political process in order to increase the confidence of affected interests in the independence of their administration (see e.g. Cabinet Office (Office of Public Service) 1997*c*: ch. 2).

The official definition stresses that NDPBs are not departments or part of departments. In this respect they differ from agencies, which as we have seen are normally administrative arrangements within departments rather than separate entities. Executive NDPBs by contrast are legally separate entities. Executive NDPBs also differ from agencies in that their functions are vested directly in them rather than in their parent or sponsor department. In this respect they are like departments. Where they differ from departments is in the fact that they are subject to a higher authority in the shape of their sponsor departments, which are ultimately responsible for them, and which may retain specific powers of control over them.

> Conferring functions on an NDPB involves recognition that a degree of independence of Ministers in carrying out those functions is appropriate. . . . Nevertheless the responsible Minister is accountable to Parliament for the degree of independence which an NDPB enjoys, for its usefulness as an instrument of Government policy, and so ultimately for the overall effectiveness and efficiency with which it carries out its functions. (Cabinet Office and Treasury 1992: para. 2.11.1)

Being subordinate to the ministerial department therefore, NDPBs do not detract from its primacy in the legal organization of government. With few exceptions they also lack Crown status and hence access to the privileges of the Crown (Cabinet Office and Treasury 1992: para. 3.3.1).

The public service reforms of the last twenty years have generally been applied to NDPBs as to departments, though with some time-lag and with appropriate adaptation. The Labour Government's policy, which in several respects mirrors that of its Conservative predecessor, is directed towards keeping the number of NDPBs to a minimum and improving the efficiency of those that remain. A new NDPB will therefore only be set up where it can be demonstrated that this is the most cost-effective and appropriate method of achieving the Government's aims. It is also committed to making those that remain more open and accountable (Cabinet Office (Office of Public Service) 1998*b*, 1998*c*). *Public Bodies*, an annual Cabinet Office publication, contains summary information on NDPBs and other public bodies (Cabinet Office (Office of Public Service) 1997*a*). The Cabinet Office has also published the first of what is intended to be a series of annual reports summarizing the main objectives and achievements of the larger executive NDPBs (Efficiency Unit 1997).

V THE CABINET AND MINISTRY

> The minister has great power. The Cabinet, like public opinion, rarely knows enough to supervise or direct him in the working of his own department. Consequently he wields the theoretically supreme power of the Sovereign in a vast variety of matters. If he himself is capable, and if he is really working in constant consultation with capable permanent advisers, the Prime Minister and the Cabinet will do well to trust him freely. Mistakes will occur; but I think that they occur much less frequently when this course is taken by the supreme authority than when the alternative method is adopted of a futile attempt at supervision in detail.
>
> (Haldane 1923: 8)

> There is a will to have a stronger centre without encroaching on the formal constitutional position.
>
> (Public Administration Committee 1998*b*: Evidence, q. 187, Sir Richard Wilson)

1 The Cabinet

As well as being individually responsible, ministers are collectively responsible to Parliament and must resign as a government should they cease to command the support of a majority in the House of Commons. The fact that ministers are collectively as well as individually responsible to Parliament indicates the need for some means of reconciling their individual responsibilities with their collective responsibility. The mechanism by which this has traditionally been done in the United Kingdom is the Cabinet, which 'remains the crystallisation of government as a collective entity' (Mount 1992: 133). Like the executive itself, the cabinet is an extra-legal organization. It has no formal powers of control or direction over departments. Its decisions, however, are binding on departments (Wilson 1976: 59–60). It is 'the ultimate arbiter of all government policy' (Cabinet Office 1997*e*: p. 2).

The composition of the Cabinet as the supreme executive authority reflects the internal organization of the executive. It is made up of the ministerial heads of departments in whom the executive functions of government are vested. Cabinet membership provides an additional guarantee of departmental autonomy within the executive branch. It means that no one department is in a position to exercise unilateral control over another. As a member of the supreme authority the ministerial head of a department can always appeal to the Cabinet (Beer 1957: 110) (though as we shall see the scope for appeal may be limited). Beer saw the problems of a plural executive as being in practice considerably offset by 'a strong tendency to reach agreement' at the official level, and by the structure of the executive itself, with its presumption of collective decision-making, which makes it easier for a minister to acquiesce in a decision than would be the case were the executive power to be vested in a single set of hands. 'Formally and psychologically the decision will be his to an extent it could not be if he were overruled in whole or in part by another person possessing the whole executive power' (1957: 112, 118). Nevertheless it is inherent in the Cabinet's status and composition that it may serve as much to reinforce the position of departments as of the centre in government. Besides the principle of a single civil service, Greaves comments, there was

> the competing principle of ministerial responsibility, which makes the political head of each department its complete master accountable for its every official and his every act; and besides the chieftainship of the Prime Minister and the First Lord of the Treasury, there is the supreme authority of the Cabinet consisting of all such department heads and therefore reinforcing their individual authority. (Greaves 1956: 104)

The implications for the internal control function of the fact that the 'central authority' is not embodied in a unitary executive but in 'a group of ministers with shifting loyalties and views' (Lee 1977: 28) we explore in the following chapters. For the moment we note that the plural character of the central executive means that both the Cabinet 'agenda' and the way in which it is handled are heavily influenced by the search for consensus. The doctrine of collective responsibility, Wakeham explains, 'means that the process of Cabinet government has to work by building consensus. Colleagues must be able to support decisions. It is not possible to conduct business by putting them in a position where the only options they have are to submit or resign' (1994: 475).

1.1 'Cabinet business'

There are no hard and fast rules about what decisions must be approved by Cabinet and what may be settled by individual ministers singly or after consulting other ministers relevant to the decision (Mount 1992: 118). Essentially, Cabinet business is business which has the potential to engage the collective responsibility of the government. The *Ministerial Code* defines it as consisting mainly of two types of question:

those which 'significantly engage the collective responsibility of the Government, because they raise major issues of policy or because they are of critical importance to the public'; and those on which there is an 'unresolved argument' between departments. (Cabinet Office 1997*d*: para. 3).

Matters 'wholly within the responsibility of a single Minister and which do not significantly engage collective responsibility', on the other hand, need not be brought to cabinet or to a ministerial committee 'unless the Minister wishes to have the advice of his colleagues' (Cabinet Office 1997*d*: para. 3). In deciding whether to seek the advice of his colleagues, a minister will have in mind the need to carry colleagues with him. 'Every Minister in framing his proposals, has to bear in mind what his colleagues will and will not tolerate. This is a matter not so much of constitutional propriety as of political prudence' (Mount 1992: 133). 'Occasionally in the past some ministers (not of my party of course!) have decided to keep colleagues in the dark. That is extremely unwise. If things go wrong the lack of enthusiasm of colleagues called on to defend policies which they knew nothing about beforehand can be only too painfully obvious' (Wakeham 1994: 477). Given that collective responsibility is capable of covering any aspect of government policy, 'a precise definition of matters that need not be brought to cabinet cannot be given', but 'in borderline cases a Minister is advised to seek collective consideration' (Cabinet Office 1997*d*: para. 3). 'We are always ready to advise on individual proposals' (Cabinet Office 1997*e*: p. 3).

Cabinet business may be transacted in a variety of ways—by ministerial committees of the Cabinet, by informal groupings of ministers, as well as by the Cabinet itself. Ministerial committees serve two purposes.

> First they relieve the pressure on the Cabinet itself by settling as much business as possible at a lower level; or failing that, by clarifying the issues and defining the points of disagreement. Second, they support the principle of collective responsibility by ensuring that, even though an important question may never reach the Cabinet itself, the decision will be fully considered and the final judgement will be sufficiently authoritative to ensure that the Government as a whole can be properly expected to accept responsibility for it. (Cabinet Office 1997*d*: para. 4).

Committees act by implied devolution of authority from the Cabinet itself and their decisions therefore have the same formal status as decisions of the full Cabinet (Cabinet Office 1997*e*: p. 2). They may be overturned by decisions of the full Cabinet, but rights of appeal to the full Cabinet are limited. 'The only automatic right of appeal is if Treasury Ministers are unwilling to accept expenditure as a charge on the reserve (below, pp. 186–7); otherwise the Prime Minister will entertain appeals to the Cabinet only after consultation with the Chairman of the Committee concerned' (Cabinet Office 1997*d*: para. 5; Wilson 1976: 65–6).

1.2 The Cabinet Secretariat

Ministers are supported collectively in the conduct of Cabinet business by the Cabinet Secretariat, which forms part of the Cabinet Office. The Secretariat is 'the key agent of central co-ordination in the cabinet system' (Burch and Holliday 1996: 17). Its aim is 'to ensure that the business of government is conducted in a timely and efficient way and that proper collective consideration takes place when it is needed before policy decisions are taken' (Cabinet Office 1997*e*: p. 2). In particular, it aims to ensure that decisions taken are ones which ministers may be expected to support. It is divided into four Secretariats—Economic and Domestic Affairs, Constitution, Defence and Overseas, and European. The Economic and Domestic Secretariat deals with legislative and parliamentary matters. The Secretariat observes a convention of strict neutrality in its dealings with departments. 'It is essential that we are impartial and retain the confidence of all Ministers and officials' (ibid.: p. 2). 'We brief those who chair the meetings, on handling issues and the options available. In doing so, we are bound to brief impartially' (ibid.: p. 8). Were it to be seen as partial its ability to act as an honest broker between departments would be compromised. For the same reason it has traditionally been reactive rather than proactive. 'The purpose of the Cabinet Office is to make Cabinet government work, not to be an *imperium in imperio*' (Wilson 1976: 94).

2 Strengthening the 'centre'

The 'centre' is the expression used to refer to the two central departments—the Cabinet Office and the Treasury—and the Prime Minister's Office, which supports the Prime Minister in his or her role as the head of the government. A recurrent theme of machinery of government reform for much of this century has been need to strengthen the centre in order to better equip it to make 'a reality of collective responsibility' (Anderson 1946: 156). The corollary of departmental autonomy within the executive branch is a centre which even under the most forceful of the post-war Prime Ministers was described as 'fragmented and as lacking a single voice of authority' (Efficiency Unit 1988: Annex B, para. 38).

Various reforms have been adopted to this end. These include the introduction of the existing permanent but flexible system of Cabinet committees; the strengthening of the machinery of the Cabinet Secretariat ('though how long the Cabinet Office can go on riding this double bicycle—providing the sort of service which the prime minister wants and at the same time preserving its neutrality policy and playing its "honest broker" role as a service to departments—I do not know' (Hunt 1987: 70)); and the unification of functions across departmental boundaries by means of the creation of 'giant departments' such as the Department of Trade and Industry or the Department of the Environment, now the Department of Environment, Transport, and the Regions (Cabinet Office 1970). Reforms that have not found favour, or have been opposed, include the appointment of a system of supervising ministers, which has been rejected as inconsistent 'both with the parliamentary responsibilities of departmental ministers and with departmental control. Authority over departments must be undivided and unquestionable. A supervising minister would mean, in practice, a supervising staff with endless possibilities of friction and clash' (Anderson 1946: 150). Also strongly opposed on the grounds that it would involve a shift in responsibility from ministers and the Cabinet to the Prime Minister has been the creation of a Prime Minister's Department (Jones 1987; Hunt 1987).

The most recent of these efforts to strengthen the machinery of central co-ordination and control has followed a review of the effectiveness of the centre of government carried out in early 1998 by the Cabinet Secretary at the request of the Prime Minister. The Cabinet Secretary identified a number of weaknesses. He concluded that the linkage between policy formulation and implementation needed further improvement. He found that cross-departmental issues of policy and service delivery were often not handled well. He diagnosed a weakness in looking ahead to future opportunities and threats, and in reviewing the outcome of government policies and the achievement of government objectives. He also found there was scope for improving the performance of the centre of government in promulgating best practice and innovation in government and in the corporate management of personnel, IT, government communications, and scientific advice.

In a House of Commons written answer on 28 July 1998 the Prime Minister announced, in response to the Cabinet Secretary's review, the merger with immediate effect of the Office of Public Service with the Cabinet Office to provide the Government with a stronger capability to review major cross-cutting policies, and to strengthen the link between policy formulation, its implementation and evaluation, and the modernization of government. The Office of Public Service, which was 'the largest single member of the Cabinet Office family of organisations' (House of Lords Select Committee on the Public Service 1998, Evidence, p. 151), was the 'direct descendant' of the Civil Service Department, which took over responsibility for the central management of the Civil Service, including control of structure and organization, and the promotion of efficient methods of work, from the Treasury in 1968, following the recommendation of the Fulton Committee (Committee on the Civil

Service 1968: para. 244; Minister for the Civil Service Order 1968). Its responsibilities included helping departments find ways to improve the implementation and delivery of policies and services on the ground. A unified organization would thus help ensure that concerns about policy implementation were properly analysed in the process of developing policy, and help contribute to more effective follow-through when policies were agreed (317 HC Debs., cols. *132–4*, written answers 28 July 1998).

In addition to its responsibility for the promotion of 'better government', the Office of Public Service was also responsible for 'the central strategic supervision for the Civil Service' (Cabinet Office 1998*a*: para. 3.1). Its responsibilities were pursued through a flexible arrangement of units and groups, which remain in being pending reorganization. Among these units and groups are:

the Better Regulation Unit, which works to ensure that regulation across government is transparent, accountable, consistent, proportionate, and targeted, and the Service First Unit, the successor to the Citizen's Charter Unit, which aims to improve public services and make them more responsive to the needs of their users;

the Efficiency and Effectiveness Group, made up of the Efficiency Unit and the Next Steps Team, which helps departments (and their agencies and other public bodies) to improve their performance by securing better value for money from the resources they use and by improving management of their business; and

the Civil Service Employer Group, which works with other departments and agencies to promote 'best practice' in the employment of people across government; the Senior Civil Service Group, which is responsible for the management and development of the upper echelons of the service; and the Machinery of Government and Standards Group, which is responsible for the maintenance of the ethical and professional standards of the civil service and NDPBs. Since the Prime Minister's statement the Machinery of Government and Standards Group has been reconstituted as the Central Secretariat. Its precise role is still being worked out, but it is expected to have a more active role in policy formulation than the other Secretariats.

The Prime Minister also announced the establishment of a Performance and Innovation Unit in the Cabinet Office to complement the Treasury's role in monitoring departmental programmes (below, pp. 191–2). It has two principal functions: first, to focus on selected issues that cross departmental boundaries and propose policy innovations to improve the delivery of government objectives; and secondly, to select aspects of government policy that require review, with an emphasis on the better co-ordination and practical delivery of policy and services which involve more than one public sector body.

Although its responsibility for public service reform gave the Office of Public Service something of the air of an embryonic super department—a department of departments—like the rest of the Cabinet Office it lacked formal powers of control or direction over other departments, save in the specific context of the civil service (below, pp. 66–9). In the absence of such powers, 'guerrilla units' (Treasury and Civil Service Committee 1994*a*: para. 234) such as the Efficiency Unit or the Citizen's Charter Unit were heavily reliant on Prime Ministerial backing. Important though this is—'The only asset I had, never to be underrated, was a weekly meeting with the Prime Minister' (Young 1991: 131)—it is not without its limitations. The strength of the Efficiency Unit, for example, was that it had 'the support and enthusiastic backing of the Prime Minister', but it lacked 'organisational power, such as that possessed by the Treasury through its constitutional responsibility for expenditure'; given that weakness it had no choice but to rely, in a manner not dissimilar to the centre as a whole, on 'the active co-operation of the departments' (Thain and Wright 1995: 67).

Nothing in the Prime Minister's statement, we should note, changes this. Although the creation of a strengthened Cabinet Office represents in the eyes of some observers the most determined effort yet to forge a coherent centre and overcome the problem of 'departmentalitis', the reforms leave the foundations of departmental power within the executive branch unaltered. 'I think it is very important to be clear that in the non-constitution which we operate, the executive powers are vested in government departments. The laws which Parliament passes give operational responsibility, legal power, to Secretaries of State, not to the Prime Minister', the Cabinet Secretary reminded MPs. 'This is not about taking over the job of departments as I have described it. It is about making sure that the Government is pulled together in a way which conveys the themes and messages of the Government and gets across its overriding philosophy. . . . There is a will to have a stronger centre without encroaching on the formal constitutional position' (Public Administration Committee 1998, Evidence q.186, Sir Richard Wilson).

VI CONCLUSION

Departments have always enjoyed a measure of autonomy in the exercise of their functions. 'According to the theory of the eighteenth century, the King appointed a minister to administer certain services on his behalf; the minister alone was responsible for the administration of these services; the appointment and dismissal of the staff, the handling of the funds placed at his (or the King's) disposal for those services, and the general control of the establishments under his charge. This idea', Jennings wrote, 'has never completely disappeared. A department is a separate unit in which, in principle, the minister is responsible for providing the staff out of moneys provided by Parliament, for maintaining efficiency among that staff, and for advising the Queen about the decisions to be taken or, if necessary, for taking the decisions himself in the Queen's name' (1959*a*: 134). On the basis of our analysis we can go further. Not only has this idea not disappeared, it remains the central idea on which the internal ordering of the executive branch is based. The autonomy of departments in the United Kingdom continues to be protected through a combination of law, which vests functions in ministers; convention, which makes them responsible for those functions to Parliament; and organization, through their membership of the central executive authority. The problem which the collective interest of government in the United Kingdom accordingly faces is not one of controlling a group of powerful but nevertheless subordinate departments as in the United States, but rather one of imposing collective disciplines on a group of parallel departments (Self 1977: 128). It is to the question of how this problem is tackled and the controls to which departments are subject that we now turn.

3
The Civil Service

I INTRODUCTION

In this chapter we turn our attention from the internal structure of the executive branch to its staffing, the men and women who make up the personnel or human resources of departments and agencies. On 1 April 1998, there were 463,300 permanent civil servants in post, a fall of 287,900 from the post-war peak of 751,000 reached in 1976 (House of Lords Select Committee on the Public Service 1998: Appendix 6). Significant though this number is, the executive is not alone in employing large numbers of staff. Two things, however, are commonly said to distinguish the civil service from other employments (Padmore 1956: 124–5). The first, is the fact that it is a largely *permanent* service, in the sense that its members are not liable to lose their jobs on a change of government. The United Kingdom never developed an equivalent of the spoils system in the United States, for example, under which the senior echelons of the administration are liable to be replaced on a change of government by the new government's own supporters (Parris 1969: ch. I; contrast public appointments where a spoils system did develop (Jennings 1959*a*: 132–3)). Instead the tradition which developed was of

> an efficient body of permanent officers, occupying a position duly subordinate to that of the Ministers who are directly responsible to the Crown and to Parliament, yet possessing sufficient independence, character, ability, and experience to be able to advise, assist, and to some extent, influence those who are from time to time set over them. (Northcote–Trevelyan 1854)

The usual justification offered for a permanent service is that it secures continuity through changes in government (Cabinet Office 1994*a*: para. 2.2). It is also said to be a more 'efficient' means of securing continuity than the alternative, which would involve some sort of ministerial *cabinet* system.

> We believe intensely that a non-political Civil Service such as ours makes for a more efficient system of government than one in which changes in the top posts have to be made whenever a Government of a different political complexion takes over. (Sir Edward Bridges, quoted in Chapman 1988: 94)

Be that as it may, there are no constitutional guarantees of the principle of permanence. In the absence of statutory backing, the principle depends on the forbearance of an incoming administration, and the 'accepted wisdom' that the potential victims of a purge are possessed of 'a peculiarly British conception of neutrality which involves the chameleon-like ability to identify with successive governments of quite different political complexions' (Treasury and Civil Service Committee 1986*b*: para. 5.10). One of the questions raised by the outcome of the 1997 general election was whether the principle would survive a change of government after 18 years of Conservative rule. It did.

The second thing that has been said to distinguish the civil service from other employments is that it presents 'a unique combination of unity and diversity. It is a single unified service, but its members serve under some scores of separate and partially independent employing authorities, and the duties which they perform are of almost limitless variety' (Padmore 1956: 124–5). The concept of the service as unified is of relatively recent origin. It was only after the end of the First World War that it became accepted that the service 'should be organised and staffed more as a unit than as a collection of heterogeneous departments each with its own way of handling and grading its employees' (O'Halpin 1989: 25). Before then the 'service' was made up of a group of independent departments over which the Treasury exercised 'only an uneasy suzerainty' (Smellie 1937: 262). An important part of the Northcote–Trevelyan prescription had been for measures to mitigate the evils resulting from the fragmentary character of the service, as well as for the replacement of patronage by competition, but it took seventy years for their prescription to be realized.

The orthodoxy that emerged after the end of the First World War—that the service should be organized and managed as a single organization—was to survive effectively unchallenged for the next fifty years. As Greaves presciently observed, however, no description of the service

> can be realistic which overlooks either the historical fact that there were once as many services as there were establishments and that it is on these that the principle of integration has been superimposed, or the political fact of the continuing powerful pulls in the direction of maintaining or reverting to the principle of severalness. (Greaves 1956: 103)

In recent years, it is the continuing pull in the direction of severalness which has been most apparent. Under devolution civil servants working in Scotland and Wales will remain members of the Home Civil Service (Scotland Act 1998, s. 51(2); Government of Wales Act 1998, s. 34(2)), but devolution represents potentially the most serious challenge yet to the concept of a unified civil service. For Ibbs, as we saw, the service was too big and too diverse to be run as a single rigid organization with common rules for financial and personnel management. Centralized rule-making was criticized for being insufficiently discriminating and for denying managers the flexibility they needed in order to manage. 'Many managers told us that central rules were acting as a constraint on good management and taking away their scope to do things which would be sensible in terms of their own organisation' (Efficiency Unit 1988: paras. 10–11, Annex B paras. 40–5). With the setting up of Next Steps agencies, therefore, came pressure for the devolution of central management functions to departments and agencies. Decentralization was effectively completed in 1996 when responsibility for the pay and grading of staff below senior levels was delegated to departments and agencies.

Decentralization clearly carries with it the risk of a return to the 'fragmented and disjointed' service of the mid-nineteenth century when relations between departments were as 'remote and prickly as those of separate States' (Smellie 1937: 262). One way in which the Conservative Government sought to counter this risk was through the creation of a Senior Civil Service. The Service, which was established on 1 April 1996, at the same time as the decentralization of central management functions to departments and agencies was completed, is made up of the 3,000 or so most senior staff in departments and agencies (roughly equivalent to the former grades 1–5). In the first of two Civil Service White Papers, the Government argued that such staff must continue to be seen as a 'cohesive Service, as well as a departmental resource'. Among other reasons this was important in order to promote 'an understanding of the collective interest of Government, in support of collective Cabinet responsibility, by encouraging movement between organisations, particularly for those with the potential for top posts' (Cabinet Office 1994*a*: para. 4.16). As well as serving the needs of collective Cabinet government, the Service is also intended to 'give a lead in sustaining key Civil Service values and necessary continuity and the corporate wisdom that can only be developed over a number of years' (Cabinet Office 1994*a*: para. 4.13).

No less significantly from our point of view, the Civil Service White Paper also insisted that the 'defining principles and standards of the Civil Service' would continue to be 'centrally prescribed and mandatory for all departments and agencies' (Cabinet Office 1994*a*: para. 1.3). These principles, which are laid down in the Civil Service Order in Council 1995 and the Civil Service Management Code, are designed to safeguard

> a non-political, permanent Civil Service which sets high value on integrity, impartiality, and objectivity, which serves loyally the Government of the

day—of whatever political persuasion—and which recruits staff on the principles of fair and open competition on the basis of merit. (Cabinet Office 1994*a*: para. 2.33)

In this chapter then we concentrate on the internal regulation of the civil service, with particular reference to the values of permanence, loyalty, honesty and integrity, impartiality, and selection (and promotion) on merit. As we shall see these are not the only values that feature in the regulation of the civil service. Confidentiality, effectiveness, and value for money are also prominent.

The discussion falls into four parts. In the second part we look at who is involved in the contemporary regulation of the civil service, and in particular at the division of responsibility between the centre in the shape of the Cabinet Office and the Office of the Civil Service Commissioners, on the one hand, and departments and agencies, on the other. In the third we look at the central requirements that apply in respect of the recruitment of staff, before looking in the final part at the requirements that apply in respect of the conduct of civil servants (and of ministers in their dealings with civil servants). We begin, however, by recalling the legal basis of the regulation of the service.

II THE LEGAL BASIS OF CONTROL

> It is common knowledge that the public service in Britain is in high degree non-political. By contrast with other countries, it is also in a high degree non-legal.
>
> (Schwartz and Wade 1972: 22)

Like the internal organization of the executive branch, the constitution treats the regulation of the civil service as a matter for the executive itself.

> The management of the Civil Service is one of the aspects of the Prerogative which is exercised by Ministers on behalf of the Crown. It follows that it is for Ministers alone to issue instructions concerning the management of the Civil Service, and that they do not require Parliamentary authority to do so. (Cabinet Office 1995*a*: para. 2.15)

Wade rejects the view that the management of the civil service is an aspect of the prerogative (see e.g. 1985: 190–4). His concern, however, is that the indiscriminate use of the label 'prerogative' may lead to the denial of remedies, for example, in contract, whose availability ought not to be in doubt, not to deny that the management of the service has been treated as a matter for the executive itself. Not all civil servants are so managed. The staff of Her Majesty's Customs and Excise, for example, are appointed, and their terms and conditions of service determined, under statutory provisions (Customs and Excise Management Act 1979, s. 6). But the prerogative is the starting point for the regulation of the service as a whole.

That the constitution should treat the regulation of the civil service as a matter for the executive itself was in the beginning at least as much a matter of accident as design. In retrospect the implementation of the Northcote–Trevelyan Report was a decisive moment in the history of the regulation of the service. Fearing the effects of departmental opposition to their proposals, Northcote and Trevelyan recommended that they be implemented by legislation:

> It remains for us to express our conviction that if any change of the importance of those which we have recommended is to be carried into effect, it can only be successfully done through the medium of an Act of Parliament. The existing system is supported by long usage and powerful interests; and were any Government to introduce material alterations into it, in consequence of their own convictions, without taking the precaution to give those alterations the force of law, it is almost certain that they would be imperceptibly, or perhaps avowedly, abandoned by their successors, if they were not even allowed to fall into disuse by the very Government which had originated them. (in Committee on the Civil Service 1968: p. 118)

In the event parliamentary legislation was beyond the reach of the Government. It was therefore compelled to rely on its prerogative powers, a course urged upon it by those who, while by no means favouring the Northcote–Trevelyan proposals, were nevertheless opposed to any further erosion of the prerogative. 'Why add yet another to the many recent sacrifices of the royal prerogative? Why advise the Queen to ask Parliament to aid her to do that which she can do as effectually without their aid?', asked Sir James Stephen (1854: p. 79). The extent of the opposition to the Northcote–Trevelyan reforms was underlined when the House of Commons voted down the Order in Council implementing the Report. However, the result did not affect the Government's decision to proceed (Wright 1969: 64; rejection by the legislature would of course have been fatal to parliamentary legislation). There was thus preserved (or established) a 'tradition' of the regulation of the civil service in the exercise of the royal prerogative, which has been maintained to the present day.

The perception that relations between the executive and its staff—the Crown and its servants—were a matter for the executive itself was reinforced by the attitude of the courts. The judicial orthodoxy that prevailed essentially unbroken from the nineteenth century until the

GCHQ case (*Council of Civil Service Unions v Minister of the Civil Service* 1985) was summed up by Jennings thus: 'The courts recognise that relations between the Queen and her servants are matters within the [unreviewable] discretion of the Queen. Accordingly, if she makes rules for her servants, they are not the concern of the courts' (1959*b*: 110). Even where, as in the case of pensions, relations were based on statute rather than the prerogative, the courts declined to intervene. According to Vice-Chancellor Malins, the civil servant's right to a pension was a 'very peculiar' right. 'As I read the Acts of Parliament, it is a right which can never be enforced in the civil tribunals of this country' (*Cooper v The Queen* 1880: at 314; *Nixon v AG* 1931). The foundations were thus laid for the development by the executive of its own internal law of the civil service, untrammelled by Parliament or the courts.

The non-statutory basis of the regulation of the civil service has meant that the difficulties entailed in passing parliamentary legislation have been less of a barrier to civil service reform than they might otherwise have been. Nevertheless the Government found it necessary to promote legislation in the shape of the Civil Service (Management Functions) Act 1992 to authorize the delegation of centrally held management functions to departments and agencies. Why legislation should have been regarded as necessary to authorize their delegation is not immediately obvious given the prerogative status of the functions involved. The explanation is that as these functions had been formally delegated by the Crown to the central departments, i.e. the Treasury and the Minister for the Civil Service, there was thought to be a risk that their further delegation without express authorization might be struck down by the courts as unlawful. Such authorization could not be provided under the prerogative: the fact that they had been transferred by statutory transfer of functions order since 1968 when they were transferred from the Treasury to the Civil Service Department following the recommendation of the Fulton Committee (see below, pp. 65–6) was regarded as having effectively extinguished the prerogative power of transfer (*Attorney-General v De Keyser's Royal Hotel Ltd* 1920; Pollitt 1984: 13). Nor could authorization be provided under the Ministers of the Crown Act, which makes provision only for the transfer of functions between 'Ministers of the Crown', i.e. between holders of offices in Her Majesty's Government (s. 8(1)), not for their transfer between ministers and persons such as agency chief executives not possessing that status (or for the attachment of conditions to a transfer).

Notwithstanding their prerogative status, therefore, the statutory transfer of the executive's central management functions had the effect of compelling the Government to secure statutory authorization for their delegation to departments and agencies. Pending the enactment of legislation, the central departments instituted a system of 'delegated authorities' in respect of the management of staff, but according to the Chancellor of the Duchy of Lancaster this was a 'pretty poor substitute for real delegation' and was 'hedged about by all kinds of obscure legal restrictions' (213 HC Debs., col. 458, William Waldegrave, 5 November 1992).

Given the far-reaching changes that have taken place in the civil service over the last ten years it was inevitable that there should have been calls for its regulation to be put on a statutory footing. For proponents of a Civil Service Act one of its principal merits was that it would create precisely the legal obstacle to the abandonment of fundamental principles that Northcote and Trevelyan had sought more than a century earlier. (We have become so persuaded of the sovereignty of the executive, i.e. that the sovereignty of Parliament is the sovereignty of the executive, that we have forgotten that the need to change the law may serve as a restraint on government.) It would also provide an opportunity to consider whether the responsibilities of civil servants ought to be owed exclusively to ministers.

One proponent of legislation in the last Parliament was the Treasury and Civil Service Committee, which called for statutory backing to be given to its proposals for strengthening the methods for upholding the essential values and standards of the civil service (Treasury and Civil Service Committee 1994*a*: paras. 116–17). In its response, the Conservative Government, while not ruling out legislation, made clear its opposition to a statutory approach were it to inhibit the 'effective and efficient' management of the service (Cabinet Office 1995*a*: paras. 2.15–2.17). At the same time, however, it accepted the importance, in the interests of 'maintaining public confidence in the impartiality and integrity of the service', of the widest possible agreement, outside the service as well as inside, on the rules governing the role and conduct of civil servants, and of confidence in the safeguards which existed to ensure that civil servants were not asked to act improperly. It therefore accepted the Committee's recommendations for a new Civil Service Code and for an independent line of appeal to the Civil Service Commissioners in cases of alleged breaches of the Code or issues of conscience which could not be resolved through internal procedures (Cabinet Office 1995*a*: paras. 2.6–2.7; see below, pp. 91–4, 98–101).

III THE ORGANIZATION OF CONTROL

1 The Treasury

For much of this century the Treasury was responsible for the central management of the civil service. Treasury control over the numbers and grading of staff employed by departments and their pay and other conditions of service was based on the theory that the control of establishments was an integral part of the control of public expenditure (Beer 1957: 9–10). The Treasury's authority over the service was consolidated after the end of the First World War as part of the general restoration of Treasury control that took place at that time (Roseveare 1969: 246–9; for the early history, see Wright 1969; Bridges 1966: 108–10). The Permanent Secretary to the Treasury took on the additional role of Permanent Head of the Civil Service, with responsibility for advising the Prime Minister on senior appointments, which were made on a service-wide rather than departmental basis; and the Treasury itself was given the power by prerogative Order in Council to make regulations 'for controlling the conduct of His Majesty's Civil Establishments, and providing for the classification, remuneration, and other conditions of service of all persons employed therein, whether permanently or temporarily' (Civil Service Order in Council 1920).

In 1968, following the recommendation of the Fulton Committee, responsibility for the central management of the service, including control of staffing and remuneration, was transferred from the Treasury to a new Civil Service Department (Minister for the Civil Service Order 1968). After the Civil Service Department was abolished in 1981, its functions were divided between the Treasury, which resumed the bulk of its former responsibilities, and a residual Management and Personnel Office in the Cabinet Office (Transfer of Functions (Minister for the Civil Service and Treasury) Order 1981). With the decentralization of responsibility for the pay and grading of staff to departments and agencies, and the introduction of control of departmental running costs in place of manpower controls, however, the Treasury ceased to play a role in the central management of the service, and its responsibilities were transferred to the Minister for the Civil Service, i.e. the Prime Minister, in 1995 (Transfer of Functions (Treasury and Minister for the Civil Service) Order 1995).

2 The Cabinet Office

Following the disengagement of the Treasury, the Office of Public Service within the Cabinet Office assumed the central role in relation to the civil service until it was merged with the Cabinet Office on 28 July 1998 following a review of the effectiveness of the centre of government undertaken by the Cabinet Secretary (above, pp. 54–7). The Cabinet Office's role in a decentralized service, like its predecessor's, is defined as one of 'strategic supervision' (Cabinet Office 1998*a*: para. 3.1). It is responsible for maintaining the 'essential coherence' of the service, while securing the benefits of devolution and management delegation, and for maintaining and enhancing its professional and ethical standards. It is also responsible, following its merger with OPS, for the promotion of 'better government which provides high quality efficient and effective public services and regulation, delivered in an accountable, open, accessible, and responsive way', and the promotion of 'high standards of accountability and openness in the wider public sector' (Cabinet Office 1998*a*: para. 3.5), as well as for its traditional task of supporting ministers collectively in the conduct of Cabinet business.

Under the Civil Service Order in Council 1995 and the Civil Service (Management Functions) Act 1992, the functions which the Cabinet Office exercises in relation to the civil service are vested in the Prime Minister, in his capacity as Minister for the Civil Service. The Prime Minister was first appointed Minister for the Civil Service in 1968 when responsibility for the central management of the service was transferred from the Treasury, of which the Prime Minister is First Lord, to the Civil Service Department (Minister for the Civil Service Order 1968). Before then he had taken the major share of responsibility for the general supervision and control of the service in his capacity as First Lord of the Treasury (Jennings 1959*a*: 149). The vesting of the central functions in relation to the civil service in the Prime Minister allows the arrangements for supporting the Prime Minister in carrying out those functions to be altered without the need for legislation—in this respect the device of the Minister for the Civil Service performs the same role as that of the Secretary of State—while at the same time underlining that responsibility for the civil service is a matter ultimately for the Prime Minister acting on behalf of the government as a whole. 'No other Minister can assert the needs of the government service as a whole over the sectional needs of powerful departmental Ministers' (Committee on the Civil Service 1968: para. 261). The Prime Minister is supported in carrying out his responsibilities as Minister for the Civil Service by the Minister for the Cabinet Office and Chancellor of the Duchy of Lancaster.

The Civil Service Order in Council 1995 empowers the Minister for the Civil Service to make regulations and give instructions for the 'management' of the Home Civil Service. It also empowers the Minister to make regulations and give instructions for controlling the conduct of the service; relating to the recruitment of staff; and prescribing qualifications for appointment (art. 10). This power is the direct successor of the power first formally delegated to the Treasury by the Civil Service Order in Council 1920. (The equivalent power in respect of the Diplomatic Service is conferred on the Secretary of State for Foreign and Commonwealth Affairs by the Diplomatic Order in Council 1995.) The bulk of the Minister for the Civil Service's functions in relation to the management of staff have been delegated to departments under the Civil Service (Management Functions) Act 1992 (see below, pp. 72–3).

The Cabinet Office is also responsible for the Civil Service Management Code. The Code, which is issued under the authority of the Civil Service Order in Council, sets out the 'key principles' which apply to the recruitment and management of staff throughout the service, together with 'a minimum framework of centrally-determined rules', which all departments and agencies are required to apply directly to their staff (Cabinet Office 1994*a*: para. 2.35). It was first issued in 1993 with the aim of providing a clear and accurate statement of the centrally issued terms and conditions to be applied by management to all civil servants, regardless of the department or agency in which they worked. In this respect it has been superseded by the delegation of authority to departments and agencies. Now, instead of prescribing terms and conditions, it sets out the framework within which departments and agencies may determine terms and conditions of service for their own staff. It replaced and rationalized the old Establishments Officers' Guide and Civil Service Pay and Conditions of Service Code, together with 'a multitude of circulars and guidance notes, which sought to regulate in detail from the centre the requirements placed upon departments and staff' (Cabinet Office 1994*a*: para. 2.34).

The central responsibilities in relation to the civil service are carried out by the Civil Service Employer Group, the Senior Civil Service Group, and the Central Secretariat (formerly the Machinery of Government and Standards Group) within the Cabinet Office. The Civil Service Employer Group works with other departments and agencies to promote 'best practice' in the employment of people across government. It aims to promote the 'essential coherence' of the service, while seeking the benefits of management delegation, and to develop management standards which reflect best practice in the wider economy. Within the Group, the Personnel Management and Conditions of Service Division is responsible for the Civil Service Management Code, and for the policy of delegating management functions to departments and agencies, while the Conduct and Discipline Branch, which is part of the Personnel Management and Conditions of Service Division, is responsible for conduct and discipline within the service, including political activities, duty of confidentiality, standards of propriety, discipline and appeal arrangements. The Senior Civil Service Group is responsible for the framework within which members of the Senior Civil Service are paid, managed, and developed. The Central Secretariat is responsible for the maintenance of the ethical and professional standards of the civil service and NDPBs. The Standards and Propriety Team within the Central Secretariat is responsible for the Civil Service Code.

In addition to the merger of the Cabinet Office and OPS, the Prime Minister also announced in response to the Cabinet Secretary's review of the effectiveness of the centre of government that there was a need for more emphasis on 'the corporate management of the civil service as whole. My objective is to meet the corporate objectives of the Government as whole, rather than just the objectives of individual departments.' The reorganization of the Cabinet Office consequent upon its merger with OPS would thus give it a new focus as 'the corporate headquarters of the Civil Service'. A Management Board for the Civil Service is to be established, whose membership will include a number of Permanent Secretaries, as a means of involving departments in the work of the Cabinet Office in its corporate management role (317 HC Debs., cols. *132–4*, written answers 28 July 1998).

3 The Office of the Civil Service Commissioners

No organization has been more dramatically affected by the delegation of central responsibilities to departments and agencies than the Civil Service Commissioners. Commissioners were first appointed in 1855 to test the qualifications of candidates nominated for appointment to departments (Order in Council of 21 May 1855). For almost the whole of their history they served as 'a central recruiting, examining and certifying body under Treasury regulation' (Greaves 1956: 103). But following the delegation of the bulk of their recruitment functions to departments and agencies, and the transfer of the remainder to an executive agency, the Recruitment and Assessment Service Agency, which was later privatized, they have now been recast as the custodians of the principle of selection on merit on the basis of fair and open competition, as part of a series of reforms aimed at 'revitalising' the principle in civil service recruitment (Cabinet Office 1994*c*: para. 3.24).

The reinvention of the Commissioners as the custodians of the principle of selection on merit on the basis of fair and open competition followed an internal review of recruitment responsibilities commissioned by the Head of the Home Civil Service. The review was critical of the division of responsibility between the centre, including the Commissioners, and departments and agencies under the then Civil Service Order in Council 1991. It concluded that 'a generally understood and accepted balance' had yet to be struck between 'maintaining the principle of fair and open competition on merit' and 'giving managers more autonomy in the use of resources' (Cabinet Office 1994*c*: para. 3.18). It recommended that a clear distinction be drawn between regulatory and executive functions, with the Commissioners being assigned responsibility for regulation and departments responsibility for recruitment (Cabinet Office 1994*c*: para. 4.12). The review's recommendations were accepted by the Government and given effect by the Civil Service Order in Council 1995, which places the Commissioners under a duty to maintain the principle of selection on merit on the basis of fair and open competition in relation to selection for appointment (art. 4 (1)). They are also required to issue a recruitment code on the interpretation and application of the principle by appointing authorities, and to audit recruitment policies and practices to establish whether the code is being observed by appointing authorities (art. 4(2),(3)). They have power to require appointing authorities to publish summary information about their recruitment, including the use made by them of the permitted exceptions to the principle of selection on merit (art. 4(4)).

The Commissioners have also been given responsibility for hearing and determining appeals under the Civil Service Code (art. 4(5)). Under the Armstrong Memorandum an appeal on matters of conscience lay to the Head of the Home Civil Service, but the Government accepted the Treasury and Civil Service Select Committee's recommendation that it should be replaced by an appeal to the Commissioners where alleged breaches of the Code or issues of conscience could not be resolved through internal procedures (Treasury and Civil Service Committee 1994*a*: paras. 108–12; Cabinet Office 1995*a*: paras. 2.10–2.12; below, pp. 98–101). For the Commissioners, this appellate role was 'very different' from their traditional responsibilities, but one which nevertheless fitted well with the 'regulatory body' they had now become (Civil Service Commissioners 1995: p. 6).

The Commissioners are appointed directly by the Crown by Order in Council under the prerogative. They lack any formal guarantees of their independence akin to those enjoyed by the judiciary or the Comptroller and Auditor General, but they are nevertheless independent of ministers in the exercise of their functions (Civil Service Commissioners 1997: 3). Their independence within the executive branch is founded on their status as office holders under the Crown rather than servants of the Crown, which is said to put them 'in a very real sense beyond the reach of ministerial interference'; and on the fact that their functions are vested directly in them under the prerogative, with no provision for ministerial direction or control over them in their exercise. It is also reflected in the fact that their annual report is made directly to the Queen rather than via the Prime Minister (Treasury and Civil Service Committee 1994*a*: para. 113). Traditionally they were drawn from the ranks of the civil service, but since 1995 no Commissioner has been a serving civil servant.

The Treasury and Civil Service Select Committee recommended that the Commissioners be reconstituted as a statutory body (Treasury and Civil Service Committee 1994*a*: para. 116), but the Government saw no need to reconstitute them either to confer new functions on them or to secure their independence. New functions could be conferred on them by Order in Council, on which basis their 'independence' had been sustained for more than a century (Cabinet Office 1995*a*: para. 2.15).

4 Departments and agencies

The traditional orthodoxy holds that civil servants are employees of the Crown rather than departments: they are servants of the Crown who are 'assigned' to particular departments (Cabinet Office 1994*c*: para. 4.12). The main role in the management of staff, however, has always been played by departments. When the relationship between the Crown and its servants was not thought to be contractual in nature, a civil servant's 'contract' of service was said to be with his department, 'the head of which alone has over him the essential powers flowing from the employer–employee relationship—transfer, promotion, discipline, retirement. . . . It is the employing department which assigns the civil servant to his duty, trains him for it, supervises him, pays him, watches his performance, promotes him and so on' (Padmore 1956: 127). The devolution of responsibility for the recruitment and management of staff to departments and agencies over the last decade or so has underlined the extent of the gap between the theory and practice of Crown employment. For practical purposes civil servants are employed in particular departments and agencies rather than by the government as a whole.[1]

4.1 The Principal Establishment Officer (PEO)

The permanent head of the department is responsible for its overall organization, management and staffing. He is required to appoint as one of his advisers a Principal Establishment Officer (PEO), with primary responsibility for the staffing of the department (Treasury 1989*a*: para. 6.2.1). PEOs were made responsible, under the permanent head of department, for economy in all matters of staff, organization, and office management as part of the arrangements for strengthening Treasury control of expenditure after the First World War. Their appointment and removal from office was also made subject to the consent of the Prime Minister, who was advised by the Head of the Civil Service (Treasury circular of 12 March 1920, *Control of Expenditure*; O'Halpin 1989: 46–55). These reforms were a key element in the development of

[1] The doctrine that the employer is the Crown and not the department was reaffirmed in *Berko v SAFE* 1998; cf. *Department of Health v Bruce* 1992.

closer collaboration in staffing matters between the Treasury and departments (Roseveare 1969: 248).

The PEO's responsibilities are no longer defined in terms of economy in staffing. Instead he or she is responsible for the provision of an assurance to the head of department that there are 'efficient personnel systems in place across all the parts of the department which will ensure that people with the skills and experience are available to carry agreed responsibilities in support of Ministers' policies' (Treasury 1989*a*: para. 6.2.28). He or she also carries primary responsibility for ensuring that the requirements of centrally prescribed rules are made known and observed across the department. The Establishment Officers Meeting (EOM) network provides a means whereby PEOs may develop links with other departments and agencies for the exchange of good practice and to ensure that practice across their department is consistent with centrally prescribed requirements (ibid.: para. 6.2.33, Appendix 6.2). In some cases the post of PEO may be combined with that of Principal Finance Officer (see below, pp. 129–30), the holder being the Principal Establishment Finance officer (PEFO). Cabinet Office approval used to be but is no longer required for appointments to PEO and PEFO posts at Grade 3 equivalent level and above.

4.2 Delegated responsibilities

The role of departments in the management of staff has increased as a result of the delegation of central management responsibilities to them under the Civil Service (Management Functions) Act 1992. The current delegations are set out in the Civil Service Management Code. They include the authority:

to determine the number and grading of posts outside the Senior Civil Service in departments; and

to determine the terms and conditions of employment of home civil servants relating to the classification of staff (with the exception of the Senior Civil Service); remuneration (with the exception of the Senior Civil Service); allowances; expenses; holidays, hours of work and attendance; part-time and other working arrangements; performance and promotion; retirement age and redundancy; and the re-deployment of staff within and between departments.

Departments have also been delegated authority to prescribe the qualifications (so far as they relate to age, knowledge, ability, professional attainment, aptitude and potential) for the appointment of home civil servants in departments (Civil Service Management Code 1996: Introduction, para. 3).

The delegations that have been made under the Civil Service (Management Functions) Act are to ministers and office holders in charge of departments, not to agency chief executives. Where departments have agencies, the presumption is that delegated functions will be exercised by agency chief executives, but the precise extent to which ministers may wish to allow the exercise of their powers by chief executives is a matter for them to determine (Civil Service Management Code 1996: Introduction, para. 5). The functions that are delegated to agencies are set out in agencies' framework documents. The chief executive of the Valuation Office Agency, for example, has delegated responsibility for all Agency 'human resource' matters, including responsibility for pay and grading systems for all Agency staff outside the Senior Civil Service; while the chief executive of the Benefits Agency is responsible for all personnel matters affecting staff outside the Senior Civil Service, consistent with general civil service staffing arrangements and the DSS Personnel Guiding Principles. Agency chief executives are required to appoint their own equivalents of PEOs to assist them (Treasury 1989*a*: para. 6.2.1).

4.3 'Cabinet Office requirements'

Departments and agencies are obliged to comply with the provisions of the Civil Service Management Code as a condition of the delegation of functions to them under the Civil Service (Management Functions) Act (Civil Service Management Code 1996: Introduction, para. 4). The Code, for example, stipulates that terms and conditions of service must be determined with regard to the general practice of large employers; value for money; and the provisions of *Government Accounting* (Civil Service Management Code 1996: Introduction, para. 5). Departments and agencies are required to define terms and conditions of service clearly and to make them available to staff, for example in a departmental or agency (staff) handbook. Where departments and agencies have delegated powers or discretion, they must make clear to staff how these will be exercised by setting out the relevant rules and procedures in their handbooks (ibid.: Introduction, para. 6).

Delegation of responsibility for pay and grading is subject to the condition that departments develop arrangements for the grading of posts and for the remuneration of staff, which are appropriate to their business needs, are consistent with the Government's policies on the civil service and public sector pay, and observe public spending controls (ibid.: paras. 6.1.2 and 7.1.2). The arrangements for the remuneration of staff must also reflect a number of 'key' principles—value for money from the pay bill, financial control of the pay bill, flexibility in pay systems, and a close and effective link between pay and performance (ibid.: para. 7.1.2). A department or agency proposing major changes to its pay and grading arrangements must submit a restructuring business case to the Cabinet Office (ibid.: para. 7.1.3).

Other central requirements exhibit a similar concern with performance. Departments are thus required to have in place procedures for dealing with inefficiency and limited efficiency. The former may arise from poor performance or poor attendance. Where neither improves, and medical retirement is inappropriate, staff may be dismissed on grounds of inefficiency. Limited efficiency is defined as performance which is not sufficiently poor to be considered inefficient, but which no longer measures up to the requirements of the post or which involves a failure to carry out duties satisfactorily. It may lead to an invitation to retire early or to compulsory early retirement (Civil Service Management Code 1996: paras. 6.3.1–6.3.4). Performance review systems must be capable of clearly identifying performance which is unsatisfactory or unacceptable; they must also be capable of contributing to a department's arrangements for making decisions on performance-related pay (ibid.: paras. 6.2.1–6.2.3).

An appeal lies to the Civil Service Appeal Board against dismissal on grounds of inefficiency, or the non-payment of compensation under the Principal Civil Service Pension Scheme to civil servants dismissed on inefficiency grounds (ibid.: paras. 12.1.26 and 12.1.35). The Board reports that appeals on grounds of inefficiency have increased, most notably since 1991 as a consequence of organizational changes within the service which have called for a 'strong focus' on performance and results. The devolution of authority for personnel matters to line management is also reported to have had a marked influence on the seriousness with which both misconduct and inefficiency are regarded (Civil Service Appeal Board 1997: Introduction).

As well as being under an obligation to comply with central requirements as a condition of the delegation of functions to them under the Civil Service (Management Functions) Act, departments and agencies are also under a 'catch all' obligation to submit to the Cabinet Office proposals or arrangements which are 'contentious, or raise questions of propriety' (Civil Service Management Code 1996: Introduction, para. 4). This obligation, which mirrors the obligation to submit spending proposals which are 'novel or contentious' to the Treasury (Treasury 1989*a*: para. 2.4.6), is designed to give effect to the Cabinet Office's continuing responsibility for the oversight of the service, enabling it to consider difficult cases and if necessary to revise the central framework in the light of them. Compliance with the Code is monitored by the Cabinet Office, which retains the right to inspect and monitor observance of the Code in departments and agencies. Its aim is to keep inspection and monitoring to the 'minimum level consistent with central responsibilities' (Civil Service Management Code 1996: Introduction, para. 8).

4.4 The Senior Civil Service

Like the rest of the civil service, Senior Civil Service staff are managed by departments, but within a common framework laid down by the centre. The main features of the common framework are:

a 'central pay framework' of nine overlapping bands;

the introduction of personal contracts for members of the service;

a common appraisal scheme; and

a greater emphasis on open competition in the filling of vacancies.

Here we concentrate on the central pay framework and the introduction of individual contracts. The greater emphasis on competition as a means of filling vacancies is discussed below (pp. 80–1).

4.4.1 The central pay framework

Below the Permanent Secretary level, the nine overlapping pay bands, broadly linked to levels of responsibility, within which members' pay is individually determined, are designed to provide some cohesion across the Senior Civil Service, while offering a good deal of flexibility to departments (Cabinet Office 1994*a*: para. 4.38). Departments must have regard to the job-weight ranges appropriate to each band when allocating staff to pay bands, but have discretion to decide which of the available bands to use. Departments also have discretion to determine the detailed operation of their pay schemes, including the progression of staff within and between bands. However, the minimum and maximum levels for each band are set each year by the Government, taking into account the recommendations of the Senior Salaries Review Body (Civil Service Management Code 1996: paras. 7.1.12–7.1.14).

The Nolan Committee was concerned that the performance pay arrangements for the Senior Civil Service should be structured so as not to undermine the political impartiality of the service.

> Many, though not all, of the senior civil servants will be in contact with Ministers and will handle sensitive policy matters. A perception that reward and promotion may depend in any way on commitment to Ministerial ideology inconsistent with the impartiality required of a civil servant would of course be wholly unacceptable. (Committee on Standards in Public Life 1995: para. 3.48)

As in other areas where there is a risk of 'politicization', such as decisions about appointments or early release, the primary safeguard takes the form of the exclusion of ministers from the decision-making process. Below Permanent Secretary level, pay is determined by heads of departments i.e. permanent secretaries, subject to the oversight of the Senior Salaries Review Body, while the pay of Permanent Secretaries, in which ministers have a say, is determined by the Government on the recommendation of an independent Permanent Secretaries Remuneration Committee, chaired by the Chairman of the SSRB, 'which the Government normally expects to accept' (Civil Service Management Code 1996: para. 7.1.11).

4.4.2 Personal contracts

Civil servants are required to sign a personal contract before taking up a first appointment in the Senior Civil Service or on moving within it (Civil Service Management Code 1996: para. 5.3.2). The introduction of personal contracts for members of the Service was one of the principal recommendations of an Efficiency Unit study of the policies and practices required for ensuring an adequate supply of suitably qualified people to fill senior posts in departmental and agency headquarters, whether from internal sources or after open competition, which was commissioned by the Head of the Home Civil Service and the Prime Minister's Adviser on Efficiency and Effectiveness in July 1992 (Efficiency Unit 1993*a*). The study was at pains to dismiss the suggestion that civil servants had no contracts of employment, or that they had jobs for life. At the same time, however, it found that departments were inhibited in their use of the existing early release provision, partly as a result of uncertainty over whether staff whose performance was fully satisfactory could nevertheless be compulsorily retired, for example, in order to remove promotion blockages (ibid.: paras. 7.10 and 7.21). It therefore proposed a 'significant shift' towards normal employment practice elsewhere, i.e. in the private sector, including a 'sharpening' of contract terms as 'a signal of management intent' to make greater use of the existing provision for early release (ibid.: pp. 4–5). In its view it was not sufficient or appropriate to secure an acknowledgement from staff that they understood and accepted the implications of the current terms. Instead, 'more explicit' contract terms should be introduced, which would give 'a convincing signal that Civil Service employment terms generally had altered, and that outstanding achievement could be properly rewarded, and poor performance and organizational issues directly addressed' (ibid.: para. 7.24). The Government accepted the study's recommendation. The introduction of individual contracts, it argued, would 'remove any lack of clarity' in the terms and conditions of employment of members of the service, while at the same time putting them 'more on a par with their counterparts in other walks of life' (Cabinet Office 1994*a*: para. 4.32).[2]

The introduction of individual contracts of employment for members of the Senior Civil Service is part of a more general shift towards the 'contractualisation' of Crown employment (*R v Lord Chancellor's Department, ex parte Nangle* 1992). This shift followed a reappraisal of the relationship between the Crown and its servants, which was prompted by the rapid increase in legislation and decided cases in the employment field (*R v Civil Service Appeal Board, ex parte Bruce* 1988: at 694). Another factor has been the extension of the power of judicial review to relations between the Crown and its servants, with the consequence that those relations are no longer automatically immune from review (*Council of Civil Service Unions v Minister of the Civil Service* 1985; *R v Civil Service Appeal Board, ex parte Bruce* 1988, 1989). It has been suggested that treating the employment relationship as contractual is potentially disadvantageous to civil servants (Fredman and Morris 1988), but doing so is not thought to offer the executive any additional remedies against civil servants or to reduce its vulnerability to challenge by way of judicial review proceedings. It does, however, allow terms of contracts to be tailored to the circumstances of individual civil servants. In this respect it is the logical outcome of the original critique of centralized rule-making—that it was insufficiently discriminating—which set in motion the decentralization of responsibility to departments and agencies.

The model contract which has been introduced for members of the Senior Civil Service follows the Efficiency Unit's preferred option of a contract for an indefinite term subject to specified periods of notice, up to a maximum of six months. The contract reflects the Government's view that it cannot exclude or restrict the prerogative power to dismiss at will by contract, and cannot therefore bind itself contractually to give notice, but makes it clear that in practice notice will normally be given. Where notice is not given, compensation may be payable. Contracts are based on a standard model with scope for department and agency variation.

The Cabinet Office assists departments and agencies to develop expertise and promote cohesion across the Senior Civil Service, through the common management framework and by encouraging mobility between departments and agencies. Much of this is achieved through provision of central programmes, support, and co-operation rather than by applying central rules or requirements (Civil Service Management Code 1996:

[2] Despite the Efficiency Unit's comments on the need for the alteration of contract terms, the general view is that contracts have formalized rather than altered senior civil service terms and conditions of employment.

para. 5.1.3). The Senior Civil Service Group within the Cabinet Office is responsible for the pay, contracts and general framework within which departments manage members of the Senior Civil Service.

IV RECRUITMENT

1 Audited self-regulation

The system for the regulation of civil service recruitment established under the Civil Service Order in Council 1995 may be characterized as one of 'audited self-regulation'. There are over 3,000 'recruitment units'—parts of departments or agencies which are authorized to undertake their own recruitment (Cabinet Office 1994*c*: para. 5.1). Under the system of audited self-regulation, departments and agencies are made responsible for the regulation of their recruitment in accordance with centrally prescribed requirements, compliance with which is then 'audited' by the Civil Service Commissioners (and by the Cabinet Office in the case of Cabinet Office requirements). Audit does not detract from the responsibility of front-line managers for ensuring that the central requirements are met.

2 The recruitment principles

'Good Government needs a Civil Service which is highly competent, politically impartial and has high standards of integrity' (Recruitment Code 1996: para. 1.1). The recruitment principles underpin this need. The principles are set out in the Civil Service Order in Council and the Civil Service Commissioners' Recruitment Code. The Order in Council provides that 'no person shall be appointed to a situation in the Service unless the selection for appointment is made on merit on the basis of fair and open competition' (art. 2(1)(a)). This has been the governing principle of civil service recruitment since the Civil Service Order in Council 1870 established open competition as the normal method of entry to the service. As the internal review of recruitment responsibilities pointed out, the language has changed over the years, but the underlying intent has remained the same since Northcote–Trevelyan: 'to guard against patronage, political or otherwise; to render jobs in the civil service accessible to people who may wish to apply for them; and to ensure that people appointed to those jobs are competent to do them' (Cabinet Office 1994*c*: para. 4.1). The review saw no cause to abandon a principle which had provided the foundation of an 'effective, non-political' civil service for more than a century. On the contrary, the devolutionary trends now affecting the service made it all the more important that it be reasserted and maintained (ibid.: paras. 2.1 and 4.6).

Like the Order in Council itself, the Recruitment Code is binding on departments and agencies. As well as the fundamental principle of selection on merit on the basis of fair and open competition, it sets out four other recruitment principles which must be followed when any post is opened to competition from outside the civil service:

prospective applicants must be given equal and reasonable access to adequate information about the job and its requirements, and about the selection process;

applicants must be considered equally on merit at each stage of the selection process;

selection must be based on relevant criteria applied consistently to all candidates; and

selection techniques must be reliable and guard against bias. (Recruitment Code 1996)

The proposal for a mandatory recruitment code came from the internal review of recruitment responsibilities. In recommending that the Commissioners should be required to issue guidance to departments and agencies, the review argued that it was important that the guidance should not just be given the force of (prerogative) law, by means of a general reference in the Order in Council, but that it should also incorporate 'a positive and coherent account of the purpose of the principles and the rationale behind the exceptions' (Cabinet Office 1994*c*: para. 4.19). The feedback received by the review suggested:

that the rules and procedures are seen by some, particularly by people in Agencies who look to private sector models of recruitment practice, as irritating bureaucratic constraints. Some procedural rules are essential, since procedure will be fundamental to openness and fairness especially. But the rationale for—and value of—the principles of openness, fairness and merit do not sing out of, say, the Minister's Rules and Advice. Those who are charged with applying the principles are more likely to do so with commitment if they understand their purpose. (Cabinet Office 1994*c*: para. 4.17)

As well as setting out the principles governing recruitment, therefore, the Code sets out 'the reasons behind them to enable individuals to make sound decisions in every case instead of mechanistically following rules which can never be comprehensive' (Civil Service Commissioners 1995: p. 5).

3 Commissioners' approval

In contrast to other civil service appointments, appointments to the Senior Civil Service, and to a number of other senior posts, including those of agency chief executives, the Government Actuary, and the Prisons Ombudsman, require the specific written approval of the Civil Service Commissioners (Civil Service Order in Council 1995, art. 5(1) and Schedule 2). The retention of the requirement of the Commissioners' approval for these appointments partly reflects the risk of political patronage that may attach to individual appointments: in this respect it serves as 'a form of guarantee that the normal principles have been observed where an appointment is seen to be susceptible to Ministerial influence' (Cabinet Office 1994*c*: para. 5.20). At the same time, it acknowledges that the principle of a non-political service, and with it the principle of permanence, would be fatally compromised were senior appointments seen to be open to ministerial influence at a time when the scope for such influence has increased as a result of the extension of open competition to senior appointments (Cabinet Office 1994*a*: para. 4.30). Although the Order in Council appears to require the Commissioners' written approval for all appointments to the Senior Civil Service irrespective of whether they are made from within or outside the civil service ('no appointment . . . shall be made to any situation in the Senior Civil Service . . . without the written approval of the Commissioners'), the Commissioners treat the requirement of their approval as being confined to appointments to the Senior Civil Service and to the scheduled list of appointments which involve recruitment from *outside* the civil service. They do not therefore scrutinize appointments which are made internally as a result of promotions or transfers.

Traditionally, open competition was confined to the lower echelons of the service. Recruitment to the upper echelons was from within the service itself. This gave rise to the criticism that the system remained essentially one based on patronage—'open competition to get in, but patronage once in' (Treasury and Civil Service Committee 1994*a*: para. 275). The last few years, however, have seen the steady extension of the principle of open competition to senior appointments to the point at which any appointment may now potentially be the subject of open competition. The Efficiency Unit study of the policies and practices required for ensuring an adequate supply of suitably qualified people to fill senior posts recommended a more structured approach to the filling of senior appointments, with greater use being made of open competition where this was necessary and justifiable in the interests of producing a strong field or of introducing new blood (Efficiency Unit 1993*a*: paras. 6.35–6.41). Now before filling any vacancies in the Senior

Civil Service, departments are required to address a number of prior questions (the 'Oughton checklist'), including whether it is necessary to fill the vacancy at all or at the proposed level; whether there is a sufficient field of candidates already within the department, or whether in order to get a strong field it is necessary to extend the search to the wider civil service or to full open competition; and whether there are reasons in the departmental interest or the corporate interest of the civil service as a whole to provide the opportunity for new blood to be brought into the department or the civil service through the vacancy (Cabinet Office (OPS) 1996*a*: Annex D).

Guidance issued by the Commissioners to departments and agencies on the procedures which must be followed in order to secure their approval for recruitment from outside the civil service to senior appointments recognizes that there are a small number of very senior posts in which ministers will be closely interested because of their importance for 'the setting and delivery of their policies'. It insists, however, that the legitimate interest of ministers in appointments to those posts 'must be accommodated within a system which produces appointments which can last into other Administrations and are free from personal or political bias.' Accordingly, although the minister may see the names on the long list and the short list, he or she may not interview the candidates. The minister may also meet the lead candidate before deciding to approve the appointment, but cannot pick and chose among the reserve candidates. And should the minister not want to appoint the lead candidate, the competition would normally need to be re-run before a legitimate appointment could be made (Civil Service Commissioners 1996*b*: paras. 19–22).

This guidance was first issued in July 1994, following the controversy which surrounded the appointment of the Director General of the Prison Service. The controversy centred on the fact that the Home Secretary had interviewed the three candidates the selection board considered suitable for appointment and had then expressed a view to the board. The board then made a recommendation to the Home Secretary, which he accepted (Treasury and Civil Service Committee 1994*a*: para. 279; Lewis 1997: pp. 10–12). Although the guidance for the most part encapsulated existing procedures, it discontinued the 'rarely used' procedure under which the board adjourned to allow the minister to see candidates placed above the line. This procedure had not carried public confidence, and it had therefore been decided that it should not be available in the future (Civil Service Commissioners 1995: pp. 8–9).

Under the Civil Service Order in Council, the Commissioners' decision to grant or withhold their approval is expressed to be 'final', which in this context means not subject to challenge within the executive rather than the courts. The Treasury's unwillingness to entertain 'appeals' against the refusal of the Commissioners' certificate was an important factor in the initial establishment of their independence within government (Wright 1969: 70–1). In a stand-off between the Commissioners and a minister therefore it is the Commissioners who appear to hold all the cards.

4 'SASC Group' appointments

The 'SASC Group' is made up of the most senior posts in the civil service, currently around 130 posts at the equivalent of the old grades 1, 1A, and 2 (listed in Cabinet Office (OPS) 1996*a*: Annex A). Permanent Secretaries are appointed by the Prime Minister on the recommendation of the Head of the Home Civil Service, while other appointments to the Group are approved by the Prime Minister on the recommendation of the Head of the Home Civil Service (Civil Service Management Code 1996: para. 5.2.1). The principle of requiring the consent of the Prime Minister to the appointment of permanent heads of departments, their deputies, principal finance officers, and principal establishment officers was 'affirmed' by Treasury circular in 1920 (Treasury circular of 12 March 1920, *Control of Expenditure;* Royal Commission on the Civil Service 1929–31: para. 20). The appointments procedure has been described as 'a peculiarly British process: the Cabinet Secretary cannot make an appointment without the approval of the Prime Minister. The Prime Minister cannot approve an appointment which has not been presented by the Cabinet Secretary. They therefore need each other' (Richards 1996: 656).

The Senior Appointments Selection Committee (SASC) advises the Head of the Home Civil Service on the senior staffing position across the service as well as on individual appointments. The Committee is made up of a small number of Permanent Secretaries, normally five, one of whom will always be the Permanent Secretary to the Treasury, one external member, and the First Civil Service Commissioner. Meetings are chaired by the Head of the Home Civil Service. It considers the basis on which appointments should be filled (whether the post is necessary, whether it should be filled within the department concerned, go to Civil Service-wide competition or full open competition). Where posts are not filled by open competition, SASC advises the Head of the Home Civil Service on candidates to be recommended to the Prime Minister (Efficiency Unit 1993*a*: Annex H; Richards 1996).

The First Commissioner attends meetings of SASC. He is responsible for helping to ensure that the best person for the job is selected in every case and that open competition is considered where it is likely to contribute to that end (Civil Service Commissioners 1996: p. 4; for the background, see Cabinet Office 1995*a*: p. 40). He is able to comment directly to the minister concerned or to the Prime Minister, if he so wishes, on the choice between open competition and internal appointment. The Conservative Government's second Civil Service White Paper anticipated that he would also be able to draw attention in the Commissioners' annual report to any ministerial decision which, should it ever arise, appeared to depart from the principle of selection on merit (Cabinet Office 1995*a*: para. 2.13). In the Commissioners' annual report he sets out the balance between open competition and internal appointment in filling senior civil service vacancies, and comments on the development of senior selection processes. The proportion of appointments going to open competition is about 30 per cent.

5 Exceptions

The principle of selection on merit on the basis of fair and open competition is subject to a number of exceptions. It does not apply to appointments made directly by the Crown, such as the Governor and Deputy Governors of the Bank of England, rather than by ministers (Civil Service Order in Council 1995, art. 3(1)). Nor does it apply to 'special advisers' whose appointments end with an administration (art. 3(2)). Special advisers are subject to a strict 'advice-only requirement', but following the 1997 general election the Order in Council was amended to allow the appointment in the Prime Minister's Office of a maximum of three special advisers with executive responsibilities, i.e. with civil servants working directly for them, in addition to their advisory role (Civil Service (Amendment) Order in Council 1997). Two appointments have been made under this provision—the Prime Minister's Chief of Staff and his Chief Press Secretary. The Civil Service Commissioners, noting that the number of appointments that could be made under this provision was strictly limited, and that it was confined in its application to the Prime Minister's Office, accepted that it did not call into question the continuing general validity of the principle of selection on merit on the basis of fair and open competition (Civil Service Commissioners 1998: p. 5).

The principle also does not apply to a number of categories of appointment set out in the Civil Service Order in Council itself (art. 6). The permitted categories include short term appointments (not exceeding five years), and extensions or conversion to permanency; secondments; re-appointments of former civil servants; transfers into the civil service; and 'surplus acceptable candidates', i.e. the appointment of a candidate of an acceptable standard who was unsuccessful in one competition to a situation for which there is a demonstrable shortage of suitable candidates. Provision is also made for the principle to be relaxed in the case of the appointment of disabled candidates (art. 7). The permitted exceptions are amplified in the Recruitment Code, which stresses that their purpose is to 'provide flexibility where it is genuinely necessary to meet the needs of the Civil Service'. Departments and agencies are under no obligation to allow recruitment under the exceptions, and they are free to set stricter limits on flexibility where they see fit (Recruitment Code 1996: para. 2.2).

Two further exceptions are specific to appointments which require the Commissioners' written approval. The first permits the appointment of a candidate of 'proven distinction'; the second the appointment of a candidate who has been assessed in open competition as suitable for appointment but not as the best candidate. In either case the appointment must also be justified for 'exceptional reasons relating to the needs of the Service' (art. 6(2)). The guidance on recruitment to senior posts expressly excludes 'personal chemistry' and 'political stance' as acceptable reasons for the appointment of a candidate other than the best candidate (Civil Service Commissioners 1996*b*: para. 48). Use of both exceptions is expected to be 'very rare', with decisions being taken collectively by the Commissioners and recorded in their annual report (Recruitment Code 1996: para. 2.34).

The Commissioners are responsible for policing the boundary between the principle of selection on merit on the basis of fair and open competition and the permitted exceptions through the audit of departmental and agency recruitment. The audits conducted so far have revealed a lack of departmental and agency guidance on the use and recording of the permitted exceptions (Civil Service Commissioners 1998: p. 19). A 'topic' audit of the recruitment and retention of casual staff also found that, although breaches of the letter of the Recruitment Code were rare, in more than one case very large numbers of casual staff were being recruited, without fair and open competition, to undertake a high proportion of continuing routine tasks. Appointments for which the principles had been suspended were the normal means of staffing these tasks. After the lessons learned from the audit were drawn to the attention of departments and agencies, fewer instances of problems in this area were reported to have been found (Civil Service Commissioners 1997: pp. 17–19).

6 Compliance and audit

Responsibility for ensuring that individual recruitment units undertake their recruitment in line with the Recruitment Code rests on the Permanent Secretary or the chief executive of each department or agency (Recruitment Code 1996: para. 1.8). (The internal review recommended that framework documents should continue to specify the extent to which recruitment authority has been delegated to the chief executive

(Cabinet Office 1994*c*: para. 4.13).) Departments and agencies are required to publish summary information about their recruitment, including the use made by them of the permitted exceptions. As well as improving transparency and accountability, disclosure is intended to underline the responsibility of departments and agencies for recruitment standards. Departments and agencies are also required to certify that there are systems in place to ensure that recruitment is carried out on the basis of fair and open competition and selection on merit and in accordance with the Recruitment Code, and that they are subject to internal check (Recruitment Code 1996: para. 3.3.a). The Commissioners' audits conducted so far have revealed very few departments or agencies with systems in place to carry out an internal monitoring programme of recruitment procedures and practices, and that in many cases departments and agencies had not considered how to collect information or how to bring it to the notice of the general public (Civil Service Commissioners 1997: p. 17; Civil Service Commissioners 1998: p. 19).

Departmental and agency compliance with the principles is monitored by the Commissioners who audit departmental and agency recruitment systems and practices to ensure that they comply with the centrally prescribed requirements. The internal review concluded that if the principles were to be made to stick it was not sufficient for the Commissioners to publish guidance and for departments to certify that they complied with it. Some form of independent review of internal monitoring was also required (Cabinet Office 1994*c*: para. 5.8). Commissioners' audit is expressly stated not to detract from the front-line responsibility of managers with responsibility for recruitment for giving effect to the recruitment principles (Recruitment Code 1996: para. 1.11). The emphasis is on helping departments and agencies to meet the requirements rather than fault-finding. As well as a systems audit every three years, the Commissioners may also carry out occasional 'topic' audits, examining issues of current concern in depth across departments and considering whether there are lessons of wider application to be learned; and *ad hoc* investigatory audits, where something appears to have gone seriously wrong. The Commissioners are required to publish an account of their audits in their annual reports. The internal review anticipated that this would provide the Commissioners with the opportunity to draw attention to any policies or practices which gave them particular concern. 'This may not seem to be a particularly sharp set of teeth, but the deterrent effect of prospective embarrassment in a publicly accountable service is real enough' (Cabinet Office 1994*c*: para. 5.18). So far the Commissioners have not found it necessary to resort to 'naming and shaming'. After the first three years of operation of the new system, their annual report reveals that minor 'technical' breaches of the Code are fairly widespread, but they are nevertheless confident that 'sound recruitment systems have been introduced and are being maintained consistently across the Civil Service' (Civil Service Commissioners 1998: p. 18).

No formal appeal lies to the Commissioners against an alleged failure to comply with the Code. The internal review concluded that it would be a potentially expensive arrangement, with little clear benefit (Cabinet Office 1994*c*: para. 5.13). The Commissioners do, however, hold themselves out as being willing to consider complaints (Recruitment Code 1996: para. 1.12), which may trigger an audit study if they suggest sufficient cause for concern.

7 'Central requirements'

Departments and agencies are also subject to 'central requirements' in the exercise of their delegated responsibilities for the recruitment of staff (including their responsibility for the prescription of qualifications for appointment to positions in their organizations relating to age, knowledge, ability, professional attainment, aptitude, and potential). The central requirements underline the need of good government for a civil service which is *competent*. They stipulate that departments and agencies must ensure that their recruitment systems 'deliver recruits who are appropriate to their needs and who are able to do the work required' (Civil Service Management Code 1996: para. 1.1.2). Departments and agencies are required to retain records for at least three years of the recruitment criteria in use and of the performance of successful candidates, which will enable compliance with the competence principle to be checked if necessary.

V CONDUCT AND DISCIPLINE

1 Standards of conduct

The conduct of civil servants is governed by a number of long-standing duties. As set out in the Civil Service Management Code and the Civil Service Code, the essential expectations of civil servants are that they should:

serve loyally the government of the day—of whatever political persuasion;
carry out their duties with honesty and integrity;
carry out their duties impartially; and

treat as confidential information to which they have had access in the course of their official duties.

A fifth expectation—that they should remain anonymous—has been effectively abandoned in recent years. (The expectation was not so much as to their conduct as that their anonymity would be preserved (by ministers) lest their ability to work for another government be impaired by reason of their identification with a particular policy or advice. The tradition of anonymity has been substantially eroded in recent years, however, without the fears expressed materializing.) Effect is given to these expectations or principles through a combination of a 'central framework' and departmental and agency staff handbooks.

1.1 The central framework

The central framework, for which the Cabinet Office is responsible, is set out in the Civil Service Management Code. The framework consists of a mixture of 'core' principles of conduct and amplifying rules. The core principles replace an earlier statement of general principles of conduct, which were first formulated and circulated in the wake of what became known as the *Francs* case, which arose out of allegations made in *Ironmonger v Dyne* (1928) of speculation in currency futures by Foreign Office officials. The principles laid down by the Board of Enquiry chaired by Sir Warren Fisher, the Head of the Civil Service, which investigated the allegations, insisted that the service exacted from itself 'a higher standard' than that required by normal standards of personal honesty and integrity, 'because it recognizes that the State is entitled to demand that its servants shall not only be honest in fact, but beyond the reach of suspicion of dishonesty' (Board of Enquiry 1928: para. 56). The principles embodying this 'Caesar's wife' standard (Mackenzie and Grove 1957: 151) were circulated to all departments by the Treasury (Treasury circular E 19377 of 13 March 1928), and for many decades served as a 'definitive statement' of the obligations of civil servants (O'Halpin 1989: 162); they became 'a sort of civil service code of conduct' (Chapman 1988: 147).

The core principles set out in the Civil Service Management Code derive from 'the need for civil servants to be, and to be seen to be honest and impartial in the exercise of their duties.' They stipulate that civil servants must not

allow their judgement or integrity to be compromised in fact or by reasonable implication;

misuse information which they acquire in the course of their official duties, or disclose official information without authority;

seek to frustrate the policies, actions, or decisions of government;

take part in any political or public activity which compromises, or might be seen to compromise, their impartial service to the government of the day or any future government;

misuse their official position or information acquired in the course of their official duties to further their private interests or those of others; or

receive gifts, hospitality, or benefits of any kind from a third party which might be seen to compromise their personal judgement or integrity. (Civil Service Management Code 1996: para. 4.1.3)

These core principles are elaborated by more detailed rules in respect of confidentiality and official information, standards of propriety, and political activities; three matters which for Mackenzie and Grove were significant as 'marks of the character of the Service' (1957: 150). Those in respect of confidentiality and official information require departments and agencies to remind staff on appointment, retirement, or resignation that they are bound by the provisions of the criminal law, including the Official Secrets Acts, and by their duty of confidentiality owed to the Crown as their former employer (Civil Service Management Code 1996: para. 4.2.1). Departments and agencies must also ensure through their local staff regulations that civil servants do not, without relevant authorization, disclose official information which has been communicated in confidence within government or received in confidence from others; or seek to frustrate the policies or decisions of ministers by the use or disclosure outside the government of any information to which they have had access as civil servants (ibid.: paras. 4.2.2 and 4.2.6).

The detailed rules in respect of propriety cover such matters as the letting of contracts to departmental and agency staff, and the employment of staff who are bankrupt or insolvent on duties which might permit the misappropriation of public funds, as well as the acceptance of gifts, hospitality, or benefits in kind. They have recently been supplemented by guidance on contacts with lobbyists (Cabinet Office 1998*b*).

They also include the Business Appointments Rules, which make the acceptance of appointments which former Crown servants propose to take up in the first two years after they leave the service conditional upon departmental or central approval depending on seniority. The rules were first laid down in 1937 (Prime Minister 1937), following the recommendation of the Royal Commission on the Private Manufacture of and Trading in Arms (Royal Commission . . . Arms 1936: para. 110). The year before, in July 1936, the Permanent Secretary to the Air Ministry, Sir Christopher Bullock, had been sacked for soliciting a job with Imperial Airways (Board of Enquiry 1936; Prime Minister 1936;

O'Halpin 1989: 206–15; Chapman 1988: ch. 4). The purpose of the rules is to ensure that the acceptance of outside appointments by former Crown servants (separate versions of the rules apply to the armed forces, the Diplomatic Service, and certain office holders) does not create any suspicion that an appointment might be a 'reward for past favours', or that a firm might gain an unfair advantage over its competitors by employing someone who had access to what they might legitimately regard as their own 'trade secrets' or to information about developments in government policy which might affect that firm or its competitors (Civil Service Management Code 1996: Section 4.3, Annex B para. 1). An Advisory Committee on Business Appointments advises on applications at the most senior levels and reviews a wider sample in order to ensure consistency and effectiveness (Advisory Committee on Business Appointments 1998; the Committee also advises former ministers on the propriety of their business appointments). Following the recommendation of the Nolan Committee (Committee on Standards in Public Life 1995: paras. 3.62–3.70), the operation, observance, and objectives of the rules were reviewed by an inter-departmental working group, which concluded that there was a continuing need for them but that formal monitoring of their observance was both unnecessary and impractical—serious breaches should, by definition, come to the attention of departments.

The purpose of the political activities rules is to maintain public confidence in the political impartiality of the service. They are intended to avoid public identification of individual civil servants with a party-political stance that could call into question an individual's impartiality, or more generally the neutrality of the service as a whole; and to avoid criticism that people paid from public funds are being used for party-political purposes (Cabinet Office (OPS) 1996*b*: *Political activities*).

The convention of political neutrality is of course a corollary of the fact that the service is a permanent service. As Mackenzie and Grove explain, the maintenance of a permanent administration, in the interests of orderly government, requires that ministers should not be free to eject civil servants. But such

> self-limitation on the part of Ministers is possible only if leading civil servants refrain scrupulously from identifying themselves publicly with any of the competing parties: and party supporters in the country are not likely to accept Ministerial forbearance unless they see that minor civil servants whom they meet in daily business are equally impartial. (1957: 155)

The Masterman Committee, which was appointed in 1948 to review the restrictions on the political activities of civil servants, which at that time varied from department to department, saw the political impartiality of the service as critical to the efficient operation of government. The need to maintain public confidence in the impartiality of the service

> is, we think, axiomatic and will not be disputed. On the contrary, we believe it will be generally agreed that the efficient and smooth working of democratic government depends very largely on maintaining that confidence and on people believing that, notwithstanding political change, the Civil Service will give completely loyal service to the Government of the day. (Committee on Political Activities of Civil Servants 1949: para. 38)

Were that confidence not to exist, it would be impossible to avoid the introduction of something like a spoils system. 'A democratic system of government requires that its citizens be satisfied that those they elect are enabled to govern without hindrance. If there were a general belief that political motivation existed within the Civil Service on a large scale, not only would the system be placed under strain but it would in fact need to be fundamentally altered' (Committee on Political Activities of Civil Servants 1978: para. 69).

The core of the political activities rules consists of restrictions on the freedom of civil servants to participate in political activities. For the purpose of the rules the service is divided into three categories. The 'politically free' category, which covers civil servants in industrial and non-office grades, can participate in any political activity. Those in the 'politically restricted' category, which includes members of the Senior Civil Service and civil servants at levels immediately below the Senior Civil Service, are banned from national political activities, but may be given permission to take part in local political activities. The 'intermediate' category, which is composed of all other civil servants, may be given permission to take part in national as well as local political activities. Following the incorporation of the European Convention on Human Rights, the compatibility of these restrictions with 'Convention rights' may be tested before the domestic courts (for the compatibility of restrictions on the political activities of local government officers with the Convention, see *Ahmed and others v The United Kingdom* 1998).

The implications of political impartiality for the conduct of civil servants more generally were considered by the Armitage Committee, which was appointed in 1976 to examine whether there was any scope for relaxing the rules. For the Committee what was of 'central importance' was that whatever views the individual civil servant may hold

> should not constitute so strong and so comprehensive a commitment to the viewpoint of one political party as to inhibit loyal and effective service to Ministers of another party. A Minister coming into a department must be able to rely on the loyalty and integrity of all civil servants and especially those with whom he or she comes into contact . . . Advice must be given with candour and

the maximum possible objectivity. Policies must be executed as the Minister intends, whether his officials agree with them or not: and the Minister must not be embarrassed by political comments from civil servants. Civil servants must not be so politically committed that they cannot easily comply with these basic constitutional requirements. (Committee on Political Activities of Civil Servants 1978: para. 67)

These stipulations are reflected in the standards of conduct departments and agencies must require of civil servants not in the politically free category, i.e. civil servants other than those in industrial or non-office grades. Such civil servants must not allow the expression of their personal political views 'to constitute so strong and comprehensive a commitment to one political party as to inhibit or appear to inhibit loyal and effective service to Ministers of another party'. They must also 'take every care to avoid any embarrassment to Ministers or their department or agency which could result, inadvertently or not, from bringing themselves prominently to notice, as civil servants, in party political controversy.' And where they have not been given permission to engage in political activities, they 'must retain at all times a proper reticence in matters of political controversy so that their impartiality is beyond question' (Civil Service Management Code 1996: paras. 4.4.13–4.4.15).

1.2 The Civil Service Code

The United Kingdom civil service tradition has relied as much on unwritten as on written rules. 'Much had been left unsaid previously which was made explicit when the Service grew large, but the "code" (if such it can be called) still le[ft] a great deal to personal honour and common sense' (Mackenzie and Grove 1957: 8). The Board of Enquiry in the *Francs* case was strongly of the view that 'practical rules for the guidance of social conduct depend as much upon the instinct and perception of the individual as upon cast-iron formulas', adding its hope that the 'surest guide' would always be found in 'the nice and jealous honour of Civil Servants themselves' (Board of Enquiry 1928: para. 59). This hope became one of the basic assumptions upon which the regulation of the service was based. According to the former Establishments Officers' Guide, the 'distinctive character' of the British civil service depended on 'the existence and maintenance of a general code of conduct which, although to some extent intangible and unwritten, is of very real influence' (1976: para. 4060, reproduced in Royal Commission on Standards of Conduct in Government 1976: Appendix 11).

Where rules have been reduced to writing, the preference has been to express them in the form of general principles rather than detailed rules. The preferred model has been that of the 'Ten Commandments' rather than the 'Justinian Code' (Kernaghan 1975: 11–12; the recent guidance for civil servants on contacts with lobbyists is an exception). One argument has been that there is no need for a detailed code because, as the Establishments Officers' Guide put it, civil servants 'jealously maintain their professional standards' (quoted in Royal Commission on Standards of Conduct in Government 1976: Appendix 11). At the same time there has been a fear that were a detailed code to be adopted not only would it be a source of unwelcome rigidity but it would also detract from the responsibility of civil servants to think through the consequences of their own actions. 'It is the duty and the responsibility of civil servants—and indeed of Ministers—to think for themselves how to apply the principles to any particular case or situation, and then to act responsibly. We should do nothing to absolve them from that duty or relieve them from that responsibility'. Were a detailed code to be introduced, propriety would be reduced to a matter of following the rules; while the more detailed the rules laid down, 'the greater would be the temptation for the barrack-room lawyer to claim that what he was proposing to do must be all right because there was nothing in the rules explicitly forbidding it' (576 HL Debs., col. 1644, Armstrong of Ilminster, 19 December 1996).

The latest addition to the central corpus of norms—the Civil Service Code—is firmly in this tradition. The Code, which came into force on 1 January 1996, was introduced on the recommendation of the Treasury and Civil Service Committee, which saw a code as a means of strengthening the existing arrangements for upholding the essential values and standards of the civil service.

> It would enable civil servants themselves and those they serve—both Ministers and the public—to know what was expected of the Civil Service. It would strengthen the hands of those who sought to maintain essential values in the face of perceived threats to those values. It would make more tangible the values which civil servants hold in common. (Treasury and Civil Service Committee 1994: para. 105).

The Government accepted the Committee's recommendation 'in the interests of maintaining public confidence in the impartiality and integrity of the Civil Service' (Cabinet Office 1995*a*: paras. 2.6–2.7). The Code is not, however, a detailed compendium of rules. Instead its purpose is to set out 'with greater clarity and brevity than existing documents the constitutional framework within which all civil servants work and the values which they are expected to uphold' (ibid.: para. 2.8). It defines 'the constitutional and practical role' of the service as being 'to assist the duly constituted Government . . . in formulating policies of the Government, carrying out decisions of the Government and in administering public service for which the Government is responsible' (Civil Service Code 1996: para. 1). Civil servants are servants of the Crown, who 'owe their loyalty to the duly constituted Government' (para. 2; see also Civil Service Management Code 1996: para. 4.1.1). They should conduct themselves with 'integrity, impartiality and honesty. They should give honest and impartial advice to Ministers without fear or favour, and make all information relevant to a decision available to Ministers. They should not deceive or knowingly mislead Ministers, Parliament or the public' (para. 5). They should also conduct themselves in such a way as 'to deserve and retain the confidence of Ministers and to be able to establish the same relationship with those whom they may be required to serve in some future Administration.' Their conduct should be such that 'Ministers and potential future ministers can be sure that confidence can be freely given, and that the Civil Service will conscientiously fulfil its duties and obligations to, and impartially assist, advise and carry out the policies of the duly constituted Government' (para. 9). They should not 'without authority disclose official information which has been communicated in confidence within Government, or received in confidence from others.' Nor should they 'seek to frustrate or influence the policies, decisions or actions of government by the unauthorised, improper or premature disclosure outside the government of any information to which they have had access as civil servants' (para. 10, re-stating Civil Service Management Code 1996: para. 4.1.3a).

Part of the pressure for the adoption of a code has been based on the argument that there is a need to define the relationship between civil servants in terms other than the traditional undivided loyalty test. 'Tying the official's loyalty unconditionally to the Crown's representative, the Minister, legitimises degrees of Ministerial discretion bordering on absolution (*sic*)' (Public Service Committee 1996*a*: para. 169). Civil servants should therefore be regarded as having a wider duty than simply to the government of the day. This argument has made little headway. Like the Armstrong memorandum before it, the Code was conceived as a restatement of the existing constitutional position rather than a revision of it (Cabinet Office 1995*a*: para. 2.8). It does not replace the traditional undivided loyalty test with some version of a public interest test. It does, however, acknowledge that civil servants' duty of loyalty to the government of the day is not unqualified, but has to be read subject to 'the duty of all public officers to discharge public functions reasonably and according to law'; 'the duty to comply with the law . . . and to uphold the administration of justice', and 'the ethical standards governing particular professions', as well as the accountability of civil servants to the Minister or office holder in charge of their department (para. 4). The duty to comply with the law, it should be noted, extends to 'international law and treaty obligations' (ibid.). This was thought to represent a radical step forward, but it is intended to reflect the fact that, regardless of their status in domestic law, the United Kingdom is bound to comply with its international obligations and it does so by means of its officers.

The Treasury and Civil Service Committee recommended that the Civil Service Code be given statutory backing, but the Code was introduced by way of an amendment to the Civil Service Order in Council (Civil Service (Amendment) Order in Council 1997). Strictly speaking there was no need for prerogative authorization to issue the Code, but it was felt desirable to have a reference to the Code on the face of the Order in Council. The opposition to statutory backing was pithily summed up by a former Head of the Home Civil Service: 'We have codes enough, and we shall not help by making them statutory. These matters do not lend themselves to statutory coding. What we need is for people to read, mark, learn and inwardly digest the principles which are already enshrined in the code and other documents . . . and then for them to live their lives in accordance with the principles' (576 HL Debs., col. 1644, Armstrong of Ilminster, 19 December 1996). Departments and agencies must incorporate the Code in the conditions of service of their staff (Civil Service Management Code: para. 4.1.5). In the Treasury and Civil Service Committee's view, the impact of the Code 'could be particularly strong if it were a condition of employment for all civil servants that they read the Code and conduct themselves in accordance with its provisions' (Treasury and Civil Service Committee 1994: para. 105). It seems, however, that awareness among civil servants of the Code's provisions cannot be taken for granted (Civil Service Commissioners 1998: p. 23). The Labour Government is committed to giving statutory backing to the Code.

1.3 The Armstrong Memorandum

The sources on which the Civil Service Code is based include the 'central framework' set out in the Civil Service Management Code, Questions of Procedure for Ministers (now the Ministerial Code), and the Armstrong Memorandum on the duties and responsibilities of civil servants in relation to ministers (73 HC Debs., cols. *128–30*, written answers 26 February 1985). The latter is 'remarkable' for being the first note of guidance on the duties and responsibilities of staff to have been issued by a Head of the Home Civil Service since Sir Edward Bridges had recourse to the same device in the aftermath of Crichel Down thirty years earlier (Seldon 1990: 106; it has now been followed by the guidance for civil servants on contacts with lobbyists issued on 27 July 1998). A number of incidents of unauthorized disclosure of information culminated in the controversial Ponting case in 1985. Ponting, a middle-ranking civil servant in the Ministry of Defence, was tried under the Official Secrets Acts after the disclosure of documents relating to the attack on the Argentine cruiser *General Belgrano* in the course of the Falklands War. His defence was one of justification rather than denial, and he was acquitted in the face of a summing up pointing clearly to conviction. Like the subsequent Civil Service Code, the Armstrong Memorandum was conceived as a 're-statement' of the essential precepts governing relations between ministers and civil servants. The Treasury and Civil Service Committee summarized its import thus:

> [it] asserts that all civil servants are servants of the Crown; that the Crown appoints Ministers; that Ministers are answerable to Parliament; and that civil servants owe their allegiance 'first and foremost to the Minister.' Any civil servant whose loyalty is put under strain is advised to refer his complaint to his superiors, even up to his Permanent Secretary if necessary, but in no circumstances to seek by his actions to frustrate Ministers' policies or decisions. (Treasury and Civil Service Committee 1986*b*: para. 2.2)

The note was issued with the consent of the Prime Minister, after consultation with Permanent Secretaries in charge of their departments, and with their agreement. It therefore represented a consensus among permanent heads of departments about the duties and responsibilities of civil servants to ministers. It was revised and reissued in December 1987 (123 HC Debs., cols. *572–5*, written answers 2 December 1987). Following the introduction of the Civil Service Code, the Memorandum no longer forms part of the Civil Service Management Code. However, it remains an 'authoritative text' on the duties and responsibilities of civil servants to Ministers (Cabinet Office (OPS) 1996*b*).

1.4 Departmental and agency rules

The central framework set out in the Civil Service Management Code is designed to deliver, through departments and agencies, 'the standards expected of civil servants individually and of the civil service as a whole' (Cabinet Office 1994*a*: para. 2.35). Departments and agencies are responsible for defining the standards of conduct they require of their staff, but the standards they require must 'fully reflect' the Civil Service Code and the standards of conduct described in the central framework set out in the Civil Service Management Code (Civil Service Management Code 1996: para. 4.1.2). They must also incorporate any additional rules necessary to reflect local needs and circumstances (Civil Service Management Code 1996: para. 4.1.6). The system is therefore one which tries to combine uniformity with regard for local needs and circumstances.

The Nolan Committee noted that the responsibility of departments and agencies for defining the standards of conduct they require of their staff created the possibility that, over time, detailed rules on conduct might diverge, depending on the circumstances of the department or agency making them. One way in which the Civil Service Management Code tries to guard against this risk, which is inherent in a decentralized system of rulebooks, is through the obligation it imposes on departments and agencies to draw difficult cases to the attention of the Cabinet Office, in the light of which the central framework can if necessary be revised. The Cabinet Office also monitors observance of the Code in departments and agencies. The Nolan Committee recommended that the OPS as it then was should continue to survey and disseminate best practice on maintaining standards of conduct to ensure that basic principles of conduct were being properly observed (Committee on Standards in Public Life 1995: para. 3.59).

2 Discipline

Discipline is a matter for departments and agencies. The central framework governing disciplinary procedures requires departments and agencies to ensure that staff are aware of the disciplinary procedures that apply to them and the circumstances in which they may be invoked. The circumstances in which the application of disciplinary procedures may be considered must include breach of the organization's standards of conduct or other forms of misconduct; and any other circumstances in which 'the behaviour, action or inaction of individuals significantly disrupts or damages the performance or reputation of the organisation' (Civil Service Management Code 1996: para. 4.5.5). Decisions concerning senior staff must be taken by the permanent head of the department or agency chief executive; decisions concerning the permanent head or a head of department are reserved to the Head of the Home Civil Service, after consultation with the minister of the department concerned and, as appropriate, the Prime Minister (ibid.: para. 4.5.10). Where staff are dismissed as a result of disciplinary proceedings, an appeal may lie to the internal Civil Service Appeal Board (Civil Service Management Code 1996: para. 12.1.26). Staff who are not dismissed, or who are dismissed but ineligible to appeal to the Board, may appeal under the department or agency's personal grievance procedure.

3 Ministerial conduct

A corollary of the principle of neutrality is that ministers should not require civil servants to act in ways which make it difficult or impossible for a future administration to have confidence in their loyalty. The convention of permanence is as vulnerable to ministerial misconduct as to misconduct or an excess of zeal on the part of civil servants. The obligations of ministers have undergone a process of codification parallel to that undergone in relation to civil servants. The Nolan Committee concluded that there was a need for greater clarity about the standards of conduct expected of ministers (Committee on Standards in Public Life 1995: paras. 3.14–3.17). Following its recommendation a set of 'principles of ministerial conduct' were introduced. The principles are set out in the first paragraph of the Ministerial Code, formerly Questions of Procedure for Ministers, which follows closely the text of resolutions of both Houses on ministerial accountability to Parliament adopted in the dying days of the last Parliament (291 H.C. Debs., cols. 273–93, 19 March 1997, 579 H.L. Debs., cols. 1055–62, 20 March 1997). In relation to the civil service they provide that: 'Ministers must not use public resources for party political purposes. They must uphold the political impartiality of the Civil Service, and not ask civil servants to act in any way which would conflict with the Civil Service Code' (Cabinet Office 1997*d*: para. 1(ix)). These duties are restated in the Civil Service Code (para. 3).

The Ministerial Code itself contains a fuller statement of the duties of ministers in relation to the civil service, from which the principle set out in the first paragraph is derived. The Code provides that:

> Ministers have a duty to give fair consideration and due weight to informed and impartial advice from civil servants, as well as to other considerations and advice, in reaching policy decisions; a duty to uphold the political impartiality of the Civil Service, and not to ask civil servants to act in any way which would conflict with the Civil Service Code; a duty to ensure that influence over appointments is not abused for partisan purposes; and a duty to observe the obligations of a good employer with regard to terms and conditions of those who serve them. Civil servants should not be asked to engage in activities likely to call into question their political impartiality, or to give rise to the criticism that people paid from public funds are being used for Party political purposes. (Cabinet Office 1997*d*: para. 56)

The original version of this statement was published in 1986 in response to a recommendation from the Treasury and Civil Service Committee that the Prime Minister should formulate and publish guidelines for ministers which would set out their duties to Parliament and responsibilities for the civil service (Treasury and Civil Service Committee 1986: para. 3.13; Cabinet Office 1986: para. 11). It was subsequently included in the revised version of the Armstrong Memorandum issued in 1987, which stated that the memorandum fell to be read in the wider context of ministers' own responsibilities as set out in the Government's response to the Treasury and Civil Service Committee's Report. The Civil Service Code, which has effectively replaced the Armstrong Memorandum, likewise operates within the framework of ministerial duties set out in the Ministerial Code (para. 3).

The resolutions of both Houses in the last Parliament on ministerial accountability to Parliament also impose duties on ministers with respect to parliamentary accountability, which have implications for the work of civil servants. These are reflected in the Ministerial Code, which asserts that it is of 'paramount importance that Ministers give accurate and truthful information to Parliament . . .' They should be 'as open as possible with Parliament and the public, refusing to provide information only when disclosure would not be in the public interest . . . ' (Cabinet Office 1997*d*: para. 1(iii)–(iv)). The Civil Service Code summarizes the obligations on ministers as being to give Parliament 'as full information as possible about the policies, decisions and actions of the Government, and not to deceive or knowingly mislead Parliament and the public' (para. 3). Guidance has been issued to officials on drafting answers to parliamentary questions in the light of these obligations. Under the guidance it is the civil servant's responsibility to Ministers to 'help them fulfil these obligations'; and the Minister's 'right and responsibility to decide how to do so' (Public Service Committee 1996*b*: Annex C).

The Nolan Committee proposed that it should be for the Prime Minister to determine whether ministers had acted in accordance with 'the highest standards of constitutional and personal conduct' required by the Code, but in the Government's view this went too far towards suggesting that the Prime Minister's relationship with his colleagues should be that of 'invigilator and judge'. It is therefore for ministers to judge how best to act in order to uphold the highest standards, in the knowledge that they are responsible for justifying their conduct to Parliament, and that their remaining in office depends on their retaining the confidence of the Prime Minister (Committee on Standards in Public Life 1995: para. 3.13; Cabinet Office 1995*c*: p. 3).

4 Appeals

This leaves the question of what a civil servant should do when faced with a request or instruction which appears to contravene accepted standards of propriety. Special provision is made in respect of expenditure in breach of the requirements of regularity, propriety, or value for money. Where an accounting officer is instructed to take action which he considers involves such expenditure, he is under an obligation to inform the Treasury and the Comptroller and Auditor General (Treasury 1989*a*: para. 6.1.5, see further below, pp. 128–9). Irregular or improper expenditure apart, however, the only means by which traditionally conflicts or concerns over instructions could be resolved was by upward referral within a department. According to the original version of the Armstrong Memorandum, a civil servant faced with 'a fundamental issue of conscience' should consult a superior officer, 'or in the last resort the Permanent Head of the Department, who can and should if necessary consult the Head of the Home Civil Service'. If that did not enable the matter to be resolved on a basis which the civil servant was able to accept, he or she must either carry out his or her instructions or resign the service. Resignation was subject to the express stipulation that it did not release a civil servant from the obligation to keep the confidences to which he or she had become privy as a civil servant.

The Armstrong procedures were later amended to allow a civil servant faced with a fundamental issue of conscience to have the matter referred to the Head of the Home Civil Service. The Treasury and Civil Service Committee, however, was of the view that this procedure did not command sufficient confidence among civil servants, partly because it required a civil servant to go back up the chain of command down which the original instruction had come (Treasury and Civil Service Committee 1994*a*: para. 110). Only one case had been referred to the Head of the Home Civil Service in nine years, and that did not involve a minister. It therefore recommended that the procedure be replaced by an appeal to the Civil Service Commissioners under its proposed Civil Service Code. This recommendation was accepted by the Government. Under the Code a civil servant who believes he or she is being required to act in a way which:

> is illegal, improper or unethical;
>
> is in breach of constitutional convention or a professional code;
>
> may involve possible maladministration;
>
> raises a 'fundamental issue of conscience'; or
>
> is otherwise inconsistent with the Code,
>
> or who becomes aware that others are acting in such a way, can report the matter to the Civil Service Commissioners if departmental procedures do not resolve his or her concerns. (Civil Service Code: paras. 11–12)

The Government had long opposed the introduction of any form of independent appeal as likely to undermine the relationship between ministers and civil servants; it 'would enshrine distrust between Ministers and officials' (Treasury and Civil Service Committee 1994*a*: para. 109). The Treasury and Civil Service Committee's proposal for an appeal to the Civil Service Commissioners in its view, however, met some of the difficulties previously identified (Cabinet Office 1995*a*: para. 2.11). It did not expand on the nature of these difficulties, but an appeal to the Parliamentary Ombudsman, for example, would involve Parliament in the determination of questions of propriety, while an appeal to the Civil Service Appeal Board would involve representatives of trade unions as well as management. The advantage of an appeal to the Commissioners from the point of view of the Government, it may be thought, is that they were suitably independent, but part of the executive branch.

The internal departmental or agency procedures for the resolution of concerns must first be exhausted before the Commissioners will consider an appeal. In both the Select Committee and the Government's view it should continue to be possible to resolve the majority of doubts about conduct, legality, and propriety within departments. In the Government's view it was also important to 'avoid any steps which weaken confidence between staff and their line managers or the confidential relationship and trust between civil servants and Ministers' (Cabinet Office 1995*a*: para. 2.11). The Commissioners aim to investigate cases as quickly as possible consistent with a thorough examination of the case and, where possible, to resolve the issues raised by agreement with those concerned. Their power is one of making recommendations rather than binding decisions, but they may make such reports on appeals 'as they think fit', which would enable them, for example, to report to Parliament a refusal by a department or agency to accept a recommendation (Civil Service Order in Council 1995, arts. 4(5), 8(2)). No appeal lies against their recommendation. If the matter cannot be resolved by the procedures laid down on a basis which the servant concerned is able to accept, he or she must either carry out his or her instructions or resign from the service. Resignation is expressly stated as before not to relieve civil servants of their obligation of confidentiality (Civil Service Code: para. 13).

The Nolan Committee saw the introduction of an independent line of appeal as a step forward, but remained concerned that the minimal use made of the possibility of an appeal to the Head of the Home Civil Service would be replicated under the new system because of the requirement that the internal procedures for the resolution of concerns must first be exhausted before recourse could be had to the Commissioners (Committee on Standards in Public Life 1995: para. 3.53). A parallel procedure has therefore been introduced on its recommendation which allows staff to raise concerns in confidence through someone nominated for the purpose outside their normal management line (Civil

Service Management Code 1996: para. 12.1.7); the Public Interest Disclosure Act 1998 has also strengthened the protection afforded public interest whistleblowers against victimization. By 31 March 1998, five appeals had been made to the Commissioners. Two had been investigated and upheld, one was resolved within the department, one had not resulted in a further appeal to the Commissioners after the internal departmental procedures had been concluded, and the other was still the subject of internal procedures (Civil Service Commissioners 1998: pp. 22–3). Against a background of continuing uncertainty over whether civil servants feel any inhibitions about raising matters under the Code, the Civil Service Commissioners are to work with the Cabinet Office to review the operation of the appeal arrangements and to raise awareness among civil servants of the Code and the mechanisms for raising possible breaches of it (ibid.: p. 23).

VI CONCLUSIONS

Against the background of the plural character of the central executive outlined in the previous chapter, what conclusions should we draw about the internal control function in its application to the civil service? First, that in contrast to the pattern outlined in the previous chapter legal primacy in the regulation of the civil service is enjoyed not by departments through their ministers but by the centre in the form of the Minister for the Civil Service. At the same time, however, control is exercised, as it has always been exercised, through departments and agencies. The primary role, in practice, is played by departments within an overall framework laid down and monitored by the centre. Of the regimes that we have looked at in this chapter it is that in respect of recruitment that illustrates the division of labour between the centre and departments most clearly.

Second, the 'law' of the civil service has undergone extensive changes in recent years. Existing codes have been rationalized and replaced, while new codes have been issued (on recruitment, on the conduct of civil servants, and on the conduct of ministers), and new machinery devised for settling disputes arising out of their application. Of the three historically impelling reasons that have been put forward for codification—clarification, unification, and law reform—it is the first two that are most revealing of this trend towards the 'codification of what might once have been assumed to be common ground' (Committee on Standards in Public Life 1995: para. 3.11). Codification has been in large measure about making existing standards (of recruitment and conduct) explicit consequent upon the changes that have taken place in the organization of government in recent years. The argument was put succinctly by the Nolan Committee. Against a background of decentralization and greater interchange between the public and private sectors 'it cannot be assumed that everyone in the public service will assimilate a public service culture unless they are told what is expected of them and the message is systematically reinforced' (Committee on Standards in Public Life 1995: para. 1.10). In the second of its Civil Service White Papers, the Conservative Government acknowledged that if the values on which the civil service was based were to be maintained it was essential that they be 'clearly expressed, effectively communicated within the Civil Service and upheld by civil servants at all levels and by Ministers in their dealings with them' (Cabinet Office 1995*b*: para. 2.5); in a more 'pluralist and less hierarchical' service it was vital to ensure that 'rules of conduct and messages about standards were communicated, inculcated and audited effectively' (Treasury and Civil Service Committee 1994: para. 77).

Codification has also been conceived as a way of maintaining the unity of what in the opinion of one interlocutor is 'no longer a service but a series of cadres'. The argument here is that one of the things that defines the service is its adherence to certain shared values; that despite the changes that have taken place the service will nevertheless continue to be held together by certain 'common codes and principles of doing business and by the unity of its purpose in serving collective Cabinet government' (Efficiency Unit 1991: Foreword). Like 'core competences' in business, 'core values' are thus conceived as a means of holding together what has become 'a conglomerate organisation—a confederation of Departments and Agencies undertaking widely different businesses' (Efficiency Unit 1993*a*: para. 3).

That law reform has not been a major factor, on the other hand, should not occasion surprise. As we saw, in the absence of any constitutional guarantees, the principle of permanence depends on ministerial forbearance, and that forbearance is likely to be called into question by any attempt to revise the understandings on which relations between civil servants and ministers have traditionally been based. As the last Conservative Government made clear, its commitment to a permanent civil service was predicated upon the loyalty of that service to the government of the day. Were civil servants to be made directly accountable to Parliament, they would become 'effectively another political force', a development which the Government could not view as 'compatible with its commitment to a permanent, non-political civil service' (Public Service Committee 1996*b*: para. 7). At the same time, it would be surprising if the opportunity presented by codification had not been taken to iron out infelicities in the existing rules. It may be no accident, for example, that the statement that civil servants owe a duty of undivided allegiance to the 'state' has been replaced by less awkward references to ministers, which leave no room for drawing a distinction between the interests of the state and those of ministers.

The executive's hand in all of this of course has been considerably strengthened by the fact that the civil service continues to be regulated under the prerogative. For Jennings, the civil service was in many respects the 'most peculiar of the institutions of the British constitution' (1959*b*: 200). At the root of its peculiarity lay the fact that the law governing the service was made by the executive itself, as part of a self-contained system of law, which was not subject at that time to the jurisdiction of the courts (1959*b*: 207). Since Jennings wrote, the barriers between the executive's own law and the law of the land—Dicey's ordinary law—have broken down as a result of the contractualization of civil service employment and the growth of judicial review. The barriers between civil service law and the legislature by contrast remain intact, though it may be that they too will diminish. The Government is committed to giving statutory backing to the Civil Service Code (Joint Consultative Committee on Constitutional Reform 1997: paras. 83–4; House of Lords Select Committee on the Public Service 1998: para. 412). More fundamentally, devolution to Scotland and Wales poses a new challenge to unity and neutrality which perhaps only legislation can meet. Under devolution arrangements the staff of the Scottish and Welsh Executives will remain members of the Home Civil Service (Scotland Act 1998, s. 51 (2); Government of Wales Act 1998, s. 34 (2)); yet administrations of different political complexions could simultaneously be sitting in London, Edinburgh, and Cardiff. For a single service to command the confidence of such administrations may be a more severe test of permanence, unity, and neutrality than any presented by the need to give loyal service to successive administrations led by opposing parties. It would not be surprising if this produced stresses leading to calls for legislative guarantees of neutrality and other characteristics of the service, or for other legislative solutions. For the moment, however, the constitution continues to look to the executive's own law for the maintenance of the values—of permanence, loyalty, honesty and integrity, impartiality, confidentiality, and recruitment and promotion on merit—on which the service is based.

4

The Financial Resources of Government: Institutions

I INTRODUCTION: THE CONSTITUTIONAL DIMENSION

This chapter, and the two which follow it, are about internal control of the financial resources of government. Such control, generally identified with the action of the Treasury, has been the subject of an extensive literature, with landmark treatments appearing at regular intervals: Samuel Beer's *Treasury Control* in the nineteen-fifties (Beer 1957); Heclo and Wildavsky's *The Private Government of Public Money* in the nineteen-seventies (Heclo and Wildavsky 1973); and Thain and Wright's *The Treasury and Whitehall* appearing most recently as the likely text for the nineties (Thain and Wright 1995). Faced with such accessible richness of treatment elsewhere, we asked ourselves what could be the justification for anything more than cursory reference here.

The answer lies in the relative indifference of these works to the constitutional dimension of this financial control. Beer writes, at least in part, in this dimension; his successors focus rather on the politics of public expenditure, on its functions as the instrument and accompaniment of policy, or view it as a policy problem in its own right. For the constitutional lawyer, however, the Treasury's financial planning and control function must surely be viewed primarily by reference to the central place occupied by Parliamentary financial powers in the design of our constitution. Parliament's supremacy, as all the books tell us, is built on its successful assertion first of the control of taxation, and second of the power of appropriation, the determination of the purposes for which government might spend its money, whether raised by taxation or otherwise. The argument over taxation may fairly be seen as closed in Parliament's favour by the Revolution Settlement of 1689 (Bill of Rights 1689, art. 4). The argument over appropriation took considerably longer to win, and Parliament's success in it has never been capable of encapsulation in the sort of simple phrases that make up the Bill of Rights. None the less, the fact that government can neither tax the citizen, nor expend any of its own funds, without Parliamentary approval of the rules and levels of taxation on the one hand, and of the broad purposes of expenditure, and the amounts to be applied to such purposes, on the other, remains the fundamental support for the central position of Parliament within our constitution. Were the scope of that requirement of approval to be narrowed, or its significance attenuated, nothing too drastic might occur in the short term; but in the long term it can hardly be doubted that the existing democratic mechanisms of our constitution would be fatally weakened.

The effectiveness of this central support for the democratic control of executive power in the United Kingdom has always depended upon the way in which government organizes its financial resources for its own purposes. Effective parliamentary control cannot come into being unless government itself possesses properly functioning systems for relating overall revenue and expenditure needs, determining how revenue is to be raised, setting limits on expenditure, allocating it between functions, and ensuring that those limits and functions are respected. In relation to these basic requirements, there is little or no difference between the interests of Parliament in financial control and those of the people within government entrusted with these tasks. In consequence, in our discussion of the development of Treasury powers later in this chapter, we shall find that at least since the end of the seventeenth century there has existed an alliance between Parliament and Treasury—albeit one whose significance to the parties has varied with their respective enthusiasm for economy in public expenditure—directed toward the control and containment of such expenditure, and grounded in a mutual dependence. The Treasury has depended on Parliament for the public ventilation of its control problems and the marshalling of political pressure in favour of the adoption of more effective systems of control. Parliament has in its turn depended on the Treasury to deliver systems which, as well as being effective, are transparent: that is to say, they incorporate the specific virtue of generating sufficiently detailed and consistent information about financial decisions to enable a body outside the administration to maintain a genuine process of supervision. Not surprisingly, Parliament and Treasury have not always wholly agreed as to how these requirements might best be met—for example, when the end of the old Exchequer system was in sight in the mid-nineteenth century Parliament favoured a legislatively based process of audit, the government an executive-based one (Chester 1981: 208–20)—but such divergences have not impaired the long-term pursuit of the common interest.

This partnership is of the greatest continuing importance to our democratic structure, because the processes—and indeed the goals—of internal control are constantly changing, and such changes could easily produce an attenuation of the significance of parliamentary controls. The impact of internal changes on constitutional fundamentals is a complex one. The fact, loudly lamented for most of the twentieth century, that

Parliament does not now 'control' government financial decisions by substituting different ones of its own is not in itself too important. What matters more, in terms of protection of democratic rights in general, is not what decisions Parliament takes, but the fact that its decision is needed and thereby may represent a roadblock to the adoption or implementation of unacceptable government policies. If the road gets moved, by the adoption within government of new financial decision-making processes, the roadblocks need to be moved too if that democratic protection is to be maintained. This dissociation between parliamentary form and executive substance in financial decision-making has in fact been a continuing concern since government started moving away, in the nineteen-fifties, from the one-year cash planning cycle on which Parliamentary control had been based since 1861. Since that time, as we shall see, there has been a constant dialogue between the Treasury and the relevant House of Commons Committees, addressed to the question of how the Treasury may exercise financial control, in the forms it considers most apt to promote economy, efficiency, and a proper economic relationship between the public and private sectors, without impairing Parliament's capacities to understand, to criticize and, ultimately, to control the government's financial decisions.

In this relationship, we should note, there continues to be an element of Treasury dependence on Parliament, to furnish a discipline which will support its own task of internal control. In 1998 the Chancellor of the Exchequer brought forward, without parliamentary prompting, a new normative, and partly legislative, long-term framework for fiscal policy, in the shape of a Code for Fiscal Stability (Treasury 1998*e*). The Code, laid before Parliament and approved by resolution of the House of Commons, commits the government to the observation of principles of transparency, stability, responsibility, fairness, and efficiency in its fiscal and debt management policies (Finance Act 1998, s. 155). It spells out the practical implications of these principles in some detail (below, pp. 153–4). The Act also requires the Treasury to lay before Parliament a range of budgetary and economic information, some traditionally provided, such as the Financial Statement and Budget Report (below, pp. 152–3), some new, such as the consultative Pre-Budget Report first produced in 1997 (s. 156). What looks like a fiscal hair shirt has been explained by the Treasury (1998*a*: 9) in terms of a desire both 'to strengthen the credibility of fiscal policy' (sc. impress the money markets, cf. Strange 1996) and 'to ensure that it is always conducted in the United Kingdom's long-term interest' (sc. reinforce the Treasury's position in arguments with spending Departments). Legislation is advantageous for these purposes not only because it expresses the right intentions in suitably solemn form

(Daintith 1997*a*: 38), but also because it brings into play external mechanisms of control, Parliamentary and perhaps even judicial (below, pp. 199–206), to supplement those of the executive itself.

A major theme of these three chapters is thus the strong interdependence between external and internal controls in the field of finance. Most of the remainder of this chapter will be devoted to description and analysis of the internal institutions of the executive with competences in this field: the Treasury; other bodies concerned with efficiency and economy; the structures within departments which interact with the Treasury; and the position of the new executive agencies deriving from the Next Steps programme. In the following two chapters we explore the ways in which these different bodies interact in the performance of the different tasks of planning and control, both with each other, and with Parliament—in particular, the Comptroller and Auditor-General and National Audit Office acting on behalf of Parliament—and the courts. Special importance attaches here to the recent Treasury–Parliament dialogue from the adoption of cash limits in the nineteen-sixties to the current discussion of resource accounting and budgeting and the new framework represented by the Code for Fiscal Stability.

II THE CONSTITUTIONAL STRUCTURE

These relationships function within a constitutional framework established well before the advent of responsible government and the assumption by the government of the day of the traditional role and powers of the Crown. As Erskine May, the leading authority on Parliamentary powers and procedures, puts it, 'The Crown demands money, the Commons grant it, and the Lords assent to the grant' (1997: 732).

This basic maxim calls for some elaboration. First, the granting of 'supply'—putting funds for public expenditure in the hands of the executive—is conceived of as something distinct from the granting of 'ways and means'—the ability to collect funds, whether through taxes, borrowing, or the application of funds flowing into the executive's purse by other routes (such as fees). These two types of grants attract different parliamentary procedures which have not generally been synchronized within the annual financial cycle. Our main focus in these chapters will be with the 'supply' or expenditure side of finance. Revenue functions, both policy and implementation, are largely concentrated within what are now known collectively as the Chancellor of the Exchequer's Departments—principally Treasury, Inland Revenue, and Customs and Excise—and associated bodies like the Bank of England. Expenditure functions, on the other hand, are disseminated across the whole of government, and their internal and external control is thus much more problematic.

Second, and a further source of complexity in the annual financial cycle as seen in Parliament, the assent of Parliament to the grant of supply and of ways and means must, constitutionally, be given by way of legislation, and not merely by way of resolution of one House or the other (Erskine May: 1997: 736). This is the case despite the privilege asserted by the Commons in financial matters; and it extends beyond the annual financial procedures to any case where a 'charge' is to be made either upon public funds (i.e. national public expenditure) or upon the people (i.e. taxes and duties) (ibid. 734–5). This means that multi-stage processes are involved in the parliamentary cycle, with parliamentary approvals being framed first in the form of resolutions and subsequently in the form of legislative provisions. The proposals which are the subject of resolutions may be much less detailed than the eventual legislation (as is the case with the ways and means resolutions which form the basis of the annual Finance Bill); or they may be much more detailed (as will be seen when the annual estimates, presented to the House of Commons for approval by resolution, are compared with the Appropriation Act which gives supply decisions legislative form and force). The legislative basis for executive financial functions means that, in principle, their discharge is subject to the scrutiny and control of the courts. In practice, while courts have applied the same processes of review to revenue raising functions as to administrative activity generally, they have been much more reticent in relation to the control of expenditure (Elliot 1981*a*), with the result that external control functions have been operated almost wholly by Parliamentary institutions. This may change (below, pp. 199–206).

The third point is that the right of initiative, both as to what the level of public expenditure shall be (supply) and as to what kinds and levels of taxation are to be imposed to pay for it (ways and means), rests firmly with the executive. The right is formally expressed only in relation to proposals for specific new expenditure, in Standing Order 48 of the House of Commons (reprinted in Erskine May 1997: Appendix), which dates from 1706 and became a standing order in 1713, and requires the Crown's recommendation for any such proposal. Erskine May asserts, however (1997: 737–8), that the Order reflects much older practice long built into the annual procedures of supply and ways and means, invariably initiated by the Crown in the form of resolutions moved by ministers. But the Order also represents the recognition by Parliament of its own innate incapacity to act as the manager of public funds. As a result, Parliament may do no more than disapprove or reduce items of public expenditure, or restrict or reject taxes. Its role in financial matters is thus one of criticism, not construction; and it acknowledges that it can hope to 'control' the government's acquisition and use of financial resources only to the extent that government is capable of controlling those processes for itself and informing Parliament about them. Parliamentary control, and internal governmental control, thus exist, and have developed, in a relationship of interdependence, in which the relevant parliamentary institutions and procedures simultaneously function as the critic and the support of the executive's own control institutions.

A fourth point is closely related to this one. Supply is granted, as Erskine May indicates, to the Crown: that is to say, to the government as a whole. In making its grant Parliament will indicate, in the Appropriation Act, the maximum that may be spent on each of a number of activities ('Votes') which tend to correspond with the scope of activities of departments; but the grant is not made to those departments, nor do these maxima connote any obligation on the Crown to spend those sums on the activities described (Beer 1957: 126–8; though see below, p. 203). (Spending obligations may, of course, be imposed by permanent legislation.) It follows from this that the Appropriation Act does not, itself, authorize departmental expenditure. Such authorization is a matter to be determined under the executive's internal arrangements, and is, as we shall see in discussing the powers of the Treasury, the root of central control over departments in this field.

III THE INSTITUTIONS OF THE EXECUTIVE

1 The Treasury

> I can't blow my nose without asking the Treasury.
>
> (Tony Benn, Secretary of State for Trade and Industry (Benn 1990: 328))

The Treasury is by tradition *the* central department of government in the United Kingdom: it has been called the 'department of departments' (Wright 1969: 1); and hailed as 'almost certainly the most powerful single government department in any Western country' (Normanton 1966: 371). Its nominal head is the Prime Minister, who also always holds the office of First Lord of the Treasury; it is responsible for raising by borrowing or taxation the funds that government needs to do its work; its overall concern with expenditure means that no policy initiative of any department is without interest for it; and has also meant that for much of the last hundred years, it has had the primary responsibility for the civil service as a whole. It is, as already noted, the subject of a large literature, and we shall here look only at those aspects of its tasks, organization, history, and powers which are relevant to its position as an agency of intra-governmental control. One word of warning to the reader: consistently with its commitment to economy, the Treasury is a ferocious user of acronyms. Confusing as these may be for the outsider, they represent the way the Treasury thinks and are often the only precise and unambiguous means of describing a notion. We have followed Treasury practice, and hope that with the help of a table of abbreviations (above, pp. *xv–xvi*) and initial definitions in our text, the reader will be able to keep up with us.

1.1 Tasks and organization

As a central department the Treasury constantly seeks to exercise leadership in the improvement of Government performance, to show by example what can be done. When Parliament pressed strongly in the early nineteenth century for economies in public expenditure to reflect the return to normality after the conclusion of the Napoleonic Wars, which had massively inflated both military and civil establishments, the Treasury substantially cut its own establishment and remunerations, in the hope—largely vain—of inducing other departments to volunteer similar economies (Roseveare 1973: 92, 161–2). Likewise, when in February 1993 the Treasury came up with the idea of Fundamental Expenditure Reviews, through which all departments should examine long-term spending trends on their programmes to see if they were sustainable and appropriate (Treasury 1994*b*: 10–11), it felt that it had to go through the exercise itself in 1994 despite the fact that quite radical changes were already taking place in the department (Burns 1995: 13). As it turned out, this review took the process of change much further, with the result that the organization of the Treasury today (1999) is different in major respects even from that reported in Thain and Wright's comprehensive 1995 treatment (1995: ch. 6, especially at 90), as is the language used to describe its aims and objectives.

The Treasury now expresses its overall aim as 'to raise the rate of sustainable growth, and achieve rising prosperity, through creating economic and employment opportunities for all' (Treasury 1998*f*: 113). In pursuance of this aim, it has defined a number of objectives, which range from 'maintaining a stable macroeconomic framework with low inflation' to 'arranging for cost effective management of the government's debt and foreign currency reserves and the supply of notes and coins' (ibid.). Each of its seven directorates is assigned responsibility for one or more of these objectives or for activities in support of them. Three of these directorates pursue objectives which imply effective control, or at least influence, over the actions of other departments as reflected in their expenditures.

The *Budget and Public Finances Directorate* has overall responsibility for fiscal policy, expressed in the objectives of 'maintaining sound public finances in accordance with the Code for Fiscal Stability' and 'promoting a fair and efficient tax and benefit system with incentives to work, save and invest'. To this general concern with financial aggregates, notably the setting of annual spending totals and policy relating to annual estimates, are added direct responsibility for the revenue side (tax and borrowing policy), as well as an interest in seeing that the financial control system delivers continuing improvements in the efficiency of government, a task which involves 'oversee[ing] the Treasury's remaining interests in the efficiency and management of the civil service' (Treasury 1994*a*: 2; for the interests transferred in 1995 to the Office of Public Service see above, pp. 65–6). Control of departmental running costs, examined in Chapter 6 below, is now the main device through which this objective is pursued.

Next, the *Spending Directorate* is the lead directorate for 'improving the quality and cost effectiveness of public services'. The reference to quality and effectiveness, as well as to cost, derives directly from the Fundamental Expenditure Review and may be seen as an attempt to address a complaint about Treasury control that is at least a century old—that an obsession with cheeseparing blinds it to the necessities of rational policy (Wright 1972; Castle 1993: 342). The Directorate continues the work of the former expenditure divisions in monitoring departmental spending to ensure that it remains within planned limits (Thain and Wright 1995: 95–7) but this objective also implies a much greater involvement in the substance of departmental policy-making and administration than has been acknowledged by the traditional image of a Treasury rigorous in financial control but at arm's length from policy-making (Wright 1972). In recent years the Treasury has regularly recorded its contributions not just to the efficient use of public money but also to the improvement of public sector decisions and, indeed, the setting of policy priorities (e.g. Treasury 1998*a*: 20–3), and has described its style of involvement as shifting from control to co-operation, a shift associated with attempts to withdraw from detailed within-year monitoring of expenditure (Treasury 1996*a*: para. 1.2.22; 1998*a*: para. 1.2.26). These new patterns of involvement have now been formalized and put at the forefront of government policy through the device of Public Service Agreements between departments and Treasury, developed out of the Comprehensive Spending Review (see Chapters 5 and 6 below).

Third, the *Financial Management, Reporting and Audit Directorate* leads in 'maintaining an effective accounting and budgetary framework and promoting high standards of regularity, propriety and accountability'. Again this appears as a distinct key objective only following the Treasury's Fundamental Expenditure Review (Treasury 1995*a*: 3; see now Treasury 1998*f*: 113). The current major preoccupation of the Directorate is the switch to resource accounting (below, pp. 164–8), but its work is also of particular constitutional salience, encompassing as it does the Treasury's concerns with the regularity and propriety of public expenditure in general. The Directorate incorporates the Treasury Officer of Accounts (TOA) and his team, the established contact on accounting matters both with Parliament (through the Public Accounts Committee, where he is in attendance), with the National Audit Office (below, pp. 193–9), and with departments. It also has advisory responsibilities for government accounting, and government internal audit, generally, in relation both to resources and to advice (below, pp. 137–9).

Under the overall supervision of the Chancellor of the Exchequer, the chief Treasury Minister, these directorates work with different members of the Treasury's ministerial team. The size of this team, and the allocation of responsibilities within it, may vary from month to month. Currently (1999) there are five Treasury Ministers besides the Chancellor. First comes the Chief Secretary, who is ordinarily a member of the Cabinet. This is the key figure in terms of Treasury control, with responsibilities for public expenditure planning and control, public sector pay, and value for money in the public service generally. Other 'control' responsibilities are divided among the Financial Secretary (responsibility for the Treasury's Parliamentary financial business, including its powers under the Exchequer and Audit Acts), and the Economic Secretary (Treasury interest in general accounting matters). The Paymaster General, currently the minister responsible for the Treasury's tax business, and the Minister of State presently have no role in expenditure control.

All the directorates are organized in small teams. Within *Spending*, for example, there are currently teams for each functional group of departmental activities, sometimes involving one department, as with the Agriculture, Social Security, and Health teams, sometimes several, as with the Home and Legal team. These teams are the first line of contact with the departments, in all the phases of expenditure planning and control that we describe in the next chapter. In addition there are standing teams which cut across directorates, such as the Management Committee for the Public Expenditure Survey, and a policy of creating *ad hoc* cross-directorate teams as needed. 'Open and accountable conduct of policy' is presented in the Treasury's aims as a general value of the organization (Treasury 1998*a*: 1).

While the range of Treasury responsibilities has been significantly modified in recent years—thus in 1998 it lost practical control over interest rates to the Bank of England's new Monetary Policy Committee (Bank of England Act 1998, Part II) but took over from the Bank day-to-day management of government debt—the central task of control and supervision of the public finances does not change. For the most effective performance of that task, the recent structural reforms seek to preserve, in 'today's fast-moving information-intensive world' (Burns 1995: 17), the Treasury's character as a compact supervisory élite, rather than as an *executive* department. Such a concept of the Treasury was clearly articulated at the beginning of the nineteenth century by Sir George Harrison, its first Assistant (i.e. permanent) Secretary (Torrance 1968: 64–9; Wright 1969: 1–4). This was a bold vision: when he held office Parliament was only beginning to awake, at the urgings of Burke and Shelburne and the movement for Economical Reform, from its long eighteenth-century indifference to good financial management (Roseveare 1973: 56–9), and the constitutional and legal bases of the Treasury's authority were obscure and perhaps incomplete. Obscure they still remain, and in the rest of this section we try to uncover the hidden links and levers of control.

1.2 History

Though the Treasury was among the first departments to acquire statutory powers (below, p. 116), its origins lie in the prerogative (above, pp. 32–9), and there exists no comprehensive legislative description of its functions. While requirements of Treasury consent to departmental decisions are scattered through the statute book, for the core powers of the Treasury we have to look to established and accepted practice, and to formal internal law of the executive in the shape of prerogative Orders in Council. As with much of what is important in the British constitution, therefore, we cannot explain the bases of Treasury control without reference to history.

The office of Lord High Treasurer is one of the great offices of state in the United Kingdom: but it has not been occupied since 1714 (Baxter 1957: ch. 1; Roseveare 1969: 77). At all times since then, and during some important periods before (Roseveare 1973: 17–45 on the vital period 1667–72) it has been 'in commission': that is to say, entrusted to a collective body, the Lords Commissioners of the Treasury, or Treasury Board. These Lords Commissioners exist today, and their names will be found, for example, at the foot of statutory instruments made by the Treasury; but with the exception of the Chancellor of the Exchequer, they have nothing to do with Treasury business. The Prime Minister, as we saw above, always holds the office of First Lord, an office which may have some symbolic significance in placing the Treasury at the centre of government but which involves no day-to-day contact; and the remaining Lords Commissioners are in fact the Government's Whips in the House of Commons (the Chief Whip, paradoxically, holding the title of Parliamentary Secretary to the Treasury and not being a Commissioner). The link between the Treasury and party discipline is, however, in no way arbitrary. The eighteenth-century House of Commons may not have been enthusiastic for financial discipline but it was very interested in securing the fruits of patronage. The Treasury controlled the lion's share of the spoils of government. In the second half of the century, 14,000 out of the 17,000 people engaged in civil government service held posts connected with the revenue, under Treasury supervision (Roseveare 1969: 84), and it was the energetic use of this patronage which shaped and maintained a government majority in the House with the First Lord of the Treasury at its head. The political strength which this conferred upon the Treasury has never been lost, and there is nice irony in the fact that the nineteenth-century search for financial control and rectitude, which could not have been carried through without that strength, involved stripping away the sources of patronage on which it had been built (Roseveare 1973; Chester 1981).

From Norman times, the Lord High Treasurer, as superintendent of the Exchequer, looked after the King's treasure, held in the so-called Lower Exchequer. The key processes were receipt, safe custody, and release or payment against proper authorization (Binney 1958: 220–33). So long as the King defrayed from his own resources the costs of his government and household—largely synonymous terms in medieval times—the responsibility was a relatively simple one, though not undemanding. Even at this period royal resources would be scattered in different landholdings and estates, whose stewards needed to hold the balances of the estate's expenditure and income and account for them at regular intervals. In England this accounting process was carried out through the Upper Exchequer, an institution which continued in separate existence until 1834. But it was the Treasurer who required to take an overall view of the King's financial position, to protect his resources against dissipation, and who therefore strove to exercise control over all income and outgoings. Matters grew more complex as the demands of war meant that, at first very occasionally, then with increasing frequency in Tudor and Stuart times, the King had to seek additional income through taxation and other means. Ensuring that this income flowed into the Exchequer, not round it, and keeping watch on the separate courts set up in Tudor times to administer specific types of funds (the Courts of Wards and Liveries, of Augmentations, of First Fruits) was a challenge to which Treasurers were not always equal (Dietz

1928). None the less it was the essence of the task of protecting the King's Treasure—and the King himself against his liberality with it—that the Treasurer should be aware of all royal expenditures, whether out of the Exchequer or not, and whatever the source of the revenue which might meet them.

The first significant modern statement of the Treasury's rights and powers in this respect dates from 1668, when the young and energetic group of Lords Commissioners to whom Charles II had entrusted the Treasury secured an Order in Council, dated 31 January 1668, confirming the need for their consent or countersignature for financial decisions such as the issue of warrants for expenditure. Roseveare (1973: 113) calls this 'the fundamental statement of Treasury authority, appealed to and re-asserted in the face of all challenges'. A little earlier another Order in Council had asserted (albeit in the emergency of hostilities with the Dutch) the ability of the Treasury to control the week-by-week details even of expenditure already authorized in general terms (Roseveare 1973: 118). In their time these Orders could be seen as essentially a matter of royal housekeeping, though their political significance, as subordinating the powerful Secretaries of State to Treasury authority in financial matters, should not be underestimated. The Orders predate by more than a century any practice of regular Parliamentary appropriation, yet they underpin the position the Treasury was to assume in executive–Parliament relations, by legitimizing its *comprehensive* control over expenditure, even by those parts of the executive which had their own Treasurers, such as the navy.

The significance of these Orders, it is important to appreciate, lay in their confirmation of a right of control in the Treasury, not in the establishment of an enduring system for the operation of such control. Royal backsliding, administrative inertia, and the joys of political patronage all played their part, in the next hundred years, in wearing away the achievements of Sir George Downing and his fellows, but when from about 1780 onwards Parliament began to develop its interests in public finance, it was able, in demanding 'the establishment of an effectual control in the hands of the Treasury', to present this as 'nothing more than the restoration to the Treasury of its ancient authority' (Select Committee on Income and Expenditure, 1828, cited in Roseveare 1973: 160). The Treasury, in the person of Sir George Harrison (above, p. 113), probably helped the Committee to reach this conclusion, which echoed his own views as to the Treasury's status as the 'legitimate and only constitutional advisers of the Crown' in all matters relating to 'the powers and authorities which the Crown, by its ancient prerogative, might exercise with regard to its revenues', and as 'the sole constitutional judge of the propriety and expediency of expenditure' (Torrance 1968: 64–5, cited in Chester 1981: 204).

While Harrison's Treasury ultimately lost to Parliament some measure of the discretion he claimed for it, notably through the replacement of executive-based by Parliament-based audit in the Exchequer and Audit Departments Act 1866, the whole course of parliamentary development over the years from the institution of Economical Reform in 1780 may in retrospect be seen to have been guided by the idea that an effective Treasury was a precondition of Parliamentary control of public finance (Chester 1981: 200). This perception accompanied, for example, the somewhat confused attempts to secure parliamentary control over the civil expenditures of the Crown, by moving away from the concept of a civil list payment voted for the king's whole reign. Though the practice of appropriation of naval and military expenditures was already well-established by 1780, it was not until 1850 that an Appropriation Act arranged civil service expenditures into orderly groups. Parliament's getting to this position depended entirely on the steady exercise and refinement of Treasury control, in getting departments to make timely and uniform presentation of their estimates to it for consolidation and presentation to the House. Such control was not, however, grounded upon legislative mandates provided by Parliament. The idea of exclusive royal responsibility for the management of the executive had by the late eighteenth century weakened sufficiently for Parliament to single out the Treasury as a part of the executive on which it wished to confer specific legal powers in relation to certain salaries and offices and, later, in relation to pensions generally (Chester 1981: 198–9, 207). But the idea that inter-departmental relations within the executive, and hence Treasury control in general, might be legislatively ordered seems never to have occurred to the parliamentary reformers, who relied on the recommendations of its numerous Select Committees inquiring into these matters, and on the general political climate of concern about public expenditure, to give sufficient political reinforcement to the Treasury's own efforts to reassert its 'ancient authority'.

1.3 Powers

This Parliamentary delicacy towards the prerogative could be embarrassing for the Treasury, especially when MPs themselves lost sight of it and pressed Treasury officials to cite legislative chapter and verse for the powers of control they claimed over departmental expenditure. George Arbuthnot, an Assistant Secretary to the Treasury, was given a rough ride on this issue by the newly formed Public Accounts Committee in 1861 (Public Accounts Committee 1862: Evidence, qq. 638 ff.). Prompted by a defiant Admiralty, the Committee seemed reluctant to be convinced either by the Treasury's 'ancient authority' (q. 665), or by the idea that Treasury control had 'very much the effect of the common law of England, which you cannot find in written statutes' (q. 760), especially when they heard that the control was ineffective because the Admiralty refused to recognize it (qq. 763–4). Yet even when the process of centralizing financial administration was effectively completed in 1866 by quite elaborate legislation (Exchequer and Audit Departments Act 1866) introducing appropriation accounting, under the direct supervision of a parliamentary officer, as the main guarantee of regularity of government expenditure, the underlying Treasury powers, steadily reinforced since the beginning of the century, were evoked by way of reference rather than being formally restated. In consequence, though Treasury powers are at the core of the financial part of our constitution, their scope and basis remain almost wholly obscure. This obscurity has been deepened by the modern rhetoric of the Treasury, developed by Sir Warren Fisher as its Permanent Secretary in the years between the two World Wars as a means of laying the ghost of a negative and obstructive 'Treasury control' (Hamilton 1951: 26–7). Fisher and his successors have emphasized co-operation and teamwork between Treasury and Departments in the search for economy almost to the point of denying that the Treasury has anything in the nature of constitutional powers at all, which may be one reason why the modern literature (with the notable exception of Beer (1957)) largely neglects them and tends to focus instead on variables like the relative power and prestige of Treasury and spending Ministers (Wright 1969; 1972). Certainly the Treasury is a Department among others, but the fact that the Cabinet collectively can overrule the Treasury does not mean that it has no powers of its own. We think that such powers are not dependent on such political accidents, but derive from three long-established (but not immutable) constitutional roles played by the Treasury: as issuer of public funds; as supervisor of the expenditure of funds once issued; and as gatekeeper of the executive's financial access to Parliament.

1.3.1 Issuance of public funds

The first of these roles is arguably the most fundamental, and is also the most fully stated in the 1866 Act. This is the Treasury's necessary participation in the issuance of public funds to Departments. Such issuance in relation to services charged directly to the Consolidated Fund is dealt with by section 13; in relation to services which are the subject of appropriation, by sections 14 and 15 of the Act. In each case, on the requisition of the Treasury, the Comptroller and Auditor-General grants a credit to it, on the Exchequer account at the Bank of England, out of which the Treasury may make the requisite issues to departments; but in the case of issues for supply expenditure, the requisition may only be made with the authority of a royal order under the Royal Sign Manual countersigned by the Treasury, that authority referring to and being limited by the sums voted or granted by Parliament for the purposes stated. It is the Treasury, rather than the Comptroller, that is responsible at this stage (of issue of funds) for ensuring that the amounts issued are consistent with the relevant legislative appropriations or supply resolutions approving estimates. While the documentation is somewhat simpler now than it was in the eighteenth century (compare the procedure as described in Binney 1958: 172–6 with the sample documents in Select Committee on Procedure (Supply) 1981: Evidence 24–7), and the procedure now has a statutory base, the crucial constant is the royal act of ordering the Treasury to distribute 'the sums . . . granted to us by Resolution of Our House of Commons'.

The personal participation of the monarch in this process is strongly symbolic of the constitutional idea that funds are granted by Parliament to the government as a whole, with the Treasury being entrusted with their management. This trust is where the Treasury's 'ancient authority' truly resides. While funds must be allocated and used subject to the limits stipulated by Parliament, the long-standing arrangements for their issuance make it impossible to suggest that there can be any departmental claim to the *ownership* of the funds they expend or, analogously, the income they receive. The importance of this has been pointed out by Beer (1957: 129) when he asks: 'Suppose appropriations were to be made not to the Crown but directly to Departments. . . . It is hard to believe that the power of requiring prior approval would not be gravely impaired.' In the field of finance, therefore, the United Kingdom executive is unitary, not pluralist.

1.3.2 Supervision of expenditure of funds

The second function is generally linked with 'Treasury control', that is to say, the Treasury's power to control the details of expenditure by departments even within the scope of annual Parliamentary appropriations and the issues of funds made in pursuit of them. This power does not derive from the 1866 Act. The Treasury always maintained that it was part of its 'ancient authority'; departments as regularly contested it. What the 1866 Act did was to furnish a new instrument, in the shape of appropriation audit conducted by the Comptroller and Auditor-General, to reinforce that authority. In effect, appropriation audit—checking that expenditure fell within the headings and limits approved by Parliament in the Votes in the Appropriation Act—incorporated and subsumed the 'administrative audit' which had up to that time been carried on on behalf of the Treasury by the Commissioners for Auditing the Public Accounts. The job of that audit was to check that the money had been spent in accordance with the relevant Treasury authorities, which derived from a wide variety of sources, such as statutes, Orders in Council, and Treasury Minutes, and was ultimately grounded on that all-embracing authority to control and supervise expenditure asserted by Sir George Harrison (above, pp. 115–16) and by George Arbuthnot (above, p. 117). The mode of transition from one system to the other was clearly set out in a memorandum prepared in 1865 for the Public Accounts Committee by Charles Macaulay, the Secretary of the Board of Audit (Public Accounts Committee 1865: 113–48 (Appendix 1)).

The Act, which closely followed the plan set forth by Macaulay (ibid.), reflects this position by simply referring to Treasury control as something pre-existent. The relevant phrase occurs in what was section 27 of the Act, dealing with the examination of appropriation accounts by the Comptroller and Auditor-General. As re-enacted, with slight modification, by the Exchequer and Audit Departments Act 1921, section 1(3), the reference is to 'any material expenditure [in a departmental appropriation account] requiring the authority of the Treasury which has been incurred without such authority.' Such expenditure is to be reported by the Comptroller to the Treasury, which may decide either to authorize it retrospectively or to report it to the House of Commons as improperly charged. The Acts (of 1866 as of 1921) say nothing more about this 'authority'. The Treasury's general view of it immediately after the Act is to be found in a Treasury Minute of April 1868 (Roseveare 1973: 172–3; Epitome I: 20–1). It is worth quoting this verbatim, since the Minute still remains the baseline from which departures and relaxations are made (below, pp. 177–83), and its language is expressive of the Treasury's own general view of its position.

. . . my Lords have taken under their consideration the question as to how far the expenditure included in these Appropriation Accounts should be supported by the direct authority of the Treasury.

It appears to my Lords that it would be beyond the functions of this Board to control the ordinary expenditure placed under the charge of the several Departments, within the limits set forth under the subheads of the several grants of Parliament, and that it is only in exceptional cases that the special sanction of the Treasury should be held to be necessary.

My Lords consider that such sanction should be required for any increase of establishment, of salary, or of cost of a service, or for any additional works or new services which have not been specially provided for in the grants of Parliament.

. . .

Add, that my Lords at the same time do not wish to limit the discretion of the Comptroller and Auditor General in reporting to this Board upon any item of expenditure which, in his opinion, should be the subject of special Treasury authority.

Departments did not regard this view as being beyond contest, and certainly did not see the 1866 Act as putting a statutory *Finis* beneath the argument (Wright 1969: 344–5). Arguments about the scope and nature of Treasury authority continued well into the twentieth century (Epitome I: *passim*). Eventually the Treasury prevailed, and we shall see that the idea of *prior authority* invoked by this Minute remains the principal lever in the Treasury's hands to keep moving departments towards greater efficiency and economy, even against the current background of decentralization of administrative functions. Indeed it may be seen as underlying the Treasury's role in the financial co-ordination of all central Government action (Beer 1957: 20), though this is also buttressed by the rules, in the *Ministerial Code* (Cabinet Office 1997*d*: para. 10) and elsewhere (Office of Public Service 1996*b*), requiring clearance with the Treasury of proposals with financial implications, before they enter the Cabinet system.

1.3.3 Control of access to Parliament

The third role performed by the Treasury is that of government's interlocutor with Parliament in financial matters—in particular, in the annual financial cycle. The House of Commons looks to the Treasury both to present the government's requests for funds, through the estimates, and to ensure that the Comptroller and Auditor-General has the materials to permit an audit which can certify that funds have been expended according to its appropriations. The 1866 Act is explicit about the Treasury's functions in relation to accounts and audit. These include the duty to prepare accounts for the Consolidated Fund and National Loans Fund (s. 21, now replaced by National Loans Act 1968, s. 21); the power to direct departments to prepare appropriation accounts (s. 22); the power to prescribe how departments keep and present their accounts (s. 23); and the power to resolve arguments between a department and the Comptroller and Auditor-General as to how disputed items should be entered into the appropriation account (s. 31). These powers, notably that in s. 23, are basic to the Treasury's concern with the accountancy function within government, and to its contemporary responsibilities for regularity and transparency.

While expansive on the topic of accounts, the Act says nothing about estimates. It did not need to; the Treasury's responsibility for presenting the civil estimates, and the power to review the military estimates and those of the revenue departments,[1] were established as a matter of practice well before the accounting system under the 1866 Act. Chester links this responsibility, and the influence it gave the Treasury over the annual expenditure total, with the House of Commons Standing Order requiring the Crown's recommendation for expenditure (Standing Order 48, above p. 108) on the one hand, and on the other, the growing perception that the Chancellor of the Exchequer's revenue-raising activities could and should be informed by an overall view of the government expenditure they had to sustain (Chester 1981: 205; cf. Ministry of Reconstruction 1918: 18–19). The main contribution of the Act in this area was to give the Treasury a control over the *structure and form* of estimates, which naturally needed to reflect the structure of appropriation accounts, as determined by the Treasury under section 23.

The ability to cut a department's financial lifeline is clearly a nuclear deterrent among powers, and in an age where parliamentary democracy has replaced limited monarchy it is natural that the likeliest moment for bringing that deterrent to bear should be that of the request to Parliament for funds, rather than that of allowing or denying departmental access to funds already granted by Parliament to the executive—though as we have seen, the Treasury could still lawfully exercise control at this later stage (above, pp. 117–18). Bodies as eminent as the Haldane Committee (Ministry of Reconstruction 1918: 17) and the Royal Commission on the Civil Service (1931: 6) have consequently seen the Treasury's control over the presentation of estimates as the most significant aspect of its 'power of the purse'. If this appreciation was ever correct—the Commission for its part appears to have heard no evidence in direct support of its assertion—it needs some qualification today. It has always been difficult to exercise any effective control at this stage, as Treasury officials themselves have acknowledged from time to time (Public Accounts Committee 1862: Evidence, q. 638 f. (George Arbuthnot); Royal Commission on Civil Establishments 1887: Evidence, q. 12 (Sir Reginald Welby)). From the departmental point of view, it has been acknowledged that estimates are sent to the Treasury at a moment when it is too late for their examination in detail, but that this is unimportant because Treasury authority for new or exceptional items will already have been obtained piecemeal over the preceding months (Durell 1917: 254). The only estimate the Treasury is known to have held back was not from a department, but from the House of Lords in respect of its employees (Heath 1927: 131). Estimates hardly rate a mention in the latest work on the Treasury (Thain and Wright 1995), since the 'real' decisions are taken

[1] At this time these Departments presented their estimates to Parliament directly, not through the Treasury; but Treasury approval was still required.

in the course of the Public Expenditure Survey (below, pp. 143–55). And the Treasury itself has in this decade been leading a process of reform which dilutes its control over departmental access to Parliament, by gradually transforming the estimates into a mere outline framework for the departmental reports which are to carry the bulk of public expenditure detail (below, pp. 143–55). Important as the gatekeeper role is, therefore, it should not be seen as the only fount of Treasury authority.

1.3.4 Conclusion

We have taken some time over tracing the constitutional and historical roots of Treasury power because of the obscurity which continues to surround them, despite the copious modern Treasury literature. These underpinnings of Treasury action will doubtless, save in the most extreme circumstances, remain invisible and unmentioned in day-to-day discussion, and even controversy, about public expenditure. Their significance, and still less their existence, are not to be put in doubt by this invisibility or by the fact that Treasury power does not always prevail. What a constitutional analysis may do is to disclose the formal bases on which that power reposes and thereby to permit its being related to other types of power, such as that which a department might derive from a legal mandate empowering it, or requiring it, to take decisions with financial consequences. In doing this we can in fact begin to sketch a *constitutional* explanation for the outcomes analysed in political or sociological terms by the general literature. The controls over issue, expenditure, estimates, and accounts make Treasury power comprehensive; it cannot be evaded (though hiving off and contracting out (above, pp. 46–50) may be seen as restrictions on this scope). At the same time it is never definitive. There is always a possibility of further recourse: *ex ante*, to the Cabinet system, and *ex post*—in the case where the department pushes resistance to the limit and incurs expenditure in face of refusal of Treasury consent—to the House of Commons (below, p. 157). This combination of features makes the Treasury very strong in the creation and application of systems and structures, in fields ranging from determination of overall levels of expenditure (below, pp. 143–55), through departmental financial organization (below, pp. 126–32), to forms and principles of accounting (below, pp. 164–8). Such systems may be seen as modes of organizing the Treasury's potentially inchoate financial power. Conversely, it makes the Treasury weak on substantive spending issues in which the department, or government as a whole, has an overriding interest. Wartime difficulties in expenditure control offer the obvious case, but much greater general significance attaches to the way in which, over the years since 1866, more and more departmental spending competences have been given the hard edge of legislative definition—and in particular, of legislative obligation. Such specific parliamentary authority is a powerful weapon against the generalities of Treasury control, and we shall see in Chapter 6 how the development of such departmental powers within the framework of the welfare state has been even more of a threat to the financial authority of the Treasury than to the legal authority of the courts.

2 Control of resources otherwise than by the Treasury

These powers of the Treasury, as supported by the Commons during the nineteenth century, enabled it to achieve a comprehensive control over departmental establishments, both as to their size, and as to the terms and conditions on which departmental staff were employed. Theoretically complete—'Not one additional clerk or cleaner was to be engaged by a department without Their Lordships' authority' (Beer 1957: 10)—though not in practice necessarily strong (modern scholars argue that departments got their way if they pushed hard enough (Wright 1972)), this control operated only negatively, and at the beginning of new programmes. Once departments were staffed for additional functions, Treasury controls were ill-adapted to secure continuing economy and efficiency, still less the discharge of staff when functions became obsolete or unnecessary. In government, what went up did not come down. The purely financial powers of the Treasury were far too blunt an instrument to attack waste in departments while protecting efficient services.

A search for mechanisms which would operate to increase efficiency and promote economy in administration has consequently preoccupied government in general, and the Treasury in particular, for many decades. Over much of the last century the emphasis of external recommendations on this question has been on the simultaneous strengthening of the Treasury's capacities in this field, and the adoption of more co-operative approaches to the problem between departments themselves and the Treasury (Royal Commission on the Civil Service 1914: para. 99; Ministry of Reconstruction 1918; Committee on Staffs 1919; Royal Commission on the Civil Service 1931: paras. 594–7). In the nineteen-sixties, against the background of scepticism, reflected in recommendations of the Fulton Committee (Committee on the Civil Service 1968: Vol. 1, para. 244), about whether Treasury concern for efficiency could ever go beyond candle-ends, responsibility for the central management of the civil service, including control of structure and organization and the promotion of effective methods of working, was transferred from the Treasury to a new Civil Service Department (CSD). Though the Civil Service Department had a short and not very happy life—it was abolished in

1981—its creation signalled the abandonment of the assumption, not since revived, that Treasury–Department co-operation, if properly structured, could by itself secure efficiency in administration.

New impulses towards economy, efficiency and effectiveness arrived with the coming to power in 1979 of a Conservative government convinced that 'rolling back the frontiers of the state' would produce positive economic and social results, and hence that a reduction in the size and functions of the civil service should be pursued as a matter of policy. The Treasury certainly played a crucial role in the long march towards the goal of a smaller more efficient state initiated by the Conservative Party's 1979 manifesto; but not always a leading one. Other bodies—such as the CSD, while it lasted, and later the Cabinet Office—marched alongside; but to mark the route and spur the flagging column the government, once elected, called into being a body as different from the Treasury as can be imagined. This was the Efficiency Unit attached directly to the Prime Minister's Office and headed by a businessman imported from the private sector (Gray and Jenkins 1985: 114–22; and above, p. 37). The Unit's stimulus to change, applied to spending departments through efficiency 'scrutinies', quickly affected the Treasury (and CSD) themselves, which soon asserted a more active interest in departmental systems for management, and in particular financial management, than they had shown in the nineteen-seventies (Thain and Wright 1995: 59–60).

The watchword of the Efficiency Unit was 'accountable management'. While this concept is closely associated with the idea of the importation of business disciplines and techniques into government, it antedates the Thatcher programme: the report of the House of Commons Expenditure Committee in 1977 saw the introduction of accountable units of management within departments as the crux of their recommendations for increased efficiency and linked this idea back to the Fulton Report (1977: paras. 93–4). The basic ideas involved have been summarized as

> the pursuit of efficiency, effectiveness and value for money: responsibility is to be decentralised, lower level operatives made aware of and accountable for the costs of their operations, targets are to be established and individuals assessed according to their ability to achieve them. (Gray and Jenkins 1986: 171)

This was a programme that went far beyond pure questions of expenditure. As developed into the Financial Management Initiative (FMI) (it was apparently the Treasury which insisted on the qualification 'Financial') (Gray and Jenkins 1991: 47), it contained three major elements: top management systems to provide ministers and senior civil servants with the information needed to guide programme and policy choices; decentralized budgetary control within departments; and instruments of performance appraisal, with particular initial emphasis on a range of indicators of both operational achievements and their costs. Launched personally in May 1982 by the Prime Minister through a minute to Ministers, the FMI was carried forward on a day-to-day basis through the traditional framework of department–Treasury co-ordination in Treasury expenditure divisions, but with stimulation, practical assistance, and monitoring provided by a small Financial Management Unit (later Joint Management Unit) set up and funded jointly by the Treasury and the Management and Personnel Office of the Cabinet Office, the organizations to which the functions of the CSD had been redistributed on its abolition in 1981.

The reader must look elsewhere for a detailed history of FMI and for evaluation of its results (Gray and Jenkins 1991; Comptroller and Auditor-General 1986; Metcalfe and Richards 1990: ch. 9). FMI, we should note here, was a central initiative which aimed at changing the ways departments went about their work; differences in departmental functions and structures meant that each department would need to carry forward the general purposes of the initiative in its own way, with a central role confined to stimulus, monitoring, and review of existing central procedures to ensure that they supported, rather than hindered, the process of change. The effects of FMI, however, extended beyond departments in a number of directions. Most dramatically, it led first to changes in the structure of government, through the creation of executive agencies as the 'next step' in securing accountable management (Efficiency Unit 1988, and see above, pp. 39–46, below, pp. 133–7). Second, it produced changes in control relationships between the Treasury and departments, through the development of better controls over administrative costs and outputs which permitted the Treasury effectively to dismantle control over manpower, which it had regained with the abolition of CSD. We deal with this in the next chapter (below, pp. 188–90). Third, it contributed to further reshuffling of central departmental responsibilities.

Initially, the effective control that the Treasury had gained over FMI was recognized in 1987 by the winding up of the Management and Personnel Office and the transfer of its management responsibilities back to the Treasury (Thain and Wright 1995: 68). When, however, the government accepted the recommendation of the Ibbs report (Efficiency Unit 1988) and initiated 'Next Steps', it entrusted this task not to the Treasury but to a Project Team headed by a Permanent Secretary in the Office of the Minister for the Civil Service within the Cabinet Office. This began a process of evolution whose current state of development we have described in Chapter 2 (above, pp. 37–46), with the Cabinet Office directly incorporating the variegated teams and units built up within the

Office of Public Service and its predecessor bodies during the nineteen-eighties and nineties. The Cabinet Office is a very different type of central department from that represented by the Treasury, but one with increasingly overlapping concerns. Here there are no 'ancient authorities', rather the strength of new ideas conceived and disseminated in the closest possible proximity to the centre of political, as opposed to legal, power in government: the Prime Minister. While this significantly reinforces central impulsion to change in government, it appears that the older, more deeply rooted Treasury powers have a continuing role in sustaining the impulse to change. A striking example of how impulsion and control can come together is provided by the integration of OPS-inspired Departmental efficiency plans (Cabinet Office 1994*a*) into the Treasury's running costs control system, so as to produce public service agreements. We shall see in Chapter 6 how these work (below, pp. 191–2).

3 The spending Departments

> The essence of Treasury control is really the control of the Department within itself, reinforced by the Treasury.
>
> (Durell 1917: 258)

Despite the remarkable variety of structure and function displayed by central government departments, the Treasury has succeeded, through long decades of effort, in securing a common system in departments for dealing with financial matters. 'Common system' does not imply uniformity, and variations in the organization of the financial function will naturally occur according to the size of departments, the degree to which their functions are now undertaken by executive agencies, and other such factors (Thain and Wright 1995: ch. 8). All, however, allocate key financial functions, as required by the Treasury, to two identified officers: the Accounting Officer; and the Principal Finance Officer.

3.1 The Accounting Officer

The Accounting Officer for a department is appointed by the Treasury under section 22 of the Exchequer and Audit Departments Act 1866. 'It is the long-standing practice,' says the Treasury (1989*a*: para. 6.1.2),

> that the permanent head of a department is appointed as its principal Accounting Officer. This reflects the fact that under the Minister he or she has personal responsibility for the overall organisation, management and staffing of the

department and for department-wide procedures, where these are appropriate, in financial and other matters.

Even this measure of uniformity was not easily won, however. The Treasury had asserted by Minute in 1872 that the Accounting Officer should normally be the permanent head, but in 1920, when the Public Accounts Committee examined the matter in detail, 37 out of 98 Accounting Officers were not heads of department: 16 were Accountants-General (the equivalent of the modern Principal Finance Officer), and 21 held other subordinate posts (Epitome I: 610–20). In the view of Sir Warren Fisher it was vital to the achievement of a general commitment to economy across government that financial responsibilities in the department should be lodged in its permanent head and not in some separate officer who might be seen as an emissary of an alien Treasury (Hamilton 1951: 18–22). Still less should the function be reposed in the Treasury itself, acting through its own officials placed in each department, as the Select Committee on National Expenditure had recommended the previous year (Epitome I: loc. cit.). It was not at first easy to convince the Public Accounts Committee that permanent heads, especially of large civil departments, would possess the necessary time or objectivity to ensure the kind of control with which it was familiar, but Fisher's views prevailed, and his approach, emphasizing shared responsibility and informal relationships between department and Treasury, was endorsed by the Committee on the occasion of subsequent reviews in 1937 (Epitome I: 760) and 1951 (Epitome II: 184, and see Treasury Memorandum at 189–95).

Government Accounting sets out the responsibilities of Accounting Officers, in the form communicated to each new appointee by an Accounting Officer Memorandum (printed at Treasury 1989*a*, following para. 6.1.7, and last revised 1997). Key tasks (Memorandum, para. 5) are to ensure that there is a high standard of management in the department as a whole; that financial systems and procedures promote the efficient and economical conduct of business and safeguard financial propriety and regularity throughout the department; and that financial considerations are fully taken into account in decisions on policy proposals. The Accounting Officer takes responsibility for the appropriation, trading and other accounts of the department, and may be called upon to explain them before the House of Commons Public Accounts Committee. 'Particular' responsibilities emphasized by the Memorandum (paras. 10–15) are for ensuring compliance with parliamentary requirements in the control of expenditure, ensuring that specific Treasury sanction is obtained where requisite, and for seeing that appropriate advice is tendered to Ministers on all matters of financial propriety and regularity, and of economical administration more generally. Information and advice is regularly conveyed from the Treasury (TOA) to Accounting Officers by means of 'Dear Accounting Officer (DAO)' letters, whose content may, in appropriate cases, later be incorporated in *Government Accounting*.

Relationships with ministers are a problem of particular delicacy. As Permanent Secretary, the Accounting Officer is at the orders of his minister as the responsible head of the department. What if these orders conflict with the requirements of regularity, propriety, or value for money? The Memorandum distils the results of more than a century of practice and debate on such issues, reflecting (as does *Government Accounting* generally) views established as a result of dialogue between Treasury, Public Accounts Committee, and others: though not necessarily shared by the ministers whose policies are challenged (see Benn 1990: 296–7). The development of practice is well illustrated by the 'Pergau Dam' affair, in which the decision to grant aid to Malaysia for the construction of the dam, based on an informal understanding between the respective Prime Ministers, was the subject of a value-for-money investigation by the National Audit Office (White, Harden and Donnelly 1994; Harden, White and Hollingsworth 1996; see further below, pp. 204–5). The critical conclusions of the Comptroller and Auditor-General led to enquiries by both the Public Accounts Committee and the House of Commons Foreign Affairs Committee. It emerged that the Permanent Secretary of the Overseas Development Administration, as Accounting Officer, had taken the view that to grant aid for the project as promised would not be consistent with the economical and efficient administration which it was his duty, under the Accounting Officer Memorandum, to secure; and as was his right under the then text of the Memorandum, he asked the Minister for a written instruction overruling his advice; which the Minister provided. Had the Accounting Officer's objection been on grounds of regularity or propriety, it would then have been his obligation to inform the Treasury and communicate the papers to the Comptroller and Auditor-General; but the objection being on grounds of economy, no further step needed to be taken beyond informing the NAO if it happened to undertake a relevant inquiry (Memorandum, 1992 version, paras. 13, 14). In a critical report on the matter, the Public Accounts Committee recommended that the distinction between disputes on regularity and disputes on economy of expenditure should be abandoned, and that the Accounting Officer should be required to pass the papers to the Comptroller in all cases, so that the Committee's ability to inquire into the matter should not be dependent, as here, on the fortuitous undertaking of a value-for-money audit (Public Accounts Committee 1994*b*). This recommendation was accepted by the

Treasury (Treasury 1994*c*: para. 13), and the Memorandum accordingly amended (Memorandum, 1997 version, paras. 13–15). In addition, when the official guidance for ministers was reissued at the outset of the Blair Government as the *Ministerial Code,* it was thought worthwhile, for the first time, to summarize the terms of this vital relationship (Cabinet Office 1997*d*: paras. 57–9).

Sometimes it may be appropriate for more than one Accounting Officer to be appointed in a department, where, for example, there are additional senior managers responsible for areas of a department's work covered by a distinct Vote (Memorandum, para. 5). In fact it is unusual to appoint such Additional Accounting Officers outside the framework of executive agencies. The special arrangements for these agencies are discussed below.

It is inherent in the nature of the Accounting Officer role that the post is not held by a financial specialist, but by the person, in the department as a whole or some discrete part of it, who has the overall responsibility for management under the minister, and is therefore in a position (subject to countermand by the minister or, where not Permanent Secretary, by the latter) to ensure that the requirements of good financial management, as defined by the Treasury, are so far as practicable met. Traditionally, financial management has probably not ranked high on the scale of interests of Accounting Officers. The politically-led concern with efficiency and value for money in the public service, which has been a major preoccupation of government as a whole since the nineteen-eighties, may well have increased the sensitivity of Permanent Secretaries to this aspect of their work—Pergau Dam was one of fifteen cases since 1979 where an Accounting Officer had required a written direction from his Minister on value-for-money grounds (White, Harden and Donnelly 1994: 529)—but specialist responsibilities for departmental financial management must continue to lie elsewhere.

3.2 The Finance Division, and the Principal Finance Officer (PFO)

The PFO is the person who deals with the department's finances, and with its relations with the Treasury. Every department should have one; though it may be appropriate—for example in smaller departments—for the post to be combined (under the acronym 'PEFO') with that of Principal Establishment Officer (PEO), whose work has already been discussed in Chapter 3 (Treasury 1989*a*: para. 6.2.1). A sign of the Treasury's 'lighter touch' in dealings with departments is that Treasury approval is no longer required for the appointment of any departmental PFO or other senior finance official (Treasury 1989*a*: paras. 6.2.40–42, removed by amendment no. 7, March 1997). Whether the posts are separate or combined, the Treasury advises against their being held in combination with operational responsibilities to an extent that would call into question their ability to advise impartially (para. 6.2.35); where this happens—as in the Welsh Office—it may well be the cause of tensions within the department (Thain and Wright 1995: 150). The Treasury does not seek to stipulate how the functions of the PFO (and PEO) should fit into the overall organization of any particular department; that would hardly be appropriate in an era of encouragement for organizational variation, through agencies and otherwise, to meet the specific needs of departmental activities. Consider two major spending departments which have reorganized significantly in recent years so as to put some or all of their major day-to-day functions in the charge of executive agencies.

The *Lord Chancellor's Department*, once a small (but highly influential) cadre linking the judiciary with the executive, now manages a Vote of over £2.5bn per year, putting it in the same spending bracket as departments like the Foreign and Commonwealth Office, Trade and Industry, or Northern Ireland (Treasury 1996*c*: 7). Its major administrative task and expense, running the court system, has since 1992 been the responsibility of the Court Service, a Next Steps agency. The remainder of the Department's functions, such as judicial appointments, legal aid policy, and its responsibilities regarding magistrates' courts are still run within the traditional departmental framework. It has brought its Finance and Personnel Divisions into a Corporate Services Group, along with Planning, Communications, Accommodation, and Internal Audit. The head of this Group functions as the Department's PFO. The Court Service, for its part, has its own Resources and Support Services Directorate, which provides it with some of these services, such as personnel, training, resources planning, and accommodation.

The *Department of Social Security* has taken a different line. Here, four agencies carved out from the Department—the Benefits Agency, the Contributions Agency, the Child Support Agency, and the War Pensions Agency—have taken on the overwhelming mass of its work, with a fifth agency, the Information Technology Services Agency, providing information technology services to them and to the Department. 98 per cent of the Department's staff worked in these agencies in 1996. Each agency has its own responsibilities, closely defined, in the case of the first four, by legislation, and objectives based on a framework document. Each has its own finance and personnel directors. Centrally, the Department has a PFO who heads a Planning and Finance Division, and a PEO heading Personnel and Support Services. Great stress is laid on coherence in departmental activity, achieved through a Departmental Board, on which all agency heads sit, along with the Head of the Department's

Policy Group, its Solicitor (see below, pp. 224–5), the PEO, the Head of Corporate Management, and the PFO, under the Chairmanship of the Permanent Secretary. There are also three members from outside the Department. The Board is strategic; agency heads are there to participate in steering the whole Department, not to represent their agencies (House of Lords Select Committee on the Public Service 1997: Evidence p. 71, qq. 173, 419). The Permanent Secretary supervises a range of cross-departmental bodies, including groups of finance officers and personnel officers.

Whatever the departmental structure, the Treasury is still concerned to see that key financial functions are carried out by an officer with sufficient status and power, and to this end it sets out in some detail, in *Government Accounting*, the range of possible responsibilities of PFOs. These cover public expenditure planning and control, including PES and estimates bids; assuring propriety and regularity of expenditure; accounts; respect for expenditure control totals (cash limits, running costs limits); banking and cash management; fees and charges; value for money; procurement arrangements; relations with NAO and the Comptroller and Auditor General; internal audit; relevant controls on the actions of the department's executive agencies, and of any non-departmental public bodies for which it may be responsible; and last but not least, relations with the Treasury (Treasury 1989*a*: paras. 6.2.12–27).

As things are presently organized in Whitehall, this last responsibility is indeed crucial, since both the Treasury, and most departments,[2] operate what has been termed a 'single window' system for organizing communications, in which Treasury contacts with a department will be expected to pass through the Finance Division, or at least to be notified to it, while the department's contacts with the Treasury will be with the relevant team in the Spending Directorate, even where the matter is being driven by other Directorates within the Treasury (Thain and Wright 1995: 182–7). Close and regular contacts between PFOs and their Finance Divisions, and the members of Treasury spending teams, produce shared values, understandings, and practices, which have been described as linking Treasury and departmental Finance Divisions in an 'expenditure policy community' that transcends institutional dividing lines and divergences of interest, and has survived numberless public expenditure reforms since the first half of the nineteenth century (Thain and Wright 1995: ch. 9). That community, it is argued, may both support and be sustained by a variety of 'rules of the game' of public

[2] The 'territorial Departments' (the Scottish Office, the Welsh Office, and the Northern Ireland Office) have operated differently, because of their complex internal organization and the multiple activities for which they are responsible. Devolution may of course produce further changes.

expenditure management, from formal policy rules such as those contained in the Exchequer and Audit Acts, through internal rules such as the *Guidelines* prescribing the mode of operation of the Public Expenditure Survey, to unwritten and uncodified policy rules, and norms of behaviour to regulate transactions between community members (ibid. 171–4).

We explore these rules and their operation in more detail in the next chapter, but it is worth a reminder here that no matter how strong this community and how effective its rules, it must co-exist with other departmental and government-wide communities with their own priorities and values: the departments' policy groups, with their responsibility for delivering the political programmes of ministers; the departments' executive branches or agencies, often committed, by legislative prescription, to the provision of particular services; and the departments' legal advisers, who are concerned to see that such legislative and other legal requirements are fully respected and who now operate in ways which offer greater scope for the formulation of interdepartmental legal consensus on such issues (below, Chapter 9).

4 Executive agencies and trading funds

4.1 History

Executive agencies, often known as 'Next Steps' agencies after the title of the report that proposed their creation (Efficiency Unit 1988), are themselves the progeny of a centrally-driven programme to ensure efficiency across government, the Financial Management Initiative (above, pp. 124–5). We have already described the general purposes, execution, and effects of the programme (above, pp. 37–46). The conception of increasing the efficiency and effectiveness with which government discharged its routine administrative tasks, by entrusting them to distinct units within departments whose heads would assume broad managerial responsibility for the achievement of defined performance targets, immediately raised concerns within the Treasury that this pursuit of two of the three 'Es', efficiency and effectiveness, might seriously jeopardize the third, economy. In particular, the Treasury feared that the delegation of responsibility within departments that was a core element of the Next Steps proposals would make its control tasks more difficult: if, as was envisaged, agencies had responsibility for their own pay arrangements, leapfrogging claims might occur, and more generally, the fact that demand for their services was not controlled by price meant that problems of expenditure control would not be eliminated in these areas, but diffused across a larger and more variegated population (Thain and Wright 1995: 73–5). While these fears did not have the effect of blocking the Next Steps initiative or even of substantially modifying its content, they led the Treasury to an initially cautious attitude which involved addressing the financial regime of each agency on a case-by-case basis 'according to the needs of that agency in improving its efficiency, the rigour of the policy and resource framework in place and the adequacy of the necessary internal control systems' (Treasury 1988: 68). Subsequent experience has allowed that caution to be relaxed.

4.2 Creation

A case-by-case approach is hardly unreasonable when it is considered that agencies range in size from the twenty-five persons employed at the Treasury's Debt Management Office (a 1998 creation) to the Benefits Agency of the Department of Social Security, the Prison Service under the responsibility of the Home Office, and the Employment Service of the Department of Education and Employment, with 66,295, 39,365, and 28,610 employees respectively in 1998. The Treasury has thus been involved, with the Next Steps Team within the Cabinet Office and the departmental minister, alike in the process of 'prior options' review which considers agency status for departmental functions along with alternatives such as privatization, contracting out, cessation of the relevant functions (are they needed at all?), and the status quo; in the eventual decision to create the agency; and in the approval of the agency's framework document (above, pp. 41–2). It continues to be involved in the process of agency review. *Ex ante* Treasury control is further extended by the fact that the Chief Executive will need to be appointed as an Accounting Officer, directly by the Treasury, if the agency is also a trading fund (see below) or has its own Vote; by the departmental Accounting Officer, by letter in a form approved by the Treasury, in other cases (Treasury 1989*a*: s. 6.1.3). This being so, the department will need to ensure that the Treasury approves of its choice of Chief Executive.

Nor did the Treasury stop at case-by-case review. Once it was satisfied about the general policy structure for agencies, it applied its energies to the elaboration of general rules and guidance for their conduct in financial matters. The Agency Chief Executives' Handbook (Office of Public Service 1996*a*: Section D) seems at first sight to have little to say on the subject; but while its fourteen paragraphs on financial management occupy a mere three pages, they refer to no less than ten other guidance documents, seven of which are 'too large to reproduce here', but which 'Chief Executives are advised to consult as necessary'. Eight of the ten documents emanate from the Treasury. They comprise the Accounting Officer Memorandum, discussed above (pp. 127–8), and guidance documents on the preparation of agency reports and accounts; on strategic planning and control in government departments; on setting targets and measuring performance in agencies; on establishing and operating trading funds (see further below); on the costing and pricing of agencies' services (the *Fees and Charges Guide*); on selling government services into wider markets; and on private finance.

Several of these documents are of quite general application in government, but others represent attempts by the Treasury to apply general principles of financial accountability to the circumstances of executive agencies as a class. The original Treasury work on targets has been superseded (above, pp. 42–3), but general principles of agency accountability and finance as still to be found in the White Paper *The Financing and Accountability of Next Steps Agencies* (Treasury 1989*b*, and see Treasury 1989*a*: paras. 16.1.8–15), including the system of accruals accounting to which, pending the general introduction of resource budgeting (below, pp. 164–8), only executive agencies are subject. All agencies, save for exceptional cases where there are few fixed assets or stocks in hand and little recourse to credit transactions, are expected to produce such commercial-style accounts within two years of launch (Treasury 1989*a*: para. 16.1.12).

The satisfactory operation of these general controls, leading to confidence that the agency regime has no deleterious effects on financial control, has meant that the Treasury now feels able to apply a much 'lighter touch', in consideration of proposals to set up agencies and of the terms of their framework documents, than in the early days of agency creation (House of Lords Select Committee on the Public Service 1998: Evidence qq. 1390–6, 1439). These processes now form part of the ordinary work of spending teams.

4.3 Types

With well over a hundred agencies doing everything from running conferences to providing subsistence for the poor there is much innocent amusement to be gained from trying to classify them in various ways. For a couple of years the annual Next Steps Review attempted a classification by function (services to the public; services to departments; research establishments; regulation), and within these groups by activity to facilitate comparison (Cabinet Office (OPS) 1997*a*: 35–7; compare Efficiency Unit 1991: 22–5), but this has been abandoned in favour of a listing arranged by responsible departments, seemingly in a deliberate attempt to emphasize ministerial responsibility (Cabinet Office (OPS)

1998*a*: vi; see above, pp. 41–5). In financial management terms, agencies may most easily be classified according to their treatment for accounting purposes, treatment which reflects the financial characteristics and self-containedness of their activity. There are three groups: agencies constituted as government trading funds; agencies not so constituted but which have their own Vote; and agencies which fall into neither of these classes.

4.3.1 Government trading funds

Government trading funds were introduced in 1973, as part of an earlier round of management changes in the civil service deriving from the Fulton Report (Committee on the Civil Service 1968). The Government Trading Funds Act 1973 identified five trading activities of government as suitable for financing through a distinct trading fund, rather than under the ordinary system of annual supply: these included the Royal Ordnance Factories and Dockyards, the Royal Mint, the Stationery Office, and a government supply agency. The list might be extended by order, on the joint proposal of the responsible minister and the Treasury, to include any other services with trading functions (s. 1). The relevant Crown assets and liabilities were vested in the fund, the transfer being remunerated by an appropriate balance of 'public dividend capital' and a loan from the National Loans Fund (s. 2). Receipts and payments on the relevant activity would not pass through the estimates or the appropriation accounts (s. 3), but would be separately accounted by an accounting officer appointed by the Treasury and in a form fixed by the Treasury, and subject to audit by the Comptroller and Auditor General and presentation to Parliament (s. 4). Save for the named activities (all of which have since been privatized), the Act was little used until 1990, when the government invited Parliament to enlarge its scope so as to permit the creation of a fund where any operations of a department, whether strictly speaking trading activities or not, were 'suitable to be financed by means of a [trading] fund . . . and . . . to be so managed that the revenue of the fund would consist principally of receipts in respect of goods or services provided in the course of the operations' and this would conduce to 'improved efficiency and effectiveness' (Government Trading Funds Act 1973, s. 1(1), as substituted by Government Trading Funds Act 1990). This enlargement brought within the scope of the 1973 Act operations, like those of the Vehicle Inspectorate, Companies House, and the Passport Office, which were funded by statutory fees, and meant that some executive agencies, at least, could be given a more 'commercial' financial regime, with identifiable capital, the remuneration of which might be one indicator of performance (Treasury 1989*b*).

The 1990 legislation somewhat elaborated the 1973 regime, but did not change its general principles, one element of which was the close control exercisable by the Treasury over the whole operation. Every discretionary power conferred by the Act on the minister responsible for the fund is to be exercised with Treasury concurrence or subject to Treasury approval or requirements. Moreover the Act makes clear, and preserves, the financial unity of the Crown in relation to these new operations: any revenue surplus, in a loan-financed fund, may go (with Treasury concurrence, of course) either for 'purposes of the funded operations' or to the Consolidated Fund (s. 4(4))—but *not* to help out the department's general budget. An important respect in which the Act extended Treasury control was in empowering the Treasury to fix the form of reports by trading funds as well as of accounts, thus providing a statutory basis for the stipulation of performance indicators (1973 Act, s. 4(6A), as amended).

These 1990 amendments were very much part of the Next Steps programme, and have produced a considerable expansion in the number of trading funds—sixteen in 1996. In addition to the Royal Mint, sole survivor of the original group of funds, such varied activities as the Central Office of Information, the Fire Service College, the Hydrographic Office, and the Medicines Control Agency are now organized in this way. The population is a shifting one, as fund status has in several cases been a step on the road to privatization (Royal Dockyards, Crown Suppliers, HMSO), and agencies are encouraged to work towards trading fund status.

4.3.2 Agencies with their own Vote

These agencies share with trading funds some important characteristics, notably the appointment of their Accounting Officer by the Treasury, with a personal responsibility for the accounts, including responding to any inquiries by the Public Accounts Committee (Treasury 1989*a*: paras. 16.1.7, 6.1.5, and Accounting Officer Memorandum paras. 18–21). Some 25 to 30 agencies fell into this group in 1998. They will likewise have accruals-based accounts, including a balance sheet, but these will be in addition to the estimates and appropriation accounts that the agency must prepare in relation to the Vote, not in substitution for them. Unlike trading funds, these agencies are not conceived of as having an endowment of financial capital which will produce returns for the Crown in the form of dividends or loan interest. The form of accounts is chosen for economic reasons—the better to show how resources, including capital resources—are being used—than for financial ones—demonstrating the capacity to remunerate capital. The same motivation lies behind the government's current switch to accruals accounting as the general form of accounting for all government expenditure (below, pp. 164–8); once it is accomplished, the financial regime of these agencies will be less distinctive than at present.

4.3.3 Other agencies

Other agencies are those which provide services within the department which either fall within one or more sub-heads of a Vote or are spread among several. Some of these agencies may be large: in the Department of Social Security, only the Benefits Agency has its own Vote (House of Lords Select Committee on the Public Service 1997: Evidence, qq. 465–8), but the Contributions Agency employs 7,380 staff, and the Child Support Agency another 7,910. Here, as already noted, the appointment of the agency's Chief Executive as an Additional Accounting Officer is a matter for the department, but under forms approved by the Treasury. It remains a device to fix on the Chief Executive personal accountability for the agency's use of resources (Treasury 1989*a*: para. 6.1.3). Save in exceptional cases these agencies will also be required to prepare their own accruals-based accounts, as well as contributing to the preparation of estimates and appropriation accounts for the Votes under which they are funded.

The differences between this kind of agency and the departments that incorporate them may in many respects be more apparent than real so far as financial management and control are concerned. In some departments, in which agencies play only a marginal role, virtually the whole department is organized on what are called 'Next Steps lines', that is to say, with the specific functions within the department having formal obligations of the nature contained in framework agreements and fully devolved budgets. The Inland Revenue is an example. Even in departments not so organized, changes pioneered in agencies, such as delegated responsibility for pay and pay-related conditions of service, have subsequently been applied, and other such examples, such as the general adoption of accruals-based accounting, will follow. Increasingly, agencies represent less a significantly different mode of organization from departments generally than a formalized expression of certain quite general trends.

5 Central responsibilities for accountancy and internal audit

We have seen that in the nineteen-twenties the Treasury firmly rejected the idea of exercising a direct control over departmental spending by means of a financial control service answering to it but distributed across departments, on the Continental model represented, for example, by the *Ragioneria dello Stato* in Italy (Cassese 1996) or the *comptables publics* in

France (Saunier 1993; above). The absence of an executive-wide financial control function did not, however, mean that there should be no communication or sharing of problems and solutions between those charged with financial discipline in departments, and between them and the Treasury. The emphasis, in such cross-departmental communication, has been on the professional and technical aspects of this work, and notably on the application of general accountancy standards within the specialized framework of government. The Treasury plays a leading role in this process, but the nature of that role is, now, purely one of advice and co-ordination.

Within the Treasury, the relevant functions are concentrated in the *Financial Management, Reporting and Audit Directorate (FMRA)* (above, pp. 110–13), whose Director is the Head of the Government Accountancy Service ('HOTGAS' in internal Treasury-speak), consisting of all professionally qualified or trainee accountants, and 'accounting technicians', within central government departments and executive agencies. The Treasury has, however, no central managerial functions in relation to the Service, which aims to help departments to make the best use of professional accountants, to provide information on best accountancy practice, and to furnish information about employment opportunities across government. In contrast to the position now reached in relation to the Government Legal Service (below, p. 218), the Service does not have any influence on the career patterns of accountants within departments.

Within the Directorate, two small teams have advisory and information responsibilities relevant to the accountancy function in government as a whole (HM Treasury: Financial Management Reporting and Audit Directorate [nd]). Central Accountancy (CA) helps the rest of the Treasury, and other departments, with accountancy advice and promoting better financial management. An important part of this task is maintaining close links with the process of development and adaptation of general accountancy standards, such as the Practice Notes of the Audit Practices Board, a private body jointly established by the various professional accountancy organizations. The Development of Accountancy Resources Team (DART) supports the aim of the Government Accountancy Service to promote best practice in managing accountancy resources in the civil service, undertaking, under a series of plans approved by the Head of the Home Civil Service, 'a programme of projects which could not be better done within departments and which departments agree should be undertaken' (ibid. 11). These tasks include the co-ordination of a government-wide finance training network, and the publication of the journal of the Service, *Gasette*.

Another team within the Directorate with related functions is

Resource Accounting and Budgeting (RAB), whose work we examine in some detail in the next chapter. Also of major importance is Audit Policy and Advice (APA), now a part of the Treasury Officer of Accounts team, which performs in relation to internal audit functions analogous to those of CA and DART for accountancy. It is responsible for the Government Internal Audit Manual (Treasury 1996*f*), which 'sets the professional standards to which all government internal auditors, whether in departments, agencies or NDPBs, are expected to work' (ibid. 4). Internal audit, it should be noted, goes well beyond financial systems. It is concerned with all administrative systems in departments and operates to provide assurance to Accounting Officers that those systems are operating effectively. Internal auditors are not necessarily accountants, and the work is different in nature from that of external auditors. Some of the functions once exercised through Treasury establishment divisions, such as organization and management work (O & M), or staff inspection (Treasury 1993*c*), may now be carried on through the internal audit function in departments, with the support of Treasury advice and training. APA organizes an annual Government Internal Audit Conference, disseminates good practice and information through 'HIA (Head of Internal Audit) letters' analogous to the 'Dear Accounting Officer' letters of the Treasury Officer of Accounts (above, pp. 127–8), and publishes a news magazine, *Auditorium*.

5
The Financial Resources of Government: Allocation and Appropriation

Expense governs everything.

(Durell 1917: 1, citing Fourth Report of Select Committee on Navy Estimates 1888)

I INTRODUCTION: A PLURALITY OF SYSTEMS

It is time to consider how the institutions described in the previous chapter function together as a system of financial control. This is no simple task, because there arguably exist today three such systems, laid down at different times, superimposed upon one another, interpenetrating to a considerable extent, and by no means fully stabilized.

The *first* of these is constituted by the Treasury's 'ancient authority' within the executive, as the department to which the general management of government funds has from the earliest times been entrusted (above, pp. 113–16). The aims which have shaped this system are those of ordinary housekeeping, albeit on the grand scale appropriate to what was once the royal household: the application of funds to their intended purposes, economy, and the avoidance of waste and fraud. While these purposes have effectively been subsumed in those of the second system (below), as have some of the instruments—such as audit—through which they were secured, the most basic control powers of the Treasury, notably that of prior approval of expenditure, are still grounded in this first system.

The *second* system is that of appropriation of Parliamentary grants and of ensuring that expenditure complies with those appropriations. Its bedrock is the Exchequer and Audit Departments Act 1866, its leading personage the Comptroller and Auditor-General. However, long before the passing of that Act or the institution of that office, Parliamentary concerns about appropriation were becoming increasingly congruent with Treasury concerns about housekeeping, so that the real effect of the 1860s reforms was to bring about a partial merger between two systems which up to that time had been distinct but mutually reinforcing. For about a century thereafter, the most visible frame for the

Treasury's action was the 1866 Act, and the Comptroller and Auditor-General laboured (until 1983) on behalf of both Parliament and Treasury. This second system did not, however, have the same aims as the Treasury housekeeping which it largely subsumed. Parliament's interest was and remains one of securing democratic control of executive action. We have already noted that under our constitution, the executive enjoys at common law all the capacities for action of an ordinary private individual, save where Parliament has expressly restricted them. Legislative constraints on executive behaviour are of course important, but they are not comprehensive. If, therefore, Parliament wants to achieve any systematic oversight of government's actions outside the rather limited sphere of its coercive powers, it needs to control the resources which make those capacities real. Appropriation of funds has since the eighteenth century been the principal and ever-developing control for this purpose. The power to say how much may be spent, and on what, determines more effectively than anything else what may and may not be done. Transparency and regularity, assuring clarity as to what is to be spent and as to whether spending has accorded with the authorities given, are accordingly the key values of this system.

Over the years since 1866, however, Parliament's concerns, expressed through the Comptroller and Auditor-General, steadily expanded so as to encompass good housekeeping as well as transparency and regularity, despite much departmental doubt and resistance (Durell 1917: 189–200, 224–40), to the point where the congruence with traditional Treasury concerns was effectively complete. The National Audit Act 1983 formally marks this moment through its statutory recognition of value-for-money audit by the National Audit Office (NAO), while simultaneously introducing a new institutional separation between the actors in the system (below pp. 193–9). The result is that legislature and executive now have the same concerns about the regularity and economy of public expenditure, but that the Comptroller and Auditor-General, and NAO, now act for Parliament alone. We consider later the impact of this separation on Treasury control.

Meanwhile a *third* system of control had been developing out of the recognition of a new economic task for the executive, and in particular the Treasury: that of relating public expenditure as a whole, and the main functional and economic categories within it, to the overall state of the economy. There are, as we shall see, different ways of translating this broad idea into an operational objective, but there has for nearly forty years existed a continuously evolving framework within which such objectives have been pursued: the Public Expenditure Survey (PES) system, initiated in 1961. While PES has changed substantially over the years, in response to the ideas of the party in power, to economic crises, to shifts in economic theory from Keynesianism to monetarism, and to new structures of government, it has always provided a framework for taking a centralized view about the government's total spending over a future period of years (currently three) and about how that spending might be apportioned between the various functions for which different departments are responsible. PES is wholly internal to the executive. Parliament hears of its results once they have been arrived at; it is not invited to approve or disapprove them, as such (below, pp. 152–5). All public expenditure decisions are, however, now related to PES, and as we shall see, an ever-widening range of control and monitoring procedures now refer back to it.

The PES system, superimposed on the 'Parliamentary' system of estimates and accounts, is at present slowly absorbing that system in much the way Parliamentary appropriation gradually incorporated Treasury control in the nineteenth century. We shall see, for example, how the presentation of information is increasingly taking place within the structures of the new system rather than the old one, and how the old structures, such as supply estimates, are being reshaped to the logic of the new system (below, pp. 152–5). Similarly, the new system has steadily expanded its concerns so as to incorporate the values and purposes of the old, while using established machinery (such as Treasury authorization) to support this enlarged range of objectives. Analysis of this process is at the present time further complicated by the government's programme, which extends into the third millennium, to change the accounting and budgeting basis on which all these systems have hitherto rested, from a 'cash' basis to an 'accruals' basis which will clearly distinguish current and capital expenditure (below, pp. 164–8). That programme is now explicitly linked to the way the government frames the overall objective of the PES process. Most recently, the government has invited Parliament, not to legislate for the process itself, but to furnish a legislatively-based framework of fiscal principle and procedure within which the PES system will in future need to be set (below, pp. 153–4).

The interpenetration of these historically distinct systems produces a complex pattern of interdependence of internal and external controls, which is reflected in the organization of this chapter and the next. In the remainder of this chapter, we examine the process of planning and allocating public expenditure, distinguishing clearly for this purpose between the PES system (part II), in which all important decisions are taken, and the system of Parliamentary appropriation and supply (part III), which now simply reflects, in forms suitable for its purposes, the substance of PES decisions. We conclude the chapter by considering the impact of the switch to resource accounting and budgeting (part IV). In the next chapter, dealing with monitoring and control within these frameworks of allocation and appropriation, we show how the concepts and mechanisms rooted in the different systems interact in aid of the objectives of both internal and Parliamentary control of expenditure.

II THE PUBLIC EXPENDITURE SURVEY SYSTEM

1 History

The progenitors of PES, in the Treasury, in the House of Commons Estimates Committee, and in the Plowden Committee which formally articulated the concept (Treasury 1961), saw it as a planning mechanism, not a control tool. Rational policy-making, they thought, was being hampered by an estimates system which had a one-year time horizon and could not deliver a comprehensive view of government expenditure (including local authority and nationalized industry expenditure). French economic planning was quietly admired; something analogous was needed here to break out of the 'stop-go' cycle of short-term decision-making which characterized British economic policy in the nineteen-fifties. PES thus sought to set public expenditure plans over the coming five years against expectations about resources, as an aid to better economic management (Pollitt 1976).

This thinking certainly implied taking a view about the desirable level of total public expenditure and its relationship with the general level of national economic activity expressed as GDP (gross domestic product). As yet, however, there was no ideological conviction that the level of public expenditure must necessarily be constrained or reduced, nor was there a sense that the forecasts generated by the PES process should function as instruments for the control of departmental spending. These elements appeared only after financial crises in 1966–67 and 1973–76, in each of which it appeared that despite the operation of PES, public expenditure was effectively out of control, with large-scale overshoots of PES forecasts. While the first crisis produced only some greater emphasis on control and monitoring arrangements, the second led directly to the supplementation, in 1976, of PES figures with cash limits on most departmental expenditure, and then (1981) to the substitution of a cash basis for a real resources basis for all PES activity. This was a fundamental shift which emphasized the control function of PES at the expense of planning (Thain and Wright 1995: ch. 3). Forecasting expenditures in cash meant that departments now had an interest in restraining inflation, including restraining public pay settlements which might contribute to it. Cash limits (on broad departmental blocks of expenditure) present departments with the prospect of actually running out of money, a risk which simply did not arise under the earlier system, where the problems of measuring cash expenditures against 'real' plans meant that supplementary estimates were freely allowed where cash overruns appeared likely. Control elements have been further tightened since 1981, notably with the introduction, in 1986, of a separation, for control purposes, between departmental programme costs and running costs (below, pp. 188–90); in 1993, of a 'top-down' system of allocation under which a figure for total public expenditure for each of the next three years is arrived at in advance of the determination of the associated departmental allocations; and in 1998, of the separate handling of current and capital expenditure, the fixing of most departmental expenditure for three years at a time rather than through a process of annual review, and the incorporation of specific performance targets into the system.

Today, therefore, it is reasonable to regard PES as an instrument of control through which the spending plans—and hence the activities—of departments are so far as is possible brought into line with the overall constraints on public expenditure dictated by general government policy. It is a system internal to the executive, and the frequent and sometimes major changes it undergoes are neither expressed nor constrained by formal legislative rules. Its development is however evolutionary: at no time since 1961 has a government decided to throw the whole system away and start again. Instead, significant changes—the cash basis, the control total, the triennial fixing of expenditure—have been introduced into a structure whose other elements have been largely held constant. What we have in 1999 is as different from what was conceived of in 1961 as is an adult from the baby s/he once was: yet it is still the PES system. In the paragraphs that follow, we look in turn at its principal elements: the setting of overall expenditure totals; the fitting of departmental expenditures to those totals; and the disciplining of departmental expenditure within the system.

2 The public expenditure total

Setting a total for public expenditure involves defining it; and how you define it depends on the reasons for setting that total. Over time these reasons have varied substantially: observing and planning the share that public expenditure would take in the process of economic growth (1961–76); bringing public expenditure growth under control (1976–80); linking public expenditure levels to government revenue levels, and holding down public expenditure as a percentage of gross domestic product (GDP) (1980–97); and currently (1997–) holding public expenditure to levels consistent with two 'strict fiscal rules': borrowing only to invest and not to fund current spending (which implies that current spending cannot exceed tax revenue plus other receipts) (the 'golden rule'); and keeping net public debt, as a proportion of GDP, at a stable and prudent level (which implies some restriction of investment expenditure) (Treasury 1998*b*: s. 3.2). Ever since 1976 the emphasis has been on setting totals which will represent targets and instruments of control, and not merely projections. Since 1980 or so there has been an increasing emphasis on defining guidelines—such as the public expenditure/GDP ratio—for setting overall public expenditure totals 'from the top down'; and since 1997, on presenting these guidelines as part of an economically rational long-term strategy. The reasoning behind the current government's 'strict fiscal rules', notably the emphasis on inter-generational equity (Treasury 1998*b*: s. 3.2.3), differs little in nature from that which has been deployed in the United States to support constitutional reforms such as the adoption of a 'balanced budget' amendment (Buchanan 1987). It seems, however, too early to say whether this new emphasis on codes and rules signals any consensus on the principles of fiscal policy strong enough to put their content beyond day-to-day politics and hence to justify a claim that they might have 'constitutional' value of the kind that we might willingly attribute to, say, the principles of freedom of speech or of movement (cf. Dearlove 1989). From our point of view, in any event, it is PES's character as a steadily evolving system of rules for resource allocation, rather than as a vehicle for the implementation of constitutional values, that gives it constitutional salience.

The new fiscal rules are felt to require the control of the whole of public expenditure, not just that of central government. Government has long had an overall expenditure total, general government expenditure (GGE), which is simply the combined expenditure of central and local government. GGE is not used as a control device within government, but the way that it is constructed reflects national accounting conventions (Office for National Statistics 1997). Such conventions, while not (subject to what is said below) legally binding, are highly influential in terms of the way government is able to present its financial decisions: whether a particular set of financial transactions counts as public expenditure or not may be of major political significance. 'Brown accused of "fiddling the books" in tax credit row' (Timmins 1998) is how such a classification issue may well be reported. Treasury concern to exclude from government expenditure totals liabilities and assets in projects under the Private Finance Initiative, the Treasury-led policy for attracting private capital to the support of public projects (Freedland 1998), has been a source of dispute with the Accounting Standards Board, the guardian of commercial accounting standards (Kelly 1998*a*, 1998*b*). In particular circumstances the conventions may acquire legal force. In the Maastricht Treaty the European Community adopted criteria for economic convergence by which member-States' eligibility for membership of Economic and Monetary Union would be judged: a general government annual deficit of not more than 3 per cent of GDP, and total government debt of not more than 60 per cent (EEC Treaty, art. 104C, as substituted by Treaty on European Union (TEU) 1992 Title II, art. G; TEU Protocol on the excessive deficit procedure, art. 1; generally, Italiener 1997). Applying the rules entails common and binding accounting definitions for such terms as 'government', 'debt' and 'deficit', which have been adopted, by Regulation, from the Community's European System of Accounts (ESA) (Council Regulation 3605/93/EC). Despite the government's unwillingness to commit itself on EMU in 1992 and indeed up to the time of writing, the National Accounts have been presented in accordance with the ESA as from 1998. The eventual application of the Regulation should thus not occasion difficulty.

The latest control aggregate has been christened Total Managed Expenditure (TME), which is the total of public sector current expenditure and public sector net investment (Treasury 1998*b*: s. 3.4). TME's immediate antecedent was called GGE(X), the measure by which the previous government judged its performance in relating public expenditure to other macro-economic measures such as GDP. GGE(X) was GGE less privatization proceeds, expenditure out of National Lottery proceeds, and net receipts of interest and dividends from public corporations and the private sector (Treasury 1992*b*). Somewhat similarly (but not exactly—that would deprive financial commentators of one of their principal opportunities to display their expertise and earn their keep), TME excludes various financial transactions such as privatization and receipts from loan sales (Treasury 1998*c*: para. 4).

GGE(X) was not the expenditure aggregate that government sought actively to control through the operation of the PES system. That aggregate, which covered a narrower range of expenditure, was in the nineteen-eighties and nineties variously termed the 'Planning Total' and the 'Control Total' and its composition likewise varied. Each total was set annually, for the coming three years.[1] In 1990, and again in 1992, government changed its view as to which elements of hard-to-forecast or hard-to-control expenditure it could usefully seek to bring within the

[1] PES, even more than the annual Parliamentary supply cycle, involves decisions and discussions extending a considerable distance in time on either side of the financial year (1 April–31 March) to which they relate, and we shall therefore adopt the convention whereby the financial year of actual expenditure is described as year 0, with prior years numbered as −1, −2 and so on, and subsequent ones as years +1, +2, +3 etc.

PES system of control (Treasury 1992*b*; Heald 1991; Heald 1995). The 1992 switch to a new, narrower 'Control Total' was generally seen as part of an attempt to derive a clearer—and hence less flexible—path for public expenditure growth. While projecting a real growth of general government expenditure (GGE) of no more than 2 per cent per annum, government excluded from its Control Total variable and hard-to-predict expenditure like unemployment benefit and other cyclical elements of social security expenditure, privatization proceeds, and debt interest, and limited that total to a maximum permitted growth of 1.5 per cent per annum (Treasury 1992*b*).[2] The hope was that by this means it would be possible—as it had proved not to be over the previous period—to hold fast to the control figure in the face of departmental claims which in aggregate always exceeded it. The 1998 changes continue in the direction of more ambitious control. They involve the government in the attempt to manage the whole of TME, but within TME there continues to be an aggregate which is to be tightly controlled (and reviewed only once every three years), made up of the sum of Departmental Expenditure Limits (DEL), and a second spending aggregate, Annually Managed Expenditure (AME), covering spending such as social security benefits (both cyclical and non-cyclical) and other spending such as local authority self-financed expenditure, and payments to EU institutions, which cannot properly be made subject to firm limits placed on departments (Treasury 1998*b*: s. 3.4 and Annex 3A; Treasury 1998*c*: paras. 16–23).

None of these totals, it should be noted, old or new, corresponds with the total of expenditure allocated and controlled within the framework of Parliamentary supply procedure: we explain the relationship below (pp. 162–4). All of them include expenditures—such as local authority expenditures—which are not, in legal terms at least, under the direct control of central government.

We have already noted the relevance to national accounting definitions of the 'Maastricht' criteria of economic convergence adopted by the European Community in 1992. The government's refusal hitherto to commit to the project has not stopped it using these criteria as a useful means for the enhancement of domestic control over the spending aggregates forming one side of the equation through which the key Maastricht figure of general government financial deficit is calculated. The 1998 Economic and Financial Strategy refers expressly to compliance with the Maastricht criteria and with the Community's Stability and Growth Pact (Treasury 1998*b*: s. 3.2).

[2] Growth in the Control Total might need to be held to a lower figure than this if other elements of GGE grew at excessive rates.

3 Fitting Departmental activities to public expenditure plans

One way of reading the history of PES is in terms of a steady shift from a 'bottom-up' to a 'top-down' method of total expenditure determination. The shift is reflected in the increasing precision of the overall objectives of public expenditure control; in the move from 'planning' to 'control' totals and the extension of the types of expenditure to be so controlled (above); and perhaps most important in practical terms, in the procedures through which the plans and related expenditure needs of departments have been related to the overall judgement as to the appropriate level of public expenditure.

For most of the life of PES departmental inputs have been the dominant factor in determining the public expenditure total. Up to 1976 this was the natural consequence of the structuring of the system in terms of constant prices and of the procedures used (Pollitt 1976). The shift to control objectives which followed the introduction of cash limits in 1976, the switch to a cash basis in 1981, and the introduction of annual planning totals, did not radically change this situation. It meant that departmental needs and plans were balanced against overall calculations of 'affordability', but it has been argued (Thain and Wright 1995: 229–42; ch. 22) that even over the period 1976–92 departmental demands continued to be the principal force shaping public expenditure aggregates, though one significantly constrained by the planning totals inherited from previous years' PES exercises: a position not inconsistent with the then medium-term objective of reducing public expenditure as a proportion of GDP (Treasury and Civil Service Committee 1988*a*: paras. 22–30, Evidence, q. 100).

Until 1992, PES procedures were essentially a matter of bilateral dialogue and negotiation, conducted annually between the Treasury and each department against the background of the previous years' planning totals for public expenditure as a whole and for the department's own share of it, and according to *Guidelines* prepared by the Treasury and 'cleared' by the Cabinet, usually without discussion (Thain and Wright 1995: 257–61; for an example, Treasury 1996*d*). The *Guidelines* addressed such issues as the timetable for the Survey, the form of departmental bids and the information to be provided in their support, and the arrangements for updating or reclassifying the baseline expenditures laid down for departments as the result of previous Surveys. Once baselines were agreed for the years covered by the Survey (years 0, +1, and +2), departments could bid for additional resources, whether to finance new, approved policies, to meet increased costs of an existing programme (for example by reason of changes in relative prices, the application of higher standards, or demographic changes); or to sustain a new programme not yet the subject of Cabinet approval. Treasury and department prepared joint papers setting out bids and identifying possible off-setting savings. Bids were resolved largely by negotiation, over the summer months of year −1, between the Chief Secretary to the Treasury, working to a planning total provisionally agreed by Cabinet in July, and each departmental minister (Thain and Wright 1995: 264–87). The results of these negotiations would be put to Cabinet for formal approval in November, at which time significant changes could hardly be made save at the risk of the collapse of the entire set of results. Only if particular Treasury–department negotiations became deadlocked would a collective decision-making machinery be brought into operation, in the shape of an *ad hoc* Cabinet Committee of senior non-spending Ministers. This was the so-called 'Star Chamber', named by Whitehall insiders after the prerogative court which became notorious for its harshness in Stuart times.

The Star Chamber was brought into operation by the Prime Minister in six of the eleven years between its invention in 1981 and its demise in 1992. Its style may have been intimidating, particularly for ministers, who found themselves appearing alone before colleagues in company with a Chief Secretary to the Treasury who might well know more about their department's finances than they did themselves. Its substance, however, hardly lived up to its nickname: it has been described as 'a conciliation service for settling disputes between Ministers and the Treasury' (Thain and Wright 1995: 303), and it certainly did not function as a mechanism for setting or revising expenditure priorities or for implementing deep cuts in programmes. Even when the Star Chamber was operating, therefore, it was really only the Treasury which was in a position to take an overall view of total 'affordable' public expenditure for the year and of how the bundle of departmental claims might be shaped and trimmed to fit within this figure; and that knowledge could, in practical terms, only be deployed tactically to juggle cuts and claims amid the changing pressures of multiple negotiations, not strategically to favour specific priorities. The absence of collective decision-making on priorities was a regular topic for adverse parliamentary comment (e.g. Treasury and Civil Service Committee 1986*a*).

PES took on a more genuinely collective character in 1992, when the introduction of the new Control Total was accompanied by the creation of a Cabinet Committee on public expenditure (known as EDX up to 1997, PX in 1997–98, and PSX since, and which we shall call the Public Expenditure Committee). This Committee's task has not been the resolution of 'hard cases' but the presentation to Cabinet of a package of decisions of spending allocations to departments within the Control Total. It did not wholly displace Treasury–department bilateral discussions, but it changed their nature and diminished their importance, in that agreement need not be reached; instead, the discussions helped to define the issues for decision by the Committee, which received papers jointly prepared by departments and Treasury, hearing oral representations from spending ministers when necessary. The collective approach was not adopted at the expense of Treasury influence in the PES process, but rather in reinforcement of it. In contrast to the Star Chamber, chaired throughout its life by a senior non-spending Minister, the Public Expenditure Committee has been chaired by the Chancellor of the Exchequer, with the Chief Secretary as a full member, sometimes 'the handmaiden and at other times the rapporteur' for the Committee, as a former Chief Secretary poetically if puzzlingly asserted (Treasury and Civil Service Committee 1992: paras. 174–6, Evidence, q. 369). Effectively this enabled the Treasury to set the Committee's agenda.

The evolution of PES took a different turn in 1998, with the introduction of the distinction between Departmental Expenditure Limits and Annually Managed Expenditure. Departmental Expenditure Limits have been firmly set for three years (1999–2002), on the basis of a Comprehensive Spending Review (CSR) of all the government's spending programmes, undertaken in 1997–98. The CSR, completed in July 1998 (Treasury 1998*d*), involved departments in 'scrutinising their programmes and producing recommendations for change, to refocus their policies and spending on the government's key priorities, as set out in its Manifesto' (Treasury 1998*b*: s. 4.1). The aim has been to conduct a more radical review of activities and their expenditure implications than has occurred within the PES annual cycle, and to destroy, through the fixing of this expenditure for three years ahead, any lingering assumption in departments of year-by-year accommodation to changing circumstances. The change of approach is reinforced by the integration, into the process of future decision-making on public expenditure, of departmental plans, covering the periods for which DELs are set, and 'tied to key outputs and efficiency targets, against which performance will be monitored' (Treasury 1998*c*: para. 24, and below, p. 189). The plans have since been presented, with great fanfare, in the form of a set of Public Service Agreements concluded between the Treasury and departments (Treasury 1998*f*); we consider in Chapter 6 the significance of this new language (below, pp. 191–2). A further review will take place in 2000, producing new triennial DELs operative from 2001–2004 (Treasury 1998*c*: para. 25). 'Illustrative' DEL figures produced in June 1998 showed them covering about half of Total Managed Expenditure (Treasury 1998*b*: Annex 3A). The other half, Annually Managed Expenditure, will clearly require, as its name indicates, some form of annual review. Again, the nature of such review is not clear: an internal PES document promises 'tough annual scrutiny by the Treasury' of the relevant programmes (Treasury 1998*c*: para. 51), and the government has publicly promised not to take policy measures which would have the effect of increasing social security or other elements of AME without taking steps to ensure that the effects of these decisions could be accommodated prudently within its fiscal rules (Treasury 1998*b*: s. 3.4). A further change, likewise suggestive of tighter Treasury control (or at least, of the desire to exercise it), derives from the strict separation of capital and current expenditure for planning and management purposes. Departments are required to submit Departmental Investment Strategies to the Treasury for approval; movement of funds from capital account to current account will be strictly regulated (Treasury 1998*c*: paras. 6–15).

Hennessy (1999: 9) reports that the Public Expenditure Committee 'Definitely did not figure as the locus of decision-taking' on the Comprehensive Spending Review. Officially, however, the process remains collective. The Committee, now titled the Public Services and Public Expenditure Committee, continues to oversee the whole process, including the monitoring of commitments under the Public Service Agreements, and to be chaired by the Chancellor of the Exchequer, though the presence of two Cabinet Office ministers reflects the new significance of that office in the process of spending review (below, pp. 191–2).

4 Results

Until 1997 the Cabinet's November decision on the Public Expenditure Committee recommendations marked the end of the planning and allocation part of the PES process, and produced a set of public spending figures which could be translated into the terms of the annual Parliamentary supply process. The effect of the 1998 reforms is to break up PES into annual and triennial elements, and into capital and current provision. The idea of a single annual spending 'round' is thereby considerably weakened. Placing too much emphasis on the increasingly formalized PES annual cycle of discussions and decisions probably always represented a distortion of the real decision-making process on spending. The annual cycle was never a self-contained process. It went on against the background of continuous discussion, between each department and its team in the Treasury's Spending Directorate, on a wide variety of issues arising out of the department's expenditure and the policies it reflected. Such discussion addressed issues like the evolution of spending in the current year, the economy, efficiency and effectiveness of past expenditure, the expenditure implications of policy proposals, considered between Treasury and department both prior to and after Cabinet approval, and the longer-term possibilities of changes to departmental policies, or the mode of their delivery, with a view to achieving value-for-money improvements. The intention of the 1998 reforms is clearly that such discussions should be much more strongly structured by departmental plans and, within these plans, by Departmental Investment Strategies. But while different elements of expenditure will thus be the subject of more variegated forms of discussion relating to different periods, it remains the case that a comprehensive series of spending figures for year 0 will still be generated by PES by November of year −1 or thereabouts, some just determined, others (DELs) possibly dating back some time, depending on the point reached in their three-year cycle.

5 PES in Parliament

5.1 In general

These year 0 spending figures have generally been brought to the notice of Parliament in November or December in year −1. Up to 1993 the vehicle was the Chancellor's Autumn Statement, setting out general spending plans for year 0 and followed up in February or March with detailed plans, presented from 1969 to 1990 as a single Public Expenditure White Paper (latterly in a number of volumes), since then as a series of Departmental Reports (below). In March also the Chancellor would present, through the Budget, the revenue side of the government's plans. From 1993 to 1996, the government switched to a 'unified' Budget presented in November, and containing both the revenue and expenditure sides of the Budget arithmetic, a change which in part reflected the claim that public expenditure was revenue-driven (Treasury 1992*a*). The Labour Government which took office in May 1997 introduced a July Budget, following it with a Budget in March 1998 on the pre-1993 pattern. Whatever the date of the Budget, the Chancellor's oral Budget statement in the Commons is supported by a hefty volume of written material, the annual Financial Statement and Budget Report ('Red Book'). The Statement incorporates the overall Budget judgement, the government's medium-term financial strategy, analyses of the state of the economy and of the public finances, global expenditure plans, and explanation of the tax and national insurance measures proposed. From 1999 this material is, in effect, being divided between two documents: the Red Book, containing the Budget judgement, the short-term outlook, and an explanation of proposed fiscal measures; and an Economic and

Fiscal Strategy Report, dealing with longer-term strategy, and normally, but not necessarily, presented at the time of the Budget (Treasury 1998*e*: paras. 15–19).

While the Red Book gives MPs plenty of material for reflection and debate, they are not asked to reach any *decision* about the broad judgements it reflects; they vote at the end of the Budget debate only on a series of financial resolutions which provide the basis for bringing in the Finance Bill and which relate exclusively to tax and national insurance measures. There is no opportunity to express approval or disapproval of the results of the PES process itself, nor of the assumptions and decisions relating to financial strategy which furnish the background both to PES decisions and to tax policy. No parliamentary decision on the overall budget balance is taken at any stage, and votes on the estimates, within the framework of the traditional parliamentary supply cycle (below, pp. 155–64) continue to provide the basis for approvals of expenditure.

5.2 The Code of Fiscal Stability

In consequence, and notwithstanding the constitutional requirements for legislative authorization of both tax and spending decisions (above, pp. 107–9), the central strategic and tactical decisions taken by government about the relationship between revenue and spending have remained legally invisible and inaccessible to the law. This is changing, for two reasons: the introduction of a legislatively-based Code of Fiscal Stability (Treasury 1998*e*); and the full interlocking of PES arrangements and parliamentary supply which should be made possible by the switch to resource accounting and budgeting (below, pp. 164–8). While the Code, and the legislation on which it is based, compel the government to state clearly and accurately the context within which its spending decisions are set through documents such as the Pre-Budget Report, the Red Book, and the Economic and Fiscal Strategy Report (Finance Act 1998, s. 156; Code, paras. 15–19), they impinge little on the substantive discretion which surrounds spending decisions, restricting it only by reference to general principles of transparency, stability, responsibility, fairness, and efficiency (Code, paras. 3–8). So far as Parliament is concerned, transparency, rather than any substantive constraint, will continue to be the most important guarantee of effective critical involvement in the PES process. The Code defines 'transparency' to mean that

> the Government shall publish sufficient information to allow the public [not, be it noted, Parliament itself] to scrutinise the conduct of fiscal policy and the state of the public finances, and shall not withhold information except where publication of that information would substantially harm

a range of interests (national security, defence, international relations, criminal prosecutions, civil proceedings, privacy, third party confidential communications, and government commercial activity),

> or harm the integrity of the decision-making and policy advice processes in government. (para. 4)

The precision of the wording here, reflecting the distinction drawn in the government's Freedom of Information proposals between information of different degrees of sensitivity (Chancellor of the Duchy of Lancaster 1997: ch. 3), attests to the unlikelihood of any greater exposure of the internal process of decision-making on public spending.

Among other principles, the one which most directly addresses public spending is that of efficiency, which

> means that the government shall seek to ensure that it uses resources in ways that give value for money; that public assets are put to the best possible use and that surplus assets are disposed of. The Government shall also have regard to economic efficiency and compliance costs when forming taxation policy. (para. 8)

The first clause is hardly new, but the second reflects a new concern with capital assets in line with resource accounting and budgeting reforms (below, pp. 164–8), and may be a helpful future point of reference for the Treasury in discussions with departments.

5.3 Departmental reports

Parliamentary involvement with the results of the PES process is, however, prolonged, and its information very substantially amplified, by the presentation of departmental reports. These reports today form the principal practical expression of this commitment to transparency. As already noted, they replaced the detailed Public Expenditure White Paper with effect from 1991. Since then each department produces annually, in February or March, a document which both *reports on its activity*, particularly over the previous year and the year in progress (i.e. years −2 and −1), and *presents its spending plans* for years 0, +1, and +2. The move to departmental reports, like other recent changes, is a reflection of the Treasury's desire to accentuate the responsibility of departments for their own finances. Departments write their own reports, though they are jointly presented to Parliament by the departmental minister and the Chief Secretary to the Treasury, and are required to incorporate a series of common core elements laid down in Treasury guidance (Treasury 1990*a*: 5–7; Public Accounts Committee 1996: Evidence, Appendix C) and kept under regular review by the Treasury Officer of Accounts team. These cover matters like the structure and content of the cash plans and out-turn tables, performance indicators, Citizen's Charter achievements, executive agencies, and value for money initiatives. A member of the TOA team is also responsible for checking the reports in draft, both generally and for compliance with the common core requirements. The process represents a delicate compromise (Treasury 1997*b*: paras. 3.1–3.5; Treasury and Civil Service Committee 1994*b*: Evidence, qq. 25–40). On the one hand, departments must take responsibility for their own reports and account to their own parliamentary select committees for their contents. On the other, the reports, individually and in aggregate, must present an accurate and consistent picture of expenditure plans and performance, and must be properly linked to the supply estimates and provide the detail which these no longer present (below, pp. 159–64). The House of Commons Treasury Committee looks to the Treasury to ensure that the reports are consistent with the general requirements for financial reporting to Parliament, and has indeed expressed concern about whether this goal is being achieved (below, pp. 163–4; Treasury Committee 1996: xx–xxiii). Significant changes to the format of reports have been suggested as part of the process of modifying supply procedure to reflect resource accounting and budgeting, such as the separation of the material into a departmental plan and a departmental annual report, presented at different times of year, and the incorporation into the former of the department's estimate (Treasury 1995*b*: para. 2.15; Public Accounts Committee 1996: para. 58 and Appendix B, para. 5.4).

III THE SUPPLY SYSTEM

1 The supply cycle

The presentation of the Budget, over the last decade or so, at different times of the financial year has not affected the formal Parliamentary processes, of ways and means and of granting supply, which reflect the basic constitutional principles already discussed. The revenue proposals for year 0, put forward by the Chancellor in his Budget Statement and provisionally approved by the financial resolutions passed after the Budget debate, are debated in detail in the proceedings on the Finance Bill, which ordinarily take place between January and March. Finance Bill proceedings have a number of special features (Erskine May 1997: ch. 32), but these need not delay us here. Expenditure proposals are taken forward through the presentation to Parliament of Departmental reports, and through the presentation to, and approval by, the House of Commons, of estimates of supply expenditure for the year (ibid.: ch. 30). Both these processes currently take place at the very end of year −1, in March, but the House does, in November of year −1, approve a Vote on Account which is designed to provide legal cover for that proportion of expenditure by goverment departments, by the House of Commons itself, and by the National Audit Office, which will be incurred between the beginning of year 0 in April and the time of the approval of that year's Appropriation Act (normally in July). The amount voted is generally based on a standard proportion (45 per cent) of the amount so far voted for the corresponding services in the current year (year −1); it does not, therefore, imply any decision as to the level of funding in year 0. This Vote is given legislative force by a Consolidated Fund Act (ibid.: 758–9).

The estimates 'form the basis of the statutory authority for the appropriation of funds to specific services' (National Audit Office 1986: 7). As such they require to be approved by the House of Commons by way of vote. All estimates are laid before the House of Commons by the Chief Secretary to the Treasury. Since 1982 the time available for considering the main estimates has been restricted, under Standing Orders 54 and 55, to three days between the presentation of the estimates and the summer recess, on which debates may be held on those estimates selected for this purpose by the Liaison Committee established under Standing Order 145. This Committee consists of the Chairmen of the House's Select Committees, thus enabling Committees which are dissatisfied with aspects of Departmental reports to seek further debate on the floor of the House (Griffith and Ryle 1989: 248–51). The remainder of the estimates are put to the vote without the possibility of debate. In the rest of this section we consider the scope, form and effect of the estimates in the light of the continuing development of the PES system and of the move to resource accounting and budgeting.

As already noted (above, p. 108), the resolutions approving the estimates are not themselves, under the constitution, a sufficient authority for expenditure. Despite the Commons' jealously guarded financial privileges (Erskine May 1997: ch. 33), which exclude any substantive consideration of supply by the Lords, supply is constitutionally granted by the whole of Parliament acting by way of legislation. Accordingly the estimates resolutions are translated into legislative form through the annual Consolidated Fund (Appropriation) Act (usually called the Appropriation Act). The Act, which is not subject to debate, is ordinarily passed shortly before the summer recess. Spending prior to this date will have been covered by the Consolidated Fund Act which implements the November Vote on Account.

Supplementary estimates are ordinarily presented on at least two occasions as the year 0 runs forward: in the winter, when the decisions will be given statutory force in the Consolidated Fund Act which also incorporates year +1's Vote on Account; and in early spring, when another Consolidated Fund Act will be needed. Summer supplementaries may also be introduced, even before consideration of the main estimates has been concluded, in order that the Appropriation Act may be as accurate as possible (Griffith and Ryle 1989: 249).

The year comes to a close at the end of March, but the financial cycle continues, with the focus switching to reporting and auditing procedures. Executive agencies, which will ordinarily be subject to distinct reporting and accounting requirements, will be presenting accounts for the year to Parliament before the summer recess (Treasury 1989*a*: para. 16.1.13) as well as providing information for inclusion in their department's report which will be presented the following March. Departmental accounts, audited by the National Audit Office and with commentary, where appropriate, by the Comptroller and Auditor-General, will be laid before Parliament in October, and will become the subject of investigation by the Public Accounts Committee, leading to the preparation, with the assistance of the Comptroller and Auditor-General, of a series of reports based *inter alia* on evidence and explanations from departments, and followed up by Treasury responses. Particular attention is paid to any case in which the Comptroller and Auditor-General has reported an excess of expenditure over the Vote (and any additional Vote stemming from supplementary estimates), or where for any other reason he has been unable to give unqualified approval to the appropriation account (Erskine May 1997: 751–2). Such excesses are the subject of a special report by the Committee to the House. A Statement of Excesses is prepared by the Treasury, and having been approved by vote ('Excess Votes'), will be given effect in the March Consolidated Fund Bill (which also implements the spring supplementary estimates for the year in progress (year +1)). Only at this point, twelve months after the close of the year, may its financial cycle be said to be complete.

Complex as these procedures are, they do not exhaust the occasions of parliamentary interest in questions of financial resources. Taxes, for example, may be imposed outside the framework of the annual Finance Act; a number of significant fiscal innovations, such as Petroleum Revenue Tax (see the Oil Taxation Act 1975), have been introduced in this way. Most expenditure falling within the framework of regular programmes will have been authorized in general terms by permanent legislation, not just by the annual Appropriation Act: indeed, there is a well-established convention to the effect that such legislation *must* ordinarily be introduced (Treasury 1989*a*: paras. 2.2.6–10 and annex 2.1; above, pp. 34–6 below, pp. 173–5). The general rules of financial initiative apply to these extra-cyclical measures in the same way as to the financial cycle itself.

Before looking in more detail at the allocation elements of the supply cycle, we should say something about its general significance for both external (parliamentary) and internal (Treasury) control of finance. This involves cutting through a layer of debate about parliamentary functions in order that we may properly perceive the internal impact of the cycle. While debate on the detail of taxation proposals continues to be lengthy, demanding, and effective (Griffith and Ryle 1989: 252–4), the 1982 reforms (above, p. 156) have brought to completion (or nearly so) a process of *formalization* of the spending side of the parliamentary cycle. Parliamentary control over expenditure through the estimates has long been regarded by commentators as ineffective, despite the invention of a variety of mechanisms of committee inquiry and floor debate, and the current system seems to acknowledge this through the reduction of days of debate to three, with the mass of spending and accounts decisions called for by the cycle going through as undebated votes.

Parliamentary spending decisions might thus seem to have become one of Bagehot's 'dignified' parts of the constitution (Bagehot 1905: 4; and Elliott 1981*a*: 60–3). From the House of Commons' point of view, however, the need for these decisions, however they may be taken, continues to provide the lever which it can use, through the inquiries and recommendations of committees such as the Public Accounts Committee, the Treasury Committee, and the Procedure Committee, to obtain the information and the opportunities for debate about the larger issues of public finance, economic management, and administrative performance. These are issues which cannot be adequately ventilated on the basis of the information contained in the estimates themselves. The House's appreciation of this point has emerged clearly from recent debate about the simplification of estimates and the transfer of much of their detail to departmental reports which are outside its formal apparatus of control (compare Treasury and Civil Service Committee 1994*b*: paras. 15–20 with Public Accounts Committee 1994*b*, and see below, pp. 163–4). The Treasury and Civil Service Committee noted that estimates documentation formed part of the formal process of granting supply, a process in which, as its specialist adviser put it, 'the myth (that the House of Commons can deny supply) [is] far more important than the reality (that this will not happen when a Government enjoys the confidence of the House of Commons)' (Treasury and Civil Service Committee 1994*b*: 40). Departmental reports, however, were no more than executive documents for the information of Parliament, and enjoyed no such formal status, with the consequence that Parliament lacked any institutional control over their form analogous to the requirement that the Treasury consult the Public Accounts Committee and the Treasury Committee before making significant changes to the form of the estimates (Erskine May 1997: 744–5). So far as the Treasury is concerned, the need to negotiate this procedural obstacle course is one of the sources of its power, in that Parliament—as a matter of long-established custom, rather than explicit rules (Roseveare 1973: 68–74; Chester 1981: 205)—expects the Treasury to present the government's proposals (for estimates, excess votes, Consolidated Fund Bills, and so on), thereby giving it the gate-keeping role that we have already discussed (above, pp. 120–2).

In addition, even those procedures which do *not* offer the House of Commons' formal decision-making opportunities help to reinforce the Treasury's position vis-à-vis departments. Parliament's desire to discuss economically significant decisions enables the Treasury to use Parliament's information needs to buttress budgeting and planning disciplines in government, within frameworks such as the Financial Statement, the Public Expenditure White Paper and, now, departmental reports. In consequence, while the Commons' procedures for decision and debate on spending matters can do little in themselves to assure economy, effectiveness and efficiency, they have been a useful reinforcement of central, primarily Treasury, influence in this field.

2 The Estimates

2.1 Structure and control

The estimates lay out the expected cash expenditure of central government over the year. Beside the expenditure, and receipts, of departments and their executive agencies, they also include sums dispensed by way of grants to other public sector bodies, such as local authorities and non-departmental public bodies like the Arts Council or the Research Councils; but their total does not correspond with any of those used in the PES process. Those totals all include expenditure which is outside the estimates (such as local authority self-financed expenditure and expenditure—like judges' salaries and EU contributions—which is charged permanently to the Consolidated Fund and thus does not require annual appropriation) (Treasury 1989*a*: para. 3.2.7a), and they have in the past excluded expenditure falling within them, such as spending on unemployment benefit, which was outside the Control Total. By way of introduction to the estimates, therefore, the Treasury provides a reconciliation, with a chart showing how the estimates total relates to the Control Total (Treasury 1996*c*: 6). Such reconciliation needs to be carried through to the departmental level if Parliament is to have a clear understanding of expenditure decisions and plans at that level, and the degree to which the information distributed between departmental reports and estimates permits such understanding has been an important issue for the House of Commons in recent years, as we shall see.

Treasury power to determine the form of estimates—and the way they are divided into Votes each covering a broad functional block of expenditure—derives indirectly from the powers to fix the form of appropriation accounts and the departments responsible for them conferred by sections 23 and 22 of the Exchequer and Audit Departments Act 1866. The overall structure of Votes and sub-heads has not changed in its essentials since the 1860s, when the Treasury formulated its original plan of accounts, though the nature of the information provided within this structure has, as we shall see, undergone regular changes, of which those currently in progress are perhaps the most radical of all. By convention, as already noted, the Treasury consults the House of Commons, through the Public Accounts Committee and the Treasury Committee, in advance of making any significant change to the form of estimates (Durell 1917: 266; Erskine May 1997: 744–5). Far-reaching changes, such as those introduced in 1996, or the planned switch to resource accounting and budgeting, are the subject of elaborate and lengthy dialogue involving both the Public Accounts Committee and the Treasury Committee, and extending where appropriate to the Select Committee on Procedure and to departmental Select Committees also. This conventional consultation now far outstrips in significance the formal power the House possesses to reject estimates on grounds of defects of presentation.

Today, the estimate for each Vote is presented in three parts. Part I indicates the net amount of money sought under the Vote as a whole; the formal description of the services to be financed from the Vote (known as the 'ambit'); the department, or person(s), who will account for the Vote; and the amount already allocated in the Vote on Account (Treasury 1989*a*: 11.3.6). Part II contains more detailed information, under a series of sub-heads, as proposed by the department and approved by the Treasury (in practice, by the relevant spending team). Part III gives details of receipts expected in connection with estimate services, but which are to be paid into the Consolidated Fund rather than being appropriated in aid of the estimate (Consolidated Fund Extra Receipts). The estimate is completed by a variety of explanatory notes and tables. It clearly identifies the parts of the Vote that are cash-limited, and the part represented by running costs (below, pp. 183–6, 188–90). The only parts of the estimate that are subsequently incorporated in the Appropriation Act, and thereby acquire legislative force, are Part I, and the total figure of appropriations in aid (which, added to the (net) amount of the Vote in Part I, shows the gross level of expenditure).

We leave until later consideration of the significance, to control of public expenditure generally, of this partially legislative status of approved estimates (below, pp. 199–206). The point for notice here is that the legislative status of the scope and overall quantity of expenditure under a Vote means that any expenditure on matters outside this scope, or in excess of the overall quantity, must be legally authorized by other means: by being charged to another Vote whose ambit covers it; by a Consolidated Fund Act following upon a supplementary estimate; by temporary resort to the Contingencies Fund. From this it follows that the larger the number of Votes into which annual supply expenditure is divided, the greater the opportunities for formal control offered to Parliament, by reason of the need for approval of supplementary estimates and their consequential Consolidated Fund Acts (Durell 1917: 278–82). Between 1900 and the end of the Second World War the enlargement of state activity brought about a substantial increase in the number of Votes, from 144 in 1900 to 196 in 1946. Since then there has been a downward trend far outpacing reductions in supply expenditure's share of GDP. Beer counted 180 Votes in 1957 (1957: 38–9); in 1996–97 there were 110. In contrast to the position in the early nineteen-hundreds, when Durell could state that 'The Public Accounts Committee is always opposed . . . to any diminution in the number of votes' (1917: 281), the House of Commons and its committees have in recent years offered little resistance to such reduction, apparently on the footing that if transparency of estimating and accounting were maintained, gains through the creation of more rational blocks of expenditure would greatly outweigh any loss of purely formal decision opportunities. Encouraged by the NAO, however, Parliament has now called a halt: while the introduction of resource accounting is likely to reduce the number of Votes to around 60 (White and Hollingsworth 1997: 439), Public Accounts Committee and Treasury have broadly agreed that there should be separate 'requests for resources' to Parliament for major blocks of expenditure within the new Votes, blocks generally corresponding to the existing Votes (Public Accounts Committee 1996: para. 3(xix); Treasury 1997*e*: para. 16; Select Committee on Procedure 1998*a*: para. 26).

Similar considerations, however, apply also to the estimates material which does not receive legislative benediction, particularly so far as Treasury control is concerned. We saw that in Part II of the estimate, detailed spending information is arranged under sub-heads. There can be no doubt that expenditure in excess of a sub-head, incurred without Treasury consent or delegated authority, is irregular, and unless within the overall total of the Vote and subsequently authorized by an exercise of virement (below, pp. 180–1), will give rise to a qualification of the account by the Comptroller and Auditor-General and to the need for an Excess Vote. The more detailed, therefore, the structure of sub-heads, the greater the Treasury's opportunity for control. The greater, also, is the amount of information available to Parliament, both in the estimates themselves and in the appropriation accounts which mirror them. As with Votes, however, the long-term trend has been in favour of a simplification of sub-heads, and it has accelerated markedly in recent years. This began with some relatively minor moves in 1988 (Public Accounts Committee 1989), but major change occurred only in the 1996–97 estimates, when much of the detail previously found in estimates was eliminated. Most but not all of it was transferred to the departmental reports produced as part of the government's annual public expenditure documentation. The content and management of this change merit consideration in a little detail, in so far as they show the ever closer interlocking of PES decisions and documentation (departmental reports) with supply procedure; change in the style and focus of Treasury control through the allocation process; and the effects of such change on parliamentary capacities for control and influence.

2.2 Simplification and alignment with PES

To get a sense of these changes we can compare the way the Lord Chancellor's Department's main Vote appeared in the 1991–92 estimates (Treasury 1991*c*: 11–19), which was the first year of publication of departmental reports, with its appearance in those of 1996–97, after the reforms (Treasury 1996*c*: 138–40). In 1991–92 the Vote covered almost all its activity with the exception of the legal aid budget (which had its own Vote). It was divided into eight sections (A: Headquarters and miscellaneous services; B: Court business; C: Other legal services (such as the Law Commission and some administrative tribunals); D: Administration of private assets; E: Other miscellaneous services; F and G: the Court building programme; and H: Legal aid administration). Each section was further divided into subheads, 34 altogether, including one in each section for appropriations in aid (that is, receipts applied to offset expenditure under the Vote). Expenditure subheads varied in size from the £284.9m provided for the running costs of the courts to the £38,000 to be paid for the Permanent Bureau of the Hague Conference on Private International Law.

Look now at the Vote in 1996–97. It occupies three pages of text as opposed to the nine required earlier. Yet it is much larger (£2.2bn as opposed to £397m), because the legal aid budget is now absorbed in this Vote instead of having one of its own. It also includes a new responsibility, magistrates courts, taken over by the department from the Home Office in 1992. Despite these additions, the eight sections of 1991–92 have been reduced by amalgamation to three, to which are added new sections for legal aid and magistrates courts grants. Each section now appears as a single line in the estimate, as part of a matrix whose six columns represent economically distinct forms of expenditure: direct expenditure (running costs, other current, and capital); grants and transfers (capital and current), and appropriations in aid. These six columns, plus totals and information from the previous two years, are the same in every estimate. Subheads now appear, without further description, simply as cells in the matrix, each of which has a cash figure or a blank as appropriate. It is still possible to see the figure for the running costs of the Court Service (now £366.2m in this estimate), but the Hague Conference, and other minor functional subheads, have disappeared altogether from sight. There are twenty-two subheads in lieu of thirty-four.

This new form of estimate is both more economical, and more economic. There is much less information, but what is there is designed to be more significant in economic terms, and to present the cash provisions which Parliament is invited to grant by way of supply in a way which is consistent with the expenditure plans emerging from the PES process by way first of the Financial Statement and Budget Report, giving the global expenditure picture, and then through the departmental reports which translate it into departmental plans. This is the external face of an increasingly refined Financial Information System within government, now incorporating a data-base which can generate, from departmental inputs, figures for supply estimates and appropriation accounts as well as PES figures (Treasury 1997*b*: 43–7). These presentational changes were accompanied by a substantive relaxation of Treasury control over virement between subheads (below, pp. 180–1). When proposals for these changes were put by the Treasury to the relevant Parliamentary Select Committees, the Public Accounts Committee was broadly sympathetic, seeing them as implementing demands it had earlier made for, *inter alia*, an exchange of detail for information of greater value (Public Accounts Committee 1994*c*). The Treasury and Civil Service Committee was much more reserved. While it acknowledged that the effectiveness of estimates as a basis for Parliamentary scrutiny of expenditure had long been the target of justified criticism, it expressed serious doubt about the adequacy of Departmental reports as a substitute vehicle for the detail previously carried by the estimates (Treasury and Civil Service Committee 1994*b*).

At the heart of the Treasury Committee's worries was the sense that the Treasury itself was abandoning a measure of its control over the financial information presented to Parliament, and that Parliament would be the loser by this. Despite the Treasury's control over departmental reports, through monitoring for the proper presentation of 'core elements' (above, p. 154–5), significant variations were occurring in the way departments presented information. Since departmental reports are considered primarily by the Select Committees which shadow individual departments, with the information provided in each case being the subject of negotiation between a department and 'its' Select Committee, there was a real risk that considerable disparities could develop in the amount and type of financial information provided to Parliament from different parts of government. A subsequent survey of Select Committee experience furnished evidence of such variation (Treasury and Civil Service Committee 1995: Evidence, Appendix 3). The Committee's concern, which has been taken up by the Procedure Committee (Select Committee on Procedure 1998*a*), closely echoes that voiced a century earlier by the Public Accounts Committee, which in 1887 strongly reproved the Treasury for permitting the Admiralty to put forward a new form of accounts to the Committee even though it objected to them itself (Durell 1917: 265). So far, the Treasury has been unwilling to modify its current preference for a more relaxed role in relation to departmental information to Parliament. This may suggest that while Parliament's sense of reliance on the Treasury is undiminished, the Treasury may be finding, in the disciplines of electronic information management (the Financial Information System), an effective substitute for the mechanical disciplines engendered by formal parliamentary control.

IV RESOURCE ACCOUNTING AND BUDGETING

1 In general

Resource accounting and budgeting (RAB) represents the most far-reaching change in government expenditure arrangements since the introduction of appropriation audit and the passage of the Exchequer and Audit Departments Act 1866. Instead of accounting and budgeting in cash, departments are starting to prepare, over a period running from 1998 to 2002, accounts and operating budgets on the accruals basis which is standard in commercial life and is already operated by government trading funds and some executive agencies (above, pp. 132–7). The core differences between cash and accruals accounting are two (Treasury 1995*b*: 5):

cash accounts record payments and income as they are actually made and received, regardless of when the obligation to pay arises and of the period over which it may extend, whereas accruals accounts record current expenditure and income in the year to which that obligation relates, even if the cash was not paid or received in that year, also recording the difference between the accruals measure and the actual cash paid or received, usually as a creditor or debtor;

for capital expenditure, cash accounts record the payment as and when made, regardless of the life of the asset; accruals accounts do not record the whole expenditure as operating cost in the year in which the asset is acquired or built, but spread the expenditure over the useful life of the asset in the form of an annual depreciation charge.

The simplicity and immediacy of cash accounts have long been prized by Parliament, but as the Comptroller and Auditor-General has pointed out to the Procedure Committee, 'they are so straightforward . . . they tell you essentially nothing' (Select Committee on Procedure 1998*a*: Evidence, q. 22). For example, cash accounts, in themselves, give no information about contractual commitments which a department might have taken on and which might extend over many years. Nor do they distinguish between current and capital expenditure. Most critically for the Treasury, they give little sense of the true cost of activities—notably, the cost of holding capital assets such as buildings and equipment.

2 Resource accounting

The switch to RAB was launched in 1994 and has been pursued without interruption despite the change of government in 1997. The first stage was the introduction of *resource accounts* by all departments, in the general form set out in the Government's White Paper (Treasury 1995*b*). This part of the process has been essentially internal to the executive, and could have been managed without parliamentary consent or even consultation, had government been content to continue to account to Parliament on the old cash basis. This option was however rejected at an early stage (Treasury 1994*d*: para. 3.34), so that the development of resource accounts has at all stages taken account of their use in Parliamentary accountability. The new accounts, which are designed eventually to replace appropriation accounts and are being published for the first time for 1999–2000, are to include an operating costs statement, showing administrative and programme costs for the department's activities; a balance sheet; a cash flow statement; a statement of resources, analysed by reference to the aims and objectives of the department; and of particular importance to eventual parliamentary scrutiny, a summary of resource out-turn, comparing out-turn with estimate by Vote, in both resource and cash requirement terms.

The development of the new system, led by the Treasury, has involved the preparation by the Treasury's RAB team of a *Resource Accounting Reference manual* for the guidance of Departments, and the appointment of a Financial Reporting Advisory Board, including external, departmental, and NAO membership, to give independent advice and ensure that the highest appropriate accounting standards are applied. Both Treasury and departments have had to rely heavily on the expertise of the NAO in this process, the Treasury for advice on the principles and policies involved, the departments for help with the practicalities of implementation (National Audit Office 1996). These should not be underestimated: switching to RAB involves the inventory and valuation of an enormous range of assets. One military aircraft, alone, constitutes hundreds of systems each of which requires separate inventory and valuation. Considerable attention has been paid by the Treasury to keeping Parliament informed through consultations with the Public Accounts, Treasury, and Procedure Committees. Generally, all three committees have welcomed the reform, while drawing attention to a variety of concerns, notably that of whether the timetable set by the Treasury allows enough opportunity for consideration by Parliament of the adequacy of the new system before the old one is abandoned (Treasury Committee 1996; Public Accounts Committee 1996; Select Committee on Procedure 1998*a*). Legislation is needed in order to change what Parliament votes, under section 22 of the 1866 Act, from cash to resources, and could be extended to secure a more extensive up-dating of the 1866 Act. The Treasury has however argued, in dialogue with the Public Accounts Committee, that RAB does not involve changing any of the fundamental principles of supply, such as annual legislative approval of expenditure, terms of operation of the Contingencies Fund (below, pp. 186–8), or procedure for consideration of excesses (Public Accounts Committee 1996: para. 3; Treasury 1997*e*: paras. 14–17). Formally speaking, this may well be true; but the switch from cash to resources and commitments, when coupled with the longer time horizons introduced into PES (above, pp. 150–1), arguably represents a change in basic thinking about control of public finance which could have ramifying constitutional effects (below, p. 206).

3 Resource budgeting

The second element of RAB is *resource budgeting*, that is, the use of resources rather than cash as the 'currency' for government expenditure planning and control through the PES system. For the reasons already mentioned, resources are seen as providing a better measure than does cash of the full cost of departments' activities, and it is therefore natural to seek to get PES on to this new footing. This will involve getting departments' running costs (below, pp. 188–90) on to an accruals basis, providing separate treatment for capital expenditure, and deriving cash financing requirements from the department's resource budget (Treasury 1995*b*: paras. 1.9–1.33). The 1998 changes to PES (above, pp. 150–1) are in line with this process of adjustment, notably in the way they reflect RAB's concern with accounting for resources in terms of objectives through tying Departmental Expenditure Limits to three-year plans with performance targets (Treasury 1998*c*: para. 24), and through their separation of current and capital expenditure at departmental level, creating the conditions for an overall capital spending total within TME. The first PES to be carried out on the resource basis will take place in 2000.

RAB will call not only for separate capital budgeting, but also for departments to be charged for their use of capital, so as to 'focus attention throughout the financial planning cycle on the cost of holding assets as well as on new capital spending' (Treasury 1995*b*: para. 1.21). Capital charges can provide an incentive to dispose of assets, and the government has deliberately drawn attention to this possibility through the creation of a National Asset Register (Treasury 1997*d*) and by inviting departments to look critically at their asset portfolios. White and Hollingsworth (1997: 440) have noted that analogous New Zealand reforms distinguished between 'working assets', which might be sold, and 'custodial assets', like national parks and forests, which could not be; but that operating this distinction was not easy. Our constitution offers little support for the idea, common elsewhere, that capital assets may be held by government in trust for the nation. Under the civilian tradition, possession of particular assets (roads, ports, sea-shore, fortifications, court-houses) has for centuries been regarded as a necessary incident of legitimate government, and as a public interest to be protected against improvident rulers by legal restrictions on disposition, reflected in the classical distinction between the (alienable) *regalia minora*, and the (inalienable) *regalia majora*. This distinction has been received in Scots law, but has been significantly weakened over the last century or so (*Stair Memorial Encyclopedia* 1993: tit. Property, paras. 309–11). English common law has no concept of inalienability of Crown land and other capital assets, so that disposals fall within Ministers' inherent or 'prerogative' powers unless there is restrictive legislation. Thus the Crown Lands Act 1702 was needed to check improvident dissipation of the Crown Estate by William III. Present legislation, while recognizing that ministers may take certain property on terms envisaging its upkeep in perpetuity (Historic

Buildings and Ancient Monuments Act 1953, ss. 8, 8A), never itself restricts disposal by the Crown. Property in the hands of the Crown Estate is subject to broad and flexible powers of management (Crown Estate Act 1961).

6
The Financial Resources of Government: Monitoring and Control

I IN GENERAL: CRITERIA, CONSTRAINTS, CONCEPTS

1 Introduction

The Public Expenditure Survey and the parliamentary supply process are two elements of the disciplines against which the spending behaviour of departments and other public bodies is judged. The third is provided by the permanent legislation which defines departmental programmes, functions, and powers. Though all three elements are centrally orchestrated (we deal with control of the legislative process in Chapter 8 below), there is ample scope for disharmony in their operation. We have already reviewed the considerable efforts made over the last decades to integrate the Survey with the supply cycle, and shall see in this section how that integration is expressed in the monitoring and control regime for public expenditure. Less effort has been devoted to considering their relationship with permanent legislation. Yet that relationship has always been a potentially awkward one, as departments brandish their statutory functions as a defensive weapon against Treasury control; and it is likely to get more awkward if courts follow the precedent of the *Pergau Dam* case (*R v Secretary of State for Foreign Affairs, ex parte World Development Movement Ltd* 1995) and embroil themselves in issues of the legality of central government spending. In this section we shall try to explain how the spending patterns set by the Survey and the supply cycle are monitored and controlled by the Treasury, through authorizations and delegations on the one hand (part II) and through PES-derived mechanisms of cash control on the other (part III). We go on to consider the way in which internal Treasury controls relate to those exercisable by Parliament (and on its behalf by the NAO), and by the courts (part IV). First, however, we look at the conceptual apparatus of control: the *status* of the rules on which control is based; and the *key concepts* around which it is articulated.

2 Legislative, parliamentary, and internal rules

The criteria for spending and the constraints upon it, and the monitoring and enforcement competences associated with those criteria and constraints, do not all have the same legal status. Some are undoubtedly *legislative* in origin. Permanent rules governing spending, laid down in the legislation creating a department, or enacting a spending policy, plainly fall into this category. So too do the annual parliamentary Votes of supply, as enacted in the Appropriation Act; the rules regarding the use of the Consolidated Fund (Exchequer and Audit Departments Act 1866, as amended by the National Loans Act 1968); the determination of the size of the Contingencies Fund (Contingencies Fund Act 1974), though not the rules for its use; and the myriad statutory provisions requiring the consent of the Treasury to financial decisions taken by a department. Since 1983, when his long-standing concern with efficiency audit was recognized by the National Audit Act, the competences of the Comptroller and Auditor-General have been wholly statutory.

Other criteria and competences are not so easy for the lawyer to characterize. Some, which may conveniently be called *parliamentary* rather than legislative, originate in the centuries-long financial conversation between the executive and Parliament, as now conducted between Treasury and Public Accounts Committee, with the Comptroller and Auditor-General in attendance, and the Commons Treasury and Procedure Committees occasionally putting a word in. They function to support the effectiveness of the parliamentary supply mechanism. Included here are the customs and expectations about who in government presents financial proposals to Parliament, requirements about consultation on the form of estimates, and perhaps most important, the understandings about the use of the Appropriation Act as the legal authority for public expenditure in the absence, or as a means of extension, of relevant permanent spending legislation. This group of rules and practices can hardly be reduced to legislative form, since they are pre- or supra-legislative, addressed to the way Parliament (albeit on the initiative of the executive) should exercise its own legislative power. This puts them close to the core of our constitutional order yet, paradoxically, it means that unless they are the subject of judicial scrutiny, they are likely to be of low visibility and uncertain status. Traditionally, these expectations have been considered under the rubric of the 'propriety' of government spending, and we examine Appropriation Act understandings under that heading (below, pp. 173–5).

Other non-legislative rules may properly be regarded as being, in their nature, *internal* to the executive, notwithstanding the fact that some of them are among the most important in the field, and underpin external controls. The whole apparatus of prior Treasury approval is of this nature. Since 1866, and even more clearly since 1921, the exercise of that competence may have legal consequences, in that unauthorized expenditure 'shall be regarded as not being properly chargeable to a Parliamentary grant' (Exchequer and Audit Departments Act 1921, s. 1(3)), but as already argued (above, pp. 118–20), this legislation does not create the power, but attaches new consequences to one already existing. Prior approval is at the base of the whole structure of rules and powers whereby each department's discretion in expenditure matters is determined. We would argue that just as it underpinned the apparatus of establishments control, now largely dismantled, it also supports the monitoring and enforcement of the PES system. When that was invented, and when it was redesigned in 1976 to incorporate the completely new discipline of cash limits, and in 1998 so as to displace, at least in part, annual review of expenditure, no legislation or Order in Council was needed to enable the Treasury to enforce it. The various control devices adopted—cash limits, end-year flexibility, running costs control, public service agreements—have all been fitted smoothly into an existing control pattern, in which the general principle of prior approval is buttressed by the powers enjoyed by the Treasury in the annual PES process and as gatekeeper of access to Parliament (above, pp. 120–2).

These internal controls are visible—so far as they are visible at all—very largely through the Treasury's own documentation: *Government Accounting* (Treasury 1989*a*), the *Fees and Charges Guide* (Treasury 1992*e*), the PES *Guidelines* (e.g. Treasury 1996*d*), the *Guide to Expenditure Work* (Treasury 1997*b*), and other such documents. While in formal terms the Treasury's 'own' rules, they may derive support and legitimacy from other sources: Parliament, especially the Public Accounts Committee, in the case of *Government Accounting*; the Cabinet in the case of specific disciplines adopted from time to time within PES. Only rather rarely do we come across documents which suggest that support from elsewhere within the executive was needed to articulate an effective control structure. The provisions of the *Ministerial Code* (Cabinet Office 1997*d*) and of the *Guide to Legislative Procedures* (Office of Public Service 1996*b*) ensuring early Treasury notice of expenditure implications of policy proposals perhaps attest to specific past difficulties in this area (Lee 1986).

3 Regularity, propriety, and value for money

3.1 Regularity

This threefold scheme of control—legislative, parliamentary, and internal—reflects a lawyers' approach to public expenditure which is not readily visible in the discourse of practitioners in the field. Despite the importance of legislative provisions, 'legality' is not a core concept in the practice of public expenditure control. In this field, the terminology derives not from consideration of the legal status of expenditure, but from the operation of parliamentary audit. It is the language of the auditor's certificate, not of the judge's opinion. So far as appropriation accounts are concerned, the certificate is concerned first and foremost with the substantive accuracy and proper presentation of the account, but the Comptroller and Auditor-General will not give his certificate unless he is satisfied also

> that the money expended has been applied to the purpose or purposes for which the grants made by Parliament were intended to provide and that the expenditure conforms to the authority which governs it. (Exchequer and Audit Departments Act 1921, s. 1(1))

In auditor's language, this is to express satisfaction as to the 'regularity' of the expenditure. 'Regularity' is defined by the Treasury as

> the requirement for all items of expenditure and receipts to be dealt with in accordance with the legislation authorising them, any applicable delegated authority and the rules of Government Accounting. (Treasury 1989*a*: para. 6.2.14; Treasury 1997*c*: 4; cf. Auditing Practices Board 1997: 5).

The professional advice on regularity, largely drafted by NAO, gives guidance on the content of regularity by examining the authorities which govern the actions and expenditure of government entities: authorizing legislation (including European legislation); regulations under governing legislation (including delegated legislation and Ministerial directions provided for by statute); parliamentary authority (supply procedure and the Appropriation Act); and Treasury authority. 'A material breach of any of these authorities would lead auditors to qualify their opinion on the regularity of transactions' (Auditing Practices Board 1997: 18). Clearly, such material breaches, of relevant legislation or delegated legislation, could also lead to judicial findings of illegality, which auditors will respect. Thus when the High Court decided in the *Pergau Dam* case (*R v Secretary of State for Foreign Affairs ex parte World Development Movement Ltd* 1995) that government financial assistance to the Pergau Dam project in Malaysia was outside the scope of the Overseas Development and Co-operation Act 1980, and therefore unlawful, the Comptroller and Auditor-General, who had passed the relevant account in 1992–93 without comment, promptly qualified the expenditure as 'irregular' in his report on the 1993–94 account (Comptroller and Auditor-General 1995: para. 13, and see further below, pp. 204–5). To say that expenditure is 'regular' is not quite the same thing as to say that it is 'lawful'. 'Regularity' may be a concept of broader scope. As we have seen, the general requirement of prior Treasury authority (as opposed to specific legislative requirements for Treasury consent), is nowhere clearly established as a legal rule, but is still referred to as 'long established custom and practice' (Auditing Practices Board 1997: 26). Conversely, illegal conduct may not always entail irregular expenditure. Departments are subject to general regulations, on matters like occupational health and safety and equal opportunities. They may breach such regulations, but this is unlikely to have a material impact on the regularity of expenditure which supports the offending activities, because those regulations do not provide authority for financial transactions of the department.

3.2 Propriety

There is also a close match between the parliamentary element of control, and the auditors' concept of 'propriety' of expenditure, which is likewise a concern of certification audit, but is less readily susceptible to objective verification and is not referred to in the central government auditor's opinion on financial statements. Propriety is

> the further requirement that expenditure and receipts should be dealt with in accordance with Parliament's intentions and the principles of Parliamentary control, including the conventions agreed with Parliament (and in particular the Public Accounts Committee). (Treasury 1989*a*: para. 6.2.14)

Until recently this definition referred principally to specific principles such as those governing the use of the Appropriation Act as the sole or overriding authority for expenditure. This has been an area of particular delicacy for the Treasury, in that in presenting the estimates and the Consolidated Fund (Appropriation) Bill it invites Parliament to exercise its legislative function in a particular way (and without the benefit of ordinary legislative debate, so that executive choices are likely to determine the issue completely).[1] Since the beginning of the modern system in the eighteen-sixties, the Comptroller and Auditor-General and the Public Accounts Committee have regularly complained to the Treasury both about the use of the Appropriation Act, year after year, to support particular continuing expenditures for which there was no permanent statutory authority, and about its use to support spending which was beyond limits set in relevant permanent legislation, or for purposes which such legislation did not cover or, indeed, appeared to exclude (e.g. Epitome I: 50, 79, 170, 206, 497, 711–12, 723–6). One repeated

[1] For internal executive rules as to the proper content of legislative proposals more generally, see below, pp. 248–50.

complaint of this kind, about the payment to certain special magistrates in Ireland of salaries exceeding such statutory limits, led to increasingly heated correspondence between the Treasury and the department over several years until the Irish Law Officers, belatedly invited to advise, suggested that the relevant officials did not need to be sworn in as magistrates anyway and could thus be paid on different scales (Epitome I: 148–9, 167–8, 219–21).

The issue of expenditure undertaken in the absence of permanent legislation came to a head again in 1930–31 after the Ministry of Labour introduced emergency schemes of relief of unemployment without prior legislative sanction. Eventually the Treasury and the Public Accounts Committee agreed in 1932, in a document known as the 'PAC Concordat' that as a matter of general principle

> where it is desired that continuing functions should be exercised by a Government Department, particularly where such functions may involve financial liabilities extending beyond a given financial year, it is proper that the powers and duties to be exercised should be defined by specific statute. (Treasury 1989*a*: Annex 2.1)

In 1984 the Treasury adopted a '*de minimis*' principle in relation to this understanding, advising departments that a threshold of £0.5m per annum might appropriately be applied as a guide to whether a new and continuing service was significant enough to require specific statutory provision, and in 1997 announced its intention to raise this threshold to £2m per annum (Public Accounts Committee 1998: Memorandum by HM Treasury, Treasury Controls, Annex, paras. 48–52).

On the related issue of inconsistency between the Appropriation Act and the permanent statute, the Treasury and the Committee have generally shared the view that while 'it is undoubtedly within the discretion of Parliament to override the provisions of an existing Statute by a Vote on Supply confirmed by an Appropriation Act' (Epitome I: 497 (1908)), such 'extensions' of powers specifically limited by statute should, in the interests of 'constitutional propriety', 'be regularized at the earliest possible date by amending legislation, unless they are of a purely emergency or non-continuing character' (Epitome I: 725 (Treasury Minute, 1932, reprinted in Treasury 1989*a*: annex 2.1)). 'Parliament should be made aware of the position by a clear statement of the facts on the face of the Estimate' (Epitome I: 725), so that there is no doubt as to its deliberate intention to override the existing limitation (Treasury 1989*a*: Para. 2.2.10). We shall argue later that there now appears to be some uncertainty in government as to the capacity of the Appropriation Act to produce these effects (below, pp. 203–6).

This highly technical understanding of propriety has come to seem strange in a period when failings in propriety in the conduct of public business have been highlighted both by the first report of the Nolan Committee, *Standards in Public Life* (Committee on Standards in Public Life 1995), and by an admonitory report by the Public Accounts Committee, *The Proper Conduct of Public Business* (Public Accounts Committee 1994*a*), insisting that 'fundamental changes in the way in which government departments and public bodies . . . carry out their work' must not have the effect of impairing 'a proper concern for the sensible conduct of public business and care for the honest handling of public money.' 'Propriety' in government business is thus now understood by the Auditing Practices Board[2] as including 'matters such as the avoidance of personal profit from public business, even-handedness in the appointment of staff, open competition in the letting of contracts and the avoidance of waste and extravagance' (Auditing Practices Board 1997: 5). Reflecting these sentiments, the Treasury, in its Handbook on *Regularity and Propriety* prepared for government departments and related bodies, now understands 'Parliament's intentions' in the *Government Accounting* definition as encompassing much broader expectations than formerly: expectations as to the way in which public business should be conducted, and the way in which public servants should behave when managing public funds (Treasury 1997*c*: 9).

3.3 Value for money (VFM)

The third key concept is 'value for money' (Harden, White, and Hollingsworth 1996). 'Value for money examination' is the second main branch of public audit, now carried out by the Comptroller and Auditor-General in pursuance of his statutory power to examine 'the economy, efficiency and effectiveness with which any department, authority or other body . . . has used its resources in carrying out its functions' (National Audit Act 1983, s. 6(1)).

This is an external control, today carried out as a distinct procedure on behalf of Parliament rather than, as was the case up to 1983, as an integrated part of an appropriation audit serving both Parliament and Treasury. Clearly, it addresses issues of profound concern to the Treasury. 'Prudent and economical administration', 'the avoidance of waste and extravagance', and 'the efficient and economical use of all the resources in his charge' are all described, in the Accounting Officer Memorandum (Treasury 1989*a*: para. 6.1.5, section 6), as part of the

[2] The Board is a professional, not a public body. It is a committee of the Consultative Committee of Accountancy Bodies, established in 1991 with the task of 'leading the development of auditing practice in the United Kingdom and the Republic of Ireland' (Auditing Practices Board [nd]).

'essence' of the Accounting Officer's role, along with propriety and regularity of departmental finances, and the Accounting Officer has only recently been strengthened in that role by the amendment to the Memorandum, following the *Pergau Dam* investigations (Public Accounts Committee 1994*b*; White, Harden, and Donnelly 1994). Now he must report to the Comptroller and Auditor-General any case where he has sought and obtained a written instruction from his minister by reason of concerns about questions of the economy, efficiency, or effectiveness of departmental action, no less than of those about regularity and propriety (above, pp. 125–6). None the less, while VFM examinations by the NAO are clearly of importance in indicating possible departures from these standards, their occasional nature, and the fact that the Treasury has no formal role in the determination of subjects for examination mean that the Treasury can hardly rely on them—as it can still rely on certification audit in relation to regularity and propriety—to discharge the main weight of its own concerns about value for money. Distinct structures for assuring value for money now exist in the external and internal control systems: we look at the Treasury's principal instruments in part III below.

3.4 Conclusion

The principles of regularity, propriety, and value for money represent both the standards by which Parliament will judge the conduct of public expenditure, and a set of internal standards towards which Treasury control must always aim. But it is important to understand that they do not themselves function as controls, and that the Treasury has an additional, and quite distinct, control aim, which is that of keeping public expenditure, both generally and Vote by Vote, within the limits laid down by PES and the supply cycle. Regularity, propriety, and value for money thus function as criteria for *ex post* judgements on Departmental and Treasury performance by the Comptroller and Auditor-General and the Public Accounts Committee, judgements which may often reflect the success with which internal Treasury controls (such as monitoring delegations of expenditure authority) have functioned. As standards they can, of course, in principle also be applied *ex ante* within the executive, and it is, within the bounds of practicability, the function of departmental Principal Finance Officers and Accounting Officers, and of spending teams and the Treasury Officer of Accounts within the Treasury, to see that this happens. So far as the Treasury is concerned, all these standards should inform the running dialogue between departments and their spending teams; in addition, regularity and propriety may be seen as a special concern of the TOA, to be protected through his casework and advice (below, p. 196): advice which may not always be welcome. As Thain and Wright put it, '[t]his official "holds the rule book for the Expenditure Divisions" and frequently a sympathetic and supportive Expenditure Division is obliged to say "no" to a [departmental] Finance Division because of his ruling' (1995: 219).

II TREASURY AUTHORIZATIONS AND DELEGATIONS

1 Introduction

According to *Government Accounting*, 'No expenditure can properly be incurred without the approval of the Treasury' (Treasury 1989*a*: para. 2.4.1). Since it has never been feasible for the Treasury to give approval to each separate item of expenditure across government, its constant preoccupation has been to define sensitive expenditures on which to concentrate its efforts. Over most of the period since the passing of the Exchequer and Audit Departments Act 1866, the general tests have been those laid down in its Minute of 1868 (above, pp. 119–20), stipulating prior approval for expenditure

exceeding sub-heads within the Vote;

for an increase of establishment, of salary, or of cost of a service; or

for additional works or new services.

The first of these is the source of the Treasury's power over virement, whereby funds may be moved from one sub-head to another to reflect changes in needs and circumstances over the year. The second sustained the Treasury's detailed apparatus of control over the size and conditions of service of the Civil Service, now dismantled, and provided, through its reference to cost of service, a platform for Treasury concerns with the general efficiency of departmental services. The third reflected the Treasury's particular sensitivity to new demands for expenditure, whether within or outside the ambit of existing Votes. It knows, from daily experience, the falsehood—when applied to public spending—of the maxim 'What goes up must come down,' and has traditionally tried to stop things going up.

2 From approvals to delegations

These tests have formed the basis of an elaborate system of rules and precedents about Treasury approval, much of it developed, since 1866, as a kind of financial 'common law' (to borrow George Arbuthnot's metaphor, above, p. 117) issuing from the permanent dialogue between the Public Accounts Committee and 'My Lords' at the Treasury. The indexes to the Epitomes of the Public Accounts Committee's Reports (Epitome I 1938; Epitome II 1970) enable us to trace the elaboration, through a process of accumulation and distinguishing of specific instances, of criteria and concepts of control: of the notion, for example, of what might constitute a 'new work' or a 'new service', or of the circumstances in which losses might properly be written off. The intervention of the Committee both provides the Treasury's requirements with a supplementary source of legitimacy, and calls for firmer and more precise formulation of rules than the Treasury, left to itself, might have been inclined to provide (see Wright 1969: 332–5).

Beside the 'case law' of the Public Accounts Committee, specific prior approval requirements, related to particular departmental powers or policies, have been multiplied through legislative provision and are now to be found scattered all over the statute book. Despite the tendency to relax detailed Treasury controls, legislation passed in 1996 introduced 42 new requirements of this kind, in relation to matters ranging from the Humber Bridge to schools inspection. The Treasury's ability to secure their insertion is protected by the consultation requirements enjoined on departments by the Cabinet's procedures for scrutiny of legislative proposals (see Office of Public Service 1996*b*, and below, pp. 246–8). The requirements relate not only to expenditure, but also to the income taken into the estimates in the form of Appropriations in Aid. When, for example, petroleum deposits in the United Kingdom were nationalized in 1934, and provision was made for the President of the Board of Trade, as responsible minister, to issue production licences to oil companies, the form and level of payment (in the event, a royalty payment on the petroleum produced) had to be approved by the Treasury (Petroleum (Production) Act 1934, s. 2(2)). When this regime was extended offshore, after the first North Sea gas discoveries, by the Continental Shelf Act 1964, we find the department (then the Ministry of Power) needing to convince the Treasury that its proposed royalty levels were appropriate and that, in the particular circumstances of the North Sea, it should not follow the American practice of obtaining additional revenue by auctioning the right to obtain a licence through payment of a cash premium (Ministry of Power 1964). Treasury consent was thus vital to the adoption of a fundamental element of North Sea oil policy which has since given rise to considerable controversy (Public Accounts Committee 1973; Dam 1976).

The system of approvals, as shown in action through the Epitomes, has, however, undergone radical revision in recent years, when the Treasury's concern has been to reduce detailed control and increase departmental responsibilities, while at the same time asserting firmer supervision over expenditure aggregates and departmental finance and management systems. We have seen how this approach has been manifested in the new shape of estimates and the development of departmental reports (above, pp. 154–64). Not much can be done, in this process, about the specific legislative requirements for Treasury authority (which anyway, numerous as they may be, seldom touch on merely trivial or routine matters). In regard to the general principles of prior approval, however, the picture is now one of extensive *delegations* of spending authority: not across the board to all departments and agencies, but individually settled in the light of the activities undertaken and a range of other factors (Treasury 1989*a*: paras. 2.4.5–2.4.10; Thain and Wright 1995: 336–8). Such delegations are likely to allow the department or agency to spend up to certain levels on defined items in particular PES programmes or estimate subheads without prior approval. They will be conditioned by requirements about the methodology of decision-taking by the department, such as techniques for investment appraisal and project evaluation, as now presented in Departmental Investment Strategies (Treasury 1998*c*: paras. 11–15); by arrangements for the Treasury to run checks on the quality of decisions; and by expectations about the adoption of financial management systems which will secure effective intra-departmental delegation of authority—a major concern of the Financial Management Initiative (above, pp. 123–6).

Other controls and associated delegations refer to spending-related matters such as the making of gifts, the writing-off of losses and the making of *ex gratia* payments, and the assumption of contingent liabilities. Here too the Treasury continues to aim for the relaxation of its own control and (with the consent of the Public Accounts Committee) of reporting requirements to Parliament (Public Accounts Committee 1998: Memorandum by HM Treasury, Treasury Controls). Perhaps in response to parliamentary concerns expressed elsewhere about the loss of Treasury control (above, pp. 163–4), we find the Treasury accompanying these proposed relaxations with the argument that accountability to Parliament will thereby be improved, since there will be less scope for departments to cloud their own responsibility by suggesting that the need for Treasury consent affected their decision (ibid., para. 17). Questioning by the Committee suggested scepticism on this score and continuing worry about consequential loss of control by Parliament (ibid., Evidence). A supplementary argument, not made on this occasion by the Treasury, might have referred to the considerable injustice which has stemmed in the past from the rigorous application of low Treasury limits on *ex gratia* payments, which have led both to departmental reluctance to identify people who might benefit retrospectively from legal changes in benefits eligibility rules (investigated in Civil Service Department 1979) and to fierce criticism from the Parliamentary Commissioner for Administration (below, pp. 361–5, where earlier relaxations are discussed, and see now Treasury 1989*a*: paras. 36.3.1–39).

The scope of delegation is also affected by the structure of departments, and in particular, the degree to which their activities are carried on through executive agencies or consist in the administration of grants to other public bodies, such as NDPBs and local authorities, or the supervision of contracted-out services. Where agencies are concerned, the acceptance of the case for agency status, the determination as to whether it is to be constituted as a trading fund or Vote-holding agency, and the drawing up of its framework document (above, pp. 37–46, 132–7) will offer the main opportunity for Treasury assessment of the performance indicators that are appropriate and the amount of delegation to allow. To the extent that departments function as grantors or contractors, the Treasury will expect the grant regime—as expressed, for example, through the financial memorandum of an NDPB—or the contract itself to reflect and secure the financial discipline appropriate to what is, in effect, institutionalized delegation.

3 Virement

Despite the radical changes in the style of Treasury control which have occurred since, the categories of control identified in the 1868 Minute remain distinct. They have evolved in line with these changes, without losing their identity. Virement remains an arena for Treasury control, but one vastly reduced in importance by reason of the steady enlargement of Votes, and of the sub-heads within them, culminating in the major simplification of estimates effected in 1996 (above, pp. 162–4). Since then, Treasury consent has been required only for virement between lines in the estimates (for example, in the Lord Chancellor's Department, between the legal aid budget and the court buildings budget) (Treasury 1996*c*: 16). Within lines, such consent is at present only required for virement into running costs provision from other heads. This control supports the new, PES-derived discipline over establishments, and is operated according to principles set out in *Government Accounting* (Treasury 1989*a*: para. 11.7.8, revised in 1997; below, pp. 188–90). Otherwise, departments can switch funds around as they wish between the sub-heads in the same line: from capital to current expenditure, for example, though this freedom will doubtless be curtailed as a result of the clear division drawn since 1998 between current and capital spending (above, pp. 150–1). Virement is not permissible, however, as a means of transferring excess receipts from appropriations-in-aid to spending heads (ibid.: para. 11.7.4). Whether it is the Treasury or the department that is to exercise the power of virement, it must not, of course, result in expenditures or appropriations-in-aid which are in excess of the *totals* under the Vote.

Since the practice of virement makes for economy in the estimates, the Treasury does not view virement requests negatively. But it will not approve virement in cases where the proposed reallocation is thought to be of such importance or so great a departure from the original estimate that it should be brought specifically before Parliament by means of a token supplementary estimate (a 'token' estimate is one which involves no request for additional net public spending). Detailed tests are laid down in *Government Accounting*: the Treasury will not agree to virement where the additional expenditure would be on a new service of which Parliament should be made aware; would be novel or contentious; would arise from a major change in policy; would be large in relation to the original provision in the subhead; would be likely to lead to heavy liabilities in later years; or does not meet the specific rules regarding virement into running costs (Treasury 1989*a*: section 11.7). The 1996 changes do not exempt departments from these tests; they make departments themselves, rather than the Treasury, the judge of whether they are satisfied. The switch to resource accounting and budgeting (above, pp. 164–8) is likely to raise difficult questions as to how an effective discipline over virement can be maintained by the Treasury and the Comptroller and Auditor-General.

Within the Treasury it is the spending teams that operate these rules. Once the pattern of the year's spending is clear, however, the Treasury's virement decisions need to be formally confirmed, with precise figures, by letter to the Comptroller and Auditor-General. This is prepared by the Treasury Officer of Accounts, who can therefore exercise some oversight of whether the formal virement rules have been respected by his colleagues.

4 Establishments

Since 1995 the Treasury no longer has responsibilities relating to civil service establishments, pay, grading, and the like. The circumstances of their delegation and transfer are detailed in Chapter 3 (above, pp. 65–6). The Treasury, as guardian of public expenditure, could countenance this striking loss of a traditional control because it had by 1991 installed and tested a new 'strategic' control instrument with similar purposes: running costs control (below, pp. 188–90). Keeping clear of detailed intervention in the area is not necessarily easy. Public Accounts Committee pressure after learning of excessive 'jollifications' under a Ministry of Defence staff incentive scheme (Treasury 1997*c*: 11–12) led the Treasury to impose a prior approval requirement in relation to certain categories of staff benefits, which it rather quickly sought to withdraw in favour of Office of Public Service guidance on staff benefits and a spread of responsibilities (OPS, Ministry of Defence, etc.) for approving benefits in kind (Public Accounts Committee 1998: Memorandum by HM Treasury, Treasury Controls, Annex, paras. 36–8). It is clear, though, that the effective demise of establishments control shows the capacity of the PES system for development, refinement, and the shouldering of control burdens previously supported by other powers.

5 New works and services

Much greater continuity appears in the evolution of powers relating to new works and services. The pattern is one of steady relaxation of approval requirements and enlargement of delegations. Consideration of issues of detail is steadily driven downwards: from Parliament to the Treasury, as when specific new projects, even major ones, disappear from the estimates in 1969–70, which henceforward recorded only new 'programmes' (Epitome II: 558–9); and from the Treasury to departments, as delegation ceilings move into eight figures (Thain and Wright 1995: 336–8). None the less, the Treasury still maintains a set of overriding criteria which demand submission of expenditure for approval even though delegations and the conditions attached to them will not be breached and where no specific requirements for consent obtain. Having conducted a general review of its controls, the Treasury still regards these criteria as essential for the achievement of its objectives (Public Accounts Committee 1998: Memorandum by HM Treasury, Treasury Controls, para. 14). They demand prior approval for any proposal which

could put pressure on current estimates provision, cash limits or running costs limits, or on future expenditure plans;

could 'set a potentially expensive precedent';

could 'cause repercussions for others';

exceeds current general capital expenditure ceilings; or

is 'novel or contentious.' (Treasury 1989*a*: 2.4.10)

These criteria are unlikely to satisfy the standards of the parliamentary draftsman; indeed, they are so indeterminate in scope as to present serious risks for any department which hazards a unilateral interpretation in preference to a frank exploration with its spending team of whether approval might be necessary. All the headings save the fourth seem open to the broadest discretion in interpretation, and though there may be safe areas for departmental decision (to do in Nottinghamshire in 1998 what the department did in Derbyshire in 1996 can hardly be 'novel') one sympathizes with the Principal Finance Officer who must reconcile these warnings with the requirement of large-scale and effective devolution of budgetary decisions urged on him under the Financial Management Initiative.

Whether the criteria, or the delegations in general, are capable of effective monitoring and enforcement, at least at Treasury level, is another matter entirely, and one which we explore in part IV.

III CASH CONTROL

1 Cash limits and supplementary estimates

When cash limits were introduced in 1976 they were considered an important reinforcement of the government's controls over public expenditure (Public Accounts Committee 1977), though one which might have significant impacts on parliamentary control and sovereignty. Since the parliamentary supply system has itself operated on a strict cash basis since the Appropriation Act of 1862, and is only now being converted to the resource basis (above, pp. 164–8), this seems a little puzzling: what exactly was being done?

What happened in 1976 was that the Treasury convinced the government that the combination of a volume-based PES and a cash-based parliamentary supply system was, in a time of rapid inflation, not just useless, but worse than useless, as a mechanism for expenditure control. The volume basis of planning built inflationary growth automatically into departmental expectations; and with double-digit inflation, the cash figures of the estimates, settled some months before the beginning of year 0, were bound to be seriously out of date before the end of it. Supplementary estimates were thus a routine necessity, occasioning neither departmental embarrassment nor parliamentary interest.

Cash limits, therefore, were introduced as a device for executive self-control, each such limit representing an undertaking *not* to seek a supplementary estimate at any time of year on a particular Vote. 'Where voted expenditure is subject to a cash limit the government is stating that it intends to avoid, if possible, seeking any non-token supplementary provision even if there are unexpected fluctuations in costs or other influences on expenditure' (Treasury 1996*c*: 9). Not all expenditure could properly be subject to such a commitment, even of a purely administrative nature. In particular, spending reflecting the exercise by individuals of their statutory rights—as to unemployment benefit—and spending disbursed, even in the absence of such individual rights, to meet individual needs by reference to prescribed standards, was not so limited (Treasury 1976: para. 8 and Appendix 1).

When cash limits were first introduced, they may well have decreased, rather than improved, the transparency of the financial system, in that Parliament had three sets of figures to deal with: the volume-based planning totals; the estimates on a current cash basis; and the cash limits which would incorporate predictions about the rate of inflation and its effect on spending under the relevant Vote in year 0. Moreover the blocks of cash-limited expenditure did not at first map accurately on to the Votes (Public Accounts Committee 1977: paras. 3–4). But with the switch of PES itself to a cash basis, the fitting of cash blocks to Votes, and the alignment of estimates and PES figures (aided by much lower inflation), the same cash figures could represent both the cash limit and the relevant estimate total. The continuing process of merging smaller Votes (above, p. 161) has created a problem in that it might become appropriate for a single Vote to encompass both expenditure suitable for cash-limiting and expenditure which was not suitable. Accordingly, since the simplification of estimates in 1996–97, mixed Votes have been introduced, in which some lines may be cash-limited and others not (such as legal aid payments within the Lord Chancellor's Vote—but legal aid *administration* is cash-limited). The limit applies to the total expenditure on the cash-limited lines within the Vote, which are clearly marked in the new estimates format.

A cash limit is an internal control, so no parliamentary authority is required for the changing of a cash limit; Parliament will ordinarily be informed by way of a written answer to a parliamentary Question. Since a cash limit will ordinarily be the same as a Vote, or the total of the relevant lines in a Vote, its increase also implies the presentation of a supplementary estimate in the ordinary way, but it can happen that a cash limit is subsequently *reduced* to a figure less than the original Vote provision. Under the logic of supply procedure there is no possibility for a Vote to be reduced, so special arrangements are made to record the disparity, and the relationship of expenditure out-turn to the two different figures.

The practice and effects of the system have been analysed by Thain and Wright (1995: ch. 17). They note that exceeding a cash limit is regarded as a serious matter, always receiving the attention of the departmental minister and of the Chief Secretary, and sometimes of the Prime Minister, and that it rarely happens. Since departments can hardly hit such targets exactly, small but consistent underspendings occur: a highly satisfactory result for the Treasury. But this high degree of compliance cannot simply be attributed to the sanctions available for breach (which we examine below, pp. 190–2). Two other factors are more important. First, there are efficient cash monitoring arrangements under the Treasury's General Expenditure Monitoring System (GEMS), which provides for monthly and quarterly returns in standard Treasury formats, enabling both the department's Finance Division and the Treasury spending team to make regular comparisons between an expected spending pattern over the year and what is actually happening (Treasury 1997*b*: 39–41). Second, the Treasury, contrary to a rhetoric emphasizing the rigidity of the limits, has in fact been willing to make changes on a regular basis. According to Thain and Wright, '[b]etween a third and a half of the 120 cash limits set for central government blocks are changed each year, slightly more being raised than lowered' (1995: 361). Along with substantial policy changes, unexpected financial costs and consequences of existing policies (pay awards, incorrectly projected levels of uptake of service, and so on) appear also to be significant factors. Only limited information is published about changes in limits, in an annual Public Expenditure Out-turn White Paper (though this is sufficient to show that complex trade-offs may be involved between different cash blocks), and unsuccessful departmental requests for changes are not publicized. This policy of setting tight limits and being prepared to vary them has furnished the Treasury with an effective instrument for influencing departmental policy choices at spending margins.

This general instrument has also been a productive source of more specific controls. For example, the year-by-year discipline on spending imposed by cash limits before 1998 created real difficulties for departments (like the Ministry of Defence) with important capital programmes. The need to avoid any mistiming of payments under such programmes in order to ensure respect for cash limits could greatly complicate contingency planning. After a period of argument in Whitehall the Treasury introduced a number of end-year flexibility arrangements, under which limited carry-forward of certain kinds of spending is permitted (Thain and Wright 1995: ch. 19; Treasury 1988). Save in relation to running costs, for which there are special arrangements (see below), the limits have been removed as a consequence of the 1998 PES reforms, setting three-year rather than annual limits for the more controllable parts of departmental expenditure. Almost all such expenditure is cash-limited. To provide incentives to improve efficiency, unlimited carry-forward of such expenditure is now allowed; but not (save in one or two special cases) any anticipation of next year's budgeted expenditure (Treasury 1998*c*: paras. 39–48). Sums carried forward (which are quantifiable only after the end of year 0) are viewed as savings on the year 0 total of Departmental Expenditure Limits, and as priority charges against the year +1 Reserve (see sect. 3.2, below).

Take-up of carryovers in a subsequent year is subject to ordinary Treasury scrutiny of supply and will require a supplementary estimate (since year 0 estimates will have been approved before eligible carry-overs are quantified).

2 The Reserve and the Contingencies Fund

As we have noted, cash limits can go down as well as up, and the power exercised by the Treasury in making these decisions is thus not simply the old power—of keeping the gateway to the pleasures of supplementary estimates—in a new guise. We can explore this further by considering how the Treasury deals with the consequences of varying cash limits. How can a cash limit be varied during the year (or, now, the triennium) without throwing the PES settlement into disarray? How can a department carry on its business if it runs out of cash on a Vote line *before* the vote of a supplementary estimate, or of the Consolidated Fund Bill giving that estimate legislative effect?

The first of these questions concerns the operation of the PES system, and its answer lies in the use of the Reserve (once called the Contingency Reserve) provided for under that system (Thain and Wright 1995: ch. 16).[3] According to Thain and Wright, '[t]he Reserve is a sum of unallocated money provided for each financial year of the Survey to enable the Treasury to finance increases in public expenditure without revising the Planning/Control Total' (1995: 341). To call the Reserve 'money' may, however, mislead. What is involved here is a decision as to how much *planned* expenditure under the PES should be left at large, rather than allocated to departments. This is an important question with significant expenditure and policy consequences. From 1984 to 1998 the Reserve was kept large enough to cope both with the expenditure effects of new policies, and with changes in estimated costs of existing policies. Under the 1998 PES reforms, the Reserve has been split into two: a Reserve within the Departmental Expenditure Limits (DEL) aggregate, and a 'margin' within Annually Managed Expenditure (AME) (Treasury 1998*c*: paras. 24–32). The DEL Reserve has been kept deliberately small on the assumption that—as was the policy before 1984—no Reserve claims based on changes in estimates of the cost of policies will be allowed save, says the Treasury, in the sort of extraordinary circumstances represented by the bovine spongiform encephalopathy (BSE) emergency

[3] The Reserve is not to be confused with the Contingencies Fund, which permits expenditure not yet voted by Parliament to be incurred on a temporary and urgent basis: see Contingencies Fund Act 1974; Treasury 1989*a*: s. 11.6; below pp. 187–8.

in 1996 (ibid., para. 31).[4] Discretionary claims, resulting from new policy decisions, will apparently still be allowed where the relevant policy initiatives have been agreed with the Treasury, as will claims arising from the use of end-year flexibility (above). Decisions are taken by the Chief Secretary to the Treasury on the basis of applications which must ordinarily be signed by the spending Minister, and are considered as part of the process of preparing supplementary estimates (Treasury 1997*b*: 21–3).

Calls on the Reserve or on the AME margin will only occur where a desired increase in expenditure, cash limited or not, cannot be offset by reductions elsewhere in a department's PES allocation. Rules about acceptable offsets for new discretionary expenditure are strict, and broadly correspond to the continuing limitations on virement by departments. Use of the Reserve ordinarily entails the loss of end-year flexibility, since the expenditure which might have been carried forward will have been used up for such offsetting purposes. Even if new expenditure can be wholly offset, so that no claim on the Reserve is needed, the excess expenditure is still likely to give rise to the need for a supplementary estimate before it can lawfully be incurred. This is where the second question arises. Parliament does not refuse such supplementary estimates; but their preparation and presentation takes time. Real money may need to be spent before approval is granted and regular expenditure can take place.

This exigency is met by the use of the Contingencies Fund, established in 1862 and currently resting on the statutory authority of the Contingencies Fund Act 1974, which fixes its capital at 2 per cent of the authorized supply expenditure of the previous financial year (Select Committee on Procedure (Supply) 1981: Evidence, Appendix 10). The Treasury can make advances to a department from the Fund for urgent expenditure in advance of the approval—or indeed the presentation—of the supplementary estimate needed (or if there is no further opportunity to present a supplementary estimate during the year, of the Excess Vote). These are strictly temporary advances, to be repaid from the relevant estimate or Vote once granted, and since they breach the basic general principle of prior appropriation of supply, they are subject to strict Treasury rules (Treasury 1989*a*: para. 11.6); the 1974 Act itself, like its predecessors, lays down no rules. Resort to the fund may be occasioned by the creation of a new service (whether under the authority of specific new legislation or otherwise); by the need for urgent unexpected

[4] The example is an odd one, in that the slaughter and other payments then made amounted to some 0.5 per cent of the 1996–97 Control Total and far exceeded what even the then larger Reserve could handle, producing an overrun of £500m on the Total (Treasury 1997*a*: para. 1.2.20).

expenditure on existing services, in anticipation of unexpectedly delayed payments; or by other urgent requirements. While an unplanned policy or service may necessitate resort both to the Reserve and to the Contingencies Fund, it is important to note that the tests are different. A call on the Reserve may not provoke demands on the Contingencies Fund if there is not sufficient urgency; use of the Fund may be dictated by urgent inter-Vote or even intra-Vote transfers which can be absorbed by the department without a call on the Reserve. The case illustrates the fact that despite their current convergence, and the Treasury's control role in both, the parliamentary supply system and the PES system have different underlying purposes.

3 Running costs control

Like the provision for end-year flexibility described above, running costs control is also a component of the system of cash control invented in 1976 and absorbed by the PES system in 1982. It deserves a section of its own because of its distinguished lineage. So far as the Treasury is concerned, running costs control is the direct successor of the control of establishments which at one time occupied a major part of the Treasury's staff and was at the origin of most of the opprobrium heaped on it by departments and commentators. The development of running costs control can be traced to the same search for efficiency in government as shaped the Financial Management Initiative (above, pp. 123–6). Attempts to measure the effectiveness of expenditure programmes quickly made clear the need to be able to distinguish the costs of administering programmes (running costs) from the inputs and outputs of the programmes themselves. The devolution of financial management responsibilities that became a core element of the Financial Management Initiative appeared then as a prerequisite to the isolation, and hence control, of running costs. Once this process had sufficiently advanced the government could contemplate placing its main reliance for achieving efficiency in the use of manpower on a financial instrument—the measurement and control of running costs—rather than approaching its value-for-money goals from the opposite direction: that is to say, by attempting to bear down directly on the numbers of civil servants and the levels at which they were paid. The first of these policies had in fact been pursued with considerable success as a Prime Ministerial initiative from 1980 to 1988 (Dunsire and Hood 1989), the second attempted with rather uncertain success by publishing the pay norms that were reflected in general cash limits (Thain and Wright 1995: 374–9).

Running costs control was introduced in 1986 and its basic concept is simple (Treasury and Civil Service Committee 1986*a*: pp. xv–xvi). A running cost is identified for each of the lines in a departmental Vote and a cash-limited figure is attached to it. This covers wage and salary costs, personnel overheads (like travel and training); accommodation costs; office services; and costs of related services provided by other public agencies and departments. This means that a department is free to spend on whatever combination of these factors best suits its purposes within the financial envelope agreed with the Treasury; but this freedom is purchased at a price, as we see below. As with any other cash limit, the rhetoric is one of strict application; this is emphasized by the omission of running costs sub-heads from the general enlargement of departmental powers of virement between sub-heads effected in 1996 (above, p. 180). Detailed indications about how the Treasury would exercise its power of virement in relation to running costs sub-heads had, however, already been provided in *Government Accounting* in 1989 (Treasury 1989*a*: para. 11.7.8).

The process of agreeing running costs limits enables the Treasury to bring considerable pressure to bear on departments. From 1986 to 1998 the Treasury operated on the assumption that departments should achieve annual 'efficiency gains' equal to 1.5 per cent of running costs, which might be in the form of cash savings or increased output. Most departments sought these gains within the framework of firm three-year running cost settlements based on management plans agreed with the Treasury (Treasury 1991*a*: 43). The 1998 reforms strengthened this system by requiring *all* departments to enter into a basic three-year running cost 'deal' involving fixed provision for running costs over the period, a set of targets to be derived from that provision over the period, underpinned by management and control systems and appropriate monitoring arrangements, and agreement not to review provisions and targets for three years (Treasury 1998*c*: Annex C). These arrangements effectively incorporate into the running costs regime the Departmental Efficiency Plans introduced at OPS initiative following work by the Efficiency Unit (above, p. 126). They involve detailed discussions between each department, the relevant Treasury spending team, and the Efficiency and Effectiveness Group in the Cabinet Office as to the performance targets to be set, the gains both in efficiency, and in effectiveness of service delivery, to be achieved, the departmental management and control systems to be employed, and the arrangements for monitoring by the Treasury and the department itself. Their results have been expressed in formal Public Service Agreements concluded between the Chief Secretary to the Treasury and the Secretary of State as head of the department (below, pp. 191–2). Performance will be subject to continuous scrutiny overseen by the Public Services and Public Expenditure Committee (above, p. 151). Provision is also made for what is called a 'comprehensive deal' under which departments which can demonstrate the strength of their established management and control systems or of their record in performance measurement may obtain additional advantages such as protection of their running cost end-year flexibility against Reserve claims elsewhere on the Vote, and the scope to negotiate with the Treasury to 'front-load' running costs expenditure in order to achieve greater efficiency gains.

In addition to these general arrangements, a specialized system continues for use where an agency or a department provides services which generate receipts on a scale sufficient to make a significant impact on its total net cost. In this case it may be permitted by the Treasury to operate running costs control on that part of its activities on a net rather than a gross basis; if demands for its services (and hence income from them) go up, it will thus be able to increase staffing resources proportionately without an increase of the running costs figure. The Treasury Solicitor's Department, whose costs are largely covered by fees from other departments, is the sort of department that would benefit from such a regime (below, pp. 217–20). Such flexibility will, however, be granted only if the Treasury is satisfied that the applicant bodies 'have suitably robust monitoring and management systems' (Treasury 1991*a*: 43; Treasury 1990*b*).

IV CONTROL AND SANCTIONS

1 A self-enforcing system?

One of the European Commission's best defences to charges of excessive bureaucracy is to remark that its total workforce is no bigger than that of a single national government department—though this of course means that it must rely on others for virtually all its enforcement work. Similarly, the Treasury has always emphasized the leanness of its staffing. Today it has fewer than 900 staff, covering functions from public debt management to international monetary negotiations, of which the frontline manpower in the spending teams is only a part. It is, by far, the smallest ministerial department (Civil Service Yearbook 1998: pp. cvi–cvii). Plainly there is no capacity here for any day-to-day policing of departmental and agency compliance with the range of controls that we have just been describing. The modern view, however, is that day-to-day policing is not the point. As we have seen in the preceding sections, the broad thrust of development throughout this century has been to move away from detailed control decisions and hence from a situation in which a high level of compliance with such specific decisions was necessary, and had to be guaranteed, if the overall management of the system was to be assured. This has been done both by delegation (sect. III.2 above) and by the increasing dominance of controls based on cash limits, keyed first to the PES system alone, subsequently to both PES and Estimates (sect. III.3 above).

The resulting structure plays effectively on the Treasury's strength in creating and sustaining *systems* for expenditure control, while minimizing the impact of its weakness in curbing *specific* increases in departmental spending (above, pp. 122–3). Where departmental controls and systems are satisfactory, these PES-based controls are relatively easy to police through the Treasury's expenditure management (GEMS) and financial information (FIS) systems (above). It is only where departmental control systems break down, or where there is deliberate deception or fraud, that this control by cash blocks and expenditure plans may lose its bearings. It is in this kind of case, as we shall see, that the Treasury still needs to rely on other agencies to help it achieve its own objectives. Otherwise, PES-based controls have the great merit of providing constraints on departmental spending which, while broad, are not only clear but also very powerful. Within the PES system, delinquencies like the breach of a cash limit can be automatically and painfully penalized by corresponding reductions in the limit for the next period, as well as by the risk of withdrawal of valuable flexibilities if the breach evidences failure of departmental management systems (Treasury 1997*b*: 26). The fact that they may often need adjustment or relaxation in order to avoid such results (a need which seems unlikely to disappear, despite the new multi-year Departmental Expenditure Limits) has from the Treasury's point of view the great advantage of bringing the department to the Treasury to confess its difficulties with the system and to demand relief, rather than the Treasury's having to go out and hunt down misfeasance.

This structure of control was in 1998 given a very public aspect by the announcement, following the Comprehensive Spending Review, of the Public Service Agreements, already mentioned, between the Treasury and each department (Treasury 1998*f*; and above, pp. 150, 180). The Agreements give formal expression to the results of the hitherto private process under which ameliorations and flexibilities in the cash limit discipline are traded by the Treasury for additional obligations to be assumed by beneficiary departments and agencies, in terms of satisfactory plans, financial controls, and management systems. The new substantive element is the integration into the expenditure management process of departmental commitments about the substantive outcomes of spending. The idea of such commitments may be traced back at least as far as the Financial Management Initiative (above, pp. 123–6), but a stronger emphasis on measurement and specificity has produced, particularly for departments which were gainers from the Comprehensive Spending Review, clear and demanding targets for outcomes (e.g. that 50 per cent of 16-year-olds should get five 'good' GCSE examination results by 2002) as well as for running cost savings. Success in achieving targets, however expressed, and whether relating to programme outcomes or to efficiency in administration, is clearly something that one would expect to see taken into account when results under three-year departmental spending plans are reviewed. Does the idea of an express agreement, or even 'contract' (Chancellor of the Exchequer, 316 HC Debs., col. 188, 14 July 1998), between department and Treasury add anything to the ramifying PES and cash limit discipline?

We may certainly see this contractual language as giving apt expression to the long-term process whereby the Treasury has fashioned a capacity to negotiate with departments about controls, systems and, latterly, plans and outcomes, out of traditional powers of detailed and *ad hoc* intervention. In so doing, the idea of a Public Service Agreement seems to carry into the heart of government the general shift, in all areas of social and economic life, from coercive or unilateral modes of regulation to 'economic' instruments operating through 'consensual' incentives (Howse, Prichard, and Trebilcock 1990). In terms of the general arguments of this book, the terminology also offers striking evidence of the plural character of the executive, as seen from within: if departments were not seen as distinct and, in some significant degree, autonomous, there would be no sense in their making agreements or contracts with each other. The analogies between Public Service Agreements and the 'real' contracts the lawyer recognizes, or even the consensual incentives favoured by the economist, should not however be pressed too far. Quite apart from the anomaly of the Treasury's entering into an elaborate agreement with itself (Treasury 1998*f*: 113–17), these 'contracts', while strong on commitments, are short on sanctions: 'should a target not be met there is no question of money being deducted from the budget for that department' (or, for that matter, automatically added to it) (Treasury 1998*f*: 2).

We may conclude that PSAs do not, any more than did agency framework agreements (above, pp. 41–2), reflect a fundamental shift in the nature of relationships within the executive. Rather, they express an enlargement of the ambitions of central control, and an executive-led attempt to enhance accountability by specification of expected performance. That a government—and a Labour government at that—should describe such changes to its core allocation and control system for public expenditure in terms of contracts and agreements is, nonetheless, a remarkable tribute to the current dominance of market-based thought and discourse in public administration.

2 Links with external controls: Parliament

2.1 The Comptroller and Auditor-General and the National Audit Office

The policing of the financial behaviour of departments has traditionally been a matter not for the Treasury itself but for specialist bodies acting under its supervision: the Exchequer, the Commissioners of Accounts, and from 1866 to 1983, the Comptroller and Auditor-General assisted by the Exchequer and Audit Departments. While the Comptroller and Auditor-General's functions have, since the creation of the office by the Exchequer and Audit Departments Act 1866, been exercised on behalf of the House of Commons, to which he reports through its Public Accounts Committee, and while he has since that time been an officer possessed of judicial independence, removable only on an address by both Houses of Parliament (1866 Act, s. 3), he has also at all times worked closely with the Treasury, whose concerns for the regularity, propriety, economy, efficiency, and effectiveness of public expenditure are not different in kind from those of the House as the government's purse holder. Indeed, while the 1866 Act is generally regarded as marking the shift from executive to parliamentary audit (Chester 1981: 214–20), it also reinforced the powers of the Treasury and left the Treasury with considerable influence over the Comptroller and Auditor-General's activity. The Exchequer and Audit Departments, over which the Comptroller presided, continued until 1983 to be civil service departments subject to Treasury establishments rules and expenditure restrictions (Exchequer and Audit Departments Act 1921, s. 8); and a considerable number of powers of direction of the process of audit were still confided to the Treasury (Normanton 1966: 293–4). Normanton indeed suggests that it would be 'a gross over-simplification' to suggest that the 1866 Act established legislative audit; rather, it set up 'an audit on behalf of both the legislature and the executive, under the detailed direction of the latter' (ibid. 372).

The National Audit Act of 1983 completed the formal separation of the Comptroller's functions from the executive, turning the Exchequer and Audit Department into a National Audit Office (NAO) funded on the basis of an estimate prepared by the Comptroller and laid before Parliament not by the Treasury but by the Chairman of the Public Accounts Commission, a House of Commons body (1983 Act, ss. 2–4). This new status and structure have not made the Comptroller and NAO more aloof from executive concerns: indeed, the reverse is true. NAO clearly regards itself as part of the process of securing more effective control of public expenditure pursued throughout the nineteen-eighties and nineties (National Audit Office [nd]), and as one of the leaders, rather than followers, in the establishment of the 'new public management'. As such it has laid the same kind of emphasis on service and value for money as has been sought through the Next Steps programme: while it recognizes Parliament as its primary client, it emphasizes that 'all the bodies we audit are clients'. 'They . . . look to us to provide them with assurance that their accounts are sound and to give advice on related matters such as internal controls' (National Audit Office 1996: 6).

NAO's work, it should be noted, extends over a field far broader than that of central Government Departments: NAO's formal 'certification' audit (see above, pp. 171–3) in 1996–97 covered 166 departmental expenditure, revenue, and government borrowing and lending accounts, 93 executive agency accounts, 208 other United Kingdom public bodies, and 53 accounts of international organizations (National Audit Office 1997*b*: 12). These extensions derive from the terms of specific enactments, from Treasury directions under section 3 of the 1921 Act, and most commonly, from agreement. In addition, the Comptroller, while not their auditor, has 'inspection rights' in relation to a large number of additional accounts, generally of non-departmental public bodies, arising either by agreement or as an incident of audit of a relevant appropriation account (Treasury 1980: 11–18 and Annex B; Treasury 1989*a*: para. 8.1.48–9), and these rights have recently been considerably extended, now covering some 4000 bodies and engendering 290 specific examinations in 1996–97 (National Audit Office 1997*b*: 42). In consequence, NAO assists departments and agencies to maintain control of their satellite organizations and beneficiaries, as well as of their own finances.

A more direct result of the 1983 Act has been a clearer division among the types of work that NAO does. From the earliest years of the Comptroller's office he and his auditors were taking an interest in the economy of government expenditure, as well as its strict regularity. Though contested at first, particularly by the Service departments, such value-for-money audit was fully established before the Second World War; it had no statutory basis, but since the 1866 and 1921 Acts provided no guidance on the scope of audit of appropriation accounts, it was possible for changes to take place without the need for amending legislation (Normanton 1966: 104–9; Treasury 1980: 7–10). By the beginning of the nineteen-eighties the attention of Parliament and the Public Accounts Committee had for many years been concentrated almost entirely on value-for-money audit concerned with economy and efficiency, as a comparison of the contents of the two Epitomes of Public Accounts Committee reports (1857–1937; 1938–1969) will readily show (Epitome I; Epitome II). More recently, a concern for effectiveness—in the sense of whether policy instruments were achieving the results intended to a degree justifying the manpower and other costs involved—was also added (Treasury 1980: 7–10). The 1983 Act gave this form of audit statutory sanction in the form of 'economy, efficiency and effectiveness examinations' (1983 Act, Part II). This has helped the Comptroller to approach this work as a distinct function, appropriately organized as a programme of investigations through annual strategic audit plans growing out of NAO's continuous monitoring of the bodies it audits.[5] The choice of which bodies and activities should be subject to this form of investigation is for the Comptroller alone, though the Public Accounts Committee is given the opportunity to comment on the draft programme (National Audit Office [nd]: 9–10).

2.2 Treasury–NAO relations

While the 1983 Act made the Comptroller and the NAO independent of the Treasury, it did not change their respective roles in control of expenditure. In particular, it did not alter the Treasury's reliance on the NAO as the United Kingdom's state audit body. The Treasury has no audit capability of its own and must look to NAO, with its staff of 750, for assurance both on the reliability of the accounts it requires of departments and on the operation in practice of the efficiency and effectiveness devices which it, and other bodies like the Efficiency Unit, so tirelessly develop, refine, and promulgate. Its dependence in matters of regularity is exemplified by that provision of the Exchequer and Audit Departments Act 1921 which invites the Comptroller to tell it about any expenditure improperly incurred without its authority (s. 1(3)), but extends much more broadly to all questions both of regularity and of value for money. No matter how intensively the Treasury probes departmental proposals for expenditure, the auditor 'sees something the Treasury does not see, namely the departmental records and deliberations which form the background to the correspondence, and he can therefore ensure that the department under audit has presented its facts to the Treasury with reasonable exactitude' (Normanton 1966: 372 n.). Prior to 1983 the auditor might have been seen as the Treasury's agent in the performance of these functions. Now the preferred conception, at NAO, is that of partnership with the Treasury, but the essence of the job has not changed.

Treasury–NAO relations can be considered under four headings: the operation of the disciplines of regularity and propriety; investigations of

[5] The idea that monitoring of departmental financial transactions should be a continuous process, not just an end-year investigation, goes back to 1866: see Exchequer and Audit Departments Act 1866, s. 28 (as extended by s. 9(2), 1921 Act)).

value for money; general accountancy and audit advice; and their respective roles in the operation of Parliamentary scrutiny.

With regard to *regularity and propriety*, while only the NAO can do the actual policing, departments may look either to the Treasury or to the NAO itself for advice. The Treasury Officer of Accounts has an annual case-load of some 3000 inquiries as to the detailed interpretation of *Government Accounting* and other questions of regularity and propriety, coming both from departments and agencies and from other parts of the Treasury, notably the spending teams. TOA also offers training, and has published a handbook of guidance for departments, executive agencies and NDPBs on *Regularity and Propriety* (Treasury 1997*c*). At the same time the contemporary culture of the NAO sees departments under audit as clients, to be served and assisted, not just policed. Bilateral contacts between departments and NAO are intense and do not ordinarily involve the Treasury. Irregularities discovered during the continuing process of audit will be referred in the first place to the department, with advice as to whether they can be retrospectively corrected by a grant of Treasury authority—not to the Treasury itself. Departments may prefer to address queries on regularity and propriety direct to the NAO, rather than to the Treasury; for its part, the NAO gives frequent advice to departments, both wholly informally, and in its 'management letters' sent to the responsible officer or body at the conclusion of each audit (Treasury 1989*a*: paras. 7.1.20–23) (but not normally seen by the Treasury). Though NAO no longer provides an analysis of their subject-matter (it did so up to 1992) it seems clear that while accounting systems and policies are the main topics of concern, issues of regularity are frequently raised. NAO treats changes introduced by departments as a result of these letters and other advice as a measure of its own performance. More general guidance from NAO on regularity has appeared in the form of an Auditing Practices Board Practice Note on the subject, which NAO largely prepared and which it regards as the 'definitive description' of the topic (Auditing Practices Board 1997).

Liaison between NAO and Treasury in the performance of these parallel functions is secured by general discussion meetings, at least twice a year, between NAO and TOA; and by prior Treasury consultation of NAO on appropriate interpretations of new Treasury authorities and guidance. NAO may liaise with the Treasury in the course of audit if it wants a Treasury view as to the meaning of its own authorities; but it is not bound by that view in deciding whether there are grounds to qualify the account. NAO has discontinued both the practice of collecting key Public Accounts Committee rulings in the Epitomes, and its own internal record of rulings which did not go to the Committee (Conspectus), but its Financial Audit Support Team does still maintain a set of precedents giving guidance in discretionary areas. TOA, too, keeps a set of precedents for the same purpose; but the two sides do not directly share this knowledge with each other.

In the now distinctive area of *value-for-money* inquiries, changes have perhaps been more noticeable. The Treasury is not a party to the process whereby NAO develops its programme (though there is likely to be informal consultation with spending teams at an early stage), and these enquiries can therefore hardly function as an instrument of Treasury control. None the less, VFM investigations address exactly the same concerns as have driven Treasury- and Efficiency Unit-led reforms in recent years, and their reports clearly provide independent support for the Treasury's efforts. From time to time NAO has also conducted VFM-type studies at the Treasury's request, rather than as part of its own programme, but these so called 'Culpin studies' are viewed with suspicion by departments. To advance its own priorities in this field, the Treasury therefore now relies rather on the pressures for efficient departmental management systems engendered by the system of cash-based controls, coupled with a variety of efficiency monitoring and targeting devices (above, pp. 183–92).

NAO further assists the Treasury by promoting best practice and high standards in *public sector accounting and auditing*, working with the Treasury, for example, to develop accounting guidance for resource accounting (above, pp. 163–6). The Treasury can lay down the principles, but it needs NAO to provide the detailed advice to departments on how to bring their accounting systems into line with them. Similarly, the Treasury looks to NAO to tell it whether an executive agency's accounts are up to standard before it issues an accounts direction (above, p. 134).

Parliamentary scrutiny of appropriation accounts, by the House of Commons Public Accounts Committee, is initiated by the presentation of the Comptroller and Auditor-General's reports on each account. An account which is qualified will always attract a report, but other accounts may also do so. The results of NAO VFM investigations are likewise reported to the Public Accounts Committee. The Committee will almost invariably follow up these reports with examination of the relevant Accounting Officer, leading to its own report. The Treasury participates in this process through the attendance of the TOA at the Public Accounts Committee hearings. Responses to the report (as to all Public Accounts Committee reports) are prepared by departments in close consultation with the Treasury and published as a Treasury Minute. Further investigation by the Public Accounts Committee, or follow-up work by NAO, may ensue (Treasury 1989*a*: paras. 7.1.43–45).

In this process, the Committee, supported by the NAO, and the Treasury have a considerable, but not complete, identity of interest, and find themselves in a situation of mutual, but perhaps not equal, dependence. Public Accounts Committee and Treasury share a concern for economical and effective public spending, but the Committee, despite its long tradition of bipartisanship, functions as an external and very public critic of the governments of which the Treasury forms part, and the Treasury may not always agree with the strictures and recommendations of the Public Accounts Committee nor with the findings of the Comptroller and Auditor-General on which they are based. The Treasury may act as a 'shop steward' in supporting departmental responses to audit queries, and Treasury Minutes will frequently mount a robust defence of departmental behaviour; though this need not prevent an acceptance for the future of the essence of Public Accounts Committee recommendations, and of a general responsibility to disseminate those recommendations across government.

At the same time, the Treasury draws strength from the sanctions of publicity and embarrassment that can be deployed through the processes of reporting by the Comptroller and Auditor-General to Parliament, of public discussion of his reports, and public interrogation of Accounting Officers by the Public Accounts Committee. This exposure to Parliamentary criticism is clearly seen by the Treasury as an important incentive for compliance. Its handbook on *Regularity and Propriety* (Treasury 1997*c*) is largely composed of cautionary tales of the Public Accounts Committee excoriating departments, agencies, and NDPBs for a variety of financial delinquencies. If NAO did not exist, the Treasury would certainly have to invent a central state audit capability of another kind. The very scope for political debate and disagreement offered by the legislative forms of United Kingdom state audit arguably means that reliance on Parliament in this field puts the Treasury in a stronger position vis-à-vis politically-led spending departments than an executive-based state audit could secure.

On the other hand, criticisms by the Public Accounts Committee count for little unless they attract Treasury acquiescence and implementation. If the spending complained of is irregular or illegal, then the Treasury must, with the department, deal specifically with the matter by way of an Excess Vote. In other kinds of case no such Vote may be needed, and the Vote does not in itself entail any adverse internal results. The changes we have chronicled in the Treasury's control approach, involving a large-scale absorption of control tools into the PES system with its broad delegations and large cash blocks, significantly affect the question of whether and how parliamentary strictures are followed up. If a negative report from the Comptroller casts doubt on the robustness of departmental financial systems, it may well occasion the restriction of Treasury delegations of spending authority (as occurred following the Public Accounts Committee's enquiry into Ministry of Defence staff benefits) or of flexibility under cash-limit disciplines. It may even negatively affect future PES allocations and cash limits. But where systems are sound and the incident or decision complained of is an isolated one, there may be neither means nor interest for the Treasury to intervene: the logic of a Treasury control focusing on systems is to leave such matters to the attention of departments. A clear sign of this is the Treasury's suggestion that responses to the Committee's reports should no longer take the form of Treasury Minutes, save where the Treasury's own business is concerned, but should be submitted directly over the signature of the departmental minister (Public Accounts Committee 1998: Memorandum by HM Treasury, Treasury Controls, Annex, paras. 30–3; Evidence, qq. 6–8, 50–2). The result might well be to leave Parliament facing the kind of variations in departmental response—and attitude—that have been manifest in relation to the content and discussion of departmental reports (above, pp. 163–4).

3 Links with external controls: the law and the courts

It will have become apparent that there is plenty of law surrounding the public expenditure process in the United Kingdom. While significant expenditures may still be undertaken in support of prerogative powers, as in the area of foreign policy, and while the power to spend on the basis of the annual Appropriation Act alone is still carefully safeguarded (Treasury 1989*a*: 2.2 and Annex 2.1), the great bulk of central government spending will be referable not just to one, but to two legal enactments: the Appropriation Act, and the permanent legislation organizing the relevant function or programme. The Treasury's planning of public expenditure, within the PES and supply processes, has therefore to be conducted within the framework provided by such permanent legislation; and the processes of monitoring and control which we have just described have to be carried out with regard both to the permanent legislative structure and to that provided, year by year, by the Appropriation Act. In such a highly legalized environment, it is at least plausible that the Treasury might have developed, in the pursuit of public expenditure goals, a relationship of interdependence, or at least of interaction, with the courts, analogous to that with Parliament which has so strongly shaped the United Kingdom's financial history.

Nothing like this has ever happened. Today, despite the fact that the Treasury Solicitor is the head of the Government Legal Service, and that his department undertakes most of the government's litigation, the

Treasury is among the departments which have the least contact with the courts. While issues involving the legality of public spending decisions probably come before the courts today more often than ever before, it is the spending departments, not the Treasury, which are involved. How did this situation come about? and what is its significance for Treasury control of expenditure?

Up to the end of the nineteenth century the Lords Commissioners of Treasury appeared quite frequently as respondents to litigation (Elliott 1981*a*). Usually, the purpose of the action was to secure payment of a civil or military pension, or of compensation for loss of office, or some other pecuniary advantage, to which the applicant felt himself entitled under statute or Royal Warrant but which the Treasury was refusing to pay. Usually, the action was unsuccessful, either because the court found that the plaintiff had no legal right to the claimed payment (*R v Lords Commissioners of the Treasury, ex parte Hand* 1836; *Ex parte Napier* 1852), or because the right was a right not against the Treasury, but against some other public officer (*R v Lords Commissioners of the Treasury, ex parte Walmsley* 1861), or because the claimed remedy (usually the prerogative writ of *mandamus*, ordering the performance of a legal duty by a public officer) was not available against the Crown, on whose behalf the Treasury was acting (*R v Lords Commissioners of the Treasury* 1872). Only in one early case, *R v Lords Commissioners of the Treasury, ex parte Smyth* 1835, do we find the applicant successfully leaping all these hurdles; and this was a decision which subsequent courts went to some lengths to distinguish.

Over the following decades, the hurdles were gradually removed by the legislation through which the welfare state was built. Clear legal rights to various forms of payments, such as state pensions or unemployment insurance, were established. Specific statutory duties to make such payments were created, thus imposing on the relevant officials and agencies duties distinct from those they might possess as agents of the Crown, so that remedies like *mandamus* might not be excluded; and new and more flexible remedies, like declaration (*Dyson v Attorney-General* 1911) made their appearance. These developments gave disappointed claimants their day in court (though often only on appeal from the decision of a specialized statutory tribunal), but they also put the Treasury on the sidelines, since in accordance with the principles of legal decentralization which we argue are fundamental to United Kingdom government, both the statutory payment obligations, and the funds to meet them, were put in the hands of the different departments. Today, therefore, it is generally the minister or the Secretary of State who is sued; the argument ordinarily focuses wholly on the situation of the individual applicant having regard to the way in which the statutory duty of payment is framed; and considerations of the relationship between the specific payment in issue and broader issues of allocation of resources, whether as between this applicant and other applicants, or this scheme and other schemes of spending, are only presented in exceptional cases.

This course of development has not simply produced an absence, as between Treasury and courts, of the kind of interaction and interdependence that have characterized its relationship with Parliament. It has also made the legal structuring of public expenditure part of the problem for Treasury control, rather than part of the solution. The argument that expenditure is required in order to meet legal obligations has always been a powerful defensive weapon for departments when the Treasury has attempted to bear down on spending, whether in routine discussions or at moments of unexpected financial difficulty. Thain and Wright (1995: 218) give an idea of the sensitivities in this area, suggesting that one of the ways in which Treasury spending teams might be seen as overstepping the bounds of a 'reasonable approach' is by disputing the legal inevitability of spending, a move which is liable to 'irritate' departmental Finance Divisions. The Treasury may none the less sometimes push a department to test the applicability of general rules in particular cases, or dispute a department's costs of complying with a compensation obligation. Disputes of this type may quickly escalate to ministerial level and draw in the Treasury Solicitor or the Law Officers (see generally below, pp. 297–315). In times of financial crisis, it is clear that departments with major statutory spending obligations have regularly been able to plead legal obstacles as a means of diverting the Treasury's attention to other targets (Pliatzky 1982: 155–6; Parker 1997). One structural response by the Treasury might be to try to influence the design of legislation so as to move departments back towards cash-limited, discretionary schemes. A well-known move of this sort was the Social Security Act 1986, section 32, which established the cash-limited Social Fund in place of an open-ended commitment to make rule-determined 'single payments' to the needy. The Treasury supported this change, but it was the Department of Health and Social Security that initiated it (Lawson 1993: 587, 593–4; and see Drabble and Lynes 1989); and it is hard to see how the Treasury could force the redesign of legislation on an unwilling department.

The Treasury's difficulties in this area should not be underestimated. Dramatic battles have from time to time been won, but the war continues, and departments currently appear to be in the ascendant. Commentators who see ouster of judicial review clauses as expressing an *executive* determination to avoid judicial control—that is, in simple separation of powers terms (above, pp. 10–12)—should be aware of the ferocity with which the same kind of issue has been contested *within* the executive. In the early eighteen-eighties, for example, the Comptroller and Auditor-General questioned the Education Department's administration of payments to schools, designed to ensure that all children had access to primary education. He suggested that certain payments were not in accordance with the Education Code, which set out the payments scheme, that the Code itself might not be consistent with the governing legislation, and that payments incorrectly made ought to be recovered. The response of the Department was robust. The Code, it said, was approved by Parliament and had the force of legislation. The Department had exclusive competence as to its interpretation, which prevailed over anything the Comptroller or the Treasury might say. Its views as to eligibility were correct and it had no power to recover monies incorrectly paid. It was for the Department to decide how the Code should be changed, and to seek parliamentary approval for such changes, whatever contrary opinion might have been expressed by the Treasury or Public Accounts Committee (Public Accounts Committee 1884: Evidence, qq. 289–482). A Treasury threat to introduce legislation to curtail the Department's claimed powers soon brought the Department to accept, 'in friendly conference', a series of 'resolutions' which essentially denied it the position of sole and final arbiter of its own legal spending regime (Public Accounts Committee 1885*a*: Appendix, p. 10; 1885*b*: paras. 47–9). But these resolutions did not give the Treasury the last word in such cases. The Law Officers were to determine future disputes about the legality of the Code; the Public Accounts Committee would be the arbiters of whether expenditure complied with it.

It is hardly surprising, therefore, that the Treasury had to fight similar battles with the Ministry of Pensions in 1918 and with the Board of Education in 1921, in each case with the Department claiming wide discretion in interpretation (Epitome I: 588–90; 632). The fact that the Treasury and Public Accounts Committee again emerged victorious from these engagements could have no definitive effect so long as the Treasury had no special authority in the legal interpretation of spending powers. Yet it never seems to have sought such a position. It stated in 1893 that it '[did] not claim to be a final and conclusive interpreter of the law which it puts in motion' (Epitome I: 312); and while it energetically promoted the centralization of legislative drafting in the late nineteenth century, in part with a view of keeping the costs of legislative proposals under review (Ilbert 1901: 83–4), it never seems to have put much weight behind the Treasury Solicitor's efforts to centralize government legal advice in his office (below, pp. 214–7). In consequence, today as in 1885, an argument which the Treasury might have with a department about legal aspects of spending is likely to be referred to the Law

Officers in the same way as any other inter-departmental legal dispute (Cabinet Office 1997*d*: para. 22; below, pp. 297–315).

While the courts have had little opportunity to develop a coherent body of doctrine on legal aspects of public expenditure, the general tenor of their occasional interventions has tended to favour the spending, rather than the Treasury, interest. They have not been ready to make any general assumption that financial constraints are a relevant consideration in the exercise of executive discretion. Where the powers, and issues, are broad enough, it may be proper to invoke them (*R v Criminal Injuries Compensation Board, ex parte P* 1995, a case of prerogative rather than statutory powers); but lack of resources cannot be an excuse for failing to perform an otherwise clear statutory duty (*In re T, a minor* 1998; compare *R v Gloucestershire County Council, ex parte Berry* 1997). On more technical expenditure issues, courts have shown little deference to Treasury views. We have seen that the 'concordat' between the Treasury and the Public Accounts Committee as to the use of the Appropriation Act either as the sole support for a programme of spending, or to override limitations in the permanent legislation sustaining such spending (above, pp. 173–5), was based on the assumption that the Act was sufficient authority for supply expenditure and could indeed impliedly, no less than explicitly, repeal *pro tanto* and *pro tempore* any plainly inconsistent provision in permanent legislation. We have also seen that it is a core element of Treasury doctrine—and indeed, we have argued, of Treasury power (above, pp. 117–18)—that the money appropriated under the Act is *not* legally transferred to the relevant departments along with an instruction to apply it to the designated purposes, but is simply 'appropriated as between the Crown and the House of Commons; there is no obligation on the Treasury to pay any sums; but they may pay them' (Sir George Jessel, Solicitor-General, in argument in *R v Lords Commissioners of the Treasury* 1872: 390).

Neither of these fundamental pieces of public expenditure doctrine has ever, so far as we can discover, been accepted by the courts. All three opinions delivered by the Queen's Bench in *R v Lords Commissioners of the Treasury* 1872 explicitly rejected the Solicitor-General's proposition, saying that the Appropriation Act imposed a duty on the Treasury to pay the sums in issue. Technically these remarks did not have the force of binding precedent, since the case turned on the question of whether *mandamus* could issue to the Treasury in this case, and the court held, with evident regret, that it could not (above, p. 200); but the judicial view could not have been more clearly expressed. So far as the capacity of the Act to override inconsistent prior legislation is concerned, the Supreme Court of Victoria, in a judgment sustained by the Privy Council (*R v Fisher* 1903), has said that it would be unwilling to find such a repeal unless express language were used (*Fisher v R* 1901); even this would be an 'unconstitutional expedient', albeit an effective one (per Madden CJ at 793).

United Kingdom courts have never ruled expressly on this point, but it is noteworthy that in the *Pergau Dam* case in 1995 counsel for the Crown apparently did not even think it worthwhile to argue that the coverage of the disputed payment in the Overseas Development Administration Vote under the Appropriation Act might 'override' the restrictions which the court, to ODA's surprise, found to inhere in section 1(1) of the Overseas Development and Co-operation Act 1980. The government seemed to be adopting a similar position in the *Fire Brigades Union* case (*R v Secretary of State for the Home Department, ex parte Fire Brigades Union* 1995), in which the House of Lords found it to be unlawful for the Home Secretary to bring forward a new scheme for criminal injuries compensation under common law powers, supported like the old scheme by the Appropriation Act alone, at a time when a statutory scheme had been enacted, but not yet brought into force. Lord Justice Hobhouse pointed out at some length in the Court of Appeal (*Fire Brigades Union* 1995: 903–6), that the new, allegedly unlawful scheme had been funded by a Vote in the Appropriation Act 1994, based on an estimate explicitly referring to that scheme (the estimate also satisfied the terms of the 1932 'concordat'), but the House dismissed this argument on the basis of a concession by the Lord Advocate, who led the argument for the government in the House, that if the decision to introduce the tariff scheme was unlawful, the fact that Parliament had voted funds for it in the Appropriation Act could not cure the invalidity. Unremarkable in the abstract (see above, pp. 33–6), the concession seems striking when it is considered that the unlawfulness of the scheme had to depend on a finding that Parliament could not have intended to permit the Home Secretary to disable himself, for the future, from bringing the statutory scheme into force. If the Appropriation Act is too feeble a vehicle even to displace judicial assumptions about Parliament's implied intentions, it is hard to see how the courts could, in the future, attribute to the Act the effects of temporary repeal of legislation actually in force contended for under the 'concordat' and in many earlier Treasury Minutes.

In dealing with the aftermath of the *Pergau Dam* case, however, the government relied on precisely these effects. Examination of the aid budget disclosed two other continuing projects which might, in terms of the court's decision, be *ultra vires* the 1980 Act, and which could not be funded under other permanent legislation such as the Export and Investment Guarantees Act 1991. Since funding was not expected to be needed beyond 1997–98,

> [t]o provide statutory authority for this expenditure in 1994–95 and in subsequent years the Administration chose to introduce a new sub-head in a Supplementary Estimate and seek Parliamentary approval to extend the ambit of the External Assistance Vote through the Appropriation Act. The Administration's legal advice was that this would be an acceptable course of action provided that Parliament was clearly informed in advance of what it was being asked to approve. (Auditing Practices Board 1997: 49; Comptroller and Auditor-General 1995: para. 34)

In other words, the Appropriation Act's broader definition of lawful expenditure was used to override, for the continuing duration of these projects, the 1980 Act's narrower one (see also Harden, White, and Hollingsworth 1996: 679). As the Comptroller and Auditor-General pointed out, this case was not even on all fours with those which underlay the concordat of 1932, where there had been no formal declaration of illegality (Comptroller and Auditor-General 1995: para. 40).

In these circumstances it is hardly surprising that the Treasury's internal guidance on expenditure appears to face two ways on this issue. In *Government Accounting*, the authoritative internal text, and one revised twice since 1995, the Treasury continues to maintain that, so far as ministers (as opposed to statutorily created bodies) are concerned, 'statutory authority for the payment of expenditure out of moneys provided by Parliament must be, *and can only be*, given year by year by means of the Supply Estimates and the confirming Appropriation Act' (Treasury 1989*a*: para. 2.2.5, emphasis supplied), so that, even in the presence of permanent legislation apparently authorizing (and limiting) ministerial expenditure, 'the Appropriation Act is . . . the sole legal authority for voted expenditure' (para. 2.2.6) and 'in a legal sense . . . sufficient authority for expenditure' (para. 2.2.8). In consequence, using it to override permanent statutory limits raises issues, not of legality, but of 'propriety' (ibid.). Elsewhere, however, the Treasury now uses language which—to say the least—puts the Appropriation Act in a less prominent position. According to its *Handbook* on *Regularity and Propriety* (Treasury 1997*c*: 5):

> First, expenditure must be consistent with the specific legislation providing for the activity or service. This legislation expresses Parliament's intention as to when and how public money should be used. . . . Second, expenditure must fall within the ambit of the relevant Vote. The ambit of each Vote records Parliament's intentions as to the purposes of the expenditure. Expenditure which is outside the ambit of the relevant Vote *or* outside the specific legislation is automatically 'irregular' (emphasis supplied).

If, as that little word 'or' requires, both the permanent legislation and the ambit of the Vote must be respected, there is no room for the principle asserted in *Government Accounting* that in the event of conflict, the latter overrides the former.

This is, of course, an informal and rather elementary document, and perhaps the author did not want to bother—or tempt—his departmental readers with possibilities of overriding legislation. The Treasury has disclaimed any intention of saying anything new about regularity in the pamphlet. None the less, the different executive utterances of the mid-nineteen-nineties are certainly capable of suggesting a plurality of opinion on this issue.

Indeed, the legal nature of expenditure legislation has been a problem for a variety of different legal systems. It is, after all, an odd kind of law that consists—as does the Appropriation Act—only of description and numerical maxima, and is addressed only to members of the executive; in some civil law jurisdictions, there has been considerable doubt as to whether such legislation can really be called law at all (Orlando 1940; Baade 1974; Daintith 1997*a*: 54–6). How one answers the question of whether it does or does not prevail over permanent spending legislation reflects, however, quite fundamental assumptions or beliefs about the purpose and effects of legislation (are all laws of equal force?) and about the primacy of commitments to policies over flexibility in meeting immediate needs (or vice versa). Yet we seem to possess no means for the coherent discussion of such preferences, whether in official or academic *fora*. There is little shared knowledge or understanding between practitioners of legal and Parliamentary systems of control of public finance; in terms of the discussion in our first chapter (above, pp. 4–5), there is no effective communication between these systems.[6] And by reason of the academic lawyer's obsession with case-law, the gap has not been filled by scholarly writing and debate (brave exceptions are Elliott 1981*a*, 1989, and the recent work of the team formed by Harden, e.g. Harden, White, and Hollingsworth 1996). In consequence, executive decisions can freely shape the constitution in this area—though, as we have seen, not necessarily coherently or even consciously. The move to resource accounting and budgeting, like that to multi-year spending plans, commitments, and ceilings, expresses a vigorous executive preference for stable policy commitments and may already be having echoes in its expenditure legislation practice (above): yet the Treasury could tell Parliament that the switch to RAB involved no change in the basic principles of supply (Public Accounts Committee 1996: para. 3).

[6] NAO has no in-house legal advice. Until recently it relied on the Treasury Solicitor. When it took the view that it needed advice which could be seen to be wholly objective, it contracted two firms of solicitors to provide it with advice.

7
The Organization of the Legal Function in Government

I INTRODUCTION

1 The salience of legality

A well-instructed conscience is no longer an adequate guide to legally correct conduct. In this age of complex social and economic regulation, the question 'Is this legal?' presents itself with increasing frequency to individuals and corporations alike, and may be impossible to answer without reflection, research, or even professional advice. A concern for legal rectitude, supported by expert advice, is however of peculiar importance to government, for at least three reasons. *First*, the executive relies, for much of its capacity to govern, on legal powers which exceed those enjoyed by other persons, notably the power to coerce and control its citizens. It claims to be a monopolist so far as the resource of force is concerned, and must accept the associated legal constraints. *Second*, the use of the resources which it does share with others—notably the financial power that it possesses in common with any wealthy subject—is, as we have just seen (above, pp. 199–206) subject to special and sometimes obscure legal restrictions. *Third*, illegal conduct, or even oppressive or unusual use of lawful powers, is likely—quite aside from any litigation it might engender—to provoke damaging political criticism, in the media, the legislature, or elsewhere.

These considerations, of course, only operate on that minority of governments that profess to operate, and do in fact operate, according to the tenets of democracy and the rule of law. Among this minority is the United Kingdom's. Accordingly, the government has long needed, and still needs today, to determine how this pervasiveness of issues of legality is to be reflected in its internal operations. In this chapter, and in the three which follow, we explore this question in two stages. This chapter deals with the structures through which the executive deals with legal issues. It sets out who undertakes legal work, how their activities are fitted into the general action of the executive, and what structures exist to control and co-ordinate their work. Chapters 8 to 10 are concerned with the operation of this structure. The first concentrates on the executive's activity in relation to law-making: both its preparation of legislation for passage by Parliament, and in its own exercise of delegated and original law-making power. The second discusses legal advice relating to administrative action and to litigation, both within and outside the context of litigation. In the third of these chapters, we shall be asking whether the government's legal advice produces, or discloses, anything in the nature of an 'executive view' of legality as a value, or of the substantive content of the law. Or is it simply a mechanism of response to external stimuli, such as judicial decisions and political pressures? Is it subject to strong central control, or can it tolerate—and provide—diversity of opinion and action?

2 Whose legality?

As Chapter 2 showed, the Glorious Revolution of 1689, whose effects were extended to Scotland by the Union some twenty years later, left little scope for the development by the executive of a distinctive and independent view of the law in the areas of concern to it. The King's courts were recognized as the only authoritative interpreters of the law, even in cases in which the Crown, or its ministers, or other organs of government, were directly involved. This did not mean—as Dicey was to claim (Dicey 1959: 188–95)—that the law was the same for public servants as for private persons, for many legal immunities persisted. It did however choke off the possibility of development of an internal executive jurisdiction on the basis of the internal control powers exercised in pre-Revolution times by the Privy Council (and within it, the Star Chamber), and by the Privy Council in Scotland; these bodies were swept away at the Revolution, condemned by their own excesses and arbitrariness (Mitchell 1965: 96–8). On the law-making side, the victory of the Parliamentary interest left minimal scope for executive legislation, not even a general power of seeing to the proper execution of the laws.

In these respects the United Kingdom stands in clear contrast to a country such as France, where adherence to a 'strong' version of the separation between executive and judicial powers (Vile 1967: 188–9) has meant that the law most closely affecting the executive has in large measure been developed within the executive itself, both through executive legislation (of varying scope in the different Republics, but always wider than that permitted in the United Kingdom), and through the development of the *Conseil d'Etat* from an authority of internal supervision into a genuine executive jurisdiction with co-ordinate authority with that of the regular courts (Kessler 1958: 27–52). Law for the executive is thus in origin very much law of the executive, a feature noted, and disapproved of, by Dicey (Cosgrove 1980: 91–102). A co-ordinate executive jurisdiction, and an extensive power of executive legislation, are not, however, essential prerequisites for a distinctive executive legality. Even in systems where judge or legislator can always have the last word, constitutional recognition as a distinct 'power' within the state may be all that is needed to enable the executive to build a jurisprudence of its own, as the example of the United States demonstrates. Opinions of the Attorney-General may only have binding force for the Federal Government for as long as no incompatible pronouncement issues from the Supreme Court or (possibly) Congress, but in some areas, such as the internal ordering of the executive branch and its relations with the other branches, the occasions for such pronouncements may not readily arise, and a body of legal opinion of some weight and consistency may thus be established within the executive (McGinnis 1993*a*; 1993*b*; 1997).

In United Kingdom constitutional law writing the emphasis on parliamentary sovereignty as the supreme, if not the only, constitutional tenet has commonly made it difficult for us to see the executive as a distinctive 'power' under the constitution at all (Daintith 1994: 210–12). Even today, when the significance of parliamentary sovereignty is being eroded by the multiplication of extra-national centres of economic and political power, most visibly the European Union, some commentators continue to insist that by reason of its subordination, not just to Parliament, but to the courts also, 'the executive cannot be one of three sovereign and equal elements of the State' (Sedley 1994: 289–90). Subordinates can, however, be powerful people, and the ability of the executive to control the levers of parliamentary action may offer it more power and discretion to take, hold, and enforce a view on legal questions than its formal position vis-à-vis Parliament might suggest. Indeed, even its formal position is stronger than is generally recognized: in financial matters its right of initiative in relation both to taxes and spending makes it the partner, not the subordinate, of Parliament (above, pp. 108–9). The executive lacks, however, any analogous influence over judicial decisions (or at least, any overt influence: see Stevens 1993: 92–6); the locus of authority for the declaration of the law has since 1689 been firmly established outside the executive, in the King's courts, not just in form but in fact.

Against these constitutional data, can government legal work be very different from the legal work of any large organization, with the job of the lawyer necessarily focused, ultimately, on the interpretation and prediction of judicial actions, no matter what the context of decision—rule-making or institution-building, day-to-day decision-making, or litigation? Or is there greater room for manoeuvre in preparing legislation or delegated legislation, by reason of the deference enjoined on courts by parliamentary supremacy? Does there remain any space for executive action—in relation, say, to its internal management—where, in a period of burgeoning judicial review, the oversight of the courts still does not reach? Both the distinctiveness and the autonomy of the executive as a legal subject are in issue here.

3 Legality as a professional specialism

In France, one result of the outgrowth of administrative law from within the executive is that there is no profound distinction, in terms of training, outlook, or career, between functionaries with a particular concern for legal matters and the general body of administrators. The members of the *Conseil d'Etat*, which combines the functions of supreme administrative court and expert adviser on legislation, make up one among several 'grands corps d'Etat' along with the *Ingénieurs des Ponts et Chaussées, et des Mines*, the *Inspection des Finances*, the *corps préfectoral*, and the *Cour des Comptes* (Kessler 1968, especially 57–69 and Part II, 'Le phénomène de corps'; Armstrong 1973: 213–23). Even in countries where the law regulating the executive is seen as originating from outside the executive itself, a common way of holding courts and executive together, and of minimizing difficulties of interpretation, has been to staff the executive government in large measure with lawyers, or at least with people having a legal training (Le Sueur and Snyder 1992: 371–2). Germany may be the case best known to us (Armstrong 1973: 161–8), but is certainly not unique (e.g. Jarvad 1996: 24–5 for Denmark).

This bridge between courts and executive does not exist in the United Kingdom, but the reasons for its absence are obscure. Legally-trained people played a significant administrative role in the first half of the nineteenth century, and continued to do so in the second half, as central administration simultaneously expanded, was professionalized, and became 'legalized' as it rapidly shifted from a prerogative to a statutory base. In the first years of this century, for example, three of the four top civil servants in the Home Office were legally-trained; yet by 1913 this number was reduced to one (Pellew 1988: 71) and about the same time, the 'rule that Home Office juniors should take their law examinations and should be called to the Bar' fell into disuse (Armstrong 1973: 161). Within government, lawyers were, in Drewry's words, slipping 'sideways, and perhaps slightly downwards, into the all-too-familar role of specialists in a predominantly generalist system' (Drewry 1988: 39), though whether this was because legal training did not fit well into the post-1870 pattern of administrative recruitment by examination (Armstrong, ibid.), or because routine administrative work replaced the legal innovation of the mid-nineteenth century (Torrance 1968), is not easy to say.

The restriction of legally-trained people to the role of specialist legal adviser (a role which of course they had at all times occupied), despite the fact that legal considerations had become all-pervading in government, clearly caused some unease even in the heyday of the generalist senior administrator, which may perhaps be dated from the civil service reforms immediately following the First World War (Jacob 1996: 90–110). Sir Francis Floud, in a 1923 paper later cited with approval by the Royal Commission on the Civil Service (1931), held up to specialists in the civil service the example of the 'wise, experienced and tactful legal adviser' who exercises influence 'over the whole range of policy of a Department without having any executive power'. Other specialists should aspire to this status; but they should not assume that it meant that their advice on policy would necessarily be accepted (Floud 1923).

Even in 1923, a representation of legality in government as *merely* a matter for specialist advice which might or might not be accepted would have been a caricature. Law was seen to impinge on government not merely as a factor relevant to the determination of policy, but also as an instrument of its implementation and enforcement, processes in which—the generalist of 1923 was ready to acknowledge—the specialist might have a considerable say (Floud 1923: 123). In addition, of course, government as an occupier of land and buildings, a purchaser of goods and services, an employer of labour, even a provider of public services, entered into the same kinds of legally-structured commercial transactions as did large private enterprises, and was, like them, likely to find that its activities gave rise from time to time to legal disputes, both contractual and non-contractual. In these latter respects government's legal relations were in formal terms distinctive by reason of certain legal privileges and immunities then enjoyed by the Crown (Jacob 1992); more practical importance may, however, have attached to the degree of public or political censure to which their erroneous conduct might expose the government. As a government lawyer put it in 1926, 'in public affairs there is hardly such a thing as an unimportant matter' (Dennis 1926: 153). Once enforcement and 'ordinary' legal affairs were taken into account, it was clear that the government lawyer would be not just adviser, but executant also, at least where formal legal process was involved. This did not mean, though, that the nature of government legal work was seen as unique. When Sir Henry James QC, MP led a Treasury inquiry into the operations of the Treasury Solicitor's Department in 1888, he looked to the Solicitor's Office of the London and North-Western Railway as a model whose efficiency the Department might seek to emulate (James 1888).

4 Legal tasks in government

Today, the ways in which law impinges on the conduct of government and the action of the executive remain broadly the same, though significant changes of emphasis have occurred. Sir Robert Andrew, in the Review of Government Legal Services he conducted in 1988, began by distinguishing between the needs of government for legal services which it shared with any other large organization, and those reflecting the special powers, position, and activities of government (Andrew 1989: 9). 'Ordinary' legal work, of the type common to government and other large organizations, has if anything become more ordinary, as government privileges have been eliminated or generalized: first by the Crown Proceedings Act 1947 (which removed many of the Crown's privileges in civil litigation), more recently by such changes as the generalization of the Crown privilege to withhold documents in litigation into a broad public interest immunity (*D v NSPCC* 1978), or the drastic restriction of Crown's tax privileges in bankruptcy by the Insolvency Act 1985 (s. 89 and Sch. 4). Within the area special to government, the role of law and lawyers has been made much more visible by the growth of judicial review as a tool for the control of administrative and even legislative action; and the very nature and scope of the law relevant to policy decisions have been profoundly modified by the increasing importance and penetration of international legal obligations and by our membership of the European Union.

The major constitutional importance of these latter developments should not distract us from the fact that the organization of the government's internal legal services (and indeed the way it uses external services) reflects the full range of legal work, in which much is 'ordinary' in the sense used above, and much that is peculiar to government—such as prosecution of offences—is routine in nature. The way government perceives and ensures its own respect for legality must be traced across an organization which thinks in terms of the legal jobs to be done. These chapters will accordingly range over the whole activity of lawyers employed in central government, with the exception only of two types of function from the list provided by the Andrew Report (Andrew 1989: 10): these are the administration of justice, through the provision of the civil and criminal court systems, a function now concentrated in the Lord Chancellor's Department (LCD) (ibid.: 12); and the provision of specialist legal services to the public, as through the Land Registry, the Charity Commission, the Office of Fair Trading, and other such bodies (ibid.: 13). Lawyers, unusually, play a major role in the administration of these departments, offering an exception to our earlier generalization about their specialized and subordinate role. The exception proves the rule: this is administration which has—unlike all other administration—been seen as especially 'legal' in nature, though it is unlikely to remain so. The courts are currently seen as a public service to be efficiently managed like any other (Stevens 1993); the requirement of a legal qualification for the Permanent Secretary to LCD has been removed (Supreme Court (Offices) Act 1997), and the first non-lawyer appointed. In this discussion, however, we confine our attention to lawyers in their normal, non-administrative roles. These are listed by Andrew as legal advice; preparation of legislation; civil litigation; conveyancing; criminal prosecution; international affairs; and law reform (Andrew 1989: 10).

Within these roles a further distinction has been developed as a result of government interest in the scope for privatization and contracting-out of legal services. This was one of the tasks given to the Andrew review, and was considered in some detail (see Andrew 1989: 24–30). Andrew concluded that there was little if any scope for privatization, and that while contracting-out was 'a more promising method to pursue' (Ibid: 25), it was ordinarily unsuitable for any of the functions we have been discussing other than conveyancing and litigation, and even there it was likely that in-house lawyers would usually provide a cheaper service. He did however recommend (ibid. 92) that departments should be ready to contract out legal work if the necessary expertise did not exist in government, if government did not have the resources to do the work without undue delay, or if it were more cost-effective for the work to be done in the private sector. In 1991 the Attorney-General responded to the Andrew Report by issuing guidance to departments on the issue; similar guidance for work in Scotland was issued by the Lord Advocate in 1993 (Attorney-General 1991; Lord Advocate 1993). While the general tone of the guidance was perhaps more friendly to contracting-out than that of Andrew's report, it introduced a new division of governmental legal work for this purpose: one between 'core governmental work', not appropriate for contracting out even where Andrew's criteria might be seen as satisfied, and other work. 'Core governmental work' covers the area where 'there will be a continuing relationship of close confidence between Ministers and their legal advisers who need to understand the implications of policy options and the public interest factor in the consideration of particular aspects of the work of the department or Agency' (Attorney-General 1991: 3). It cuts across the categories of types of legal work identified by Andrew, and includes

work with national security or other especially sensitive implications;

work relating to major policy or constitutional issues;

government-to-government and other international non-commercial work;

work affecting the long-term interests of more than one Department, such as public interest immunity (PII); and

work where Cabinet Office co-ordination is necessary (Attorney-General 1991: 3–4).

These matters, as we shall see, bear a strong resemblance to those on which departments may be expected to seek central legal advice (below, pp. 302–9).

In the body of this chapter, therefore, we shall look first at the evolution of the structure through which the different legal functions are performed (part II). Next, we shall examine the different legal services presently operating within government, both in what may be called central legal departments (such as the Treasury Solicitor's Department), and in the main ministerial departments of government (part III). Finally, in part IV, we shall look at the history and general functions of the Law Officers. It may seem odd to discuss the relevant ministers only after examining the work of the legal service departments they supervise. It is odd; but so is their supervisory role, as we shall see. Just how, and how effectively, that role is carried out forms one of the main concerns of Chapter 9.

II THE DEVELOPMENT OF THE STRUCTURE FOR GOVERNMENT LEGAL WORK

The first thing the enquirer notices about the structure of government legal services is how untidy and piecemeal it appears. Some departments have their own legal services; others rely on central services, which themselves are not organized according to the ordinary principles of ministerial responsibility. The second is that it has remained untidy and piecemeal despite frequent attempts at reform, which have been going on for more than a hundred years. Powerful countervailing forces are at work here: on the one side, the desire of departments to control their own legal services; on the other, pressure for a rational, centralized system in which a single corps of lawyers services all the needs of government. We may see the struggle between these forces as emblematic of that general tension between departments and centre which has influenced both the behaviour of the executive and the content of our constitution. This does not mean that the significance of the struggle is merely managerial, a question of the location of power within the executive, of who controls what or whom. It bears also on the issue of how law affects the action of the executive. A unified corps of lawyers, providing advice and other services to all departments, is likely to have a different outlook, and a different influence (both within and outside the executive), from those of distinct groups of lawyers each serving a single departmental 'client', operating under that department's financial and managerial control, and in continuous contact with its work.

The balance of forces in the battle about how legal services were to be provided in government was established early. By the middle of the nineteenth century, at the time of the Northcote–Trevelyan reforms of the civil service, there already existed both a centralized legal service, and some departmental ones. The Treasury Solicitor, whose office was 'first officially defined' in 1661 (Treasury Solicitor's Department [nd]), was acting for a number of departments beside the Treasury; but departments like Customs, the Admiralty, the Inland Revenue, and the Post Office had had their own solicitor for some time. When the Jessel Committee was asked to review government legal work in the eighteen-seventies, it concluded that despite the degree of centralization already attained (the Treasury Solicitor was by then acting for seventeen departments), and the arguments it had heard about its effectiveness, there should not be a single office for legal work. In consequence, the Treasury Solicitor would not, in his relations with the other departments, 'in any degree interfere between the departmental solicitors and the chiefs of their several offices, but . . . he would be the head of their class, would act as a referee in all matters of practice, and would be the adviser of the government in all that concerned the organization of the legal departments of its offices' (Jessel 1877: 62).

One hundred and twenty years later, this remains an accurate description. Changes have occurred meantime, but they have not occurred easily. Conveyancing has been concentrated in the Treasury Solicitor's Department (which will hereinafter be referred to, following internal practice, as 'TSol') for a number of years (for the current situation see below, p. 220), and civil litigation was largely unified there by 1972, in pursuance of proposals first made (by the Treasury Solicitor, naturally) in the nineteen-twenties (Drewry 1981: 21–8).

Only very gradually has meaning been given to the Jessel Committee's view of the managerial role of the Treasury Solicitor. Progress in this has been bedevilled by the entanglement of the issue with that of the recruitment and retention (and hence pay and status) of government lawyers. Departmental resistance to change has thus reflected both fear of loss of control, through centralization, over what they clearly regarded as 'their' ancillary resources and fear that lawyers were getting above themselves with pretensions to equality of treatment with administrators (Drewry 1981: 23). Treasury Solicitor responsibility for the co-ordination of legal service recruitment and career management was proposed by the Barlow Committee in 1944, and though it met with vigorous departmental disapproval, the Treasury felt able to commend the idea, 'somewhat tentatively' (Drewry 1981: 24) to the Fulton Committee on the Civil Service in the mid-nineteen-sixties. Fulton accepted it; the Government did not (Drewry 1981: 25), though a Legal Groups Management Committee chaired by the Treasury Solicitor was apparently set up at this time (Andrew 1989: 36). The establishment of further co-ordinating arrangements, including a Legal Career Panel chaired by the Treasury Solicitor, was recommended by a further enquiry in 1971 by Sir Edmund Compton, who had been asked to resolve disputes as to the proper consequences of the merger of departments, some serviced by TSol, some with their own legal services, into the giant departments of Trade and Industry and of Environment. There was a price to be paid for this gain in co-ordination. The new departments kept the legal services they had inherited from their predecessors, which were strengthened by a transfer of lawyers *from* TSol (though TSol's litigation pre-eminence was reinforced by an inverse transfer of the departmental litigators) (Drewry 1981: 25–8).

The next enquiry, that of Sir Robert Andrew in 1988–89, found low morale in the government legal service, recruitment and retention problems, and precious little mobility, and concluded that these co-ordinating committees had 'signally failed' in the job of providing effective management of the service (Andrew 1989: 34). It recommended the creation of a Central Management Unit for personnel management across the service, answering to a small Legal Management Board chaired by the Treasury Solicitor (36–7). Andrew placed this suggestion in the framework of what—in the light of the past hundred years of history—were bold proposals to create a Law Officers' Department incorporating TSol and the other 'central' legal departments (see below) under the direct ministerial responsibility of the Law Officers with the Treasury Solicitor as Permanent Secretary (Andrew 1989: 31–3). Resistance to such radical proposals was as effective as usual, the Prime Minister, in her parliamentary response on the implementation of the Andrew report, rejecting it without expressly saying so (145 HC Debs., cols. *262–3*, written answers 19 January 1989). None the less, the personnel management idea survived as the Lawyers' Management Unit, which answers to the Treasury Solicitor and has since 1997 been part of TSol (below, p. 218).

Despite a century of centralizing effort, however, the principle of control by departments of their own legal staffs and functions remains unimpaired. If anything, it may have been reinforced in recent years both by frequent changes in departmental structure and by the kind of thinking about efficiency that underlies the 'new public management'. We have seen that on the creation of the giant Department of Trade and

Industry (DTI) and Department of Environment in 1970 the existing departmental legal services extended their competence. This process was not reversed in 1974, when the departments were split up again: the Solicitors of the Departments of Trade and of Environment continued to act for the new Departments, of Industry and of Consumer Protection in the first case, of Transport in the second (Archer 1978: 29). DTI is now once more a single department with its own legal service; so too, since 1997, is Environment, under the title of the Department of Environment, Transport and the Regions (DETR).[1] Likewise, when the Department of Health and Social Security split in 1989, the Solicitor to the new Department of Social Security continued to provide legal services for the Department of Health, and he has since taken over TSol's former role in providing litigation services in health matters.

The general cast of mind in government that favours privatization, contracting-out, and the separation of policy from administration through the creation of executive agencies is likely to produce at best suspicion, at worst hostility, should proposals for further centralization of services *within* government be offered. The remit given to Sir Robert Andrew's review in 1988 pointed clearly towards privatization or contracting-out, asking how the legal service needed by government could most economically and effectively be provided and organized in the light of those policies (Andrew 1989: 5). In fact, as we have seen, he found little fresh scope for this, certainly not in terms of value for money (above, p. 213). He heard strong pleas for centralization (Andrew 1989: 34); but even the compromise he offered was considerably watered down (above, p. 216). 'New public management' has since arrived in legal services in a variety of ways which we shall explore (see below, Chapter 9), the most notable being the constitution of TSol as an executive agency, but a TSol which must continue to co-exist with a number of powerful departmental legal services.

III THE CURRENT STRUCTURE OF LEGAL SERVICES

1 The Treasury Solicitor's Department

The Treasury Solicitor's Department is the principal central legal department in England and Wales. It provides all the legal services (other than drafting of primary legislation) required by a number of departments (see sect. 6 below), and some of the services used by almost all others. It is the government's main litigator, handling most domestic civil litigation and

[1] Transport, as a separate department, was serviced by TSol from 1983 to 1997.

having exclusive, United Kingdom-wide, competence in European Community litigation; the government's conveyancer, through the Government Property Lawyers, an executive agency of TSol; and the legal adviser to the central Departments of government (Cabinet Office, Treasury).

The head of the Department is the Treasury Solicitor, whose office, as we have seen, has existed since the middle of the seventeenth century. One hundred and twenty-two years after the Jessel Committee described him as 'head of [the] class' of departmental solicitors (above, p. 215), he was in 1989 formally recognized as Head of the Government Legal Service (GLS) (see 145 HC Debs., cols. *262–3*, written answers 19 January 1989). As such he is responsible for the career structure of lawyers throughout this service, being assisted in this by the Lawyers' Management Unit (LMU) set up after the Andrew Report. GLS includes a number of lawyers who work outside what are ordinarily thought of as government departments, such as the lawyers employed by regulators like OFWAT and OFTEL, and it excludes many who do work in central government: thus it does not extend to Scotland or Northern Ireland; it does not include the Parliamentary Counsel Office (PCO) or the Crown Prosecution Service (CPS) (though it does include the Serious Fraud Office (SFO)); nor does it cover Foreign and Commonwealth Office lawyers who, in common with most other FCO staff, are not part of the Home Civil Service at all, but of the Diplomatic Service. None the less, its career competences mean that GLS has much more significance, as a career group within the civil service, than does the similarly-titled Government Accountancy Service (above, pp. 137–9). GLS still works, however, essentially by co-ordination and advice, with LMU functioning as a repository of information (it holds, for example, CVs of all GLS lawyers) and provider of services (for example, in organizing common recruitment exercises for GLS departments and internal promotion competitions). This role of Head of GLS is seen in departments as involving functions quite distinct from those of the Treasury Solicitor. LMU formally became part of TSol in 1997, but as a self-standing unit with distinct objectives which 'supports the TS in his role as Head of the Government Legal Service' (Lord Chancellor's and Law Officers' Departments 1996: 66).

Until 31 March 1996 TSol could properly be described as a non-ministerial department. The Treasury Solicitor was legally constituted as a corporation sole by the Treasury Solicitor Act 1876, essentially for the purposes of his functions in relation to unclaimed estates. The Attorney-General was answerable to Parliament for the efficiency and effectiveness of TSol, an arrangement formalized, following the Andrew Report, by a nomenclature under which TSol, along with the Crown

Prosecution Service, the Serious Fraud Office, and the Legal Secretariat to the Law Officers, would henceforward be known as the 'Law Officers' Departments' (see 145 HC Debs., cols. *262–3*, written answers 19 January 1989). Yet he was not its ministerial head as, say, was the Home Secretary in respect of the Home Office. Decisions in TSol were not taken in the Attorney-General's name, nor did he even have the power of appointment of the Treasury Solicitor; this rested with the Lords Commissioners of the Treasury, the Attorney-General being one of the ministers consulted.

On 1 April 1996 TSol became an executive agency. This was expected to produce significant change in the internal culture of the department, by reason of the need to establish a clear corporate and business plan, to market-test services, and to develop performance indicators such as recovery of full operating costs, reductions in unit costs, evidence of levels of customer satisfaction, and minimum levels of chargeable hours (Lord Chancellor's and Law Officers' Departments 1996: 67; Treasury Solicitor's Department 1996). Even in advance of obtaining agency status, however, TSol acted on a commercial basis in the sense that it billed departments for its services much as a firm of solicitors would (including the charging of VAT).[2] TSol is thus a likely candidate for the operation of a net running costs regime (above, pp. 188–90). Agency status involves the creation of a ministerial Advisory Board, set up to oversee the agency on behalf of the supervising minister, who remains the Attorney-General. Ordinarily such a Board would include the Permanent Secretary of the department, but since the Attorney-General, as we shall see, has no department of his own (below, p. 222–3), the initial composition of the Board is an appointee from the private sector, the Permanent Secretary to the Lord Chancellor's Department, and the Treasury Solicitor himself. The Board meets three times yearly and reports to the Attorney-General through his Legal Secretary.

Agency status is as likely to make TSol's relationship with the Attorney-General closer as to put more distance between them. The Attorney-General's ministerial responsibilities are not affected, though he follows the now standard practice for executive agencies of referring written Parliamentary Questions for reply by the Treasury Solicitor as Chief Executive of the agency, and is responsible for the appointment of

[2] In the interest of fair competition between public and private suppliers, and of the protection of the revenue, there exist elaborate rules determining when government departments must charge VAT for services they provide, including services to other government departments, and when government departments in receipt of services, including services provided by other departments, may reclaim the VAT they have paid. See Value Added Tax Act 1994, s. 41, and for their current application, *London Gazette* April 1, 1993 as amended April 12, 1996, and June 21, 1996. Legal services provided by one department to another attract VAT, but this VAT can be reclaimed from Customs and Excise. Allocations of funds to government departments take these VAT liabilities into account.

the Treasury Solicitor as Chief Executive. Agency status may, perhaps, more accurately reflect the relationship, notably by emphasizing the operational independence of TSol within the framework of the Attorney-General's supervision. As the latter put it to the Scott Inquiry, 'I would not expect . . . anybody in my small team to start jumping in and either second-guessing or substituting themselves for, for example, here Treasury Solicitor's Department *qua* instructing solicitor on PII [public interest immunity]' (Scott 1996: paras. G13.123–4). The status may also emphasize the fact that responsibility for asking for and using the services of TSol lawyers lies with the departments it serves, and that it is their departmental ministers who are responsible to Parliament for the decisions they take in the light of its advice, not the Attorney-General. Oddities, however, remain. The Government Property Lawyers are a unique example of an agency within an agency. The funding for the Legal Secretariat to the Law Officers (which used to be known until 1989 as the 'Law Officers' Department') is carried on the TSol vote; it is unusual for an executive agency thus to fund the officials closest to its supervising minister.

TSol's internal organization reflects its particularly close relationship with those departments for which it provides the full range of legal services. Thus it has separate advisory divisions for Culture, Media and Sport; Defence; Education and Employment; the Cabinet Office; and Treasury. Other divisions include the Government Property Lawyers, constituted as an executive agency and undertaking conveyancing for all departments on a competitive basis; and a Bona Vacantia division, dealing with a specific responsibility of the Treasury Solicitor to administer the Crown's prerogative in relation to unclaimed estates and other property. Most important for our purposes, perhaps, are the two further divisions dealing respectively with TSol's general responsibilities for European matters and for litigation. The first of these, European Division, we deal with in detail in Chapter 9. The second, Litigation Division, conducts civil and criminal litigation not only for TSol's regular client departments but also for a number of others (below, p. 223). As such it represents the main repository of expertise in civil litigation within government, a situation of especial importance today in the light of the dramatic growth in the volume and range of legal challenges to government action in recent years. TSol was a pioneer in attempting to communicate this expertise to administrators in a form which they could use in their own decision-making, through its 'child's guide' to judicial review, *The Judge over your Shoulder* (1987; 1995). Departmental legal services have followed suit in seeking to raise legal awareness by publications of this kind (below, p. 227–8).

2 The Parliamentary Counsel Office

The other central legal department providing services is the Parliamentary Counsel Office (PCO), responsible for the drafting of all government-sponsored legislation in England and Wales. Parliamentary Counsel also provide advice and support as government Bills pass through Parliament. In addition, they draft or vet a certain amount of delegated legislation (below, pp. 259–60). The Office has expanded substantially in recent years, and now numbers thirty-eight draftsmen, who generally work in Bill teams of two, one senior, one junior. At its head is First Parliamentary Counsel, who is appointed by the Prime Minister and enjoys Permanent Secretary rank. Lines of responsibility, and of accountability to Parliament for the Office, are complex. In terms of finance and management, the Office forms part of the Cabinet Office complex, for which the Prime Minister as Minister for the Civil Service is responsible. The Cabinet Secretary is its Accounting Officer. This fits with PCO's conception of itself: 'Serving the Cabinet, i.e. ministers collectively, is what we do.' In the Office's day-to-day work, its relationship with the departments whose Bills it drafts may be seen in professional terms as one of provider and client. Unlike TSol, the Office does not charge departments for its service. Constitutionally, the departmental minister is responsible for the results of PCO's work on his Bills much as he is responsible for action taken on the advice of his departmental legal service.

The Office also answers to, and advises, the President of the Council, the minister responsible for the government's legislative programme, and the current chair of the Cabinet's Legislation Committee. The Office is not one of the Law Officers' Departments, though a transfer of general responsibility to the Attorney-General has been suggested both by the Andrew Report (1989: 33) and the Hansard Commission (Hansard Society 1992: 51), partly as a means of giving ministers a clear channel of recourse if they are dissatisfied with PCO's performance on their Bills. It does, however, keep the Attorney-General and the Lord Chancellor fully briefed on the legislation it drafts and may call for the Attorney's intervention in the event of disagreements over legal policy with its departmental clients (as indeed may the departments themselves). We deal fully with its work in Chapter 8.

3 The Crown Prosecution Service and the Serious Fraud Office

The Crown Prosecution Service was established in 1986, under the Prosecution of Offences Act 1985, to take responsibility for most public prosecutions in England and Wales, on a pattern already long established in Scotland. It is headed by the Director of Public Prosecutions (DPP), an office dating back to 1879 which has always had close links with the Attorney-General (Prosecution of Offences Act 1879, s. 2; Edwards 1984). The creation of CPS has of course radically changed the role of the DPP, from a specialized office dealing with serious and sensitive crime either in general or by virtue of special statutory competences to one of managing the entire criminal prosecution system. Special arrangements were made under the Criminal Justice Act 1987, Part I, for the prosecution of serious fraud, and the SFO, with its own Director, was set up in that year. Its remit extends to England and Wales and Northern Ireland (but not Scotland). The DPP and the Director of SFO are both appointed by the Attorney-General, though from 1879 to 1985 power to appoint the DPP resided in the Home Secretary (Edwards 1984: 7–11). CPS and SFO are both 'Law Officers' Departments', but the role of the Attorney-General is, as we shall see (below, pp. 287–90), one of statutory superintendence rather than hierarchical authority on the usual Departmental pattern. Unlike TSol, they are not executive agencies, though they 'operate on Next Steps lines' (above, p. 38 n. 2).

4 The Legal Secretariat to the Law Officers

The Attorney-General is the senior of the two English Law Officers and the government's 'chief legal adviser' (Attorney-General's Chambers 1996*a*: 1). Despite this pre-eminent position in the field of legal services, the Attorney-General (who is assisted by a second minister, the Solicitor-General) does not head a ministerial department in any conventional sense. We have seen that the proposal of the Andrew Report to give him one, with the Treasury Solicitor as its Permanent Secretary, was not accepted (above, p. 216), but that his supervisory responsibilities were subsequently formalized by referring to the relevant departments (TSol, CPS, SFO, and the Legal Secretariat) as the 'Law Officers' Departments'. Bracketing the Legal Secretariat (which was formerly known simply as the 'Law Officers' Department') together with these other bodies may be misleading. The Secretariat is a small group of lawyers (currently a dozen or so) and supporting staff which works directly to the Attorney-General and Solicitor-General and functions much as would a minister's private office elsewhere (Andrew 1989: 14; Silkin 1979: xxviii). Its legal staff are normally all on secondment from TSol or other Departments. They do not function, as do civil servants elsewhere, as the *alter ego* of the Attorney-General, under the *Carltona* principle (above, p. 40). The Attorney-General acts personally, though the Solicitor-General may, since 1997, exercise any of his functions, statutory or other (Law Officers Act 1997), without the need for the case-by-case delegation previously required under the Law Officers Act 1944. We trace the evolution of the Legal Secretariat in more detail below, as part of our discussion of the work of the Law Officers.

5 Law reform

General responsibility for law reform in England and Wales rests with the Law Commission, which is a central function but is chaired by a judge and acts independently of ministers (Andrew 1989: 13–14; Law Commissions Act 1965). Each department will, however, have responsibility for the reform of the law within its specific sphere of competence and in implementation of departmental policy, and the Home Office has a particular concern with reform of criminal law and justice, and a distinct Criminal Law Revision Committee to advise it. The function of considering what changes are needed in the law is, therefore, widely disseminated among lawyers in government.

6 Departmental legal services

The most helpful way of classifying the legal services of ministerial departments is to indicate the extent to which they rely on the services of the Treasury Solicitor's Department. On this criterion departments may be divided into three classes:

—those for which TSol provides all services: currently these are the Treasury; the Cabinet Office; the Department for Education and Employment (DfEE); the Department of Culture, Media and Sport; and the Ministry of Defence. Its services to DfEE, MoD, and Treasury are provided by means of outstations located in those departments;

—those for which it provides services of litigation and conveyancing only: these are currently the Departments of Environment, Transport and the Regions, and of Trade and Industry (though the latter does its own criminal prosecutions, in relation to company law and insolvency offences and related matters), the Home Office, the Foreign and Commonwealth Office, and the Welsh Office;

—those which do all their own legal work save for conveyancing: currently these are Customs and Excise; Inland Revenue (which does some specialized conveyancing of its own and contracts out the rest to private firms, not the Government Property Lawyers); the Ministry of Agriculture, Fisheries and Food; and the Departments of Health and of Social Security. These last two share a common Solicitor's Office.

The range of legal work undertaken by legal services of departments in these second and third categories is wide. It includes legal advice on the whole gamut of departmental business; preparing instructions for legislative draftsmen;[3] drafting subordinate legislation; ordinary commercial-type legal work; and in departments with a litigation section, undertaking criminal prosecution work, sometimes of considerable volume, as with Customs and Excise and Social Security; representing the department in tribunal hearings; and civil litigation. The largest of these legal services, that of Customs and Excise, had a complement of 97 lawyers in 1996; in early 1997 TSol's lawyers numbered 177.

Given the variation in their size and in their range of work—to say nothing of their traditions of independence—it should not be surprising to find that no two of these departmental legal services are organized in the same way. In 1995–96 the two largest services, Customs and Excise and DSS/DH, were both extensively reorganized in the interests of greater efficiency (and in the case of Customs and Excise, after a Fundamental Expenditure Review exercise (above, p. 110) following up an internal review conducted by the Solicitor's Office). The Customs reorganization produced a structure with three groups: the first dealing with advice on customs and international, VAT and excise matters, preparation of legislation, and tribunal work; the second with all corporate affairs of Customs and Excise itself, including personnel issues, civil litigation, and judicial review; and the third (the largest) with prosecutions (including criminal policy advisory work). There is also an administration section. Customs and Excise has a large staff spread around the country (known as the 'Outfield'), and legal services reflect this, with some members from all three groups operating from Manchester.

In the Departments of Health (DH) and of Social Security (DSS), where the Solicitor's Office has the status of a Headquarters Group within DSS, the reorganization followed a Senior Management Review, and produced what the Office has itself described, in an internal document (1996), as 'a legal practice with two legislative/policy-supporting wings (one serving DSS, one DH) and several enterprises in between which serve DSS and DH jointly': prosecutions, commercial law advice (with industrial tribunal work divided between these two), and civil litigation (including judicial review). The equivalent of the Customs and Excise administration unit is a Practice Management Group. The Solicitor also has 'stewardship' functions in relation to independent statutory bodies such as the Independent Tribunal Service, the Office of the Pensions Ombudsman, and the Central Adjudication Services. His role is to provide assurance to the Department's Accounting Officer regarding the expenditure of voted money on and by these bodies. His functions

[3] See Ch. 8 below, and note that in the Inland Revenue and the Northern Ireland Civil Service instructions are drafted by the responsible administrators, not the departmental lawyers.

involve reviewing and monitoring their expenditure and performance, approving their business plans, and so on.

While there are some important differences here, such as the different location of tribunal work in the two departments and the close association, in Customs and Excise, of criminal advisory work with prosecution practice, it is worth noting the similarity of overall pattern in the two services, notwithstanding the fact that the Solicitor to DSS deals with two distinct departments (with considerable differences of subject-matter and of administrative style), and also with two of the largest executive agencies, the Benefits Agency and the Child Support Agency. We shall see that the existence of agencies has relevance to the way legal services work (below, pp. 332–4), but it does not appear to have impinged on general structures.

The other 'full service' departments, the Ministry of Agriculture, Fisheries and Food (MAFF), and Inland Revenue, follow different approaches, having more in common with the structure of the TSol, albeit on a smaller scale. MAFF's fifty or so lawyers are organized in two main groups, one of which is concerned with legal tasks across the department, such as prosecutions, while the other is functionally organized, to cover different areas of departmental concern such as health or animal welfare. The division is not a rigorous one: the first, 'horizontal' group covers fisheries, while the functional group deals with the department's concerns with European Court of Justice cases. A small number of lawyers are outstationed with bodies like the department's Animal Health Group. The Inland Revenue takes this functional principle further, with most of its lawyers working in subject-related teams, each covering a range of topics or a specialized function, and undertaking all types of work (notably including both advice and litigation, often involving advocacy work) within that area.

Another area of variation is to be found in the position of the Solicitor's or Legal Adviser's Office within the department as a whole. Though the heads of each of the legal offices in departments with their own services are alike in ranking directly below Permanent Secretaries in the Senior Civil Service structure (the Treasury Solicitor, DPP, and First Parliamentary Counsel have Permanent Secretary rank), the degree to which they may participate in the general management of the department, and the range of responsibilities they undertake, will vary. The Solicitor to Customs and Excise is a member of its statutory governing Board, and as such participates in general discussions at the highest levels of the department. Inland Revenue, likewise a non-ministerial department, has a structure similar to Customs and Excise, but here the Solicitor is not a member of the Board: he participates, however, in weekly 'Deputies' meetings attended by Board members. In more orthodox departments under direct ministerial control, the Solicitor or Legal Adviser will commonly be a member of the department's management board or other top management structure, and will have a reporting line direct to the Permanent Secretary. 'Ministers have collectively recognised that their legal advisers must be involved in the development of policy in order to minimise the risk of adverse judicial review of administrative decisions' (Attorney-General 1991: 3). Beyond this, however, it is difficult to generalize about departmental lawyers' input—otherwise than through responding to requests for advice—into policy-making, even at the highest level.

Some heads of legal services may have additional responsibilities. We have noted the 'stewardship' role of the Solicitor to DSS; for his part, the Solicitor to the DTI has responsibilities going beyond legal services, being the Head of DTI's Investigations Division, which conducts company investigations (and has a significantly larger staff—250 or so—than the Solicitor's Office proper—about 70 lawyers and 40 support staff), and of a Business Law Unit which has policy responsibility for international business law and co-ordinates the Department's legislative programme. The Solicitor and Legal Adviser to the Department of the Environment, Transport and the Regions oversees two administrative divisions in the Department, one responsible for servicing its Management Board, for central policy initiatives, and for 'change management', the other for liaison with the Health and Safety Commission and Executive, which now falls within DETR's responsibilities.

The financial situation of departmental legal services also varies across Whitehall. We have seen that TSol, as a central service department, charges its 'client' departments for its work. Conveyancing and litigation are charged on a 'billable hours' basis; advisory services to those departments which rely wholly on TSol are remunerated by agreed annual payments; but in all cases, as noted, VAT will be payable. This approach is to varying degrees followed in departments having their own legal services, as a matter of internal financial control. At the DTI, 'hard charging', under which the charges made by the Solicitor's Office for its work actually determine the funding available to it, was introduced in 1995, simultaneously with a degree of freedom for administrators to look elsewhere for legal advice. (The freedom is in fact quite heavily circumscribed, in part by the Attorney-General's veto on contracting out core work (above, pp. 213–14), in part by a variety of control and advisory functions reserved to the Solicitor, including the power to say what is and is not core work.)

No other department has gone as far as this. The DSS/DH Solicitor's Office works on the basis of service level agreements with the agencies in DSS and DH such as the Contributions Agency, the Benefits Agency, and the Child Support Agency, which account for a substantial proportion of its work; funding is fixed annually in relation to these service levels, and a form of 'hard charging' appears if an agency wants work done beyond what has been specified. The Office is also moving towards 'hard charging' for DH work. Other offices are more conventionally funded: the Solicitor to Customs and Excise, for example, agrees annually, with the Chairman of the Board of Customs and Excise, the level of the budget and, in global terms, what this will cover; time recording has only just been introduced, but might be a first step towards more explicit charging arrangements. In the Home Office, the smallest of the separate legal services with only eighteen lawyers, the Legal Adviser's Branch is only a part of a larger 'services' group for budgetary purposes, and shares in any cuts imposed on that group, regardless of its relative workload. Again there is at present no recording within the Branch of time spent on particular matters, though this is expected to follow necessarily from the introduction of resource accounting across government, and would make possible a switch to a 'hard charging' approach.

'Hard charging', along with possibilities of contracting out, can be seen both as a means of matching legal resources more closely to a department's legal needs, and of alerting administrators (and indeed legal services themselves) to the real costs of legal advice, both generally and from different providers. The introduction (or consideration) of these charges has been accompanied by careful attention to the risk that they might inhibit the readiness of administrators to take legal advice. When DTI introduced 'hard charging' the President of the Board of Trade, then Michael Heseltine, warned that civil servants would still be 'culpable' if they did not seek legal advice in appropriate circumstances, a view reflected in instructions on the new regime jointly circulated by the DTI Finance Department and Solicitor's Office. This particular minister was perhaps unusually sensitive to the need for convincing legal advice of high quality (Scott 1996: paras. G13.59–71, and G18.97–100; Defence Committee 1986), but the idea that cost should not be the determining factor in any decision to seek legal advice or take legal action appears to be widely shared, by administrators no less than by ministers and by lawyers themselves. Greater importance should probably be attached here to more general attitudinal factors: awareness by administrators of the legal context in which they work, the degree to which legal considerations permeate administrative decision-making in a department or a particular part of it, and the consequent confidence (or lack of it) of administrators in handling legal material; and the attitude of administrators to the running of legal risks.

We look at all these issues in Chapter 10. Here, however, it may be useful to finish this description of departmental legal services by pointing to the growing tendency for them to issue general guidance to administrators about the services they provide and how best to use them. At least four legal services now publish such guidance: DETR (Legal Directorate, DoE, *Is it Legal? How to use your Lawyer* (1997)); DSS/DH (The Solicitor's Office, DSS/DH, *How to get The Best out of Your Lawyer* (1994)); DTI, *A Guide to the Solicitor's Office* (1995)); Home Office, Legal Adviser's Branch, *Getting the best out of your lawyer* (1995)). These combine very basic legal information—'Delegated legislation . . . is not capable of being passed subject to amendments' (DSS/DH 1994: 29); 'The European Treaties and legislation made by European Union institutions can have the force of law within the UK without further domestic legislation' (DTI 1995: 11)—with description of what the legal service does, statements of approved practice—such as when it will be appropriate for the department to use external legal advice or to make a reference to the Law Officers, or whom to consult in relation to delegated legislation—and practical guidance—such as who should ask for advice and how, and how long to allow for the preparation of statutory instruments or the obtaining of counsel's advice. They may be seen as complementing advice like that prepared by TSol on judicial review, *The Judge over your Shoulder* (Treasury Solicitor's Department 1987, 1995). In so far as they present, in a departmental context, guidance centrally generated (for example by the Cabinet Office, below, pp. 204, 303), they provide valuable evidence of departmental lawyers' attitudes to it and of the way it is effectively disseminated through government.

7 Scotland and Wales

Arrangements in Scotland have long been different, partly by reason of the distinctive character of Scots law and the Scottish legal system, partly as the result of the way devolved administration has developed in Scotland (Andrew 1989: 80–4). The legislative devolution currently (1999) in train will of course accentuate the special characteristics of government in Scotland, with most Scottish Office functions being transferred to the new Scottish administration responsible not to Parliament at Westminster but to the Scottish Parliament. This will be a new kind of executive, not necessarily operating according to the same rules as those of the United Kingdom government, and we do not seek to explore here how its legal services will be organized. The pre-devolution position may be briefly summarized as follows.

The broad range of activities of the Scottish Office (with Agriculture, Environment and Fisheries; Development; Education and Industry; Health; and Home Departments) means that the Solicitor to the Secretary of State for Scotland performs what would in England be a multi-departmental role. The organization of the Solicitor's Office reflects this, with four client-based divisions each dealing with the work of one or more departments, and three divisions dealing with specific legal functions such as conveyancing, contracts, employment, and litigation (Solicitor to the Secretary of State for Scotland 1997). In addition, some Great Britain departments, such as DSS, the Home Office, and DTI, use the Office for their Scottish work, though others use private solicitors or the Lord Advocate's Department or—the case of the Inland Revenue—have their own Scottish branch. The Office is treated for budgetary purposes as part of the Scottish Home Department, operating under an annual grant rather than a charging system. It does, however, seek to charge Great Britain departments for its services, but since the Treasury has been unwilling to install a net running costs regime in respect of the Office's work (above, pp. 188–90), it cannot apply the payments to increase its staffing for this purpose, so that there is a disincentive to continue offering such services. Their withdrawal might, of course, have the effect of further weakening the coherence of Scottish legal advice on United Kingdom matters.

Scotland has its own Law Officers, the Lord Advocate and the Solicitor-General for Scotland, who will, with devolution, become part of the Scottish apparatus of government. There will be an Advocate General for Scotland as a United Kingdom Minister (below, p. 236). The Parliamentary Draftsmen for Scotland, who draft purely or mainly Scottish Bills as well as the Scottish provisions of British or United Kingdom Bills, form part of the Lord Advocate's Department; indeed, the First Parliamentary Draftsman for Scotland is also the Lord Advocate's Legal Secretary. The Scottish equivalent of the Crown Prosecutor is the Procurator Fiscal, an office of much greater antiquity in Scotland—its origins can be dated to the sixteenth century—whose holders are organized into a prosecution service—the Crown Office—headed by a senior, legally-qualified civil servant, the Crown Agent, and under the direction of the Lord Advocate, to whom the Crown Agent is responsible (Paterson and Bates 1993: 73–82). Along with the Scottish Courts Administration, for which he has joint responsibility with the Secretary of State for Scotland, the Lord Advocate's Department and the Crown Office comprise the 'Lord Advocate's Departments'. Scotland has its own Law Commission.

Welsh devolution will produce comparable effects against a less complex background. The Welsh Office, like the Scottish Office, has multi-functional territorial competences, which shape the work of its legal advisers, but the absence of a distinct Welsh legal system means that in other respects, the work is not different from that of Great Britain departments' legal services.

8. Northern Ireland

The structure for Northern Ireland is also distinctive, reflecting the existence of a separate Northern Ireland Government which continued notwithstanding the disappearance of a Northern Ireland legislature as a result of the introduction of direct rule by the Northern Ireland Constitution Act 1973 (Andrew 1989: 84–9), and which will now, under the Northern Ireland Act 1998, be responsible to the new Northern Ireland legislative assembly. Thus United Kingdom supervision of Northern Ireland affairs is the responsibility of the Northern Ireland Office, which gets its legal advice, for historical reasons, from the Home Office. The Northern Ireland departments themselves, however, have a centralized legal service, but one divided between advisory work, done very largely by the Departmental Legal Service of the Department of Finance and Personnel, and civil litigation, done normally by the Crown Solicitor for Northern Ireland. While the Head of the Service is responsible ultimately to the Secretary of State for Northern Ireland, the Crown Solicitor is appointed by the Attorney-General, acting as Attorney-General for Northern Ireland. Northern Ireland has its own Office of Legislative Draftsmen, its own Director of Public Prosecutions, and a Law Reform Office which functions not as an independent statutory commission but as a branch of the Department of Finance and Personnel.

9 General comments

The structure we have described appears as a 'mixed' system of departmentally and centrally provided legal services. The existence of central elements should not, however, hide from view the fact that these services, whether departmental or central, are in almost all cases provided to departments, and not to the government as a whole. A department such as the Treasury functions as an agency of co-ordination or control on behalf of the whole government, and some legal advice (notably, advice by TSol on European legal matters) is given direct to Cabinet Office, to the Prime Minister, or (by the Attorney-General and the Lord Advocate) to Cabinet itself. Otherwise, legal advice and other legal services are an input to decisions taken in departments in the context of departmental agendas, concerns, constraints, styles, and politics. This is as true of the Litigation Division of TSol as of any departmental legal service. The Scott Report on Iraq arms exports referred sympathetically to the difficulties under which the Division laboured in the *Matrix Churchill* case, in seeking to prepare for counsel a brief on public interest immunity, when the departments for which it was working had quite different views, ranging from a strong desire, at

FCO, to disclose nothing, to an equally strong one in the President of the Board of Trade that some material, at least, should not be the subject of a public interest immunity certificate. The Treasury Solicitor and counsel, said Scott, were placed in 'an impossible position' (Scott 1996: paras. G13.104–22, especially at G13.119).

The implications of this departmentalism for 'legality' within government are important. First, the majority of government lawyers are civil servants of departments, serving the department's ministers, and probably still see themselves primarily as such, rather than as 'government lawyers'. Their ideas of legality are developed within the framework of an advice function whose confidentiality is protected by the double veil of ministerial responsibility on the one hand, and legal professional privilege on the other. Legal advice, along with law enforcement, is one of the very few areas for which government has proposed *complete* exclusion from Freedom of Information legislation (Chancellor of the Duchy of Lancaster 1997: paras. 2.21–2.22; Public Administration Committee 1998*a*: Report, paras. 31–2). The scope for public testing of these ideas is therefore limited, in ways we explore more fully below (pp. 340–4). Second, the fact that any common, or *governmental,* sense of 'legality' must be articulated and made operative through the advice and actions of a number of different groups of departmental legal advisers places a heavy burden on processes of dissemination of opinion and co-ordination of approach among legal advisers, coupled with whatever central powers of control the system may offer. The Scott Report may be read as suggesting that these processes and powers have little force; this is an impression we test in Chapter 9. To conclude our structural survey, however, we need to look more closely at the history and status of the Law Officers, the most visible agents of central control and co-ordination.

IV THE LAW OFFICERS: HISTORY AND STATUS

1 The English Law Officers

Anyone who relishes the United Kingdom constitution's capacity to contain contradictions should take a look at the position of the Attorney-General. Here is a politically-appointed minister who must act 'wholly independently of Government' in performing some of his major functions (in criminal prosecutions) (Attorney-General's Chambers 1996); an officer who on appointment receives a summons to attend on the House of Lords which it would be constitutionally improper for him, as a member of the Commons, to obey (Jones 1969: 43–4); a minister responsible to Parliament for the conduct of not one, but several departments (the 'Law Officers' Departments'), but who has no department of his own; a minister who has as one of his main roles the function of chief legal adviser to the government, but who is not responsible to Parliament for this advice, which is treated as strictly confidential not just as to its content, but even as to its existence (below, pp. 309–13). The constitution must accommodate these contradictions; the Attorney must day by day straddle a bewildering range of roles: not just as chief legal adviser to the government and superintendent of criminal prosecutions, but as protector of charities; as representative of the public interest in such areas as relator actions and contempt of court; as occasional adviser to Parliament; and as the Head of the Bar of England and Wales. And until 1992, when a Minister of State was appointed, the Attorney-General also answered in the Commons for administration of justice matters on behalf of the Lord Chancellor, though taking no ministerial responsibility for his decisions. Every so often the discomfort of this position is made apparent when public controversies erupt around actions of the Attorney-General: the *Campbell* prosecution in 1924 (Edwards 1964: 199–225; Edwards 1984: 310–18); the *Gouriet* action in 1977 (*Gouriet v Union of Post Office Workers;* Edwards 1984: 129–46; Rawlinson 1977; Archer 1978: 15–18); the *Matrix Churchill* inquiry in 1996 (Scott 1996; Bradley 1996; Birkinshaw 1996: 422). How did the Attorney-General come to occupy this position? and what is its significance for our theme?

The Attorney-General's office, under that title, dates back to 1461 (Shawcross 1953: 4; Edwards 1964: 27; Jones 1969: 43; Archer 1978: 3, however, suggests 1315), though the function of acting in litigation as the general or regular attorney to the King had developed over the previous two centuries. 1461 was also the date when his 'political' functions clearly began, with a summons to the House of Lords to advise on legal matters. The title of Solicitor-General was first used in the same year (Edwards 1964: 27), and whatever his role before this time, he was then seen as effectively the number two to the Attorney, the role he has played ever since. The difference of title has nothing to do with the division between the two branches of the legal profession, and both Attorney-General and Solicitor-General have always been members of the English Bar. The Solicitor has no special area of competence defined either by convention or statute; while generally providing support for the Attorney, he may from time to time be given specific jobs to do within government. Sir Geoffrey Howe, when Solicitor-General, was entrusted with the preparation and parliamentary passage of the European Communities Act 1972 and other major legislation (Howe 1994: 55–69); a recent successor was charged, *inter alia*, with the handling of 'green issues' in the Law Officers' Departments, such as recycling waste paper and saving water (Lord Chancellor's and Law Officers' Departments 1995: 64). The Solicitor may also exercise any statutory or other powers of the Attorney (Law Officers Act 1997). Given the lack of any distinctiveness in the Solicitor's functions, we shall speak no further of him, but refer to the Attorney-General or to the Law Officers as appropriate.

From the time of his first appearance until around the time of the Reform Acts the Attorney-General was seen as having a peculiarly close relationship with the Crown: one that led to great parliamentary suspicion of holders of the office, whose acceptability as members of the House of Commons (even if they were sitting there prior to appointment) was not clearly established until 1670 (Edwards 1964: 35–8). By 1688 membership was, however, expected, and it became the custom, until 1832, for the Treasury to lay out £500 to purchase a seat for any appointee who did not have one (ibid.: 38 n.). Throughout this period Attorneys-General performed the functions of Crown prosecutor with a vigour often thought excessive, earning themselves such epithets as the 'bloodhounds' (Shawcross 1953: 3) or 'bulldogs' (Jones 1969: 44) of the Crown, or (this as late as the beginning of the nineteenth century) as 'a sort of Ministerial spy . . . whose business it is to ferret out and prosecute all who either by their actions or writings are endeavouring to misplace the personages to whom he is indebted for his situation or who are attempting to promote any reform in the system they support' (Shawcross 1953: 3, who does not cite his source).

At some time in the nineteenth century the Law Officers managed a remarkable transformation from ferocious prosecutors to eminent legal advisers whose objectivity was guaranteed by their position in the highest reaches of the Bar, a position they maintained through continuing in private practice even while occupying their state functions. How far individuals managed to accommodate both sets of qualities, and how far the change was due simply to the consolidation of parliamentary democracy and to changes in the conduct of politics consequent upon the enlargement of the franchise, are matters which remain obscure. Even as these characteristics of professional independence were being established, countervailing pressures were arising from the increasing volume of advisory business being brought to the Law Officers from departments. An embarrassing argument about remuneration broke out in the eighteen-seventies, and was the first matter taken up by the Jessel review of government legal business. In 1871 a Treasury Minute, reflected in the Law Officers' Fees Act 1872, had put their pay on a new footing, whereby fees were only paid for contentious business, while non-contentious work was remunerated by a fixed salary. The Jessel Committee heard loud complaints from the Attorney-General,

Baggallay, that the consequence had been a large increase in non-contentious business, much of it of a trivial nature and some of it improperly so classified (Edwards 1964: 82–6; Jessel 1877: 3–59, esp. at Evidence, qq. 162–81). The situation was improved by a new Treasury Minute in 1875, implementing the Committee's recommendation that the scope of 'contentious business' should be clarified and somewhat enlarged (Edwards 1964: 88).

The remuneration issue was, however, only a symptom of the underlying tension between a conception of Law Officers as detached professionals and a contrasting view of them as full ministerial participants in government, at the service—for legal matters—of the other departments of state (Edwards 1964: 85–6): 'servants of servants', in the phrase of the nineteenth-century commentator cited by Shawcross (1953: 3). The tone of Baggallay's evidence to the Jessel Committee was much more like that of an aggrieved contractor with Government than of a participant in its decisions. Since then, however, it is the second of these views that has steadily gained ground (though its proponents, including several Attorneys-General, have not necessarily phrased it in this way). In 1894 the Law Officers lost the right to engage in private practice (Archer 1978: 3); in 1893 they obtained, following a Treasury Minute, a staff of four clerks (incorporating their own two chambers clerks) with a view to bringing some order into their government work and the recording of it. The staff slowly grew in subsequent decades, though an increase (to four), and the creation of the post of Legal Secretary, were only obtained in 1931 in return for the Law Officers' accepting a reduction in their own salaries (Edwards 1964: 141–6, 151). Today the professional establishment of the Legal Secretariat to the Law Officers stands at 12. We have seen that the Andrew Report's recommendation that the Attorney-General should become a full-fledged departmental minister, presiding over a Law Officers' Department incorporating TSol, CPS, SFO, and the Legal Secretariat, with the Treasury Solicitor as Permanent Secretary according to the usual departmental pattern, was too radical to find acceptance; but the *de facto* growth in the Attorney-General's Ministerial responsibilities, in the sense of formal superintendence of criminal law enforcement and of TSol, was signalled by the new collective title of 'Law Officers' Departments' adopted in 1989 (above, p. 218–19). Contrast this with the position as late as 1978, when the Attorney-General could say that 'the Law Officers have no Ministerial responsibilities in the wide sense in which their two colleagues [the Lord Chancellor and the Home Secretary] have them' (Silkin 1979: xxviii).

The lack of formal responsibilities and hierarchical authority, particularly towards what is now GLS, should not be taken to imply a history of indifference. If we look back at the century-long series of stand-offs which constitute the process of reform and development of government legal provision (above, pp. 214–17), we find that it is intervention by the Attorney-General which has sometimes (not always) been the most proximate cause of further enquiry. In this century, the Treasury Solicitor appears to have been the prime mover for change (Drewry 1981: 21–3), but it was the Attorney-General's interventions at ministerial level, grounded essentially in concerns about levels of recruitment and retention of legal service staff, which were responsible for the setting up both of the Barlow Committee in 1943 (Drewry 1981: 23) and of the Andrew Review in 1988 (Andrew 1989: 5). Both of these inquiries produced some improvements on the pay front, but as we have already noted their suggestions for more far-reaching structural changes, which would have benefited the unity of the government legal service and must thereby have strengthened the position of the Attorney-General, were in each case emasculated by departmental opposition. Even so, the position now occupied by the Attorney-General, as the minister to whom the Head of the GLS reports, gives him an explicit interest in the general health of the Service, both centrally and departmentally. His guidelines on contracting-out (Attorney-General 1991) may be seen as one expression of this.

Another change in the direction of ordinary Ministerial status, which some will have seen as being of considerable symbolic significance, was the physical removal in 1990 of the Attorney-General's chambers from the Royal Courts of Justice in the Strand to premises in Buckingham Gate within easy reach of Whitehall and Westminster. According to Sir Peter Rawlinson, writing in 1977 as a former Attorney-General, the then physical separation of the Law Officers from other ministers served to emphasize the dual (advisory and public-interest) roles of the Law Officers and their separation from the ministry in which they serve. He saw the Attorney-General as someone who should be in court regularly and 'aloof from his colleagues in the Ministry to a quite formidable extent' (Rawlinson 1977). Silkin for his part took the opposite view, stressing the importance of the Attorney-General's active participation in affairs of government if he was to exercise, in the interests of legality, a sufficient influence on his colleagues (Silkin 1978: 156–7). Silkin may also be seen as a supporter of the more explicit responsibilities of administration and control now signalled by the 1989 changes referred to above (Silkin 1984: 184). We shall see, in looking at the Law Officers' current work in more detail, that his is the view which has found favour with succeeding Law Officers.

The accretion of these small changes of practice and nomenclature is almost certainly of much greater importance than the seemingly more 'constitutional' issue of whether the Attorney-General should be a member of Cabinet or not. This was a matter of considerable controversy during the quite short period early this century (intermittently between 1912 and 1928) when Attorneys-General were appointed to Cabinet. MPs and the Bar alike complained of the risks to objectivity that this entailed, though paradoxically it was the actions of an Attorney-General *not* in Cabinet in this period, Sir Patrick Hastings, in relation to the Campbell prosecution, which led to accusations of political influence and to a political crisis for the then Labour Government (Edwards 1964: 165–226). The reasons for the innovation were purely *ad hominem* (Isaacs, the Attorney-General in 1912, was disappointed at being passed over for the Lord Chancellorship, and Cabinet membership was offered as a consolation prize), and its disappearance in 1928 does not seem to have been regretted, even by an Attorney-General who describes himself as 'interventionist' and stresses the Attorney-General's voice in the formulation of policy (Silkin 1979: xxix).[4] In any event the Attorney-General attends Cabinet whenever his advice is required on legal or constitutional issues.

2 The Scottish Law Officers

The constitutional status of Scottish Law Officers will change substantially as a result of the Scottish devolution legislation. Essentially, they will cease to be ministers of the Crown and become instead members of the Scottish Executive (Scotland Act 1998 ss. 48(6), 44(1)), but the need for Scottish legal advice to the United Kingdom government will continue and will be met by a new ministerial appointment, that of the Advocate General for Scotland (section 87). It remains valuable, however, to evoke the distinctive history and functions of the Scottish Law Officers, since this has produced a structure and environment for the performance of their advisory functions different from that in England and Wales, and serves to demonstrate the possibility of alternative approaches to this role.

The precise origins of the office of Lord Advocate are obscure, but the practice of appointing an advocate to the King to argue in certain trials

[4] Though it is interesting to note that Silkin (who thinks the Attorney-General should always be present in Cabinet, though not a member (1978: 157)) gives a different reason for absence from that offered by other holders of the office such as Shawcross and Jones. For Silkin, there is a convention that the Attorney not be a member, and this is for the protection not of him, but of his colleagues, who 'cannot share responsibility for a wide range of Law Officers' decisions, particularly in the sphere of prosecuting policy' (1979: xxix). For Shawcross, who is followed by Jones, 'it has been considered more appropriate that the independence and detachment of his office should not be blurred by his inclusion in the political body which may have to take decisions on policy after receiving the legal advice that the law officers may give' (Shawcross 1953: 6–7; Jones 1969: 47).

appears to have been established by the end of the fifteenth century (Edwards 1984: 271). The Solicitor-General for Scotland came later, in the eighteenth century, though 'King's Solicitors' had been appointed since 1587 (Edwards 1984: 286–90). As in England there has been no very clear delineation of functions between the two offices, and the Law Officers Acts 1944 and 1997 likewise apply, although not in exactly the same terms. The dual location of the Scottish Law Officers' functions, however, in London and Edinburgh, led to the practice whereby the Lord Advocate tended to spend more time in London than the Solicitor, at least when Parliament was in session, leaving the latter to devote particular attention to the Crown Office work carried out in Edinburgh.

The early associations of the Lord Advocate's office were, like that of his English counterpart, with the function of criminal prosecution, with his right of initiative in all cases recognized by an Act of the Scottish Parliament of 1587. In the criminal field the Lord Advocate secured, centuries before the Attorney-General, comprehensive control of the criminal prosecution system, exercised through Advocates-Depute and local Procurators Fiscal (above, p. 229). Outside the criminal sphere, the Lord Advocate also secured—but later lost—something the Attorney-General has never had: real executive power. Established by the mid-sixteenth century as the holder of one of the great Offices of State in Scotland, the Lord Advocate, following the Union of 1707, gradually gathered to himself *de facto* responsibility for the entire civil government of Scotland as the other offices fell into desuetude or irrelevance and the English departments maintained an attitude of indifference and inertia. The consequent power and prestige of the Lord Advocate lasted well into the nineteenth century and was only definitively ended by the creation of the office of Secretary for Scotland by the 1885 Act of that title. By a later Secretary for Scotland Act (1887), a number of law and order functions for Scotland were transferred from the Home Secretary to the Secretary for Scotland, with the effect that from that time the core functions of the Lord Advocate—the criminal prosecution system, and legal advice—have reverted to being purely legal and have broadly resembled those of the Attorney-General (Edwards 1984: 275–80).

While granting this broad resemblance, we should note some differences both of functions and of status which will need to be taken into account in the discussion that follows. As to functions, the Lord Advocate's scope was broader in three respects. His London office combined the functions of Legal Secretariat and of Parliamentary Draftsman's office for Scottish government Bills; however, the Scottish Law Officers maintained a hands-off approach to the drafting role (not, for example, having access to the department's instructions to the draftsman) and in practice could thus provide the sort of 'independent' support to the draftsman on legal issues offered by the English Law Officers to Parliamentary Counsel (below, pp. 254, 256–8). Second, under arrangements in place since 1972 the Lord Advocate acquired, from the Secretary of State for Scotland, responsibilities for the civil law and for law reform similar to those held, in England, by the Lord Chancellor (Edwards 1984: 280 n.). Third, the Lord Advocate, likewise from 1972, shared responsibility for the court system in Scotland with the Secretary of State, as one of the two ministerial heads of the Scottish Courts Administration.

As to status, the Attorney-General has formal precedence over the Lord Advocate (*Attorney-General v Lord Advocate* 1834) and of course tends to have much the wider, and weightier, range of governmental issues on which to advise. But by reason of his functions, the Lord Advocate has had no real rival as the minister for legal affairs in his own jurisdiction, whereas the Attorney-General must share legal responsibilities with the Lord Chancellor, a minister of senior rank who today presides over the seventh-largest department. The English Law Officers enjoy a much closer relationship with Parliament, being almost always members of the House of Commons, whereas it has often been impossible, particularly in recent years, for the government to find among its Scottish supporters in the House lawyers of sufficient standing to fill even one of the Scottish offices. The most common recent situation, therefore, has been for the government to appoint senior and sympathetic members of the Faculty of Advocates (the Scottish Bar), elevating the Lord Advocate (and sometimes the Solicitor-General also) to the House of Lords. A curious result of this divergence in the recruitment of the two sets of Law Officers has been the greater ease with which truly high-calibre Scots lawyers may be appointed as Law Officers than may English ones, by reason of the increasing difficulty of combining a first-class practice with the modern demands of the House of Commons. The disparity may have been reinforced by the fact that Lords Advocate, and even Solicitors-General, still appear to have some claim to judicial preferment in Scotland, whereas the former claims of Attorneys-General to fill vacancies as Lord Chief Justice or Lord Chancellor now appear to have lost most if not all of their weight (Edwards 1964: ch. 15; 1984: 284–6).

These differences, in functions, background, and perhaps professional status also, should caution us against assuming that the changes we have described in the nature of the English Law Officers' tasks and situation (above, pp. 231–6) necessarily apply in the same way to their Scottish counterparts.

3 Conclusion

Multifarious as their functions are, the core roles which the Law Officers discharge, both north and south of the Border, may be reduced to two: the oversight of the criminal prosecution system; and the task of being the government's chief legal adviser in the relevant jurisdiction. These are the two roles in which the Law Officers might be capable of controlling and co-ordinating government legal work and opinion, whether in the interest of effective implementation of judicial control and parliamentary constraints; or of some distinct conception of legality internal to the executive; or of some combination of both. In the next two chapters, we explore the practice of control and co-ordination, looking both at how the Law Officers perform these functions, and at what other mechanisms of control and co-ordination exist alongside them. We deal separately with legislation and delegated legislation on the one hand, where control and censure of the government's actions have traditionally come from Parliament; and at crime, general legal advice, and litigation on the other, where it is the interpretations offered by the courts that government must respect.

8
Legislation

I INTRODUCTION

Money and staff are not unique to government. The power to change the law is. Under the constitution the power to make and unmake laws is vested in Parliament, strictly speaking the Queen in Parliament, but in practice it is exercised by the executive. It was during the nineteenth century that the executive appropriated the legislative power to itself—in substance though not in theory or form. The century, Walkland wrote, 'essentially saw a nationalisation and centralisation of legislative initiative in the hands of the government, a massive supplementation of Private Bill procedure by government-introduced Public General Acts, and a marked diminution in the opportunities for private members to legislate' (1979: 247). By the end of the century the transformation was complete. 'Only in form was parliament a law-making body: in substance the law was made elsewhere' (Parris 1969: 184).

The control exercised by the executive over legislation does not mean, as is sometimes suggested, that Parliament is simply a rubber stamp. The translation of the executive's wishes into law is a complex and time-consuming process which requires the repeated mobilization of a majority. It does, however, mean that, in the United Kingdom tradition, getting the legislation needed to give effect to its policies, to clothe them with the force of law, has not normally been a problem for the executive. Only where the executive has lacked an overall majority or its majority has been in doubt has it struggled. The executive's possession of the initiative in relation to legislation also means, as Foster and Plowden point out, that, in contrast to, say, the United States, legislation is more likely to be 'single-minded and capable of rational explanation than the largely inexplicable result of legislative compromise' (1996: 212).

As legislation came to be seen as a function of government, the legislative machinery of executive government expanded. It is with that machinery and the purposes it serves that we are concerned in this chapter. We begin by outlining the basic machinery of internal control, distinguishing between primary and secondary legislation, before concentrating on two developments which have given rise to an increase in central co-ordination and control in recent years. The first of these is the United Kingdom's membership since 1973 of the European

Communities, now the European Union. The second is concern with the burdens imposed on business by legislation. More recently concern with burdens on business has become part of a more general concern with improving the quality of legislation. The new Labour Government identified 'better legislation' as one of four parliamentary modernization themes (294 HC Debs., col. 904, Ann Taylor, 22 May 1997). We note the impact of that concern on the machinery of internal control at appropriate points in the chapter.

II MACHINERY AND PURPOSES

1 Primary legislation

Not surprisingly, given their status as the highest recognized form of law under the constitution, the legislative machinery of government is most highly developed in relation to Acts of Parliament. Since their inception, central controls over primary legislation in the form of Acts of Parliament have been directed to three broad purposes:

first, towards ensuring that what is introduced by way of legislation reflects the *priorities* of the government of the day, a task made specially important by reason of the fact that there are almost always more proposals for legislation than there is time in which to enact them;

second, towards ensuring that what is introduced is *consistent* with government policy overall, a task made more difficult by reason of the need to ensure consistency with 'European' as well as domestic law; and

third, towards ensuring that draft legislation is prepared *on time* and that it is *effective*, both in the sense of being capable of withstanding parliamentary scrutiny—in Lord Thring's aphorism 'Bills are made to pass, as razors are made to sell' (Ilbert 1901: 24; Engle 1983)—and in the sense of being capable once it is enacted of withstanding judicial scrutiny. The latter consideration, we may note in passing, has been one of the most powerful influences on the United Kingdom style of statutory drafting. Because Parliament jealously reserved to the ordinary courts 'the exclusive right and power of interpreting all enactments', Ilbert suggested, it was regarded as essential that they 'be expressed with such technical accuracy and precision as [would] enable them to survive the ordeal of judicial interpretation' (1901: 222). More influential, arguably, than Parliament's insistence on exclusively judicial interpretation was the idea that legislation constituted an exception to or gloss on the common law. In Sir James Stephen's view it was not enough 'to attain a degree of precision which a person reading in good faith can understand; but it is necessary to attain, if possible, to a degree of precision which a person reading in bad faith cannot misunderstand. It is all the better if he cannot pretend to misunderstand it' (quoted in Thring 1902: 9). There thus emerged a practice of seeking certainty through detailed provision which continues to form the basis of the United Kingdom approach to statutory drafting.

1.1 Determining legislative priorities

If time is money the executive might also say it is legislation. Although the House of Commons sits for more days each year than any other comparable legislature, and devotes the single greatest proportion of its time to legislation, there are invariably more proposals for legislation than there is time in which to enact them. As Secretary of State for Social Services, Barbara Castle reflected on 'how totally unaware our party rank and file are of the barriers to rapid action in a democracy. It is not just money; it is parliamentary time' (Castle 1980: 447). This in turn indicates the need for some machinery for adjudicating between competing claims on the limited time available. At one time the Cabinet itself drew up the legislative programme for each session, but that machinery is now provided by two Cabinet business (as opposed to policy) committees—the Queen's Speeches and Future Legislation Committee (QFL), which is concerned with legislation in future sessions, and the Legislation Committee (LEG), which is concerned with legislation in the current session.

The QFL Committee's terms of reference are 'to prepare and submit to the Cabinet drafts of the Queen's Speeches to Parliament, and proposals for the Government's legislative programme'. Herbert Morrison, Leader of the House of Commons and Lord President of the Council in the first post-war Labour Government, saw QFL's predecessor, the Future Legislation Committee, as a 'small and impartial planning tribunal' which would decide between competing departmental claims; departmental ministers should therefore be excluded as 'possible competitors for places in the programme' (Morrison 1964: 234). This principle is reflected in the composition of the Committee. Its key members are those responsible for getting the Government's business through Parliament—the President of the Council, who chairs the Committee, the Lord Privy Seal, and the two Chief Whips. Its other members include the Minister for the Cabinet Office and Chancellor of the Duchy of Lancaster, the Chief Secretary to the Treasury, the Minister of State at the Cabinet Office, the Attorney General, and the Lord Advocate. The two exceptions to the Morrison principle under the current administration are the Lord Chancellor, who chaired the Committee during the first session of the new Parliament, and the Deputy Prime Minister, who is also Secretary of State for the Environment, Transport and the Regions.

The LEG Committee's terms of reference, on the other hand, are 'to examine all draft Bills; to consider the Parliamentary handling of Government Bills, European Community documents, and Private Members' business, and such other related matters as may be necessary; and to keep under review the Government's policy in relation to issues of Parliamentary procedures'. Its membership overlaps substantially with that of QFL. Also chaired by the President of the Council, its other members include the Lord Chancellor, the Lord Privy Seal, the Secretaries of State for Scotland and Wales, the Financial Secretary to the Treasury, the Attorney General, the Lord Advocate, the two Chief Whips, Ministers of State at the Foreign and Commonwealth Office and the Home Office, and the Parliamentary Secretary to the Cabinet Office.

The formulation of the legislative programme for the next parliamentary session begins with an invitation to departments from QFL in the November or December of the preceding year for bids for legislation. Departments are normally requested to complete a pro-forma for each bid indicating among other things the priority they attach to the Bill and whether it is 'essential, contingent, programme or uncontroversial'. Similar classifications have been employed since the Cabinet Home Affairs Committee first took on the task of recommending a provisional programme to the Cabinet between the wars (Wilson 1975: para. 521), their purpose being to help the Committee rank bids in some order of priority. An 'essential' Bill is defined as one which *must* be enacted in the forthcoming session, for example to meet treaty obligations, or because existing powers or finance would otherwise expire. A 'contingent' Bill is one which would become essential, for example, were litigation to which the government was a party to go against it. Provision was therefore made for the inclusion of an emergency Bill in the 1984–85 legislative programme in anticipation of a successful challenge to the Government's reliance on the war-time Import, Export and Customs (Defence) Act 1939 to restrict the import of bananas from dollar area countries (Scott 1996: C.1.58–1.60). A 'programme' Bill, on the other hand, is one which will form a central element of the legislative programme, while an 'uncontroversial' Bill is one which it is desirable should be enacted but which is unlikely to be demanding in terms of parliamentary time. Departments are also requested to give their best estimate of the likely length of the Bill; their opinion of the most appropriate parliamentary procedure; and their assessment of the likely political reaction to the Bill. They are also asked to state when instructions will be ready to send to Parliamentary Counsel, and when the Bill is expected to be ready for introduction (Office of Public Service 1996*b*: Appendix A).

After the QFL Committee has considered departmental bids, in discussion with ministers concerned, it draws up a draft programme for submission to the Cabinet. In deciding how many Bills can sensibly be included in the next session's programme, the primary constraint is the number of days on the floor of the House they may be expected to occupy (Engle 1983: 12). Other factors that QFL are likely to take into account in deciding the programme to recommend to Cabinet, in addition to the time available, include the political content and urgency of the proposed Bills and how well prepared for introduction individual Bills are likely to be (OPS 1996*b*: para. 3.8). The internal *Guide to Legislative Procedures,* which is intended mainly for officials taking part in work on a Bill for the first time,[1] emphasizes the importance of allowing sufficient time, e.g. for settling detailed points of policy, for the preparation of drafting instructions, and for drafting, in estimating the timetable according to which a Bill is to be prepared. 'No estimate of the time required should be offered to Ministers without consulting the legal adviser, who, where appropriate, should consult First Parliamentary Counsel' (Office of Public Service 1996*b*: para. 3.10).

'[B]ills and budgets—legislation and loot—are the two things departmental Ministers fight for with the greatest zest'; although QFL occupies a strategic position in relation to access to the legislative process, it is only the 'first skirmishes in the annual battle of the bills' that take place in QFL (Hogg and Hill 1995: 112–13). When the programme for the 1975–76 session was discussed at Cabinet, Barbara Castle's complaint was that she had nothing.

> Ted Short [the Lord President of the Council] gave us his best headmaster's head shaking act. The legislative pressure this year had been 'intolerable', he said. Colleagues really must accept that they could not put in the kind of legislative bids they had done last time. We then all fought passionately for our own bids again. It was a fight with no quarter given by anyone. When I pointed out that DHSS hadn't got a single piece of legislation accepted for the essential bills list this year, there were derisory cheers of approval. So I made their blood curdle with warnings of the industrial action health unions would take if I wasn't allowed to legislate for the phasing out of pay beds. (Thank God for the unions!). (Castle 1980: 446–7)

In the end she got her Bill.

The legislative programme at this stage is provisional. It may need to be revised because an additional Bill has become necessary or a Bill

[1] The *Guide* was originally issued by the Civil Service Department in 1976 in the wake of 'one of the most formidable legislative programmes since the war' (Wilson 1979: 123). The impetus came principally from Parliamentary Counsel, who saw it as a means of avoiding having to explain the procedures anew to each and every Bill team.

needs to be dropped because its preparation has fallen behind. It is usually not until October that the programme is finalized. The fact that a Bill has not been included in the programme does not exclude its introduction in the forthcoming session. A minister wishing to include a Bill in the programme once it has been finalized, however, would have to show an 'exceptionally strong case' (Office of Public Service 1996*b*: para. 3.13).

Once the new session has begun, responsibility for the programme passes to LEG. Its role is essentially that of 'a monitor and spur' (Wilson 1976: 129). When he was Lord President of the Council, Crossman recorded:

> At Legislation Committee I had to play my traditional role as controller of the legislative timetable and haul the ministers over the coals. Each of them had promised me six months ago that if I gave their Bill a place in the programme it would be ready to go to Second Reading before Christmas yet now we come to the end of the Queen's speech and there are fewer Bills ready than ever before. All the big Bills are teetering over and it looks as though they won't start till after the Christmas recess. I told the Committee that their Bills would be lost if they weren't ready by the end of the Session. (Crossman 1976: 557–8; see too Howe 1994: 646–7)

As well as monitoring progress in the preparation and enactment of Bills, the Committee is responsible for authorizing the introduction of measures the need for which was not anticipated when the programme was drawn up; determining the Government's attitude to private Members' Bills; and the final clearance of Bills and the authorization of their introduction in Parliament.

1.2 'Better legislation'

Traditionally, the legislative programme has been planned a session in advance only. This is changing. Following the recommendation of the Modernisation Committee (Modernisation Committee 1998*a*), the House of Commons has accepted that, in principle, it should be possible to carry Bills over from one session to the next, opening up the possibility of introducing one or two big Bills late in a session, which can then complete their parliamentary stages in the course of the following session. In recent years, too, a number of Bills have been approved for publication in draft during the next session on the basis that legislative time is likely to be found for them in a subsequent session. The purpose of this procedure, which has been adopted in relation to Bills the drafting and substance of which are likely to benefit from public consultation (Office of Public Service 1996*b*: para. 3.6), is to contribute to improving the quality of legislation. It is hoped that if comments are made before rather than after introduction, it will be less frequently necessary to distort the structure of Bills as they go through Parliament. In 1994–95 five Bills were published in draft, which were included in the 1995–96 legislative programme; while the Labour Government committed itself to publishing seven Bills in draft form in the first session of the new Parliament. In the event only three were published. Nevertheless, the foundations have been laid for a system of pre-legislative scrutiny, which may be expected in time to affect the way in which the legislative programme is planned—with provision being made for the publication of a number of Bills in draft—and managed. The decision of the Government to publish explanatory notes (combining the material previously provided in the explanatory memorandum and the notes on clauses) with all Bills and Acts (305 HC Debs., cols. *253–4*, written answers 28 January 1998; 288 HL Debs., col. *217*, written answers 22 April 1998) is also expected to have an impact on the planning and management of the programme (as well as make a significant contribution in helping to understand the law).

1.3 Policy clearance

The process of gaining a place on the legislative programme is to be distinguished from the process of securing collective approval for the policy proposals which the legislation is to enact. Before the Parliamentary Counsel Office was established in 1869

> there was no security for uniformity of principle in measures for which the Government was collectively responsible. Different Departments introduced inconsistent Bills, and there was no adequate means by which the Prime Minister, or the Cabinet as a whole, could exercise effective control over measures fathered by individual Ministers. [In addition,] there was no check on the financial consequences of legislation. There was nothing to prevent any Minister from introducing a Bill which would impose a heavy charge on the Treasury, and upset the Chancellor of the Exchequer's Budget calculations for the year. (Ilbert 1901: 83–4)

The need for some guarantee of uniformity of principle and for a check on the financial consequences of legislation is now mainly met, not through the Parliamentary Counsel Office, but through the machinery of Cabinet policy approval. The *Guide to Legislative Procedures* stipulates that the content and timing of primary legislation are matters that 'significantly engage the collective responsibility of the Government' (Office of Public Service 1996*b*: para. 3.1). Both must therefore be agreed by Cabinet or by its committees before legislation is introduced.

The lead department is responsible for ensuring that interested departments are consulted and that policy clearance is obtained. A non-exhaustive checklist of departmental interests is contained in the *Guide to Legislative Procedures*. As we would expect, the Treasury must be consulted on any proposal involving actual or potential public expenditure or reduction in revenue, while the Inland Revenue must be consulted on any proposal which could have direct or indirect effects on tax charges or reliefs. So, too, the territorial departments must be consulted on any proposal which may have implications for their areas of responsibility, which in practice means the great majority; the Department of the Environment, Transport and the Regions on any proposal which has implications for local authorities, or which will have an impact, positive or negative, on the environment; the Lord Chancellor's Department on any proposal which would confer additional functions on the courts or tribunals, or which would be likely to increase the civil litigation or the number of criminal prosecutions; and the Deregulation Unit, now the Better Regulation Unit, on any proposals which would have an impact, positive or negative, on business (Office of Public Service 1996*b*: para. 4.2).

Among the matters on which the Home Office and the other home departments must be consulted are proposals to create or re-enact powers of entry by public authorities to private premises. This requirement was first introduced in 1980 following complaints from the Adam Smith Institute and the National Federation of Self-Employed and Small Businesses that a 'growing army' of inspectors possessed excessive powers of entry (Adam Smith Institute 1979). Under the 'Mitchell principles', which anticipated elements of the Conservative Government's later Deregulation initiative, but which also possess a strong 'civil liberties' flavour, proposals to create or re-enact such powers require clearance by the appropriate home department to ensure they impose the minimum of constraints and burdens on owners and occupiers of premises (Office of Public Service 1996*b*: Appendix B). A feature of the clearance procedure, which was also employed in the Deregulation initiative, is that ministers in both the originating and the appropriate home department must *personally* approve proposals to create or re-enact such powers. As well as reducing the likelihood of such powers being casually assumed—because of the need for ministerial approval—this procedure also reduces the likelihood of ministers being caught unawares by opposition to proposals for such powers.

It is only when a legislative proposal actually begins to take shape that the policy considerations with which it has to be made consistent can be properly identified. The range of possible subjects of legislation makes the identification of policy considerations in the abstract largely meaningless. The *Guide to Legislative Procedures,* however, identifies a number of considerations as being of *continuing* relevance to the decision to grant or withhold policy clearance to a proposal:

EU implications

It is treated as being of paramount importance that proposals for domestic legislation should be consistent with the United Kingdom's obligations as a member of the European Union. We return to this consideration below in examining the impact of EU membership on the legislative machinery of government.

The risk of legal challenge

It is government policy that legislative proposals should be scrutinized with a view to reducing the vulnerability of decision-making to challenge before the courts by way of judicial review proceedings. Cabinet Office guidance (Office of Public Service 1996*b*: Appendix E), first circulated in 1987 at the same time as *The Judge Over Your Shoulder* (Treasury Solicitor's Department 1987), provides that the lead in scrutinizing proposals for likely subjects of challenge should be taken by ministers and their policy advisers, since the source of challenge to legislative provisions 'often lies in opposition to the provision on policy grounds'. 'It is for them to alert their legal advisers and Parliamentary Counsel to those aspects of the policy which are liable to be principally opposed, so that the draftsman can focus on the likely areas of technical challenge.' Where there is thought to be a risk of challenge, this should be drawn to the attention of the relevant Cabinet policy committee, with any steps taken to reduce the risk being drawn to the attention of the Legislation Committee. Among the means the guidance identifies of reducing the risk of challenge is by making the government's intention as clear as possible, 'even at the cost of drafting in terms that are presentationally or politically unattractive'. The risk may also be reduced by making decisions subject to parliamentary procedures, since the courts are 'reluctant to go against something which is clearly the express wish of Parliament', and by the provision of avenues of appeal for those affected, which must first normally be exhausted before recourse will be permitted to judicial review. Departments should ensure that ministers are aware of these possibilities, so that they can make informed decisions on the shape of legislation.

Open Government

In its White Paper on Open Government the last Conservative Government committed itself to subjecting future restrictions on the disclosure of information to a 'harm test' rather than framing them as unqualified prohibitions. It also committed itself to subjecting existing restrictions on disclosure to such tests as and when legislative opportunities arose, unless there were compelling public interest arguments against doing so (Cabinet Office 1993: para. 8.40). Bill teams were required to have regard to these commitments in the preparation of proposals (Office of Public Service 1996*b*: para. 4.9). These commitments continue to apply, but they have been largely overtaken by the Labour Government's announcement that it intends to repeal or amend many of the existing restrictions on disclosure to bring them into line with the policy underlying its proposed Freedom of Information Act (Chancellor of the Duchy of Lancaster 1997: para. 3.20).

Equal opportunities

The last Conservative Government also committed itself to a policy of 'mainstreaming' equal opportunities across Whitehall. Instead of relying on specialist agencies such as the Equal Opportunities Commission to identify possible breaches of the law and to take appropriate remedial action, departments are required, under guidance originally issued by the Cabinet Office, which was later amplified by guidance prepared by the DfEE and circulated to all departments in August 1996, to ensure that policy proposals for which they are responsible will not result in unlawful discrimination or unjustifiable inequality between, for example, men and women or people of different religious beliefs or political opinions (DfEE 1996; Office of Public Service 1996*b*: Appendix D; the current guidance is to be superseded by guidance being prepared by the Women's Unit attached to the Cabinet Office). Where policy options and proposals are put forward for ministerial consideration, confirmation must be provided that the implications for all aspects of equal treatment and non-discrimination have been identified and taken into account. Besides its commitment to equal opportunities, a factor behind the adoption of the policy of mainstreaming appears to have been a desire to avoid inadvertently breaking the law. 'The Government must also, of course, comply with the law and, in line with the new Civil Service Code, it should not be advised to take a course of action that is unlawful' (DfEE 1996: Foreword; it may be no more than coincidence that the guidance was issued following *R v Employment Secretary, ex parte Equal Opportunities Commission* 1995). Set in this context, a potential drawback of specialist agencies such as the Equal Opportunities Commission is that their existence may divert attention from the need for departments to ensure that their policies are compatible with the requirements to which the executive is subject. Mainstreaming seeks to guard against this risk by placing the responsibility for promoting fair treatment and non-discrimination squarely on departments.

Departments are therefore required to have regard to these requirements in framing legislative proposals. Where they do not, and this is picked up, they risk being denied policy clearance for their Bill.

Consultation with interested departments is not a substitute for formal policy approval, which must be obtained from the relevant Cabinet policy committee. It is not a condition of securing a place on the programme that policy clearance has in fact been obtained, but in the case of Bills of any size it is expected that the process will have begun, and whether clearance has been obtained is one of the matters on which information is sought by the QFL Committee; departments are required to list all the measures which they propose to include in the Bill, stating in each case whether policy clearance has been obtained from the relevant Cabinet Committee (Office of Public Service 1996*b*: Appendix A). Clearly, the less far-advanced consultations are on a measure on which it is likely to be difficult to secure internal agreement, the less likely it is to be included in the programme. Whether or not collective agreement has been achieved in advance, it will need to be secured before the Bill can proceed.

1.4 Drafting

As we have seen, the Parliamentary Counsel Office is responsible for the drafting of government Bills, except for those relating exclusively or mainly to Scotland and the Scottish provisions of United Kingdom Bills, which are drafted by the Lord Advocate's Department. A few (but not all) Bills relating to Northern Ireland are drafted by Legislative Counsel in Belfast. The Office defines its aim as being 'to ensure the highest standards, in terms of both quality and timeliness, in the drafting and the procedural handling of the Government's legislative programme'. Parliamentary Counsel's essential task is to give effect to the government's intentions in a form capable of withstanding Parliamentary and later judicial scrutiny. Because the legislative timetable is tight, it is equally important that they deliver Bills on time. 'The government must get its Bills on time and they must be in a form which will first stand up in Parliament and then stand up in court' (Bennion 1990: 22), though Bills may be introduced in the knowledge that more text will be added later or that certain clauses will be altered by government amendment. As well as drafting Bills, Counsel also assist their progress through Parliament, advising departments on parliamentary procedure (the Public Bill Office in the Commons also advises departments), drafting amendments, and where other amendments are accepted or carried against the government invariably re-drafting them in a form consistent with the Bill.

1.4.1 *The PCO's monopoly*

When the PCO was first established it was not intended that it should assume responsibility for drafting all government legislation (Ilbert 1901: 85), but by the end of the First World War it had become established practice for government Bills, other than those relating to Scotland, to be drafted by the Office. From time to time it has been suggested that the Office's almost complete monopoly of the drafting of primary legislation is inherently undesirable and ought therefore to be broken (e.g. Mather 1994). The drafting of parts of the Finance Act 1996 was contracted out, but the conclusion that would seem to have been drawn from this exercise is that the advantages of centralized drafting arrangements continue to outweigh their possible disadvantages.[2] In particular, they make it more likely that legislation will be 'ready' on time, a consideration of paramount importance in a system in which time is at a premium. The fact that Bills are drafted in one office, Ellis observed, 'enables the order of their preparation to be controlled, and the time at which they will be ready to be predicted, as would not otherwise be possible' (Ellis 1949: 178). Centralized drafting arrangements are also conducive to a general consistency of method and style in the drafting of legislation, and with it the likelihood that measures will be interpreted as the government intends (Andrew 1989: p. 50; Dale 1977: 337). One of the results of the system, or want of system that obtained before the PCO was established, Ilbert pointed out, was the lack of any 'security for uniformity of language, style, or arrangement, in laws which were intended to find their place in a *common* Statute Book' (Ilbert 1901: 83–4, emphasis added). The Renton Committee would have deprecated any large-scale transfer of drafting work away from the Government draftsmen as being liable to result in a return to the legislative 'jungle' of the eighteenth and early nineteenth centuries when different Bills were drafted by different people 'who neither knew nor cared how the other performers were framing their legislation' (Committee on the Preparation of Legislation 1975: para. 8.18; see also Andrew 1989: pp. 26–7; Hansard Society 1992: para. 187).

1.4.2 *Ministerial responsibility*

The Parliamentary Counsel Office has been described as 'unique in the Civil Service, inasmuch as, though it is directly and essentially concerned with matters of the first political consequence, its distinctive functions are not under the control of any one Minister' (Ellis 1949: 176). As we have seen, it now forms part of the Cabinet Office, for which the

[2] As well as being very expensive the contractors' work was thought to be opaque and 'over-drafted'.

Prime Minister is responsible. So far as its drafting work is concerned, individual Counsel are responsible to the ministers on the preparation of whose Bills they are engaged, while the First Parliamentary Counsel works with QFL and LEG on the planning and implementation of the legislative programme as a whole. Like their English counterparts, Scottish Parliamentary Counsel consider themselves responsible to the minister in charge of the Bill for their drafting work on that Bill. The Lord Advocate has, however, taken responsibility in Parliament for matters relating to the drafting of Scottish Bills (489 HL Debs., cols. 1441–9, Lord Cameron of Lochbroom, 11 November 1987).

1.4.3 Drafting authority

The Review of Government Legal Services thought the absence of single ministerial responsibility for the Office not altogether surprising in view of its 'unique position at the interface between the executive and the legislature' (Andrew 1989: p. 14). The co-ordination of its services to different ministers is secured through a combination of the centrally-determined legislative programme and the requirement of drafting authority before Parliamentary Counsel will undertake the drafting of a Bill (Ellis 1949: 176). The requirement of drafting authority was first introduced in 1935 (Miers and Page 1990: 50). The lack of any attempt before then effectively to co-ordinate the demands for legislation stemming from different departments had resulted in 'continual pressure upon the Parliamentary Counsel for the output of bills quite beyond his powers' (Graham-Harrison 1935: 44). Bills intended for introduction in a future session which have a place in the programme approved by Cabinet and which have secured policy approval from the appropriate Committee automatically have drafting authority. 'Special' drafting authority, on the other hand, must be obtained from the chairman of LEG Committee where a Bill is proposed to be added to the programme for the current session, or a significant amendment is planned to a Bill which has already been agreed by LEG, or a large number of amendments is necessary for a particular stage of a Bill, so affecting the handling or timing of that stage (Office of Public Service 1996*b*: para. 6.4). Departments should not send instructions until drafting authority has been given for the legislation and the policy to be enacted by it has been collectively agreed (ibid.: para. 6.2). Although drafting authority for Scottish Bills is frequently sought and given, it is thought to be unnecessary. The great majority of Scottish Bills are drafted separately in the Lord Advocate's Department for only one instructing department—the Scottish Office. Pressures on the Scottish draftsmen for competing Scottish Bills need not, therefore, be moderated in the same way as those on Parliamentary Counsel.

1.4.4 Relations with instructing departments

The theory on which the relationship between the PCO and the instructing department is based is that the policy is for the department, but the form in which it is expressed is for Parliamentary Counsel. The department has the final say on policy; the draftsman the final say on the wording, as distinguished from the substance, of a Bill (Kent 1979: 236). Although departments should therefore satisfy themselves that the intention of their instructions has been met, 'it may emerge that the intention is best given legislative form in a manner which is not quite as they originally contemplated; that is normal and to be expected' (Office of Public Service 1996*b*: para. 6.10). Parliamentary Counsel have, the Guide points out, 'besides their professional skill, far wider experience of legislation than any department is likely to have' (ibid.: para. 6.8).

In the final analysis though, the Bill is the minister's Bill, and if he insists on the Bill being drafted in a particular way, 'he must in the last resort have his way' (Kent 1979: 236). Ministers often want 'positive' language for political reasons; they also need to be 'comfortable' with the language in 'their' Bills. This is not to say that the point will be easily conceded. One kind of dispute in which the Law Officers have sometimes found themselves called upon to adjudicate is over the instructing department's insistence on a particular form of words. 'It has come to be recognised that someone within Government should protect the Statute Book from purely cosmetic exercises and this task has fallen to the Law Officers' (Archer 1978: 18). In practice, there are said to be very few cases of ministers insisting on a form of words against the advice of Parliamentary Counsel.

Short titles provide a sometimes revealing glimpse of the relationship in practice. It is for Counsel to give a Bill its short and long titles (Office of Public Service 1996*b*: para. 6.18), the convention or working rule in relation to short titles being that they should be short and not misleading. Sometimes therefore the draftsman has been able to use the short title as a way of indicating his view of a measure. Such was the case with the Health and Safety at Work etc. Act 1974, the rebarbative 'etc.' being added by the draftsman who disliked the admission of the 'unwelcome cuckoo' of Part III of the Act, which dealt with the quite separate topic of building regulations, into an 'otherwise homogeneous nest' (Engle 1983: 13). Faced with ministers who want to make a political impact, however, the draftsman may find himself forced to give ground. Perhaps the most striking example in recent years is the Crime and Punishment (Scotland) Act 1997. Parliamentary Counsel has been more successful in holding the line in England and Wales; even so the title of the parallel Crime (Sentences) Act 1997 was not his first choice.

When Nigel Lawson proposed the 'Oil and Gas Enterprise Bill' as the title of his Bill to privatize the British National Oil Corporation it was rejected by Parliamentary Counsel as possessing a 'vector quality', a euphemism Lawson took for being 'too political'; eventually the 'masterly compromise' of the 'Oil and Gas (Enterprise) Bill' was struck (Lawson 1992: 212).[3]

1.4.5 Counsel as guardians of legal values

Parliamentary Counsel are more than just instruments of the executive's will, a specialist cadre whose professional skill lies in translating the government's intentions into legislative form. They also act as the internal guardians of values customarily regarded as integral to the legal order such as those of non-retrospection, proper use of delegation, and respect for the liberties of the subject. Faced with a conflict between their instructions and what they interpret as their duty to the law and the statute book, they have the power to refer their instructions to the Law Officers, who have a special responsibility for 'legislative policy' within government (Mayhew 1990: 2), and who can if they agree with Counsel take up the matter with the minister whose Bill it is.

The legal values of which Counsel act as the internal guardians are impossible to state with precision. One legal adviser described the concept of 'legal policy' as 'not terribly well-defined' but as apt to cover, in addition to non-retrospection, proper use of delegation and respect for individual liberties, 'unusually draconian' powers of entry, or the restriction of expected powers of scrutiny of subordinate legislation. Other principles which tend to recur in discussions of the concept include those of compliance with international law, clarity, and proportionality in the sense of the avoidance of excessive interference with personal or property rights (for an attempt to codify the concept, see Thornton 1996: 134–7). Nor is the concept necessarily uniform across departments. The Inland Revenue, for example, has its own rules on retrospection—the so-called 'Rees rules', named after the Financial Secretary to the Treasury who first announced them to Parliament (St Committee A, cols. 719–20, 6 June 1978). But in the absence of a higher law by which a sovereign Parliament is bound, the concept of legal policy as interpreted by Parliamentary Counsel is as close as our system has traditionally come to a check on the 'constitutionality' of legislation.

[3] The classic illustration of the importance politicians may attach to short titles is provided by the innocuously titled Environmental Protection Act 1990. This began life as the Environment Protection Bill, but shortly before its introduction, a Private Member's Bill with the same title was introduced. The Prime Minister was understood to be apoplectic that a flagship 'Green' initiative would as a result be the 'No 2' Bill. The difficulty was overcome when the Public Bill Office simply suggested calling it the Environmental Protection Bill.

Counsel regard the power to refer matters arising on Bills to the Attorney-General as a 'very powerful weapon' in the defence of such values. It is not one which is lightly used. Before referring a matter Counsel will invite the instructing department to reconsider. If the department declines to do so, Counsel will inform the department that he proposes to refer the matter to the Law Officers. Most disputes are resolved without a reference, if only because the clock by this time is running against the department. Should the Attorney be called in, he may take up the matter with the minister after obtaining clarification of the views of Counsel. Whether the matter is taken up will obviously depend on whether Counsel's views are shared, but in one former First Parliamentary Counsel's experience he had never received less than 100 per cent support from the Law Officers. It is impossible to be categorical about the weight that will attach to the Law Officers' opinion. One view has it that it would take a decision of the whole Cabinet to overrule the Attorney. This may go too far. What seems clear though, is that, while not necessarily the last word, their advice is unlikely to be lightly, or easily, disregarded.

In Scotland, a similar system operates. There, too, the draftsmen are 'disciplined to spot questions of legal policy', and will informally raise them with the instructing department, with the implicit threat that if the department does not respond they will be drawn to the attention of the Law Officers. In this way 'our conscience becomes their conscience'. The fact that the Law Officers are in the same department as the draftsmen is said in no way to diminish the potency of the threat to involve them.

Parliamentary Counsel's role as the watchdogs of legal policy may be rationalized as a means of protecting individual ministers, and the government as a whole, from the difficulties that may be encountered before Parliament and the courts should such matters be ignored. The combination of independence from the instructing department and unmatched experience of legislation, including legislative procedure, means that Counsel are uniquely placed to undertake this role. It is only a short step from here to the argument that it is Counsel's duty 'to prevent the Minister getting into difficulties', and that 'If the Minister or his department are obdurate in resisting him on a legal point, he must do what is necessary to get, if he can, the support of the Law Officers' (Graham-Harrison 1935: 44). The prospect that a Bill will encounter difficulties before Parliament and the courts should such matters be ignored undoubtedly increases the seriousness with which they are treated by departments and the Law Officers, but it seems clear that the importance attached by Parliamentary Counsel to the protection of legal values is not solely attributable to the risk of such difficulties. It also reflects their own conception of their role and in particular the belief that they owe a responsibility to the law and statute book as well as to the minister whose policy they are responsible for translating into statutory form.

As well as their duty to the law, Counsel also owe a duty to Parliament: 'the Office stands, by accepted and salutary practice, in a position of trust to the House and its officials, in the discharge of which a duty devolves on Parliamentary Counsel to be meticulous in securing avoidance of any circumvention of the rules of Order and of any framing of a Bill in a form which would embarrass effective debating of its provisions' (Ellis 1949: 176–7). This does not mean that it is any part of Counsel's job to make it easier for opponents of a measure to attack the policy on which it is based. The 'adamantine quality' of the drafting of the Education (Student Loans) Bill 1990, for example, made it extremely difficult, as ministers no doubt wished, to address the working of the proposed scheme by means of amendment (see too Miers and Page 1990: 79–80). Counsel's position of trust in relation to the House authorities does mean, however, that they are under a duty, akin to that owed by a lawyer to the court, not to mislead the authorities and to provide advice which is 'frank and impartial', for example, on the meaning and effect of an amendment or on whether it cannot be debated because it falls outside the scope of the Bill. Their utility as advisers to ministers is dependent upon their retaining the trust of Parliament. Were they felt to be acting as 'mere spokesmen' for departments, they would soon lose that trust.

1.4.6 The role of the Law Officers

The Law Officers may be seized of questions relating to legislative proposals by means other than a reference from Parliamentary Counsel. Departmental legal advisers are expected to consult the Law Officers where they are in doubt about 'the legality or constitutional propriety' of proposed legislation (or the *vires* of proposed subordinate legislation) (Cabinet Office 1997*d*: para. 22). As part of the formal machinery of consultation they must be consulted on any proposal for a provision in a Bill to apply retrospectively (Office of Public Service 1996*b*: para. 4.2); accordingly, although Counsel may draw such proposals to their attention, they would normally expect to be consulted before Counsel is asked to give effect to them. It is also possible for departments to approach the Law Officers over a disagreement with Counsel; less commonly, ministers may approach the Law Officers directly.

The Law Officers also scrutinize draft Bills before they are examined by the Legislation Committee, for which purpose they are briefed by Parliamentary Counsel, who also brief the Lord Chancellor, with whom the Law Officers have a shared responsibility for the 'form and quality' of legislation (Edwards 1984: 186; Silkin 1978: 154), and by their own secretariat, who can take up matters with the department concerned (Edwards 1964: 146–8). In Scotland the procedure for the scrutiny of draft Bills is less formal, the Lord Advocate's Department having either drafted them or collaborated in their drafting. Occasionally, however, it is found helpful to arrange that the lawyer assisting the Lord Advocate with a question on a draft Bill is someone other than the draftsman.

The Attorney-General and the Lord Advocate are both members of the Legislation Committee. The Committee's examination of a Bill once it has been drafted provides a last opportunity to raise legal policy questions. Agreement to the introduction of a Bill in Parliament and its subsequent handling is sought on the basis of a memorandum prepared by the department. Approval is normally subject to 'any minor or drafting amendments'. If there are any unresolved problems the Committee may decide that the Bill must be re-submitted after they have been dealt with. The expectation, however, is that such problems should arise only exceptionally at this stage (Office of Public Service 1996*b*: para. 10.5). At one time the Committee did examine Bills closely 'not normally from the point of view of policy but from the standpoint of general structure, proper legal wording, fairness, good sense in carrying out the intentions of the Government, and general acceptability as a workable measure' (Morrison 1964: 250), but the questions with which it is now concerned are primarily those of parliamentary handling, tactics, and timing (Office of Public Service 1996*b*: para. 10.3). Nevertheless, the need to obtain clearance creates an incentive for departments to resolve differences over legal policy before they get to the Committee. Otherwise the Bill may be delayed or lost.

It has been proposed with a view to improving the quality of legislation that the Committee should resume its former practice of closely scrutinizing draft Bills. The Hansard Commission, for example, recommended that the Committee should be given the wider and longer-term role of ensuring that Bills conform with 'the best constitutional principles' and, where appropriate, that they have been prepared after full and genuine consultation (Hansard Society 1992: para. 195). How practicable such suggestions are is doubtful. For one adviser, the Committee could not be expected to give effective legal scrutiny to Bills; it was quite impossible for them to look at everything as thoroughly as they would have to do for that purpose. For another, the volume of business and the late stage in the process at which the Committee typically becomes involved both made it unlikely to hold back legislation on technical drafting grounds. If the problem of the quality of legislation is to be successfully tackled, it must be at an earlier stage than the eve of a Bill's introduction.

2 Subordinate legislation

'Everywhere in our statute book the same process is visible. The action of our Acts of Parliament grows more and more dependent upon subsidiary legislation', wrote Cecil Carr in 1921 (Carr 1921: 1). Despite its importance as a source of law, however, subordinate legislation has never attracted the same degree of central co-ordination and control as its primary counterpart. There have been exceptions. For some time after the Second World War, though no longer, clearance was required from the Legislation Committee for 'important' instruments, including all those 'involving any departure from precedent, e.g. in relation to the type of penalties imposed, in the procedure relating to such matters as appeals, or in encroachment upon the liberty of the subject' (Select Committee on Delegated Legislation 1953: para. 40; Morrison 1964: 250). But as a general rule, the exercise of subordinate law-making powers has been treated as a matter for departments.

We do not have to search far for an explanation for this difference in treatment. The principal reason is that subordinate legislation for the most part has no implications for time on the floor of the House. One of the main impulses to central co-ordination—the need to allocate scarce parliamentary time—has therefore been missing. At the same time subordinate legislation has been conventionally understood, and practice at least until recently has substantially conformed to this understanding, as being both politically and legally of a lesser order of importance than its primary counterpart, being confined to the detailed application of principles laid down in Acts of Parliament, while not enjoying the latter's traditional immunity from judicial review. Being on the face of it less important than primary legislation, and having no implications for parliamentary time, it has therefore been treated as a matter for departments themselves.

2.1 The Statutory Instruments Act 1946

In the absence of the pressures of parliamentary time, the main central involvement in secondary legislation has arisen as a result of the need to arrange for the registration and publication of instruments in accordance with the Statutory Instruments Act 1946. The Act, which 'owed as much to backbench agitation as to executive enlightenment' (Lee 1977: 129), introduced a greater degree of uniformity in the procedure for laying instruments before Parliament and made provision for their publication.

At one time the Statutory Publications Office was responsible for receiving instruments for registration and numbering in accordance with the Act (s. 2(1)), but that function is now undertaken by Her Majesty's Stationery Office, a residuary body, headed by a Controller, within the Machinery of Government and Standards Group of the Cabinet Office (now the Central Secretariat), which was established to administer HMSO's statutory functions and Crown copyright following the privatization of its trading functions in September 1996. Before registering instruments the Statutory Instruments Registrar within the Office checks that the requirements of the Act are complied with: for example, in the case of instruments which require to be laid before Parliament, that each instrument bears on its face a statement showing the date of its laying and the date of its coming into operation (s. 4(2)). The Office also advises departments on the requirements of the Act.

Her Majesty's Stationery Office is also responsible for *Statutory Instrument Practice* (Cabinet Office 1987), a manual compiled for the use of departments with power to make statutory instruments which provides guidance on the preparation and making of instruments and the parliamentary procedures relating to them. The manual, a new edition of which has been in preparation for some time, replaced the earlier *Handbook on Statutory Instrument Procedure*, which was first issued in 1964, and which consolidated Treasury statutory instrument circulars issued since 1947. It also provides a means by which points of general concern can be brought to the attention of departments. SI (98) 2, for example, reminds departments of their responsibilities for checking the layout and accuracy of the text of instruments proofed by the Stationery Office Ltd.

2.2 Departmental practice

It is in the nature of what is effectively a decentralized system of law-making that the procedures followed by any two departments in making subordinate legislation will not be exactly the same. The normal practice, however, 'is for the administrative division concerned with the subject-matter of the enabling enactment to take the lead on the preparatory work, undertaking such consultation as necessary, obtaining Ministerial instructions, and co-operating with the legal staff on the drafting itself' (Joint Committee on Delegated Legislation 1972: Appendix 8, para. 8). Once a draft has been settled, a timetable is agreed for the printing, signature, laying, publication, and bringing into operation of the instrument. All but routine instruments are signed, or approved before signature, by ministers.

Departments which make extensive use of subordinate legislation usually have their own manuals setting out the procedures to be followed departmentally in the preparation and making of instruments. The Department of Health's *Preparation and Making of Statutory Instruments* (December 1995), which is addressed to administrators as well as lawyers, for example, provides a comprehensive statement of departmental procedures in relation to the making of instruments. HM Customs and Excise's *Statutory Instruments: Practice and Procedure* (1997), by contrast, is primarily intended for the use of lawyers in advisory teams who have little or no experience in the preparation and making of statutory instruments. Manuals intended for the use of lawyers usually address points of style as well as procedure.

In contrast to primary legislation, most secondary legislation is drafted by the legal branches of departments rather than by the PCO; the exceptions are those instruments, such as transfer of functions orders under the Ministers of Crown Act, which are drafted on behalf of the Cabinet Office by Parliamentary Counsel (or Scottish Parliamentary Counsel). Responsibility for ensuring legal effectiveness thus rests with departmental legal advisers. As a safeguard, instruments are usually subject to some form of scrutiny within departments, which may extend beyond strict questions of *vires* (on which the validity of instruments as law depends) to more general questions of structure and style. In the Home Office, the practice, which is said to be typical of practice across Whitehall, is for lawyers at former Grade 5 level to take responsibility for all instruments drafted in their teams. In the DTI another lawyer takes a 'second look' at instruments, while a senior lawyer acts as a source of advice on drafting issues. Instruments drafted by the Office of Solicitor to the Secretary of State for Scotland are scrutinized by a 'stylist' who is responsible for checking their *vires* and that they conform to the Solicitor's Office style. Where legal advisers are in doubt about the *vires* of proposed instruments, they are expected to consult the Law Officers (Cabinet Office 1997*d*: para. 22).

In the absence of centralized drafting arrangements, a measure of consistency in the structure and style of secondary legislation has been achieved through *Statutory Instrument Practice*, which provides a means of communicating best practice to departments, and through the work of the Joint Committee on Statutory Instruments and its predecessors (below).

2.3 Parliamentary scrutiny

The degree of parliamentary scrutiny to which instruments are subject depends largely on the provision made in the parent Act. It is therefore a matter for departments, subject to the approval of Parliament when the parent Act is before Parliament as a Bill. Successive governments have denied the possibility of laying down any hard and fast rules fettering departments' discretion in the choice of procedure to which instruments should be subject, insisting that the decision must be made in the light of all the circumstances, a position recently endorsed by the House of Lords Select Committee on the Scrutiny of Delegated Powers (1993: para. 30) (below). The *Guide to Legislative Procedures* advises departments that the experience of Parliamentary Counsel may prove helpful in deciding whether instruments should be subject to some form of parliamentary control and, if so, the form of that control. It warns that since both Houses are likely to consider carefully the nature and extent of Parliamentary control, the department should ensure that the Minister is content with what is proposed, where it may prove controversial (Office of Public Service 1996*b*: paras. 6.12–6.13).

Instruments laid before Parliament are examined by the Joint Committee on Statutory Instruments, which also has power to examine general instruments in respect of which there is no laying requirement. The Committee is solely concerned with 'technical' scrutiny, i.e. the legality and drafting of instruments, not their political merits (House of Commons Standing Order No. 151(1)). It is empowered to draw the special attention of both Houses to an instrument on any of a number of technical and 'legal policy' grounds, which do not impinge on the merits of the instrument or the policy behind it. Among the grounds on which attention may be drawn to an instrument are that its drafting appears to be defective, that there appears to be a doubt whether it is *intra vires,* that it appears to make some unusual or unexpected use of the powers conferred by the parent Act, that it is made under an Act excluding the instrument from challenge in the courts, or that it purports to have retrospective effect despite the absence of express provision in the parent Act. Before drawing attention to an instrument the Committee must seek an explanation from the department concerned.

Although Parliament has an interest in policing the exercise of delegated law-making powers to ensure that they are exercised within the limits laid down, there is an obvious overlap between technical scrutiny of the kind undertaken by the Committee and the sort of scrutiny which might have been conducted centrally within the executive branch. In the absence of such scrutiny, the Joint Committee may be seen as providing a partial substitute. (Where the Joint Committee differs from the Public Accounts Committee is in its lack of any obvious central interlocutor akin to the Treasury within the executive.) As a parliamentary committee the Joint Committee is in the relatively unusual position of being heavily dependent upon its professional advisers, who are usually former government legal advisers or have experience of the government legal service, for the expertise needed to carry out its task (Select Committee on Procedure 1996: p. 28). Extensive informal consultation takes place between departmental lawyers and Counsel to the Speaker and Counsel to the Lord Chairman of Committees, the counterpart to the Speaker in the Lords, who advise the Committee. Consultation may be especially valued on complex instruments, where a department may seek Counsel's views in advance in order to protect against possible Committee objection. 'I know in the past our advisers have actually been asked how could a particular drafting problem be solved. As one of them remarked at the time, when is the gamekeeper the poacher and is our job to get it right or impose our or our advisers' view?' (ibid.: p. 29). This does not mean that their opinion, e.g. as to the *vires* of an instrument, will always be accepted. 'Questions of *vires* being questions for the law courts, the views of laymen are inconclusive' (Carr 1956: 207). It has not been unknown therefore for a legal adviser to prefer his view to that of Counsel. On one occasion no objection was apparently taken to an *'ultra vires'* instrument in order to allow the Government to buy time and a pressure group to claim a victory in the courts (Select Committee on Procedure 1996: p. 29, a reference apparently to *R v Secretary of State for Social Services, ex parte Cotton* 1985).

In theory an adverse report could give rise to problems. The lack of time available for the consideration of instruments in Parliament, however, has meant that the Committee's work has become a largely self-contained exercise which depends for its impact more on the Committee's standing in the eyes of departments than on effective voting in Parliament. 'Its work is painstaking, unglamorous and goes largely unregarded within the House' (Select Committee on Procedure 1996: para. 19). The Committee has traditionally been regarded as a useful deterrent: 'by its very existence, [it] has undoubtedly a salutary effect upon the Government Departments who realise that their work will have to be considered by the Committee' (Select Committee on Delegated Legislation 1953: para. 87). Together with its predecessors, it has also had some success in establishing canons of good law-making, which are communicated to departments through circulars and amendments to *Statutory Instrument Practice;* but from the evidence of the Joint Committee's own reports compliance with its recommendations is patchy. In a recent special report, the Committee drew attention to a number of complaints which *regularly* arise on statutory instruments under consideration (Joint Committee on Statutory Instruments 1996). As we would expect in a decentralized system, departments differ sometimes quite markedly in the attention they pay to its recommendations. 'I have heard from a variety of sources how upset [departments] are at having to give oral evidence. On the other hand some memoranda to our inquiries suggest some departments could not care less' (Select

Committee on Procedure 1996: p. 29, Andrew Bennett (Chairman of the Joint Committee)). The Committee now requests from all departments a return on instruments reported to both Houses during the calendar year (Joint Committee on Statutory Instruments 1998).

2.4 The changing character of subordinate legislation

In the next two sections of the chapter we examine two developments which have had a major impact on the legislative machinery of government—the United Kingdom's membership of the European Union and the concern with burdens on business. Quite apart from these developments, however, subordinate legislation became controversial in the course of the nineteen-eighties in a way in which it had more or less ceased to be following the report of the Committee on Ministers' Powers (1932) and the reforms introduced at the end of the Second World War (Miers and Page 1990: 108–9). The growing controversy surrounding subordinate legislation prompted two developments, which may be conveniently dealt with here.

The first of these was the setting up, in 1992, of the House of Lords Delegated Powers Scrutiny Committee, on the model of the Scrutiny of Bills Committee of the Australian Senate, 'to report whether the provisions of any bill inappropriately delegate legislative power or whether they subject the exercise of legislative power to an inappropriate degree of parliamentary scrutiny'. The Committee was set up on the recommendation of the Jellicoe Committee in response to criticisms of the increase in the number of so-called 'Henry VIII' clauses empowering ministers to modify primary legislation by order (House of Lords Select Committee on the Committee Work of the House 1992: paras. 59–62, 133 and 185; for the criticisms, see Rippon 1989, 1990). The Committee, which was made permanent in 1994, sees its primary aim as being 'to inform debate with a view to saving time on the floor of the House' (House of Lords Select Committee on the Scrutiny of Delegated Powers 1993: para. 32). It considers each Bill in the light of a memorandum from the relevant department identifying provisions for delegated legislation in the Bill, describing their purpose, explaining why the matter has been left to delegated legislation, and explaining the level of parliamentary scrutiny to which it is proposed the exercise of the powers be subject. It aims to submit a report on the appropriateness of the Bill's provisions for delegated legislative powers before the beginning of the Bill's committee stage. The use made of its reports is a matter for the House.

Like the Joint Committee on Statutory Instruments, the Delegated Powers Scrutiny Committee's main significance is as a deterrent. Its experience has been that 'the number of bills which cause concern has diminished; and that Ministers appear to have been taking into account the Committee's likely reaction to their Bills. The mere presence of a parliamentary watchdog may make it unnecessary for it to bite too often' (Select Committee on Procedure 1996: Appendix 2, para. 29). From an internal control perspective, there is no reason why the centre should be opposed to a mechanism which provides an additional check on the powers departments seek by way of delegated legislation. Its attitude, however, is likely to be as much influenced by the prospect of getting its legislation more easily as by that of the Committee's ensuring that measures that should be in primary legislation are not slipped through in secondary legislation.

The second development was the extension in 1991 of the existing machinery of PCO scrutiny of draft instruments (below) to include all secondary legislation which amends or repeals primary legislation, regardless of whether or not it is made for the purpose of giving effect to EC obligations. Previously this machinery had been confined to instruments which were made in the implementation of Community obligations. As was the case with the establishment of the original machinery, the purpose of this extension was to guard against the risk that legal effectiveness might be compromised as a result of the possession by departments of much greater powers to amend or repeal primary legislation than in the past. The PCO has also assumed responsibility for the vetting or drafting of deregulation orders (below) whether or not they amend primary legislation, though virtually all do.

III THE IMPACT OF EUROPE

Jacques Delors, the former President of the European Commission, once famously predicted that, within ten years, 80 per cent of the laws affecting the economy and social policy would come from Brussels. Whatever the exact percentage ten years later there is no question that the negotiation and implementation of EC legislation now accounts for a significant proportion of the overall legislative activity of the executive. An efficiency scrutiny commissioned by the President of the Board of Trade to examine ways of minimizing the burden on business imposed by EC law estimated that over a third of existing UK legislation (including subordinate legislation) arose from an obligation to implement EC obligations, and that this proportion was likely to increase (DTI 1993: Introduction, para. 1). At the same time EU membership creates a need, as we have noted, to ensure that domestic legislation is consistent with the UK's obligations as a member of the Union.

1 The negotiation and implementation of EU law

1.1 EC law-making

The European Secretariat of the Cabinet Office is responsible for co-ordinating policy on EU matters, including proposals for legislation. It is also responsible for co-ordinating the parliamentary scrutiny of European Community documents (Bender 1991: 19). This is in contrast to parliamentary scrutiny generally where relations between departments and Parliament are treated as matters for departments themselves (other exceptions include the Osmotherly rules, and the rules on answering Parliamentary questions). The explanation for this difference is that the executive is under a 'self-imposed' obligation, embodied in a Commons resolution the principle of which is extended to the Lords, to give Parliament an opportunity to express its views on proposals for EC legislation before decisions are taken. It therefore has an interest in ensuring the smooth operation of the scrutiny system in order to ensure that scrutiny is cleared before the consideration of proposals reaches its final stages. Guidance has been issued to departments on scrutiny policy and procedures, but despite reminders from the Cabinet Office (Select Committee on European Legislation 1996: para. 237), departments' handling of scrutiny business falls some way short of the requirements to which the executive has committed itself, testifying to a more general neglect of parliamentary relations on the part of departments over the last twenty years. The European Legislation Committee's Report on the Scrutiny of European Business included an 'illustrative list' of scrutiny and handling problems ranging from the apparently trivial (documents sent to the wrong address) to the much more serious (accidental lifting of a scrutiny reserve) (Select Committee on European Legislation 1996: Annex H; for an up-date, see Modernisation Committee 1998*b*: Appendix 1, Annex G). Following the Committee's Report, efforts were made by the Lord President to improve matters, but the Committee reported that, after a general improvement, the performance of almost every department had declined (Ninth Report 1997–98: para. 7.11); the Select Committee on Procedure described the level of service between Whitehall and Westminster as 'unacceptably poor' (1997: para. 8). The Modernisation Committee has now recommended that a designated senior civil servant in each department should be responsible for the smooth running of scrutiny business and for taking corrective action when errors occur (Modernisation Committee 1998*b*: paras. 44–7).

1.2 Giving effect to EC obligations

The machinery of Cabinet Office co-ordination also extends to the implementation of EC obligations. The adverse consequences that may attach to a failure to implement obligations timeously or correctly provide an obvious incentive to such co-ordination. In theory, obligations could be implemented by means of primary legislation. In practice they are almost invariably implemented by secondary means, principally because successive governments have preferred to devote the parliamentary time available to other purposes. Page estimates that no less than 92 per cent of Community obligations are implemented by statutory instrument (Page 1998; see also 289 HC Debs., col. *131*, written answers 28 January 1997), made under either section 2(2) of the European Communities Act 1972 ('ECA') or other subordinate law-making powers specific to the subject-matter of the directive or regulation in question. (As well as empowering 'designated' departments to legislate in the implementation of Community obligations, section 2(2) provides that regard may be had to Community obligations in the exercise of other subordinate law-making powers. Absent this provision, Community obligations might be considered to be extraneous matters that ministers were obliged to ignore.)

1.2.1 Central co-ordination

The practice of relying on secondary legislation in the implementation of EC obligations gives rise to a central interest in such legislation, which has no parallel in relation to its purely domestic counterpart. One way in which that central interest has been given expression is through the institution of a system of what may be described as 'negative clearance' in respect of subordinate implementing legislation, which serves the purpose of ensuring that the Cabinet Office is kept informed about developments in the implementation of obligations and in particular about difficulties that may be encountered, whether in individual cases or more generally, which may have implications for other departments or the executive as whole. Under this system departments are not required to obtain the clearance of the European Secretariat of the Cabinet Office for implementing legislation, but they are expected to consult the Secretariat over a number of matters, including:

the appropriateness of using section 2(2) ECA;

doubts about the adequacy of the proposed method of implementation, which must normally be by binding means;

especially sensitive provisions, e.g. provisions imposing onerous duties on the subject; and departures from 'precedent', i.e. previous practice with regard to the parliamentary procedure to which an instrument made under section 2(2) ECA is to be subject—instruments made under section 2(2) may be subject to the negative or affirmative resolution procedure at the discretion of the designated department (Sched. 2, para. 2), with most instruments being subject to negative resolution procedure.

Departments are also expected to inform the European Secretariat where difficulties are anticipated in meeting deadlines for the implementation of obligations; and to draw to its attention any use of powers—and any dealings with the Joint Committee—which contain novel elements or raise questions of a general nature (note the analogous provision in respect of staff, above p. 74, 96). The Secretariat is thus in a position to take a view of the government-wide implications of developments and if necessary to issue advice to departments in the light of them.

The Secretariat has also issued guidance on giving effect to Community obligations by subordinate legislation. An earlier version of this guidance, which was first issued shortly after accession, had become outdated, but it was revised and reissued in 1995, 'at the cost of considerable effort', mainly in an attempt to reduce the number of requests from departments for advice on questions of implementation. The guidance, which covers the obligation to implement, methods of implementation, the drafting of statutory instruments and so on, represents the collective view of departments as to 'best practice' in the implementation of Community law. It is based on drafts circulated to departments and developed or amended on the basis of lawyers reflecting on their own experience and practice. It also includes Law Officers' opinions (e.g. as to the implementation of prospective obligations (as to which see 368 HL Debs., cols. *399–417*, 17 February 1976)), which are flagged and which enjoy special authority within the compilation. Although the guidance was collectively agreed, departments are free to raise for further consideration matters covered by it. Guidance on the drafting of statutory instruments which give effect to EC obligations (based on the original Cabinet Office guidance) is also contained in *Statutory Instrument Practice* (Cabinet Office 1987: paras. 2.97–2.102).

1.2.2 PCO scrutiny

Provision has also been made for the vetting by Parliamentary Counsel of instruments which amend or repeal statutory provisions—subordinate legislation made under section 2(2) ECA may include 'any provision (of any such extent) as might be made by Act of Parliament' (ECA s. 2(4)). As its restriction to instruments which amend or repeal statutory provisions indicates, the purpose of this requirement, which was introduced in the early years of Community membership, is not to provide a check on the legal effectiveness of instruments, which remains a matter for departments, although the vetting of instruments may involve 'reconstructive surgery', but rather a check on their impact on the statute book. By ensuring that the PCO is informed of changes which departments propose to make to the statute book, and given an opportunity to resolve any ambiguities beforehand, it guards against the risk that legal effectiveness generally may be compromised as a result of a failure to take account of changes made to primary legislation by departments. It also affords the Office the opportunity to maintain a measure of consistency in the style of amendments to primary legislation. In 1991, as we have seen, this system was extended to all instruments which amend or repeal primary legislation, regardless of whether or not they are made in the implementation of EC obligations (above).

2 The impact on domestic law-making

2.1 European Community law

Given the scope of EC law and the consequences that may attach to its breach, it would be surprising were the *Guide to Legislative Procedures* not to include the EC implications among the issues which need to be addressed in deciding whether to grant policy clearance to proposals for domestic legislation. The *Guide* suggests that at the earliest possible stage in the preparation of a Bill 'consideration should be given to the EU implications of what is proposed and legal advice should be obtained on whether there is any potential conflict with EC law' (Office of Public Service 1996*b*: para. 4.8). Departments are advised to consult the European Secretariat of the Cabinet Office, 'who can provide detailed guidance', for which purpose as we have seen it has its own sources of legal advice available to it, no later than the time at which instructions are sent to Parliamentary Counsel. Cabinet Committee memoranda are also expected to set out the EU implications of proposals (Cabinet Office 1997*e*). While, as we would expect, therefore, departments retain the lead responsibility for scrutinizing their legislative proposals for consistency with EC obligations, the role of the centre being essentially one of the provision of expert advice and assistance, the fact that the centre has its own sources of advice available to it, as well as to departments, means that it is in a position to assure itself that the EU implications of domestic legislative proposals have been properly addressed. And should it emerge that they have not been addressed, the fact that primary legislation is involved, which requires policy clearance, means that it is in a position to insist that the issue is properly ventilated before policy clearance is granted.

2.2 The European Convention on Human Rights

What is true of the European Union—that account has to be taken of its law in framing proposals for domestic legislation—is true of the United Kingdom's international obligations more generally, though the impact on the executive's legislative machinery is less immediately apparent, with the consequence that correspondingly greater reliance is placed on the role of Parliamentary Counsel and the Law Officers as the guardians of legal policy. A case in point is the ECHR where departments have been responsible from the outset for scrutinizing their own legislative proposals for conformity with ECHR law, seeking advice from the Foreign and Commonwealth Office as the 'guardians of the Convention' or the Law Officers as necessary. Cabinet Office guidance circulated in 1987 at the same time as *The Judge Over Your Shoulder*, reminded departments that it should be 'standard practice' when preparing a policy initiative for officials in individual departments, in consultation with their legal advisers, to consider the effect of existing (or expected) ECHR jurisprudence on any proposed legislative or administrative measure. If departments were in any doubt about the likely implications of the Convention in connection with a particular measure, they should seek *ad hoc* guidance from the FCO, with copies to the Law Officers and the 'home' departments (Office of Public Service 1996*b*: Appendix E, para. 8). Cabinet documents should also include an assessment of the impact, if any, of the ECHR on the action proposed (ibid.: Appendix E, para. 9).

The record of the United Kingdom before the ECHR has inevitably provoked considerable scepticism about the effectiveness of these arrangements. Kinley calculates that of the 28 cases decided against the UK between 1960 and 1991 no fewer than 22 involved direct violations of Convention-protected rights by domestic legislation (Kinley 1993: Appendix 1). The fact that so many items have slipped through the net when a system of internal scrutiny, albeit an informal one, is said to have been in operation, Kinley regards as 'indeed damning' (1993: 113 n.). In reply departmental lawyers argue that the width of the Convention combined with the generality of many of its provisions and the confusion of its jurisprudence make it very difficult to predict whether a particular provision of domestic law is likely to lead to a breach of the Convention, and they point with pride to the many unrecorded occasions when they have persuaded ministers (with difficulty) away from policies 'which sailed too close to the Strasbourg wind'. There is no doubt a great deal in this. Drawing on Kinley's analysis, however, Ryle asks whether the smaller number of cases in which Acts of Parliament have been found to be incompatible with EC law does not nevertheless indicate that the pre-legislative search for possible infringements has been taken more seriously and carried out more thoroughly in the EC field than in the ECHR (1994: 193 n.).

Kinley acknowledges that executive-based systems of pre-legislative scrutiny may have the effect of making policy-makers consider the human rights implications of proposals, and that in time this may prove to be 'the single most valuable instrument of prevention possessed by *any* scrutiny system' (1993: 114, original emphasis). He nevertheless regards such systems as 'fundamentally flawed . . . by the very positions they occupy. Ultimately, their location within the governmental machine places political pressures on them which allow the Government to have its way' (1993: 113). Leaving aside the question of what *is* the government for the purpose of 'having its way', an equally plausible interpretation of the evidence he assembles is not that such systems are fundamentally flawed, but rather that they are more likely to be fallible in the absence of the kind of central oversight exercised in relation to EU matters by the European Secretariat of the Cabinet Office. This in turn would seem to point to the necessity of such oversight if compatibility is to be assured.

The decision to make Convention rights directly enforceable in UK law will lead to a strengthening of the system of internal scrutiny along these lines. In the White Paper that preceded the Human Rights Bill the Government observed that it was 'highly desirable for [it] to ensure as far as possible that legislation which it places before Parliament in the normal way is compatible with the Convention rights' (Home Office 1997: para. 3.1). When the Act is brought into force the minister in charge of a Bill will be required to certify that its provisions are compatible with the Convention (s. 19). This statement of compatibility will be included alongside the explanatory notes which accompany a Bill when it is introduced in Parliament. The Government anticipated that this requirement would in turn have 'a significant and beneficial impact' on the preparation of draft legislation within government. It will ensure that ministers, departments, and their officials 'are fully seized of the gravity of the Convention's obligations in respect of human rights' (ibid.: para. 3.4). The onus will therefore be firmly on departments to ensure that proposals they bring forward are compatible with Convention rights.

At the same time, however, the Government also intends 'to strengthen collective Government procedures so as to ensure that a proper assessment is made of the human rights implications when collective approval is sought for a new policy as well as when any draft Bill is considered by Ministers' (ibid.: para. 3.4). It saw no need, however, to follow the example of deregulation initiative, for example, and make a particular minister responsible for promoting human rights across government, or to set up a separate new unit for this purpose, as recommended by the Constitution Unit (1996: para. 162). The responsibility for complying with human rights requirements 'rests on the Government as a whole' (Home Office 1997: para. 3.5). As the example of mainstreaming equal opportunities discussed earlier indicates, a potential drawback of making a minister or unit responsible is that it may detract from the front-line responsibility of departments for compliance. This does not mean that specialist units have no part to play. The Civil Service Commissioners, for example, play a vital role in securing compliance with the Recruitment Code (above, pp. 85–6). There is less need for such policing, however, where as in the case of primary legislation there are existing filters by means of which an effective check can be exercised over departmental proposals.

There is thus a double thrust to the Government's proposals—better equipping departments, by way of training, advice and assistance, to 'ECHR proof' their legislation, while at the same time strengthening the machinery of co-ordination and control at Cabinet Office level along lines similar to those in respect of the EU. An inter-departmental group of administrators and lawyers, chaired by the Cabinet Office (Constitution Secretariat), has been established with the task of co-ordinating advice to departments on policy and other issues arising from the legislation. It will also consider what training on ECHR proofing can be arranged for departments, which will retain responsibility for scrutinizing their own draft legislation. It will be interesting to see whether this new system of scrutiny will prove more effective than its predecessor.

IV BURDENS ON BUSINESS

The Conservative Government's Deregulation initiative was launched in 1985, following an inter-departmental scrutiny of the costs to business of complying with regulatory requirements (Minister without Portfolio 1985; DTI 1985). Annual reports on progress were published between 1986 and 1988, two in the form of White Papers, but after three years the attention and resources devoted to the initiative declined, while expectations that a deregulatory culture would become embedded in departments proved to be over-optimistic (DTI 1993: para. 5.2). In 1992 the initiative was re-launched. Following its re-launch, renewed emphasis was placed on the repeal or simplification of allegedly unnecessarily burdensome regulation, with powers being taken under the Deregulation and Contracting Out Act 1994 (above, pp. 47–8) for this purpose. Under the banner of 'fewer, better, simpler', the initiative in its later stages aimed to improve competitiveness and encourage enterprise, by reducing the burden of existing regulation, minimizing the burden of new regulation, making enforcement more business-friendly and improving communication with business and others.

Following the change of government in May 1997, the initiative was re-named Better Regulation. Although the Labour Government claims to be less hostile to regulation than its predecessor, there are substantial elements of continuity between the two initiatives. Like its predecessor, the Labour Government's aim is to regulate

> only where necessary and to ensure that those regulations—both European and domestic—affecting business and citizen alike—are targeted at the problem at hand, clear and simple to understand, applied consistently, proportionate to the problem and the circumstances of individual businesses, voluntary groups and others, and enforced effectively and constructively by a body accountable for its conduct. These principles reflect the commitment in the Government's business manifesto not to impose burdensome regulations on business, to cut red tape and build a regulatory framework which is transparent and simple, in which there will be fewer government demands for data and one in which the benefits of regulation outweigh the costs. (Better Regulation Unit's Website)

1 Machinery

When the initiative was first launched a central Enterprise and Deregulation Unit, later the Deregulation Unit, drew up a 'concordat' between departments setting out how deregulation should be tackled (Department of Employment 1986: Annex 3). The first annual report on progress explained that because this was 'the first major, Whitehall-wide, exercise to control the flow of regulations' departments had found it 'helpful' to have 'clear guidance' in this new area of work (ibid.: para. 3.4). Under the concordat the 'prime' responsibility for ensuring that burdens on business were reduced was placed on regulatory departments in consultation with the departments that sponsored the business sectors concerned. The original White Paper had underlined the importance, 'managerially and constitutionally', of regulatory departments retaining responsibility for assessing regulations. A central task force would be set up to co-ordinate the initiative throughout government, but the determination of policy issues and their regulatory consequences would remain the 'prerogative' of departmental ministers (Minister without Portfolio 1985: paras. 8.5–8.6). To help overcome the problem of departmental resistance or inertia, the concordat suggested that each department establish a deregulation unit, answerable to a minister, responsible for pursuing deregulation across the field of the department's activities (Department of Employment 1986: para. 3.5). Their activities would in turn be co-ordinated and monitored by the Enterprise and Deregulation Unit, which was responsible for driving the initiative forward across government—ensuring that procedures were complied with, spreading best practice, initiating reviews of existing regulations, consulting business, and keeping the needs of business and employment to the fore across government (Department of Employment 1987: para. 1.2).

This basic machinery was later strengthened by the addition, in July 1994, of an advisory body—the Deregulation Task Force—to help ensure that the process of review maintained momentum. In the view of the efficiency scrutiny set up to examine ways of minimizing the burden on business imposed by EC law the Deregulation Unit's effectiveness as an instrument of change depended on the political climate in favour of deregulation. While there remained an important role for it in seeking to bring about cultural change in Whitehall, some additional mechanism was needed. It recommended the establishment of an independent Regulatory Review Commission with the power to conduct reviews of existing legislation which affects business, to call for evidence, to examine official documentation, to make recommendations and to publish reports (Department of Trade and Industry 1993: paras. 5.4– 5.6).

Under the Better Regulation initiative this machinery has been retained. The Deregulation Unit's successor, the Better Regulation Unit, is responsible for the central co-ordination of the initiative, while the Better Regulation Task Force is responsible for advising 'on action which improves the effectiveness and credibility of government regulation by ensuring that it is necessary, fair and affordable, and simple to understand and administer taking account of the needs of small businesses and ordinary people' (Better Regulation Task Force 1998*b*).

2 Mechanisms

In its bearing on the legislative machinery of government the Deregulation initiative had two aspects: preventing departments imposing 'unnecessary' burdens on business, and the systematic scrutiny of existing burdens with a view to the repeal or simplification of those that were unnecessarily burdensome. The first of these aspects led to the introduction of a system of regulatory appraisals and the formulation of a set of principles of good regulation; the second to the power to repeal unnecessary burdens by ministerial order under the Deregulation and Contracting Out Act. Under the Better Regulation initiative, the system of regulatory appraisals has been replaced by a system of regulatory impact assessments, and the principles of good regulation have been revised.

2.1 Regulatory appraisal and regulatory impact assessments

The system of regulatory appraisal which was in place from 1996 to 1998 involved the systematic assessment of the costs and benefits of proposed regulatory options with a view to ensuring that any regulation was necessary, aimed at the right target, and proportionate to the problem. The objective was not to 'reduce the risk at all costs, but to ensure that there is an appropriate balance between costs and benefits' (Deregulation Unit 1996*b*: para. 1.2). It was made up of two elements:

a compliance cost assessment, which was conceived as a 'structured appraisal of the cost impact of all primary, secondary, and EC legislative proposals likely to affect business. Its purpose is to inform ministers, MPs, business and other interested parties of the likely costs to business of complying with new or amended legislation so that these costs can be assessed, and unnecessary burdens to business identified, *well before a decision is taken to go ahead with the proposals'* (Deregulation Unit 1996*a*: para. 1.1; original emphasis); and

a risk assessment, which is a 'technique for considering the various risks associated with a particular situation, procedure or operation and examining whether controls are necessary, and if so, what form they should take' (Deregulation Unit 1994). It involves specifying the problem or situation and the scale of the resulting harm; estimating the risk; identifying options to reduce the risk; and assessing the impact of these options on the risk.

Regulatory appraisal thus went further than compliance cost assessment in that it considered the costs of a range of options and included costs additional to those faced by business such as those to consumers and government. Guidance on regulatory appraisal was contained in *Checking the Cost of Regulation* (Deregulation Unit 1996*a*) and *Regulation in the Balance* (Deregulation Unit 1996*b*).

The requirement to prepare a compliance cost assessment for regulatory proposals which could affect business was a feature of the Deregulation initiative from the outset. Some commentators have suggested that the requirement was initially confined to secondary legislation (Froud and Ogus 1996: 226), but this is mistaken. The requirement applied to all proposals by departments for new regulations, or amendments to existing regulations, affecting business, including proposals for primary legislation (Department of Employment 1986: para. 3.9; see also Annex 3 Appendix A—'regulations' is being used here not in the specialized legal sense of secondary legislation but in the sense of requirements regardless of their source). Until 1992 the only check on whether assessments were in fact completed appears to have been by Departmental

Deregulation Units, some of which had been run down to little more than postboxes (Department of Trade and Industry 1993: para. 5.2), and the central Deregulation Unit, but when the initiative was relaunched in 1992 efforts were made to integrate the requirement into the machinery of collective decision-making. At the request of the Prime Minister, all Cabinet papers and minutes to the Prime Minister's Office for collective discussion which dealt with proposals that might have an impact on business, and all bids for legislation under the annual legislative bids procedure that might have an impact on business, had to spell out clearly the likely compliance costs; the President of the Board of Trade was charged with drawing attention to cases where this was not done properly (Deregulation Unit 1992). In the following year assessments were required to be published alongside all primary legislation introduced into and secondary legislation laid before Parliament which had an impact on business.

The requirement to undertake a risk assessment was introduced in 1996 following a recommendation from the Deregulation Task Force (Deregulation Task Force 1995). To tighten the system further, the Task Force recommended that ministers should be held 'personally accountable for acts of over-regulation that destroy jobs' (Deregulation Task Force 1995). When a bid was made for legislation therefore the minister had to certify that he had seen the compliance cost assessment and the risk assessment and was satisfied that the Bill struck an appropriate balance between cost and benefit (Office of Public Service 1996*b*: Appendix A para. 2.5). Permanent Secretaries were also asked by the Prime Minister to take personal responsibility for all assessments prepared by their departments (Deregulation Unit 1996*a*: Introduction).

Under a government whose members are ideologically opposed to regulation it is not difficult to see the potential of a requirement of ministerial certification as a check on the imposition of regulatory burdens. Even so, one suspects, the temptation for ministers was to certify that the balance struck was an appropriate one. Perhaps for this reason the Task Force in its second annual report recommended the establishment of a control regime for new regulatory proposals similar to that in respect of public expenditure, under which the sanction of the regulatory equivalent of the Chief Secretary to the Treasury would be required for new regulatory 'expenditure' (Deregulation Task Force 1996). Under this system regulation would have been treated as a collective resource which could only be 'spent' with the approval of a Ministry of Regulation with presumably the same parsimonious approach to regulation as traditionally characterized the Treasury's approach to expenditure. The history of public expenditure control indicates, however, that the establishment of such a system in a plural executive would face formidable obstacles in the absence of the traditional authority on which the Treasury was able to draw (above, pp. 113–16); moreover, it is only with the willing co-operation of 'spending' departments that it could be made to work.

The Labour Government initially continued to operate the system of regulatory appraisals, but in August 1998 it was replaced by a system of regulatory impact assessments. A regulatory impact assessment is—

> a short, structured document which is published with regulatory proposals and new legislation. It briefly describes the issue that has given rise to a need for regulation and compares various possible options for dealing with that issue. One or more non-regulatory options will normally be included. The costs and benefits of each option are identified—and quantified wherever possible—to assist informed public debate about regulation. (Better Regulation Unit 1998: p. 28)

Like the system of regulatory appraisal it replaces, regulatory impact assessment is intended to ensure that any regulation is necessary, aimed at the right target, and in proportion to the problem or issue being addressed (ibid.: p. 28). One of the ways in which it is said to differ from regulatory appraisal is in taking 'a more rounded view of costs and benefits, with clearer recognition of non-business costs (such as damage to the environment) and a wider acknowledgement of different kinds of benefits that regulation can bring when used wisely' (ibid.: p. 31). A full regulatory impact assessment must accompany any new legislation (including legislation implementing EU obligations) or consultation papers on regulatory proposals. Where inter-departmental clearance is being sought for proposals which have an impact on business, charities, or voluntary bodies, departments are required to provide a 'robust assessment' of the costs and benefits; a clear analysis of who will be affected; and an explanation of why non-regulatory action would be inadequate. The intention is that without such an assessment clearance should not be given (Better Regulation Unit 1998, Foreword). As before, the responsible minister is required to certify that he or she has read the assessment and is satisfied that 'the balance between cost and benefit is the right one in the circumstances.' A *Better Regulation Guide* (ibid.) contains guidance on the preparation of regulatory impact assessments and a description of good practice at all stages of regulating.

Some commentators have seen the significance of the original system of compliance cost assessments as largely symbolic, its purpose not so much to increase the rationality of regulation as to underline the government's commitment to a deregulatory strategy (Froud and Ogus 1996). From an internal control perspective, however, the significance of these 'tripwires' is that they are intended to prevent regulation being introduced 'without sufficient scrutiny, or "by default" ' (Deregulation Task Force 1996: p. 4). They may also of course have the effect of making it more difficult to introduce regulation even where it is 'necessary'; which, too, may be part of their purpose (Mashaw 1996: 420), particularly when as in the United States they are combined with the possibility of judicial enforcement.[4] Boden and Froud come closer to it when they suggest that 'we are witnessing an elaborate public sector quadrille in which deregulation of the private sector can only be achieved by increasing regulatory control over the extent and nature of public administration' (Boden and Froud 1996: 530). On this interpretation, deregulation and its successor better regulation are 'a manifestation of a new culture of control over regulators' (1996: 545).

2.2 Principles of good regulation

The Conservative Government also endorsed three 'principles of good regulation' formulated by the eight Sainsbury Task Forces which were set up to review existing regulation after the initiative was relaunched in 1992. The three principles were:

Think Small First—because small businesses are most vulnerable to over-regulation they should be consulted on every new regulation to make sure that they are able to cope;

Proportionality—make sure that the benefits of regulation outweigh the costs; and

Go for Goal-Based Regulation—tell business *what* it should do, if you must, but let them work out *how* they should do it.

These principles were incorporated in a booklet, *Thinking About Regulating: A Guide to Good Regulation* (Deregulation Unit 1994), designed to help policy-makers to improve the quality of regulations, which also contained a ten-point summary of 'good regulatory practice'. Both the principles and the summary of good practice were later set out in a separate *Good Regulation Checklist,* which also included a *Compliance Cost Assessment Checklist.*

The Sainsbury Task Forces' example has now been followed by the Better Regulation Task Force, which has published its own *Principles of Good Regulation* (Better Regulation Task Force 1998*a*) setting out what it believes to be 'the key principles of all good regulation', as a template against which to evaluate the quality of regulations. The five principles

[4] It has been suggested that because regulatory appraisal in the United Kingdom is based on 'internal administrative directives' it does not impose 'any formal constraints on what regulators may lawfully do' (Froud and Ogus 1996: 226), but in a world of 'legitimate expectations' this conclusion would by no means seem to follow. The possibility cannot be excluded therefore that the requirements set out in the current *Good Regulation Guide* will prove to be judicially enforceable.

of good regulation identified by the Task Force, which incorporate the Sainsbury principles, are:

Transparency—policy objectives should be clearly defined; regulations should be simple, clear and easily understood;

Accountability—regulators should be accountable; there should be proper consultation, and a fair and efficient appeals procedure;

Targeting—the approach taken should be aimed at the problem; a goals-based approach should be used where possible; regulations should be periodically reviewed;

Consistency—new requirements should be consistent with existing requirements; requirements should be evenly enforced; and

Proportionality—the right balance should be established between risk and cost; no needless demands should be imposed on those being regulated—think small first.

2.3 Deregulation orders

The scrutiny of existing requirements with a view to the removal of those which imposed unjustifiable burdens on business initially proved less tractable. A major problem was lack of legislative time. As the efficiency scrutiny reported later, 'radical examination of existing legislation was rare, in part because resources had not been allocated for such activity and also because any change would often require primary legislation which was not expected to be available' (Department of Trade and Industry 1993: para. 5.2). When the initiative was relaunched in 1992, departments were required 'to identify and set up programmes to review comprehensively all existing legislation'. At the same time, the business task forces already mentioned were set up to advise ministers 'on priorities for the repeal or simplification of existing regulations and enforcement methods so as to minimise the costs on business . . . bearing in mind the considerations of public health, safety and security which underlie the regulatory system'.

The task forces made over 800 recommendations for reducing the burden on business and the voluntary sector, over 500 of which were accepted by the Government. The immediate difficulty the Government faced in giving effect to the proposals it accepted was the need in many cases for primary legislation. The solution it adopted was to take the power, which the House of Lords Delegated Powers Scrutiny Committee described as 'unprecedented in time of peace' (1994: para. 1), to amend or repeal by ministerial order primary legislation passed before the end of the 1993–94 session which imposed a burden on business, provided that necessary protection was not removed (Deregulation and Contracting Out Act 1994 s. 1). In order to reduce burdens on business the Government thus found itself compelled to increase the law-making powers of departments.

As well as representing an advance for the Government in its efforts to promote deregulation at minimum costs to itself in terms of parliamentary time, the deregulation order-making power appeared at first blush to put the review of existing regulations on a new footing by removing the 'excuse' of lack of legislative time. In practice, the scope for restructuring regulatory regimes under the 1994 Act has been limited by the strictness with which its criteria have been interpreted. Equipped with the order-making power, however, the Conservative Government was able to embark on the deregulatory equivalent of the main legislative programme. By agreement between the House of Commons Deregulation Committee, which scrutinizes proposals, and the Deregulation Unit, it brought forward deregulation proposals at the rate of approximately one a week. In contrast to normal subordinate legislation, all such orders are drafted or vetted by the PCO, whether they amend primary legislation or not, though virtually all do. They are also considered by the Legislation Committee.

2.4 Secondary legislation

Burdens on business may be as easily imposed by secondary legislation as by Act of Parliament. One of the more striking features of the Deregulation initiative in its later stages was the lengths to which the Government found itself compelled to go in its efforts to curb the burdens on business imposed by secondary legislation. Although secondary legislation is subject to the same requirements in respect of regulatory appraisal and ministerial certification as apply to Acts of Parliament, it does not pass through the same collective filters, making its control more difficult than the control of primary legislation, notwithstanding the requirement of ministerial certification. In the absence of the same collective filters as apply to Bills, ministers were 'required' to submit monthly reports to a Cabinet Committee on Competitiveness, chaired by the Deputy Prime Minister, giving details of all the regulations they had introduced in the previous month, identifying those which affected business, and giving full details of the costs or savings involved (Deregulation Unit 1996*b*: p. 5). According to the Chancellor of the Duchy of Lancaster, the result of this requirement (which is no longer in operation) was that only 228 statutory instruments affecting business were made in 1996 (Cabinet Office (OPS) Press Notice 23/97). A 'hit list' of about 1000 'regulations' was also drawn up for repeal or amendment. In October 1996 the Government announced that over 750 'regulations' had been repealed or amended in the last three years, 420 in the last year, with about 350 further regulations to be repealed or amended by the end of 1996 (282 HC Debs., cols. *1086–7*, 17 October 1996). At the same time departments were exhorted to 'Make One, Drop One' (Cabinet Office (OPS) Press Notice 23/97).

The increasing decentralization of the legislative process as a result of the greater willingness of Parliament to delegate law-making power to a wider range of bodies than would have seemed possible only a few years ago meant that the Government found itself also compelled to try and extend these disciplines to other law-making bodies, notably financial services legislators to whom City legislation had been effectively 'contracted out' under the Financial Services Act 1986 (see e.g. Deregulation Task Force 1996).

2.5 EC legislation

Concern with burdens on business also led to persistent concern with the alleged over-implementation or 'gold-plating' of EC obligations. The efficiency scrutiny that investigated ways of minimizing the burdens of business imposed by EC law was commissioned against the background of claims 'that the UK may have tended to exceed its obligations under EC law, imposing as a consequence unnecessary burdens on business and damaging international competitiveness' (Department of Trade and Industry 1993: Introduction, para. 1). It found little evidence to show that 'officials deliberately hide behind Brussels to add-in additional requirements for which they would otherwise have been unable to find legislative time' (ibid.: para. 4.6). It did, however, find that implementing legislation tended to go beyond the requirements of directives for two main reasons.

First, where EC law had been integrated into existing UK law there was 'a tendency to carry over existing national provisions, wider scope and tougher penalties than in other Member States' (Department of Trade and Industry 1993: Executive Summary, para. 2). A weakness of relying on subordinate law-making powers, including section 2(2) ECA, in the implementation of obligations, the scrutiny argued, was that it could normally not be used to remove existing requirements which might be unnecessary in the light of the obligation to which effect was being given. Under section 2(2) ECA the scope of amendments to domestic legislation is confined to matters 'arising out of or related to' the requirement to implement the directive. This resulted, the scrutiny suggested, in 'a strong tendency to retain existing requirements and just add on new EC requirements', which the scrutiny identified as one cause of over-implementation (Department of Trade and Industry 1993: para.

4.6–4.9). How serious a problem this was and continues to be is uncertain. On a broad interpretation of section 2(2) ECA, for which judical support now exists (*R v Secretary of State for Trade and Industry, ex parte Unison* 1996), it was less of a problem that the scrutiny appears to have assumed. The scrutiny, however, recommended that section 2(2), which had traditionally been used as the method of implementation of last resort, should be used where it provided 'a more coherent route' to implementation, and that consideration should be given to increasing its scope to allow it to be used for 'minor, non-controversial amendments to domestic law resulting from the implementation of EC law' (Department of Trade and Industry 1993: para. 4.10). Consideration was apparently given to amending the Act before the 1992 election, but its amendment was rejected as politically impossible. With judicial support now for a broad interpretation of section 2(2) the need for its amendment may be less keenly felt.

The scrutiny also recommended that more consideration should be given to the possibility of using primary legislation in the implementation of obligations. Departments, it noted, were 'encouraged whenever possible to use secondary legislation, no matter how cumbersome, to implement EC law' (Department of Trade and Industry 1993: para. 4.7). It acknowledged that a disadvantage of primary legislation was that it raised the potential of a debate going beyond the scope of the obligation assumed, but pointed out that an Act of Parliament may be the only sensible means of enabling EC requirements and existing domestic legislation to be presented in a 'coherent and non-burdensome way' (ibid.: para. 4.11). The presumption, however, would appear to remain firmly against using primary legislation to give effect to obligations. A department bidding for a place in the legislative programme to give effect to EC obligations is required to explain why delegated legislation is not considered suitable and whether the opinion of the Law Officers has been sought (Office of Public Service 1996*b*). Partly because it prefers to use the available parliamentary time for other purposes, and partly because of the political difficulties which stand in the way of amending the European Communities Act, the executive thus finds itself relying in the implementation of Community obligations on subordinate law-making powers, which are not ideally suited to the purpose.

The second reason the scrutiny identified why implementing legislation tended to go beyond the requirements of directives was because the domestic tradition of detailed drafting led departmental draftsmen to elaborate upon EC texts which were often drafted in considerably less detailed or precise terms than had traditionally been the case with legislative texts in the United Kingdom (above, pp. 241–2). The UK legal system was based on 'a tradition of precise drafting which aims to eradicate doubt in contrast with the purposive approach on which EC law and that of other Member States is based' (Department of Trade and Industry 1993: Executive Summary, para. 2). In transposing requirements, therefore, a departmental gloss might be added which took the implementing legislation beyond the 'strict' requirements of the directive.

One way of reducing the scope for over-implementation which arises as a result of this difference in drafting traditions is through the adoption of the 'copy out' as opposed to the more traditional 'elaborative' approach to implementation. Under the copy out approach the implementing legislation 'simply refers to or literally adopts the same, or virtually the same, language as the directive itself', whereas under the elaborative approach the directive is re-written in the style of traditional domestic legislation (Department of Trade and Industry 1993: para. 4.17). But while a merit of the copy out approach is that it guards against over-implementation (and under-implementation), its potential drawback is it may leave unclear the effect of the implementing legislation on the statute book, exposing it to the criticism that it represents 'an abrogation of a duty to make legal obligations clear and unambiguous without having to resort to the courts for interpretation' (ibid.: para. 4.18). Individuals are put to the expense of finding out what their obligations are, while the courts are afforded a greater measure of latitude in the interpretation of statutory requirements than has traditionally been regarded as acceptable in the UK (Bennion 1990: 23–6).

The scrutiny acknowledged that there were difficulties in using the copy out approach where a directive had to be fitted into a substantial body of existing UK legislation, but where there was no existing domestic legislation on a topic it recommended that copy out should be considered as an option (Department of Trade and Industry 1993: para. 4.19; Annex D, paras. 33–5). In practice, as we have seen, instruments that amend the statute book are vetted by the PCO. As the guardians of the statute book, Parliamentary Counsel may be expected to oppose the copy out approach where it threatens to leave the effect of EC law on the statute book unclear, or less clear than would be the case were the more traditional elaborative approach to be used, but while the Office may be said to have an institutional tendency to oppose the copy out approach, individual views within the Office are also said to vary quite considerably. Other government lawyers, while opposed to the evangelical zeal with which the Deregulation Unit urged the adoption of the copy out approach as the sole approach to the implementation of Community obligations, take the view that it is usually to be preferred, and that elaborative re-drafting is better reserved for particular cases involving, for example, the creation of criminal offences, where ambiguity is both unfair to the individual and unworkable.

Among the recommendations of the efficiency scrutiny was that the

Deregulation Unit prepare a 'concise and readily accessible' guide to the formulation and implementation of EC law in the UK (Department of Trade and Industry 1993: para. 3.33). *Getting a Good Deal in Europe . . . Deregulatory Principles in Practice* sets out the way UK ministers and officials will negotiate, implement, and enforce European Community law 'to ensure that it does not impose unnecessary regulation' (Department of Trade and Industry 1994: Foreword). The guide identifies subsidiarity and proportionality as critical issues at the outset. It enjoins officials to question whether legislation is needed at all at the Community level. They should be ready to challenge the need for legislation and ensure alternatives are considered. If Community action is appropriate they should ensure that any proposed legislation does not go beyond what is necessary to achieve its objectives. Ministers should be involved early in addressing these issues (see further Department of Trade and Industry 1993: para. 3.8). Once it has become clear that legislation is to be put forward, the guide suggests that departments try to ensure continuity throughout the process of negotiating EC law and implementing it in the UK. Departmental lawyers should be involved from the outset so they can be alert to how EC legislation should be implemented in the UK if it is adopted (Department of Trade and Industry 1994: p. 3). As soon as it is clear that legislation is likely to be adopted, departments should start planning how to implement and enforce it. Implementing legislation should be based on the principle that it should 'impose least costs and provide greatest certainty consistent with the UK's implementation obligations'. The guide does not express any preference between the copy out and elaborative approaches. 'In practice, these approaches will be combined to some extent in most cases. Both have their place, their advantages and disadvantages' (ibid.: p. 6).

The guide was followed by the issue, in May 1996, of a checklist on *Implementing European Law.* The checklist, which is modelled on the *Good Regulation* checklist, is designed 'to assist ministers and officials in avoiding any over-implementation of EC legislation'. Under the checklist departments are required to ensure:

that 'double banking' is avoided; i.e. that existing domestic law is not duplicated as a result of the implementation of a directive. If existing domestic law is insufficient, it suggests using the European Communities Act or a deregulation order to dispense with it;

that 'gold plating' is avoided, so that, for example, obligations are implemented from the latest possible date, unless the UK benefits of early implementation clearly outweigh the costs; the substantive requirements 'follow exactly the wording of the directive'—in other words, the elaborative approach is not employed without good reason and the compliance costs implications of doing so being taken into account; and unnecessary statutory codes or non-statutory guidance are not proposed, and any necessary code or guidance is as short, simply expressed and as non-prescriptive as possible;

that all implementing measures are properly integrated and expressed in plain English; and

that it is clear when and by whom the actual impact of the implementing measures will be monitored.

When submitting bids for legislation under the annual legislative bids procedure ministers must certify that the checklist has been applied (Office of Public Service 1996*b*: Annex A, para. 2.5). Ministers must also certify that it has been applied in the case of secondary legislation—the normal means of implementing EC obligations.

Ultimately, however, the problem of the alleged over-regulation can only be tackled at source. Action at the national level to reduce burdens on business has therefore been complemented by efforts to pursue deregulation at the European Union level. Since the beginning of the 1990s the number of proposals for new Community legislation has in fact been in steep decline. The decline in the number of new proposals is partly a consequence of the completion of the single market programme, but it also reflects the adoption of the principle of subsidiarity, and the commitment of the present Commission, which took office in 1995, 'to do less, but to do it better'. The Commission has also embarked on a programme of legislative (and administrative) 'simplification' aimed at identifying ways in which single market legislation can be simplified without decreasing the level of protection for citizens, workers or the environment (COM (97) 626 final, 26 November 1997).

A striking feature of the growth of these disciplines is the lack of executive emphasis on external as opposed to internal scrutiny of the implementation of EC obligations. The Select Committee on Procedure in the last Parliament regarded as unsatisfactory 'the lack of continuity between the scrutiny of draft European legislation and its implementation' (1997: para. 73). It concluded that the implementation of EC obligations by means of secondary legislation 'might never or only rarely raise legal doubts as to *vires*, and might also produce less "gold-plating" than was sometimes suggested: but there was every reason to believe that there was "silver-plating", and every reason for Parliament to ascertain what was happening' (1997: para. 79). It proposed scrutiny by some parliamentary body before the laying of parliamentary legislation, with the power to ensure a debate in cases of inappropriate or onerous implementation' (1997: para. 80). The Committee saw this as a potentially highly productive area of scrutiny. No action has yet been taken on its recommendation (for the views of the Select Committee on European Legislation, see Modernisation Committee 1998*c*: Appendix 1, paras. 94–5).

V CONCLUSIONS

The collective interest in government has traditionally exercised (or possessed the capacity to exercise) close control over primary law-making, much less control over secondary law-making. The fact that under the constitution primary law-making power is centralized in Parliament makes its control a relatively straightforward matter. It is a matter of controlling access to it through the machinery that has been put in place for that purpose. The exercise of collective control over secondary law-making by contrast is much more difficult by reason of the fact that the powers are vested in departments rather than the centre. What we see in this chapter is the collective interest in government being driven to seek closer control over departmental law-making in order to ensure conformity with 'European' law, to ensure that legal effectiveness is not compromised as a result of the increasing scope of the legislative powers in departmental hands, and to reduce regulatory burdens on business.

These efforts have met with mixed success. On the available evidence, the centre has been more successful in ensuring conformity with EC law and in securing legal effectiveness than it has been in ensuring conformity with ECHR law or in reducing burdens on business imposed by way of secondary legislation. Two factors may be adduced in explanation of this difference. The first is conflict or its absence. The extension of PCO scrutiny to departmental law-making has not provoked departmental opposition because the interest in legal effectiveness is one which is shared by departments as well as by the centre. Where agreement is lacking, however, as over burdens on business, there is much greater scope for departments to resist the urgings of the centre and pursue their individual conceptions of the public interest: witness the increasingly desperate lengths to which the last Conservative Government found itself driven in its efforts to curb the burdens imposed on business by secondary legislation.

Conflict cannot be the whole of it, however. On the face of it there is no scope for disagreement over the need to comply with the ECHR to which the United Kingdom has been a party from the outset, yet the UK has been less successful in complying with the ECHR than with the law of the European Union of which it has been a member only since 1973. Here it is arguably the lack of central oversight which has been crucial. Present in relation to EC law, its absence in relation to ECHR law may be thought to go some way towards explaining the United Kingdom's relatively poorer showing in relation to ECHR law than its EC counterpart. As one lawyer put it to us, exhortations to civil servants to have regard to certain matters do not by themselves produce effective results. It is crucial to the success of any system of internal control that there be built into it the capacity to monitor and if necessary second-guess departments. That capacity exists in relation to the EC; and, as we have seen, it is in the course of being developed in relation to the ECHR.

The delegation of law-making powers to departments is only one aspect of a wider fragmentation of law-making power under the constitution, which has also involved the transfer of law-making power to the institutions of the European Community. This has in turn required the extension of the internal machinery of co-ordination and control to include the making of EC law and its implementation. As the Conservative Governments quickly discovered, there is little point in exercising closer control over departmental law-making in order to stem the growth of burdens on business if at the same time the executive as whole is being compelled to increase these burdens in order to give effect to EC obligations. The shift to qualified majority voting, however, makes the control of EC law-making even more difficult than the control of domestic law-making. What we have seen in the last few years, however, is a growing harmonization of legislative agendas which for the moment at least has drawn much of the sting from this issue. The subordination however remains.

Looking to the future, the fragmentation of law-making power now also includes the devolution of functions to a Scottish Parliament and executive with their own law-making capacities. The implications for the existing machinery of co-ordination and control are two-fold. On the one hand there is the need to ensure that the Scottish Parliament and executive observe the limits on their powers imposed by the devolution legislation. On the other hand there is the need to ensure that they take action including legislative action where necessary to give effect to the United Kingdom's international and European obligations. There will also be a need in some cases to ensure the co-ordinated exercise of legislative powers across national boundaries, as well as a continuing need to take the Scottish dimension into account in United Kingdom legislation (and a residual liability to meet Scottish legislative needs that cannot be met through Edinburgh). Following the general pattern we have encountered in other contexts we would expect the lead responsibility for these matters to fall to the Scottish Executive, but we would also expect its performance to be closely monitored by the Scottish Office or its successor and by the Advocate General within the United Kingdom government. Like the extension of the machinery of internal co-ordination and control to include the ECHR, how successful their efforts will be remains to be seen.

9

Litigation and Legal Advice: Co-ordination and Control

Legislation and delegated legislation are distinctive governmental products, sources of law which are themselves constructed according to familiar, in some cases ancient, rules and processes. Outside this sphere government lawyers function in an environment which is at once less structured, more varied, and less amenable to their control. We have already looked, in Chapter 7, at the complex set of arrangements through which legal advice and action may be delivered. Here we ask how such advice is co-ordinated and controlled; in other words, who, in government, says what the law is? Is there one voice, or are there many? Where and by whom may these voices be heard? And are the arrangements for the formulation and expression of executive legal opinion adequate to the present stage of development of our constitution?

I THE LAW OFFICERS, PROSECUTORS, AND CIVIL LITIGATION

1 The general constitutional position

Such a discussion must start with the Law Officers. In considering how the Law Officers act to give content and force to ideas of legality within the executive it is best to distinguish between their functions in relation to criminal law and prosecutions and their functions as the government's legal advisers. The reason is that the Law Officers are now recognized, in England and Wales no less than in Scotland, as having genuine Ministerial responsibilities for the criminal prosecution system. When the Crown Prosecution Service and the Serious Fraud Office were created in England in the nineteen-eighties, clear lines of political responsibility needed to be established, even if the nature of the work required two kinds of departure from ordinary departmental arrangements in order to secure, and to be seen to secure, the necessary objectivity and independence.

The first departure is that the Attorney-General's relationship with the DPP, as head of CPS, and with the Director of SFO, is a statutory one.

These officials are not *alter ego*s of the Attorney-General in the same way as is the Permanent Secretary (and the other staff) of the ordinary ministerial department, but have their own statutory responsibilities, which they exercise under the superintendence of the Attorney-General.[1] The Legal Secretariat supports the Attorney-General in managing what is essentially a personal relationship with the Directors. Within this framework of statutory superintendence, the Attorney-General, as minister, has three kinds of interest.

In the first place he is responsible for administrative superintendence of areas of operation such as budgets, structure, and the efficiency and effectiveness of these departments. For their part they look to him to fight their corner within government on both policy and budgetary issues, and to answer for their activities in Parliament.

Second, he is concerned with policy work, both within and beyond the remit of CPS and SFO themselves. Within this remit, he needs to be sure that the prosecution policies being pursued by CPS and SFO are such as he could happily defend to Parliament should the need arise. In addition, however, he is concerned with what might be called 'Whitehall policy' in criminal matters, that is to say with Home Office and Lord Chancellor's Department policies as they might affect CPS and SFO, and regular trilateral consultation arrangements exist between his departments, represented by the Legal Secretary, Home Office, and LCD.

The third interest is in case-work. CPS and SFO 'routinely tell the Attorney-General about cases of particular difficulty' (Attorney-General's Chambers 1996*a*: 2). This practice prolongs, within the new statutory framework, the Attorney-General's overall responsibility for prosecutions. Until 1978 he had explicit power to direct the DPP in the performance of his functions (Prosecution of Offences Regulations 1946 and 1978; Edwards 1984: 11); that power is now understood as subsisting as an element of 'superintendence'. It was presumably in the exercise of such superintendence that the Attorney-General, in 1997, instructed the DPP not to make a prosecuting decision (positive or negative) relating to deaths in police custody without taking advice from Treasury Counsel (Halliburton 1997). Overall responsibility is now rooted both in statute and in the common law: the DPP has power to take over any prosecution commenced by others (Prosecution of Offences Act 1985, s. 6(2)). Alternatively the Attorney may prevent any case being prosecuted through the procedure known as *nolle prosequi* (Edwards 1964: 227–37 and 1984: 444–8; Shawcross 1953: 8–11; Anon. 1958 (an article in fact written by the

[1] Prosecution of Offences Act 1985, s. 3; Criminal Justice Act 1987, s. 1; on the relationship of the DPP and the Attorney-General before the Prosecution of Offences Act 1985 see Edwards 1984: ch. 1; Silkin 1978: 151.

then Legal Secretary to the Law Officers)). Some kinds of prosecution, however, have long been reserved by statute for the Attorney-General or DPP, or require the Attorney-General's consent, notably prosecutions of offences which are of an essentially public character and of such importance as to affect the life of the community; of offences liable by their nature to provoke vexatious legal proceedings; and of regulatory offences (often created in wartime) where the regulatory policy has been expressed in broad terms (Attorney-General 1958; Edwards 1964: 237–46).

These interests arising through the superintendence of CPS and SFO do not exhaust the Attorney-General's concern with criminal prosecutions. There are other public prosecutors besides these agencies; as we saw above (pp. 223–5), several departments retain their own prosecution functions, despite the 'nationalization' of public prosecution by the 1985 Act (Lidstone, Hogg and Sutcliffe 1980). Thus MAFF prosecutes on a variety of matters including agricultural censuses, fisheries offences, and animal health; DSS prosecutes social security fraud and like offences; DTI prosecutes company law offences; Inland Revenue and Customs and Excise prosecute revenue offences (and, in the case of Customs and Excise, the import and export control offences which were central to the Scott Inquiry on the export of arms to Iraq (Scott 1996)). While a direct result of the Scott Inquiry was increased supervision by the Attorney-General of certain customs prosecutions (below, pp. 294–5), he does not superintend these other prosecuting authorities, who answer to their own Ministers. His function in relation to their prosecutions has been described by Sir Patrick Mayhew as one of 'overall purview' (Trade and Industry Committee 1992: Evidence, q. 3436; and see Attorney-General's Chambers 1996*a*: 1) and rests very largely on his powers to discontinue prosecutions by *nolle prosequi* or to cause the DPP to take them over—possibly in order to discontinue them—under the Prosecution of Offences Act 1985, s. 6.

The other departure from departmental norms is represented by the long-established conventions about the behaviour of the Law Officers themselves in the exercise of these powers of superintendence and overview. In the words of a press release from the Attorney's Chambers: 'When the Attorney-General intervenes in criminal proceedings he acts wholly independently of Government and is not subject to collective ministerial responsibility' (Attorney-General's Chambers 1996*a*: 1). A more elaborate statement of his position was given by Shawcross in a House of Commons adjournment debate in 1951 after extensive consultation with executive and judicial authorities, and would still appear to be accurate (483 HC Debs., cols. 681–8, 29 January 1951), largely repeated in Shawcross 1953: 11–12; Edwards 1984: 316–24; cf. Silkin

1978: 149–52; Legal Secretariat to the Law Officers 1996: 2–3). For the Attorney-General, the only issue is whether a prosecution would be in the public interest, including the interests of justice. In determining this, he should take all relevant facts into account, including, for example, the effect the prosecution might have on public morale, public order, or international relations, but excluding effects on the political fortunes of the Attorney, his party, or the government; for such purposes he may properly consult colleagues in the government; those colleagues may not, however, give him orders as to whether he should prosecute or not, nor should they put him under any pressure to take a decision in one sense or another; the decision is that of the Attorney-General alone and the responsibility is not shared with his colleagues. Since these decisions are 'unreviewable, unappealable and unbypassable' (Silkin 1978: 150; Feldman and Miller 1997), a culture of respect within government for the Attorney-General's independence in this field assumes the highest constitutional importance, and the political and parliamentary concern in 1992–96 about the circumstances leading to the *Matrix Churchill* and other prosecutions relating to exports to Iraq can be readily understood. But from the standpoint of our inquiry as to how concepts of legality are given content and force within government, what matters most about the position of the Attorney-General in this area is not whether the convention of total independence is ever breached, but how it bears on Crown prosecutions in general and on the Law Officers' control of them. For this purpose we look next at how their powers have been exercised in criminal matters.

2 The exercise of the Law Officers' powers

The Home Secretary, not the Attorney-General, is the minister generally responsible for the state of the criminal law in England and Wales. Similarly in Scotland, the Scottish Office Home Department, not the Lord Advocate's Department, has hitherto carried these responsibilities. It is the Home Office that brings forward legislative proposals for reform of all aspects of criminal law, including procedure, enforcement, and penal practice: a Criminal Justice Bill appears at least every two or three years. Police and prisons alike fall within the Home Secretary's sphere of power and responsibility; magistrates' courts were transferred to LCD in 1992. When these powers and competences are considered in conjunction with the procedural and evidentiary rulings of the courts, the limited space left within which the Attorney-General may develop enforcement policy becomes apparent. None the less, prior to the creation of the CPS the Attorney-General had developed a practice of issuing prosecution guidelines on a variety of topics, providing prosecutors with general statements of good practice drawn either from the considerations which would guide his own decisions or from authoritative external opinion or advice. Thus his 1981 guidelines on disclosure of documents by the prosecution which figured largely in evidence to the Scott Inquiry, were based on the report of the Royal Commission on Criminal Procedure (1981: para. 8.19). Other examples of such guidelines are those relating to the decision to prosecute (1982), to jury vetting (1980, revised 1986 and 1989: Attorney-General 1989; Edwards 1984: 476–90), and to identification evidence (1976, revised 1979) (912 HC Debs., cols. *287–9*, written answers 27 May, 1976; 971 HC Debs., cols. *236–7*, written answers 25 July, 1979).

With the creation of CPS, a structure within which prosecution practice can be much more readily standardized than before, the function served by such guidelines is being taken over by the Code for Crown Prosecutors, issued by the CPS under section 10 of the Prosecution of Offences Act 1985, but based on principles endorsed by the Attorney-General (Crown Prosecution Service 1994); and by elements of the CPS Service Manual. Guidance on when prosecution is proper is the main concern of the Code which, while a CPS document, expresses principles which are equally applicable to prosecutions by other departments. Such departments were invited by the then Attorney-General, in 1986, to adhere to the Code, and by 1992, he thought, all had done so (Trade and Industry Committee 1992: Evidence, q. 3412). Alternatively guidelines may be overtaken by changes in the law itself, whether originating in case-law or statutory reform. Thus the disclosure guidelines were effectively overtaken by the decisions in *R v Maguire* 1992 and *R v Ward* 1993, and the matter is now covered by the Criminal Procedure and Investigations Act 1996, Part II. The Crown's right to object to jurors, the subject of the jury vetting guidelines, is of much reduced practical importance following the abolition of the defence's right of peremptory challenge by the Criminal Justice Act 1988, s. 118.

While the effective scope of the Attorney-General's guidelines is therefore likely to diminish, they and successor documents like the Code continue to be an important point of reference for his functions of superintendence and overview of prosecutions. The Scott Report shows the use of the Code in the 'Supergun' prosecution, in which Customs and Excise planned to prosecute persons thought to be exporting parts for an Iraqi long-range weapon. Consulted by Customs and Excise, the Attorney-General, Sir Patrick Mayhew, supported the view of Treasury Counsel as to the application of the 'reasonable prospect of conviction' test in paragraph 4 of the Code. Counsel was very doubtful if the test was satisfied. Customs and Excise argued for a flexible application of the test; failure to prosecute would be a blow to the credibility of enforcement in the area of export control. The Attorney-General advised that if an acquittal was likely, such failure, and any consequent political embarrassment, was no justification for proceeding, given the fact that prosecution was of itself invasive of individual liberty (Scott 1996: paras. J1.17–22, 32–3, 39).

This case should be set alongside the subsequent, and much more notorious, *Matrix Churchill* case, another Customs and Excise prosecution for an export control offence relating to the Iraq arms embargo. Here prosecuting counsel was happy about prospects of conviction, and the Attorney-General—now Sir Nicholas Lyell—was not consulted by Customs; he took the initiative in reviewing the prosecution after becoming aware of possible difficulties in the case through discussions about ministers' public interest immunity certificates protecting documents from disclosure (above, pp. 230–1). His concern was with the overall soundness and fairness of the prosecution, and on the basis of the assurances of prosecuting counsel, he allowed it to go forward (Scott 1996: paras. G13.64, 76–80).

We learn a lot from these cases about the control of prosecutions in practice. The first thing to note is that these were Customs and Excise prosecutions, not CPS or SFO prosecutions. The Attorney-General was therefore not responsible for them, whether directly or in respect of any power of superintendence; responsibility lay only with the Commissioners of Customs and Excise.[2] This was not a proposition the Attorney-General found easy to put over to the public or Parliament in the aftermath of the Scott Report (Attorney-General's Chambers 1996*a*: 1–2; 1996*b*), and it is noteworthy that his predecessor felt it necessary to explain the position to Customs and Excise in the course of the 'Supergun' prosecution (Scott 1996: paras. J1.29, 36). The Attorney-General's powers in the cases were not powers of superintendence or hierarchical control, but powers to *intervene*, either by taking the cases over or by discontinuing them through a *nolle prosequi*.

These powers of intervention, we should recall, do not have their origin in any allocation of powers among ministers for the purposes of

[2] The Attorney-General, in Evidence to the Trade and Industry Committee (1992), q. 3411, stated that this responsibility was exclusive, so that Treasury ministers' general powers of control over the Revenue Departments do not operate in this respect, and such ministers have 'no responsibility whatsoever for any prosecuting decision brought by the Commissioners'. The statutory position of the two departments is not identical. The Commissioners of Customs and Excise are subject only to 'the general control of the Treasury' (Customs and Excise Management Act 1979, s. 6(2)); but the Commissioners of Inland Revenue are subject to 'the authority, direction and control of the Treasury' and must obey its 'orders and instructions in that behalf' (Inland Revenue Regulation Act 1890, s. 1(2)). The Attorney's statement may thus represent law in relation to Customs and Excise, but convention only in relation to the Inland Revenue.

ensuring the enforcement of export control or any other policy. (The Attorney-General has power to prosecute export control offences under section 145(5) of the Customs and Excise Management Act 1979, but has never done so in recent times (Scott 1996: Appendix A, Part B(x), p. 10).) They form part of the Crown's general control of the administration of justice, which until 1986 applied principally to police and private prosecutions. It is a paradoxical result of the creation of CPS and SFO that their main application should now be in respect of prosecutions brought by other government departments. The nature of the powers, however, has not changed, and though the Scott Report confirms that in their exercise successive Attorneys-General did in fact operate according to the apolitical principles enunciated by Sir Hartley Shawcross in 1951, their effectiveness as a means of controlling government prosecutions outside CPS and SFO remains open to question, for several reasons.

First, the Attorney-General is clearly heavily reliant on the views of prosecuting counsel as to the propriety of the prosecution. The cases signal the importance of the Attorney-General's powers of appointment of members of the Bar to represent the government in the courts, an issue we discuss in the next section.

Second, though Customs and Excise described itself to Scott as an independent prosecuting authority, which should act without regard to political considerations, and was free of 'improper political influence' (Customs and Excise 1996: 1), it operates very differently from CPS and SFO. While ministers have no role in prosecutions, the function of the department's lawyers is restricted to one of as to whether there is sufficient evidence to proceed. It is administrators who, on the basis of this advice, take the prosecution decision, in export control as in other areas. Though they regard the Code for Crown Prosecutors as applicable to them in this respect (Scott 1996: App. A, Part B(x), p. 3), the cases show that they took a different approach from that of the Law Officers to the balance between firm enforcement of policy (or the appearance of it) and the liberty of the subject. In the non-revenue prosecuting departments, lawyers are in control of the decision to prosecute, either directly or (as with DSS for summary prosecutions) by way of review of an administrator's decision. At the same time, in one department (DTI), ministers may, if very exceptionally, be involved in the prosecution decision. The Code for Crown Prosecutors is applied in all departments, but by choice, not obligation, and in some cases with modification to suit departmental circumstances. The whole context to which it is applied is, indeed, significantly different in these departments which, unlike the police and Crown prosecutors, are 'not engaged in law enforcement as a primary function, but rather fulfil a specialist enforcement role as one means of fulfilling other primary functions' such as revenue collection, the integrity of the benefits system, or the protection of animal health (Lidstone, Hogg, and Sutcliffe 1980: 34). Amid this autonomy and diversity the scope for the Attorney-General, through his purview powers, to produce any real impact on departmental prosecution practice appears limited indeed.

Third, aside from specific statutory competences, the common law powers of the Attorney-General are of only limited reach so far as general government behaviour in relation to criminal prosecutions is concerned. The 'Supergun' case shows that advice he gives which is backed by the threat of a *nolle*, no matter how unpalatable, will not easily be rejected. Departments may, however, behave very differently when his advice cannot be so backed. There is ample evidence in the Scott Report that departmental legal advisers either did not share, or did not act upon, the Attorney-General's view of how his Guidelines on Disclosure of Documents should be applied in the context of the *Matrix Churchill* prosecution. According to him they should 'examine [papers] which, having regard to the information provided to them [by the prosecutor, here Customs and Excise] might be expected to contain documents of significance. . . .', should disclose material thought likely to be relevant, even in the absence of a specific approach, and 'were under a duty to respond fully and positively to inquiries' by the prosecution (Scott 1996: para. G9.6, reporting the Attorney-General's written statement to the inquiry). The FCO, through its Permanent Secretary, took explicit issue with this statement, saying that departmental officials without legal training could not take responsibility for sifting and selecting documents (para. G9.10); the DTI, through its Legal Adviser, did all it could to avoid the application of the guidelines by trying to keep its documents out of the hands of Customs and Excise, and to get them back once they had been passed over (see paras. G5.59–62, G6.11, G10.13–25).

The broad acceptance by the government of the recommendations on prosecution practice made by Sir Richard Scott at the close of his inquiry does very little to strengthen the position of the Attorney-General in relation to prosecutions. The recommendation which went most directly to the position of the Attorney-General in the regulation of the power of criminal prosecution was that Customs and Excise prosecutions in support of export control, being analogous to CPS or SFO prosecutions in support of general policing, should—as the Attorney-General had himself argued in evidence—be the subject of his statutory superintendence, not just overall purview (para. K4.6–10).[3] The changes announced

[3] Other recommendations were that the relationship between investigators and lawyers within Customs and Excise should be reviewed (Scott 1996: para. K4.15; for acceptance see 280 HC Debs., cols. 490–1 (written answers 4 July 1996); and that the procedure for obtaining documents from departments in connection with prosecutions should be reviewed (para.

by the government in June 1996 were the minimum consistent with a positive response. The Attorney-General would be enabled to exercise 'supervisory control' over certain prosecutions by Customs and Excise (Treasury 1996*e*). This control would, however, be confined to offences concerning the export of defence material and requiring *mens rea* (i.e. where guilty intent has to be proved). He would be consulted by Customs and Excise on such prosecutions and would be accountable to Parliament for prosecution decisions. Treasury Ministers would, however, retain responsibility for investigations, for enforcement policy, and for general aspects of prosecution policy in these as in all other cases.

When coupled with a simultaneous statement reasserting the Attorney's independent and objective role in relation to all prosecutions, and advising ministers outside prosecuting departments to refer public interest issues to him (Legal Secretariat to the Law Officers 1996), the change may be seen as reaffirming the pre-eminence of the Attorney-General in relation to the public interest aspects of prosecutions, but hardly as strengthening it. Notwithstanding the weaknesses of the Attorney's position as documented in the Scott Report, no breach of any significance is made in the principle of departmental responsibility, and erosion of departmental autonomy in this field has been effectively resisted.

3 The appointment of counsel

We have seen that the Attorney-General, in exercising his supervisory powers, must rely heavily on the advice, and hence on the professional probity, of counsel for the Crown. The selection of such counsel, in civil no less than in criminal matters, is in fact an exclusive privilege of the Attorney-General, and a significant source of his influence. Arrangements differ on the civil and criminal sides.

On the civil side, the key appointments are those of First Treasury Counsel, one for common law matters, one for Chancery matters: the 'Treasury Devils'. The common law appointee will enjoy for some five years a general retainer for all government common law work (Woolf 1990: 3–7), which has placed him in a central position so far as the development of judicial review is concerned. First Treasury Counsel are backed up by several panels of barristers from whom counsel are drawn as need arises for general civil work and some forms of specialist work, and there are standing counsel in several specialist areas. Appointments to these panels are by the Attorney-General.

K5.1): this will now be undertaken in the light of the Criminal Procedure and Investigations Act 1996, Part II, which makes fresh provision on the matter.

On the criminal side, the main prosecuting departments—Customs and Excise, Inland Revenue, DTI—maintain their own lists, panels, or standing counsel, which are kept under review by, and changes to which are made with the approval of, the Attorney-General, who also directly appoints Treasury Counsel to prosecute serious crime on behalf of the Crown.

Departments, or the Treasury Solicitor, may also ask the Attorney-General to make appointments *ad hoc*, for example where they desire to retain a Queen's Counsel or where some specialist competence not represented on a panel is needed. Finding counsel more sympathetic to the department's position is not a good reason. The Attorney-General gave short shrift to Customs and Excise when it attempted in the 'Supergun' case to get counsel who might take a more positive attitude than had senior Treasury Counsel: he did not approve, he said, 'of a prosecuting authority shopping around for an opinion' (Scott 1996: paras. J1.14–15). In civil cases, the need for *ad hoc* appointments may diminish, but will not disappear, as a result of the adoption of a structured, enlarged, and more open system of panels of ascending order of seniority. Such a system has been recommended by a working party chaired by the Solicitor-General and set up following suggestions that the existing system gave insufficient assurance of equality of opportunity among barristers (Legal Secretariat to the Law Officers 1998).

All Crown Counsel, not excluding First Treasury Counsel, continue to be independent members of the Bar. This independence of situation should substantially reinforce the internal legal control of government deriving from the professionalism of its in-house lawyers, or where necessary, and one hopes exceptionally, correct for its absence. There are ample signs of this independence and of its self-conscious preservation. Treasury Devils, who go straight to the bench at the end of their tenure, have in recent years been among the boldest exponents of the extension of judicial review (e.g. Lord Woolf in *R v Secretary of State for the Home Department, ex parte Fayed* 1996; Sir John Laws in *R v Lord Chancellor, ex parte Witham* 1997; Sir Simon Brown in *R v Commissioners of Inland Revenue, ex parte Unilever plc* 1996). Lord Woolf, having become a judge, recalls his successor as First Treasury Counsel commenting to him that now that he had been on the bench a year, it was no longer necessary always to give judgment against the Crown (Woolf 1990: 7 n.). This separation from the executive is emphasized by the fact that the Attorney-General is assisted in the appointment process not by the Legal Secretariat but by his clerk in chambers (though the Treasury Solicitor's Department may in future play a more prominent role in the preliminary stages).

II THE LAW OFFICERS AS THE GOVERNMENT'S CHIEF LEGAL ADVISERS

> The House did not want the Attorney-General to blaze forth in rhetoric and eloquence. They wanted a plain, solid, simple man who knew the law, and . . . who would be perfectly ready to do the business, and who would do the business perfectly well, for a salary of £5000, and the chance of gravitating into a judgeship afterwards.
>
> (Henry Labouchere, 92 HC Debs. col. 1482, 26 April 1901)

1 Introduction

To 'act as the Government's Chief Legal Adviser' is described by the Attorney-General as his other main role alongside superintendence of the CPS and SFO (Attorney-General's Chambers 1996*a*: 1). When so acting he 'gives his objective analysis of the law as he sees it' (ibid.); but he does not, as with his criminal work, act independently or outside the scope of collective responsibility. This role of adviser must be seen as encompassing more than the giving of opinions on the law: it also extends to participation in a number of Cabinet Committees (Burch and Holliday 1995: 41); to his relationship with the Treasury Solicitor and, in this context, to a concern with the quality of government legal services in general; and likewise to the relationship with First Parliamentary Counsel, and concern with 'legal policy' in the drafting of legislation, which we discussed in the previous chapter. While 'advice' is thus a broader term than might appear at first sight, the self-description of chief legal adviser to government also risks an over-generous interpretation. As earlier discussion will have made apparent, 'chief' does not mean that the Attorney-General is at the head of a unified corps of legal advisers. There is no such corps, and he does not even occupy this position in relation to TSol, of which he is the superintendent rather than the director (Scott 1996: paras. G13.123–4). 'Chief' refers not to organizational position but to status: in essence the Attorney-General is an individual legal adviser functioning, when giving advice, much as does a departmental legal adviser or, for that matter, Treasury Counsel. *Mutatis mutandis* these remarks have applied with equal force to the Lord Advocate in Scotland. What marks out the Attorney and the Advocate, along with the other Law Officers, is that unlike all other such advisers they are Ministers of the Crown. As politically responsible lawyers (though not necessarily, in Scotland at least, career politicians: above, p. 238), their advice thus has a special quality and status. In particular, this means that when the Cabinet, as such, wants legal advice it will be the Law Officers, with the Attorney-General pre-eminent among them, who give it. In the words of Lord Howe, Solicitor-General from 1970–72, 'The two [*sic*] Law Officers are *the* source of considered legal opinions for the Cabinet.' The word 'considered' here should be given full weight: in Howe's time, Hailsham as Lord Chancellor apparently often gave impromptu legal opinions (Rawlinson 1989: 105), and it is clear that other Lord Chancellors have been ready to advise from time to time, notably Lord Chancellor Kilmuir on the legality of the Suez invasion in 1956, on which the Law Officers were not consulted (Elwyn-Jones 1983: 149; Rawlinson 1989: 70). The primacy of the Attorney-General as legal adviser is thus closely connected with the collective aspect of government.

In the following sections we examine in detail the advisory work of the Law Officers, considering particularly how far (if at all) it furnishes that governmental view of legality which forms the elusive object of this inquiry. The focus will be on the Attorney-General, but the position of the Lord Advocate often differs in thought-provoking ways, and we shall draw attention to those differences. We ask first what Law Officers' opinions are; next, how they come to be given; next, what is the position with regard to the confidentiality of this advice; and finally, what is its significance and effect.

2 Law Officers' opinions: their nature

Law libraries with good international collections will hold the impressive runs of volumes of Law Officers' opinions on questions of international law: a set edited by Sir Arnold McNair, containing opinions up to the end of the nineteenth century (McNair 1956); and two edited by Clive Parry, carrying matters forward to 1939 (Parry 1970–3; 1976). Contemplation of the body of legal opinion on international law laid out there could easily lead to a threefold misconception as to current practice: that opinions are published (they are not); that opinions are at least collected and relied upon within government (practice varies); and that advice takes the shape of formal opinions (it hardly ever does). It is the last of these points that we deal with now, reverting to the others later.

In these days, 'Law Officers' advice' has no formal identity. It could refer to anything from a bulky file of correspondence to the content of a telephone call. Edwards (1964: 151–2) records the decline of the formal opinion: a constant level of rather less than 200 per year from the late nineteenth century till the First World War; a doubling during and immediately after the war; then a fairly precipitate decline to figures like 20 (in 1955) and 12 (in 1962). Today formal opinions are only given in special circumstances: for example, when the subject-matter makes it appropriate for an opinion to be given jointly by the English and Scottish Law Officers, or where, exceptionally, the Attorney-General enlists a specialist practitioner to give a joint opinion with him on a recondite point.[4] The gradual decline of the formal opinion, over a period when the demanding and varied nature of the advisory function is regularly stressed (Shawcross 1953: 5–6; Jones 1969: 46–7; Archer 1978: 3–6; Silkin 1979: xxvii–xxix) is probably to be attributed to that change in the status of the Attorney-General, from distinguished but somewhat detached adviser to fully-integrated Whitehall player, that we have already charted over the same period (above, pp. 233–6).

Along with the shift from the formal to the informal expression of advice there appears a more subtle change in its character. Naturally, that character will tend to vary according to the nature of the matter in hand. In circumstances like litigation, where time is of the essence, advice on individual points may need to be given from moment to moment, with little opportunity for deliberation or consultation outside the Legal Secretariat. The Scott Report documents these pressures in the *Matrix Churchill* case (Scott 1996: chs. G12, G13). From time to time we glimpse similar pressures arising within Parliamentary or commercial contexts: as when the Attorney-General tells the House of Commons he prepared his opinion on the effects of the opt-out clauses of the Maastricht Treaty within the space of 24 hours or so, after the FCO legal advisers had worked up their own, contrary, opinion over several months (219 HC Debs., cols. *683–744*, 22 February 1993); or where we see the Solicitor-General advising by telephone as to the legal effect of a minister's letter, and following up by letter written after 'refreshing his memory of the documents' for a couple of hours (Defence Committee 1986: paras. 134–41). It should be noted, though, that urgency does not necessarily preclude consultation; the Lord Advocate joined in the Maastricht opinion (and see Silkin 1979: xxviii for another example). In other cases, a relatively leisured approach can be taken to considering all aspects of a complex problem.

While making allowances, therefore, for these situational variations, what may be perceived is a change in the nature of the Attorney-General's advice. Although his advisory work is still organized on the barristers' chambers model (the term 'Attorney-General's Chambers' is still used from time to time in preference to 'Legal Secretariat' (Attorney-General's Chambers 1996*a*, and see Archer 1978: 4 for the symbolic

[4] For an example, almost unique in recent years, of a contemporaneously published formal opinion, see Attorney-General 1971. A formal joint opinion of the English and Scottish Law Officers was given on the Maastricht opt-out clause (below) but not published.

significance of this)), with the bright young secondees of the Secretariat devilling his opinions, it is not the personal authority of leading counsel that gives his advice its weight. Given the central place of the courts' decisions in shaping government's legal thinking, experience as senior counsel certainly continues to be of great importance to the job; but there appears to be little dispute about the fact that today's difficulties of combining legal practice and a parliamentary career are such that the English Law Officers, at least, are now unlikely to be drawn from the very highest reaches of the Bar (Bawdon 1996; Anon. 1978; Jenkins at 569 HL Debs., cols. *1242–3*, 26 February 1996); but cf. Rawlinson, ibid., cols. 1295–6). This may not be true of their Scottish counterparts, for reasons already examined (above p. 238 and below pp. 315–22).

Within government, while the Law Officers' forensic experience was stressed to us, we found no one to say that their advice was likely to be qualitatively better than that which might be obtained elsewhere. Today its distinctive nature resides rather in the two features of *process* and *status*.

Process is of particular salience in England and Wales. Edwards remarked in 1984 that the Law Officers 'can mobilise at short notice the full range of legal expertise from within the government itself, from outside counsel and from academic lawyers, which may be demanded in dealing with a complex situation' (1984: 188; cf. Rawlinson, 569 HL Debs., col. *1296*, 26 February 1996).

In matters of any weight this mobilization now appears to be assuming an institutional aspect, albeit within the highly flexible and pluralistic structure which characterizes executive action. Through suggestions and requests by the Legal Secretariat, the Attorney-General's involvement is placed at the end of a co-ordinated process of opinion-gathering. This may involve 'a well-researched and well-argued request'; consultation with Treasury Counsel and the provision of their opinion(s) as part of the request for advice; consultation with other specialist counsel; inter-departmental consultation. While this approach has clearly been developing for some time (Silkin 1979: xxviii; Rawlinson, supra), it appears to have been reinforced by the other co-ordination arrangements—to be examined later (below, pp. 315–22) which have developed in recent years, under the aegis of the Cabinet Office (for European issues) and of the Treasury Solicitor, as head of the Government Legal Service (for general legal issues of inter-departmental concern). While these mechanisms may produce a common view which makes reference to the Law Officers unnecessary, they may also operate as a platform for the preparation of such references, when they disclose and clarify departmental disagreements about the law which need to be resolved; or they may be the means of organizing, on major issues such as public interest immunity, a continuing dialogue between departmental lawyers, counsel, and the Law Officers, *en route* to the production of a definitive opinion (Scott 1996: paras. G13.90–98).

The Scottish approach is different, both more direct and more personal. The great majority of requests to the Lord Advocate will arise from the multi-functional Scottish Office; a direct relationship is established in each case between the appropriate Scottish Office lawyer and the lawyer in the Lord Advocate's Department who will be 'devilling' his opinion; there is a high degree of personal involvement by the Law Officer, which may extend to direct contact with the administrators concerned; and there exists no equivalent to Treasury Counsel nor any practice of reference to specialist counsel.

The English process of refining issues and obtaining various kinds of opinion could obviously go on without the Law Officers being involved at all. Often they are not, as where a departmental legal adviser both takes counsel's opinion and consults opposite numbers elsewhere, without troubling the Law Officers. What makes their advice different in such cases is the second factor, of status: that is to say, their status as ministers. By advising, the Law Officers take the issue out of the framework of intradepartmental relationships between civil servants (the legal advisers) and their ministers, and into—at least potentially—that of inter-ministerial discussion. Whatever the extent or quality of the Law Officers' personal input, this necessarily gives the advice a political dimension, even while it remains 'an objective view of the law as he sees it' (Attorney-General's Chambers 1996*a*: 1). Ideally, the advice will reflect

> professional politicians' . . . understanding of the problems confronting the politicians whom they are advising . . . the need to pursue a coherent policy, the tactical problems of introducing legislation to deal with a technical snag and the need to express advice in a way which can be passed on intelligibly to the public. (Archer 1978: 6)

Whatever its style or content, it may be discussed in Cabinet or Cabinet Committees; it may need to be defended in Parliament (though not necessarily, or even normally, by the Law Officer who gave it—below, pp. 309–13). We shall see in the next section that this character is intimately linked to the reasons for which references are made to the Law Officers, particularly from departments; and we shall consider later (pp. 325–6) what its significance is for the formation of government's own concepts of legality.

Here, we may summarize our discussion on the nature of the Law Officers' advice simply by saying that, in marked contrast to the opinions of leading counsel which its history evokes, it is informal in character, pluralistic in inspiration, and political in authority.

3 Asking for advice

'I'm only here to help you' is, as often as not, a formula of control, and this is certainly true of the arrangements through which the Law Officers' assistance with points of law may be sought or supplied. It follows from the political nature of their involvement just described: this is a means by which a legal issue may be transformed from a matter of merely departmental concern to one of which the Cabinet as a whole can take cognizance. Sometimes, of course, the need for advice arises directly out of discussions at Cabinet level, on issues in relation to which no one department may have been expected to be in previous communication on legal issues with the Attorney-General: issues on which the Prime Minister, for example, has taken the policy lead. Such issues are, however, likely to be both rare and of major importance (Mount 1992: 122–3 (British assistance to US bombing of Libya in 1986)). Ordinarily, Cabinet level discussions have as their basis the plans or actions of particular departments. If departmental proposals are seen by other ministers as raising legal issues, they will want to be assured that the department's legal advice is adequate, and in case of doubt may want the reassurance of the Law Officers' opinion. *A fortiori*, if a Law Officer in Cabinet Committee expresses such a doubt. Again, if actions of a department become the object of Cabinet discussion by reason of legal problems they have raised, thus putting the department's legal advice in question, ministers will want to know whether the Law Officers, as their collective legal advisers, were consulted *ex ante* on the matter. If they were not, intra-governmental embarrassment may be added to the public embarrassment already being suffered. A salutary example is offered by the case of Mr Patrick Jenkin, whose action in 1979 as health minister in suspending a local health authority without, apparently, taking the Law Officers' advice about the legality of such a grave decision turned out to be invalid (*R v Secretary of State for Social Services, ex parte Lewisham, Lambeth and Southwark LBCs* 1980), making it necessary for the government to obtain an Act of indemnity from Parliament (National Health Service (Invalid Direction) Act 1980).

These considerations appear to furnish rather good reasons why departments, whether in the persons of their ministers (who will take the heat at Cabinet level), their senior administrators, or their legal advisers, should make frequent references of legal difficulties to the Law Officers, if only to guard their backs. Certainly the consistent rhetoric of the Law Officers themselves, ever since Baggallay's complaints to the Jessel Committee (above, pp. 233–4), has been suggestive of a consequent need to keep trivia off their doorstep, making reference to the 'special importance' (Shawcross 1953: 6) which should attend matters referred to the Law Officers. But if trivia are the only problem, it is curious that the only wholly new element to appear between 1946 and 1976 in the *Ministerial Code* should be a section explaining when departments ought to seek the Law Officers' opinion. As Lee (1986: 348) points out, modifications get made to this document when issues arise on which the Prime Minister of the day has to make a decision.

In the current version of the *Ministerial Code* (Cabinet Office 1997*d*), the key paragraph states:

> 22. The Law Officers must be consulted in good time before the Government is committed to critical decisions involving legal considerations. It will normally be appropriate to consult the Law Officers in cases where:
> a. The legal consequences of action by the Government might have important repercussions in the foreign, Community or domestic field;
> b. A Departmental Legal Adviser is in doubt concerning
> (i) the legality or constitutional propriety of legislation which Government proposes to introduce; or
> (ii) the vires of proposed subordinate legislation; or
> (iii) the legality of proposed administrative action, particularly where that action might be subject to challenge in the courts by means of application for judicial review;
> c. Ministers, or their officials, wish to have the advice of the Law Officers on questions involving legal considerations, which are likely to come before the Cabinet or Cabinet Committee;
> d. There is a particular legal difficulty which may raise political aspects of policy;
> e. Two or more Departments disagree on legal questions and wish to seek the views of the Law Officers.
>
> By convention, written Opinions of the Law Officers, unlike other Ministerial papers, are generally made available to succeeding administrations.

While more elaborate, the text differs little from the criteria for reference mentioned by Shawcross in 1953: legal difficulty, considerations of policy or public relations, or there being a large amount at stake (1953: 6). The message must, at least in 1976, have been felt to need reinforcement (though it clearly had little immediate effect on the Department for Social Services: above, p. 302). Since its first insertion in the *Code*, the Legal Secretariat has been given the opportunity, at each revision, to comment on the wording, and would be likely to do so if it felt that the right kinds of cases were not being referred. No recent comment has been felt necessary, and the current sense in the Secretariat is that departments, though not necessarily having a copy of the *Code* 'always to hand', comply fully with the paragraph. What is departments' view of the matter?

Among the evidence reported by the Jessel Committee in 1877 was the result of an enquiry among the solicitors to departments about the number of matters their respective offices had handled in the three years 1872–75, and the number of references they had made to the Law Officers for their opinion. The replies gave little support to Baggallay's complaints of a flood of trivia, but showed major differences of practice. The Solicitor to the Office of Woods, for example, replied that he had dealt with 2,937 matters, and had consulted the Law Officers in 30 of them, and other counsel in 53. The Solicitor to the Inland Revenue for his part had had seven times as much business (18,693 matters), but had gone to the Law Officers in only ten of them; while the Solicitor to Customs and Excise reported with some pride that despite handling 11,154 cases he had never needed the advice of the Law Officers over the three years. The Treasury Solicitor, handling, then as now, the contentious business of a large number of government departments, gave no overall figure, but had consulted the Law Officers on 202 occasions, other counsel on 3,863 (Jessel 1877: 71–2, 79–84, 86–9).

Things seem little changed today, though it is impossible to be as precise. The Legal Secretariat, despite the fact that the motivation for its first beginnings in 1893 was, 'having regard to the much more frequent reference of late years by public Departments to the Law Officers . . . to secure a complete record of the opinions given by successive Law Officers' (Treasury Minute January 12, 1893, cited in Edwards 1964: 141–5), is now not able to say (other, perhaps, as the stock parliamentary answer goes, than at disproportionate cost) how many references the Law Officers receive each year department by department. Its database is simply not organized that way. The variety of forms in which advice is rendered puts further difficulties in the way of emulating the precision of the replies to the Jessel Committee. For their part, and often symptomatically of more general attitudes in the matter, departmental legal advisers seldom appear to keep detailed or systematic information on the question either.

It can, however, be said that the frequency of reference varies both as between departments at any given time, and within departments over time. Writing in 1984, Edwards sought to discern some kind of pattern, suggesting a rank order in terms of frequency of reference, with DPP, LCD, Home Office, FCO, and Northern Ireland authorities at the top, in contact on a day-to-day basis, followed a little way behind by the Cabinet Office, DTI, and TSol (Edwards 1984: 186–7); and also distinguishing subject-matter where the Attorney-General's views on legal policy might be paramount, such as international law and human rights, from that where they might be viewed as 'more peripheral than central', such as trade, social security and defence (ibid.: 190). While Edwards appears to have been making no very clear distinction between advisory and prosecution functions (hence the appearance of DPP at the top of the list), his ordering certainly does not reflect our impression of current practice. Over recent years DTI, while probably one of the more frequent seekers of Law Officers' advice, has been making around thirty or so references a year; Home Office references are said to have increased over the last five or six years to around that figure; the FCO sees itself as more 'self-reliant' than many other departments and tends not to 'trouble' the Law Officers (it did not, for example, consult them on the implementation in United Kingdom law of the Maastricht Treaty: Woodhouse 1993; Rawlings 1994). Across departments the quantitative variations of 1876 are reproduced with remarkable fidelity today. Reported current annual rates of reference, in very approximate terms, from some of the major departments of state (Home Office, FCO, DSS/DH, MAFF, Customs and Excise, Inland Revenue, DTI, TSol) ranged from 'not more than two per year' (Inland Revenue) to 'substantially in excess of 50' (TSol). About 30–40 written references a year go from the Scottish Office to the Lord Advocate, a figure that perhaps reflects its broad span of action.

More important than these numbers are the attitudes they reflect. Here the interests of three separate groups of actors within departments have to be taken into account: those of ministers, senior administrators, and legal advisers. These interests may pull in different directions: ministers may set particular store by the political assurance flowing from the provision of an opinion from the Attorney-General; administrators may be anxious about possible effects of delay flowing from elaborate consideration of legal issues; legal advisers may wish to avoid any impression that their service cannot provide (or find for itself) the necessary legal expertise.

At the same time behaviour within these groups will also vary. Not all ministers are the same: one will go to the Attorney-General 'at the drop of a hat'; another may hold him, or his office, in low esteem and go only when pressed to do so by his own legal adviser. Some ministers may be highly responsive to the degree of political controversy surrounding the department's work, others less so: for example, references from the Department of the Environment, as it then was, rose significantly when control over local authority spending became a major issue in the mid-nineteen-eighties, and dropped when the issue cooled; but controversy over Home Office policy on prisons and sentencing in the nineteen-nineties apparently did not produce the same effect. From time to time Ministers, whatever their general approach, may find themselves in situations where they do not like the legal advice they are getting within the department and want something different—which the Law Officers may or may not supply (Howe 1994: 57).

Departmental legal advisers, likewise, are not an undifferentiated breed. Some clearly value the advisory work of the Law Officers and their Secretariat more highly than do others, and their departmental practice must be likely to reflect in some measure these varying appreciations. Another influence which may be just as important, perhaps more so, is the fact that their services consist of groups of professionals, some of considerable seniority, who in their advisory work will have their own 'clients' among administrators and even ministers. In relation to specific matters the outlook of the individual adviser may be just as important as that of the head of the legal service. Frequency of references to the Law Officers (and possibly also to other outside lawyers) may thus be as much a function of the degree of control the Departmental Solicitor or Legal Adviser can exercise or wishes to exercise over his own colleagues' case-work as of his own policy in the matter. The DSS/DH Solicitor's Office guide for administrators states that a request to the Law Officers 'will as a general rule be submitted by the Solicitor himself' (1994: 18); this is also the rule in the Scottish Office. In the Home Office the practice is that the Legal Adviser should be informed that the request, usually prepared by a lawyer of at least Grade 5 equivalent level, was going in; though this does not always happen. In DETR a reference 'will always have the blessing of the Legal Adviser or a Deputy Solicitor' (DoE 1997: 23). In Customs and Excise, and the TSol outstation at MoD, the Solicitor or Head of the outstation is not necessarily involved in the making of a request at all.

While we should keep in mind these important variations, the handbooks prepared by departmental legal services disclose some general lines of approach which effectively gloss the rather open-textured criteria of the *Ministerial Code*. (That departmental legal advisers feel themselves free to modify and restate these criteria is itself surely significant.) The first of these is the particular value placed on the political input of the Law Officers, making their advice especially helpful where 'the point at issue involves political risks as well as legal ones' (DTI 1995: 9 (para. 3.1.1), adopting the wording of DSS/DH 1994: 16) or 'where the problem has a political dimension and advice is needed . . . on the political wisdom of pursuing the strategy notwithstanding [any legal] risks' (DSS/DH 1994: 18) (cf. DoE 1997: 24 to the same effect; Home Office 1995: 24, referring to 'constitutional or political risks'). This obviously reflects ministers' sensibilities, but it is important to appreciate that the political position of the Law Officers may be of service to departmental legal advisers also. Their advice may help to 'stiffen the spine' of a minister in defence of departmental positions on legal issues; it may be essential if ministers are to be convinced of the legal need to follow a course of action when they are unconvinced of its political wisdom, or even ethical correctness (Scott 1996: ch. G13, on how PII certificates came to be signed in the *Matrix Churchill* case). We should also notice that the term 'political' here is capable of bearing a broad meaning, covering not only matters of party political controversy, but also those on which any powerful interests, including commercial ones, are capable of bringing uncomfortable pressure to bear on government.

Second, the Law Officers are commonly viewed in departments as one of a number of 'external' sources of legal advice to which the department, through its own legal advisers, may turn (see DTI 1995: 9–10; DSS/DH 1994: 16–20; DoE 1997: 21–4; Home Office 1995: 23–4), and will not be seen as the most suitable ones in all cases. Obviously this is true of routine litigation, but there may also be specific types of difficulty on which other lawyers will be preferred. Highly specialized matters such as intellectual property problems or tax questions may be best taken to specialist counsel (DSS/DH 1994: 18, though the Attorney-General will need to be involved if this is an 'off-panel' appointment, above, pp. 295–6). Judicial review issues may be best taken initially to First Treasury Counsel (if only because the Law Officers are likely to send them on there anyway). At least one department, DSS/DH, applies this principle much more widely (1994: 18). Within Whitehall FCO has been the first point of reference on European Convention on Human Rights issues, though practice is likely to be modified under the Human Rights Act following incorporation of the Convention rights into United Kingdom law (above, pp. 269–71). For EU law problems, the European Secretariat machinery functions both as a source of expertise and as an important staging post for an important flow of references to the Law Officers (below, pp. 316–19). This selective approach is not simply a matter of preservation by departmental Solicitors of their prerogatives of choice, but has clear ministerial support. In the words of a recent Lord Chancellor (admittedly, one with whom the Law Officers of his day had a certain amount of difficulty: above, p. 298):

> [T]here are other alternatives [to the Law Officers] and one must exercise one's wisdom about them if one is a Minister. . . . When I was Minister of Education and then Secretary of State for Education and Science, we had a very competent legal staff, and I am bound to say that on matters which were directly within the field of education I should probably have preferred their advice to that of any other available lawyers. . . . It depends very much on the kind of question one is asked. (Lord Hailsham LC, 407 HL Debs., cols. *202–3*, 18 March 1980)

Third, subject to what has just been said about EU law issues, there is little indication that particular kinds of substantive legal difficulties should be taken to the Law Officers rather than elsewhere. One or two of the departmental guides to using lawyers refer specifically to international law questions and matters of constitutional or other general legal principle (DTI 1995: 9; DoE 1997: 23; Home Office 1995: 24). Edwards suggested in 1984 (1984: 189) that the Law Officers had a particular concern with questions of legal policy, such as form of legislation, definitions, retrospection, indemnities, and so on. This undoubtedly remains true, but issues of this kind are mostly likely to arise within the processes of preparation of legislation and delegated legislation, in which, as we have seen (above, pp. 254–8, 259–60), PCO and the Lord Advocate's Department (or Scottish Parliamentary Counsel) act as the particular guardians of these legal policy principles, with the Law Officers appearing essentially as a source of support at ministerial level. Such questions may also cause difficulty in relation to proposed administrative action (Civil Service Department 1979), but with the increasing propensity to challenge such action on a wide variety of legal grounds, through judicial review or otherwise, they are no longer so clearly defined, as a class, as once they were. The historical record, in any event, shows that diversity has always been the order of the day. The Solicitor to the Admiralty could not provide the Jessel Committee in 1876 with the statistics of references to the Law Officers they had sought, but he did list the sorts of matters he had referred, which ranged from contractual disputes on dockyard development to the question whether the Hong Kong administration could seize a naval officer's clothing as a means of enforcing payment of a debt (Jessel 1877: 77–9). As earlier Attorneys-General have remarked, their advisory practice addresses 'every conceivable kind of matter, from the law relating to international affairs to the law relating to intoxicating liquors' (Shawcross 1953: 6).

Three more comments should be added if these features of the advisory relationship between departments and the Law Officers—political pre-eminence; lack of a monopoly of external advice; absence of legal specialism—are to be given their proper weight.

The first is that no argument exists about the role of the Law Officers as umpire or 'final court of appeal' (Edwards 1984: 185) in cases where departments differ from each other on the law (Cabinet Office 1997*d*: para. 22; DoE 1997: 24; DTI 1995: 9; Home Office 1995: 24; and see above, pp. 256–8). Theirs is the last word on such questions, though not necessarily the first one, particularly now that an increasing range of *fora* exists for inter-departmental settlement of such issues. Second, the Law Officers do not necessarily have to take a wholly passive attitude to being asked for advice. Their powerful position in Cabinet Committees means that they have the opportunity to comment on many policy issues whether previously consulted or not; the Scottish Law Officers have been able recently to reverse what they saw was a growing tendency of Great Britain departments to neglect to take their advice on the Scots law aspect of legal issues; and the presence of the Legal Secretary, or other Secretariat staff, on most of the newer co-ordinating mechanisms we shall describe later (below, pp. 319–22) provides a supplementary source of information about legal issues being considered by departments. Intervention through either ministerial or official avenues is likely to be couched in the form of suggestions that the Law Officers be duly approached by the relevant department: suggestions which it will be difficult or impossible to refuse. Third, and always to be remembered, the quality of the work a Law Officer does will affect the amount of business he gets: the elements of structure and process we have described greatly constrain, but do not eliminate, the professional choice of government lawyers as to where the best advice is to be had—a choice sometimes even manifested as between one serving Law Officer and another.

4 Confidentiality, dissemination, and impact

The general rule relating to the confidentiality of Law Officers' advice can be stated very shortly: such advice is confidential. But for whose benefit is confidentiality imposed? who may waive it? and in whose favour? The answers to these questions are of great relevance to the way legal opinion is formed and diffused in government.

4.1 Disclosure outside government

So far as disclosure to Parliament—which in practice means general publication—is concerned, the answer appears at first sight to be stated clearly by the standard authority, Erskine May's *Parliamentary Practice*:

> The opinions of the law officers of the Crown, being confidential, are not usually laid before Parliament, cited in debate or provided in evidence before a Select Committee, and their production has frequently been refused; but if a Minister deems it expedient that such opinions should be made known for the information of the House, he is entitled to cite them in debate. (1997: 389)

At first sight, this passage seems to apply the general idea that while advice should in the ordinary way be confidential to the adviser and the decision-maker, it is the decision-maker (here the minister), and not the adviser (here the Law Officer), who can determine whether to make public his reasons for action, including any advice he has been given. Thus Edwards, in his two authoritative works on the Law Officers, reviews practice up to 1984 in some detail and concludes that this statement is correct and, specifically, that there is no convention prohibiting disclosure by ministers (1964: 257–9; 1984: 213 n. 22 and 207–35 *passim*). He is contradicted, however, by internal instructions about appearances before Select Committees issued to civil servants in 1980 (the so-called 'Osmotherly Rules', since reissued (1997) but without this paragraph):

> There should not be disclosed to a Committee any advice that may have been given by the Law Officers. There is a well-established convention that the advice which Law Officers give to Ministers is confidential. It is only where Law Officers expressly authorise the disclosure of that advice, or themselves report to or advise Parliament or a Committee, that such advice is revealed. (Civil Service Department 1980)

This instruction is not incapable of reconciliation with Erskine May, which may be read as reflecting solely the Parliamentary rules on the matter, and not the internal government requirements to be satisfied before a minister may deem publication expedient. Earlier evidence of this 'well-established convention' is, however, elusive. In 1964 Edwards thought that a minister who proposed to cite a Law Officer's advice in Parliament should obtain his consent simply as an 'ordinary courtesy' (Edwards 1964: 259), not as a matter of obligation. What is apparent, however, is a determined and successful attempt by the Law Officers, in the following years, not just to confirm this as a convention, but to extend its scope.

Edwards noted twenty years later that there was 'support in modern times . . . for the imposition of an impregnable moat around Law Officers' opinions' (1984: 226), and some vigorous digging was done in a circular of 11 August 1983 from the Law Officers' Department to all departments (cited in Defence Committee 1986: para. 171) which stated:

> The basic rule is that it is not permissible, save with the express prior authority of the Law Officers, to disclose to anybody outside UK Government service what advice the Law Officers have given on a particular question *or whether they have given any advice on that question or even whether their advice on it has been or is going to be or may be sought*. Such prior authority is occasionally given but only in very exceptional circumstances (emphasis supplied).

This seemingly unilateral extension of the Law Officers' prerogative was repeated in a parliamentary answer in 1986 after the DTI leaked advice given by the Solicitor-General to the Ministry of Defence in the Westland affair (Defence Committee 1986; 92 HC Debs., col. *279*, written answers 20 February 1986), and obtained Cabinet Office recognition in the Code of Practice on Access to Government Information (Cabinet Office 1994*d*: paras. 4.15–16). Finally, the Prime Ministerial accolade was given with the appearance of the rule in the 1997 *Ministerial Code* in the form

24. The fact and content of opinions and advice given by the Law Officers, including the Scottish Law Officers, either individually or collectively, must not be disclosed outside Government without their consent. (Cabinet Office 1997*d*)

The words 'The fact and content of' are not to be found in the 1992 version.

Two questions are prompted by this rapid process of rule-development, from courteous usage to blunt prohibition. Why have the Law Officers been striving so mightily for invisibility? and what is the constitutional significance of their success?

A variety of explanations for the width of the rule have been aired within government. Some echo the grounds cited for the general exclusion of legal advice from the scope of Freedom of Information legislation (Chancellor of the Duchy of Lancaster 1997: paras. 2.21–2.22): possible disclosure might impair candour of communication; disclosing even the fact of consultation might signal the importance, or legal fragility, of the relevant decisions. More frequently evoked is the fear that if Parliament knew whether or not Law Officers' advice had (or had not) been sought, and might thus criticize ministers on this ground, questions would be referred to the Law Officers which are at present properly left to departmental lawyers. Baggallay's flood of trivia would rise again to inundate the Law Officers. Departmental comment and practice (above, pp. 303–8) makes one wonder whether this would really be such a big problem. An alternative rationale is that it would be impossible to debate legal advice effectively or usefully in Parliament, or to keep it separate from the policy issues to which it related, so that if the content or fact of Law Officers' advice became public, that advice would itself be opened to political challenge, by ministers no less than by MPs, with consequent risks for its independence.

Whatever the reasons for its existence and extension, the necessary implication of the 'convention' is that the Law Officers, though ministers with advisory functions, are not responsible, in the parliamentary or public sense, for the advice they give. Indeed, so much has expressly been claimed by the Attorney-General: 'The Law Officers are not answerable to Parliament for the legal advice which they give to the Government . . . ' (92 HC Debs., col. *279*, written answers 20 February 1986); and see Mr Balfour, as Prime Minister, in 1901, likewise denying any responsibility for advice on the part of the Law Officers: 92 HC Debs., col. 1479 26 April 1901). The claim now finds some reflection in House of Commons Standing Orders. What is now Standing Order 152, establishing Departmental Select Committees, was in about 1991–92 amended to bring the administration and expenditure of the Attorney-General's

Office within the remit of the Home Affairs Committee, but this was expressed to exclude 'individual cases and appointments and *advice given within government by Law Officers*' (emphasis supplied) (Erskine May 1997: Appendix). In effect, therefore, the Law Officers are wholly veiled in the collective responsibility of the government, unless they choose to allow that veil to be drawn aside by giving 'prior authority'. Otherwise, the minister advised must behave as if the decision were his alone.

How may we fit this notion of an irresponsible minister into our constitution? Arguably this is simply an example of the way in which collective responsibility commonly works in practice. Ministers will often find that departmental plans are modified or even rejected by Cabinet or its committees; when this happens they are not entitled to go to the Commons and say, in a matter falling within their departmental responsibilities, 'the Cabinet made me do it' (Cabinet Office 1997*d*: para. 16). Likewise, perhaps, with Law Officers' opinions. These may not often be discussed in Cabinet, but they have the implicit authority of the Cabinet behind them, in the sense that a Law Officer who gave advice to a minister in categorical terms ('You must not do that') would expect the Cabinet's backing if challenged, and if denied it, might well feel it incumbent on him to resign (cf. Shawcross 1953: 7). This of course does not preclude a minister's taking less categorical opinions—pointing, say, to legal risks rather than clearly asserting illegality—to Cabinet to argue about them, or for that matter simply taking a departmental decision to run the risks signalled by the Law Officer. It need not even preclude Cabinet decisions to act contrary to legal obligations, at least if the obligations are owed to foreigners (compare Benn 1989: 155, on cancellation of sale of Wasp helicopters to South Africa in 1974 with Elwyn-Jones 1983: 194 and Howe 1994: 56 on how successive Attorneys-General prevented cancellation of the Concorde project on legal grounds).

If Law Officers' advice is thus to be taken as imputable to the Cabinet unless Cabinet decides otherwise, the rule may be seen as one expression of the general principle that the collective acts and views of government are to be accepted and defended by the minister with the responsibility for the specific matter in issue. Such a principle protects Parliament's need for clear lines of responsibility for government decisions, by rejecting any attempt to move them away from the departmental minister, whatever the means by which they were arrived at (Woodhouse 1993). This does not, however, explain why it should be the Law Officers, rather than Cabinet itself, who may determine whether to move away from this principle or not. No other ministers claim such a privilege.

The rule has another important effect. It reflects and reinforces legal pluralism in government. By denying responsibility the Law Officers also deny to their advisory function, and to their view of the law, any constitutional legitimacy beyond that conferred by the expectation of Cabinet support. That support is based on political calculation, not on the recognition of a central source of opinion as inherently authoritative. The publicly authoritative opinion, on law as on other elements of decision, is that of the departmental minister, and the law itself, in its application to government, is seen as divided into parcels corresponding to departmental competences.

4.2 Dissemination within government

Given this effect of the confidentiality rules, there is no paradox in the fact that the Law Officers' claim to control the publication of their advice does not appear to extend to its dissemination *within* the executive. Here the position is inverted: 'Advice', according to a former Treasury Solicitor, 'belongs to the department requesting it.' This being so, the question must arise as to whether rulings by the Law Officers which might be of significance to more than one department might not risk obscurity and neglect, if the recipient department, for good or bad reasons, does nothing to disseminate them through Whitehall. No system for avoiding this risk appears to exist. It is left to the good sense and perceptiveness of government lawyers to ensure that any other interested departments are associated in the formulation of a request (and therefore naturally also receive the advice afterwards), or to perceive their interest *ex post* once advice has been received. The Legal Secretariat plays an important role here in prompting such perceptions and thus in ensuring that advice reaches the places where it is most needed. This should obviously happen automatically where the reason for the reference is a difference between departments on a legal issue. The co-ordinating arrangements recently developed or institutionalized (below, pp. 319–22) must also play a supportive role in this respect.

There is no reason to believe, therefore, that departmental 'ownership' of Law Officers' advice means that it is not seen by other departments to which it is also contemporaneously, and specifically, relevant. We do, however, have real doubts about whether knowledge about the general legal implications of specific issues, and of the advice given in connection with them, is adequately disseminated across Whitehall. Not all legal advisers expressed themselves satisfied with the effectiveness of the unstructured arrangements just described. General dissemination of advice appears to be a rarity, occurring routinely only in relation to EC law (where a specialized co-ordination structure has been built up (below, pp. 316–19). Elsewhere special and quite onerous efforts appear to be needed for this purpose, such as those made by the Legal Secretariat to develop and disseminate an authoritative opinion on public interest immunity.

Given the importance attached by government lawyers to 'coherence' in executive action both as a justification for and a result of the Law Officers' advisory function, this situation appears curious. It is to be explained, perhaps, by the highly particularistic view of legal issues that appears prevalent among government lawyers. Most advice from the Law Officers is considered to be applicable primarily, if not exclusively, to the matter at hand. Outside the Law Officers' departments, and except in one or two special areas, such as international law and European law, such advice is not treated as though it constituted any kind of repository of authoritative opinion. The keeping of a full set of opinions in the Legal Secretariat, available for consultation by any government lawyer, was abandoned as early as the nineteen-twenties, on the ground that it was not of sufficient general interest. Even within individual departments, conservation of a complete and fully indexed set of opinions or advice from the Law Officers, readily retrievable, is the exception, not the rule. Departments are, however, confident that they can, if they need to, retrieve any advice they have received, and it is the expectation of the Law Officers that new departmental instructions will flag up any earlier relevant advice and that the Legal Secretariat will ordinarily run its own check if there is doubt on this score.

In this connection it is also worth considering the significance of the rules relating to access by one government to another government's papers. Here, according to a leading authority, written opinions of Law Officers form an exception to the general rule that ministers may not see Cabinet papers, or papers recording unpublished opinions of ministers, of previous administrations of a different political party (Hunt 1982; and see Cabinet Office 1997*d*: para. 22). While these sources state no limitations to this exception, which clearly works in favour of the coherence of legal advice to government over time and regardless of political affiliation, current practice appears somewhat more subtle and restrictive. Neither the current minister in the department which received the original opinion, nor the Law Officers themselves, may have sight of advice when the result would be disclosure of the kind of information about policy thinking that is protected under the general rules. Should a minister, or a Law Officer, desire to see advice under these circumstances, the Legal Secretary and the departmental Permanent Secretary would consult with a view to seeing how the necessary information might be conveyed without breaching the general rule. Perhaps it is to such a process that Edmund Dell refers when, in describing the background to the introduction of Petroleum Revenue Tax in 1975, he speaks of being 'allowed to read an edited version of [a Law Officer's] opinion' given to the previous administration about the legality of 'carried interest', a particular form of state participation in oil licences (Dell 1993: 250 n. 14). If this is so, it would not appear that the editing was very rigorous or effective: the opinion, says Dell, 'showed that carried interest was very seriously considered by the Heath Government' (ibid.). The inability even of the Law Officers themselves—who, it should be recalled, act personally and not through officials—to range freely through previous substantive advice sits uneasily with frequently reiterated claims to 'objectivity' or 'detachment' in relation to the advisory function. Moreover, this inter-temporal restriction on intra-governmental, even intra-office disclosure, even if only applicable at ministerial level, must furnish a further obstacle to the formation or preservation of any sense that there can exist a body of legal opinion within government whose authority is continuing, and not merely contingent upon the political and other circumstances which elicited it.

III CABINET OFFICE CO-ORDINATION IN LEGAL MATTERS

1 In general

As befits its situation, the Cabinet Office is responsible for a range of important co-ordinating functions in legal no less than in other fields (above, pp. 51–7). Much of the general advice and guidance which it falls to Cabinet Office to issue to government as a whole has legal elements of considerable importance, even if not addressed primarily to legal advisers in departments. In performing this function, the Office serves as a transmission belt for ideas and practices that may have originated elsewhere; while giving them the *imprimatur* of the authoritative central agency of government. An example of this type is the *Agency Chief Executives' Handbook*, first issued in 1996 (Office of Public Service 1996*a*), which sets out to provide a personal guide for agency Chief Executives on some of the key issues they face: general administration, accountability, conduct, financial management, personnel management, and agency reviews. In essence the *Handbook* is a collation of established practice: its 'general administration' section is in fact a guide to sources of intra-governmental guidance on the widest range of topics, from the Armstrong Memorandum (on civil servants' duties to ministers) to civil servants' acting as witnesses in civil actions. The guide points to sources of guidance on such legal topics as international law and treaty obligations, judicial review, Law Officers' advice (where the 'convention' against disclosure without their consent is stated as a rule), and legal entitlements (Civil Service Department 1979); it also contains a short substantive annex on legal challenges to government decisions.

Authoritative indication of when to consult, and whom to consult, appears elsewhere in more comprehensive terms in this part of the *Handbook* and also figures prominently in the internal *Guide to Legislative Procedures* (Office of Public Service 1996*b*) which we examined in the previous chapter (above, pp. 244–50). Government lawyers too lay much stress on the importance of *ad hoc* consultation, whether with colleagues in other Departments, TSol litigators, the Legal Secretariat, or others. Whereas once it might have been assumed that those who had reached positions of sufficient importance to need to consult extra-departmentally would by then have absorbed common knowledge and practice on this issue, the increasing decentralization of activity and diversity of recruitment within the Civil Service makes this assumption less reliable than in the past. Hence the formal setting forth of these procedural obligations which might once have resided, possibly in unwritten form, in the institutional memory of departments.

This general concern with appropriate and effective consultation between departments is of course the essence of the Cabinet Office's overall function. Facilitating inter-departmental contacts, getting the right people together, anticipating or, if necessary, resolving disputes: all these are its stock-in-trade. Where *ad hoc* Cabinet machinery is set up in this way, on a topic which has an important legal dimension (such as rail privatization), the Law Officers and Legal Secretariat are likely to participate: the Law Officers when the committee is at ministerial level, the Legal Secretary for official-level machinery. In some cases such machinery may acquire a degree of permanence, as with a standing committee on pay restraint which existed for several years under earlier Labour governments, and a similar committee which functioned as a co-ordination mechanism for the government's responses to the Scott Inquiry. But it is only in relation to European Union matters that a truly permanent Cabinet Office co-ordinating mechanism has been established in such a way as to centralize legal advice and other services.

2 On European law

The European Secretariat of the Cabinet Office is the government's co-ordinating agency for European Community and Union affairs (Bender

1996).[5] Despite (or perhaps because of) their day-to-day importance to every Department of government, EC/EU affairs are not handled differently from other matters: while there is a Foreign Office minister with particular responsibility for EU matters, who has a special concern with United Kingdom policy in the EU, departments handle the matters that affect them and are co-ordinated through the Cabinet Office machinery. The European Secretariat, as one might imagine, is a busy part of that machinery, generally organizing around 150 meetings of officials a year, some essentially for discussion and exploration of issues, others aiming to reach decisions (Holroyd 1989: para. 11). The United Kingdom places a high value on policy consistency across departments in EC/EU discussions and negotiations—higher perhaps than any other member. The working methods of the Secretariat aim at reaching interdepartmental agreement at official level on the basis of positions endorsed by ministers, and failing this, to crystallize areas of disagreement in such a way as to facilitate ministerial agreement through correspondence or meeting. Ordinarily the 'lead' department takes the initiative by producing and circulating a paper; if meetings are required, these are organized by the Secretariat, which may itself sometimes draft papers, and may also initiate discussions if needed consultation is not occurring (Bender 1996: 3–4).

Legal advice to the European Secretariat is provided by the European Division of TSol, which is also responsible for all United Kingdom litigation before the European Court of Justice. The advisory lawyers are functionally part of Cabinet Office machinery and are known generally as Cabinet Office Legal Advisers (COLA); the litigation lawyers are functionally part of TSol. The advisory work of the Division supports and extends general European Secretariat activity. COLA are entitled to attend all meetings, and are absent only when it is clear that there is no legal dimension to the policy under discussion. But in addition to this participation, they also run discussions among legal advisers through an *ad hoc* committee, under the aegis of a legal committee, EQO(L), the main Secretariat machinery being EQO. Like the general work of the Secretariat, this is a co-ordinating function. Each Department may come across EC/EU law questions in the course of its ordinary work; the *ad hoc* committee's function is to ensure that the lawyers of the different departments involved are of a common view on the legal issues. Just as most EQO work is initiated by departments, who perceive the need for co-ordination (though the Secretariat attaches

[5] European Community affairs are those falling within the ambit of the Community Treaties (ECSC; EEC; Euratom) and hence under the so-called 'first pillar' of the (Maastricht) Treaty on European Union (1992). European Union affairs include also those falling under the second and third 'pillars', i.e. justice and home affairs, and foreign affairs.

great importance to stimulating departmental awareness of this need (Holroyd 1989: para. 10), legal work will generally be stimulated by departmental lawyers raising legal points that they feel need collective consideration, though the Division may sometimes raise issues itself. The Foreign and Commonwealth Office naturally occupies a rather special position in these processes, having a broad-ranging concern with the constitutional and external relations aspects of EU/EC affairs, rather than a subject-based departmental interest, and sometimes acting in tandem with European Division, as in providing legal advice within the 1996–97 Intergovernmental Conference.

In policy work, the job of the Division is to ensure that a common view of the legal issues is reached. If views are irreconcilable, either because departmental lawyers are genuinely at odds as to what the law is or because their policy instructions require them to be, or if doubts persist, the lead policy department will ordinarily be asked to refer the question to the Law Officers. The institutionalized character of co-ordination on EC/EU law means that the Law Officers' work on these issues displays in a very clear form the 'process' characteristics referred to earlier (above, pp. 300–1), with elaborate inter-departmental preparation and briefing being the norm. It also affects the impact of their opinions. More than any other part of GLS, European Division works for the government as a whole. It differs even from the other 'horizontal' divisions of TSol, the Litigation Division and the Government Property Lawyers, in that its 'clients' are not departments, but the Cabinet Office. As such, it can perform a function which in other fields is deprived of institutional support: that is, to act as the guardians of the advice of the Law Officers. It has a special position in relation to that advice when given on EC/EU law matters, ordinarily receiving a copy of what is sent to departments despite the 'departmental ownership' rule. Effectively, it treats the opinions of the Law Officers as judgments, and when new issues come up, considers whether they may be regarded as covered by earlier advice. European law may itself change, of course, and a minister might insist on further reference to the Law Officers in any event, but it seems clear that the European Division machinery assures a systematic consideration of Law Officers' advice which does not obtain in other fields.

Community policy work is the Division's 'bread and butter'; but its functions in relation to implementation, and to European-level litigation and its impacts, also disclose a unique position among government legal services. Guidance on implementation has already been discussed (above, pp. 266–8). Co-ordination in policy and implementation is prolonged by its monopoly of European-level litigation. It not only runs the United Kingdom's cases in the European Court of Justice and

Court of First Instance: it also circulates information on all new cases before these courts to any department which may have an interest; co-ordinates the making of observations by the United Kingdom in any article 234 (formerly 177) case which raises issues of any breadth or complexity (the lead department can settle the United Kingdom line in the absence of cross-departmental issues); and circulates judgments and Advocate-General's opinions to interested departments. Only exceptionally, however, is the government's response to European Court judgments treated as a matter for co-ordination by the Division. The *Francovich* case (1991), where the Court held that a government might be liable in damages to its citizens for loss stemming from failure to implement a Directive, was one such exception. The Division initiated a process of reflection which began with an inter-departmental meeting of lawyers and culminated in advice from the Law Officers based on counsel's opinion on the implications of the judgment. It also organized a series of follow-up meetings to co-ordinate departmental responses to *Factortame III (Brasserie du Pecheur* 1996*)*, establishing the definitive criteria for the liability of member-states in damages. Again, after the *Fisscher* and *Vroege* judgments (1994) on equal access to pension benefits, industrial tribunals were deluged with thousands of applications co-ordinated by trade unions. There were at least three departments involved either as defendants or as sponsors of defendant public bodies like NHS Trusts. Important questions had been left by the European Court of Justice to national courts, such as what limitation period was applicable and whether arrears could be limited. The task, assumed by the Division, of co-ordinating the governmental response was a strenuous one not least because the Division lacked, in relation to domestic litigation, the authoritative role it enjoyed in litigation at the European level.

IV CO-ORDINATION WITHIN THE FRAMEWORK OF THE GOVERNMENT LEGAL SERVICE

Collective consideration of substantive legal issues may remain a rarity, as the salience of the *Francovich* and *Fischer/Vroege* initiatives testifies; but departmental legal advisers do at least now possess an institutional forum within which regular discussions—which may touch on such substantive issues—can take place. This is the Government Legal Service Liaison Group (GLSLG), set up in 1993 by the then Treasury Solicitor, Sir Gerald Hosker. The Group, which represents the formalization of earlier, more *ad hoc* meeting arrangements, comprises all the principal Departmental Solicitors and Legal Advisers (viz. Home Office, DETR, Customs and Excise, Inland Revenue, DSS/DH, DTI, Welsh Office, MAFF), the

Legal Secretary to the Law Officers, the Deputy Treasury Solicitor, and the Director of SFO. Senior lawyers from the FCO, CPS, PCO, the Scottish Office, and Northern Ireland attend as observers. Meetings take place every six weeks and are chaired by the Treasury Solicitor in his capacity as Head of GLS.

The meetings of GLSLG are mainly concerned with the sorts of issue that have prompted past enquiries into the situation of government lawyers: recruitment, retention, training, promotion, and other management questions. Its existence provides, in these fields, a collegial counterpart to the central support arrangements introduced following the Andrew Report, in the shape of the Lawyers Management Unit, which acts on behalf of GLS as a whole (above, p. 218), and it has been suggested that the Group was created to reassure departments that TSol did not intend by such means to take them over. It keeps departments informed of one another's practices, and ensures that the Treasury Solicitor, in his GLS role, knows their views. Interestingly, it is also developing into the hub of what might be seen as a GLS discussion network. Several standing sub-groups have been formed. A Prosecutors' Group was created in 1996 to enable non-CPS prosecutors (such as MAFF and the Revenue Departments) to exchange information, to encourage career moves between them, and to keep them in touch with thinking at CPS (which is represented on the Group, as is the Legal Secretariat). A Training Sub-Group considers legal training issues, in which GLS has an increasingly important role, with LMU servicing a network of departmental legal training officers, and a variety of common courses being developed. There are also sub-groups on recruitment and employment issues. In addition, a Government Litigators Group, not formally a sub-group of GLSLG, came into being in 1993, taking over the remit and membership of an *ad hoc* committee that had operated since 1985: it deals with issues of common interest arising in civil litigation (such as counsel's fees).

While management is its main concern, GLSLG does also discuss substantive legal issues. It provided the forum, for example, for a first inter-departmental discussion of public interest immunity following the Scott Report (Scott 1996). Other substantive subjects have ranged from Crown immunity (after *M v Home Office* 1994) and the interpretation of the Code of Practice on access to official information (Cabinet Office 1994; 1997*b*), to the need for justices' licences for parties on government office premises (an issue which also went to the Law Officers for advice), and the implementation of the regulations giving effect to the EC Acquired Rights Directive (Transfer of Undertakings (Protection of Employment) Regulations 1981). The individuals sitting on GLSLG may not, of course, be the departmental experts on these varied issues, but the Group provides the means whereby departmental consensus on them may be sought, whether on the basis of memoranda circulated among experts or through *ad hoc* groups in which such specialists may get together. Such groups may enjoy an extended life: the group set up to look at issues relating to industrial tribunals subsequently acquired a general employment law remit, and discussion of PII was continued within such a group. Bodies like the Litigators' or Prosecutors' Groups may also discuss substantive issues falling within their purview, such as the giving of reasons for administrative decisions.

An obvious question is whether GLSLG, albeit of recent foundation, is on the way to becoming an effective co-ordination mechanism for legal views within government, complementary to the work of the Law Officers. Could it perform, in relation to legal advice generally, the sort of role discharged by the European Division in relation to European law? There are signs that formal co-ordination may increase, though not necessarily through GLSLG. In making arrangements for the rights protected by the European Convention to operate directly in United Kingdom law, the government rejected the idea of a separate implementation unit (Home Office 1997: para. 3.5), but in addition to provision for an inter-departmental group to give policy advice on issues arising from the legislation (above, pp. 269–71), it also envisaged 'an inter-departmental group of lawyers and administrators meeting on a regular basis to ensure that a consistent approach is taken [to human rights Convention points in criminal, civil and judicial review proceedings to which a department is party] and to ensure that developments in case law are well understood by all those in Government who are involved in proceedings on Convention points' (ibid.). As things have turned out, separate groups have been set up to deal with criminal and with civil litigation (including judicial review). All three groups meet under the aegis of the Cabinet Office.

On other matters, Cabinet Office continues to organize inter-departmental legal discussions outside the framework of GLSLG (for example on the implications of the *Pepper v Hart* decision on the use of Hansard in judicial proceedings (1993), an issue felt to be of more than purely professional legal interest); and much inter-departmental discussion on legal topics of common concern, such as human rights, defamation, public appointments, public inquiries, and the PCA, goes on effectively without the benefit of GLSLG co-ordination or, for that matter, Law Officers' opinions. Among government lawyers, moreover, there is a palpable sense of resistance to all-encompassing institutional arrangements or even to privileged channels of communication. 'Responsiveness', 'instinct' (as to when and how to consult), 'flexibility', and 'variety' are repeatedly emphasized as values of the system, which must militate against the development of any central (even if collegial) forum for the formation of legal opinion. Indeed such a forum, it has been suggested, might present an additional danger: that views on legal issues there agreed and adopted might, if they became publicly known, themselves form the object of judicial review. Development of such a function for the GLSLG system is therefore likely, if it proceeds at all, to advance with great caution.

Instinct, no matter how finely honed, and flexibility, no matter how intelligently applied, still cannot assure co-ordination and coherence in the absence of adequate information by reference to which these qualities may be applied. We have already seen that the distribution of key information such as Law Officers' opinions is, with rare exceptions, itself a matter for *ad hoc* decision-making. The same is true of the process of spreading other kinds of legal information around within government, though perhaps the new human rights arrangements described above signal a change of approach. Hitherto it has been assumed that legal advisers will pick up the information that is relevant to the work of their departments, through public sources such as Hansard, the law reports, the statute book, and the press. Apart from the work of European Division in diffusing information about EC/EU law, the only central information service is the *Treasury Solicitor Digest*, which describes itself as 'a commentary on recent cases which may be of interest to Whitehall lawyers generally'. This is edited in TSol, has appeared some three or four times a year since 1992, and is distributed across the GLS, as well as to Treasury Counsel and some other 'public' lawyers. The *Digest* covers a very wide range of topics and is not confined to cases brought by or against government departments. While departments find it valuable for its selection of material and its commentary, some point out that it comes only after the event and that knowledge of pending cases is more important. A departmental legal adviser was 'as likely to become aware of significant litigation affecting other Departments by reading the newspapers' as by processes of internal dissemination of information. Bodies like the Litigators' Group and Prosecutors' Group may have an important role to play in filling this gap.

10

Executive Legality: Constitutional Background and Current Issues

I LEGALITY: PLURALISM AND CENTRALIZATION

Let us briefly review the findings of the last three chapters on the key features of executive structure and practice on legality, before trying to assess their significance.

First, legal work in government, like other work, is done within a structure which is essentially and fundamentally departmental, that is to say, in which functions and powers are allocated, on a subject-matter basis, among a number of legally co-ordinate authorities: politically-responsible ministers and their departments. Departments are diverse in their activities, their organization, and their approach to legal work and its management. While there exist important common legal services (notably the TSol litigation and conveyancing functions), centralization of legal work is exceptional, and is confined to legislative drafting and EC/EU litigation.

Second, the work of government lawyers, and in particular the formation and expression of views about the content of the law, is seen as an advisory function, albeit one increasingly integrated into departmental policy-making and administrative action. Legal services' advice to the ministers they serve is strictly confidential, and the government wishes it to remain so despite the granting of wider access to government information.

Third, central control of legal work is both patchy and weak. While most criminal work in both Scotland and in England and Wales is now under central (Law Officer) control, control over the criminal work of ministerial departments remains *ad hoc* and is often precarious. For civil legal work (and subordinate legislation) there is no legally grounded central control; control through 'authoritative' Law Officers' advice relies on conventions of political support and on a referral system which leaves broad discretion to departments. Law Officers' advice is secret.

Fourth, considerable and steadily increasing efforts are devoted within government to the co-ordination of legal work and legal opinion, through Cabinet Office guidance, specialized institutional arrangement for European matters, and the development of a formal consultation network within the Government Legal Service. With rare exceptions, however, co-ordination is grounded on correct consultative procedures, not substantive standards; 'there is no policy other than that there should be a policy'. Any substantive standards apply almost exclusively to the preparation of legislation or delegated legislation.

Fifth, increasing the 'legal awareness' of administrators is today regarded as an important function of government lawyers.

In order to discuss the significance of these findings it is helpful to consider how else things might be done. There is no difficulty in imagining an alternative model of government legal work which would contrast strongly with this picture of departmental variegation, multiple (and sometimes competing) sources of legal opinion, intermittent and politically contingent central control, and problematic co-ordination. Many countries have unified, or largely unified, structures for government legal advice and representation: Italy's *Avvocatura dello Stato* and *Consiglio di Stato* offer a convenient example (Ferri 1988; Paleologo 1998). Rather than start from foreign models, however, we can refer to a strand of domestic opinion, both within and outside government, which—to quote the latest review of the subject—has constantly favoured

> a unified legal service whose members are paid from a single Vote and can be deployed by a central authority to the areas of greatest need. Only in this way, it is argued, can parochial barriers be broken down and the most effective use made of scarce resources. Complete centralisation of the Government Legal Service would be a culmination of a process begun in the 19th century and would make possible the effective management of the Service, which the various co-ordinating committees proposed in the past have signally failed to do. It would also reinforce the independence of government lawyers by detaching them slightly from the departments they advise. (Andrew 1989: 34 (para. 5.10))

The emphasis here is very strongly upon managerial considerations, but the final sentence recognizes, at least faintly, the implications of such an alternative structure for what lawyers do within government and the way they do it. 'Independence' immediately raises the question 'independent of whom?', quickly followed by 'dependent upon whom?' Honest answers to these queries must evoke the idea of a corps of government lawyers owing a primary loyalty to their corps and its leaders rather than to the departments and ministers they serve, whether this service be on a case-by-case basis or in the framework of some more permanent attachment. Even on the latter basis, it is hard to imagine that under such arrangements, legal work could continue to be so diverse in content and organization, so strongly shaped by departmental styles and priorities. A department within which all government legal advice was centralized, whether ministerial or non-ministerial, must surely soon acquire a more unified set of working practices, and even of legal opinions, than presently characterizes our distributed system of legal work. Indeed, despite the way TSol, with its multi-departmental responsibilities, works now, one wonders if a department which was the *unique* repository of legal advice within government could long avoid taking much more visible and explicit responsibility for the advice it gave, since the ignorance which now prevails as to where the legal advice underlying any ministerial decision came from would, *ex hypothesi*, have been dissipated.

These speculations on the implications of radical centralization may help us to see more clearly what it is that has shaped, and still sustains, our present arrangements—system seems too strong a word. If we find it difficult to imagine abandoning the secrecy of advice and even of legal opinion, or the 'ownership' of legal services by departments, we need to ask just where and how deep this difficulty lies.

II CONSTITUTIONAL ROOTS OF OUR PRESENT SYSTEM

1 Ministerial responsibility

Ministerial responsibility is not a bad starting-point, so long as we do not detach the concept from the political environment—of inter- and intra-party contest—in which it is exercised. Ministers are the actors in government who bear both legal and political responsibility; government's collective decisions, no less than departmental ones, are carried out through the exercise of those responsibilities. Legal advice, like legal work more generally, forms part of the resources through which they may be discharged, and has been shaped—notably as to its confidentiality—by the same factors which have produced the idea of civil service anonymity as the counterpart to the minister's exclusive answerability to Parliament. That exclusiveness has come under heavy pressure as efforts are made, in the interests of efficiency, to fit executive branch structures better to the different kinds of work done in government, and some pointers exist—the identification of conveyancing as an early subject for an executive agency, the Attorney-General's division of legal work into 'core' and 'non-core'—as to how that kind of differentiation might be carried over into the area of legal work. The starting-point from which these changes are being made, however, is a structure in which legal work is done for the minister in his department, and in which legal opinion is put at his disposition as an element of the decisions for which he takes responsibility (whether in fact they were taken below him, by the department's administrators, or collectively, in the Cabinet system).

The political context of that decision-making ensures that the legal advice will not—save in very rare circumstances—be the only factor that contributes to the decision. Even internal legal advice which has been consistently maintained over a long period may have to yield to the requirements of a government's political programme, or to the political pressures which a minister faces. That minister may even be the Attorney-General, who in 1981 found himself compelled by a combination of popular opinion and judicial accident to use his *nolle prosequi* power in circumstances where, according to established opinion in his department, it was inappropriate or even unavailable (Edwards 1984: 445, 446 n.; Harlow and Rawlings 1992: 261).

To say that the political responsibility of ministers makes it difficult to regard legality as an absolute value within government does not imply readiness to act illegally as and when it suits politically. Advice, as indicated earlier, is seldom so clear-cut; and it may often have more to do with legally-preferred ways of doing things than with a choice between what is lawful and what is not. What *is* implied is that legal advice is given—whether by departmental legal services or by central figures like the Law Officers or Treasury Counsel—having regard to the political and administrative situation of the advisee. The situations of ministers, both across government and over time (and particularly over times that straddle changes of governing party), vary radically, and the advice given, even if fundamentally based on some set of consistent concepts, must reflect this variation, in its content (what matters need advice), in its context, and in its approach. This is the sense in which we may say that concepts of legality within government are relativistic; and this variation is, in our observation, perceived by lawyers within government as a major reason why, despite the existence of an authoritative centrally-situated legal adviser, no perceptibly coherent body of governmental legal opinion has developed, save in one or two specialized areas.

It seems unlikely, though, that this is the only reason. After all, other governments likewise live in a world of changing programmes and circumstances, and onerous political pressures, yet maintain at least the appearance of what might be termed an 'executive jurisprudence' (McGinnis 1993*a*; 1993*b*). Two further, closely interlocked elements of the situation of the United Kingdom executive need to be evoked here. The first is its subservience to the judiciary; the second, its dominance of the legislature.

2 Executive subservience to the judiciary

That the executive in the United Kingdom will abide by, and implement, judicial decisions holding its actions incorrect or illegal without delay or demur is a general expectation, maintained by courts and government alike. The case of *M v Home Office* 1994 illustrates this expectation. There the Home Secretary, under great pressure of time but having taken legal (including counsel's) advice, decided not to act in accordance with an order of a High Court judge to secure the return to Britain of a person who had just been deported in breach of an undertaking to that judge given by counsel on behalf of the Home Secretary. The Home Secretary formed the view that the order was outside the jurisdiction of the judge. The Court of Appeal and the House of Lords held that his view was wrong and that his disregarding the order constituted a contempt of court. Not all litigation against the central government will involve the making of mandatory orders (the main point of *M v Home Office* was to clarify the availability of such mandatory remedies), and only very rarely will disobedience involve such dramatic consequences as might plausibly have followed in that case (where the applicant, claiming to be a political refugee, was sent back by the Home Office to the country from which he had fled). None the less, the case was a strong one in so far as the decision ignored was made (necessarily and properly, given the circumstances) impromptu by a single judge without hearing both sides. The assumption was still one of obedience pending *judicial* reversal of the impugned decision.

Assumptions about compliance do not, however, stop at the point of executive obedience to the judicial decision in the instant case. Under the doctrine of precedent, judicial decisions, at least of the superior courts, themselves possess legal authority and form part of the law which the executive is bound to respect. Consequently a decision of a court interpreting a statutory or common law power and having value as a precedent must be treated as an authoritative statement of the meaning of the power, and a department will not be acting legally if, even in different circumstances from those which gave rise to the original ruling, it continues to adhere to, and apply, a conflicting interpretation. But what if the decision is by a lower court, and has weaker, or no, precedential value; or is by an administrative tribunal; or is a mere *obiter dictum*? Must this be applied by the relevant department, pending a successful appeal (or in the absence of any appeal)? or may the department simply say, 'We will implement the decision in this case, but continue our existing practice and see if it attracts other successful challenges in other courts and tribunals' (which will be free to reach different decisions)?

Exploration of this area is rendered difficult by the fact that clear examples of conscious maintenance of a departmental position, whether on statutory interpretation or common law principles, in the face of contrary judicial opinion, are hard to find. Sometimes they exist, but no one finds them. The clear and unanimous—but *obiter*—views of Queen's Bench in *R v Lords Commissioners of the Treasury* 1872 appear to have had no effect whatever on the Treasury's contrary opinion, explicitly argued in the case, as to the legal significance of the Appropriation Act (above, p. 203). Where they are found, they have been treated as ground for censure, at least by academic commentators. When the High Court ruled against the Supplementary Benefits Commission in 1974, holding that it should have calculated certain offsets to benefit on a case-by-case basis, in the exercise of its discretion, rather than in pursuance of a fixed rule (*R v Greater Birmingham Supplementary Benefits Appeal Tribunal, ex parte Simper* 1974), the Commission—pending corrective legislation—issued an internal circular effectively adhering to its earlier practice in relation to most offsets other than the one specifically in issue. Though the parliamentary record showed that the Commission's practice was in line with what Parliament intended, and though the Parliamentary Commissioner for Administration, after investigating the issuance of the circular, did not criticize it (Parliamentary Commissioner for Administration 1974–75: 85–8), the Commission's response was stigmatized as 'incredible' (Harlow 1976) and 'highly unsatisfactory' (Prosser 1983: 62). The Commission followed a rather similar line in response to *R v West London Supplementary Benefit Appeal Tribunal, ex parte Wyatt* 1978, issuing an internal circular designed to minimize, indeed negate, the impact of the decision, while declining to appeal it to the Court of Appeal; and again attracted criticism (Prosser 1983: 67–8; and for a later example, Sunkin and Le Sueur 1991: 169–71).

The rarity of documented cases, and the negative reactions they evoke, are strongly suggestive of a broad expectation, within and outside government, of executive deference, to judicial *dicta* no less than to decisions with unambiguous authority as precedent. This means real judicial power, of the strongest sort—the sort that people do not even see because they can hardly imagine its absence (Lukes 1974). To imagine it they only need to look across to the United States, where the phenomenon of 'non-acquiescence' by Federal executive agencies even in appellate court decisions is long-standing, formally claimed and expressed, and has been practised, in situations much like that of the *Simper* case, on a very wide scale (Maranville 1986; Estreicher and Revesz 1989). A further indicator, no less telling for being indirect, is the criticism sometimes levelled at departments—as at other respondents to judicial review—for settling cases, often only after leave has been given, with the result that while one applicant's grievance is remedied, a potentially adverse ruling which might benefit many others is avoided. In the absence of an expectation, internally as well as externally, that such rulings would be followed, rather than resisted through compelling further litigation, such complaints would make no sense.

This assumption of generous compliance is what we mean by executive subservience to the judiciary. It is an attitude of mind which has deep roots in the parliamentary and judicial victories over 'independent' royal power won in the seventeenth century against the pretensions of the Stuart Kings, and which has doubtless been further nourished in more recent times by the endless repetition, in the law schools and doubtless in the Civil Service College also, of the formulations of the rule of law offered by Professor Dicey, including the absolute supremacy or predominance of regular law, and the subjection of officials, equally with ordinary citizens, to the ordinary law of the land administered by the ordinary courts (Dicey 1959). Such an attitude of mind is reinforced by pragmatic considerations: any good lawyer keeps his client out of trouble, and retaining existing practice or interpretations when there have been indications of a significant likelihood of judicial disapproval is asking for trouble.

That executive subservience is the norm is easily obscured by occasional controversies, and there is discussion (which we seek to develop below) about whether it may currently be under threat; but for us its importance here is the way in which it undercuts the development of an 'executive jurisprudence'. Effectively it means that across that area of the activities of the executive which are liable to be the subject of judicial consideration (a term deliberately broader than 'judicial review'), even the most authoritative legal opinion within the executive is not different, in kind, from that which might be offered to any private party with complex legal business on hand. Only in those areas where the judges cannot go or do not want to go is it likely that executive interpretations of the law (or of legal principle) can be sustained for long enough, and without destabilization by external interference, to create anything in the nature of a body of internal legal opinion which amounts in effect to something more than a set of guesses about the results of future litigation.

We are not, of course, suggesting that such prediction is necessarily the purpose of internal rule-making. There are very large quantities of internal (or quasi-internal) departmental or agency working rules indicating, to their own officials, how the department or agency's powers and functions are to be exercised. These rules naturally embody or express internal legal interpretations, but were created for reasons of fair and systematic administration. None the less, they may need to be modified and developed, or sometimes relaxed, in response to judicial views suggesting different interpretations or even, now, subjecting them directly to scrutiny for their legal correctness (*R v Department of Social*

Security, ex parte Overdrive Credit Card Ltd 1991; *R v Inland Revenue Commissioners, ex parte Camacq Corporation* 1989). Cross-departmentally, there is little if anything, outside the area of legislative preparation (above, pp. 246–50), that can be pointed to as 'executive jurisprudence' of a consistent kind. In a rare case when substantive legal guidance was given outside this area, the authors were at pains to stress that 'our report does not lay down rules of law; that is a matter for Parliament and the courts' (Civil Service Department 1979: 2)—though in effect, they went on to advise as to what administrative practice might be legally questionable and what might not. We can, of course, only speculate as to what doctrinal riches may lie double-locked in the Law Officers' files. There probably is some significant learning on hitherto non-justiciable matters, like the legal status of ministerial powers (above, pp. 33–6) or the (unreviewable) public interest powers of the Law Officers themselves (above, pp. 288–90), but it surely cannot be long before the onward march of judicial review reaches even these preserves (*R v Secretary of State for Foreign Affairs, ex parte World Development Movement Ltd* (*'Pergau Dam'*) 1995; Feldman and Miller 1997).[1]

To say that legal advice to government is not, by reason of its explicit or underlying concern with what the judges will say, different in kind from that which might be given to large companies invites at least two separate charges of over-simplification (readers can probably come up with more). The first of these relates to the government's attitude to the prospect of litigation, and to the fact that it cannot resolve issues about how it should act by a simple cost-benefit calculation: risk of litigation; risk of defeat; costs of defeat and of settlement; revenue stream from the contestable behaviour, and so on. Governments have to be concerned with larger issues of principle: it may be financially cheap to settle a particular action; but if a principle is thereby lost or weakened . . . The argument raises interesting issues about the interplay between legality and other values like economy and efficiency, which we touch on below, but at root it simply reasserts that the much wider range of interests which government—as opposed even to the largest companies—must consider makes advising it a more complex and delicate matter. The subservience of the advice to anticipated judicial opinion and action is not changed.

[1] Government lawyers may of course be called upon to advise on the meaning of codes, guidance, and other such internal documents, discussed particularly in Chapters 3 and 11, and a body of authoritative internal opinion on them may be built up. This might certainly be regarded as an important area for an 'executive jurisprudence'; but it is not our concern here.

3 Executive dominance of Parliament

The second objection re-evokes the other basic relationship of the executive mentioned above: with Parliament. Executive dominance of Parliament, one might suggest, surely gives a quite distinctive coloration to the government's legal advice, since if the advice is unpalatable enough, one answer at least is to get some new law. Once this possibility appears, the law, as declared by the judges, is itself relativized; legislation can be identified as an option if desired departmental practice should meet with judicial disapproval, and its costs identified along with those of other courses of action, such as playing safe. Certainly this is an option which is peculiar to government (and one which our government can use more easily than can some other governments with less complaisant legislatures (Rose 1982: 11)). Evidently, the amount of power that the executive can exercise in this area, subject only to political as opposed to constitutional constraint, has made internal guidance about legislating a particularly prominent tool (above, pp. 246–50). Yet there is no sign that this power has been reflected in *general* attitudes of government lawyers, and of the administrators and ministers they advise, to the prospect of litigation, and in particular, of judicial review. Even if, as some are suggesting (below, p. 337), some ministers and administrators are less averse to legal risks than once they were, there seems no basis for attributing such a shift to consciousness of legislative might. Legislation is always a scarce resource (above, Chapter 8), and legislation which seeks to 'correct' adverse judicial decisions may carry unusually high political costs (Harlow 1976; McAuslan and McEldowney 1985: 28–32; James 1996), making it much less attractive than avoiding litigation or, if it cannot be avoided, winning it.

In consequence, the ultimate opportunity to have one's way through legislation has not in practice operated to sustain any body of executive opinion about what the law is or should be against contrary judicial opinion. Indeed, it might almost be argued that the opposite has happened: that one of the reasons why the executive has never bothered to develop and sustain its own view of what administrative law should look like has been the availability of the legislative escape route to get away from the consequences of those judicial decisions which are seen as presenting really dramatic and specific problems (Zellick 1985: 288–93). Another way in which the United Kingdom government's relatively easy access to legislation impairs the significance of internal opinion formation can be seen in what has been happening to the Attorney-General's guidelines relating to the conduct of prosecutions. These represent rare modern examples of independently formed, systematically diffused, executive legal opinions. Should their subject-matter become the object of judicial rulings, however (as has notably occurred with the issue of prosecution disclosure to the defence), the obvious route to the avoidance of confusion (or perhaps to the maintenance of the government's, rather than the courts', approach) is to secure the passage of legislation governing the subject—such as the Criminal Procedure and Investigations Act 1996. By these and other means, as we have seen (above, pp. 290–2), the significance of the guidelines in criminal matters has been whittled away in recent years.

The relative ease with which the government can secure the passage of legislation, and the absence (outside the sphere of European Community law and, now, Human Rights law) of any judicial apparatus for testing such legislation against a higher law, has meant that if there are to be any rules about the permissible content of legislation, it is the government that must make them and apply them to itself. Such rules, as we have seen (above, pp. 246–50), are by no means insignificant, and their existence reinforces, rather than weakens, the general point about 'executive jurisprudence' that we have been making here.

III THE CHANGING CONTEXT

Pluralism and secrecy in government legal work have thus been sustained by a variety of working practices based on well-established constitutional ideas and conventions. They have withstood the test of time: the regular attempts to create a more centralized legal service have largely failed (above, pp. 214–17); the drive for openness in government has not prevented the maintenance, nor even the tightening, of the rules protecting the secrecy of legal opinion in government (above, pp. 309–15). But these concepts will not necessarily hold firm if their constitutional supports—such as ministerial responsibility—start to slide. There is ample evidence that these supports are weakening. Two sources of erosion are particularly relevant to ideas and practice about the organization and delivery of legal advice.

1 Administrative heterogeneity

The first is the ever-accelerating decentralization and heterogeneity of the central or 'core' executive, 'now less a "service" than a series of "cadres" ', as one government lawyer put it to us. The proliferation of executive agencies (above, pp. 37–46), and the more varied nature of civil service recruitment and career patterns (above, Chapter 3), both part of this phenomenon, are already having an effect on the legal advice function.

Some of these effects are easy to see. The more varied the kinds of people recruited into the civil service at senior levels, and the more diverse the careers people have at those levels, the less easy it is to rely on a shared, almost instinctive knowledge of 'what to do'. Hence the mushrooming of written guidance across government, which these days is not just guidance by departments to their members about how to do the department's substantive jobs, but guidance about how, in general, to be a public servant, which necessarily involves a fair amount of legal material. These elements of legal advice necessarily become both more formalized, and more centralized through receiving the Cabinet Office *imprimatur.* They will also tend to become more public, if only because they appear in documents with a relatively wide circulation, such as the *Agency Chief Executives' Handbook* (Office of Public Service 1996*a*).

At departmental level, too, the nineteen-nineties novelty of generalized, widely-circulated guidance about when and how to use departmental legal services must owe something to this phenomenon of increasing variegation of the clientele with which the lawyers have to deal. Doubtless there has always been intra-, as well as inter-departmental diversity in administrators' approaches to law, particularly in those departments that have seen frequent changes of scope and structure through reshuffles of governmental functions. It would be surprising, for example, if the administrators in the Department of Trade and Industry, whose functions have, within the last thirty years, been in the hands of four separate departments, were to have the same homogeneity of outlook on the legal function as has typified Home Office administrators, undertaking a range of tasks which has not changed much over a century. The contrast is heightened by the fact that DTI's current tasks themselves have had very different legal profiles: traditionally, the business of trade regulation has been a much more legalized field of administration than has that of industrial subsidies. Largely because of European Community law, this particular difference has disappeared, but administrative differences of attitude may persist unless corrected by the more pro-active approach to advice expressed in the departmental lawyers' booklets.

'Agencification' can only increase this problem. Agencies are, after all, supposed to be different, and chief executives may well form the view that the way they get their legal work done should not simply be a carbon copy of general departmental practice. And where they provide a large part of a legal service's work (as is the case with the large DSS agencies: the Contributions Agency, the Benefits Agency, the Child Support Agency), their views will obviously carry weight, at least up to the point where a clear departmental interest intervenes, such as the need for the departmental Solicitor to retain ultimate control over litigation in respect of which he is, under the Crown Proceedings Act 1947, s. 17(1), the sole recipient of service. Large departments like DSS and DTI which have advanced some distance towards formalization and commercialization of their 'client' relationships may perhaps be able to handle this kind of variegation better—say through service level agreements—than those which have not gone down this road.

The creation of agencies, of course, brings new issues of political control of, and accountability for, their actions, issues which have been the subject of extensive public debate. Where lines demarcating responsibilities between the agency and the core department are unclear or contested, the legal advice function can easily be compromised. In 1996 an unfortunate series of misunderstandings between the Prison Service and the Home Office about the bases on which legal advice was being given and the status and purpose of meetings at which it was discussed led to the erroneous early release by the Service of a substantial number of prisoners, without prior notice to the Home Secretary, and the public identification of the Home Office lawyer involved (Travis 1996).

While this drama was the product of a problem relationship, there may also be a more widespread and insidious effect on legal work flowing from the creation of agencies and the general 'hollowing out' of the department. Many of the traditional 'horizontal' functions of departments, like establishments and finance, formerly extending across the whole range of its work, have been dispersed or devolved (above, pp. 129–32). The same has not happened to departmental legal services: agencies may contract out odd legal jobs, but as already noted, mainstream work remains centralized. The disappearing central departmental control and service functions operated, of course, as stores of wisdom, including legal wisdom in the form of practice authenticated by legal advice. Agencies, and possibly even parts of departments, are now being cut off from these resources by the distribution of these functions and flattening of management structures: the result, for some departmental legal services at least, is a considerably increased flow of requests for legal advice emanating from quite low levels—Higher Executive Officers and even Executive Officers—in the administrative hierarchy of agencies and departments. This structural factor seems likely to accentuate a tendency towards the legalization of administration which is already being driven by the attitudes of departments' clients; these days, for example, prisons are academies for litigators as well as criminals.

2 The rise and rise of judicial review

2.1 Expansion in scope and depth

More generally, such legalization of administrative work has clearly been occurring as the importance of judicial review continues to grow. In the last two decades it has grown remarkably, if unevenly, in volume (Sunkin, Bridges, and Mészáros 1993; Law Commission 1994). Equally if not more important, its ability to reach types of decision previously thought to be legally or practically unreviewable continues to expand. In recent years it has encompassed: decisions in the exercise of the executive's common law or prerogative powers (*R v Criminal Injuries Compensation Board, ex parte Lain* 1967; *Laker Airways Ltd v Department of Trade* 1977; *Council of Civil Service Unions v Minister for the Civil Service* 1985; *R v Secretary of State for the Home Department, ex parte Fire Brigades Union* 1995); decisions relating to expenditures (Daintith 1994; *R v Secretary of State for Foreign Affairs, ex parte World Development Movement Ltd* 1995 (the '*Pergau Dam*' case); decisions without direct legal consequences, such as those relating to the content of advisory or publicity material (*Gillick v West Norfolk and Wisbech Area Health Authority* 1986; *R v Secretary of State for the Environment, ex parte Greenwich London Borough Council* 1989). This sort of penetration arises in part because of a more relaxed attitude to standing, linked to the broad terms of Order 53 (de Smith, Woolf, and Jowell 1995: 99–154), which means that decisions whose harmful effects are diffuse, rather than specific, can now be questioned in court. In part it occurs because of the readiness of the judges, today, to draw legal consequences from statutory provisions which might once have been seen as too indefinite to be justiciable. Both tendencies converged strikingly in the *Pergau Dam* case, which we have discussed in relation to the basic principles of financial legislation (above, pp. 35, 204–5).

In this process of growth and penetration the increased tendency of aggrieved individuals and groups to turn to judicial proceedings for redress functions both as cause and effect, provoking the greater volume and range of judicial decisions which in turn open up new and attractive possibilities for litigious challenge to administrative action. The process has now reached the point where judicial review holds an equal place with parliamentary question and debate, resort to the ombudsman, and media pressure among the means by which both specific and general executive decisions may be routinely challenged. Often these approaches may be used in combination; in some areas judicial review holds a predominant place because of its ability to furnish, in disputes about administrative decisions, definite and—where really necessary—speedy resolution.

2.2 Positive reactions

In legal circles, and notably in academic legal circles, the general trend has been to see this growth of judicial review as a highly positive development, improving the protection of the citizen and providing a stronger legal framework within which administrators might carry out their duties. The idea has been evoked of a 'partnership' between judiciary and executive in the pursuit of these aims, notably by Lord Donaldson, when Master of the Rolls (*R v Lancashire CC, ex parte Huddleston* 1986: 245). This sort of language evokes that earlier phase in the history of judicial review when the common law courts, having seen off the prerogative jurisdiction of the Star Chamber, took over much of its function of supervision of local and subordinate administration, acting essentially as an arm of central government (Henderson 1963).

One of the things that is new about the 'new' judicial review is the degree to which it impinges on decisions at the centre of government, by ministers, not just on the actions of its subordinate parts. None the less, its initial reception within the central executive was positive, perhaps remarkably so. The broad-ranging review undertaken by a senior group of administrators and government lawyers in the mid-nineteen-eighties opted for adaptation rather than resistance, commissioning *The Judge over your Shoulder* (Treasury Solicitor's Department 1987) and seeking to revitalize training in legal awareness for administrators (Sunkin and Le Sueur 1991). *The Judge over your Shoulder*, sometimes (ironically?) referred to as 'JOYS' and now in a second, enlarged edition (Treasury Solicitor's Department 1995), is a visible expression of a concern to ensure that administrators bear in mind the possibility, in some areas even the likelihood, of legal challege to the decisions they are preparing. In retrospect the academic criticism it received for being negative in tone and somehow treating law as distinct from good administration (Bradley 1987) seems ungracious; given the intensification of judicial review of central government action which had already occurred by then, what may be seen as remarkable is that the strongest epithet it applied to what the judges were doing was 'imaginative' (Treasury Solicitor's Department 1987: 2). Its message has, as we have seen, been carried into individual departments by their own legal services, sometimes through the production of their own internal brochures (above, pp. 227–8). The involvement of lawyers in administrative decision-making has thereby been accelerated and deepened, as the administrator—with the spectral judge looming over his shoulder—calls regularly for legal advice at an early stage (cf. Blom-Cooper 1984). Doubtless the pace of this juridification of administrative process has varied from department to department. It may be slower in departments in which administration has been thought to have a very low legal content, like the former Overseas Development Administration, or in which general administration has always had strong legal elements, such as the Revenue departments and the Home Office, where administrators have been accustomed to tackle legal issues themselves. It may be more marked where departments have responded to radical changes in the nature of their work, such as those produced by the operations of the EU/EC: in the Department of Environment, Transport and the Regions, lawyers more often than not lead for the department in its international and EU/EC business. Despite these differences, the general view among government lawyers is clearly that administrators are now more conscious of the legal environment and significance of their decisions than they were a decade ago, and that judicial review is a 'working tool' for reaching this result (Hammond 1998: 39).

2.3 Negative reactions

This positive picture has subsequently been cast into shadow by a more negative and critical reading of executive/judiciary relationships. We should not, of course, assume that administrators ever fully shared the enthusiasm of their legal colleagues in government for the imposition of a tighter legal discipline. But in recent years, it is suggested, ministers too have come to see themselves and their policy-making powers as confined within an 'iron triangle' formed by EU requirements and restrictions; by increasingly powerful pressure groups; and by judicial review (which of course is used to reinforce both the other constraints) (Willetts 1997). Familiarity with judicial review, it is said, has indeed bred contempt (literally, in *M v Home Office* 1994 and above, p. 327): as judicial review becomes a regular element of administrative process, so that the stigma that once attached to being the subject of review is lost, ministers are increasingly willing to take the legal risks pointed out to them by their advisers. Rather than ensuring for themselves that they act within the law, they are ready to shift this responsibility to the judges and take the course of action that is administratively most convenient or politically most attractive. If there is no review, or review is favourable, so much the better; and an alternative approach can always be held in readiness against the risk of adverse review (McAuslan and McEldowney 1985; Le Sueur 1996; Barker 1996). Some ministers, it is suggested (Le Sueur 1996), combine this opportunistic approach with a critical, even confrontational attitude towards the judges (and see generally Woodhouse 1996; Stevens 1997).

2.4 Underlying problems

The more dramatic elements of this analysis may well prove to have reflected attitudes born of a longish spell of single-party government (1979–97). Stripping them away discloses, however, a more fundamental set of issues. At their root is the innate and necessary tension in all *judicial* review of *administrative* action: that a decision taken as part of a policy process, possibly as one of hundreds or thousands of similar decisions taken every year for the same ends, is scrutinized for legality in a context—of litigation—which isolates it from this policy framework and administrative flux and looks at it in terms of an individual legal relation between complainant and administration. There are many ways of reducing and thereby controlling this essential tension, from the nurturing of a race of judge-administrators as practised in France (above, pp. 208, 210), through the legalization and judicialization of administration in the United States (Breyer and Stewart 1992), to the abstentionist policy generally thought to have been followed by United Kingdom courts before 1964 or thereabouts (though see Sterett 1997: ch. 2). The abandonment of that policy in the United Kingdom has not been accompanied, on the judicial side at least, by the adoption of any alternative device for the management of this tension. Indeed, judicial review has been expanded at precisely the time when a smaller and smaller proportion of the senior judiciary have any experience of political activity or governmental office (Jacob 1993: 124–6).

Moreover, while judicial review has, over recent years, become so much more widespread and penetrating, it is difficult to claim that it has, in similar measure or perhaps even at all, become more predictable. It is a part of the law which is replete with judicial discretion (for example, as to the granting of leave or the recognition of standing) (de Smith, Woolf, and Jowell 805–20) and with open-textured standards (*Wednesbury* unreasonableness[2], 'irrelevant' considerations, 'fair' procedure, 'legitimate' expectations). What is striking is that the proliferation of case law seems to be doing little to move these standards towards harder-edged rules. The most prominent recent attempt to do this—the distinction between private and public law rights introduced in *O'Reilly v Mackman* (1983) to determine the availability and exclusivity of judicial review itself—appears to have led to a situation of such confusion that new rules of court have been suggested to get around the problem (Law Commission 1994: 19–30), and elsewhere there is evidence of judicial

[2] The standard for overturning a discretionary administrative decision laid down by Lord Greene MR in *Associated Provincial Picture Houses v Wednesbury Corporation* 1948: 230: that the decision is so unreasonable that no reasonable decision-maker could have reached it.

reluctance to formulate tests or adopt principles which would significantly limit the judge's ability to apply the general standards afresh to each new case (e.g. Woolf 1990: 123–4). This maintenance of open-textured standards and judicial discretion places the United Kingdom system in striking contrast with its continental counterparts (Schwarze 1992: 697), whose practitioners find difficulty with such ideas as that the assertion of a public law *right* can properly be subject to a judicial discretion to grant or withhold leave.

More seriously, the perpetuation of this general style, at a time when judicial review is more important than ever before, creates real problems of effectiveness and of efficiency. The expanding phenomenon of loosely disciplined judicial intervention in executive affairs, likened by one commentator to 'guerrilla raids' (Rawlings 1986: 142), has fuelled complaints of unpredictability over at least a decade (Kerry 1983; 1986; Rawlings 1986). It must, at the least, have contributed to those ministerial resentments that recently overflowed into public utterance (Le Sueur 1996). It is seen by administrators as making it increasingly difficult to administer policies efficiently, as adding substantially to departmental costs, and sometimes as effectively destroying the substantive effect of policies through the imposition of delay while approaches censured in judicial review are corrected (James 1996: 617–20). No less a personage than the Treasury Solicitor, while extolling the merits of judicial review, has described some recent decisions as 'interesting' and has noted the novelty of the bases on which they have rested (Hammond 1998). Academic lawyers, too, are now suggesting that this broad-brush judicial style limits the effectiveness of judicial review (Richardson and Sunkin 1996; *contra*, Feldman 1988).

Ideas have been mooted from time to time to address this malaise. A favourite is the promulgation of principles of good administration, whether in statutory or non-statutory form (JUSTICE-All Souls 1988: 7–23; James 1996: 636). Precedents exist in a variety of common law jurisdictions, and in statements of principle drawn up within the Council of Europe (and assented to there by United Kingdom governments) (JUSTICE-All Souls 1988: 376–96). Unfortunately judges have evinced no enthusiasm for this idea: they do not want to cut down the capacity to do justice in the instant case that the broad common law principles offer them (Woolf 1990: 123–4). The outlook within the executive is less clear. Administrators still express the fear that such principles, whatever their form, would effectively restrict ministers' ability to make administrative arrangements that suit the circumstances (which may be highly political) of particular types of decision. That ability, however, may already have been crippled by judicial review. In *R v Secretary of State for the Home Department, ex parte Mohamed Al Fayed* 1996, the express statutory exemption from the duty to give reasons in refusing a nationality application (British Nationality Act 1981, s. 44(2)) was effectively nullified by the Court of Appeal's holding that though the Secretary of State did not have to give reasons for a refusal, he still, to comply with the common law obligation of fairness, had to inform the applicant of the areas of concern that were making it difficult to grant the application. Simultaneously, a set of administrative standards is to be found stealing in by the back door of 'Better Regulation'. As we saw in Chapter 8, the government's Better Regulation Task Force has published *Principles of Good Regulation* (Better Regulation Task Force 1998*a*), enunciating desiderata of transparency, accountability, targeting, consistency, and proportionality which could well be applied to a wider range of decisions and could be developed so as to offer guidance to judges as well as administrators.

Different approaches have been suggested by Lord Woolf (1990). The suggestion that attracted most attention was a proposal for the appointment of a politically-independent Director for Civil Proceedings through whom public interest proceedings against the Crown—mainly by way of judicial review—might be developed and systematized (103–13). This need may already have been overtaken by the continued extension of standing, which has greatly reduced the significance both of the Attorney-General's power to consent—or not—to a relator action, and of the obvious difficulty of getting the Attorney to bring such an action against another minister. Less noticed, but much more important in terms of the tensions we have identified as inherent in judicial review, was his call for judges to get greater exposure to experience of administration, through contact with administrators and visits to government departments (115–17). Innocuous as this might seem, there is no consensus either among administrators or lawyers about the propriety or desirability even of regular dialogue between judiciary and executive, let alone any more intensive interaction (Daintith 1997*b*: 10, 12 (comments by anonymous discussants)). The contrast here between executive–legislative, and executive–judicial relations could hardly be more striking.

IV CHANGE WITHIN THE EXECUTIVE

How is the executive responding to the challenges created by the weakening of ministerial responsibility; the legalization of the environment of government stemming from judicial review, the onrush of European law, and the new law on human rights; and the continuing uncertainties in administrative litigation? All these changes have made legal advice and opinion a much more central function in the executive than was the case forty years ago. Are the key characteristics of executive legality in the United Kingdom, pluralism and secrecy, in any way being modified as a result?

1 Litigation strategy

Lord Woolf's Director of Civil Proceedings was designed to bring order and system into judicial review proceedings against the government; but government itself faces exactly this problem in carrying on proceedings. Marc Galanter, the American sociologist of law, has strikingly compared the situation of those who do not normally find themselves involved in litigation with that of the 'repeat players'; the large companies, especially in fields like insurance, for whom litigation is a regular incident of their business and who enjoy not only the advantages of corporate wealth but also the chance to improve their position both through litigation strategies and through legislative campaigning (Galanter 1974). Central government is the 'repeat player' *par excellence* in United Kingdom judicial review, and might be expected to use the opportunities this offers to make its legal situation more comfortable, notably by seeking to diminish the unpredictability of judicial decision-making by means of action both within and outside litigation. Pluralism and secrecy represent serious obstacles here.

Despite its almost daily appearances in court, central government has not in the past had anything that could be called a litigation strategy—a broad view of what it wanted to get out of fighting judicial review applications—save in the large and negative sense of defending departmental decisions already taken. 'We try,' says the Treasury Solicitor, 'not to fight bad cases nor to engage in street-fighting for the sake of it' (Hammond 1998: 39); but there is yet no obvious sign that the executive consciously seeks to choose the *best* cases to fight; to develop lines of argument which embody the harder-edged rules of administrative behaviour that might, if adopted by the judges, make it easier for the executive to cope with judicial review; and to deploy them consistently. In a departmentally-organized Government Legal Service where, as we have seen (above, pp. 319–22), there was no regular liaison machinery until the nineteen nineties, this is hardly surprising. Even were there no significant divergences of view between departments, litigation strategy could hardly be built out of the energy and intuition of the Legal Secretary to the Law Officers and the 'feel' of departmental legal advisers for when they should consult others of their own accord (above, pp. 321–2); nor could it realistically be found in the TSol Litigation Division, whose difficulties in co-ordinating the views of different departmental clients in litigation were amply documented in the Scott Report (above, pp. 230–1), nor in First Treasury Counsel, who may play an important role in offering to TSol consistent interpretation of judicial development, but are in no position, both by reason of pressure of work and of their proper distance from departments, to spend time and effort on general strategic issues (Woolf 1990: 3–7, 112).

In addition, the executive operates under the handicap, in judicial review and in much other litigation, of having to play with the black pieces, and of hence to shape its argument according to the attack chosen by the applicant. None the less it is striking how rarely, in the cases, one finds counsel for the Crown accepting a legal constraint on administrative action and seeking to reformulate it in terms more sympathetic to general administrative requirements (*R v Secretary of State for the Environment, ex parte Brent London Borough Council* 1982 is a possible example). The forms and consequences of adversary litigation constantly drive the executive into purely negative argument in the courtroom, even when internal practice and opinion suggest a more positive approach. Thus the report on *Legal Entitlements and Administrative Practices* (Civil Service Department 1979) refers throughout to 'proportionate' effort by departments in informing people of positive and possibly retrospective changes to benefits like war pensions, both as representing good administrative practice and as necessary to satisfy the courts. Similarly, the Better Regulation Task Force now actively promotes proportionality as one of its criteria for good regulation: the right balance should be established between risk and cost, and no needless demands should be imposed on those being regulated (Better Regulation Task Force 1998*a*). In litigation, however, the government's counsel have consistently argued against the adoption of a test of 'proportionality' as a measure of the legality of administrative action under domestic (as opposed to EC) law (*R v Secretary of State for Transport, ex parte Pegasus Holdings (London) Ltd* 1988; *R v Secretary of State for the Home Department, ex parte Brind* 1991; *R v Secretary of State for the Home Department, ex parte Leech* 1994). No doubt the fear here is that if the courts did treat proportionality as a distinct head of review, it would simply be added to the catch-alls like '*Wednesbury* unreasonableness' rather than providing one of several more clearly structured substitutes (Irvine 1996: 74–5).

In recent years, however, the executive has moved steadily towards a position where a positive litigation strategy is at least a feasible development. There are clear signs of a more strategic approach to litigation at departmental level, driven essentially by value-for-money considerations and by modern devices like Fundamental Expenditure Reviews to which they have given rise (above, p. 110). This is today showing signs of spreading out from the area of enforcement, where departments like the Revenue departments and the Department of Social Security have long treated prosecution as one element in an overall approach to effective enforcement (Lidstone, Hogg, and Sutcliffe 1980), to issues much closer to judicial review, such as Customs and Excise policy on appealing VAT Tribunal decisions, and in judicial review itself, such as DSS policy on seeking post-leave discussion and settlement. The question whether the approach can be extended to the inter-departmental arena, otherwise than in the fully centralized area of European Court of Justice litigation, still remains. Certainly there has occasionally been substantive co-ordination between departments when major issues have arisen. The issue of mandatory and interlocutory relief against the Crown, tested in *M v Home Office* 1994 and *Factortame* 1991, is one area where there has been such co-ordination (though hardly with positive results in terms of the arguments made on the Crown's behalf in the litigation); and other examples have been cited earlier in this chapter (above, pp. 319, 321). This process, however, works across the grain of a departmentalized legal service, and it is acknowledged, within government, that it has been a strenuous one. The new arrangements under the aegis of GLSLG (above, pp. 319–22), and notably the existence of a Government Litigators Group, may perhaps make things easier, and the desire to exploit such machinery for this kind of purpose is clearly shown by the creation of groups to monitor civil and criminal litigation on human rights (above, p. 321).

2 The executive in legal debate

The courts are not the only place where the executive might argue for a more predictable and responsive administrative law. Until very recently, however, the executive has maintained, outside the courtroom, an almost complete public silence about the evolution of judicial review, the general course it is taking, the merits and drawbacks of particular tests or rules on which it relies. Obviously the expression by ministers of views about particular cases or even lines of cases in Parliament or other political *fora* would raise questions of propriety and might well contravene parliamentary rules protecting judges from political censure. Other channels of expression are, however, open. Judges, likewise restrained until recently by the so-called Kilmuir rules, now engage freely, through extrajudicial utterance, in serious public debate, writing scholarly papers, delivering lectures, writing book reviews, and even mounting radio programmes. A search in 1996 discovered virtually no comparable activity by government lawyers. They might participate in informal and unattributable seminar discussion with academics (Barker 1996), but with very rare exceptions they did not publish in the learned journals, unless anonymously (Anon. 1958—see Edwards 1984: 445) or, if Foreign and Commonwealth Office lawyers, on international law issues. Nor did they play a visible role in processes of reform in frameworks like that of the Law Commissions; the decline, as an engine of enquiry and reform, of the Royal Commission, with its large volumes of written submissions and evidence, has choked off one of the few channels for public discussion of the law by the executive.

This reticence about a subject such as judicial review, on which government lawyers are perhaps more knowledgeable than anyone, must surely be attributable to the influence of the doctrine of ministerial responsibility and the ironclad confidentiality of legal advice. Certainly government lawyers are busy people; but should we assume that they are busier than members of the Court of Appeal? Presumably it has been thought too dangerous for any government lawyer, from the Law Officers down, to join even in scholarly debate in the journals about, say, a principle like that of protecting legitimate expectations; for what s/he says may provide a clue to advice that s/he has given, is giving, or might at some time in the future give. The danger, however, is that if the executive continues to refuse to join the intellectual argument about judicial review, it will lose it by default; and that such a loss will only reinforce the temptation—already felt in some quarters (Le Sueur 1996)—to seek to delegitimize judicial review by political means. Whether by reason of awareness of this problem, or simply as an effect of the general striving for more openness, there has been a measurable increase since 1996 in participation by executive lawyers in public legal discussion. Examples can be cited from authors of varying seniority going up to the level of the Law Officers (MacLeod, Hendry, and Byatt 1996; Hardie 1998). In the field of judicial review, the Treasury Solicitor's article, already cited here, on 'Judicial review: the continuing interplay between law and policy' (Hammond 1998), is particularly notable. While carefully avoiding any criticism of judicial decisions it none the less succeeds in giving important pointers to legal opinion within the executive on a number of issues. The multiplication of such contributions would surely improve the quality of the debate on judicial review by incorporating greater experience of its administrative significance and effects. The crucial contrast between the legal concern for the instant case and the administrative concern for the integrity of the scheme or policy will surely be better illuminated if it is publicly explored and analysed by those who live it daily.

3 The ethics of government lawyering

In the preceding sections we have shown how adaptations to the new challenges being presented by 'agencification', judicial review, European law, and other factors of change are being made within the pluralist, departmentally-based model of executive legal services, rather than by any moves towards a more centralized legal function. The coming together of lawyers and administrators within the department, which has been fostered since the mid-nineteen-eighties, has been seen in the positive light of spreading legal ideas and values to administrators (Hammond 1998). It is at least arguable that the opposite could happen; that government lawyers could find their independence of mind being eroded by more intimate involvement in, and hence commitment to, the political purposes of the department. That government lawyers should currently feel the need to discuss among themselves a possible Code of Conduct or Guidance for their own work is not, in this light, necessarily a positive development; it suggests difficulties, whether because of pressures from ministers or administrators or for other reasons, in adhering to the principles government lawyers feel should regulate their behaviour. We have already argued (above, pp. 209–14, 329–30), that most legal advice within government resembles that which might be given elsewhere—to large companies, for example—both by reason of its link with future judicial decision-making and of the increasing 'ordinariness' of much government legal work. If legal controls on administration become ever more constricting, there must be a danger that departments and agencies will follow some of their commercial counterparts in devoting increasing effort to what has been called, in tax and company law fields, 'creative compliance': 'using the law to escape legal control without actually violating legal rules' (McBarnet and Whelan 1991: 848); and that their lawyers will be conscripted to help them in this.

The prospect is not merely hypothetical. In December 1988, the ill-phrased remarks of a junior Minister for Health about the incidence of salmonella in domestic egg production provoked an immediate crisis for the industry and for MAFF as its regulating ministry. A compulsory slaughter scheme had to be introduced, but at the lowest possible cost. The Ministry went to some pains to ensure that the scheme was so framed and introduced as to conceal from poultry farmers the fact that the compensation the Ministry offered was based on a fixed proportion (60 per cent) of the estimated healthy value of any flock, notwithstanding the fact that the statutory requirement was to pay 'the value of the bird immediately before it was slaughtered' (Animal Health Act 1981, Schedule 3, para. 5(2)), implying that payment should vary according to the extent of infection in each flock. Having persuaded a substantial number of farmers—many of whom were under great financial pressure—to accept compensation on this basis, it then refused to reopen their cases after being driven to admit the true basis of compensation and the absence of any sampling of the level of infection in flocks. The average level of infection turned out to be 8 per cent, not the 40 per cent implied by the fixed-percentage basis; and the Ministry began to settle other cases on the basis of flock-by-flock sampling.

Not unnaturally, farmers who had settled for 60 per cent complained to the Parliamentary Commissioner for Administration of a serious injustice, both in the original framing and introduction of the scheme and in the later refusal to reopen cases; and unsurprisingly, he agreed with them, as did his Select Committee (Parliamentary Commissioner for Administration 1992–93; Select Committee on the Parliamentary Commissioner for Administration 1993a). What emerged from his report (paras. 9, 10) was the degree to which the Ministry's action had been guided by legal advice directed towards the concealment of its method of calculating compensation. Essentially, the Ministry's lawyers were indicating how to pursue a policy of doubtful legality while reducing the scope for judicial review. Their concern was 'creative compliance.'

If this is a glimpse of what a pro-active approach to judicial review, and close lawyer–administrator co-operation, commonly means in practice, there is cause for concern about the effects of moving away from the concept of the 'rather remote' legal adviser so strongly promoted by Rawlinson (1977; 1989: 238, 241). The taming or even castration of professional legal sensibilities that he envisaged as a consequence would appear a real risk. Where among the MAFF lawyers was that 'highly developed sense of justice', that assistance to administrators 'in taking a fair and just line apart from the strict legal position', and that 'almost judicial . . . discretion' which for Dennis (1925: 385; 1926: 153–4) provided the government lawyers' 'constitutional justification'? There is no sign of these qualities in their written communications cited by the Parliamentary Commissioner, which show them striving, on behalf of their client, to find legal cover for the cheapest solution—just like good corporate lawyers.

Are the qualities described by Dennis and evoked by Rawlinson simply out of date in a period when the executive is hemmed round with legal restrictions which are far vaguer in their effect than those a company has to put up with from the tax legislator? This does not—yet—appear to be the view of the executive itself. It is of some comfort to note that though the Ministry strenuously maintained to the end that it believed its conduct to be legally defensible (Select Committee on the Parliamentary Commissioner for Administration 1993*b*), the affair was followed by an inquiry into the Ministry's legal service, conducted by a former Counsel to the Speaker. Neither the inquiry nor its results have been made public, but at least it suggests a sense, within government, that things should have been otherwise.

4 Conclusion

A general response—such as a Code of Conduct—to ethical issues of the kind raised by the salmonella case is again likely to be found within the structures of co-ordination of departmentally-based legal activity rather than through any further centralization of the kind evoked by the Andrew Report (above, pp. 324–5). A single, hierarchically organized government legal service would probably produce more systematic and open legal advice in government, and a clear assumption of responsibility for giving it. Possibly it might also produce more 'objective' legal advice, less likely to bend to the policy imperatives of the department in the way that occurred at MAFF (Dennis 1925: 383). At the same time the work of such a service would have a more monolithic character, and while it probably would not suppress internal debate (by reason of the professional independence of the legal advisers), the fact that lawyers 'representing' administrators with different policy-based requirements were answerable not to their 'clients' but to the legal service itself would surely muffle the argument and deprive it of the vigour which now clearly characterizes inter-departmental legal discussion. Would it not be a little odd if the adversary procedures on which our system has relied to form both its common law and its legislation found no echo in the arrangements for developing legal opinion within the executive?

11

Better Government: Charter Standards, Open Government and Good Administration

I INTRODUCTION

The Citizen's Charter (Cabinet Office 1991) was launched in July 1991 as a ten-year programme to raise the standard of public services and make them more responsive to the needs and wishes of their users. John Major's 'big idea', as it quickly became known, was greeted with considerable scepticism, but in retrospect it marked a significant extension of the aims of public service reform to include the increased accountability of public services to their users, alongside the earlier and continuing drive to improve managerial accountability for the use of resources. In this chapter we concentrate on the Charter, which was relaunched in June 1998 as Service First (Cabinet Office 1998*b*). We also consider freedom of information, an issue which has long preceded notions of client or user accountability, but which in recent years has been pursued in the context of the Citizen's Charter. Under the current Labour Government both initiatives form part of a wider 'Better Government' programme, on which a White Paper is planned, and which also includes support for 'one-stop shops', the development of electronic forms, and the Better Regulation Enforcement Concordat.

From the point of view of our concern with the structure and substance of internal control, a number of features of these initiatives are of interest. The first is that they both represent a widening of the agenda of central control of the executive to include the relationship between the executive and the individual. Traditionally, the lead in defining that relationship has been taken by departments rather than by the centre. Second, both initiatives were originally pursued, and for the moment continue to be pursued, by non-statutory means. The Labour Government's proposed Freedom of Information Act will change this, but under its Conservative predecessor improvements in standards of service and in openness were both sought by administrative rather than legal means. Third, the fact that the standards laid down have not been invested with the force of law does not mean that they are necessarily unenforceable, only that they are not directly enforceable through the courts. As we shall see, service standards are enforceable in some cases through an extensive system of executive redress, with the possibility of recourse to the Parliamentary Ombudsman, while provision has likewise been made for the enforcement of the Code of Practice on Access to Government Information through the Parliamentary Ombudsman.

Our focus in this chapter is therefore on what are essentially informal systems of law, made by the executive for the control of itself, which are of direct concern to individuals, but which do not look to the familiar machinery of courts or tribunals for their enforcement or for the settlement of disputes arising out of their application. One question which this development raises, which we examine, is why the executive should prefer to rely on 'the ancient practice of government by Royal Proclamation' (*R v Criminal Injuries Compensation Board, ex parte Lain* 1967, at 886, per Diplock LJ) rather than parliamentary legislation. We also consider the extent of the parliamentary and other forms of external scrutiny to which these controls are subject. We begin, however, with the controls themselves, including the burgeoning machinery of executive redress through which they may be enforced and disputes arising out of them settled.

II THE CITIZEN'S CHARTER AND SERVICE FIRST

The Citizen's Charter has been described as 'a rare attempt to define the relationship between government and the public and to develop a dialogue between them' (Public Service Committee 1997: Evidence, p. 4 (Institute of Public Policy Research)). The accompanying White Paper described the Charter as 'the most comprehensive programme ever to raise quality, increase choice, secure better value, and extend accountability' (Cabinet Office 1991: 4). The initiative drew on a number of sources, including an earlier OMCS management study which tried to identify the essential elements of a 'service to the public strategy' (Cabinet Office 1988). It faced considerable opposition from departments, which were said by tradition to be reluctant to discuss standards or quality, the Treasury because of fears that it would be called upon to fund improvements (Hogg and Hill 1996: 93). It was little surprise therefore when the Treasury tried to undermine the initiative at an early stage by letting it be known that it would prove 'costly and inefficient' (Seldon 1997: 190). It was eventually driven through with the support of key politicians and civil servants, including the Cabinet Secretary (ibid.: 193). After the White Paper was published, a Citizen's Charter Unit was established within the Office of Public Service to maintain the momentum behind the initiative. Under the last Conservative Government, the

Charter became one of two 'key disciplines', the other being control of departmental running costs, within the framework of which further 'improvements' in civil service performance were sought (Cabinet Office 1994*a*: paras. 3.2–3.4).

Following the change of government, the Charter was relaunched, in June 1998, as 'Service First'. The change of name is said to better reflect the programme's emphasis on 'providing responsive public services that meet people's real needs' (Cabinet Office 1998*b*: para. 1.7). Its relaunch followed a consultation exercise which showed considerable support for the Charter, with most respondents of the view that it had led to significant improvements in service delivery. In its revised form the programme seeks to build on the achievements of its predecessor, while giving a new emphasis to four main themes: responding to people, promoting quality, ensuring effectiveness, and working together. The last of these reflects the emphasis on the better co-ordination and delivery of services which involve more than one public sector body (above, pp. 54–7). Like the Citizen's Charter, Service First applies to all public services, including government departments and agencies, local authorities, the National Health Service, the courts, police and emergency services, and the privatized utilities where a monopoly element remains (for example, electricity distribution and water) and to the train operating companies. It also applies whether services are delivered direct or through contractors (Cabinet Office 1998*b*: para. 2.9). The Service First Unit within the Cabinet Office is responsible for the programme. It defines its aim as being 'to promote high quality, efficient and effective public service delivered in an accountable, open, accessible and responsive way'.

1 A non-statutory initiative

A number of reasons may be identified for the Conservative Government's decision to proceed on a non-statutory basis. The first is that there was thought to be no necessity for legislation. For some commentators, the absence of a legal framework left the executive 'essentially dependent upon the goodwill of heads of agencies who may mouth the rhetoric of the Charter without ensuring that it is effectively adhered to' (Bellamy and Greenaway 1995: 483), but in the Government's view the Charter did not require 'legislative teeth' in order to achieve results (Goldsworthy 1994: 63). It did, however, take the precaution of securing statutory provision for the publication of performance information in relation to local government, education, and the privatized utilities (Local Government Act 1992, Education (Schools) Act 1992, Competition and Service (Utilities) Act 1992). Legislation was also no doubt seen as generally undesirable. As well as threatening the executive's control of the initiative by exposing it to the uncertainties of the legislative process, it was suggested that it would open up the prospect of 'judicial auditing of government performance', a prospect which was said to be 'alien to British constitutional practice' (Bellamy and Greenaway 1995: 482–3). And once enacted, legislation might be difficult to alter. According to the Deputy Director of the Citizen's Charter Unit, legislation to empower citizens to obtain their entitlements from public services could in practice become a 'constraint on developing more flexible, responsive public services that reflect what people want today' (Goldsworthy 1994: 63). Observers from countries whose administrative systems could not be reformed without legislation were said to see the United Kingdom as possessing an 'enormous advantage in being able to make change without large-scale law-making' (ibid.: 63).

The Public Service Committee in the last Parliament was cautious about putting the Charter on a statutory basis. While legislation might be useful in the long term as an enforceable statement of minimum standards of public administration, it accepted that to set standards too precisely at the outset might be 'unhelpful and bureaucratic' (Public Service Committee 1997: para. 94). The absence of any form of statutory underpinning for much of the Charter has nevertheless occasioned persistent criticism. The Government has responded by announcing that it intends, as part of its proposed Freedom of Information Act, to require public authorities to make information publicly available as a matter of course on the services they provide, the standards of service users can expect to receive, how they have performed against them, and how to complain if something goes wrong (Chancellor of the Duchy of Lancaster 1997: para. 2.18). This, however, will simply put the obligation to publish information about standards, for example, on a statutory basis. It will not alter the status of the standards themselves.

2 Principles of public service delivery

The charter process is founded on a number of principles of public service delivery to which service providers are expected to give effect. The current principles represent the Government's 'vision of what every public service should be striving to achieve' (Cabinet Office 1998*b*: para. 2.8). The principles were reviewed and updated as part of the re-launch of the Citizen's Charter. There are now nine principles in place of the six on which the Charter was based. The nine principles require each public service to:

Set standards of service
Set clear standards of service that users can expect; monitor and review performance, and publish the results, following independent validation wherever possible.

Be open and provide full information
Be open and communicate clearly and effectively in plain language, to help people using public services: and provide full information about services, their cost and how well they perform.

Consult and involve
Consult and involve present and potential future users of public services, as well as those who work in them, and use their views to improve the service provided.

Encourage access and promotion of choice
Make services easily available to everyone who needs them, including using technology to the full, and offering choice wherever possible.

Treat all fairly
Treat all people fairly; respect their privacy and dignity; be helpful and courteous; and pay particular attention to those with special needs.

Put things right when they go wrong
Put things right quickly and effectively; learn from complaints; and have a clear, well publicised and easy-to-use complaints procedure, with independent review wherever possible.

Use resources effectively
Use resources effectively to provide best value for taxpayers and users.

Innovate and improve
Always look for ways to improve the services and facilities offered.

Work with other providers
Work with other providers to ensure that services are simple to use, effective and co-ordinated, and deliver a better service to the user.

Four of these principles are new: promote access and choice; treat all fairly; work with other providers; and innovate and improve.

3 Delivering the principles

It is for individual service providers to give effect to the principles of public service delivery by issuing their own charters and charter standard statements.[1] There are now some 200 national charters and

[1] Under the Conservative Government a distinction was drawn between national charters, such as the Taxpayer's Charter or the Patient's Charter, and 'charter standard statements', which were drawn up by executive agencies and NDPBs. This distinction has now been abandoned (Cabinet Office 1998*b*: para. 4.5).

over 10,000 local charters. The Conservative Government also promulgated six minimum service standards for central government in an attempt to develop a more 'customer-focused' culture in Whitehall (Cabinet Office 1996*a*: p. 46; for the performance of departments and agencies against the standards, see 315 HC Debs., cols. *647–8*, written answers 31 July 1998). The consultation exercise that preceded the relaunch of the Citizen's Charter revealed that very few people were aware of these 'Whitehall standards', although most thought they were worthwhile (Cabinet Office 1998*b*: para. 5.18).

Exercising effective control over the charter-making process has proved difficult, considerably more so than in the case of subordinate legislation (above, pp. 285–6). According to the Deputy Director of the Citizen's Charter Unit, the original Charter principles were conceived not as 'a strait-jacket but as an enabling framework to ensure that the exercise remain[ed] focused on *results* and d[id] not get bogged down in process' (Goldsworthy 1994: 60, original emphasis). The Citizen's Charter Unit did endeavour, however, to exercise a measure of control over the making and revision of charters through a combination of guidance, which included a checklist of what charters should contain, and clearance requirements. Some national charters required central clearance, while others required clearance by departmental ministers (Citizen's Charter Unit 1997). The first version of the Patient's Charter is reputed to have been rejected, sending 'a powerful signal around Whitehall that the initiative would not go away' (Seldon 1997: 194; Pollitt 1994: 10). The Labour Government has issued revised guidance on the making and review of national and local charters in an attempt to improve their quality and consistency (Service First Unit 1998*a* and *b*). It has also announced a review by departments of the main national charters and the setting up of an audit team to monitor the quality of a cross-section; four new national charters are also planned (Cabinet Office 1998*b*: paras. 4.11–4.12, 4.22–4.26).

Although the original Charter principles stipulated that there should be 'regular and systematic consultation' with users of services and that their views about services and priorities for improving them should be taken into account in final decisions on standards, a recurrent criticism of the charter-making process has been that charters have been mostly drawn up by service providers themselves with little or no consultation with users (Bellamy and Greenaway 1995: 488). The guidance on procedures for clearing national charters now requires new and revised charters to demonstrate that users of the service have been consulted on the standards and type of service offered, and that their views have been taken into account. It has also been a requirement since April 1997 that new and revised national charters be issued in draft, so that users' views can be taken into account before final versions are published

(Cabinet Office 1996*a*: para. 3.8). The Government has also issued a guide to effective consultation (Service First Unit 1998*c*), which sets out five 'guiding principles' to be followed when carrying out written consultation exercises; and it is revising and updating a guide to improving services through consultation with users, which was first published jointly with the National Consumer Council and the Consumer Congress in 1995 (Citizen's Charter Unit 1996).

The Citizen's Charter did not just rely on exhortation to improve the quality of services and make them more responsive to users. It also created an inducement to service providers to subscribe to a 'Charter standard' for the delivery of quality in public services in the form of a Charter Mark award scheme (Cabinet Office 1991: 6). The scheme, which remains part of the programme, provides a means whereby service providers may, if they so choose,[2] signal their compliance with the Charter standard by seeking and obtaining Charter Mark status; this in turn creates the potential to use the threatened withdrawal of the status as a means of inducing providers to continue to subscribe to the standard. The idea of 'the people's mark of approval' (Public Service Committee 1997: para. 83) has proved popular, and the Government plans to expand and develop the scheme as a means of encouraging and rewarding excellence in the provision of public services (Cabinet Office 1998*b*: paras. 6.7–6.13).

3.1 Charter standards

A central part of the charter process is the setting and monitoring of service standards. The Citizen's Charter White Paper envisaged that, in addition to *courtesy and helpfulness* from staff, service standards should invariably include *accuracy* in accordance with statutory entitlements and a commitment to *prompt action* which might be expressed in terms of a target response or waiting time (Cabinet Office 1991: 5). (Accuracy is normally treated as a measure of quality of output, timeliness as a measure of procedural or processual efficiency.) An examination of individual charters reveals that the most common standards are for accuracy and timeliness, with those for timeliness being more common than those for accuracy. The Inland Revenue's current customer service standards are not untypical. They are expressed in the form of accuracy targets for dealing correctly first time with cases, as well as targets for dealing with correspondence (there are also targets for the fullness of the response to correspondence), attending to personal callers, answering

[2] The Conservative Government planned to require all service providers to apply for Charter Mark status (Public Service Committee 1997: Evidence, q. 411 (Roger Freeman)).

telephone calls, and dealing with repayment claims. The Benefits Agency follows a similar pattern with targets for benefit claim clearance times, accuracy of assessments, dealing with correspondence, attending to personal callers, and answering telephone calls. In common with several other agencies, it also has a customer satisfaction target which was set at 80 per cent for 1995–96, against which it achieved 86 per cent. The six Whitehall standards require departments and agencies to have correspondence targets and to publish performance against them, to see visitors within ten minutes of appointments, to provide information and a public enquiry point, to consult users of services and to report findings, to have a complaints procedure, and to make services accessible.

A common criticism of charters has been that they fail to make clear whether they are to be understood as a guarantee that certain standards will be met, or merely as statements of good intentions, which may or may not be fulfilled (Select Committee on the Parliamentary Commissioner for Administration 1995: para. 70; Public Service Committee 1997: para. 41). Given that the Charter was conceived primarily as a means of improving services rather than conferring rights on individuals, charter standards are probably best regarded in the absence of any contrary indication as non-enforceable statements of good intentions. The criticism is acknowledged, however, in the guidance on procedures for clearing national charters, which stipulates that charters should make clear whether they create 'rights' or 'expectations' in the users of the services to which they relate. Rights are defined as standards which users will receive all the time, expectations as standards providers are aiming to achieve, but which exceptional circumstances may sometimes prevent from being met (Citizen's Charter Unit 1997). In the later guidance on the preparation of national charters the distinction is more clearly expressed as one between 'enforceable rights', which are enforceable through the courts or some other means such as a complaints procedure, and 'targets', which are levels of service which the provider is aiming to provide, but which the user cannot always expect to receive, and for which a remedy is not necessarily available (Service First Unit 1998*a*: 20). Treasury guidance on financial redress in the context of the Citizen's Charter, which was issued following an inquiry by the Select Committee on the Parliamentary Commissioner for Administration into the practice of redress among government departments (below), also provides that charters should 'explain the nature of the commitment to the user, and, where appropriate, whether compensation may be paid and in what general circumstances' (DAO (GEN) 7/96: para. 36.3.12; now contained in Treasury 1989*a*: para. 36.3.12). But while the guidance requires the significance of charter standards to be made clear, it is for service providers themselves to determine whether they constitute enforceable rights or non-enforceable statements of good intentions.

As part of its revised guidance on national and local charters, the Labour Government has promulgated a checklist for drawing up standards. This requires standards to be 'relevant, meaningful, challenging, simple, measurable, monitored, published, and reviewed' (Cabinet Office 1998*b*: para. 4.9).

Charter standards are not set in isolation. As we have seen, the targets set by ministers for agencies include targets for financial performance, efficiency and, in some cases, volume of output or throughput, as well as quality of service (above, pp. 42–3). The precise balance to be struck between targets is a matter for ministers: 'One of the most important aspects of target setting is to ensure that targets for standards and quality on the one hand and those for efficiency on the other reflect an explicit decision by Ministers on the desired balance between these two aspects of performance' (Treasury 1992*c*: para. 8). Where ministers set quality of service targets, the targets set are usually reflected in the service standards and targets set by agencies, with the difference that the latter are commonly expressed in absolute rather than percentage terms—all applications dealt with in four days rather than 80 per cent in two days—the intention being that individuals should know what they are entitled to expect. A National Audit Office examination of the Contribution Agency's customer charters, however, found some inconsistency between the Secretary of State's targets for customer service and the standards set out in the Agency's charters. It also found that only two of the Secretary of State's four targets related directly to standards set in the Agency's charters, leading it to recommend that the Agency review the link between the customer charters and the Secretary of State's targets, to ensure greater consistency and efficiency in measuring and reporting performance to customers and to strengthen accountability (National Audit Office 1997*a*).

The Conservative Government maintained that there was no necessary contradiction between efficiency gains and improvements in service to the public—improved accuracy, for example, could lead to lower costs (Treasury 1992*c*: para. 33). Clearly, however, financial restraints may lead to reductions in levels of service (Public Service Committee 1997: para. 34). The available evidence also indicates that considerations of efficiency have taken precedence over considerations of quality. Trosa, for example, found that financial targets were given much higher priority (Trosa 1994: para. 2.22); while the consortium project on the strategic management of agencies reported that it was generally felt that most weight internally and externally was given to financial targets (Next Steps Team 1995*a*: 70). The Competing for Quality Review, an

Efficiency Unit scrutiny of the management of the last Government's Competing for Quality initiative, found that the emphasis had generally been on cost rather than quality. 'Delivering a high quality of service to users' was felt by the key players surveyed to be of less prominence as an objective than providing taxpayers with 'better value for money, producing net savings and achieving Departmental/Agency targets' (Efficiency Unit 1996: para. 4.6–4.7).

3.2 Performance audit

The Citizen's Charter White Paper envisaged that standards should be published accompanied by full and *audited* information about the results achieved (Cabinet Office 1991: p. 5). The Public Service Committee in the last Parliament, however, found little evidence of monitoring or audit of performance against charter standards, despite the vulnerability of performance data to manipulation. The Committee recommended that the Government accept proposals from the National Audit Office for the independent validation of performance data produced by departments and agencies (Public Service Committee 1997: paras. 62–3). In the specific case of the Contributions Agency, the NAO found that, apart from its target for customer satisfaction, there was no external validation of the Agency's performance against the Secretary of State's targets for customer service. It recommended that the Agency examine the costs and benefits of external independent validation of reported performance against the Secretary of State's and charter targets to reinforce accountability, to ensure the reliability and sufficiency of information used to calculate performance, and to ensure reported performance accurately reflected real achievements (National Audit Office 1997*a*). In its subsequent report on the Benefits Agency, the NAO expressed the opinion that agencies could provide greater assurance to Parliament about their reported performance by arranging for the performance information in their published annual reports to be validated by an external party (National Audit Office 1998). In its relaunch of the Citizen's Charter, however, the Government refrained from taking a firm line on the question of validation of performance against published standards. The revised 'standards' principle merely requires information on performance against standards to be published, 'following independent validation wherever possible.'

3.3 Charter standards: conclusions

One of the dilemmas in the charter process, the Public Service Committee in the last Parliament observed, is 'whether to measure very imprecisely the things that really matter, or to measure precisely the things that do not matter so much' (Public Service Committee 1997: para. 95). Like ministerial targets for executive agencies, charter standards are major 'drivers' of performance in the sense that 'what-gets-measured-is-what-gets-done' (Next Steps Team 1995*a*: 68). The risk is that by concentrating attention on certain aspects of quality of service—the measurable aspects—they divert attention from other less easily measurable but nevertheless vitally important aspects. Do patients get better, as opposed to being seen or operated on within a certain time? This underlines the importance of scrutiny of choice of standards, of the relationship between charter standards and other targets to which service providers may be subject, such as ministerial targets for executive agencies, and of actual performance against prescribed standards, issues to which we return below.

4 Complaints procedures

Complaints procedures were conceived as an integral part of the Citizen's Charter from the outset. The 'putting it right' principle required service providers to have 'well publicised and easy to use complaints procedures with independent review wherever possible'. Perhaps more so than with the setting of service standards, the Charter caught a tide which was already flowing strongly in the direction of alternative mechanisms of redress.

The principal role in the elaboration of the putting it right principle was played by the Citizen's Charter Complaints Task Force, which was set up in June 1993, after the White Paper's proposal for a lay adjudicator had proved unworkable, to draw up and publish 'a set of principles for effective public service complaints systems that people can believe in'. The Task Force, with a membership drawn from the private and public sectors, identified seven basic principles of effective complaints systems which it believed to be of widespread application. Complaints systems, it suggested, should be:

easily *accessible* and well publicized;

simple to understand and use;

speedy, with well established time limits for action, and keeping people informed of progress;

fair, with a full and impartial investigation;

confidential, to maintain the confidentiality of both staff and complainants;

effective, addressing all the points at issue, and providing appropriate redress; and *informative*, providing information to management so that services can be improved. (Complaints Task Force 1993)

The Task Force was also charged with encouraging public service organizations that did not do so already to adopt its principles. It was not equipped with statutory powers for this purpose, a fact which it emphasized in its literature, but relied instead on a mixture of advice and encouragement to secure their adoption. It also published as part of its final report a *Good Practice Guide*, which public services were encouraged to use as the 'basic building block' of their complaints handling systems (Complaints Task Force 1995; see now Service First Unit 1998*d*).

A feature of public service complaints systems is that their scope is not confined to the circumstances in which service standards are allegedly not met. The Task Force recommended that each public service develop its own definition of a complaint, and apply it consistently across all its services (Complaints Task Force 1995: para. 4). The definition chosen should be the most appropriate and least restrictive to suit its circumstances. A working definition organizations might wish to consider was 'any expression of dissatisfaction which needs a response' (ibid.: para. 5). Some commentators have claimed to detect a clear conceptual distinction between complaints procedures and other avenues of redress (Complaints Task Force 1994: 57).[3] A definition of this breadth, however, is apt to catch many complaints that might ultimately form the subject of an appeal or other form of challenge, and indeed part of the attraction of complaints systems for organizations must be that they reduce their vulnerability to other forms of challenge. Following the establishment of their own complaints machinery, there was a noticeable reduction in the number of complaints to the Parliamentary Ombudsman against the Prison Service, while the percentage of complaints relating to the Inland Revenue also fell (Parliamentary Commissioner for Administration 1997: paras. 36, 60).

Complaints systems typically make provision for some form of 'independent' *internal* review, which the Task Force defined as 'review within the organization but separate from the direct line management of the person or section complained about' (Complaints Task Force 1993: para. 5; cf. the growth of statutory internal review procedures). The Task Force found that although many systems provided a full and thorough review, there was a good deal of scepticism among the public about

[3] The compilers of the complaints literature review also assert that making a complaint is not the same thing as suing. 'Complainants want different things from litigants. They may want some form of compensation but they are more likely than are people who are turning to law to be primarily interested in an apology and an assurance that whatever is wrong will be put right' (Williams and Goriely 1994: 1164).

whether internal reviews were truly independent (Complaints Task Force 1995*b*: para. 2.57). Perhaps for this reason it has become more common for complaints systems to make provision for a review stage beyond investigation by an organization's own staff. The lead in this respect was taken by the Inland Revenue, which established an Adjudicator scheme in 1993 (see Morris 1996). Its scope now covers the three revenue-raising authorities, i.e., Customs and Excise and the Contributions Agency as well as the Inland Revenue. Adjudicators or complaints commissioners have also been established for Companies House, the Prison and Scottish Prison Services, and the Child Support Agency. The Task Force was sufficiently impressed by the Inland Revenue's adjudicator scheme to recommend that all public services providing a service direct to members of the public establish an external review mechanism appropriate to their own circumstances and their existing complaints handling arrangements (Complaints Task Force 1995*b*: para. 3.87, 1995: para. 3.23; see too Citizen's Charter Unit 1996: para. 19).

The main note of caution to have been sounded in relation to external review mechanisms came from the Select Committee on the PCA in the last Parliament, which thought it 'unacceptable for there to be no policing of the term 'complaints adjudicator'. 'The public should be able to make certain assumptions about the way their complaint is to be handled when they come across the phrase.' As well as underlining the importance of their independence, the Committee stressed that adjudicators' task was to apply 'robust criteria of fairness' to ensuring that complainants were offered appropriate redress, not to simply police organizations' compliance with their own rules, no matter how harsh. It sought clear central guidance on the essential features of an adjudicator scheme, and recommended that adjudicators' terms of reference be approved centrally in order to ensure consistency of standards among adjudicators (Select Committee on the Parliamentary Commissioner for Administration 1994: paras. 64–5).

Guidance issued by the Citizen's Charter Unit, in response to the Committee's recommendation, which has now been revised and updated, suggests ways of ensuring the independence and effectiveness of complaints review arrangements. Among the 'guiding principles' for complaints review that it identifies, derived from the Task Force's *Good Practice Guide*, are that reviewers be independent of the sponsoring service; have adequate resources to do the job properly; be free from pressure from the service about how to carry out investigations and run their affairs; have the right of access to the service's staff and documentation; and have power to make decisions binding on the service, or have a clear agreement that decisions will not be accepted only in exceptional circumstances (Citizen's Charter Unit 1997; Complaints Task Force

1995*a*: paras. 3.24–3.25; 1995*b*: para. 3.89; Service First Unit 1998*d*). The guidance emphasizes that it is for individual services to judge the merits of a complaints review system in the light of the number and nature of their unresolved complaints and their resources.

Beyond external review by some form of complaints adjudicator, the possibility may also exist, in relation to service providers subject to their jurisdiction, of a complaint to one of the statutory ombudsmen as the final rung in the public services complaints ladder. The guidance advises against the use of the term 'ombudsman' to describe public services' own complaints review arrangements in order to avoid confusion between these arrangements and the statutory ombudsmen, as 'the wholly independent part of the public service complaints system' (Citizen's Charter Unit 1997: para. 5). A persistent concern of the former Select Committee on the PCA in the last Parliament was to ensure that public services' complaints literature did not omit mention of the possibility of a complaint to the Parliamentary Ombudsman. The guidance on redress under the Citizen's Charter enjoins departments and agencies that fall within the PCA's jurisdiction to ensure that their charters refer to the PCA's involvement in independently reviewing complaints; and to explain this option for seeking redress to complainants who remain dissatisfied (Citizen's Charter Unit 1996: para 18; Citizen's Charter Unit 1997: para. 35). Guidance has also been issued on handling Parliamentary Ombudsman cases (DEO (PM) (96) 4).

4.1 Redress

The Complaints Task Force identified the provision of redress as one of the two prime purposes of a complaints system; the other purpose it identified was the provision of feedback so that services can be improved. The Citizen's Charter Unit's guidance on procedures for clearing national charters required charters to explain what remedies are available in the event that charter standards are not met. The principal question to have arisen in relation to redress is whether the 'redress menu' should feature financial compensation for sub-standard service as well as an apology, an explanation, an assurance that the same thing will not happen again, and action to put things right. The Citizen's Charter White Paper accepted the principle of financial redress, but only where it would make a positive contribution to efficiency. 'Nobody wants to see money diverted from service improvement into large scale compensation for indifferent services. But the Government intends to introduce new forms of redress where these can be made to stimulate rather than distract from efficiency' (Cabinet Office 1991: 5). It offered no insights, however, into the circumstances in which compensation might have this benign effect.

The principles governing financial compensation for sub-standard service were eventually worked out following an inquiry by the Select Committee on the PCA into the practice of redress among government departments. A leading role in securing clarification of the principles was played by the Parliamentary Ombudsman. '[B]eing aware of the need to encourage a wider consistency of approach among departments', the PCA wrote to OPSS in November 1993 to explain the view he was taking when complaints about failures to meet published charter targets were referred to him. He drew a basic distinction between what administrative lawyers would call mandatory and directory standards:

> If targets are expressed as mandatory, or a promise has been given that the citizen has an expectation to compensation should they not be met or should they be missed by a specified period, the case for compensatory redress is strong. Otherwise targets are to be taken as indicators of a satisfactory or unsatisfactory performance rather than as a firm commitment that a specific performance will be achieved in every individual case. They will be persuasive indicators, but they are not positive guarantees. (Parliamentary Commissioner for Administration 1994: para. 6)

To that 'general view' was added the important qualification that 'it will not automatically be the case that, simply because such a target has been met, a Department's performance will necessarily have been fault-free or that an argument for considering compensation can be ignored'.

The Parliamentary Ombudsman then encouraged the Select Committee to undertake an inquiry into the practice of redress among government departments. This was the first such 'thematic' inquiry undertaken by the Committee, with the Ombudsman's encouragement, into issues that recur in the course of his investigations.[4] The Select Committee's report, *Maladministration and Redress*, was published in December 1994 (Select Committee on the Parliamentary Commissioner for Administration 1994). It revealed a disturbing picture of the practice of redress in a plural executive. Central to the Committee's inquiry was guidance issued by the Treasury in its role as guardian of the public purse, governing the payment of compensation in cases involving maladministration. This guidance was contained in a 'Dear Accounting Officer' letter (DAO (GEN) 15/92) issued in August 1992, a year after the

[4] Parliamentary Ombudsman and Select Committee concern with the question of financial redress for maladministration may be traced back to the 1974 Report of the Select Committee in which it criticized the Inland Revenue's refusal to make any allowance for costs needlessly incurred by taxpayers as a result of serious error on its part as 'unjust' (Select Committee on the Parliamentary Commissioner for Administration 1974: para. 15). This led to the introduction of the so-called 'Norman Price rules', or 'Price practice', after the then Chairman of the Board of Inland Revenue, governing the reimbursement of costs arising out of serious error on the part of the Revenue (Inland Revenue 1996).

Citizen's Charter was published, and elaborated in *Government Accounting* (Treasury 1989*a*: ch. 36 (as set out in Amendment No. 4, Government Accounting 4/1992)). The Committee found that the Charter had been published without 'any concerted attempt being made to revise this guidance [the 1992 guidance replaced guidance given in an unnumbered DAO letter dated 7 June 1988] or to enunciate a philosophy of redress'; there was no 'unifying principle of redress', merely lists of kinds of cases which qualified for compensation (Select Committee on the Parliamentary Commissioner for Administration 1994: paras. 5–6). The guidance itself was 'directed more to the protection of the public purse than to the rights of the complainant', who 'by definition', the guidance reminded departments, 'has no legal right to any compensation at all' (ibid.). The Committee condemned as 'both cynical and irresponsible' (para. 36) the advice that claims for loss of earnings should be automatically reduced by 50 per cent. The 'delegated limits' set by the Treasury within which departments might pay compensation without its approval varied widely, and there was no clear rationale for the differences between them; for example, the Legal Aid Board's limit was set at £1,000, but the Scottish Legal Aid Board's limit was set at £50 (para. 19). Nor was it always the case that where maladministration was identified an attempt was made to identify all those who had been similarly affected (para. 11).

In the Committee's view, it was time to end 'the grudging and defensive culture' so evident in the current guidance (para. 71). It recommended that redress be based on the principle, proposed by the PCA, that 'the person who has suffered injustice as a result of maladministration should be put back in the same position he or she would have been had things gone right in the first place' (para. 7). As well as being based on principle, the system needed to be consistent in its application. 'Casual or unreasonable variation, in which one complainant might receive a larger payment or another speedier redress simply as a result of the department approached—that cannot be just' (para. 17). It recommended that departments follow the example of the Inland Revenue and the Department of Social Security and draw up their own rules governing the payment of compensation, which should be subject to central approval, thereby allowing the relaxation of the current 'restrictive and inconsistent' delegated limits (paras. 26, 29, and 40). It also recommended that it should be 'a clear instruction to departments and agencies to seek out others affected where maladministration comes to light and to grant them redress' (para. 12). As we have seen, the LEAP guidelines (Civil Service Department 1979) warned that economical administration must not extend to illegality, but the evidence of the Select Committee's inquiry suggests that they were largely ineffectual.

On the question of financial compensation for failure to meet service standards, the Committee agreed that the priority in expenditure should be the improvement of services. Nevertheless compensation should be payable where financial loss had been incurred as a result of service failure. 'The Guidance should be reworded to reflect positively the need for financial compensation to remedy injustice' (paras. 69–70).

In March 1996 the Treasury issued revised guidance on financial redress in cases of maladministration and in the context of the Citizen's Charter (DAO (GEN) 7/96, now incorporated in Treasury 1989*a*), which gives substantial effect to the Committee's recommendations. Where actual financial loss has been suffered as a result of *maladministration,* or costs have been faced which would otherwise not have been incurred, the guidance stipulates that 'the general position should be to restore the complainant to the position he or she would have enjoyed had the maladministration not occurred'. Where, on the other hand, there is no actual financial loss or costs, 'a greater element of judgement will be required to identify whether financial redress is appropriate'. Such redress 'should only be made in exceptional circumstances' (Treasury 1989*a*: para. 36.3.5). With regard to consistency, it enjoins departments 'to put in place suitable guidance on the handling of compensation cases, designed to achieve *inter alia* consistency in handling the same type of case throughout the organisation' (para. 36.3.15). And it provides that where, 'following a complaint or a discovery of a case, departments conclude that other individuals or bodies may have suffered in the same way, they should seek to identify wherever reasonably practicable all those affected and consider whether, in the interests of equity, they should offer redress' (para. 36.3.6; see too Citizen's Charter Unit 1996: para. 15, and DEO (PM) (96) 4: para. 53).

On the question of financial compensation for failure to meet service standards, the guidance takes as its starting point the nature of the commitment to the users of the service. After quoting the Ombudsman's 1993 statement, it states that charters should 'explain the nature of the commitment to the user, and, where appropriate, whether compensation may be paid and in what general circumstances' (Treasury 1989*a*: para. 36.3.12); the Select Committee had been critical of the language of many charters, recommending that they identify those standards, which if not met, entitled the citizen to redress, financial or otherwise (Select Committee on the Parliamentary Commissioner for Administration 1994: para. 70). It is therefore for service providers in the first instance to determine whether compensation is payable for sub-standard service, subject to the approval of the Treasury where a department or agency proposes to commit itself to financial payments as a standard part of redress procedures for failure to deliver a service (Treasury 1989*a*: para. 36.3.14).

The Treasury guidance on financial redress was reinforced by Citizen's Charter Unit guidance on redress under the Charter, which was initially prompted by a PCA case in which a farmer had sought compensation on the grounds that MAFF had failed to meet the time limit set out in its charter statement. The guidance anticipates that financial compensation following a failure to achieve a charter standard will be appropriate in relatively limited circumstances. Unless there is a legal liability to pay financial compensation, departments and agencies must bear in mind the constraints on using taxpayers' money to provide redress. Where appropriate, charters should explain whether compensation may be paid, and in what circumstances. It emphasizes that it is important to ensure that charters do not create a general expectation that compensation will automatically be paid if charter standards are not met (Citizen's Charter Unit 1996: para. 11).

More generally, the Select Committee was of the view that the Treasury had failed 'to promote a positive and consistent ethic of redress within the Civil Service'. It therefore recommended that the central role in relation to redress should be removed from the Treasury and transferred to a redress team within the Charter Unit, on which the Treasury's representation should not exceed 50 per cent of its membership (Select Committee on the Parliamentary Commissioner for Administration 1994: paras. 23–5). Not surprisingly, this did not happen. In its initial response to the Select Committee, the Government accepted the view imputed to the Committee that there should be 'close co-operation' between the Treasury and the Charter Unit, but reserved its position on the setting up of a redress team until it had received the Complaints Task Force's final report. Novel or contentious cases should, however, continue to be referred to the Treasury. In the event, while strongly supporting 'the thrust of the Select Committee', the Task Force declined to be 'prescriptive' about the setting up of a redress team, recommending instead that the Charter Unit take the lead in producing guidance on redress in public services which reflected the Charter principle of effective redress (Complaints Task Force 1995*b*: para. 3.44).

4.2 Systems improvement

The other purpose of complaints systems that the Task Force identified was the provision of feedback so that systems might be improved. The Citizen's Charter Unit guidance on redress under the Charter lays down as a general principle that, as well as putting things right for individual users, public service complaints systems must allow organizations to learn the lessons from complaints, initiate a systemic change, or make an improvement in the way a service is delivered (Citizen's Charter Unit 1996: para. 4). One of the hallmarks of effective complaints systems was that they should:

> enable public services to learn the lessons from complaints, whether they concern a failure to meet a Charter standard, or a case of maladministration. One of the most effective means of redress is to be able to assure users that failures in service will not recur. Within the constraints of resources available, departments and agencies should record and analyse complaints for trends; set targets for reducing recurring failures; look for any repetition or pattern in failures to meet standards or in maladministration; and take action to change systems or procedures where necessary. (Citizen's Charter Unit 1996: para. 5d)

To the same effect the Treasury guidance requires departments to 'ensure that defective systems or procedures are corrected where a complaint (or PCA investigation) has shown systemic faults' (Treasury 1989*a*: para. 36.3.15; see too DEO (PM) (96)4: para. 55).

4.3 Complaints procedures: conclusions

In its final report to ministers on the way in which public services handled complaints, the Task Force said there was still some way to go before all public services could be said to operate wholly effective complaints systems (Complaints Task Force 1995*b*). It recommended that public services draw up an action plan for implementing its recommendations and that the Citizen's Charter Unit commission a survey every two years of user awareness of, and satisfaction with, how public services were handling complaints to establish whether real progress was being made and to identify what problems needed addressing. The first such survey, undertaken in May 1997, showed that satisfaction with the way public services dealt with complaints was still low (Service First Unit 1998*d*: p. 5). The last Parliamentary Ombudsman, however, was sufficiently convinced of the 'general strengthening' of internal departmental complaints procedures to conclude that he should not normally investigate a complaint unless it has first been put to the department in question, a process which he felt could itself provide valuable evidence should the complainant remain dissatisfied. (PCA 1995*a*: para. 23; see also Cabinet Office 1995*b*: p. 7).

Clearly, there is a double-edged quality to complaints procedures. On the one hand, they can contribute to the speedy and effective resolution of disputes and the enforcement of standards. On the other hand, they can become just another hurdle to be negotiated—'layers of investigation that simply become an obstacle course' (Citizen's Charter Unit 1997:

para. 6)—which may have the effect of deterring individuals from pursuing well-founded complaints. The latter possibility underlines the importance of the scrutiny of the effectiveness of their operation. In its report on the *Powers, Work and Jurisdiction of the Ombudsman*, the Select Committee on the PCA recommended that its terms of reference be widened to include oversight of the assorted non-statutory or statutory complaint and redress mechanisms in the public sector as part of its 'redress of grievance' role envisaged by Parliament in 1967 (Select Committee on Parliamentary Commissioner for Administration 1993*c*: para. 130). The Public Service Committee also recommended that, following the example of monitoring officers in local government, agency chief executives should be made formally accountable for the effectiveness of complaints procedures (Public Service Committee 1997: para. 49).

III ACCESS TO OFFICIAL INFORMATION

1 The Code of Practice

Proposals to reform the traditional secrecy of British government are not new. Under the last Conservative Government a potentially significant step was taken in this direction with the promulgation of a non-statutory Code of Practice on Access to Government Information (Cabinet Office 1994*d*). The Code, which bore a striking similarity to proposals for a voluntary code developed in the late nineteen-seventies, built on the commitment to greater transparency in the aims, performance and delivery of public services under the Citizen's Charter (Cabinet Office 1993: para. 1.3). But whereas the other Charter principles were mostly left to individual service providers to elaborate, subject to the oversight of the Citizen's Charter Unit, access to official information was pursued by means of a centrally drawn code. There is no inherent reason why access to official information should not have been pursued in the same way as the other Charter principles. Indeed when steps were first take in the direction of greater openness it was on such a basis. The Croham directive, issued by the Head of Home Civil Service in 1977, was intended to secure the release of more of the background detail and information behind ministerial decisions. The failure of that approach to produce any improvement in transparency meant, however, that when the question of access to official information was reopened in the context of the Citizen's Charter a resumption of the earlier decentralized approach would have lacked credibility. Clear rules were thus identified as essential if the intentions set out in the White Paper were to be made to stick (Cabinet Office 1993: para. 4.3).

Although rules were thus regarded as essential, the Government's preference was for a non-statutory code. As with the Citizen's Charter, it did not see any need for legislation to give effect to its proposals. By embodying the basic elements of its approach in a 'series of practical steps', it argued, the 'principal objectives of those who have sought a full statutory freedom of information regime can be met without the legal complexities such regimes entail' (Cabinet Office 1993: paras. 1.7–1.8). Only in the fields of personal information and health and safety did statutory encroachment make its preferred combination of a non-statutory code and Ombudsman enforcement unworkable. A further advantage of a non-statutory code in the Government's view no doubt was that it had none of the perceived drawbacks of legislation. It did not threaten the Government's control of the final outcome as would be the case were its proposals to be pursued by means of legislation. It avoided the 'legal complexities' attendant on recourse to legislation, a prospect the Government also sought to avoid by the choice of the Parliamentary Ombudsman rather than the courts as the means of enforcement. And it could be more easily amended than a statutory code; as the Select Committee on the PCA pointed out, however, the greater flexibility of a Code cut both ways, enabling it to be used to diminish as well as to enhance individual entitlements (1996: para. 124). It may also have been easier to secure agreement among departments to a non-statutory code than to legislation. Certainly, the difficulty experienced by its Labour successor in framing a Bill suggests that the need to secure internal agreement is a considerable obstacle.

The Code, which is now in a second edition, came into effect on 4 April 1994 (Cabinet Office 1994*d*; 1997*b*). It defines its aims as being:

to improve policy-making and the democratic process by extending access to the facts and analyses which provide the basis for the consideration of proposed policy;

to protect the interests of individuals and companies by ensuring that reasons are given for administrative decisions, except where there is statutory authority or established convention to the contrary; and

to support and extend the principles of public service established under the Citizen's Charter.

These aims are balanced by the need to maintain high standards of care in ensuring the privacy of personal and commercially confidential information; and to preserve confidentiality where disclosure would not be in the public interest or would breach personal privacy or the confidences of a third party (Cabinet Office 1997*b*: Part I, para. 2).

Subject to a number of exemptions set out in Part II of the Code, the Code commits the departments and public bodies to which it applies to:

publishing the facts and analyses of the facts which the Government considers relevant and important in framing major policy proposals and decisions;

publishing or otherwise making available explanatory material on departments' dealings with the public;

giving reasons for administrative decisions to those affected (except where there is statutory authority or well established convention to the contrary);

publishing in accordance with the Citizen's Charter full information about how public services are run, how much they cost, who is in charge, and what complaints and redress procedures are available, as well as full and, where possible, comparable information about what services are being provided, what targets are set, what standards of service are expected and the results achieved; and

releasing, in response to specific requests, information relating to their policies, actions and decisions and other matters related to their areas of responsibility.

(Cabinet Office 1997*b*: Part I, para. 3)

The PCA is responsible for the investigation of complaints arising out of the Code. The White Paper envisaged that 'detached, authoritative and independent supervision' as well as clear rules were needed in order to make the intentions set out in the White Paper stick (Cabinet Office 1993: para. 4.3). Among the advantages of the PCA over the courts or a specialized tribunal, the White Paper argued, was that he could afford a 'more constructive, persuasive and informal dialogue with departments'. A 'legalistic' approach, it was suggested, might make departments 'extremely cautious. They may take a restrictive line not because of the merits of a particular case, but because they fear a precedent which would be binding in other more sensitive situations' (Cabinet Office 1993: para. 4.21). In practice, the PCA later reported, some departments took a line that was no less restrictive than that they might have been expected to adopt before a court or tribunal (below).

A further advantage of relying on the PCA, the White Paper argued, was that ministerial responsibility to Parliament was maintained. Many of the decisions on access to information would involve a 'fine balance between the public interest in disclosing information and the public interest in withholding it'. There was a case therefore for retaining an element of parliamentary accountability for such decisions. The PCA was an officer of Parliament 'and in the last analysis Ministers are accountable to Parliament for the decisions they have taken on his recommendations' (Cabinet Office 1993: para. 4.21). An advantage in ministers' eyes of relying on the PCA may therefore have been that it preserved the possibility of defying a recommendation to which they were opposed. Were the decision to be entrusted to a court or a tribunal that possibility would be denied to them. But when the Labour Government suggested in the White Paper setting out its proposals for a Freedom of Information Act that a disadvantage of the PCA was the perception that he was subject to some form of 'political override' (Cabinet Office 1993: para. 5.7), it had to assure Parliament that it had not meant to imply that he was subject to political influence or direction (Public Administration Committee 1998*c*). The fact remains, however, that the PCA has no power to make binding decisions, only a power to make recommendations.

The extension of the PCA's jurisdiction to include the operation of the Code was secured through his agreement that he was willing to investigate, as potentially disclosing maladministration, complaints that departments and bodies within his jurisdiction have failed to comply with the Code (Cabinet Office 1993: para. 1.12). Although this gave the Code teeth it would otherwise lack, one of the weaknesses of proceeding in this way is that it confines the scope of the Code to those departments and bodies that are subject to the PCA's jurisdiction; it does not apply to bodies that are outside his jurisdiction for whatever reason. At first, the Government sought to compensate for this by asking executive NDPBs to introduce their own codes of openness, taking account where appropriate of the additional measures in the Nolan Committee's Standard of Best Practice for Openness (Cabinet Office 1996*b*: para. 5), but it later abandoned this in favour of including executive NDPBs within the PCA's jurisdiction, unless there were valid reasons for continuing to exclude them; this would have the effect of subjecting them to the Code (Cabinet Office 1997: para. 183). It means also that access is not direct but through an MP (cf. the Citizen's Charter Complaints Task Force's principles, above). Before a complaint is referred to the Ombudsman, it must first be made to the department or body concerned (Cabinet Office 1997*b*: Part I, para. 11).

The Freedom of Information Unit within the Home Office is responsible for the Code as well as for the development of the policy on freedom of information legislation (below). The Unit was transferred from OPS to the Home Office following the merger of the Cabinet Office and OPS in July 1998. In addition to taking the lead in the revision of the Code, it has issued guidance on its interpretation which is intended to assist departments, agencies, and public bodies in their application of the Code to particular cases and circumstances (Cabinet Office 1997*c*). Unlike the Code itself, which is a relatively brief document, the guidance runs to almost 100 pages. The Unit may be consulted on the application of the Code in individual cases, but its application remains a matter for the department or body concerned. It also circulates summaries of Open

Government cases, produced by the Parliamentary Commissioner's office, in an effort to ensure consistency in the interpretation and application of the Code, and publishes an annual monitoring report on its operation (Select Committee on the Parliamentary Commissioner for Administration 1996, Evidence, p. 21 (Office of Public Service and Science)). Despite the Unit's efforts, the PCA reports as a matter of concern that many departments appear not to have heard of the Code four years after it came into operation (PCA 1998: para. 6.29).

The Conservative Government's approach to freedom of information was based on the belief that a 'Code-based approach' was likely to be more effective than a 'statutory, legalistic approach' (Select Committee on the Parliamentary Commissioner for Administration 1996: Evidence, q 108 (Andrew Whetnall)). The manner in which some departments responded to requests for information suggested, however, that it was the fact of the Code, not its form, that most exercised them. The tendency in some departments, the PCA reported, was to use every argument that can be mounted, whether legally-based, Code-based or at times simply obstructive, to help justify non-disclosure (PCA 1996: p. 51; 1998: paras. 6.12–6.13).

The Code generated only a small number of complaints to the PCA in its first three years of operation, leading some observers to doubt whether open government was a matter in which the public were interested. An alternative interpretation of the low number of referrals was that it reflected a low level of public awareness, the Code not having received the 'rocket launch' of publicity that would have followed parliamentary enactment (Select Committee on the Parliamentary Commissioner for Administration 1996: para. 57).[5] In the absence of that boost, departments and OPS fell to arguing among themselves about whose Code it really was and to whom therefore should fall the task of publicizing it: departments argued that it was the responsibility of the centre, the centre that it was the responsibility of departments. 'The facts to date', the Select Committee concluded, 'suggest a Government machine suspicious of its own Code and unwilling to encourage its use' (1996: para. 59). It nevertheless urged OPS to maintain its role as a monitor and advocate of open government within the public service. 'Open government', it commented, 'will perhaps inevitably not always be at the forefront of many departments' thinking. This is particularly true where the requirements are not set down in statute' (1996: para. 64).

[5] In the most recent annual monitoring report, the Labour Government notes that the continuing low number of monitored Code requests 'is almost certainly indicative of the Code's underlying limitations as a non-statutory openness arrangement whose operation is (in the eyes of many applicants) essentially dependent on the goodwill of the department or agency' (Cabinet Office 1998*c*: para. 18).

2 Towards a Freedom of Information Act

The Labour Government came to power committed to a statutory approach. 'The traditional culture of secrecy will only be broken down by giving people in the United Kingdom the legal right to know' (Chancellor of the Duchy of Lancaster 1997: Preface). A White Paper 'with green edges' setting out the Government's proposals for a Freedom of Information Act was published in December 1997. Apart from the fact that it envisaged the creation of a statutory right of access to official information, the White Paper proposals differed from the Code in a number of respects:

The Act would apply right across the public sector rather than just to those bodies subject to the PCA's jurisdiction. The Government's original intention was that it should also apply to the privatized utilities and some private sector organizations carrying out duties on behalf of government, but the privatized utilities were later reported to have been excluded.

Whereas the Code only allows access to 'information', the Act would provide access to documents as well as information.

The number of exemptions would be reduced. Instead of the Code's fifteen exemptions, public authorities would only be able to withhold information if disclosure would cause harm to one of seven specified interests. In most cases the test would be one of 'substantial' rather than 'simple' harm.

An independent Information Commissioner would investigate complaints that requests for information had been rejected. Under the original proposals it was intended that no appeal should lie from the Commissioner's decision to the courts, but this was later reported to have been revised to allow an appeal from decisions that information should be released to a tribunal composed of a mixture of judges and retired civil servants, creating a risk that the Commissioner would be inhibited in the exercise of his powers to order disclosure by the knowledge that a department would almost certainly appeal.

The crucial question is whether the statutory approach will be any more effective than its predecessor in breaking down the traditional culture of secrecy. The risk is that by going against the grain of an administrative culture which is attached to secrecy and unsympathetic if not hostile to law and legal processes, a statutory code may be less effective (if that were possible), and possibly even counterproductive. The White Paper acknowledged the need therefore to champion openness within government itself if it is to become 'part of the official culture rather than an irksome imposition' (Chancellor of the Duchy of Lancaster 1997: para. 7.1). The Freedom of Information Unit would therefore develop an action programme to support the move from a culture of secrecy to one of openness. 'It is vital that FOI should not result in a position where all the pressure for an open and positive approach to disclosure of information lies outside government, while a resulting counter-culture of reluctance develops within' (Chancellor of the Duchy of Lancaster 1997: para. 7.6).

The White Paper anticipated that a draft Bill would be published for consultation. A draft for consultation was promised before the 1998 summer recess but it never materialized. Meanwhile, following the merger of the OPS with the Cabinet Office, responsibility for freedom of information was transferred to the Home Office, where it is reported to be subject to a fundamental re-appraisal. Whether severing the link with the centre will prove detrimental to the cause of freedom of information remains to be seen. A draft Bill for consultation is now planned for the 1998–99 session. Until such time as it is enacted, the Code continues to apply.

IV EXTERNAL CONTROLS ON STANDARDS OF ADMINISTRATION

1 Parliament

1.1 The Parliamentary Commissioner for Administration

One of the main external checks on standards of administration is the Parliamentary Ombudsman. In addition to his responsibility for investigating 'complaints of injustice sustained in consequence of maladministration' (Parliamentary Commissioner Act 1967, s. 5(1)), he is also responsible, as we have seen (above, p. 369), for the investigation of complaints arising out of the Code of Practice on Access to Government Information.

Sir William Reid, Parliamentary Ombudsman between 1990 and 1996, welcomed the attention focused by these reforms on the accountability of public services to their users. He was also generally supportive of the reforms themselves. In particular, he supported the formulation of charter standards as useful but not necessarily definitive statements of good administration (Parliamentary Commissioner for Administration 1992: para. 8; see too Select Committee on the Parliamentary Commissioner for Administration 1992: para. 3). He also supported the introduction of complaints procedures, and as we have seen he played a leading role in forcing the executive to clarify the circumstances in which financial compensation is payable for maladministration and substandard service. By doing so he did much to clarify the nature of charter promises.

Sir William Reid also adopted a significantly broader interpretation of his role than his predecessors. At the start of his period of office, his aims were conventionally defined in terms of securing the redress of justified complaints (Parliamentary Commissioner for Administration 1991: para. 7), but by 1994 their definition had been widened to include:

> the identification of measures needed 'to improve systems, practices and procedures which the investigations of complaints have shown to be deficient, with a view to avoiding or reducing the repetition of maladministration', and
>
> the promotion of 'higher standards of administration by publishing evidence of bad practice to enable government departments and other bodies within jurisdiction to assess what steps they can take to improve the standards of service they offer'. (Parliamentary Commissioner for Administration 1995*a*: para. 14)

Under his successor, more emphasis has been put on the throughput of cases, but not at the expense of the investigation of systemic defects (Parliamentary Commissioner for Administration 1998: paras. 1.5, 1.8).

Commentators had long urged the PCA to devote more attention to the systemic aspects of good administration (see e.g. Harlow 1978). As we have seen, the provision of feedback is regarded as a standard purpose of complaints systems (above). The emphasis on improving standards of administration, however, appears to have come from the Parliamentary Ombudsman himself, and to have been driven mainly by fears of the effects of public service reform and in particular the fragmentation of the civil service and the attendant dilution of civil service knowledge on standards of administration. In his annual report for 1993, the PCA wrote that 'continuing changes in the public services and the way its functions are to be carried out' had heightened the 'need for best practice to be disseminated among departments in a directed and focused manner' (Parliamentary Commissioner for Administration 1994: para. 8). It was, he wrote, a 'source of great concern that my investigations reveal one department repeating unnecessarily another department's errors' (ibid.: para. 3).

The PCA undertook a number of initiatives in pursuit of his aim of improving standards of administration. He revised and expanded the original Crossman catalogue of maladministration, 'in the language of the 1990s', in order to make 'departments and others more aware of what constitutes maladministration' (Parliamentary Commissioner for Administration 1994: para. 7). He also published a booklet, *The Ombudsman in Your Files* (Cabinet Office 1995*b*), which was inspired partly by the example of *The Judge Over Your Shoulder* (Treasury Solicitor's Department 1995), explaining the PCA's role and offering civil servants advice on how to avoid complaints of maladministration. The advice takes the form of a number of 'basic principles of good practice', which are illustrated with examples drawn from recent investigations. The 'lessons' are described as 'often simple':

treat people *fairly* and *consistently*;

when giving advice, make sure it is *correct* and keep a *record* of all significant telephone calls and other conversations;

deal with things *promptly*;

if something goes wrong, investigate objectively, and if it is clear that the fault lies with the public authority, *apologise sincerely* and offer appropriate redress,

follow laid down *procedures*;

if procedures do not work, *get them changed*!

when introducing new procedures or schemes, *plan* carefully and, where practical, run *pilot tests* in advance to make sure systems work and staff are properly trained;

when responding to requests for information under the Code of Practice [on Access to Government Information], consider disclosure on the merits of the individual case, not simply against the practices which have been followed in the past.

As part of the same effort to increase departmental and agency awareness of maladministration, the PCA also arranged the circulation by OPS of summaries of the reports of his cases, produced by his office, together with notes drawing civil servants' attention to the lessons of general application that can be learned from them (Parliamentary Commissioner for Administration 1994: para. 4; 1996*a*: para. 4). The summaries are headed *Lessons to be Learned from the Ombudsman's Investigated Cases or What to Avoid*. He also made greater use of his power to issue special reports, e.g. on disability living allowance (Parliamentary Commissioner for Administration 1993*b*) or the Child Support Agency (Parliamentary Commissioner for Administration 1995*b*, 1996*b*), in order to highlight issues of redress or administrative practice raised by a particular case or group of cases; and, as we have seen, encouraged the Select Committee to undertake 'thematic' inquiries into issues that recur in the course of his investigations.

It is not so long ago that the suggestion that standards of good administration might be made more explicit was viewed with some scepticism, if not as positively inimical to the needs of good administration. Sir Cecil Clothier, Parliamentary Ombudsman from 1979 to 1984, opposed the introduction of a code of principles of good administration, on the grounds that, if they were anything more than 'pious generalisations', they could be the cause of 'undesirable bureaucratic rigidity . . . [and] the enemy of that sensitivity and flexibility which were essential to good administration' (JUSTICE-All Souls 1988: para. 2.24). What we see here, however, is not so much the introduction of a rigid code, as the PCA, in common with other watchdogs, engaged in the elaboration and illustration of the principles of which he is the guardian in an effort to make departments and agencies more aware of those principles and hence to diminish the risk of their being infringed. Clearly, however, there are limits to what such efforts alone can achieve. In his 1995 annual report, the PCA expressed his concern that further planned reductions in the number of civil servants would lead to an increased level of complaints. 'I foresee more, not less, maladministration despite the references to efficiency savings' (Parliamentary Commissioner for Administration 1996*a*: para. 6).

1.2 Other parliamentary checks

One consequence of the public service reforms of recent years has been to increase the scope for the more thorough parliamentary scrutiny of administration. Executive agencies offer perhaps the best example. By increasing the capacity of ministers to control the work of civil servants, Jones points out, agencies increase the potential accountability of ministers to Parliament for policy and performance. Trosa, too, saw Next Steps as enhancing the capacity of Parliament to discuss the relevance of targets and the quality of their implementation (1994: para. 3.5.6). But for this to happen, Jones and Burnham warn, MPs must give up their concern to raise with ministers the 'minutiae of implementation', while for their part ministers must recognize 'the relevance of framework documents, annual reports, and quality-of-service and performance targets as crucial links in the chain of accountability between civil servants, ministers and Parliament, and be prepared to answer openly about them and keep MPs up-to-date' (1995: 178).

There is little sign of this happening. As we have seen, the Public Accounts Committee, supported by the National Audit Office, has highlighted the issue of the validation of performance standards. The Public Service Committee and the Select Committee on the PCA in the last Parliament also carried out important inquiries into the Citizen's Charter and Open Government. But departmental select committees have shown little appetite for the detailed scrutiny of framework documents, the standard-setting process, department or agency self-reporting of performance against targets, and complaints procedures. One way in which it has been suggested this shortcoming might be remedied is through a Machinery of Government Committee, supported by an Assessment of Government Office modelled on the National Audit Office, for the scrutiny of non-financial administrative performance and policy (Winetrobe 1995). The Public Administration Committee in the present

Parliament goes some way in this direction. Its purposes include the examination of matters relating to the quality and standards of administration provided by departments, but it lacks the support enjoyed by the Public Accounts Committee through the NAO. There is also a risk that it will lend less effective support to the PCA than a committee dedicated to that purpose. The impression is thus of a scrutiny system which is only gradually adjusting to the changing structure of the executive branch.

One area in urgent need of scrutiny, if necessary at the expense of a continuing major involvement in the redress of individual grievances, is the effectiveness of the internal complaints procedures which have been set up under the Citizen's Charter. The report of the Select Committee on the PCA on maladministration and redress (above, pp. 362–4) graphically illustrates the contribution a select committee inquiry may make to reform. Given MPs' traditional jealousy of their largely self-assumed role in the redress of grievances, it is doubtful how positively they would respond to any suggestion that their role should be reduced. But severing or reducing the link between MPs, ministers and the redress of grievances by, for example, making access to the PCA direct rather than through an MP, would have the additional advantage of removing one stimulus to ministerial intervention to the detriment of the purposes for which Next Steps agencies were established.

2 The courts

We have already considered the role of the courts in relation to the administrative process by way of judicial review proceedings (above, pp. 335–40). Charter standards for the most part are not directly enforceable through the courts. 'Charters are not legal documents; their promises do not, by and large, constitute legal rights' (Public Service Committee 1997: para. 42). This does not exclude the possibility of their indirect judicial enforcement, though there have been few signs of the 'juridification' (Hood 1995: 179) of charter standards. There have been calls for the legalization of charter rights, but these have generated little enthusiasm. In evidence to the Public Service Committee, the National Consumer Council concluded that non-statutory entitlements could be at least as effective as statutory ones if public authorities acted as if they were under a duty, if consumers were able to act as if they had rights, and if complaints and redress procedures for enforcing their rights were effective and user-friendly (Public Service Committee 1997: Evidence, p. 34). It is of course where these conditions are not satisfied that user expectations may be disappointed.

3 The Council on Tribunals

The Council on Tribunals is responsible for keeping under review the constitution and working of administrative tribunals (Tribunals and Inquiries Act 1992 s.1). Like the PCA, the Council has been supportive of the charter movement, seeing charters as a useful means of publishing the standards that can be expected by appellants. When the Charter was first launched, it urged the issue of charters for all the major tribunals falling within its jurisdiction (Council on Tribunals 1993: paras. 2.6, 2.110). The fragmented nature of the administrative justice system, itself a reflection of the plural character of the executive branch, has made this a more difficult exercise than in relation to the court system, where it has proved possible to proceed on the basis of a single Charter for Court Users (in Scotland, a Justice Charter). But a number of tribunal systems, including the Independent Tribunal Service, have now published their own charters. The Lord Chancellor's Department has also published *Standards of Service for Tribunals,* which sets out the standards of administrative service individuals can expect from the administrative staff of tribunals supported by the Department (Council on Tribunals 1996: para. 2.191).

The Council has also been generally supportive of initiatives designed to bring about structural and organizational changes in tribunal systems which are capable of delivering benefits in terms of value for money for the taxpayer and for tribunal users. It has emphasized its concern, however, that their effect should not be to undermine the independence and integrity of the tribunal systems themselves or to interfere in the exercise of the judicial function. Amidst signs that departments were not adhering to these principles, the Council drew attention in its 1995–96 annual report to instances where the overall drive to reduce costs and to secure additional savings was being achieved at the expense of increased hearing delays, inadequate administration, and an absence of effective support to tribunals (Council on Tribunals 1996: paras. 2.2–2.6). Following a review of the organization and management of tribunal systems, the Council has now issued guidance on the essential elements of the independence and integrity of tribunals, and their implications for relations between departments and individual tribunal systems, to which it 'expects' departments to have regard whenever consideration is given to the setting up of new adjudicative structures or to a review of existing ones (Council on Tribunals 1997).

V CONCLUSION

The mechanisms considered in this chapter constitute potentially valuable additions to the traditional machinery for promoting good administration. They are additions to that machinery, however, not a substitute for it. The risk is that in the face of continuing budgetary pressures the existing checks come to be seen as an irritating constraint rather than as a crucial element of good administration. The neglect by some departments of the traditional machinery of administrative justice indicates that this risk is not without foundation. We also find it illustrated on a lesser scale by the difficulties experienced by the PCA in investigating complaints against the Employment Service in 1994. The Service wrongly understood the PCA to be a complainant's advocate rather than an independent investigator. It was also so committed to its philosophy of 'getting it right first time' that it found it difficult to accept the possibility that it might have got it wrong (Select Committee on the Parliamentary Commissioner for Administration 1995*b*: paras. 17–21). The Council on Tribunals and the Parliamentary Commissioner have sought in different ways to guard against the risk of the principles of which they are the guardians being inadvertently ignored by departments and their agencies. Guardians, however, can only do so much. In the final analysis, the responsibility for compliance with those principles rests with departments.

12
Conclusions: Internal Control in a Plural Executive

I INTRODUCTION

Executive self-restraint constitutes one of the essential underpinnings of democracy and the rule of law. 'To achieve restrained discretion, more is needed than criticism of authority and pressure upon it. The system depends heavily on self-restraint and thus on social mechanisms for building in appropriate values and rules of conduct' (Selznick 1968: 54–5). Our focus in this book therefore has been on the internal control function in modern government, as a counter to the concern with external parliamentary and above all judicial controls which provides the starting point for so much constitutional law scholarship.

The public face of internal control in executive government is largely concerned with what Ministers say. Projecting into a media-obsessed and -driven age the ideal of ministerial unanimity implicit in collective responsibility leads to an endless press hunt for evidence of ministerial disagreement or departure from the party line. Governments appear to live in constant fear of the damage to their prestige and election prospects which might flow from such disclosure, and to react by seeking ever-tighter control of ministerial utterances. The Prime Minister's Office vets speeches; the Prime Minister's Press Secretary asserts his pre-eminence in the information hierarchy; the press reports with elaboration and enthusiasm these tributes to its own power (Public Administration Committee 1998*b*).

Our story has been concerned rather with the quieter but equally diligent pursuit, at the centre of government, of control in appropriate measure over what departments do. We do not say that the control of information is without significance—indeed, information, and the authority and prestige that may be linked with it, may be seen as resources of government in themselves (Daintith 1997*a*) but it is in the sphere of the control of action and of the exercise of legally-recognized power that the basic structure of the United Kingdom executive has produced its most important constitutional results. The picture that emerges from the foregoing chapters is of a system of internal control which has been shaped by the plural structure of the executive branch, but which is in the course of significant change, largely but not solely as a result of the public service reforms pursued by successive governments over the last twenty or so years. In this chapter we draw together the threads of the changes that are affecting internal control, before examining the relationship between internal control and the external controls operated by Parliament and the courts. In the final section we offer our conclusions on the constitutional significance of the internal control function in contemporary United Kingdom executive government.

II TRENDS IN INTERNAL CONTROL

1 The traditional system

Traditionally, internal control in the United Kingdom has been treated as a departmental rather than a central function. As we saw, departmental primacy has been the central organizing principle of the executive branch since the middle years of the nineteenth century (Chapter 2). The corollary of departmental primacy was an essentially decentralized system of internal control for the operation of which the ministerial head of each department was responsible to Parliament. The permanent head of the department was in turn responsible to the minister for its overall organization, management and staffing (Treasury 1989*a*: para. 6.2.1). The role of the 'centre' within this system was one essentially of co-ordination, advice, and assistance rather than control. The traditional orthodoxy was that it was better to trust departments than to engage in 'a futile attempt at supervision in detail' (Haldane 1923: 8).

To this pattern there were exceptions. The most important were those in respect of expenditure and establishments, the latter being treated until recently as part of the control of expenditure (Chapter 3). Treasury control of money and staff in a plural executive was founded on control of access to resources (Chapter 4), reinforced in the case of staff by a mixture of mainly prerogative and to a lesser extent statutory controls, the former being reduced to writing and formally allocated to the Treasury within the executive branch for this purpose (Chapter 3). But although the Treasury has always possessed important powers of control over departments, it has never strayed far from an approach which treats the primary responsibility for financial as well as policy decisions as belonging to spending departments (Woods 1956: 113). No doubt the adoption of that approach reflected a calculation that a system in which the emphasis was on the 'conjoint and co-operative responsibility, under Ministers, of all departmental heads, including the Treasury' (Hamilton 1951: para. 86) was likely to be more effective than one in which the emphasis was on the Treasury's powers of control alone, but it also acknowledged the extent to which collective control in a plural executive depended on agreement among departments. The reason why Treasury control of public expenditure was never so complete or severe as the conventional wisdom asserts, Greenleaf reminds us, was because 'departments were important official entities in their own right and headed by ministers with their special authority and responsibility to Parliament. Against this twin array the Treasury could not ultimately stand alone and needed Cabinet support and Parliamentary follow-up' (1987: 253).

The strength of the United Kingdom approach to internal control, in contrast to one in which spending decisions must be passed by representatives of the Treasury or Ministry of Finance located in each spending department, as in France or Italy, is that it places the responsibility for compliance firmly on the shoulders of departments. Their sense of responsibility is not diminished as a result of responsibility being seen to belong elsewhere. Its weakness is that it is vulnerable to non-compliance. Where central systems of control have been established, as in the case of expenditure and establishments, reliance on the department as the primary agent of control has therefore invariably been accompanied by some form of check on the diligence with which central disciplines are applied. As we saw, expenditure control has been backed both by a powerful system of state audit and, in more recent years, by an increasingly sophisticated cash monitoring system (Chapter 6). So, too, when after the Second World War the decentralization of responsibility for much of establishments' work was formalized and made permanent, the Treasury 're-affirmed its right of inspection and of access to departments—the right to go and see for itself—and particularly the right to submit particular branches and posts to closer examination if it should seem to it desirable to do so' (Padmore 1956: 130).

This combination of delegated authority and central monitoring, however, was the exception rather than the rule. Across much of what the executive did the traditional system was one of departmental self-discipline or self-control under the individual and collective supervision of ministers. Seen in this light old problems take on a new air. The reason we have traditionally lacked a system of administrative law is not that the courts somehow failed to forge one, but that 'Parliament gave a free hand to half a hundred draftsmen and departmental solicitors to produce whatever appealed to their taste or fancy' (Cooper 1957: 269). Given that latitude the 'unsystematic encroachment upon traditional principles' about which critics complained was always the likely result.

2 Growth and change

2.1 Forces for change

Departmental self-discipline continues to form the cornerstone of internal control. Over the last twenty or so years, however, the internal control function has undergone significant growth and change. As we have suggested, the main driving force behind this development has been the public service reforms pursued by successive governments over this period. If functions are to be contracted out, if burdens on business are to be reduced, if openness is to be increased, if services are to be made more responsive to their users, if co-ordination across departmental boundaries is to be increased and so on, the centre has to find some means of inducing or compelling departments and agencies to move in the desired directions. In some cases, the increase has resulted not from any growth in the agenda of internal control but from the continued delegation of central functions to departments and agencies. The delegation of responsibility for recruitment, for example, led as we saw to a central Recruitment Code policed by the Civil Service Commissioners (Chapter 3). As we would expect, the possibility that departments should simply certify their compliance with the Code was rejected (Cabinet Office 1994*c*: para 5.1). Changes in the constitutional environment have also played a major role. In particular, EU membership has produced, in the shape of the European Secretariat, a more vigorous central co-ordination mechanism than exists for the co-ordination of purely domestic issues (Chapters 8–9).

2.2 Co-ordination versus centralization

In all these areas, therefore, new systems of control have emerged. The shape they take reflects the location of power over the resource with which they are concerned. Only rarely, in our system, has such power been centralized or even concentrated in a single department. The notable exceptions are the Treasury's 'ancient authority' over government's financial resources (Chapter 4), and the Cabinet's more recently acquired control over legislative resources, that is, over departmental access to Parliament for legislative purposes (Chapter 8). Less well known—except to ambitious barristers, perhaps—is the Attorney-General's power over the appointment of all counsel representing the Crown, and over Crown legal proceedings generally (Chapter 9). These 'resource monopolies' within the executive are all conventional in nature, though it is quite possible for such a monopoly to be created by law: the specific powers of control with which the Civil Service Commissioners are still endowed represent the remains of powers which have been in existence since the Civil Service Order in Council 1870 established open competition as the normal method of entry to the service and put the Commissioners in control of it. A body that possesses such a monopoly may use it as an instrument of control. This has always been the endeavour of the Treasury, though, as we have seen, both the purpose and the style of the control regime have changed radically over the years. Control over legislative access has likewise been the means by which the Cabinet has pursued, mainly through the Parliamentary Counsel Office, goals of consistency in legislative drafting and a discipline—admittedly limited—over aspects of legislative content. Naturally, where such monopoly power is conventional in origin, it may in the last resort be over-ridden by *ad hoc* decision within the Cabinet system, a possibility that provides an inbuilt constraint on the over-zealous use of such power. But it remains the case that its holder enjoys a privileged position in shaping the relevant control regime, whether by way of a long-term process of delegation, as with the Treasury, or through turning potential powers of obstruction to constructive use in building norms and expectations, as with the Parliamentary Counsel Office in alliance with the Law Officers.

The new control and co-ordination machinery engendered by public service reform and by changes in the constitutional environment has received little if any support from the creation or extension of resource monopolies. There come to mind only the leveraging of the Treasury's running costs control regime to support participation by the Cabinet Office (formerly OPS) in the monitoring of Departmental performance (above, pp. 188–90), and the extension of central powers of control of litigation by giving a monopoly of management of litigation in the European Court of Justice to the European lawyers in the Treasury Solicitor's Department (above, pp. 318–19).

Nor has the new machinery been based on prerogative or statutory powers, with the exception of the controls over recruitment which continue to be exercised by the Civil Service Commissioners in their new role as the guardians of the principle of recruitment on merit on the basis of fair and open competition, and the analogous controls which have been introduced in respect of public appointments. Instead of taking powers of control over departments and agencies to achieve these new ends, government has preferred to build on techniques of co-operation and co-ordination honed in the Cabinet Office over many decades, of which the Cabinet or ministerial committee and the official committees that sometimes parallel them provide the quintessential institutional expression. The process of co-operation is however increasingly driven by a variety of centrally-placed units each with a well-defined mission (and often, a set of norms and standards to go with it). The traditional Cabinet Office maxim, 'There is no policy other than there should be a policy', is being supplemented by a variety of specific policies that its component parts are pursuing—efficiency, better regulation, better government—through stimulation, exhortation, and co-ordination. These units and their policies depend for their influence directly upon consensus in their favour within the Cabinet system, at the highest political levels of the executive, a consensus which may need to be sustained, or even imposed, by the political leadership and power of the Prime Minister.

This kind of co-ordination technique is no longer confined to questions of how to conduct executive government, but is coming to be used increasingly as a means by which the centre can (seek to) influence substantive policy, through the setting up of units or groups within the Cabinet Office to address problems like social exclusion, or industrial innovation and enterprise. It is also being practised in other departments which have an acknowledged co-ordinating role, as witness the institutionalization of the Government Legal Service under the leadership of the Treasury Solicitor, the creation of the Lawyers Management Unit, and the steady elaboration of a structure of co-ordination led by the Government Legal Service Liaison Group (Chapter 9). The Treasury Solicitor has never achieved, over legal resources, the sort of monopoly enjoyed by the Treasury over financial ones, but now arguably exercises stronger leadership over the legal function in the executive than does the Treasury over its accountancy counterpart (above, pp. 137–9). Such leadership capacities, however, appear to rest rather upon professional cohesion than upon the collective political consensus sustaining the Cabinet Office role in 'directed co-ordination'.

This model of internal control, which has affinities with notions of 'co-operative implementation' (Michael 1996) and 'enforced self-regulation' (Ayers and Braithwaite 1992), continues to be based on departmental self-control, but involves a greater degree of central initiative than in the past. The role of the centre is no longer confined to advice and assistance; it is also increasingly one of encouraging and exhorting departments and agencies to move in desired directions. The foundations of departmental primacy within the executive branch, however, remain essentially intact. Their functions continue to be vested in them rather than the executive as a whole. They are as a general rule subject to no higher authority in the exercise of those functions. Their ministerial heads continue to be responsible for those functions to Parliament. They are also members of the Cabinet. The retention by departments of these guarantees of their autonomy means in turn that the exercise of collective control continues to rely heavily on agreement. Where there is agreement as in the case of recruitment we may expect it to proceed relatively smoothly. Where there is an absence of agreement or scope for disagreement as in the case of deregulation we may expect it to remain problematic. The Better Regulation Unit may have the support of the Prime Minister, but it is still powerless to prevent the Minister of Agriculture from banning beef on the bone.

2.3 Formalization

Co-ordination and control which derives from political agreement does not, however, have to be continuously sustained thereafter by the maintenance of such agreement. The articulation of such control in the form of explicit rules and procedures eventually furnishes an independent source of legitimacy. Such formalization may indeed be a useful, perhaps even essential, support for the specific control policies of the new central units in government. A document expressed in terms of standards, or principles, or rules, and hence looking rather like law, may acquire an aura of authority which usefully supplements whatever influence is possessed by the relevant Cabinet Office Unit. The need to legitimate these new control policies may be a significant factor explaining the clear recent trend to the formalization of internal control.

Such formalization is indeed frequently linked to the reform processes we have described. New internal procedures have been instituted, for example, in respect of the scrutiny of secondary legislation which amends primary legislation or legislative proposals which have a potential impact on business (Chapter 8). There has been a flood of codes, handbooks, guidance, framework documents, charters, statements of principle, and other forms of normative material stemming directly from the public service reforms of recent years. Constitutional change, too, has also played a part. The decision to make Convention rights directly enforceable in United Kingdom law, for example, is leading to provision for the more systematic consideration of the legislative implications of ECHR obligations along lines similar to that undertaken in respect of EC obligations since accession (Chapter 8).

Formalization, however, has not just been about implementing reform, and buttressing such reform is certainly not its only motive. It has also been about the restatement and reinforcement of existing expectations in the face of the challenge to those expectations represented by public service reforms in the shape of the growing fragmentation of the public service, increased budgetary pressures, and new modes of delivery of public services. Their re-statement has also been prompted by fears that the existing mechanisms of professional socialization are breaking down, a breakdown compounded by the growth in recruitment from the private sector. The proliferating codes, handbooks, and booklets all serve to increase the visibility of existing expectations in an effort to reduce the risk of their being ignored. The Civil Service Code, the Recruitment Code, and the numerous handbooks and booklets which have been produced both by external and internal watchdogs all reflect this concern. The preparation of the Agency Chief Executive's Handbook, for example, was occasioned by the 'need for even greater vigilance about standards throughout the Service'. Its purpose was to ensure that Service-wide rules on conduct and financial propriety were always available to chief executives in a 'readily accessible form' (Cabinet Office (Office of Public Service) 1996*c*: p. iv). *The Ombudsman in Your Files* (Cabinet Office 1995*b*) and *Regularity and Propriety* (Treasury 1997*c*) stem from the same impulse. *The Judge Over Your Shoulder* (Treasury Solicitor's Department (1995)), the model for these booklets, was also about alerting civil servants to requirements, but it was a response to the increasing prominence of judicial review rather than the expression of a fear that public service reform might pose any threat to legality. To find a comparable upsurge in the codification of the rules relating to government we have to go back to the inter-war period and that too followed a period, of dislocation, upheaval and uncertainty (above, pp. 87–91).

This codification of expectations has also been about maintaining or restoring public confidence in government, in which regard, too, it has been as much about reaffirming existing standards and increasing their visibility to allay the scepticism of outsiders as about laying down new and more exacting standards. The need for articulation and codification arose, the Chancellor of the Duchy of Lancaster argued in 1996, not because of any fall-off in respect for the implicit shared rules of public life, but because in 'a far more open society' it was 'right that all citizens should be able to have access to the rules by which their politicians and public servants are expected to behave' (Willetts 1996).

For some observers this increasing formalization of internal control is to be regretted. The multiplication of codes to ensure probity, Foster and Plowden argue, is leading to a system which will be less effective and more expensive than reliance on 'traditional civil service methods'. The reason for this in their view is that rules simply do not work:

> they merely stimulate ways round them, so leading to yet more rules to plug loopholes, leading to a growing climate of regulation of a kind from which the new public management saw the need to escape in the interests of efficiency. There can be no guarantee that reliance on these methods will be more effective or cheaper than relying on traditional civil service methods, based on the traditional Haldane relationship: indeed on both counts, rather the reverse. (Foster and Plowden 1996: 229)

This is an important argument, but one which needs to be approached with a degree of caution. It misrepresents the traditional system as 'a system not of rules but of advice' (ibid.: 77). The nature of the British constitution is thus said to be not 'to circumscribe matters with rules but to rely upon the more elastic safeguard of taking advice' (Thomas 1978: 6–7). Perhaps this is the way in which key actors thought of the constitution, or would have liked it to be seen, but the normative content of the traditional system was considerably greater than this suggests. For example, as we have seen, many of the key principles governing the civil service are traceable in written form to the inter-war period or earlier. The form in which they were expressed (below) may have allowed considerable latitude in their interpretation and application, but there was no question that the civil service had its own code (Chapter 3).

It also neglects the role of rules in the provision of certainty; not absolute certainty, for that is unattainable, but greater certainty than is provided by reliance on unwritten rules. For Kernaghan 'the suggestion that contemporary public servants can rely for ethical guidance simply on unwritten rules in the form of traditions, conventions, understandings and practices is naive, and even dangerous'; a dominant rationale for written rules, he points out, 'is that there is much uncertainty as to what the traditional rules are and what they mean in the day-to-day operation of government' (1993: 27). The traditional objection to codification is that the pretence at clarification is illusory and must be paid for by the loss of flexibility which is the great merit of unwritten law, but as Freund pointed out 'the layman's purpose will often be served by intelligible explicitness falling short of absolute certainty; and this gives the written rule a political and educational value which nations living under codes fully appreciate' (1932: 6).

Finally, it overlooks one of the most significant features of these codes, namely the fact they are without exception non-statutory. With this in mind we can turn to the relationship between internal control and the external controls operated by Parliament and the courts.

III INTERNAL CONTROL AND EXTERNAL CONTROLS

1 Executive reliance on external control: Parliament

Here the picture we have is of the executive relying on its own resources for the purposes of internal control rather than seeking external parliamentary or judicial support. The principal exception is in expenditure control where a relationship of mutual dependence has existed between the Treasury and Parliament from the outset, although there are signs that Treasury dependence on parliamentary disciplines may be beginning to decline (Chapter 6). The civil service, on the other hand, with the exception of civil service numbers, has always been regulated in the exercise of the executive's prerogative powers.

This pattern has not been radically altered by the public service reforms of recent years. Sometimes the executive has had no choice but to secure legislation in the implementation of those reforms, but wherever possible it has preferred to proceed on the basis of its own powers both in the narrow prerogative sense (the Civil Service Management Code, the Recruitment Code, the Civil Service Code, the Public Appointments Code) and in the sense of the power of 'any Tom, Dick or Harry' (Ferguson 1988) to issue a non-statutory code (the Code of Practice on Access to Government Information). At the same time, as we have seen, the revival of the device of the Secretary of State has had the unexpected but welcome effect of reducing the executive's dependence on legislation in matters of its own organization (Chapter 2). It is a mark of the success of its policy of avoiding legislation wherever possible that the public service reforms of recent years have generated a total of only three enactments, all directed to the removal of obstacles to the implementation of specific policies: the Government Trading Funds Act 1990, the Civil Service (Management Functions) Act 1992, and the Deregulation and Contracting Out Act 1994.

Several reasons may be suggested why the executive should prefer to rely for internal control purposes on its autonomous powers. Legislative time is in short supply: relying on its own powers wherever possible enables the available time to be devoted to other, by implication, more worthwhile purposes. It also means that at some future point valuable legislative time does not have to be devoted to amending legislation. One reason why parliamentary legislation has been so infrequent is that there have been few previously erected statutory obstacles to the implementation of public service reform. As well as being time-consuming, recourse to parliamentary legislation may also be risky: a government that relies on its own powers avoids the lottery of legislative amendment. It is also possible that, despite the fact that the executive controls access to the legislative process, parliamentary legislation may in fact be beyond it: either there is internal agreement in which case legislation is unnecessary, or there is no agreement in which case parliamentary legislation is not a practical possibility. As in the case of freedom of information, it may be easier to secure internal agreement to a non-statutory code than to an Act of Parliament.

At the same time, non-statutory regulation is commonly regarded as possessing, in this as in other contexts, a number of advantages over its statutory counterpart. It is typically expressed differently: in the form of a mixture of general principles and subsidiary rules, which those who are bound by them are expected to observe in their spirit as well as their letter, rather than in the form of detailed rules. This combination of principles and rules is said to allow the legislative project to be kept within manageable bounds, while at the same time allowing the underlying purpose of obligations to be made plain and discouraging conduct at or near the margin of unlawfulness; in contrast to the Recruitment Code we do not expect the underlying principles to 'sing out of' Acts of Parliament (above p. 79). It is claimed to be more easily adaptable to changing circumstances or new developments. New cases can be decided by reference to the general principles on which systems are based, and the rules themselves can be changed quickly and with a minimum of formality. It is also said to be quicker and more flexible in its application to individual cases; the rules can be interpreted and applied in a practical common-sense (less legalistic) manner, taking into account their spirit as well as their letter. Statutory regulation, on the other hand, is said to invite the inflexible application of rules without regard to their underlying purpose; it 'imports a rigidity into any procedure it touches' (Sisson 1966: 60). Finally, of course, non-statutory regulation in its prerogative form was for a long time not open to challenge in the courts. It thus combined certainty of effect with the avoidance of litigation.

Whether non-statutory regulation has always realized these advantages is open to question. Nor is there any inherent reason why statutory regulation should not be expressed in the form of a mixture of principles and rules. The principal objection to the executive proceeding on a non-statutory basis, however, is not that the claims made for the non-statutory approach may be exaggerated, but that by doing so it avoids the degree of parliamentary scrutiny and control attendant on the formulation and enactment of legislative proposals. This objection would not have cut much ice with Sir James Stephen who thought it beneath the Queen's dignity to ask Parliament 'to aid her to do that which she can do as effectually without their aid' (above, p. 63). Nor is it a theory which has weighed heavily with successive governments, who have preferred to exploit the latitude afforded them by the existing constitutional framework. The last Conservative Government acknowledged the view that 'additional authority' would be conferred on the proposed Civil Service Code by a 'statutory approach', but made clear its opposition to such an approach were it to inhibit the 'effective and efficient' management of the service (Cabinet Office 1995*a*: paras. 2.15–2.17). The result, however, is an area of law of increasing importance, extending for example to relations between the executive and the individual in matters such as freedom of information, which is governed by the executive own law rather than parliamentary legislation. We come back to this point in discussing the constitutional significance of the internal control function below. What it underlines, however, is how narrow in some respects is Parliament's formal dominion over the executive.

As part of its programme of constitutional reform, the Labour Government is committed to giving statutory backing to the Civil Service Code. It is also committed to a Freedom of Information Act, although a place on the legislative programme for either has yet to be secured. Regardless of whether or not the statutory element of internal control increases, we would expect the interdependence between internal and external agents and mechanisms of control to increase as a result of the expanding public scope of internal control, the fact that through initiatives like the Citizen's Charter or Better Regulation internal control now addresses the relationship between the executive and the citizen in a way in which traditionally it did not. This has brought with it a need, for example, for independent complaint-handling mechanisms, which in some cases has proved capable of being met internally—the Civil Service Commissioners for example have been reinvented as an internal appellate as well as regulatory body—but which in others has had to be addressed through external mechanisms. Prominent among these as we have seen has been the Parliamentary Ombudsman, who as well as being the final rung in the Citizen's Charter complaints ladder is also currently responsible for the investigation of complaints arising out of the Code of Practice on Access to Official Information. This extension of the subject-matter of internal control has also brought demands for the independent validation of agency performance against ministerial targets, which again can only be met externally, but which the executive has yet to concede.

2 Executive reliance on external control: the courts

Despite the executive's preference for proceeding wherever possible on the basis of its own law there are some examples, mainly in the field of finance, of parliamentary support being sought for internal schemes of control. There are no equivalent examples of executive reliance on the courts. Individual senior judges, it is true, have proved a convenient resource when the executive wants delicate jobs done in an atmosphere of impartiality (Stevens 1993), but this willingness to rely on judicial impartiality and acumen does not extend to courts as institutions. The failure of seventeenth-century experiments with a judicial power within the executive, and the undistinguished record of the ordinary courts as administrative supervisors in the eighteenth and nineteenth centuries doubtless explain, in part at least, the absence of executive recourse to the courts in support of systems of internal control. In more recent years, the attention paid to excluding possibilities of judicial review even where the executive was borrowing from judicial methods in meeting new administrative needs—as in planning and social security—betrays a deep-seated fear that executive effectiveness would be compromised by 'the inept intrusion of the law' (Sisson 1966: 71).

We may assume, therefore, that a key part of the rationale for the executive's reliance on its own law has been to keep the courts as well as Parliament out of its 'own affairs'. Following the *GCHQ* (1985) case, it can no longer be assumed that internal controls are automatically immune from review. This has not meant, however, that the executive has found itself enmeshed in judicial rulings which somehow fail to take proper account of the needs of the administration. Although judicial review of civil service regulation has been a possibility now for more than a decade, the law of the civil service continues to be made, interpreted, and applied, and disputes arising out its application settled, largely within the executive itself. Nor is it the case that where the courts have been called upon to intervene rulings have been necessarily unsympathetic to the needs of the administration: indeed the reverse appears to have been the case (*R v Lord Chancellor's Department, ex parte Nangle* 1992; *Ahmed and others v The United Kingdom* 1998).

3 The dependence of external controls on internal control

Whether or not the executive can influence their shape and development, the controls operated by Parliament and the courts depend unequivocally on the executive's own machinery for their effectiveness. The evidence of the foregoing chapters bears out Grunow's contention that internal controls are heavily influenced by the external demands—for economy, for legality, and, increasingly, for effectiveness as well as responsiveness—to which the executive is subject (Grunow 1986: 647). It is through the system of departmental self-discipline we have described here that such controls are mainly transmitted and diffused within the executive. The corollary is that the effectiveness with which they are internalized may vary from department to department, but this possibility is inherent in a decentralized system of compliance. Defenders of such a system emphasize the relative imprecision of the European Convention as a factor in the United Kingdom's relatively poor record before the European Court on Human Rights, but, as we have suggested, it is difficult to regard the lack of the central oversight that exists in relation to EC law as not also a factor (Chapter 8). Where by contrast central controls are strong, as in finance, the effectiveness with which external controls are internalized appears much greater.

At the same time, as we have seen, the system of internal control is changing. We have suggested that it is public service reforms rather than constitutional developments which are the principal factor behind the strengthening of central control, but constitutional developments have also played an important part. In particular, the expanding network of obligations to which the executive finds itself subject as a result of EU membership has resulted in a more proactive central co-ordination mechanism in the European Secretariat of the Cabinet Office and an increase in the centre's capacity to second-guess departments. Judicial influences have significantly reshaped the internal structure and control the executive's legal function in recent years. Not so long ago, judges were understanding (and often politically experienced), judicial intervention was rare and, if unfortunate, could usually be reversed by legislative means. In consequence government ran its legal services rather like those of a very loosely structured conglomerate in which each subsidiary had its own firm of solicitors who might—or might not—consult head office lawyers when things got difficult. European law, and judicial review, have changed all that. The basic structure remains decentralized, but a long-term effort of central co-ordination of legal advice, and of integrating it into policy-making, was initiated in the nineteen-eighties and still continues (Chapter 9). The incorporation of the European Convention on Human Rights, by making the domestic courts a forum in which the compatibility of executive action with Convention rights can be challenged, further increases its importance. So far that effort has been directed essentially to managing the consequences of changes in the legal environment of executive action. The executive's capacity to shape that environment remains unproven.

Changes in parliamentary, as opposed to judicial, controls have not had the same impact on the internal control function. Instead, it is the changes in its structure and functions which the executive has unilaterally determined for itself that have wrought a basic change in the subject-matter of parliamentary control. As a general rule, moreover, parliamentary relations continue to be left to departments, where there is some evidence that they are slipping down the scale of departmental priorities.

IV THE CONSTITUTIONAL SIGNIFICANCE OF INTERNAL CONTROL

For the citizen, the meaning of the constitution lies in how it affects, and reflects, the way of living a life in the country that it governs. For most people in Britain, the question is still the one that was uppermost in the minds of the framers of the constitution of the United States: how can we organize public power to give ourselves—all of us—the best chance of leading a free and prosperous life? The question may seem far removed from the enquiry conducted in this book into how the executive controls itself and the detailed examination of decision-making structures and procedures entailed in such an enquiry. Let us explain why it is not.

What a constitution does for or against basic interests like freedom, equality or prosperity it does through a combination of the structures it ratifies and the values it represents. 'Democratic' control of the executive through the legislature may be a mixed blessing if the legislature's instincts are more populist or nationalistic than those of the executive, or if the legislature's key institutional values amount to no more than expediency and survival. Judicial independence may be a curse if the courts have less respect for freedom than does the executive. Recent examples from foreign lands could be adduced to illustrate all these possibilities. We do not argue (which is not to say that we think it unarguable) that such inversions of commonplace expectations about guarantees of democracy and the rule of law exist in the United Kingdom. By contrast we would argue strongly that to say that the constitution enshrines a value like equality or openness is meaningless unless one knows what institutions under the constitution subscribe to it, what other values each such institution may need to set against it in decision-making, and how each such institution can secure respect for that balance both by the individuals and bodies of which it is made up, and by other institutions within the state that it seeks to control or influence. Our focus on 'control' has been designed to throw light in particular on this last question, of how things get done, and thus to illuminate what has hitherto been both the darkest part of the constitutional structure yet at the same time the part closest to the decisions which will affect the way the citizen lives. In consequence, and consistently with our argument in Chapter 1, the exploration here has been of the structures, processes, practices, and rules encountered within the executive branch (although always with reference to their connections with other branches), rather than with the values for which they are the vehicle. None the less, the recent changes in those structures, processes, practices, and rules, which we have chronicled in the book and summarized in this last chapter, throw up some points worthy of consideration even by those who do not particularly want to look inside the executive but only to understand evolving relationships between the traditional 'powers' in the state, or whose concern is mainly with the behaviour and impact of the state rather than with its structures.

Three points will be enough by way of conclusion. First, the reforms of public expenditure which began in the nineteen-sixties, and the public service reforms which gathered pace some ten years later, were initiatives conceived within the executive and carried through by the executive with only marginal reference to the other powers in government. They have demonstrated a fact little remarked upon in recent decades, the fact that the executive is a distinct power within the constitution which enjoys the same kind of institutional autonomy as do Parliament and the courts. While the actions of any given government require to be legitimated by parliamentary support for its leaders, and must respect the rule of law, the executive is not thereby rendered a mere mechanical contrivance for the implementation of legislative and judicial decisions. It thinks for itself and has extensive capacities, within the constitution, to translate its thoughts into action. In so doing it may be quite capable of changing the rank ordering of constitutional values. Much recent public service reform, and in particular the Citizen's Charter initiative, now tellingly entitled 'Service First', moves attention away from the special case—the sort of case which once made good material for a parliamentary question—towards normal performance: the sort of standards in administration which all citizens should be able to expect. Whether one sees this as an innately egalitarian rethinking of administration, or as a regrettable slide towards consumerism in provision of public services (as does Jacob 1991) one cannot deny that a process of real constitutional significance is going on. The same can be said of the way in which governments of either political stripe, the one under the technicist rubric of resource accounting, the other through the mystical language of the 'golden rule' (Treasury 1998*b*), have been modifying the basic financial structures of the constitution so as to accommodate a new approach to fiscal policy, one which gives more weight to medium-term results and to world market opinion and much less to responsiveness to (democratic) political pressure (above, pp. 106–7, 165–6). Of course the executive has always had its own ideas, and those ideas have been powerful and have often decided the fate of our country: Treasury and Foreign Office arrogance in the face of the European Community project, and its unfortunate results, have been well documented (Young 1998). What is new, in recent years, is the explicitness with which those ideas have been formulated, and the executive's readiness to present and operate them as its own, without wrapping itself in the gauzy platitudes of parliamentary sovereignty.

Second, looking at the constitution from the worm's eye view of internal control of the executive shows the other constitutional organs in an interestingly new light. So far as Parliament is concerned, it helps us to get behind the clichés like 'elective dictatorship' to see what is actually going on. Our constitution is one which actually demands that the leaders of the executive be able to dominate Parliament; if they could not, they would not be eligible as its leaders. It therefore seems perverse to grumble about the use of party discipline to override parliamentary doubt and dissent. Instead, understanding internal control points our attention to the narrow gateways set by parliamentary powers and procedures and through which it is essential for executive policies to pass if they are to be effective. The positioning of these gateways, and how they are operated, has as we have seen a profound influence on the internal organization of government, helping to sustain two of its key points of central control: over the legislative programme and over annual expenditures. In the long run it is more important for Parliament to ensure that these gateways are not enlarged or circumvented than itself to determine what passes through them, since real control, generally in a sense sympathetic to Parliament's concerns, is exercised centrally within the executive by reference to the gateways (see Chapters 4, 5, and 8). In fact the current situation is full of dangers for Parliament. In the legislative field, an increasing volume of important traffic is circumventing the gateway, often because of the choices as to mode of implementation of EC law offered to departments under the European Communities Act 1972 (above, pp. 266–8). Alternative control mechanisms have been devised within the executive, but do not secure the same opportunities for Parliament. In expenditure, it is the Treasury's gradual withdrawal from its role as keeper of the parliamentary gateway, in favour of other ways of performing its own job, which is making it more difficult for Parliament to exercise overall scrutiny (above, Chapter 5).

As well as suffering this attrition of the bases of its power, Parliament is also witnessing a rather radical challenge to the relevance of its activity. In the last two decades the executive has carried through, without asking Parliament's consent, a public service reform project which, even if it has not destroyed the bases of traditional ministerial responsibility to Parliament, has profoundly modified the meaning of such responsibility, by sweeping away the management and communication structures within the executive on which it relied. As part of this process, the executive has undermined the role of the ordinary MP in redress of grievances by creating a quite new context within which grievances may be framed and redressed, the Citizen's Charter programme. The ordinary MP has no privileged place within this structure; indeed, she has no place at all. There seems to be less and less difference between what an MP might do in relation to a complaint about departmental activity on the one hand, and one about local authority services on the other. These internal moves by government mean that if 'calling government to account' is to continue to be an effective parliamentary function, Parliament, and primarily the House of Commons, must find new methods of work and new points of leverage on the reconstituted executive.

By contrast the position of the courts appears much more positive. As we have seen, the expansion of judicial review, and other legal developments, have created changed conditions for the exercise of the executive's legal function, to which it has had to respond by changes in its internal control system. Developments such as the incorporation of the European Convention on Human Rights, devolution and the continuing ramification of European Union law appear likely to reinforce further the influence of judicial decisions on the substance of state policy, and to restrict executive scope to 'correct' unwelcome judicial decisions through the legislative process. None the less, the judicial function may not be impervious to change resulting from executive-led development of the constitution.

It is possible to imagine the public service reforms we have analysed impinging on the courts in two different ways. The first is under the control of the courts themselves. There seems no reason why the standards of self-regulation that the executive has been so busily developing within the Citizen's Charter programme, the Better Regulation programme, and elsewhere, should not be adopted or assimilated by the courts as elements of our judge-made administrative law. The structures of judicial action, and the principle of judicial independence, suggest, however, that this will happen only if parties regularly argue from these premises in litigation, and it is not yet clear that departments, as the key litigants, yet see advantages in going down this road. A second effect of executive self-regulation, however, may be to change the pattern of litigation coming before the courts, a process that the judiciary cannot itself control. If expectations of effective redress are displaced from judicial review to internal procedures, as they seem to have been displaced in recent decades—in part at least—from parliamentary question and complaint to judicial review, the landscape of public law litigation may again undergo significant change. If these executive programmes really work, then people who want administrative errors rectified will seek and find the private redress they offer. It is people who want to make a point, about the legality of executive action, who will continue to go to the courts. Whatever the rhetoric of administrative law, policy rather than administration may become the primary concern of judicial review.

A final point relates to the general structure and theory of the constitution. The executive has been able to play the leading role in modern constitutional development that we have charted here not because we really have no constitution, nor because we have a constitution in which anything goes, as different theorists we identified in Chapter 1 would have us believe. The executive can do this because basic principles of our constitution recognize it as an autonomous body which can manage its own resources save where Parliament ordains otherwise, and give it co-ordinate power with Parliament in the all-important area of public expenditure. While other rules subject the executive to the control of Parliament and courts in vital areas of its activity, they leave significant scope for the executive to determine how it is going to operate within those constraints. In seeking to describe and analyse the structures and internal control of the executive, we have in effect been showing how those powers and discretions are transformed by the executive itself into stable rules and procedures for the deployment of resources of government. As modes of concretizing and implementing basic principles of our constitution, those rules and procedures are no less a part of our constitutional law than the rules of legislative procedure, or the general rules of administrative jurisdiction.

Bibliography

1 Books and articles

Adam Smith Institute (1979), *An Inspector at the Door: an index of officials who can demand rights of entry* (London: Adam Smith Institute).

Alito, S. *et al.* (1993), 'Symposium: Executive Branch Interpretation of the Law', 15 Cardozo Law Review 21–523.

Allan, T. R. S. (1993), *Law, Liberty and Justice: The Legal Foundations of British Constitutionalism* (Oxford: Clarendon Press).

Allison, John (1997), 'Theoretical and institutional underpinnings of a separate administrative law', in Taggart, M. (ed.), *The Province of Administrative Law* (Oxford: Hart Publishing), 71–89.

Andenas, M. L., Gormley, L., Hadjimatheou, C., and Harden, I. (eds.) (1997), *European Economic and Monetary Union: The Institutional Framework* (London: Kluwer).

Anderson, Sir John (1946), 'The Machinery of Government', 30 Public Administration 147–56.

Andrew (1989): in Section 2 below.

Anon. (1958), 'Nolle Prosequi', Criminal Law Review 573–82.

—— (1978), 'Is there an Attorney-General in the House?' New Statesman (27 October 1978) 532–3.

Archer, Peter (1978), *The Role of the Law Officers* (London: Fabian Society).

Armstrong, John A. (1973), *The European Administrative Elite* (Princeton: Princeton University Press).

Attorney-General (1989), 'Attorney-General's Guidelines, Juries: The Exercise by the Crown of its Right to Stand By', (1989) 88 Criminal Appeal Reports 123–6.

Auditing Practices Board (1996), *Practice Note: The Audit of Central Government Financial Statements in the United Kingdom* (London: Auditing Practices Board).

—— (1997), *Practice Note: The Audit of Regularity in the Central Government Sector: A Consultation Draft* (London: Auditing Practices Board).

—— [n.d.], *Raising the Standards* (London: Auditing Practices Board).

Auster, R., and Silver, M. (1979), *The State as a Firm: Economic Forces in Political Development* (Boston: Martinus Nijhoff).

Ayres, Ian, and Braithwaite, John (1992), *Responsive Regulation: Transcending the Deregulation Debate* (Oxford: Oxford University Press).

Baade, H. W. (1974), 'Mandatory Appropriation of Public Funds: A Comparative Study', 60 Virginia Law Review 393–450, 611–63.

Bagehot, W. (1905), *The English Constitution* (2nd edn., London: Kegan Paul).

Barker, Anthony (1996), 'The impact of judicial review: perspectives from Whitehall and the courts', Public Law 612–21.

Barker, Anthony (1988), 'Political Responsibility for Prison Security—Ministers Escape Again', 76 Public Administration 1–23.

Bawdon, Fiona (1996), 'Power of Attorney', 93 Law Society's Gazette 12.

Baxter, Stephen B. (1957), *The Development of the Treasury 1660–1702* (London: Longmans, Green).

Beer, Samuel (1957), *Treasury Control: The Co-ordination of Financial and Economic Policy in Great Britain* (2nd edn., Oxford: Clarendon Press).

Bellamy, Richard, and Greenaway, John (1995), 'The New Right Conception of Citizenship and the Citizen's Charter', 30 Government and Opposition 469–91.

Bender, Brian (1991), 'Whitehall, Central Government and 1992', 6 Public Policy and Administration 13–20.

—— (1996), 'Co-ordination of European Union policy in Whitehall,' (unpublished paper given at St Antony's College, Oxford).

Benn, Tony (1990), *Against the Tide: Diaries 1973–76* (pbk edn., London: Arrow Books).

Bennion, Francis (1990), *Bennion on Statute Law* (3rd edn., London: Longman).

Binney, J. E. D. (1958), *British Public Finance and Administration 1774–92* (Oxford: Clarendon Press).

Birkinshaw, Patrick (1996), 'Government and the End of its Tether: Matrix Churchill and the Scott Report', 23 Journal of Law and Society 406–26.

Blackstone, Sir William (1783), *Commentaries on the Laws of England*, i (9th edn., London: Strahan, Cadell and Prince).

Blair, Leo (1958), 'The Civil Servant—Political Reality and Legal Myth', Public Law 32–49.

Blom-Cooper, Louis (1984), 'Lawyer and Public Administrators: Separate and Unequal', Public Law 215–35.

Boden, Rebecca, and Froud, Julie (1996), 'Obeying the Rules: Accounting for Regulatory Compliance Costs in the United Kingdom', 21 Accounting, Organizations and Society 529–47.

Bradley, A. W. (1987), '"The Judge Over Your Shoulder"', Public Law 485–8.

—— (1996), 'The Attorney-General and the Scott Report', Public Law 373–83.

—— and Ewing, K. D. (1997), Constitutional and Administrative Law (12th edn., London: Longman).

Brazier, R. (1992), 'The Non-Legal Constitution: Thoughts on Convention, Practice and Principle', 43 Northern Ireland Legal Quarterly 262–87.

Brennan, G., and Hamlin, A. (1996), 'Economical constitutions', 44 Political Studies 605–19.

Breyer, S., and Stewart, R. (1992), *Administrative Law and Regulatory Policy* (3rd edn., Boston: Little Brown).

Bridges, Lord (1966), *The Treasury* (2nd edn., London: Allen and Unwin).

Bryce, James (1901), *Studies in History and Jurisprudence* (2 vols., Oxford: Clarendon Press).

Buchanan, James M. (1987), 'The Constitution of Economic Policy', in Buchanan, James M., *Economics between Predictive Science and Moral Philosophy* (College Station, Texas: Texas A&M University Press), 303–14.

Bunnag, Jayavadh (1992), 'Thailand's Mineral Resources Crisis: A Legal Practitioner's Viewpoint', 10 Journal of Energy and Natural Resources Law 164–71.
Burch, M., and Holliday, I. (1996), *The British Cabinet System* (Englewood Cliffs, NJ: Prentice Hall).
Burns, Sir Terence (1995), *The Management of Economic Policy* (The Eleanor Rathbone Memorial Lecture, University of Manchester, 28 March 1995, mimeo).
Calabresi, Steven, and Rhodes, Kevin (1992), 'The Structural Constitution: Unitary Executive, Plural Judiciary', 105 Harvard Law Review 1153–1216.
Cappelletti, Mauro (1984), 'General Report', in Favoreu, Louis, and Jolowicz, J. A. (eds.), *Le contrôle juridictionnel des lois* (Paris: Economica) 301–14.
Carr, Sir Cecil Thomas (1921), *Delegated Legislation* (Cambridge: Cambridge University Press).
—— (1956), 'Parliamentary Control of Delegated Legislation', Public Law 200–17.
Cassese, Sabino (1996), 'Internal Control of the Executive in Italy', in Daintith, Terence (ed.), *Constitutional Implications of Executive Self-Regulation: Comparative Experience* (London: Institute of Advanced Legal Studies), 11–22.
—— and Franchini, Claudio (eds.) (1996), *I garanti delle regole* (Bologna: Il Mulino).
Castle, Barbara (1980), *The Castle Diaries 1974–76* (London: Weidenfeld and Nicolson).
—— (1993), *Fighting All the Way* (London: Macmillan).
Chapman, Richard (1988), *Ethics in the British Civil Service* (London: Routledge).
Chester, Sir Norman (1981), *The English Administrative System 1780–1870* (Oxford: Clarendon Press).
—— and Willson, F. G. (1968), *The Organisation of British Central Government 1914–64* (2nd edn., London: Allen and Unwin).
Constitution Unit (1996), *Human Rights Legislation* (London: Constitution Unit).
Cooper, Lord, of Culross (1957), *Selected Papers 1922–1954* (Edinburgh: Oliver and Boyd).
Cosgrove, Richard A. (1980), *The Rule of Law: Albert Venn Dicey, Victorian Jurist* (London: Macmillan).
Craig, James T. (1961), 'The Reluctant Executive', Public Law 45–74.
Crick, Michael (1997), *Michael Heseltine: A Biography* (London: Hamish Hamilton).
Crossman, Richard (1972), *Inside View* (London: Jonathan Cape).
—— (1976), *The Diaries of a Cabinet Minister*, ii. *Lord President of the Council and Leader of the House of Commons 1966–68* (London: Hamish Hamilton and Jonathan Cape).
—— (1977), *The Diaries of a Cabinet Minister*, iii. *Secretary of State for Social Services 1968–70* (London: Hamish Hamilton and Jonathan Cape).
Daintith, Terence (1988), 'Law as a Policy Instrument: Comparative Perspectives', in Daintith, T. (ed.), *Law as an Instrument of Economic Policy: Comparative and Critical Approaches* (Berlin: W. de Gruyter), 3–55.
—— (1991), 'Political Programmes and the Content of the Constitution', in Finnie, W., Himsworth, C., and Walker, N. (eds.), *Edinburgh Essays in Public Law* (Edinburgh: Edinburgh University Press), 41–55.

Daintith, Terence (1993), Comment on Lewis: Markets, Regulation and Citizenship, in Brownsword, R. (ed.), *Law and Public Interest* (Archiv für Rechts- und Sozialphilosophie Beiheft 55), 140–6.

—— (1994), 'The Techniques of Government', in Jowell, Jeffrey and Oliver, Dawn (eds.), *The Changing Constitution* (3rd edn., Oxford: Clarendon Press), 209–36.

—— (1997*a*), 'Regulation', in *International Encyclopaedia of Comparative Law*, xvii. *State and Economy* (Buxbaum, Richard and Madl, Ferenc (eds.), ch. 10) (Tübingen: Mohr Siebeck).

—— (1997*b*), *Judicial Review and its Impact on Government* (LSE Public Policy Group Paper, second series No. 10, London: London School of Economics).

Dale, Sir William (1977), *Legislative Drafting: A New Approach* (London: Butterworths).

Dam, Kenneth (1976), *North Sea Oil and Gas: Who Gets What How?* (Chicago: University of Chicago Press).

David, René, and Brierley, John E. C. (1985), *Major Legal Systems in the World Today* (3rd edn., London: Stevens).

Dearlove, John (1989), 'Bringing the Constitution Back In: Political Science and the State', 37 Political Studies 521–39.

Dell, Edmund (1993), 'The Origins of Petroleum Revenue Tax', 7 Contemporary Record 215–52.

Dennis, Sir Alfred H. (1925), 'The Official Lawyer's Place in the Constitution', 46 Law Quarterly Review 378–88.

—— (1926), 'The Legal Departments of the Crown', 4 Public Administration 141–55.

De Smith, S. A., Lord Woolf of Barnes, and Jowell, J. (1995), *Judicial Review of Administrative Action* (5th edn., London: Sweet & Maxwell).

Dicey, Albert Venn (1905), *Law and Public Opinion in England* (London: Macmillan).

—— (1959), *Introduction to the Study of the Law of the Constitution* (10th edn., London: Macmillan).

Dietz, Frederick C. (1928), 'The Receipts and Issues of the Exchequer during the Reigns of James I and Charles I', 13 Smith College Studies in History 117–71.

Drabble, Richard, and Lynes, Tony (1989), 'The Social Fund—Discretion or Control?' Public Law 297–322.

Drewry, Gavin (1981), 'Lawyers in the UK Civil Service', 59 Public Administration 15–46.

—— (1988), 'Lawyers and statutory reform in Victorian government', in MacLeod, R. (ed.), *Government and Expertise: Specialists, administrators and professionals, 1860–1919* (Cambridge: Cambridge University Press), 27–40, 267–9.

—— and Butcher, Tony (1991), *The Civil Service Today* (2nd edn., Oxford: Blackwell).

Dunsire, Andrew (1978), *Implementation in a Bureaucracy; Control in a Bureaucracy* (The Execution Process, Vols. 1 and 2) (Oxford: Martin Robertson).

—— and Hood, Christopher (1989), *Cutback Management in Public Bureaucracies* (Cambridge: Cambridge University Press).

Durell, A. J. V. (1917), *The Principles and Practice of the System of Control over Parliamentary Grants* (Portsmouth: Gieves Publishing).

Dyson, Kenneth (1980), *The State Tradition in Western Europe* (Oxford: Martin Robertson).

Edwards, J. Ll. (1964), *The Law Officers of the Crown* (London: Sweet and Maxwell).

—— (1984), *The Attorney-General, Politics and the Public Interest* (London: Sweet and Maxwell).

Elliott, Michael (1981*a*): in Section 2 below.

—— (1981*b*), *The Role of Law in Central–Local Relations* (London: Social Science Research Council).

—— (1989), 'The control of public expenditure', in Jowell, Jeffrey, and Oliver, Dawn (eds.), *The Changing Constitution* (2nd edn., Oxford: Clarendon Press), 165–91.

Ellis, A. E. (1949), 'The Making and Form of Bills', 2 Parliamentary Affairs 175–84.

Elwyn-Jones, Lord (1983), *In My Time* (London: Weidenfeld and Nicolson).

Engle, George (1983), '"Bills are made to pass as razors are made to sell": practical constraints in the preparation of legislation', 4 Statute Law Review 7–23.

Epitome I, Epitome II: in Section 2 below.

Erskine May, T. (1997), *Parliamentary Practice* (Erskine May's Treatise on The Law, Privileges, Proceedings and Usage of Parliament) (21st edn., by Donald Limon and W. A. McKay, London: Butterworths).

Estreicher, Samuel, and Revesz, Richard L. (1989), 'Nonacquiescence by Federal Administrative Agencies', 98 Yale Law Journal 679–772.

Feldman, D. J. (1988), 'Judicial Review: A Way of Controlling Government?' 66 Public Administration 21–34.

—— and C. J. Miller (1997), 'The Law Officers, Contempt, and Judicial Review', 113 Law Quarterly Review 36–40.

Ferguson, R. B. (1988), 'The Legal Status of Non-Statutory Codes of Practice', Journal of Business Law 12–19.

Ferri, Giorgio Piero (1988), 'Avvocatura dello Stato', in *Enciclopedia Giuridica Treccani* (Rome: Istituto dell'Enciclopedia Italiana).

Floud, Sir Francis L. C. (1923), 'The Sphere of the Specialist in Public Administration', 1 Public Administration 117–26.

Foster, C. D. (1997), 'A Stronger Centre of Government' (pre-print from Constitution Unit, Constitutional Futures, forthcoming).

—— and Plowden, Francis J. (1996), *The State under Stress* (Buckingham: Open University Press).

Fredman, Sandra, and Morris, Gillian (1988), 'Civil Servants: a Contract of Employment', Public Law 58–77.

Freedland, Mark (1995), 'Privatising Carltona: Part II of the Deregulation and Contracting Out Act 1994', Public Law 21–6.

—— (1996), 'The rule against delegation and the Carltona doctrine in an agency context', Public Law 19–30.

Freund, Ernst (1932), *Legislative Regulation: A Study of the Ways and Means of Written Law* (New York: The Commonwealth Fund).

Froud, Julie and Ogus, Anthony (1996), '"Rational" Social Regulation and Compliance Cost Assessment', 74 Public Administration 221–37.

Galanter, Marc (1974), 'Why the "Haves" Come Out Ahead: Speculations on the Limits of Legal Change', 9 Law and Society Review 95–160.

Garcia Llovet, Enrique (1993), 'Autoridades Administrativas Independientes y Estado de Derecho', Rivista di Administracion Publica, No. 131, 61–118.

Goldsworthy, Diana (1994), 'The Citizen's Charter', 9 Public Policy and Administration 59–64.

Graham-Harrison, W. H. (1935), 'An Examination of the Main Criticisms of the Statute Book and of the Possibility of Improvement', Journal of the Society of Public Teachers of Law 9–45.

Grant, Malcolm (1989), 'Central–Local Relations: The Balance of Power', in Jowell, Jeffrey and Oliver, Dawn (eds.), *The Changing Constitution* (2nd edn., Oxford: Clarendon Press), 247–72.

Gray, A., and Jenkins, W. I. (1985), *Administrative Politics in British Government* (Brighton: Wheatsheaf Books).

—— (1986), 'Accountable Management in British Central Government: Some Reflections on the Financial Management Initiative', 2 Financial Accountability and Management 171–86.

—— (with A. Flynn and B. Rutherford) (1991), 'The Management of Change in Whitehall: The Experience of the FMI', 69 Public Administration 41–59.

Greaves, H. R. G. (1956), 'The Structure of the Civil Service', in Robson, W. A. (ed.), *The Civil Service in Britain and France* (London: The Hogarth Press), 98–108.

Greenleaf, W. H. (1987), *The British Political Tradition*, iii. *A Much Governed Nation*, Part 2 (London: Methuen).

Gregory, Roy, and Hutchesson, Peter (1975), *The Parliamentary Ombudsman: A Study in the Control of Administrative Action* (London: Allen and Unwin).

Griffith, J. A. G. (1963), 'Comment', Public Law 401–2.

—— (1979), 'The Political Constitution', 42 Modern Law Review 1–21.

—— and Ryle, Michael (1989), *Parliament: Functions, Practice and Procedures* (London: Sweet & Maxwell).

—— and Street, H. (1952), *Principles of Administrative Law* (London: Pitman).

Grunow, Dieter (1986) 'Internal Control in Public Administration', in Kaufmann, F-X, *Guidance, Control and Evaluation in the Public Sector* (Berlin, New York: W. de Gruyter), 645–62.

Haldane, Viscount, of Cloan (1923), 'An Organised Civil Service', 1 The Journal of Public Administration 6–16.

Halliburton, Rachel (1997), 'DPP must seek counsel's advice', Law Society's Gazette, 30 July 1997, 4.

Hamilton, Sir H. P. (1951), 'Sir Warren Fisher and the Public Service', 29 Public Administration 3–38.

Hammond, A. H. (1998), 'Judicial review: the continuing interplay between law and policy', Public Law 34–43.

Hansard Society (1992), *Making the Law* (Report of the Hansard Society Commission on the Legislative Process) (London: Hansard Society).

Harden, I. (1991), 'Review Article: The Constitution and Its Discontents', 21 British Journal of Political Science 489–510.

—— and Lewis, Norman (1986), *The Noble Lie* (London: Hutchinson).

—— White, F., and Hollingsworth, K. (1996), 'Value for Money and Administrative Law', Public Law 661–81.

Hardie, Lord (1998), 'The Lockerbie Trial', 1998 Scots Law Times (News) 9–14.

Harlow, Carol (1976), 'Administrative Reaction to Judicial Review', Public Law 116–33.

—— (1978), 'Ombudsmen in Search of a Role', 41 Modern Law Review 446–54.

—— (1980), '"Public" Law and "Private" Law: Definition without Distinction', 43 Modern Law Review 241–65.

—— and Rawlings, R. (1992), *Pressure through Law* (London: Routledge).

—— (1997), *Law and Administration* (2nd edn., London: Butterworths).

Heald, D. (1991), 'The Political Implications of Redefining Public Expenditure in the United Kingdom', 39 Political Studies 75–99.

—— (1995), 'Steering Public Expenditure with Defective Maps', 73 Public Administration 213–40.

Heath, Sir Thomas (1927), *The Treasury* (London: Putnam).

Heclo, H., and Wildavsky, A. (1973), *The Private Government of Public Money* (London: Macmillan).

Henderson, Edith (1963), *Foundations of English Administrative Law: Certiorari and Mandamus in the Seventeenth Century* (Cambridge, Mass.: Harvard University Press).

Hennessy, Peter (1990), *Whitehall* (London: Fontana Press).

—— (1999), *The Blair Centre: A Question of Command and Control?* (London: Public Management Foundation).

Hogg, Peter W. (1989), *Liability of the Crown* (Toronto: The Carswell Company Ltd.).

Hogg, Sarah, and Hill, Jonathan (1996), *Too Close to Call* (London: Warner Books).

Holroyd, J. H. (1989), 'United Kingdom Government Structure and the Implementation of European Community Policy' (unpublished paper presented at the W. G. Hart Workshop, Institute of Advanced Legal Studies, London, 5 July 1989).

Hood, C. C. (1983), *The Tools of Government* (London: Macmillan).

—— (1995) 'Emerging Issues in Public Administration', 73 Public Administration 165–83.

—— and Wright, M. (1981), *Big Government in Hard Times* (Oxford: Martin Robertson).

Howe, Sir Geoffrey (1994), *Conflict of Loyalty* (London: Macmillan).

Howse, R., Prichard, J. R. S., and Trebilcock, Michael J. (1990), 'Smaller or smarter government?' 40 University of Toronto Law Journal 498–541.

Hunt, Lord, of Tanworth (1982), 'Access to a Previous Government's Papers', Public Law 514–18.

—— (1987), 'The United Kingdom', in Plowden, William (ed.), *Advising the Rulers* (Oxford: Basil Blackwell), 66–70.

Ilbert, Sir Courtenay (1901) *Legislative Methods and Forms* (Oxford: Clarendon Press).

Institute for Public Policy Research (1993), *A Written Constitution for the United Kingdom* (2nd edn., London: Mansell).

Irvine, Lord, of Lairg, QC (1996), 'Judges and Decision-Makers: The Theory and Practice of Wednesbury Review', Public Law 59–78.

Italiener, Alexander (1997), 'The Excessive Deficit Procedure: A Legal Description', in Andenas, M. L., Gormley, L., Hadjimatheou, C., and Harden, I. (eds.), *European Economic and Monetary Union: The Institutional Framework* (London: Kluwer), 191–237.

Jacob, Joseph M. (1991), 'Doctors go to Hospital', Public Law 255–81.

—— (1992), 'The Debates behind an Act: Crown Proceedings Reform 1920–1947', Public Law 452–84.

—— (1993), 'From Privileged Crown to Interested Public', Public Law 121–50.

—— (1996), *The Republican Crown: Lawyers and the Making of the State in Twentieth Century Britain* (Aldershot: Dartmouth).

James, Sir Henry (1888): in Section 2 below.

James, Simon (1994), 'The Cabinet System since 1945: Fragmentation and Integration', 47 Parliamentary Affairs 613–29.

—— (1996), 'The Political and Administrative Consequences of Judicial Review', 74 Public Administration 613–37.

Jarvad, Ib Martin (1996), 'Executive Self-Regulation in Denmark', in Daintith, T. (ed.), *Constitutional Implications of Executive Self-Regulation: Comparative Experience* (London: Institute of Advanced Legal Studies), 23–39.

Jennings, Sir Ivor (1959*a*), *Cabinet Government* (3rd edn., Cambridge: Cambridge University Press).

—— (1959*b*), The Law and the Constitution (5th edn., London: University of London Press).

Jessel, Sir George (1877): in Section 2 below.

Johnson, Nevil (1977), *In Search of the Constitution: Reflections on State and Society in Britain* (Oxford: Pergamon Press).

Joint Consultative Committee on Constitutional Reform (1997), *Report* (London: The Labour Party).

Jones, Sir Elwyn (1969), 'The Office of Attorney-General', 27 Cambridge Law Journal 43–53.

Jones, G. W. (1987), 'The United Kingdom', in Plowden, William (ed.), *Advising the Rulers* (Oxford: Basil Blackwell), 36–66.

—— (1992), 'Cabinet Government since Bagehot', in Blackburn, Robert (ed.), *Constitutional Studies: Contemporary Issues and Controversies* (London: Mansell), 14–31.

Jones, George, and Burnham, June (1995), 'The Environment Agencies', in Giddings, Phillip (ed.), *Parliamentary Accountability: A Study of Parliament and Executive Agencies* (London: Macmillan), 155–90.

JUSTICE-All Souls (1988), *Administrative Justice: Some Necessary Reforms* (Report of the Committee of the JUSTICE-All Souls Review of Administrative Law in the United Kingdom, Chairman: Patrick Neill QC) (Oxford: Clarendon Press).

Kantorowicz, E. H. (1957), *The King's Two Bodies: A Study in Mediaeval Political Theology* (Princeton: Princeton University Press).

Keith, A. B. (1938), *The British Cabinet System* (London: Stevens).

Kelly, Jim (1998*a*), 'New rules "revive the threat of creative accounting"', Financial Times, 30 April 1998, 13.

Kelly, Jim (1998*b*), 'Watchdog defends draft rules on PFI accounting', Financial Times, 15 June 1998, 10.

Kent, Sir Harold S. (1979), *In on the Act: Memoirs of a Lawmaker* (London: Macmillan).

Kernaghan, Kenneth (1975), *Ethical Conduct: Guidelines for Government Employees* (Toronto: Institute of Public Administration).

—— (1993), 'Promoting Public Service Ethics: The Codification Option', in Chapman, Richard (ed.), *Ethics in Public Service* (Edinburgh: Edinburgh University Press), 15–29.

Kerry, Sir Michael (1983), 'Administrative Law and the Administrator', 38 Management in Government 168–77.

—— (1986), 'Administrative Law and Judicial Review—The Practical Effects of Developments over the Last 25 Years on Administration in Central Government', 64 Public Administration 163–72.

Kessler, Marie-Christine (1968), *Le Conseil d'État* (Paris: Armand Colin).

Kinley, David (1993), *The European Convention on Human Rights: Compliance without Incorporation* (Aldershot: Dartmouth).

Lawson, Nigel (1993), *The View from No. 11: Memoirs of a Tory Radical* (London: Corgi).

Lee, J. M. (1977), *Reviewing the Machinery of Government 1942–52: An Essay on the Anderson Committee and its Successor* (mimeo).

—— (1986), 'Cabinet Procedure', 64 Public Administration 347–9.

Lessig, Lawrence, and Sunstein, Cass (1994), 'The President and the Administration', 94 Columbia Law Review 1–123.

Le Sueur, Andrew (1996), 'The Judicial Review Debate: From Partnership to Friction', 31 Government and Opposition 8–26.

—— and Snyder, Francis (1992), 'La Incidencia del Derecho de la Comunidad Europea en la Organizacion Administrativa del Reino Unido,' in Barnés Vázquez, J. (ed.), *La Comunidad Europea, la Instancia Regional y la Organzacion Administrative de los Estados Membros* (Madrid: Civitas), 365–505.

Lidstone, K. W. *et al.* (1980): in Section 2 below.

Lilley, Peter (1996): in Section 2 below.

Loughlin, Martin (1992), *Public Law and Political Theory* (Oxford: Clarendon Press).

—— (1994), 'The Restructuring of Central–Local Government Relations', in Jowell, Jeffrey and Oliver, Dawn (eds.), *The Changing Constitution* (3rd edn., Oxford: Clarendon Press), 261–93.

Lukes, Steven (1974), *Power: A Radical View* (London: Macmillan).

McAuslan, Patrick (1983), 'Administrative law, collective consumption, and judicial policy', 46 Modern Law Review 1–20.

—— (1988), 'Public law and public choice', 51 Modern Law Review 681–705.

—— and McEldowney, John F. (1985), 'Legitimacy and the constitution: the dissonance between theory and practice', in McAuslan, Patrick, and McEldowney, John F. (eds.), *Law, Legitimacy and the Constitution* (London: Sweet and Maxwell), 1–38.

McBarnet, Doreen, and Whelan, Christopher (1991), 'The Elusive Spirit of the

Law: Formalism and the Struggle for Legal Control', 54 Modern Law Review 848–73.

McGinnis, John O. (1993*a*), 'Executive Branch Interpretation of the Law: Introduction', 15 Cardozo Law Review 21–9.

—— (1993*b*), 'Models of the Opinion Function of the Attorney-General: A Normative, Descriptive, and Historical Prolegomenon', 15 Cardozo Law Review 436.

—— (1997), 'Comments', in Daintith, T. (ed.), *Constitutional Implications of Executive Self-Regulation: The New Administrative Law* (London: Institute of Advanced Legal Studies), 34–8.

McGuire, M. C., and Olsen, Mancur (1996), 'The economics of autocracy and majority rule: the invisible hand and the use of force', 34 Journal of Economic Literature 72–96.

Mackenzie, W. J. M., and Grove, J. W. (1957), *Central Administration in Britain* (London: Longmans).

Mackintosh, J. P. (1962), *The British Cabinet* (London: Stevens).

MacLeod, I., Hendry, I. D., and Byatt, Stephen (1996), *The External Relations of the European Communities* (Oxford: Clarendon Press).

McNair, A. (ed.) (1956), *International Law Opinions*, 3 vols. (Cambridge: Cambridge University Press).

Maitland, F. W. (1900), 'The Corporation Sole', 16 Law Quarterly Review 335–54, reprinted in Maitland (1936).

—— (1901), 'The Crown as Corporation', 17 Law Quarterly Review 131–46, reprinted in Maitland (1936).

—— (1908) *The Constitutional History of England* (Cambridge: Cambridge University Press).

—— (1936), *Selected Essays* (ed. Hazeltine, H., Lapsley, G., and Winfield, P.) (London: Cambridge University Press).

Maranville, D. (1986), 'Non-Acquiescence: Outlaw Agencies, Imperial Courts, and the Perils of Pluralism', 39 Vanderbilt Law Review 471–538.

Marsh, D. (1991), 'Privatization under Mrs. Thatcher: A Review of the Literature,' 69 Public Administration 459–80.

Marshall, Geoffrey (1971), *Constitutional Theory* (Oxford: Clarendon Press).

Mashaw, Jerry L. (1996), 'Reinventing Government and Regulatory Reform: Studies in the Neglect and Abuse of Administrative Law', 57 University of Pittsburg Law Review, 405–22.

Massey, Andrew (1995): in Section 2 below.

Mather, Graham (1994), *Better Legislation* (London: European Policy Forum).

Mayhew, Patrick (1990), 'Can Legislation Ever be Simple, Clear, and Certain?', 11 Statute Law Review 1–10.

Metcalfe, Les, and Richards, Sue (1990), *Improving Public Management* (2nd edn., London: European Institute of Public Management/Sage).

Michael, Douglas C. (1996), 'Co-operative Implementation of Federal Regulations', 13 Yale Journal on Regulation 535–601.

Miers, David R., and Page, Alan C. (1990), *Legislation* (2nd edn., London: Sweet and Maxwell).

Mitchell, J. D. B. (1964), *Constitutional Law* (Edinburgh: W. Green and Son).
—— (1965), 'The Causes and Effects of the Absence of a System of Public Law in the United Kingdom', Public Law 95–118.
—— (1971), 'British Law and British Membership', 6 Europarecht 97–118.
Montemartini, G. (1900), 'The fundamental principles of a pure theory of public finance', reprinted in Musgrave, R., and Peacock, A. (eds.), *Classics in the Theory of Public Finance* (London: Macmillan 1967), 137–51.
Montesquieu, Baron Charles (1989 [1748]), *De l'Esprit des Lois* (trans. and ed. Conlon, Miller and Stone) (Cambridge: Cambridge University Press).
Morris, Philip (1996), 'The Revenue Adjudicator—The First Two Years', Public Law 309–22.
Morrison, Lord (1964), *Government and Parliament: A Survey from the Inside* (3rd edn., London: Oxford University Press).
Mount, Ferdinand (1992), *The British Constitution Now: Recovery or Decline?* (London: Heinemann).
Mueller, Dennis C. (1989), *Public Choice* (Cambridge: Cambridge University Press).
Normanton, E. L. (1966), *The Accountability and Audit of Governments* (Manchester: Manchester University Press).
North, D. C. (1981), *Structure and Change in Economic History* (New York: Norton).
Northcote–Trevelyan (1854): in Section 2 below.
—— and Weingast, Barry (1989), 'The evolution of institutions governing public choice in seventeenth century England', 49 Journal of Economic History 803–22.
O'Connor, J. (1973), *The Fiscal Crisis of the State* (New York: St. Martin's Press).
O'Halpin, E. (1989), *Head of Civil Service: A Study of Sir Warren Fisher* (London: Routledge).
Oliver, Dawn (1995), 'Standards of Conduct in Public Life—what standards?' Public Law 497–503.
Orlando, V. E. (1940), 'Sul contenuto giuridico della legge del bilancio', in Orlando, V. E., *Diritto Pubblico Generale: Scritti Vari* (Milan: Giuffré).
Padmore, Sir Thomas (1956), 'Civil Service Establishments and the Treasury', in Robson, W. A. (ed.), *The Civil Service in Britain and France* (London: The Hogarth Press), 124–38.
Paleologo, Giovanni (1998), *I Consigli di Stato di Francia e d'Italia* (Milan: Giuffré).
Parker, George (1997), 'Harman sought to avoid payout', Financial Times, 31 December 1997, 5.
Parris, Henry (1969), *Constitutional Bureaucracy: The Development of British Central Administration since the Eighteenth Century* (London: Allen and Unwin).
Parry, Clive (ed.) (1970–73), *Law Officers' opinions to the Foreign Office 1793–1860* (97 vols.) (Farnborough: Gregg).
—— (1976), *Great Britain Law Officers' opinions* (microfilm) (Dobbs Ferry, NY: Transmedia).
Paterson, A. A., and Bates, T. St.J. N. (1993), *The Legal System of Scotland* (Edinburgh: W. Green/Sweet & Maxwell).
Pellew, Jill (1988), 'Law and order: expertise and the Victorian Home Office', in

MacLeod, R. (ed.), *Government and Expertise: Specialists, administrators and professionals, 1860–1919* (Cambridge: Cambridge University Press), 59–72, 272–5.

Pendlebury, Maurice, Jones, Rowan, and Karbhari, Yusuf (1994), 'Developments in the Accountability and Financial Reporting Practices of Executive Agencies', 10 Financial Accountability and Management 33–46.

Pliatzky, L. (1982), *Getting and Spending: Public Expenditure, Employment and Inflation* (Oxford: Blackwell).

Pollitt, C. (1976), 'The Public Expenditure Survey 1961–72', 54 Public Administration 127–42.

—— (1984), *Manipulating the Machine: Changing the Pattern of Ministerial Departments, 1960–83* (London: George Allen & Unwin).

—— (1994) 'The Citizen's Charter: A Preliminary Analysis', Public Money and Management 9–14.

Prosser, Tony (1983), *Test Cases for the Poor* (London: Child Poverty Action Group).

—— (1997), *Law and the Regulators* (Oxford: Clarendon Press).

Rawlings, H. F. (1986), 'Judicial Review and the "Control of Government"', 64 Public Administration 135–45.

Rawlings, Richard (1994), 'Legal Politics: The United Kingdom and Ratification of the Treaty on European Union,' Public Law 254–78, 367–91.

Rawlinson, Sir Peter (1977), 'A Vital Link in the Machinery of Justice', 74 Guardian Gazette 798–9.

—— (1989), *A Price too High* (London: Weidenfeld and Nicolson).

Renton, Lord (1990), 'Current Drafting Practices and Problems in the United Kingdom', 11 Statute Law Review 11–17.

Richards, David (1996), 'Appointments to the Highest-Grades in the Civil Service—Drawing the Curtain Open', 74 Public Administration 657–77.

Richardson, Genevra, and Sunkin, Maurice (1996), 'Judicial Review: Questions of Impact', Public Law 79–103.

Ridley, F. F. (1988), 'There is no British Constitution: A Dangerous Case of the Emperor's Clothes', 41 Parliamentary Affairs 340–61.

Rippon, Lord (1989), 'Henry VIII Clauses', 10 Statute Law Review 205–7.

—— (1990), 'Constitutional Anarchy', 11 Statute Law Review 184–8.

Robson, William A. (1950), 'Administrative Law in England, 1919–48', in Campion, Lord *et al.*, *British Government Since 1918* (London: Allen and Unwin), 85–156.

Rose, Richard (1982), *The Role of Laws in Comparative Perspective* (Glasgow: Centre for the Study of Public Policy, University of Strathclyde).

Roseveare, Henry (1969), *The Treasury: The Evolution of a British Institution* (London: Allen Lane The Penguin Press).

—— (1973), *The Treasury 1660–1870* (London: Allen and Unwin).

Ryle, Michael (1994), 'Pre-legislative scrutiny: a prophylactic approach to protection of human rights', Public Law 192–7.

Sassen, Saskia (1996), *Losing Control? Sovereignty in an Age of Globalization* (New York: Columbia University Press).

Saunier, Philippe (1993), 'Principes fondamentaux de comptabilité publique', in *Jurisclasseur Administratif* (Paris: Editions du Jurisclasseur), fascicule 113.

Schwartz, Bernard, and Wade, H. W. R. (1972), *Legal Control of Government: Administrative Law in Britain and the United States* (Oxford: Clarendon Press).

Schwarze, Juergen (1992), *European Administrative Law* (London: Sweet & Maxwell; Luxembourg: Office for Official Publications of the European Communities).

Scott, Sir Richard (1996): in Section 2 below.

Sedley, Stephen (1994), 'The Sound of Silence: Constitutional Law without a Constitution', 110 Law Quarterly Review 270–91.

Seldon, Anthony (1997), *Major: A Political Life* (London: Weidenfeld and Nicolson).

Self, Peter (1977), *Administrative Theories and Politics* (2nd edn., London: Allen and Unwin).

Selznick, Philip (1968), 'The Sociology of Law', in Sills, D. (ed.), *International Encyclopaedia of the Social Sciences*, ix (New York: Macmillan and the Free Press), 50–9.

Shawcross, Sir Hartley (1953), *The Office of the Attorney-General* (London: The Law Society).

Siedentop, L. (1990), 'Thatcherism and the Constitution', Times Literary Supplement (26 January–1 February 1990), 88–9.

Silkin, S. C. (1978), 'The functions and position of the Attorney-General in the United Kingdom', 59 The Parliamentarian 149–58.

—— (1979), 'The Attorney-General's Dilemma', 2 Malayan Law Journal xxvi–xxx.

—— (1984), 'The legal machinery of government', Public Law 179–86.

Simcock, A. J. C. (1992), 'One and Many—The Office of Secretary of State', 70 Public Administration 535–53.

Sisson, Charles H. (1966), *The Spirit of British Administration and Some European Comparisons* (2nd edn., London: Faber).

Smellie, Kingsley Bryce (1937), *A Hundred Years of English Government* (London: Duckworth).

Stair Memorial Encyclopaedia, xviii (1993), title 'Property' (Edinburgh: W. Green and Sons).

Stephen, Sir James (1854): in Section 2 below.

Sterett, Susan (1997), *Creating Constitutionalism? The Politics of Legal Expertise and Administrative Law in England and Wales* (Ann Arbor: Michigan University Press).

Stevens, Robert (1993), *The Independence of the Judiciary: The View from the Lord Chancellor's Office* (Oxford: Clarendon Press).

—— (1997), 'Judges, Politics, Politicians and the Confusing Role of the Judiciary', in Keith Hawkins (ed.), *The Human Face of Law: Essays in Honour of Donald Harris* (Oxford: Clarendon Press), 245–89.

Strange, Susan (1996), *The Retreat of the State: The Diffusion of Power in the World Economy* (Cambridge: Cambridge University Press).

Sunkin, M., Bridges, L. and Mészáros, G. (1993), *Judicial Review in Perspective* (London: Public Law Project).

Sunkin, M., Bridges, L., Mészáros, G. and Le Sueur, A. P. (1991), 'Can Government Control Judicial Review?' Current Legal Problems 161–83.

Telser, Lester (1980), 'A Theory of Self-Enforcing Agreements', 53 Journal of Business 27–40.

Teubner, Gunther (1992), 'Social Order from Legislative Noise? Autopoietic Closure as a Problem for Legal Regulation', in Teubner, Gunther, and Febbrajo, Alberto (eds.), *State, Law and Economy as Autopoietic Systems: Regulation and Autonomy in a New Perspective* (European Yearbook of the Sociology of Law, double issue 1991–92, Milan: Giuffrè), 609–49.

Thain, Colin, and Wright, Maurice (1995), *The Treasury and Whitehall: The Planning and Control of Public Expenditure, 1976–1993* (Oxford: Clarendon Press).

Thomas, R. (1978), *The British Philosophy of Administration* (London: Longman).

Thornton, G. C. (1996), *Legislative Drafting* (4th edn., London: Butterworths).

Thring, Henry (1902), *Practical Legislation* (London: John Murray).

Timmins, Nicholas (1998), 'Brown accused of "fiddling the books" in tax credit row', Financial Times, 6 July 1998, 1.

Todd, A. (1887), *On Parliamentary Government in England* (2nd edn., London: Longmans, Green and Co.).

Torrance, J. R. (1968), 'Sir George Harrison and the growth of bureaucracy in the early nineteenth century', 83 English Historical Review 52–88.

Travis, Alan (1996), 'Lawyer in jail release row named', The Guardian, 31 March 1996.

Trosa, Sylvie (1994): in Section 2 below.

Turpin, Colin (1972), *Government Contracts* (Harmondsworth: Penguin Books).

Vile, M. J. C. (1967), *Constitutionalism and the Separation of Powers* (Oxford: Clarendon Press).

Wade, H. W. R. (1985), 'Procedure and Prerogative in Public Law', 101 Law Quarterly Review 180–99.

Wade, Sir William and Forsyth, Christopher (1994), *Administrative Law* (7th edn., Oxford: Clarendon Press).

Wakeham, Lord (1994), 'Cabinet Government', 8 Contemporary Record 473–83.

Walkland, S. A. (1979), 'Government Legislation in the House of Commons', in Walkland, S. A. (ed.), *The House of Commons in the Twentieth Century* (Oxford: Clarendon Press), 247–91.

Wheare, Sir Kenneth (1953), *The Statute of Westminster and Dominion Status* (5th edn., London: Oxford University Press).

White, Fidelma, Harden, Ian, and Donnelly, Katy (1994), 'Audit, accounting officers and accountability: the Pergau Dam affair', Public Law 526–34.

—— and Hollingsworth, Kathryn (1997), 'Resource accounting and budgeting: constitutional implications', Public Law 437–45.

Wicksell, Knut (1967), 'A New Principle of Just Taxation', in Musgrave, R. A. and Peacock, A. T., *Classics in the Theory of Public Finance* (London: Macmillan), 72–118.

Wiener, Celine (1996), 'Internal Control of the Executive in France', in Daintith, T. (ed.), *Constitutional Implications of Executive Self-Regulation: Comparative Experience* (London: Institute of Advanced Legal Studies), 43–56.

Willetts, David (1996), 'Public Service Reform' (speech delivered at Civil Service College 17 July).
—— (1997), 'The perils of political power', Financial Times, 30 January 1997, 18.
Williams, Tom, and Goriely, Tamara (1994), 'Big idea—any effect?', 144 New Law Journal 1164–5.
Willson, F. M. G. (1955), 'Ministries and Boards: Some Aspects of Administrative development Since 1832', 33 Public Administration 43–58.
Wilson, Harold (1976), *The Governance of Britain* (London: Weidenfeld and Nicolson, and Michael Joseph).
—— (1979), *Final Term: The Labour Government 1974–76* (London: Weidenfeld and Nicolson, and Michael Joseph).
Wilson, J. Q., and Rachal, P. (1977), 'Can government regulate itself?' 46 Public Interest 3–14.
Wilson, S. S. (1975), *The Cabinet Office to 1945* (London: HMSO).
Winetrobe, Barry (1995) 'Next Steps and Parliamentary Scrutiny', in Giddings, Phillip (ed.), *Parliamentary Accountability: A Study of Parliament and Executive Agencies* (London: Macmillan), 33–51.
Wolf-Phillips, Leslie (1972), *Comparative Constitutions* (London: Macmillan).
Woodhouse, Diana (1993), 'Ministerial Responsibility: the Abdication of Responsibility through the Receipt of Legal Advice', Public Law 412–19.
—— (1996), 'Politicians and the Judges: A Conflict of Interest', 49 Parliamentary Affairs 423–40.
Woods, Sir John (1956), 'Treasury Control', in Robson, W. A. (ed.), *The Civil Service in Britain and France* (London: The Hogarth Press), 109–23.
Woolf, The Rt. Hon. Sir Harry (1990), *Protection of the Public—The New Challenge* (London: Sweet & Maxwell).
Wright, Maurice (1972), 'Treasury Control 1854–1914', in Sutherland, G. (ed.), *Studies in the Growth of Nineteenth-Century Government* (London: Routledge).
—— (1969), *Treasury Control of the Civil Service 1854–1874* (Oxford: Clarendon Press).
Young, Hugo (1998), *This Blessed Plot: Britain and Europe from Churchill to Blair* (London: Macmillan).
Young, Lord, of Graffham (1991), *The Enterprise Years* (London: Headline).
Zellick, Graham (1985), 'Government Beyond Law', Public Law 283–308.

2 Parliamentary and other official papers

Note: all Parliamentary papers are published by Her Majesty's Stationery Office (since 1996, The Stationery Office), London and are abbreviated in this list as follows:

HC House of Commons Paper
HL House of Lords Paper
C., Cd., Cmd., Cmnd., Cm. Command Paper (each series numbered 1–9999)

Advisory Committee on Business Appointments (1998), *First Report 1996–1998* (London: Cabinet Office).

Andrew, Sir Robert (1989), *Review of Government Legal Services* (London: Cabinet Office).

Attorney-General (1958), *Memorandum by the Attorney-General to the House of Commons Select Committee on Obscene Publications* (1958) HC 123–I, App. 1.

—— (1971), *Legal Obligations of HM Government arising out of the Simonstown Agreements*, Cmnd. 4589.

—— (1989), in Section 1 above.

—— (1991), *Use of the Private Sector for Government Legal Work: Guidance* (mimeo).

Attorney-General's Chambers (1996*a*), *The Role of the Attorney-General* (press release, mimeo).

—— (1996*b*), *The Attorney-General and Matrix Churchill* (press release, mimeo).

Auditing Practices Board (1996), in Section 1 above.

—— (1997), in Section 1 above.

—— [n.d.], in Section 1 above.

Better Regulation Task Force (1998*a*), *Principles of Good Regulation* (London: Better Regulation Task Force).

—— (1998*b*), *Annual Report 1997/98* (London: Better Regulation Task Force).

Better Regulation Unit (1998), *Guide to Good Regulation* (London: Better Regulation Unit).

Board of Enquiry (1928), *Report of the Board of Enquiry appointed by the Prime Minister to investigate certain Statements affecting Civil Servants*, Cmd. 3037.

—— (1936), *Report of the Board of Enquiry appointed by the Prime Minister to investigate certain discussions engaged in by the Permanent Secretary to the Air Ministry*, Cmd. 5254.

Cabinet Office (1970), *The Reorganisation of Central Government*, Cmnd. 4506.

—— (1982), *Efficiency and Effectiveness in the Civil Service. Government Observations on the Third Report from the Treasury and Civil Service Committee, Session 1981–82, HC 236*, Cmnd. 8616.

—— (1986), *Civil Servants and Ministers: Duties and Responsibilities. Government Response to the Seventh Report from the Treasury and Civil Service Committee, Session 1985–86, HC 92*, Cmnd. 9841.

—— (1987), *Statutory Instrument Practice* (2nd edn., London: HMSO).

—— (1988), *Service to the Public* (London: HMSO).

—— (1991), *The Citizen's Charter: Raising the Standard*, Cm. 1599.

—— (1993), *Open Government*, Cm. 2290.

—— (1994*a*), *The Civil Service: Continuity and Change*, Cm. 2627.

—— (1994*b*), *The Citizen's Charter. Second Report: 1994*, Cm. 2540.

—— (1994*c*), *Responsibilities for Recruitment to the Civil Service* (London: Cabinet Office).

—— (1994*d*), *Code of Practice on Access to Government Information* (London: Cabinet Office).

—— (1995*a*), *The Civil Service: Taking Forward Continuity and Change*, Cm. 2748.

—— (1995*b*), *The Ombudsman in Your Files* (London: HMSO).

—— (1995*c*), *The Government's Response to the First Report from the Committee on Standards in Public Life*, Cm. 2931.

—— (1996*a*), *The Citizen's Charter—Five Years On*, Cm. 3370.

Cabinet Office (1996*b*), *Second Annual Report on the Operation of the Code of Practice on Access to Government Information* (London: Cabinet Office).
—— (1996*c*), *Civil Service Code* (London: Cabinet Office).
—— (1997*a*), *The Governance of Public Bodies: A Progress Report*, Cm. 3557.
—— (1997*b*), *Code of Practice on Access to Government Information* (2nd edn., London: Cabinet Office).
—— (1997*c*), *Code of Practice on Access to Government Information: Guidance on Interpretation* (2nd edn., London: Cabinet Office).
—— (1997*d*), *Ministerial Code: A code of conduct and guidance on procedures for Ministers* (London: Cabinet Office).
—— (1997*e*), *Cabinet Committee Business: A Guide for Departments* (London: Cabinet Office).
—— (1998*a*), *The Government's Expenditure Plans 1998–99: Cabinet Office, Privy Council Office and Parliament*, Cm. 3290.
—— (1998*b*), *Service First: the new charter programme* (London: Cabinet Office).
—— (1998*c*), *Code of Practice on Access to Government Information: 1997 Report* (London: Cabinet Office).
Cabinet Office (OPS) (1996*a*), *A Checklist of Processes for Senior Appointments* (London: Cabinet Office (OPS)).
—— (1996*b*), *Guidance on Guidance* (London: Machinery of Government and Standards Group).
—— (1996*c*), *Next Steps Agencies in Government Review*, Cm. 3164.
—— (1997*a*), *Next Steps Agencies in Government Review 1996*, Cm. 3579.
—— (1997*b*), *Public Bodies 1997* (London: HMSO).
—— (1997*c*), *Opening up Quangos: A Consultation Paper* (London: Cabinet Office).
—— (1997*d*), *The Citizen's Charter: A Consultation Exercise* (London: Cabinet Office).
—— (1998*a*), *Next Steps Report 1997*, Cm. 3889.
—— (1998*b*), *Quangos: Opening the Doors* (London: Cabinet Office).
—— (1998*c*), *Quangos: Opening up Public Appointments* (London: Cabinet Office).
Cabinet Office and Treasury (1992), *Non-Departmental Public Bodies: A Guide for Departments* (London: HMSO).
Chancellor of the Duchy of Lancaster (1997), *Your Right to Know: Freedom of Information*, Cm. 3818.
Citizen's Charter Unit (1992), *Charters, Charter Standards, Explanatory Leaflets and Consultation Papers* (London: Citizen's Charter Unit).
—— (1996), *Asking Your Users . . . How to improve services through consulting your consumers* (London: Citizen's Charter Unit).
—— (1997), *Charter Checklist* (London: Citizen's Charter Unit).
Civil Service Appeal Board (1997), *Annual Report 1996–97* (London: Civil Service Appeal Board).
Civil Service Commissioners (1995), *Annual Report 1994–95* (London: Office of the Civil Service Commissioners).
—— (1996*a*), *Annual Report 1995–96* (London: Office of the Civil Service Commissioners).

—— (1996*b*), *Guidance on Civil Service Commissioners' Recruitment to Senior Posts* (2nd edn., London: Office of the Civil Service Commissioners).
Civil Service Commissioners (1997), *Annual Report 1996–97* (London: Office of the Civil Service Commissioners).
—— (1998) *Annual Report 1997–98* (London: Office of the Civil Service Commissioners).
Civil Service Department (1979), *Legal Entitlements and Administrative Practices: a report by officials* (London: HMSO).
—— (1980), *Memorandum of Guidance for Officials giving evidence before Select Committees* (GEN 80/38) (Civil Service Department 16 May 1980, mimeo).
Civil Service Yearbook 1998 (1998) (London: The Stationery Office).
Committee on the Civil Service (Lord Fulton, Chairman) (1968), *The Civil Service: Report of the Committee 1966–68*, Cmnd. 3638.
Committee on Ministers' Powers (1932), *Report*, Cmd. 4060.
Committee on the Preparation of Legislation (Lord Renton, Chairman) (1975), *Report*, Cmnd. 6053.
Committee on Political Activities of Civil Servants (1949), *Report*, Cmd. 7718.
—— (1978), *Report*, Cmnd. 7057.
Committee on Staffs (1919), *Final Report of the Committee appointed to inquire into the Organisation and Staffing of Government Offices*, Cmd. 62.
Committee on Standards in Public Life (1995), *Standards in Public Life: First Report*, Cm. 2850.
Complaints Task Force (1993), *Effective Complaints Systems: Principles and Checklist* (London: Citizen's Charter Unit).
—— (1994), *Complaints: Literature Review* (London: Citizen's Charter Unit.
—— (1995*a*), *Good Practice Guide* (London: HMSO).
—— (1995*b*), *Putting Things Right: Main Report* (London: HMSO).
Comptroller and Auditor-General (1986), *The Financial Management Initiative* (1985–86) HC 588.
—— (1995), *Report, in Appropriation Accounts 1993–94, Vol. 2, Class II—Foreign and Commonwealth Office* (1994–95) HC 100–II.
Constitution Unit (1996), in Section 1 above.
Council on Tribunals (1993), *The Annual Report of the Council on Tribunals for 1992–93*, (1993–94) HC 78.
—— (1996), *The Annual Report of the Council on Tribunals for 1995–96* (1995–96) HC 114.
—— (1997), *Tribunals: their Organisation and Independence*, Cmd. 3744.
Court Service (1995), *The Court Service Framework Document* (London: Court Service).
Crown Prosecution Service (1994), *The Code for Crown Prosecutors* (3rd edn., London: Crown Prosecution Service).
Customs and Excise (1996), *Prosecution Procedures* (Press release 15 February 1996 C&E S1/96, mimeo).
Defence Committee (1986), *Westland plc: The Government's Decision-Making* (1985–86) HC 519.
Department for Education and Employment (1996), *Equal Opportunities into the*

Mainstream: Guidance on Policy Appraisal for Equal Treatment (London: Department for Education and Employment).

Department of Employment (1986), *Building Businesses . . . Not Barriers*, Cmnd. 9794.

Department of Employment (1987), *Encouraging Enterprise: A Progress Report on Deregulation* (London: Department of Employment).

Department of the Environment, Legal Directorate (1997), *Is it Legal? How to use your Lawyer* (London: Department of the Environment).

Department of Social Security (1996), *Improving decision making and appeals in Social Security*, Cm. 3328.

Department of Social Security Benefits Agency (1995), *A Framework for the Agency* (London: Department of Social Security Benefits Agency).

Department of Social Security Contributions Agency (1994), *Framework Document* (Newcastle Upon Tyne: Department of Social Security Contributions Agency).

Department of Social Security/Department of Health, The Solicitor's Office (1994), *How to get The Best out of Your Lawyer* (London: Department of Social Security).

Department of Trade and Industry (1985), *Burdens on Business: Report of a Scrutiny of Administrative and Legislative Requirements* (London: HMSO).

Department of Trade and Industry (1988), *Releasing Enterprise*, Cm. 512.

—— (1993), *Review of the Implementation and Enforcement of EC Law in the UK* (London: Department of Trade and Industry).

—— (1994), *Getting a Good Deal in Europe . . . Deregulatory Principles in Practice* (London: Department of Trade and Industry).

—— (1995), *A Guide to the Solicitor's Office* (London: Department of Trade and Industry).

Deregulation Task Force (1995), *Report 1994/1995* (London: Deregulation Unit).

—— (1996), *Report 1995/1996* (London: Deregulation Unit).

Deregulation Unit (1992), *Checking the Cost to Business: A Guide to Compliance Cost Assessment* (London: Department of Trade and Industry).

—— (1994), *Thinking About Regulating: A Guide to Good Regulation* (London: Department of Trade and Industry).

—— (1996*a*), *Checking the Cost of Regulation: A Guide to Compliance Cost Assessment* (London: HMSO).

—— (1996*b*), *Regulation in the Balance: A Guide to Regulatory Appraisal Incorporating Risk Assessment* (London: HMSO).

—— (1996*c*), *The Government Response to the Deregulation Task Force Report 1996* (London: Deregulation Unit).

Efficiency and Effectiveness Group (1995), *Efficiency Plans: Guidance for Development and Use* (London: HMSO).

Efficiency Unit (1988), *Improving Management in Government: the Next Steps. A Report to the Prime Minister* (London: HMSO).

—— (1991), *Making the Most of Next Steps: The Management of Ministers' Departments and their Executive Agencies. Report to the Prime Minister* (London: HMSO).

Efficiency Unit (1993*a*), *Career Management and Succession Planning Study* (London: HMSO).

—— (1993*b*), *The Government's Guide to Market Testing* (London: HMSO).

—— (1995), *Resource Management Systems: An Efficiency Unit Scrutiny* (London: HMSO).

—— (1996), *Competing for Quality Policy Review* (London: HMSO).

—— (1997), *Executive Non-Departmental Public Bodies: 1997 Report*, Cm. 3712.

—— (1998*a*), *Better Quality Services: a handbook on creating public/private partnerships through market testing and contracting out* (London: HMSO).

—— (1998*b*), *Better Quality Services: Guidance for Senior Managers* (London: HMSO).

Elliott, Michael (1981*a*), 'A note on some aspects of the law relating to supply' (Memorandum submitted to Select Committee on Procedure (Supply) (1981), q.v., Appendix 18, pp. 51–63.

Epitome I: see Public Accounts Committee (1938).

Epitome II: see Public Accounts Committee (1970).

Expenditure Committee (1977), *Eleventh Report: The Civil Service* (1976–77) HC 535.

Historic Scotland (1994), *Framework Document* (Edinburgh: Historic Scotland).

Home Office (1997), *Rights Brought Home: The Human Rights Bill*, Cm. 3782.

Home Office, Legal Adviser's Branch (1995), *Getting the best out of your lawyer* (London: Home Office).

House of Lords Select Committee on the Committee Work of the House (1992), *Report* (1991–92) HL 35.

House of Lords Select Committee on the Public Service (1997), *Special Report* (1996–97) HL 68.

—— (1998), *Report* (1997–98) HL 55 (Report), 55-I (Evidence).

House of Lords Select Committee on the Scrutiny of Delegated Powers (1993), *First Report* (1992–93) HL 57.

—— (1994), *Eighth Report* (1993–94) HL 60.

Inland Revenue (1996), *Code of Practice 1: Mistakes by the Inland Revenue* (Inland Revenue: London).

James, Sir Henry (1888), *Report of the Committee appointed by the Treasury to inquire into the system of conducting the legal business of government* (James Committee) (1888) HC 239, 1888 Parl. Pap. LXXX.

Jessel, Sir George (1877), *First, Second and Third Reports of the Departmental Committee to inquire into the system under which the legal business of government is conducted* (Sir George Jessel, MR, Chairman) (1876–77) HC 199, 1877 Parl. Pap. XVIII (folio).

Joint Committee on Delegated Legislation (1972), *Report* (1971–72) HL 184; HC 475.

Joint Consultative Committee on Constitutional Reform (1997), in Section 1.

Law Commission (1994), *Administrative Law: Judicial Review and Statutory Appeals* (1994–95) HC 669 (Law Com. No. 226).

Legal Secretariat to the Law Officers (1996), *Relationship between the Attorney-General and Government Departments which have concerns about particular pro-*

secutions or which have prosecuting responsibilities but are not subject to his superintendence (June 1996, mimeo; deposited in the Library of the House of Commons and referred to in 279 HC Debs., cols. *336–7* written answers 17 June 1996).

—— (1998), *The Appointment of Counsel* (London: Legal Secretariat to the Law Officers).

Lidstone, K. W., Hogg, R., and Sutcliffe, F. (1980), *Prosecutions by Private Individuals and Non-Police Agencies* (Royal Commission on Criminal Procedure, Research Study No. 10) (London: HMSO).

Lilley, Peter (1996), *Welfare state of the art—the future of social security delivery* (London: Department of Social Security).

Lord Advocate (1993), *Use of the Private Sector for Government Legal Work in Scotland: Guidance by the Lord Advocate* (London: Lord Advocate's Department).

Lord Chancellor's and Law Officers' Departments (1995), *Departmental Report: The Government's Expenditure Plans 1995–96 to 1997–98*, Cm. 2809.

—— (1996), *Departmental Report: The Government's Expenditure Plans 1996–97 to 1998–99*, Cm. 3209.

Machinery of Government and Standards Group (1997), *Departmental Evidence and Response to Select Committees* (London: Cabinet Office).

Massey, Andrew (1995), *After Next Steps: An examination of the implications for policy making of the developments in executive agencies* (London: Office of Public Service and Science).

Minister without Portfolio (1985), *Lifting the Burden*, Cmnd. 9571.

Ministry of Power (1964), *Note of a meeting in Mr Viner's room at the Treasury, 3rd March 1964*, Public Record Office file POWE 33/2598/6/1.

Ministry of Reconstruction (1918), *Report of the Machinery of Government Committee* (Haldane), Cd. 9230.

Modernisation Committee (1998*a*), *Third Report, Carry-Over of Public Bills* (1997–98) HC 543.

—— (1998*b*), *Fourth Report, Conduct in the Chamber* (1997–98) HC 600.

—— (1998*c*), *Seventh Report, The Scrutiny of European Business* (1997–98) HC 791.

National Audit Office ([n.d.]), *Helping the Nation spend wisely: a guide to the National Audit Office* (London: National Audit Office).

—— (1986), *Report of the Comptroller and Auditor-General, Financial Reporting to Parliament* (1985–86) HC 576.

—— (1995), *Performance Measurement in the Civil Service—Experience in the Foreign and Commonwealth Office, HM Customs and Excise and Department of Education and Science* (1990–91) HC 399.

—— (1996), *Helping the Nation Spend Wisely: NAO Annual Report 1996* (London: National Audit Office).

—— (1997*a*), *The Contribution Agency's Customer Charters* (1996–97) HC 266.

—— (1997*b*), *Helping the Nation Spend Wisely: NAO Annual Report 1997* (London: National Audit Office).

—— (1998), *Benefits Agency: Performance Measurement* (1997–98) HC 952.

Next Steps Team (1995*a*), *The Strategic Management of Agencies: Full Report and Case Studies* (London: HMSO).

Next Steps Team (1995*b*), *The Strategic Management of Agencies: Models for Management* (London: HMSO).

Northcote–Trevelyan (1854), *Report on the Organisation of the Permanent Civil Service*, reprinted in Committee on the Civil Service (1968), above, Cmnd. 3638, Appendix B.

Office for National Statistics (1997), *United Kingdom National Accounts: The Blue Book 1997* (London: The Stationery Office).

Office of Public Service (1996*a*), *Agency Chief Executives' Handbook* (London: Cabinet Office).

—— (1996*b*), *Guide to Legislative Procedures* (4th edn., London: Cabinet Office).

—— (1996*c*), *Redress under the Citizen's Charter: Guidance for Departments and Agencies* (London: Office of Public Service).

—— (1997*a*), *Complaints Review Arrangements in Public Services* (London: Office of Public Service).

—— (1997*b*), *The Citizen's Charter: A Consultation Exercise* (London: Office of Public Service).

Parliamentary Commissioner for Administration (1974–75), *First Report* (1974–75) HC 49.

—— (1991), *Annual Report for 1990* (1990–91) HC 299.

—— (1992), *Annual Report for 1991* (1991–92) HC 347.

—— (1992–93), *Fourth Report, Compensation to Farmers for Slaughtered Poultry* (1992–93) HC 519.

—— (1993*a*), *Annual Report for 1992* (1992–93) HC 569.

—— (1993*b*), *Delay in Handling Disability Living Allowance Claims* (1992–93) HC 652.

—— (1994), *Annual Report for 1993* (1993–94) HC 290.

—— (1995*a*), *Annual Report for 1994* (1994–95) HC 307.

—— (1995*b*), *Investigation of Complaints against the Child Support Agency* (1994–95) HC 135.

—— (1996*a*), *Annual Report for 1995* (1995–96) HC 296.

—— (1996*b*), *Investigation of Complaints against the Child Support Agency* (1995–96) HC 20.

—— (1997), *Annual Report for 1996* (1996–97) HC 386.

—— (1998) *Annual Report 1997–98* (1997–98) HC 845.

Prime Minister (1936), *Minute by the Prime Minister on the Report of the Board of Enquiry appointed by the Prime Minister to investigate certain discussions engaged in by the Permanent Secretary to the Air Ministry*, Cmd. 5255.

—— (1937), *Memorandum on the subject of the Acceptance of Business Appointments by Officers of the Crown Services*, Cmd. 5517.

Public Accounts Committee (1862), *Third Report* (1861–62) HC 467, 1862 Parl. Pap. XI.

—— (1865), *Report* (1864–65) HC 413, 1865 Parl. Pap. X.

—— (1884), *Second Report* (1883–84) HC 237, 1884 Parl. Pap. VIII.

—— (1885*a*), *First Report* (1884–85) HC 112, 1885 Parl. Pap. VII.

—— (1885*b*), *Second Report* (1884–85) HC 267, 1885 Parl. Pap. VII.

Public Accounts Committee (1938), *Epitome of the Reports from the Committees of Public Accounts 1857–1937* (1937–38) HC 154 ('Epitome I').

—— (1970), *Epitome of the Reports from the Committees of Public Accounts 1938–1969* (1969–70) HC 187 ('Epitome II').

—— (1973), *First Report, North Sea Oil and Gas* (1972–73) HC 122.

—— (1977), *Third Report, Cash Limits* (1976–77) HC 274.

—— (1994*a*), *Eighth Report, The Proper Conduct of Public Business* (1993–94) HC 154.

—— (1994*b*), *Seventeenth Report, Pergau Hydro-Electric Project* (1993–94) HC 155.

—— (1994*c*), *Twenty-fifth Report, Financial reporting to Parliament: Changes in the Format of the Supply Estimates* (1993–94) HC 386.

—— (1996), *Ninth Report, Resource Accounting and Proposals for a Resource-Based System of Supply* (1996–97) HC 167.

—— (1998), *Minutes of Evidence, 11 May 1998, Treasury Controls* (1997–98) HC 730–i.

Public Administration Committee (1998*a*), *Third Report, Your Right to Know: the Government's Proposals for a Freedom of Information Act* (1997–98) HC 398.

—— (1998*b*), *Sixth Report, The Government Information and Communication Service* (1997–98) HC 770.

—— (1998*c*), *Fourth Special Report, Government Response to the Third Report from the Committee (Session 1997–98) on Your Right to Know: the Government's Proposals for a Freedom of Information Act* (1997–98) HC 1020.

Public Service Committee (1996*a*), *Ministerial Accountability and Responsibility* (1995–96) HC 313.

—— (1996*b*), *First Special Report. Government Response to the Second Report from the Committee (Session 1995–96) on Ministerial Accountability and Responsibility* (1996–97) HC 67.

—— (1997), *The Citizen's Charter* (1996–97) HC 78.

Royal Commission on Civil Establishments (1887), *First Report*, C. 5226.

—— on the Civil Service (Lord McDonnell, Chairman) (1914), *Fourth Report*, Cd. 7338.

—— on the Civil Service 1929–31 (Lord Tomlin, Chairman) (1931), *Report*, Cmd. 3909.

—— on Criminal Procedure (1981), *Report*, Cmnd. 8092.

—— on the Private Manufacture of and Trading in Arms (1936), *Report*, Cmd. 5292.

—— on Standards of Conduct in Government (1976), *Report*, Cmnd. 6526.

Scott, Sir Richard (1996), *Report of the Inquiry into the Export of Defence Equipment and Dual-Use Goods to Iraq and Related Prosecutions* (5 vols.) (1995–96) HC 115.

Scottish Prison Service (1993), *Scottish Prison Service Agency Framework Document* (Edinburgh: Scottish Prison Service).

Select Committee on Delegated Legislation (1953), *Report*, (1952–53) HC 310.

Select Committee on European Legislation (1996), *Twenty-seventh Report, The Scrutiny of European Business* (1995–96) HC 51.

Select Committee on the Parliamentary Commissioner for Administration (SCPCA) (1974), *Session 1974*, (1974) HC 268.

Select Committee on the Parliamentary Commissioner for Administration (SCPCA) (1992), *The implications of the Citizens' Charter for the work of the Parliamentary Commissioner for Administration* (1991–92) HC 158.

—— (1993*a*), *Third Report, Compensation to Farmers for Slaughtered Poultry* (1992–93) HC 593.

—— (1993*b*), *First Special Report, Government Reply to the Third Report* (1992–93) HC 947.

—— (1993*c*), *The Powers, Work and Jurisdiction of the Ombudsman* (1993–94) HC 33.

—— (1994), *Maladministration and Redress* (1994–95) HC 112.

—— (1995*a*), *Government Response to the First Report from the Select Committee on the Parliamentary Commissioner for Administration, Session 1994–95, Maladministration and Redress* (1994–95) HC 316.

—— (1995*b*), *Fourth Report, Report of the Parliamentary Ombudsman for 1994* (1994–95) HC 394.

—— (1996), *Open Government* (1995–96) HC 84.

Select Committee on Procedure (Supply) (1981), *First Report* (1980–81) HC 118.

Select Committee on Procedure (1996), *Fourth Report, Delegated Legislation* (1995–96) HC 152.

—— (1997), *Third Report, European Business* (1996–97).

—— (1998*a*), *Second Report, Resource Accounting and Budgeting* (1997–98) HC 438.

—— (1998*b*), *Minutes of Evidence, Financial Procedure* (1997–98) HC 848.

Service First Unit (1998*a*), *How to draw up a national charter: a guide to drawing up national charters* (London: Service First Unit).

—— (1998*b*), *How to draw up a local charter: a guide to preparing local charters* (London: Service First Unit).

—— (1998*c*), *How to conduct written consultation exercises: an introduction for central government* (London: Service First Unit).

—— (1998*d*), *How to deal with complaints* (London: Service First Unit).

Solicitor to the Secretary of State for Scotland (1997), *Solicitor's Office* (Edinburgh: The Scottish Office).

Stephen, Sir James (1854), letter in *Papers relating to the Re-organisation of the Civil Service*, Parliamentary Papers (1854–55), Vol. 20.

Trade and Industry Committee (1992), *Exports to Iraq* (1991–92) HC 86.

Treasury (1961), *Report of the Committee (Plowden) on the Control of Public Expenditure*, Cmnd. 1432.

—— (1976), *Cash Limits on Public Expenditure*, Cmnd. 6440.

—— (1980), *The Role of the Comptroller and Auditor-General*, Cmnd. 7845.

—— (1988), *HM Treasury Public Expenditure Committee, Operation of End-Year Flexibility*, PESC(88)22, PESC(WM)(88)36 (London: HM Treasury, mimeo).

—— (1989*a*), *Government Accounting: A Guide on Accounting and Financial Procedures for the Use of Government Departments* (2 vols., looseleaf) (London: HMSO).

—— (1989*b*), *The Financing and Accountability of Next Steps Agencies*, Cm. 914.

—— (1990*a*), *Financial reporting to Parliament*, Cm. 918.

—— (1990*b*), *Definition and Control of Departmental Running Costs from 1991–92*, PESC(90)3, PESC(WM)(90)1 (London: HM Treasury).

—— (1991*a*), *Public Expenditure Analyses to 1993–94*, Cm. 1520.

Treasury (1991*b*), *Competing for Quality: Buying Better Public Services*, Cm. 1730.
—— (1991*c*), *Supply Estimates 1991–92, Class X* (1990–91) HC 236–X.
—— (1992*a*), *Budgetary Reform*, Cm. 1867.
—— (1992*b*), 'A new approach to controlling public expenditure,' Treasury Bulletin, 3/3 (Autumn), 11–18.
—— (1992*c*), *Executive Agencies: A Guide to Setting Targets and Measuring Performance* (London: HMSO).
—— (1992*d*), *Payment of Ex Gratia Compensation in cases of Maladministration* (DAO (GEN) 15/92) (London: HM Treasury).
—— (1992*e*), *Fees and Charges Guide* (London: HM Treasury).
—— (1993*a*), *Guidance to Departments on Reports and Accounts for Next Steps Agencies* (London: HM Treasury).
—— (1993*b*), *Review of End-Year Flexibility for Running Costs: New Arrangements*, PES(93)35 (London: HM Treasury).
—— (1993*c*), *Staff Inspection: History and Practice* (London: Management Services Division, HM Treasury).
—— (1994*a*), *Fundamental Expenditure Review: Executive Summary* (111/94, 19 October 1994) (London: HM Treasury).
—— (1994*b*), *Departmental Report of the Chancellor of the Exchequer's Departments: The Government's Expenditure Plans 1994–95 to 1996–97*, Cm. 2517.
—— (1994*c*), *Treasury Minute on the Seventeenth to Twenty-First Reports from the Committee of Public Accounts 1993–94*, Cm. 2602.
—— (1994*d*), *Better Accounting for the Taxpayer's Money: Resource Accounting and Budgeting in Government*, Cm. 2626.
—— (1995*a*), *Chancellor of the Exchequer's Smaller Departments: The Government's Expenditure Plans 1995–96 to 1997–98*, Cm. 2817.
—— (1995*b*), *Better Accounting for the Taxpayer's Money: The Government's Proposals. Resource Accounting and Budgeting in Government*, Cm. 2929.
—— (1996*a*), *HM Treasury: Chancellor of the Exchequer's Smaller Departments: The Government's Expenditure Plans 1996–97 to 1998–99*, Cm. 3217.
—— (1996*b*), *Financial Statement and Budget Report 1997–98* (1996–97) HC 90.
—— (1996*c*), *Supply Estimates 1996–97: Main Estimates* (1995–96) HC 261.
—— (1996*d*), *Public Expenditure Survey, Guidelines for the 1996 Survey* (PES (96) 9) (London: HM Treasury, mimeo).
—— (1996*e*), *Superintendence by the Attorney-General of Prosecutions of Export Offences by HM Customs and Excise* (mimeo, placed in House of Commons Library, see 279 HC Debs., cols. 336–7 (written answers 17 June 1996).
—— (1996*f*), *Government Internal Audit Manual* (London: HM Treasury).
—— (1996*g*) *Financial Redress: Maladministration and Charter Standards* (DAO (GEN) 7/96) (London: HM Treasury).
—— (1997*a*), *Chancellor of the Exchequer's Smaller Departments: The Government's Expenditure Plans 1997–98 to 1999–2000*, Cm. 3517.
—— (1997*b*), *The Guide to Expenditure Work* (London: HM Treasury, provisional edition, mimeo).
—— (1997*c*), *Regularity and Propriety: A Handbook* (London: HM Treasury).
—— (1997*d*), *The National Asset Register* (London: HM Treasury).

Treasury (1997*e*), *Treasury Minute on the Ninth Report from the Public Accounts Committee*, Cm. 3577.

—— (1998*a*), *Chancellor of the Exchequer's Departments: The Government's Expenditure Plans 1998–99*, Cm. 3917.

—— (1998*b*), *Stability and Investment in the Long Term: Economic and Fiscal Strategy Report 1998*, Cm. 3978.

—— (1998*c*), *Public Expenditure Survey, Reform of the Public Expenditure Regime*, PES(98)14, 11 June 1998 (mimeo).

—— (1998*d*), *Modern Public Services in Britain: Investing for Reform. Comprehensive Spending Review: New Public Spending Plans 1999–2002*. Cm. 4011.

—— (1998*e*), *Code for Fiscal Stability* (London: HM Treasury).

—— (1998*f*), *Public Services for the Future: Modernisation, Reform, Accountability. Comprehensive Spending Review: Public Service Agreements 1999–2002*, Cm. 4181.

—— Financial Management Reporting and Audit Directorate ([n.d.]), *Annual Report 1996–97* (London: HM Treasury).

Treasury and Civil Service Committee (1986*a*), *Third Report, The Government's Public Expenditure Plans 1986–87 to 1988–89 (Cmnd. 9702)* (1985–86) HC 192.

—— (1986*b*), *Seventh Report, Civil Servants and Ministers: Duties and Responsibilities* (1985–86) HC 92.

—— (1988*a*), *Second Report, The Government's Public Expenditure Plans 1988–89 to 1990–91* (Cm. 288) (1987–88) HC 292.

—— (1988*b*), *Eighth Report, Civil Service Management Reform: The Next Steps* (1987–88) HC 494–II.

—— (1990), *Eighth Report, Progress in the Next Steps Initiative* (1989–90) HC 496.

—— (1992), *First Report, The 1992 Autumn Statement and the Conduct of Economic Policy* (1992–93) HC 201.

—— (1994*a*), *Fifth Report, The Role of The Civil Service* (1993–94) HC 27.

—— (1994*b*), *Third Report, The Form of the Estimates* (1993–94) HC 192.

—— (1995), *Fourth Report, Simplified Estimates and Resource Accounting* (1994–95) HC 212.

Treasury Committee (1996), *Second Report, Resource Accounting and Budgeting* (1996–97) HC 186.

Treasury Solicitor's Department (1987), *The Judge over Your Shoulder: Judicial Review of Administrative Decisions* (London: Cabinet Office).

—— (1995), *Judge over Your Shoulder. Judicial Review: Balancing the Scales* (London: Cabinet Office).

—— (1996), *Framework Document* (London: Treasury Solicitor's Department).

—— ([n.d.]), *The Treasury Solicitor—A Brief History of the Department* (London: Treasury Solicitor's Department home page).

Trosa, Sylvie (1994), *Next Steps: Moving On* (London: Office of Public Service).

United Kingdom Passport Agency (1996), *Framework Document* (London: United Kingdom Passport Agency).

Valuation Office Agency (1995), *Framework Document for the Valuation Office Agency 1995* (London: Valuation Office Agency).

Index

Access to information, *see* Freedom of information
Accountancy:
  central responsibility for 137–9
Accounting Officer:
  appointment 126
  ministers, relationships with 128
  more than one, appointment for department 129
  Pergau Dam affair, role in 128
  Public Accounts Committee, interrogation by 198
  responsibilities of 127
  status of 127
  written directions, requiring 129
Administration of justice:
  control of 293
  Lord Chancellor's Department, responsibility of 212
Attorney General:
  administrative superintendence 288
  appointments by 222
  Cabinet, as member of 236
  case-work, interest in 288
  chambers, location of 235
  see also Law Officers
  chief legal adviser, as 222; Cabinet Committees, membership of 297; functions 297; interpretation 297; opinions, giving 297
  common law powers, extent of 294
  constitutional position of 231
  counsel, appointment of 296
  criminal proceedings, intervention in 289–90
  criminal prosecution, interest in 289
  Crown, relationship with 233
  Customs and Excise cases, review of 291–5
  Director of Public Prosecutions, relationship with 287–8
  Director of Serious Fraud Office, relationship with 287–8
  export control offences, prosecution of 293
  function of 222, 231–2
  independent and objective role 295
  intervention by 235
  legal advice, giving 8
  legal work, guidance on 213
  Legislation Committee, membership of 257
  litigation, acting in 232
  Lord Advocate, precedence over 238
  matters arising on Bills referred to 255
  nolle prosequi procedure 288
  office of 232
  opinions: change in nature of 299–300; character of 299; specialist practitioner, assistance of 299
  policy work 288
  prosecuting counsel, reliance on views of 293
  prosecution guidelines, issue of 290–1
  prosecutions reserved for 289
  Treasury Solicitor, relationship with 219
Audit:
  internal, central responsibility for 137–9

Business:
  burdens on, *see* Legislation

Cabinet:
  business of 52–3
  committees 53–4
  composition 51
  control and co-ordination, political capacities of 6
  extra-legal organization, as 51
  internal control function 52
  Secretariat 53–4

Cabinet (*cont.*):
shifting styles of work 23
system, day-to-day working of 22
Cabinet Office:
Central Secretariat 68
centre, as 54
Civil Service, control of 66–9
Civil Service Employer Group 68
consultation between departments, concern with 316
co-ordinating functions: European law, on 316–19; range of 315
European Secretariat: co-ordination by 316–7, 383; legal advice to 317
general advice and guidance, issue of 315–16
inter-departmental legal discussions, organization of 321
Legal Advisers 317
Next Steps Team 133
Office of Public Service, merger with 55, 126
Performance and Innovation Unit 56
Secretariat as part of 53
Senior Civil Service Group 68
Service First Unit 350
Treasury, overlapping concerns with 126
Citizen's Charter:
aims of public service reform, extension of 348
application of 350
Cabinet Office, Unit in 350
central government, minimum service standards for 352–3
Charter Standard 354
complaints procedures: agency chief executive, accountability of 367; double-edged quality 366–7; effectiveness 377; external review mechanisms 360–1; guidance 360; independent internal review, provision for 359–60; integral part, as 358; nature of systems 358; redress, provision of 361–5; scope 359; strengthening of 366; systems improvement 365–6; Task Force 358–9
courts, role of 377
financial redress, Treasury guidance on 355
inducement to service providers 354
initiative 349
key discipline, as 350
launch of 348
national and local 352–3
non-statutory initiative, as 350–1
Office of Public Service, Unit in 349
performance audit 357
process of making, control over 353
public service delivery, principles of: delivery of 352–8; foundation on 351–2; regular and systematic consultation, stipulation of 353; statement of 352
redress: actual financial loss, where suffered 364; basis of 363; Citizen's Charter Unit guidance 365; delegated limits 363; departmental rules for 363; ethic of 365; financial compensation 362; government departments, among 362; inquiry into 362; maladministration, in case of 364; provision of 361; starting point 364
relaunch of 348, 350
Service First, as 348, 350
standards: criticism of 355; drivers of performance, as 358; isolation, not set in 356; performance audit 357; setting and monitoring 354–7
systems improvement 365–6
targets 356
Civil Service:
accountability 102–3
Armstrong Memorandum 94–5, 99
authority delegated to 64–5
Central Secretariat 68
Code: adoption of 92; general principles 91–2; purpose of 92–3; statutory backing, opposition to 94, 103
Commissioners: appeals to 100–1;

appeals, hearing 70; appointment 70; control by 69–71; functions of 69–70; history of 69; independence 70; powers of control 383–4; recruitment, approval of 79–84; recruitment compliance, monitoring 85
conduct, standards of: anonymity, abandonment of 87; Armstrong Memorandum 94–5, 99; Business Appointments Rules 88–9; central framework 87–91; Civil Service Code 91–4; confidentiality and official information 88; core principles 87–8; departmental and agency rules 95–6; long-standing duties 86; political activities 88–91; propriety 88-9; undivided loyalty test 93; unwritten rules 91
control: Cabinet Office, by 66–9; departments and agencies, by 71–8; legal basis of 62–5; management regulations 67; Office of the Civil Service Commissioners, by 69–71; organization of 65–78; Senior Civil Service, of 75–8; Treasury, by 65–6
corporate management, emphasis on 69
Crown: as employees of 71; relations with 63–4
Crown appointments 83
decentralization 61
departments, management in: Cabinet Office requirements 73–5; conduct, standards of 95–6; contentious proposals, review of 74; delegated responsibilities 72–3
efficiency, control of 74; pay and grading, responsibility for 73; Principal Establishment Officer 71–2; responsibility for 71
devolution, impact of 60, 103
discipline 96
dismissal, appeal against 74
Employer Group 68
Head of Home Civil Service, issues referred to 99
internal control function 101
internal regulation 62
irregular or improper expenditure, instruction involving 98–9
law, changes to 101–2
Management Board 69
Management Code 61, 68, 73–4, 87
management of 37, 62–5
ministerial conduct to 97–8
Next Steps agencies, see **Next Steps agencies**
Northcote-Trevelyan reforms 60, 63
Order in Council 61, 67
pensions, right to 64
permanent service, as 59–60
prerogative, regulation under 103
Prime Minister as Minister for 67
Principal Establishment Officer 71–2
principles and standards of 61
recruitment: audited self-regulation 78; central requirements 86; Code 78–9; Commissioners' approval of 79–82; compliance and audit 84–6; delegation of responsibility for 383; exceptions to principles 83–4; internal review 85; legal advice function, impact on 332–3; open competition, principle of 80; principles 78–9; proven distinction, candidates of 84; SASC Group appointments 82–3; units 78; upper echelons, to 80
reform, legislation for 64
request contravening accepted standards of propriety, appeals 98–101
Senior: central pay framework 75–6; common framework for 75; creation of 61; group 68; guidance on recruitment 81; management 75; open competition, principle of 80; Oughton checklist 80; personal

Civil Service (*cont.*):
contracts 76–8; recruitment, approval of 79–84
Senior Appointments Selection Committee 82–3
shared values, adherence to 102
single organization, management as 60
size of 59
unity and diversity, character of 60–1
White Paper 61
Civil Service Department:
functions of 123
Committee on Standards in Public Life:
role of 11
Comptroller and Auditor-General:
appropriation accounts, reports on 197
appropriation audit, conduct of 118–19
compliance of expenditure with appropriation, ensuring 140
departmental accounts, audit of 157
education payments, questioning 202
executive concerns 193
functions of 193
public discussion of reports 198
qualification of accounts 162
Treasury, working with 193
Constitution:
alternative theories of 15
British understanding of 16
citizen, meaning for 393
codified, legislative alteration of norms in 19
conventions 22
deployment and control of resources 23
development of 12
empirical record, as 16
external controls 23
fiction, as 17–18
one grand idea, as 16–17
organization of resources 22
positive theory 15–19; values and principles underpinning 20
resource-based theory, executive in 19–25
rules, empirical evidence of 20
structure and theory of 397–8
structure of values, as 18–19
true system of obligations, as 18
United Kingdom, nature of 16
Constitutional law:
executive, place of 1
Contracting out:
better value for money, offering 47
exceptions 47–8
extent of 48
functions eligible for 47
Guiding Principles 46
non-statutory functions, of 47
statutory provisions 47–8
Council on Tribunals:
responsibility of 378
Counsel:
Crown 295–6
Departments, to 296
First Treasury 295
prosecuting departments, of 296
Criminal law:
Home Secretary, role of 290
Crown:
administration of justice, control of 293
civil expenditures, parliamentary control over 116
concept of 12
corporation sole, as 13
employment, contractualizing 77
executive, as 27
land 167
one and indivisible, as 27
prerogative powers, as source of 27–8
proceedings, privileges in 212
public interest proceedings against 340
source of unity, as 27
tax privileges 212
use of term 27
Crown Prosecution Service:
Code for Crown Prosecutors 291, 293
establishment of 221
function of 221–2
Service Manual 291
Customs and Excise:
Adjudicator Scheme 360

Law Officers, reference of issues to 305–6
Solicitor 225

Democracy:
governments operating according to 207
Department for International Development:
creation of 32
Department of Agriculture, Fisheries and Food:
Law Officers, reference of issues to 305
lawyers in 225
Minister 33
statutory origins 32
Department of Education and Employment:
statutory origins 32
Department of Environment, Transport and the Regions:
creation of 54
departmental legal services 217
legislative proposals, consultation on 247
Secretary of State, transfer of functions to 32
statutory origins 32
Department of Health:
Law Officers, reference of issues to 305
Solicitor's Office 224, 226–7, 306
statutory origins 32
Department of Social Security:
agencies 130
compensation payments, rules for 363
Departmental Board 130–1
head of legal services, role of 226
Law Officers, reference of issues to 305–6
Principal Establishment Officer 130
Principal Finance Officer 130
Social Security Benefits Agency: business plan, approval of 44; relationship with 41
Solicitor's Office 224, 226–7, 306
statutory origins 32
Department of Trade and Industry:
departmental legal services 217
functions absorbed into 32
hard charging 226
head of legal services, role of 226
Law Officers, reference of issues to 305
President of Board of Trade 33
Deportation:
judicial order, disregard of 327
Devolution:
governmental functions, of 12
law-making power, of 286
Director for Civil Proceedings:
proposal for appointment of 340–1
Director of Public Prosecutions:
Attorney-General, relationship with 287–8
function of 222
prosecutions reserved for 289
prosecutions, taking over 288

Estimates:
approved, partially legislative status 161
contents of 159
control 159–62
form, Treasury power to determine 160
laying before House of Commons 156
legislative approval, parts not receiving 161–2
new form of 163
parts of 160
simplification and alignment with PES 162–4
structure 159–62
supplementary 156–7, 183–6
Votes, division into 160
EU law:
business, burdens on 280–4
compliance with 285
domestic law-making, impact on 268
legislative activity, impact on 264
making of 265
over-implementation of obligations 280–2
policy, co-ordinating 265
European Secretariat, functions of 316–19

European Convention on Human Rights:
compliance with 285
domestic law-making, impact on 269–71
internal control, system of 286
rights, enforcement in UK 270
UK record on 269
Executive:
administrative heterogeneity 332–4
allocation of powers, etc., within, lack of legal rules 13–14
autonomous body, as 398
changing legal climate: government lawyering, ethics of 345–7; legal debate 343–4; litigation strategy 341–3; reasons for 340
component parts, control of 8
constitutional law, place in 1
control and management of resources, stable rules for 22
courts, lack of bridge to 210
democratic control of 394
departmental or agency working rules, scrutiny of 329–30
departments, made up of 6
external controls 3–5; courts, by 391–2; internal control, dependence on 392–3; Parliament, by 388–91; reliance on 388–92
importance of 1
internal co-ordination and external controls 8
internal control *see* Internal control
judicial consideration, activities subject to 329
judiciary, subservience to 326–30
jurisprudence 209
law, barely known to 26
leaders, domination of Parliament by 396
legal ordering 13
legal organization, not 26
legal powers, reliance on 207
legislation, *see* **Legislation**
neglect of, political background 10
new constraints 3
norms of 9
Parliament, dominance of 331–2
plural 6–9
prerogative powers 27–8
resource-based theory of constitution, in 19–25
self-management, norms of 18
self-regulation 397
unified 6
unity, treatment as 27
Executive agencies:
independent 6
See also Next Steps agencies

Financial firms:
compliance 3–4
regulation, increasing 3
Financial resources:
accountable management 124
Accounting Officer, role of, *see* Accounting Officer
appropriation: compliance of expenditure with 140; control of 104; Parliamentary concerns 140–1; system of 140–1
Code of Fiscal Stability 106
common system for dealing with 126
executive agencies see Next Step agencies
external control: internal controls, interdependence of 107; Parliamentary institutions, by 108
Financial Management Initiative 124–5
initiative, right of 108
internal control: cash limits 184; constitutional dimension 104–7; constitutional structure 107–9; efficiency and economy, mechanisms for promotion of 123–4; external controls, interdependence of 107; literature on 104; other than by Treasury 123–6; Treasury, role of, *see* Treasury
legal restrictions 207
monitoring and control: spending patterns, of 169; supply cycle, of 169
organization of 105
Parliament, role of 108–9
parliamentary control 105–6

parliamentary interest in 157
people, charge on 108
plurality of systems 140–3
Principal Finance Officer, *see* Principal Finance Officer
public expenditure, *see* Public expenditure
public funds, charge on 108
spending behaviour, disciplines for judging 169

First Treasury Counsel:
appointment of 295
counsel backing up 295
independence of 296

Foreign and Commonwealth Office:
Diplomatic Service, powers as to 67
functions absorbed into 32

Freedom of Information:
proposed legislation 348
Code of Practice on Access to Government Information: aims, definition of 368; departments and public bodies, requirements of 368–9; investigation of complaints 369–70; issue of 367; non-statutory 368; number of complaints 371
Conservative government's approach to 371
documents, allowing access to 372
executive NDPBs, codes of 370
exemptions 372
Home Office Freedom of Information Unit 370
Home Office Unit 370
Information Commissioner 372
statutory approach 372–3

Good Administration:
courts, role of 377
legal awareness, function of 324
legal nature of 213
legalization 210
machinery for promoting 378–9
parliamentary checks on 376–7
Parliamentary Commissioner, *see* Parliamentary Commissioner for Administration:
promulgation of principles of 339

Government:
centre: effectiveness, review of 55; meaning 54; stronger, creation of 57
financial resources, *see* Financial resources
legal personification of 13
legal powers, vesting of 6
legal services, *see* Legal services
legal tasks in 212–14
legal work, departmental nature of 323
litigation strategy 341–3
powers and functions, distribution of 7
tools, distribution of 7

Government Property Lawyers:
agency within agency, as 220

Government trading funds:
financial regime 135–6
introduction of 135
trading activities 135

Home Office:
criminal law, responsibility of Home Secretary for 290
Freedom of Information Unit 370
Law Officers, reference of issues to 305–6
legislative proposals, consultation on 247
Passport Agency, relationship with 41
prisons and sentencing policy 305

Human rights:
compliance with requirements 271
legislation, implications of 270–1

Inland Revenue:
Adjudicator Scheme 360
compensation payments, rules for 363
Law Officers, reference of issues to 305
lawyers in 225

Internal control:
autonomous powers, reliance on 389
centre, role of 385
co-ordination versus centralization 383–6
codification of expectations 387
collective 382

Internal control (*cont.*):
  constitutional organs, view of 395–6
  constitutional significance 393–8
  decisions, carrying out 6
  departmental function, as 381
  departments, of 380
  effective system, commitment to 4
  executive government, function within 26
  expenditure, of 381–2
  explicit rules and procedures 386
  external control depending on 392–3
  financial resources, of, *see* Financial resources
  forces for change 383
  formal rules, lack of 14
  formalization 386–8
  new machinery, basis of 384
  non-statutory regulation 389–90
  public face of 380
  resource monopolies 383
  rules, role of 388
  substantive policy, influence on 385
  system of 380; adoption of 24
  traditional system 381–2
  UK approach, strength of 382

Judicial decisions:
  precedent 327
Judicial powers:
  constitutional control of government 5
Judicial review:
  administrative action, of 338
  administrative process, as regular element of 337
  availability and exclusivity of 338
  Crown, public interest proceedings against 340
  effectiveness and efficiency 339
  evolution 343
  executive action, of 2–3
  executive, handicap for 342
  expansion of 335, 397
  government litigation strategy 341–3
  government reticence on 344
  governmental decisions, impact on 336
  importance of 335
  legal debate 343–4
  negative reactions 337
  ouster of clauses 201
  positive development, growth as 336
  predictability, lack of 338
  pro-active approach to 346
  underlying problems with 338–40
Judiciary:
  executive subservience to 326–30
  public debate, involvement in 343

Law:
  conduct of government, impinging on 212
  executive, of 208
  immunities 208
  informal systems of 349
  interpreters of 208
Law Commission:
  function of 223
Law Officers:
  advice: access to 314; asking for 302–9; attitudes reflected by 305; Cabinet, implicit authority of 312; citing in Parliament 310; confidentiality, general rule 309; control of publication 313; departmental ownership 313; disclosure outside Parliament 309–13; dissemination within government 313–15; Freedom of Information legislation, exclusion from 311; identity of 298
  Attorney-General, *see* Attorney-General
  collective responsibility, veiled in 312–13
  considered legal opinions, as source of 298
  constitutional position 287–90
  Department 232; adoption of title 234; Legal Secretariat 220, 222; meaning 219
  draft Bills, scrutiny of 256
  English 231–6
  external source of advice, as 307
  fees 233–4
  forensic experience 300

legal advisers, as 233
legal expertise, mobilizing 300
Legal Secretariat 234
legislative proposals, role as to 256–8
Lord Advocate *see* Lord Advocate
ministerial position in government 234; ministerial responsibility 287; opinions: character of 299, formal 298–8, international law, interpretation of 298, nature of 298–301, political dimension 301, record of 304, Scottish approach to 301, specialist practitioner, assistance of 299
political position of 306
powers, exercise of 290–5
public interest powers 330
reference of issues to: attitudes reflected by 305; constitutional 308; criteria for 302–4; final court of appeal, as 308; frequency for 304–5; international law questions 308; substantive legal difficulties, types of 307–8
roles of 239
Scottish 229, 236–8
Solicitor-General 232
umpire, as 308

Law reform:
responsibility for 223

Lawyers:
administrative decision-making, involvement in 336–7
government lawyering, ethics of 345–7
independence 324
judicial review, reticence on 344
legal work of 323

Legal Advice:
administrative action, as to 208
administrative heterogeneity, effect of 332–4
asking for 302–9
collective or centralized decisions on 9
departmental advisers 305–6
European Secretariat, to 317
executive dominance of Parliament, effect of 331–2
external sources of 307
government: centralization of 324–5; spreading within 322
judiciary, subservience to 326–30
Law Officers, from, *see* Law Officers
legally-trained people, from 211
litigation, as to 208
major departments, to 8
ministerial responsibility, and 325–6
Prison Service and Home Office, misunderstandings between 334
Scots law aspects of issues, on 309

Legal services:
contracting-out 213, 217
departmental: classification of 223; Customs and Excise, in 224–5; Departments of Health and Social Security, in 224–5; financial situation 226–7; general guidance, issue of 228; hard charging 227; heads of, responsibilities 226; Inland Revenue, in 225; legality, implications of departmentalism for 231; Ministry of Agriculture, Fisheries and Food, in 225; Northern Ireland, in 230; organization 224; range of work 223–4; Scottish Office, in 228–9; Solicitor's or Legal Adviser's Office, position of 225–6; Welsh Office, in 229
government: Andrew enquiry 216; Central Management Unit 216; co-ordination within framework of 319–22; Crown Prosecution Service 221–2; departmental 223–8; departments, control by 216–17; guidance on use of 333; institutionalization of 385; Law Commission 223; Lawyers Management Unit 320; legal awareness, function of 324; Legal Management Board 216; legality, implications of departmentalism for 231; Liaison Group 319–22; needs 212; Northern Ireland, in 230; organization of 212;

Legal services (*cont.*):
  Parliamentary Counsel Office, *see* Parliamentary Counsel Office; review of 215; Scotland and Wales, in 228–9; Serious Fraud Office 221–2; structure of 230, development of 214–17; Treasury Solicitor's Department, *see* Treasury Solicitor; unified 324
  privatization 213, 217
Legal work:
  agencies, of 333–4
  central control, patchy and weak nature of 323
  co-ordination of 323–4
  constitutional roots of system: executive dominance of Parliament 331–2; judiciary, executive subservience to 326–30; ministerial responsibility 325–6
  core and non-core 325
  diversity of 324
  government: alternative model of 324; other organizations, similarity to 209; pluralism and secrecy, sustaining of 332
  lawyers, of 323
Legality:
  absolute value, as 326
  illegal conduct, criticism of 207
  institutionalized self-restraint 380
  Law Officers giving content and force to 287
  professional specialism, as 210–11
  representation in government 211
  salience of 207–8
Legislation:
  business, burdens imposed on 241, 272–84
  deregulation: Better Regulation initiative 272; Better Regulation Unit 273; burdens on business, reduction of 271; EU level, at 284; good regulation, principles of 277–8; initiative 271; machinery for 272–3; mechanisms for 273–84; orders 278–9; proportionality 342; regulatory appraisal 274–7; regulatory impact assessments 276–7; risk assessment 275; secondary legislation 279; Task Force 273
  EC obligations, giving effect to: central co-ordination 266–7; checklist 283–4; deadlines, meeting 267; Deregulation Unit, guide by 283; double banking, avoiding 283; elaboration of texts 281–2; existing UK legislation, fitting in to 282; external scrutiny 284; machinery for 266; over-implementation of obligations 280–2; Parliamentary Counsel Office, scrutiny by 267–8; primary legislation, use of 281; statutory instrument, by 266; subordinate legislation, by 267
  EU law, impact on domestic law-making 268
  European Convention on Human Rights, impact of 269–71
  European, *see* EU law
  executive 208–9; power of 240
  good regulation, principles of 277–8
  Guide to Legislative Procedures 244, 246
  higher law, judicial testing against 332
  human rights implications, assessment of 270–1
  judicial disapproval of departmental practice, overcoming 331
  law-making power: control over 285; delegation to departments 286; devolution 286
  legislative programme: essential Bills 243; formulation of 243–4; Legislation Committee 242–3, 245; policy consistency 246–50; programme Bills 243; proposals for 242; provisional 244–5; Queen's Speeches and Future Legislation Committee 242–4; session in advance, planned for 245

machinery of executive government: expansion of 240; primary legislation 241–58
Parliament, role of 240
pre-legislative scrutiny 246
primary: Acts of Parliament 241; carrying over Bills 245; central controls, purposes of 241; drafting 250–8; *see also* Parliamentary Counsel Office; equal opportunities, principle of 249–50; EU implications 248; home departments, consultation with 247; improving quality of 245–6; judicial interpretation 241; Law Officers, role of 256–8; lead department, responsibility of 247; legal challenge, risk of 248; legislative priorities, determining 242–6; Open Government principles 248–9; policy consistency 246–50; short titles 253
regulatory appraisal 274–7
regulatory impact assessments 276–7
subordinate: adverse report on 262; business, burdens on 279; central control and co-ordination, lack of 258; changing character of 263–4; departmental practice 259–60; drafting 260; EC obligations, giving effect to 266–7; Her Majesty's Stationery Office, role of 259; House of Lords Delegated Powers Scrutiny Committee 263–4; informal consultation on 262; Joint Committee on Statutory Instruments, examination by 261–3; manuals 259–60; Parliamentary Counsel Office, scrutiny by 264; parliamentary scrutiny 260–3; statutory provisions 258–9; Statutory Publications Office, role of 259; structure and style, consistency in 260

Legislative powers:
constitutional control of government 5
Lord Advocate:
drafting of legislation 250, 252
legal work in Scotland, guidance on 213
Legislation Committee, membership of 257
opinions of 301
origins of office 236
precedence of Attorney-General over 238
role of 229, 236–8
Lord Chancellor's Department:
administration of justice by 212
legislative proposals, consultation on 247
Permanent Secretary 213
spending by 130
Lord High Treasurer:
office of 113–14

Ministerial departments:
access to papers by other department 314
Accounting Officer, *see* Accounting Officer
autonomy, principle of 29–31, 57–8
board of public officials, replacing 28–9
consultation between 316
control over 380
effective unit of government, as 28
establishment of 32–3
executive, making up 6
expenditure 34–6
extent of powers 28
giant 54
internal ordering of executive, as 57
internal organization, responsibility for 40
legal advice to 8
ministerial responsibility, essence of 29
Next Steps agencies, *see* Next Steps agencies
powerful position of 31
powers 33–6
prerogative, as expression of 32–3

Ministeril departments (*cont.*):
- Principal Finance Officer, *see* Principal Finance Officer
- significance of 29
- statutory creation of 32
- transfer of functions between 32
- Treasury control over 30
- value added tax, payment of 14
- vesting of functions in, machinery for transfer 36–7

Ministerial responsibility:
- accountability by 5
- analysis of 2
- basis of 29
- collective 51–2
- departmental autonomy, underlying 31
- emphasis on 30
- extent of 30
- Law Officers, of 287
- officials, exercise of functions by 40
- Parliamentary Ombudsman, effect of appointment 31
- political environment of 325
- vesting of functions in, due to 39

Ministers:
- agents of Crown, as 34
- civil service, duties to 97–8
- common law capacities 34
- conduct, standards of 97–8
- parliamentary accountability 98
- powers, extent of 34–5
- prerogative, as creatures of 33
- statutes requiring 33
- transfer of functions between 36–7

National Audit Office:
- audit sanctions 195
- certification audit 194
- division between types of work 194
- effective control of public expenditure, securing 193
- Exchequer and Audit Department, change from 193
- executive concerns 193
- extent of work 194
- public sector accounting and auditing, promotion of best practice and high standards in 197: regularity and propriety, policing 196; Treasury, relations with 195–9; value-for-money inquiries 197

Nationality:
- refusal of applications, exemption from duty to give reasons 340

Next Steps agencies:
- accountability for 45
- business plans 43–5
- Cabinet Office, Team in 133
- chief executives 43–5
- civil service, within 38
- classification 134
- Court Service 130
- creation 37–8, 133–4
- efficiency, aim of 132
- financial control 133–4
- financial management terms, classification in 135
- framework documents 41–2, 44
- government trading funds 135–6
- legal work of 333
- management, strategic approach to 44
- ministers, intervention of 45
- mode of establishment 39–41
- own Vote, with 136
- performance, emphasis on 38
- political control and accountability, issues of 334
- responsibilities of 38
- review 45–6, 133–4
- services, providing 137
- size of 38, 133
- social security 130
- sponsor department, relationship with: chief executives 43–5; framework documents 41–2; strategic management 41; targets 42–3
- status of 39
- sub-heads of Vote, within 137
- targets: balance 356; departments, key aspect of relationship with 42; good practice principles 42–3; publication 43; setting, principles for 43; simplicity 43
- Treasury control tasks, effect on 132
- types of 134

Non-departmental public bodies:
- agencies, differing from 49–50

categories of 49
Crown status, lacking 50
freedom of information codes 370
legal separate entities, as 49
meaning 49
number of 50
old style of devolution, as 49
reasons for conferring functions on 49
Northern Ireland:
legal services in 230
supervision of affairs 230

Office of Public Service:
Cabinet Office, merger with 55, 126
Civil Service, control of 66–9
Civil Service Department, successor to 55
Efficiency Unit 56–7
formal powers, lack of 56
responsibility of 56
units and groups in 56

Parliament:
administration, scrutiny of 376
annual financial cycle 108
constitutional control functions 4
Departmental reports to 155
executive, controls on 388–91
executive dominance of 331–2
financial powers 104–9, 170; *see also* **Financial resources**
leaders of executive, domination by 396
legislation, *see* Legislation
ministerial responsibility to 2
public expenditure: assent to 108; controls 193–9; decisions 158; grants, appropriation of 140; Public Expenditure Survey system 142, 152–5
relevance of activity, challenge to 396
supply cycle 155–9
Treasury, relationship with 105–6; *see also* **Treasury**
Parliamentary Commissioner for Administration:
access to information, investigation of complaints 369–70
basic principles of good practice, issue of 374–6
broad interpretation of role 374
catalogue of maladministration 374
functions of 373
initiatives 374
ministerial responsibility, reconciliation with principle of 31
recourse to 349
reports of cases 375
standards of administration, check on 373
Parliamentary Counsel Office:
accountability 221, 252
Cabinet Office, as part of 221, 251
drafting authority 252
drafting, responsibility for 221, 250
expansion of 221
function of 221
guardians of legal values, Counsel as 254–6
instructing departments, relations with 253
instruments amending or repealing statutory provisions, scrutiny of 267–8
monopoly of 251
Parliament, duty to 256
subordinate legislation: drafting 260; scrutiny of 264
Parliamentary sovereignty:
emphasis on as constitutional tenet 209
erosion of 209
Prime Minister:
control and co-ordination, political capacities of 6
conventional power 7
legal powers, lack of 6
Minister for the Civil Service, as 67
shifting styles of work 23
Treasury, as nominal head of 109
work of government, co-ordination of 23
Prime Minister's Office:
centre, as 54
creation of 55
Efficiency Unit 124
Principal Finance Officer:
appointment 129

Principal Finance Officer (*cont.*):
Department of Social Security, of 130
Lord Chancellor's Department, of 130
possible responsibilities, range of 131
Principal Establishment Officer, combination of roles 130
Treasury, relations with 129, 131
Public Accounts Committee:
Accounting Officers, interrogation of 198
appropriation accounts, scrutiny of 197–8
critic of government, as 198
criticisms, acting on 198–9
validation of performance standards, highlighting issue of 376
Public choice theory 11–12
Public expenditure:
absence of permanent legislation, in 174
affordable, total of 149
Annually Managed Expenditure 147, 150–1, 186
assent of Parliament to 108
Budget, presentation of 155
Cabinet Committee on 149–51
carry-forward 185
cash controls: carry-forward 185; Contingencies Fund 187–8; end-year flexibility arrangements 185; limits 183–6; mistiming of payments 185; Reserve 186–7; running 188–90; supplementary estimates 183–6
Code of Fiscal Stability 153–4
conditional grant of supply 156
Contingencies Fund 187–8
control: Comptroller and Auditor-General, *see* Comptroller and Auditor-General; conceptual apparatus of 169; law and courts, link with external controls by 199–206; legal and parliamentary systems, lack of shared knowledge or understanding 206; legislative, parliamentary and internal rules 170–1; National Audit Office, *see* National Audit Office; negotiation with departments 192; Parliamentary controls, link with 193–9; principles of 176; propriety 173–5, 196; Public Service Agreements 191–2; regularity 171–3, 196; self-enforcement 190–2; structure of 191; systems for 191; Treasury, aim of 176; value for money 175–6, 197
Departmental Expenditure Limites 147, 150, 186
economic convergence, Maastricht criteria 146–7
efficiency gains, aim of 189
end-year flexibility arrangements 185
establishments, on 181–2
estimates, *see* Estimates
Excess Vote 162
Fundamental Expenditure Reviews 110
internal control, constitutional dimension 104–7
lawyers' approach to 171
legal aspects, lack of opportunity to develop body of legal doctrine on 203
legal duty to pay sums under Appropriation Act 203–5
legal obligations, meeting 201
legal structuring 201
legislation, legal nature of 206
management, rules of the game 131–2
maximum amount, Parliament indicating 109
new works and services, on 182–2
parliamentary decisions 158
plans, fitting departmental activities to 148–51
politics of 104
propriety 173–5, 196
Public Expenditure Survey system: cash basis, switch to 184; collective character 149; departmental reports 154–5;

estimates, alignment of 162–4; function of 141–2; Guidelines 148; history of 143–4; instrument of control, as 144; Parliament in 152–5; procedures 148; running cash controls 188–90
public funds, charge on 108
Public Service Agreements 150
reforms 395; result of 151–2
regularity 171–3, 196
relation to overall state of economy 141
reporting and auditing procedures 157
Reserve 186–7
resource accounting and budgeting, *see* Resource accounting and budgeting
'Star Chamber' 149
strict fiscal rules, levels consistent with 145
supply cycle 155–9
supply, granting of 107
total: Control 146–7; general government expenditure (GGE) 145; GGE(X) 146; Planning 146; setting 144; targets and instruments of control, representing 145; top-down, shift to 148; Total Managed Expenditure 146
Treasury authorizations and delegations: establishments 181–2; ex gratia payments 179; need for 177; new works and services, as to 182–2; prior, tests for 177; relaxations 179; revision of system 178–9; rules and precedents 177–8; scope of delegation 180; sensitive expenditures, definition of 177; spending-related matters, referring to 179; statutory provisions 178; virement 180–1
Treasury, role of, *see* Treasury
value for money 175–6, 197
ways and means 107
White Paper 152

Public services:
market testing, services subject to 46
principles applying across 11
reforms, impact on courts 397

Resource accounting and budgeting:
capital, charge for use of 167
cash and accruals accounting distinguished 164–5
expenditure arrangements, change in 164
inventory and evaluation of assets 166
Reference Manual 166
resource accounts, introduction of 165
resource budgeting 166–8
supply, principles of 166
switch to 165
Resources:
deployment and control of 23
pre-constitutional 22
raw materials of constitutional organization, as 24
Royal prerogative:
statutory powers, relationship with 2
Royal Proclamation:
reliance on government by 349
Rule of law:
governments operating according to 207

Scotland:
devolved executive, establishment of 29
drafting of legislation 250, 252, 255; scrutiny 257
government legal services in 228–9
Law Officers 229, 236–8; reference of issues to 306
Lord Advocate, *see* Lord Advocate
Parliament, establishment of 29
Prison Service 44
Scottish Office, activities of 228–9
Secretary of State:
functions vested in 32–3
incorporation 32
Ministers of State distinguished 33
number of 33

Separation of powers:
constitutional law, influence on 10
doctrine of 10
France, in 208
new social theories, called into question by 11
organizational blocs, allocation of powers and functions within 12
public choice theory, effect of 11–12
Serious Fraud Office:
Director, relationship with Attorney-General 287–8
establishment of 222
Service First, *see* Citizen's Charter
Solicitor-General, *see* Law Officers
State:
associative enterprise for control of territory, as 21
paramountcy of 21
powers, derivation of 21
Supplementary Benefits Commission:
judicial order, disregard of 328

Taxation:
control of 104
detail of proposals 158
Finance Acts, imposition outside 157
Treasury:
accountancy and internal audit, central responsibility for 137–9
Accounting Officer, *see* Accounting Officer
accounts and audit functions 120
acronyms, use of 110
action, underpinnings of 122
Budget and Public Finances Directorate 111
Cabinet Office, overlapping concerns with 126
central department of government, as 109
Chief Secretary 112
Civil Service, control of 65–6
Code of Fiscal Stability 106
constitutional and legal bases of authority 113
control problems, ventilation of 105
courts, contact with 200
dependence on Parliament 106
directorates 110–13
Economic Secretary 112
effective, need for 116
estimates, role as to 120–2
financial controls, delegation of 9
Financial Management Initiative 124–5
Financial Management, Reporting and Audit Directorate 111–12, 138
financial planning and control function 104
Financial Secretary 112
general management of government funds by 140
history of 113–16
internal financial control: discipline supporting 106
internal guidance on expenditure 205–6
legal duty to pay sums under Appropriation Act 203–5
Lords Commissioners 113–14; respondents to litigation, as 200
ministerial team 112
National Audit Office, relations with 195–9
nominal head of 109
objectives 110
Orders in Council 115
organization 110–13
origins of 113
overall aim of 110
Parliament, relationship with 105–6
Paymaster General 112
payments, legal battles on 202
powers: access to Parliament, control of 120–2; authority for 116–17; constitutional basis of 117; departmental establishments, comprehensive control over 123; expenditure of funds, supervision of 118–20; legislative basis for 116; public funds, issuance of 117–18; scope and basis, obscurity of 117, 122
Principal Finance Officer, relations with 131
public expenditure information, furnishing 9
public expenditure, authorisation

and delegation, *see* Public expenditure
public finances, control and supervision of 113
responsibility of 109
right of control 115
rights and powers, first modern statement of 115
single window communications system 131
Spending Directorate 111
staffing, leanness of 190
systems and structures, creation and application of 122
tasks of 110–13
teams 112
transparency of systems 105
Treasury Board 113
Treasury Officer of Accounts 112, 196
virement, power over 177, 180–1

Treasury Solicitor:
Attorney-General, relationship with 219
Chief Executive of Agency, as 219–20
corporation sole, as 218
Department: advisory divisions 220; conveyancing by 215; decisions in 219; European Division 317–19; European Secretariat, advice to 317; head of 218; internal organization 220; lawyers, instructing 220; legal services provided by 217–18; ministerial departments relying on 223; non-ministerial department, as 218; principal central legal department, as 217
Digest 322
executive agency, as 219
judicial review decisions, description of 339
litigation strategy 341–3
managerial role 215–16
ministerial Advisory Board 219
office of 218

United States:
core executive, unitary nature of 7
plural administration 7

Value added tax:
government departments, paid by 14

Virement:
meaning 177
requests, view of 181
Treasury power over 177, 180–1

Wales:
devolution 29, 229
Welsh Officer, activities of 229

Welfare state:
legal rights, establishment of 200

Ingram Content Group UK Ltd.
Milton Keynes UK
UKHW020022260723
425794UK00003B/258